BAYESIAN TIME SERIES MODELS

'What's going to happen next?' Time series data hold the answers, and Bayesian methods represent the cutting edge in learning what they have to say. This ambitious book is the first unified treatment of the emerging knowledge-base in Bayesian time series techniques. Exploiting the unifying framework of probabilistic graphical models, the book covers approximation schemes, both Monte Carlo and deterministic, and introduces switching, multi-object, nonparametric and agent-based models in a variety of application environments. It demonstrates that the basic framework supports the rapid creation of models tailored to specific applications and gives insight into the computational complexity of their implementation.

The authors span traditional disciplines such as statistics and engineering and the more recently established areas of machine learning and pattern recognition. Readers with a basic understanding of applied probability, but no experience with time series analysis, are guided from fundamental concepts to the state of the art in research and practice.

BAYESIAN TIME SERIES MODELS

Edited by

David Barber
University College London

A. Taylan Cemgil
Boğaziçi University, Bebek, Istanbul

Silvia Chiappa
University of Cambridge

CAMBRIDGE
UNIVERSITY PRESS

University Printing House, Cambridge CB2 8BS, United Kingdom

Cambridge University Press is part of the University of Cambridge.

It furthers the University's mission by disseminating knowledge in the pursuit of education, learning and research at the highest international levels of excellence.

www.cambridge.org
Information on this title: www.cambridge.org/9780521196765

First published 2011

A catalogue record for this publication is available from the British Library

Library of Congress Cataloguing in Publication data
Bayesian time series models / edited by David Barber, A. Taylan Cemgil, Silvia Chiappa.
p.   cm.
ISBN 978-0-521-19676-5 (hardback)
1. Time-series analysis.   2. Bayesian statistical decision theory.   I. Barber, David, 1968 Nov. 9–
II. Cemgil, Ali Taylan.   III. Chiappa, Silvia.   IV. Title.
QA280.B39   2011
519.5′5–dc22
2011008051

ISBN 978-0-521-19676-5 Hardback

Contents

V   Nonparametric models

VI   Agent-based models

Contributors

Cédric Archambeau, *Department of Computer Science, University College London*

Yves Atchadé *Department of Statistics, University of Michigan*

David Barber *Department of Computer Science, University College London*

A. Taylan Cemgil *Department of Computer Engineering Boğaziçi University*

Silvia Chiappa *Statistical Laboratory, University of Cambridge*

Idris A. Eckley *Department of Mathematics and Statistics, Lancaster University*

Paul Fearnhead *Department of Mathematics and Statistics, Lancaster University*

Gersende Fort *LTCI, CNRS – Telecom ParisTech*

Jurgen Van Gael *Department of Engineering, University of Cambridge*

Zoubin Ghahramani *Department of Engineering, University of Cambridge*

Simon J. Godsill *Signal Processing Laboratory, Department of Engineering, University of Cambridge*

Stefan Harmeling *MPI for Biological Cybernetics, Department Schölkopf, Tübingen*

Tom Heskes *Institute for Computing and Information Sciences, Radboud University Nijmegen*

Simon Hill *Signal Processing Laboratory, Department of Engineering, University of Cambridge*

Nick R. Jennings *School of Electronics and Computer Science, University of Southampton*

Adam M. Johansen *Department of Statistics, University of Warwick*

Hilbert J. Kappen *Donders' Institute for Neuroscience, Radboud University, Nijmegen*

Rebecca Killick *Department of Mathematics and Statistics, Lancaster University*

Risi Kondor *Center for the Mathematics of Information, California Institute of Technology*

Neil D. Lawrence *School of Computer Science, University of Manchester*

Jack Li *Signal Processing Laboratory, Department of Engineering, University of Cambridge*

Eric Moulines *LTCI, CNRS – Telecom ParisTech*

Manfred Opper *Technische Universität Berlin, Fakultät IV – Elektrotechnik und Informatik*

Michael A. Osborne *Department of Engineering Science, University of Oxford*

Sze Kim Pang *Signal Processing Laboratory, Department of Engineering, University of Cambridge*

Omiros Papaspiliopoulos *Department of Economics, Universitat Pompeu Fabra, Barcelona*

Pierre Priouret *Laboratoire de Probabilités et Modèles Aléatoires, Université P. & M. Curie, Paris*

John A. Quinn *Department of Computer Science, Makerere University*

Sarvapali D. Ramchurn *School of Electronics and Computer Science, University of Southampton*

Magnus Rattray *School of Computer Science, University of Manchester*

Stephen J. Roberts *Department of Engineering Science, University of Oxford*

Alex Rogers *School of Electronics and Computer Science, University of Southampton*

Maneesh Sahani *Gatsby Computational Neuroscience Unit, London*

François Septier *Institut TELECOM/ TELECOM Lille 1, France*

Sumeetpal S. Singh *Signal Processing Laboratory, Department of Engineering, University of Cambridge*

Amos Storkey *Institute for Adaptive and Neural Computation, University of Edinburgh*

Michalis K. Titsias *School of Computer Science, University of Manchester*

Marc Toussaint *Technische Universität Berlin*

Richard Eric Turner *Gatsby Computational Neuroscience Unit, London*

Nick Whiteley *Statistics Group, Department of Mathematics, University of Bristol*

Christopher K. I. Williams *Institute for Adaptive and Neural Computation, University of Edinburgh*

Onno Zoeter *Xerox Research Centre Europe, Meylan*

Preface

Probabilistic time series modelling

Time series are studied in a variety of disciplines and appear in many modern applications such as financial time series prediction, video-tracking, music analysis, control and genetic sequence analysis. This widespread interest at times obscures the commonalities in the developed models and techniques. A central aim of this book is to attempt to make modern time series techniques, specifically those based on probabilistic modelling, accessible to a broad range of researchers.

In order to achieve this goal, leading researchers that span the more traditional disciplines of statistics, control theory, engineering and signal processing, and the more recent areas of machine learning and pattern recognition, have been brought together to discuss advancements and developments in their respective fields. In addition, the book makes extensive use of the graphical models framework. This framework facilitates the representation of many classical models and provides insight into the computational complexity of their implementation. Furthermore, it enables to easily envisage new models tailored for a particular environment. For example, the book discusses novel state space models and their application in signal processing including condition monitoring and tracking. The book also describes modern developments in the machine learning community applied to more traditional areas of control theory.

The effective application of probabilistic models in the real world is gaining pace, largely through increased computational power which brings more general models into consideration through carefully developed implementations. As such, developing new models and associated approximate inference schemes is likely to remain an active area of research, with graphical models playing an important role in facilitating communication and guiding intuition. The book extensively discusses novel developments in approximate inference, including both deterministic and stochastic approximations.

The structure of the book

Chapter 1 gives a general introduction to probabilistic time series and explains how graphical models can be used to compactly represent classical models, such as the linear dynamical system and hidden Markov model. The chapter also discusses stochastic approximation schemes such as Markov chains and sequential Monte Carlo (particle filtering), and less well known deterministic approximation schemes such as variational methods.

The subsequent chapters are organised into six thematic parts: the first two deal with more theoretical issues related to approximate inference, while the remaining four deal with the development and application of novel models. More specifically, the parts are organised as follows.

Monte Carlo Monte Carlo methods are important and widespread techniques for approximate inference in probabilistic models. Chapter 2 gives a comprehensive introduction to adaptive Markov chain Monte Carlo methods. In time series models, a particularly relevant issue is that data often arrives sequentially, for which sequential Monte Carlo methods are appropriate. Chapter 3 gives a survey of recent developments in particle filtering. Chapter 4 presents the application of Monte Carlo methods to diffusion processes.

Deterministic approximations Chapter 5 discusses some characteristics of variational approximations, highlighting important aspects and difficulties idiosyncratic to time series models. Chapter 6 presents a novel deterministic approximate inference method for continuous-time Markov processes. Chapters 7 and 8 deal with inference in the important but computationally difficult switching linear dynamical system, and introduce specific deterministic inference schemes as improvements on classical methods.

Switching models Switching models assume that an underlying process may change from one parameter regime to another over time and may be used to model changes in the environment. In Chapter 9 switching models are applied to condition monitoring, in particular physiological monitoring. Chapter 10 reviews changepoint models, which are restricted switching models used to detect abrupt changes in time series, and gives insights into new applications.

Multi-object models A particularly active research area is the tracking of moving objects, such as crowds. In Chapter 11, a detailed discussion of a tracking model and associated stochastic inference method is given. In a similar vein, in Chapter 12 a framework for sequentially inferring how groups dynamically evolve is presented and applied to tracking the group behaviour of financial stocks. In Chapter 13 a different theoretical approach to multi-object tracking based on non-commutative harmonic analysis is discussed.

Nonparametric models In recent years flexible nonparametric models have been a particular focus of machine learning research. In this part, their extension to time series analysis is presented. Chapter 14 discusses sampling algorithms for Gaussian processes. Chapter 15 presents recent developments in nonparametric hidden Markov models, along with associated inference algorithms and applications. Chapter 16 introduces an application of a nonparametric time series model to multi-sensor time series prediction.

Agent-based models A recent viewpoint is to treat a control problem as an inference problem in an associated probabilistic model. This viewpoint is complementary to classical control theory and reinforcement learning and makes use of concepts familiar to probabilistic modellers, facilitating an entrance into this field. In Chapter 17 optimal control theory and the linear Bellman equation are discussed in relation to inference in a probabilistic model. In Chapter 18 the standard methods of learning in probabilistic models are applied to learning control policies in Markov decision problems.

Whom this book is for

This book will appeal to statisticians interested in modern aspects of time series analysis in areas bordering with engineering, signal processing and machine learning and how time series analysis is approached in those communities. For engineers and machine learners, the book has a wealth of insights into statistical approaches, particularly dealing with sampling techniques applied to difficult time series models. To follow the book, no specific knowledge of time series is required. However, readers are assumed to have a basic understanding of applied probability.

Acknowledgements

We are particularly grateful to the following people for their advice and comments on the book: Julien Cornebise, Mark Girolami, Andrew Golightly, Jim Griffin, Matt Hoffmanm, Antti Honkela, Jonathan Huang, Ajay Jasra, Jens Kober, Jan Peters, Sonia Petrone, Alan Qi, George Sermaidis, Olivier Stegle, Matt Taddy, Evangelos Theodorou, Yener Ulker.

1

Inference and estimation in probabilistic time series models

David Barber, A. Taylan Cemgil and Silvia Chiappa

1.1 Time series

The term 'time series' refers to data that can be represented as a sequence. This includes for example financial data in which the sequence index indicates time, and genetic data (e.g. $ACATGC\ldots$) in which the sequence index has no temporal meaning. In this tutorial we give an overview of discrete-time probabilistic models, which are the subject of most chapters in this book, with continuous-time models being discussed separately in Chapters 4, 6, 11 and 17. Throughout our focus is on the basic algorithmic issues underlying time series, rather than on surveying the wide field of applications.

Defining a probabilistic model of a time series $y_{1:T} \equiv y_1, \ldots, y_T$ requires the specification of a joint distribution $p(y_{1:T})$.[1] In general, specifying all independent entries of $p(y_{1:T})$ is infeasible without making some statistical independence assumptions. For example, in the case of binary data, $y_t \in \{0, 1\}$, the joint distribution contains maximally $2^T - 1$ independent entries. Therefore, for time series of more than a few time steps, we need to introduce simplifications in order to ensure tractability. One way to introduce statistical independence is to use the probability of *a* conditioned on observed *b*

$$p(a|b) = \frac{p(a, b)}{p(b)}.$$

Replacing *a* with y_T and *b* with $y_{1:T-1}$ and rearranging we obtain $p(y_{1:T}) = p(y_T|y_{1:T-1})p(y_{1:T-1})$. Similarly, we can decompose $p(y_{1:T-1}) = p(y_{T-1}|y_{1:T-2})p(y_{1:T-2})$. By repeated application, we can then express the joint distribution as[2]

$$p(y_{1:T}) = \prod_{t=1}^{T} p(y_t|y_{1:t-1}).$$

This factorisation is consistent with the causal nature of time, since each factor represents a generative model of a variable conditioned on its past. To make the specification simpler, we can impose conditional independence by dropping variables in each factor conditioning set. For example, by imposing $p(y_t|y_{1:t-1}) = p(y_t|y_{t-m:t-1})$ we obtain the *m*th-order Markov model discussed in Section 1.2.

---

[1] To simplify the notation, throughout the tutorial we use lowercase to indicate both a random variable and its realisation.

[2] We use the convention that $y_{1:t-1} = \emptyset$ if $t < 2$. More generally, one may write $p_t(y_t|y_{1:t-1})$, as we generally have a different distribution at each time step. However, for notational simplicity we generally omit the time index.

David Barber, A. Taylan Cemgil and Silvia Chiappa

(a)   (b)

Figure 1.1 Belief network representations of two time series models. (a) First-order Markov model $p(y_{1:4}) = p(y_4|y_3)p(y_3|y_2)p(y_2|y_1)p(y_1)$. (b) Second-order Markov model $p(y_{1:4}) = p(y_4|y_3, y_2)p(y_3|y_2, y_1)p(y_2|y_1)p(y_1)$.

A useful way to express statistical independence assumptions is to use a belief network graphical model which is a directed acyclic graph[3] representing the joint distribution

$$p(y_{1:N}) = \prod_{i=1}^{N} p(y_i|\text{pa}(y_i)),$$

where pa (y_i) denotes the parents of y_i, that is the variables with a directed link to y_i. By limiting the parental set of each variable we can reduce the burden of specification. In Fig. 1.1 we give two examples of belief networks corresponding to a first- and second-order Markov model respectively, see Section 1.2. For the model $p(y_{1:4})$ in Fig. 1.1(a) and binary variables $y_t \in \{0, 1\}$ we need to specify only $1 + 2 + 2 + 2 = 7$ entries,[4] compared to $2^4 - 1 = 15$ entries in the case that no independence assumptions are made.

Inference

Inference is the task of using a distribution to answer questions of interest. For example, given a set of observations $y_{1:T}$, a common inference problem in time series analysis is the use of the posterior distribution $p(y_{T+1}|y_{1:T})$ for the prediction of an unseen future variable y_{T+1}. One of the challenges in time series modelling is to develop computationally efficient algorithms for computing such posterior distributions by exploiting the independence assumptions of the model.

Estimation

Estimation is the task of determining a parameter θ of a model based on observations $y_{1:T}$. This can be considered as a form of inference in which we wish to compute $p(\theta|y_{1:T})$. Specifically, if $p(\theta)$ is a distribution quantifying our beliefs in the parameter values before having seen the data, we can use Bayes' rule to combine this prior with the observations to form a posterior distribution

$$\underbrace{p(\theta|y_{1:T})}_{\text{posterior}} = \frac{\overbrace{p(y_{1:T}|\theta)}^{\text{likelihood}}\ \overbrace{p(\theta)}^{\text{prior}}}{\underbrace{p(y_{1:T})}_{\text{marginal likelihood}}}.$$

The posterior distribution is often summarised by the maximum a posteriori (MAP) point estimate, given by the mode

$$\theta^{\text{MAP}} = \underset{\theta}{\text{argmax}}\ p(y_{1:T}|\theta)p(\theta).$$

---

[3] A directed graph is acyclic if, by following the direction of the arrows, a node will never be visited more than once.

[4] For example, we need one specification for $p(y_1 = 0)$, with $p(y_1 = 1) = 1 - p(y_1 = 0)$ determined by normalisation. Similarly, we need to specify two entries for $p(y_2|y_1)$.

It can be computationally more convenient to use the log posterior,

$$\theta^{MAP} = \underset{\theta}{\text{argmax}} \log\left(p(y_{1:T}|\theta)p(\theta)\right),$$

where the equivalence follows from the monotonicity of the log function. When using a 'flat prior' $p(\theta) = \text{const.}$, the MAP solution coincides with the maximum likelihood (ML) solution

$$\theta^{ML} = \underset{\theta}{\text{argmax}}\ p(y_{1:T}|\theta) = \underset{\theta}{\text{argmax}} \log p(y_{1:T}|\theta).$$

In the following sections we introduce some popular time series models and describe associated inference and parameter estimation routines.

1.2 Markov models

Markov models (or Markov chains) are of fundamental importance and underpin many time series models [21]. In an mth order Markov model the joint distribution factorises as

$$p(y_{1:T}) = \prod_{t=1}^{T} p(y_t|y_{t-m:t-1}),$$

expressing the fact that only the previous m observations $y_{t-m:t-1}$ directly influence y_t. In a time-homogeneous model, the transition probabilities $p(y_t|y_{t-m:t-1})$ are time-independent.

1.2.1 Estimation in discrete Markov models

In a time-homogeneous first-order Markov model with discrete scalar observations $y_t \in \{1, \ldots, S\}$, the transition from y_{t-1} to y_t can be parameterised using a matrix θ, that is

$$\theta_{ji} \equiv p(y_t = j|y_{t-1} = i, \theta), \quad i, j \in \{1, \ldots, S\}.$$

Given observations $y_{1:T}$, maximum likelihood sets this matrix according to

$$\theta^{ML} = \underset{\theta}{\text{argmax}} \log p(y_{1:T}|\theta) = \underset{\theta}{\text{argmax}} \sum_t \log p(y_t|y_{t-1}, \theta).$$

Under the probability constraints $0 \le \theta_{ji} \le 1$ and $\sum_j \theta_{ji} = 1$, the optimal solution is given by the intuitive setting

$$\theta_{ji}^{ML} = \frac{n_{ji}}{T-1},$$

where n_{ji} is the number of transitions from i to j observed in $y_{1:T}$.

Alternatively, a Bayesian treatment would compute the parameter posterior distribution

$$p(\theta|y_{1:T}) \propto p(\theta)p(y_{1:T}|\theta) = p(\theta) \prod_{i,j} \theta_{ji}^{n_{ji}}.$$

In this case a convenient prior for θ is a Dirichlet distribution on each column $\theta_{:i}$ with hyperparameter vector $\alpha_{:i}$

$$p(\theta) = \prod_i \mathcal{DI}(\theta_{:i}|\alpha_{:i}) = \prod_i \frac{1}{Z(\alpha_{:i})} \prod_j \theta_{ji}^{\alpha_{ji}-1},$$

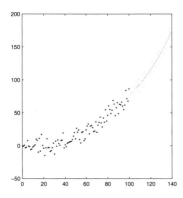

Figure 1.2 Maximum likelihood fit of a third-order AR model. The horizontal axis represents time, whilst the vertical axis the value of the time series. The dots represent the 100 observations $y_{1:100}$. The solid line indicates the mean predictions $\langle y \rangle_t, t > 100$, and the dashed lines $\langle y \rangle_t \pm \sqrt{r}$.

where $Z(\alpha_{:i}) = \int_0^1 \prod_j \theta_{ij}^{\alpha_{ji}-1} d\theta$. The convenience of this 'conjugate' prior is that it gives a parameter posterior that is also a Dirichlet distribution [15]

$$p(\theta|y_{1:T}) = \prod_i \mathcal{DI}(\theta_{:i}|\alpha_{:i} + n_{:i}).$$

This Bayesian approach differs from maximum likelihood in that it treats the parameters as random variables and yields distributional information. This is motivated from the understanding that for a finite number of observations there is not necessarily a 'single best' parameter estimate, but rather a distribution of parameters weighted both by how well they fit the data and how well they match our prior assumptions.

1.2.2 Autoregressive models

A widely used Markov model of continuous scalar observations is the autoregressive (AR) model [2, 4]. An mth-order AR model assumes that y_t is a noisy linear combination of the previous m observations, that is

$$y_t = a_1 y_{t-1} + a_2 y_{t-2} + \cdots + a_m y_{t-m} + \epsilon_t,$$

where $a_{1:m}$ are called the AR coefficients, and ϵ_t is an independent noise term commonly assumed to be zero-mean Gaussian with variance r (indicated with $\mathcal{N}(\epsilon_t|0, r)$). A so-called *generative form* for the AR model with Gaussian noise is given by[5]

$$p(y_{1:T}|y_{1:m}) = \prod_{t=m+1}^{T} p(y_t|y_{t-m:t-1}), \quad p(y_t|y_{t-m:t-1}) = \mathcal{N}\left(y_t \middle| \sum_{i=1}^{m} a_i y_{t-i}, r\right).$$

Given observations $y_{1:T}$, the maximum likelihood estimate for the parameters $a_{1:m}$ and r is obtained by maximising with respect to a and r the log likelihood

$$\log p(y_{1:T}|y_{1:m}) = -\frac{1}{2r} \sum_{t=m+1}^{T} \left(y_t - \sum_{i=1}^{m} a_i y_{t-i}\right)^2 - \frac{T-m}{2} \log(2\pi r).$$

The optimal $a_{1:m}$ are given by solving the linear system

$$\sum_i a_i \sum_{t=m+1}^{T} y_{t-i} y_{t-j} = \sum_{t=m+1}^{T} y_t y_{t-j} \quad \forall j,$$

---

[5]Note that the first m variables are not modelled.

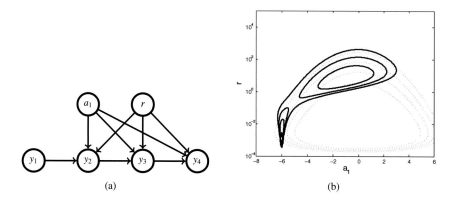

Figure 1.3 (a) Belief network representation of a first-order AR model with parameters a_1, r (first four time steps). (b) Parameter prior $p(a_1, r)$ (light grey, dotted) and posterior $p(a_1, r|y_1 = 1, y_2 = -6)$ (black). The posterior describes two plausible explanations of the data: (i) the noise r is low and $a_1 \approx -6$, (ii) the noise r is high with a set of possible values for a_1 centred around zero.

which is readily solved using Gaussian elimination. The linear system has a Toeplitz form that can be more efficiently solved, if required, using the Levinson-Durbin method [9]. The optimal variance is then given by

$$r = \frac{1}{T - m} \sum_{t=m+1}^{T} \left(y_t - \sum_{i=1}^{m} a_i y_{t-i} \right)^2.$$

The case in which y_t is multivariate can be handled by assuming that a_i is a matrix and ϵ_t is a vector. This generalisation is known as vector autoregression.

Example 1 We illustrate with a simple example how AR models can be used to estimate trends underlying time series data. A third-order AR model was fit to the set of 100 observations shown in Fig. 1.2 using maximum likelihood. A prediction for the mean $\langle y \rangle_t$ was then recursively generated as

$$\langle y \rangle_t = \begin{cases} \sum_{i=1}^{3} a_i \langle y \rangle_{t-i} & \text{for} \quad t > 100, \\ y_t & \text{for} \quad t \leq 100. \end{cases}$$

As we can see (solid line in Fig. 1.2), the predicted means for time $t > 100$ capture an underlying trend in the time series.

Example 2 In a MAP and Bayesian approach, a prior on the AR coefficients can be used to define physical constraints (if any) or to regularise the system. Similarly, a prior on the variance r can be used to specify any knowledge about or constraint on the noise. As an example, consider a Bayesian approach to a first-order AR model in which the following Gaussian prior for a_1 and inverse Gamma prior for r are defined:

$$p(a_1) = \mathcal{N}(a_1 | 0, q),$$

$$p(r) = \mathcal{IG}(r | v, v/\beta) = \exp\left[-(v+1) \log r - \frac{v}{\beta r} - \log \Gamma(v) + v \log \frac{v}{\beta} \right].$$

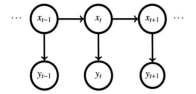

Figure 1.4 A first-order latent Markov model. In a hidden Markov model the latent variables $x_{1:T}$ are discrete and the observed variables $y_{1:T}$ can be either discrete or continuous.

Assuming that a_1 and r are a priori independent, the parameter posterior is given by

$$p(a_1, r | y_{1:T}) \propto p(a_1) p(r) \prod_{t=2}^{T} p(y_t | y_{t-1}, a_1, r).$$

The belief network representation of this model is given in Fig. 1.3(a). For a numerical example, consider $T = 2$ and observations and hyperparameters given by

$$y_1 = 1, \quad y_2 = -6, \quad q = 1.2, \quad v = 0.4, \quad \beta = 100.$$

The parameter posterior, Fig. 1.3(b), takes the form

$$p(a_1, r | y_{1:2}) \propto \exp\left[-\left(\frac{v}{\beta} + \frac{y_2^2}{2} \right) \frac{1}{r} + y_1 y_2 \frac{a_1}{r} - \frac{1}{2} \left(\frac{y_1^2}{r} + \frac{1}{q} \right) a_1^2 - (v + 3/2) \log r \right].$$

As we can see, Fig. 1.3(b), the posterior is multimodal, with each mode corresponding to a different interpretation: (i) The regression coefficient a_1 is approximately -6 and the noise is low. This solution gives a small prediction error. (ii) Since the prior for a_1 has zero mean, an alternative interpretation is that a_1 is centred around zero and the noise is high.
   From this example we can make the following observations:

- Point estimates such as ML or MAP are not always representative of the solution.

- Even very simple models can lead to complicated posterior distributions.

- Variables that are independent *a priori* may become dependent *a posteriori*.

- Ambiguous data usually leads to a multimodal parameter posterior, with each mode corresponding to one plausible explanation.

1.3   Latent Markov models

In a latent Markov model, the observations $y_{1:T}$ are generated by a set of unobserved or 'latent' variables $x_{1:T}$. Typically, the latent variables are first-order Markovian and each observed variable y_t is independent from all other variables given x_t. The joint distribution thus factorises as[6]

$$p(y_{1:T}, x_{1:T}) = p(x_1) \prod_{t=2}^{T} p(y_t | x_t) p(x_t | x_{t-1}),$$

where $p(x_t | x_{t-1})$ is called the 'transition' model and $p(y_t | x_t)$ the 'emission' model. The belief network representation of this latent Markov model is given in Fig. 1.4.

---

[6]This general form is also known as a state space model.

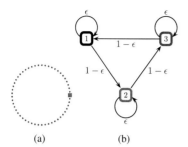

Figure 1.5 (a) Robot (square) moving sporadically with probability $1 - \epsilon$ counter-clockwise in a circular corridor one location at a time. Small circles denote the S possible locations. (b) The state transition diagram for a corridor with $S = 3$ possible locations.

(a)   (b)

1.3.1 Discrete state latent Markov models

A well-known latent Markov model is the hidden Markov model[7] (HMM) [23] in which x_t is a scalar discrete variable ($x_t \in \{1, \ldots, S\}$).

Example Consider the following toy tracking problem. A robot is moving around a circular corridor and at any time occupies one of S possible locations. At each time step t, the robot stays where it is with probability ϵ, or moves to the next point in a counter-clockwise direction with probability $1 - \epsilon$. This scenario, illustrated in Fig. 1.5, can be conveniently represented by an $S \times S$ matrix A with elements $A_{ji} = p(x_t = j|x_{t-1} = i)$. For example, for $S = 3$, we have

$$A = \epsilon \begin{pmatrix} 1 & 0 & 0 \\ 0 & 1 & 0 \\ 0 & 0 & 1 \end{pmatrix} + (1 - \epsilon) \begin{pmatrix} 0 & 0 & 1 \\ 1 & 0 & 0 \\ 0 & 1 & 0 \end{pmatrix}. \tag{1.1}$$

At each time step t, the robot sensors measure its position, obtaining either the correct location with probability w or a uniformly random location with probability $1 - w$. This can be expressed formally as

$$y_t|x_t \sim w\delta(y_t - x_t) + (1 - w)\mathcal{U}(y_t|1, \ldots, S),$$

where δ is the Kronecker delta function and $\mathcal{U}(y|1, \ldots, S)$ denotes the uniform distribution over the set of possible locations. We may parameterise $p(y_t|x_t)$ using an $S \times S$ matrix C with elements $C_{ui} = p(y_t = u|x_t = i)$. For $S = 3$, we have

$$C = w \begin{pmatrix} 1 & 0 & 0 \\ 0 & 1 & 0 \\ 0 & 0 & 1 \end{pmatrix} + \frac{(1 - w)}{3} \begin{pmatrix} 1 & 1 & 1 \\ 1 & 1 & 1 \\ 1 & 1 & 1 \end{pmatrix}.$$

A typical realisation $y_{1:T}$ from the process defined by this HMM with $S = 50$, $\epsilon = 0.5$, $T = 30$ and $w = 0.3$ is depicted in Fig. 1.6(a). We are interested in inferring the true locations of the robot from the noisy measured locations $y_{1:T}$. At each time t, the true location can be inferred from the so-called 'filtered' posterior $p(x_t|y_{1:t})$ (Fig. 1.6(b)), which uses measurements up to t; or from the so-called 'smoothed' posterior $p(x_t|y_{1:T})$ (Fig. 1.6(c)), which uses both past and future observations and is therefore generally more accurate. These posterior marginals are obtained using the efficient inference routines outlined in Section 1.4.

---

[7]Some authors use the terms 'hidden Markov model' and 'state space model' as synonymous [4]. We use the term HMM in a more restricted sense to refer to a latent Markov model where $x_{1:T}$ are discrete. The observations $y_{1:T}$ can be discrete or continuous.

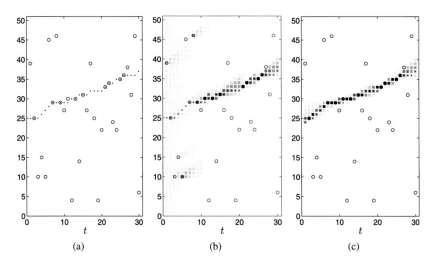

Figure 1.6 Filtering and smoothing for robot tracking using a HMM with $S = 50$. (a) A realisation from the HMM example described in the text. The dots indicate the true latent locations of the robot, whilst the open circles indicate the noisy measured locations. (b) The squares indicate the filtering distribution at each time step t, $p(x_t|y_{1:t})$. This probability is proportional to the grey level with black corresponding to 1 and white to 0. Note that the posterior for the first time steps is multimodal, therefore the true position cannot be accurately estimated. (c) The squares indicate the smoothing distribution at each time step t, $p(x_t|y_{1:T} = y_{1:T})$. Note that, for $t < T$, we estimate the position retrospectively and the uncertainty is significantly lower when compared to the filtered estimates.

1.3.2   Continuous state latent Markov models

In continuous state latent Markov models, x_t is a multivariate continuous variable, $x_t \in \mathbb{R}^H$. For high-dimensional continuous x_t, the set of models for which operations such as filtering and smoothing are computationally tractable is severely limited. Within this tractable class, the linear dynamical system plays a special role, and is essentially the continuous analogue of the HMM.

Linear dynamical systems

A linear dynamical system (LDS) on variables $x_{1:T}$, $y_{1:T}$ has the following form:

$$x_t = Ax_{t-1} + \bar{x}_t + \epsilon_t^x, \quad \epsilon_t^x \sim \mathcal{N}\left(\epsilon_t^x|0, Q\right), \quad x_1 \sim \mathcal{N}\left(x_1|\mu, P\right),$$

$$y_t = Cx_t + \bar{y}_t + \epsilon_t^y, \quad \epsilon_t^y \sim \mathcal{N}\left(\epsilon_t^y|0, R\right),$$

with transition matrix A and emission matrix C. The terms $\bar{x}_t$, $\bar{y}_t$ are often defined as $\bar{x}_t = Bz_t$ and $\bar{y}_t = Dz_t$, where z_t is a known input that can be used to control the system. The complete parameter set is therefore $\{A, B, C, D, Q, R, \mu, P\}$. As a generative model, the LDS is defined as

$$p(x_t|x_{t-1}) = \mathcal{N}\left(x_t|Ax_{t-1} + \bar{x}_t, Q\right), \quad p(y_t|x_t) = \mathcal{N}\left(y_t|Cx_t + \bar{y}_t, R\right).$$

Example   As an example scenario that can be modelled using an LDS, consider a moving object with position, velocity and instantaneous acceleration at time t given respectively by q_t, v_t and a_t. A discrete time description of the object dynamics is given by Newton's laws (see for example [11])

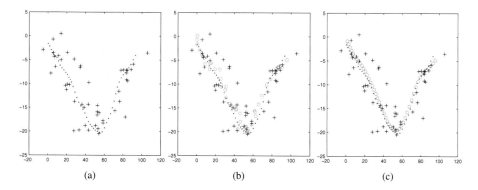

(a)   (b)   (c)

Figure 1.7 Tracking an object undergoing Newtonian dynamics in a two-dimensional space, Eq. (1.2). (a) The dots indicate the true latent positions of the object at each time t, $q_{1,t}$ (horizontal axis) and $q_{2,t}$ (vertical axis) (the time label is not shown). The crosses indicate the noisy observations of the latent positions. (b) The circles indicate the mean of the filtered latent positions $\int q_t p(q_t|y_{1:t})dq_t$. (c) The circles indicate the mean of the smoothed latent positions $\int q_t p(q_t|y_{1:T})dq_t$.

$$\underbrace{\begin{pmatrix} q_t \\ v_t \end{pmatrix}}_{x_t} = \underbrace{\begin{pmatrix} I & T_s I \\ 0 & I \end{pmatrix}}_{A} \underbrace{\begin{pmatrix} q_{t-1} \\ v_{t-1} \end{pmatrix}}_{x_{t-1}} + \underbrace{\begin{pmatrix} \frac{1}{2} T_s^2 I \\ T_s I \end{pmatrix}}_{B} a_t$$

$$x_t = A x_{t-1} + B a_t,$$

(1.2)

where I is the 3×3 identity matrix and T_s is the sampling period. In tracking applications, we are interested in inferring the true position q_t and velocity v_t of the object from limited noisy information. For example, in the case that we observe only the noise-corrupted positions, we may write

$$p(x_t|x_{t-1}) = \mathcal{N}(x_t|Ax_{t-1} + B\bar{a}, Q), \quad p(y_t|x_t) = \mathcal{N}(y_t|Cx_t, R),$$

where $\bar{a}$ is the acceleration mean, $Q = B\Sigma B^{\top}$ with Σ being the acceleration covariance, $C = (I\ 0)$, and R is the covariance of the position noise. We can then track the position and velocity of the object using the filtered density $p(x_t|y_{1:t})$. An example with two-dimensional positions is shown in Fig. 1.7.

AR model as an LDS

Many popular time series models can be cast into a LDS form. For example, the AR model of Section 1.2.2 can be formulated as

$$\underbrace{\begin{pmatrix} y_t \\ y_{t-1} \\ \vdots \\ y_{t-m+1} \end{pmatrix}}_{x_t} = \underbrace{\begin{pmatrix} a_1 & a_2 & \cdots & a_m \\ 1 & 0 & 0 & 0 \\ 0 & \ddots & 0 & 0 \\ 0 & 0 & 1 & 0 \end{pmatrix}}_{A} \underbrace{\begin{pmatrix} y_{t-1} \\ y_{t-2} \\ \vdots \\ y_{t-m} \end{pmatrix}}_{x_{t-1}} + \underbrace{\begin{pmatrix} \epsilon_t \\ 0 \\ \vdots \\ 0 \end{pmatrix}}_{\epsilon_t^x},$$

$$y_t = \underbrace{\begin{pmatrix} 1 & 0 & \cdots & 0 \end{pmatrix}}_{C} x_t + \epsilon_t^y,$$

where $\epsilon_t^x \sim \mathcal{N}(\epsilon_t^x|0, \mathrm{diag}(r, 0, \dots, 0))$, $\epsilon_t^y \sim \mathcal{N}(\epsilon_t^y|0, 0)$, the initial mean μ is set to the first m observations, and $P = 0$. This shows how to transform an mth-order Markov model into a constrained first-order latent Markov model. Many other related AR models and extensions can also be cast as a latent Markov model. This is therefore a very general class of models for which inference is of particular interest.

1.4   Inference in latent Markov models

In this section we derive computationally efficient methods for computing posterior distributions in latent Markov models. We assume throughout that x_t is discrete, though the recursions hold more generally on replacing summation with integration for those components of x_t that are continuous.

1.4.1   Filtering $p(x_t|y_{1:t})$

In filtering,[8] the aim is to compute the distribution of the latent variable x_t given all observations up to time t. This can be expressed as

$$p(x_t|y_{1:t}) = p(x_t, y_{1:t})/p(y_{1:t}).$$

The normalising term $p(y_{1:t})$ is the likelihood, see Section 1.4.2, and $\alpha(x_t) \equiv p(x_t, y_{1:t})$ can be computed by a 'forward' recursion

$$\alpha(x_t) = p(y_t|x_t, \cancel{y_{1:t-1}})p(x_t, y_{1:t-1})$$

$$= p(y_t|x_t) \sum_{x_{t-1}} p(x_t|x_{t-1}, \cancel{y_{1:t-1}})p(x_{t-1}, y_{1:t-1})$$

$$= p(y_t|x_t) \sum_{x_{t-1}} p(x_t|x_{t-1})\alpha(x_{t-1}), \qquad (1.3)$$

where the cancellations follow from the conditional independence assumptions of the model. The recursion is initialised with $\alpha(x_1) = p(y_1|x_1)p(x_1)$. To avoid numerical over/underflow problems, it is advisable to work with $\log \alpha(x_t)$. If only the conditional distribution $p(x_t|y_{1:t})$ is required (not the joint $p(x_t, y_{1:t})$) a numerical alternative to using the logarithm is to form a recursion for $p(x_t|y_{1:t})$ directly by normalising $\alpha(x_t)$ at each stage.

1.4.2   The likelihood

The likelihood can be computed as

$$p(y_{1:t}) = \sum_{x_t} \alpha(x_t), \quad \text{and} \quad p(y_{1:T}) = \sum_{x_T} \alpha(x_T).$$

Maximum likelihood parameter learning can be carried out by the expectation maximisation algorithm, known in the HMM context as the Baum-Welch algorithm [23], see also Section 1.5.1.

---

[8]The term 'filtering' is somewhat a misnomer since in signal processing this term is reserved for a convolution operation. However, for linear systems, it turns out that state estimation is a linear function of past observations and can indeed be computed by a convolution, partially justifying the use of the term.

1.4.3 Smoothing $p(x_{1:T}|y_{1:T})$

The smoothing distribution is the joint distribution $p(x_{1:T}|y_{1:T})$. Typically we are interested in marginals such as $p(x_t|y_{1:T})$, which gives an estimate of x_t based on all observations. There are two main approaches to computing $p(x_t|y_{1:T})$, namely the parallel and the sequential methods described below.

Parallel smoothing $p(x_t|y_{1:T})$

In parallel smoothing, the posterior $\gamma(x_t) \equiv p(x_t|y_{1:T})$ is separated into contributions from the past and future

$$\gamma(x_t) \propto \underbrace{p(x_t, y_{1:t})}_{\text{past}} \underbrace{p(y_{t+1:T}|x_t, \cancel{y_{1:t}})}_{\text{future}} = \alpha(x_t)\beta(x_t). \tag{1.4}$$

The term $\alpha(x_t)$ is obtained from the forward recursion (1.3). The terms $\beta(x_t)$ can be obtained by the following 'backward' recursion

$$\beta(x_t) = \sum_{x_{t+1}} p(y_{t+1}|\cancel{y_{t+2:T}}, \cancel{x_t}, x_{t+1}) p(y_{t+2:T}, x_{t+1}|x_t)$$

$$= \sum_{x_{t+1}} p(y_{t+1}|x_{t+1}) p(y_{t+2:T}|, \cancel{x_t}, x_{t+1}) p(x_{t+1}|x_t)$$

$$= \sum_{x_{t+1}} p(y_{t+1}|x_{t+1}) p(x_{t+1}|x_t) \beta(x_{t+1}), \tag{1.5}$$

with $\beta(x_T) = 1$. As for filtering, working in log space for β is recommended to avoid numerical difficulties.[9] The $\alpha - \beta$ recursions are independent and may therefore be run in parallel. These recursions also are called the *forward-backward algorithm*.

Sequential smoothing $p(x_t|y_{1:T})$

In sequential smoothing, we form a direct recursion for the smoothed posterior as

$$\gamma(x_t) = \sum_{x_{t+1}} p(x_t, x_{t+1}|y_{1:T}) = \sum_{x_{t+1}} p(x_t|x_{t+1}, y_{1:t}, \cancel{y_{t+1:T}}) \gamma(x_{t+1}), \tag{1.6}$$

with $\gamma(x_T) \propto \alpha(x_T)$. The term $p(x_t|x_{t+1}, y_{1:t})$ is computed from filtering using

$$p(x_t|x_{t+1}, y_{1:t}) \propto p(x_{t+1}|x_t)\alpha(x_t),$$

where the proportionality constant is found by normalisation. The procedure is sequential since we need to complete the α recursions before starting the γ recursions. This technique is also termed the *Rauch–Tung–Striebel* smoother[10] and is a so-called correction smoother since it 'corrects' the filtered results. Interestingly, this correction process uses only filtered information. That is, once the filtered results have been computed, the observations $y_{1:T}$ are no longer needed. One can also view the γ recursion as a form of dynamics reversal, as if we were reversing the direction of the hidden-to-hidden arrows in the model.

---

[9]If only posterior distributions are required, one can also perform local normalisation at each stage, since only the relative magnitude of the components of β is of importance.

[10]It is most common to use this terminology for the continuous latent variable case.

Computing the pairwise marginal $p(x_t, x_{t+1}|y_{1:T})$

To implement algorithms for parameter learning, we often require terms such as $p(x_t, x_{t+1}|y_{1:T})$, see Section 1.5.1. These can be obtained from the sequential approach using

$$p(x_t, x_{t+1}|y_{1:T}) = p(x_t|x_{t+1}, y_{1:t})p(x_{t+1}|y_{1:T}),$$

or from the parallel approach using

$$p(x_t, x_{t+1}|y_{1:T}) \propto \beta(x_{t+1})p(y_{t+1}|x_{t+1})p(x_{t+1}|, x_t)\alpha(x_t). \tag{1.7}$$

1.4.4   Prediction $p(y_{t+1}|y_{1:t})$

Prediction is the problem of computing the posterior density $p(y_\tau|y_{1:t})$ for any $\tau > t$. For example, the distribution of the next observation may be found using

$$p(y_{t+1}|y_{1:t}) = \sum_{x_{t+1}} p(y_{t+1}|x_{t+1})p(x_{t+1}|y_{1:t}) = \sum_{x_{t+1}} p(y_{t+1}|x_{t+1}) \sum_{x_t} p(x_{t+1}|x_t)p(x_t|y_{1:t}).$$

1.4.5   Interpolation

Interpolation is the problem of estimating a set of missing observations given past and future data. This can be achieved using

$$p(y_\tau|y_{1:\tau-1}, y_{\tau+1:T}) \propto \sum_{x_\tau} p(y_\tau|x_\tau)p(x_\tau|y_{1:\tau-1})p(y_{\tau+1:T}|x_\tau).$$

1.4.6   Most likely latent trajectory

The most likely latent trajectory that explains the observations is given by

$$x_{1:T}^* = \underset{x_{1:T}}{\operatorname{argmax}}\, p(x_{1:T}|y_{1:T}).$$

In the literature $x_{1:T}^*$ is also called the *Viterbi path*. Since $y_{1:T}$ is known, $x_{1:T}^*$ is equivalent to $\operatorname{argmax}\, p(x_{1:T}, y_{1:T})$. By defining $\delta(x_t) \equiv \max_{x_{1:t-1}} p(x_{1:t}, y_{1:t})$, the most likely trajectory $x_{1:T}$ can be obtained with the following algorithm:

$$\delta(x_1) = p(x_1, y_1), \quad \delta(x_t) = p(y_t|x_t)\max_{x_{t-1}} p(x_t|x_{t-1})\delta(x_{t-1}) \quad \text{for } t = 2, \dots, T,$$

$$\psi(x_t) = \underset{x_{t-1}}{\operatorname{argmax}}\, p(x_t|x_{t-1})\delta(x_{t-1}) \quad \text{for } t = 2, \dots, T,$$

$$x_T^* = \underset{x_T}{\operatorname{argmax}}\, \delta(x_T), \quad x_t^* = \psi(x_{t+1}^*) \quad \text{for } t = T - 1, \dots, 1,$$

where the recursion for $\delta(x_t)$ is obtained analogously to the recursion (1.3) by replacing the sum with the max operator.

1.4.7   Inference in the linear dynamical system

Inference in the LDS has a long history and widespread applications ranging from tracking and control of ballistic projectiles to decoding brain signals.[11] The filtered and smoothed

---

[11] The LDS and associated filtering algorithm was proposed by Kalman in the late 1950s [14] based on least squares estimates. It is interesting to note that the method also appeared almost concurrently in the Russian literature, in a form that is surprisingly similar to the modern approach in terms of Bayes recursions [25]. Even earlier in the 1880s, Thiele defined the LDS and associated filtering and smoothing recursions [16].

posterior marginals, can be computed through conditioning and marginalisation of Gaussian distributions. The key results required for algebraic manipulation of Gaussians are stated below.

Gaussian conditioning, marginalisation and linear transformation

A multivariate Gaussian distribution is defined in the so-called moment form by

$$p(x) = \mathcal{N}(x|\mu, \Sigma) \equiv \frac{1}{\sqrt{\det 2\pi\Sigma}} e^{-\frac{1}{2}(x-\mu)^{\mathsf{T}}\Sigma^{-1}(x-\mu)},$$

where μ is the mean vector, and Σ is the covariance matrix.

Consider a vector z partitioned into two subvectors x and y,

$$z = \begin{pmatrix} x \\ y \end{pmatrix},$$

and a Gaussian distribution $\mathcal{N}(z|\mu, \Sigma)$ with corresponding partitioned mean and covariance

$$\mu = \begin{pmatrix} \mu_x \\ \mu_y \end{pmatrix}, \qquad \Sigma = \begin{pmatrix} \Sigma_{xx} & \Sigma_{xy} \\ \Sigma_{yx} & \Sigma_{yy} \end{pmatrix}, \quad \Sigma_{yx} \equiv \Sigma_{xy}^{\mathsf{T}}.$$

The distribution of x conditioned on y is then given by

$$p(x|y) = \mathcal{N}\left(x\middle|\mu_x + \Sigma_{xy}\Sigma_{yy}^{-1}(y-\mu_y), \Sigma_{xx} - \Sigma_{xy}\Sigma_{yy}^{-1}\Sigma_{yx}\right), \tag{1.8}$$

whilst the marginal distribution of x is given by $p(x) = \mathcal{N}(x|\mu_x, \Sigma_{xx})$.

A linear transformation $y = Ax$ of a Gaussian random variable x, with $p(x) = \mathcal{N}(x|\mu, \Sigma)$, is Gaussian with $p(y) = \mathcal{N}\left(y|A\mu, A\Sigma A^{\mathsf{T}}\right)$.

Filtering: predictor-corrector method

For continuous x, the analogue of recursion (1.3) is[12]

$$p(x_t|y_{1:t}) \propto p(x_t, y_t|y_{1:t-1}) = p(y_t|x_t)\int_{x_{t-1}} p(x_t|x_{t-1})p(x_{t-1}|y_{1:t-1}). \tag{1.9}$$

Since Gaussians are closed under multiplication and integration, the filtered distribution is also a Gaussian. This means that we may represent $p(x_t|y_{1:t}) = \mathcal{N}(x_t|f_t, F_t)$ and the filtered recursion translates into update formulae for the mean f_t and covariance F_t. One can derive these updates by carrying out the integration in Eq. (1.9). However, this is tedious and a shortcut is to use the linear transformation and conditioning results above. Specifically, let $\langle x|y \rangle$ denote expectation with respect to a distribution $p(x|y)$, and let $\Delta x \equiv x - \langle x \rangle$. By using the transition and emission models

$$x_t = Ax_{t-1} + \bar{x}_t + \epsilon_t^x, \qquad y_t = Cx_t + \bar{y}_t + \epsilon_t^y,$$

we obtain

$$\langle x_t|y_{1:t-1}\rangle = Af_{t-1} + \bar{x}_t, \quad \langle y_t|y_{1:t-1}\rangle = C\langle x_t|y_{1:t-1}\rangle + \bar{y}_t,$$

---

[12] With $\int_x$ we indicate the integral with respect to the variable x.

Algorithm 1.1 LDS forward pass. Compute the filtered posteriors $p(x_t|y_{1:t}) \equiv \mathcal{N}(f_t, F_t)$ for a LDS with parameters $\theta_t = A_t, C_t, Q_t, R_t, \bar{x}_t, \bar{y}_t$. The log-likelihood $L = \log p(y_{1:T})$ is also returned.

$\{f_1, F_1, p_1\} = \text{LDSFORWARD}(0, 0, y_1; \theta_1)$

$L \leftarrow \log p_1$

for $t \leftarrow 2, T$ **do**

    $\{f_t, F_t, p_t\} = \text{LDSFORWARD}(f_{t-1}, F_{t-1}, y_t; \theta_t)$

    $L \leftarrow L + \log p_t$

end for

function LDSFORWARD $(f, F, y; \theta)$

$\mu_x \leftarrow Af + \bar{x}$

$\mu_y \leftarrow C\mu_x + \bar{y}$

$\Sigma_{xx} \leftarrow AFA^\mathsf{T} + Q$

$\Sigma_{yy} \leftarrow C\Sigma_{xx}C^\mathsf{T} + R$

$\Sigma_{yx} \leftarrow C\Sigma_{xx}$ $\Sigma_{yx}^\mathsf{T}\Sigma_{yy}^{-1}$ is termed the Kalman gain matrix

$f' \leftarrow \mu_x + \Sigma_{yx}^\mathsf{T}\Sigma_{yy}^{-1}\left(y - \mu_y\right)$ updated mean

$F' \leftarrow \Sigma_{xx} - \Sigma_{yx}^\mathsf{T}\Sigma_{yy}^{-1}\Sigma_{yx}$ updated covariance

$p' \leftarrow \exp\left(-\frac{1}{2}\left(y - \mu_y\right)^\mathsf{T}\Sigma_{yy}^{-1}\left(y - \mu_y\right)\right) / \sqrt{\det 2\pi\Sigma_{yy}}$ likelihood contribution

return f', F', p'

---

and

$$\left\langle \Delta x_t \Delta x_t^\mathsf{T}|y_{1:t-1}\right\rangle = AF_{t-1}A^\mathsf{T} + Q, \quad \left\langle \Delta y_t \Delta x_t^\mathsf{T}|y_{1:t-1}\right\rangle = C\left(AF_{t-1}A^\mathsf{T} + Q\right),$$

$$\left\langle \Delta y_t \Delta y_t^\mathsf{T}|y_{1:t-1}\right\rangle = C\left(AF_{t-1}A^\mathsf{T} + Q\right)C^\mathsf{T} + R.$$

By conditioning $p(x_t, y_t|y_{1:t-1})$ on y_t using the formula (1.8), we obtain a Gaussian distribution with mean f_t and covariance F_t given by

$$f_t = \langle x_t|y_{1:t-1}\rangle + \left\langle \Delta x_t \Delta y_t^\mathsf{T}|y_{1:t-1}\right\rangle \left\langle \Delta y_t \Delta y_t^\mathsf{T}|y_{1:t-1}\right\rangle^{-1}(y_t - \langle y_t|y_{1:t-1}\rangle),$$

$$F_t = \left\langle \Delta x_t \Delta x_t^\mathsf{T}|y_{1:t-1}\right\rangle - \left\langle \Delta x_t \Delta y_t^\mathsf{T}|y_{1:t-1}\right\rangle \left\langle \Delta y_t \Delta y_t^\mathsf{T}|y_{1:t-1}\right\rangle^{-1}\left\langle \Delta y_t \Delta x_t^\mathsf{T}|y_{1:t-1}\right\rangle.$$

The resulting recursion is summarised in Algorithm 1.1, generalised to time-dependent noise means $\bar{x}_t, \bar{y}_t$ and time-dependent transition and emission noise covariances.

    Algebraically the updates generate a symmetric covariance F_t although, numerically, symmetry can be lost. This can be corrected by either including an additional symmetrisation step, or by parameterising the covariance using a square root approach [22]. A detailed discussion regarding the numerical stability of various representations is given in [26].

Smoothing: Rauch–Tung–Striebel/correction method

For reasons of numerical stability, the most common approach to smoothing is based on the sequential approach, for which the continuous analogue of Eq. (1.6) is

$$p(x_t|y_{1:T}) \propto \int_{x_{t+1}} p(x_t|y_{1:t}, y_{t+1:T}, x_{t+1})p(x_{t+1}|y_{1:T}).$$

Due to the closure properties of Gaussians, we may assume $p(x_t|y_{1:T}) = \mathcal{N}\left(x_t|g_t, G_t\right)$ and our task is to derive update formulae for the mean g_t and covariance G_t. Rather than long-handed integration, as in the derivation of the filtering updates, we can make use of some algebraic shortcuts. We note that $p(x_t|y_{1:t}, x_{t+1})$ can be found by first computing $p(x_t, x_{t+1}|y_{1:t})$ using the linear transition model, and then conditioning $p(x_t, x_{t+1}|y_{1:t})$ on x_{t+1}. Given that $p(x_t|y_{1:t})$ has mean f_t and covariance F_t, we obtain

$$\langle x_{t+1}|y_{1:t}\rangle = Af_t, \quad \langle \Delta x_t \Delta x_{t+1}^\mathsf{T}|y_{1:t}\rangle = F_t A^\mathsf{T}, \quad \langle \Delta x_{t+1} \Delta x_{t+1}^\mathsf{T}|y_{1:t}\rangle = AF_t A^\mathsf{T} + Q.$$

Therefore $p(x_t|y_{1:t}, x_{t+1})$ has mean

$$\langle x_t\rangle + \langle \Delta x_t \Delta x_{t+1}^\mathsf{T}\rangle \langle \Delta x_{t+1} \Delta x_{t+1}^\mathsf{T}\rangle^{-1}(x_{t+1} - \langle x_{t+1}\rangle) \tag{1.10}$$

and covariance

$$\overleftarrow{\Sigma}_t \equiv \langle \Delta x_t \Delta x_t^\mathsf{T}\rangle - \langle \Delta x_t \Delta x_{t+1}^\mathsf{T}\rangle \langle \Delta x_{t+1} \Delta x_{t+1}^\mathsf{T}\rangle^{-1} \langle \Delta x_{t+1} \Delta x_t^\mathsf{T}\rangle, \tag{1.11}$$

where the averages are conditioned on the observations $y_{1:t}$. Equations (1.10) and (1.11) are equivalent to a reverse-time linear system

$$x_t = \overleftarrow{A}_t x_{t+1} + \overleftarrow{m}_t + \overleftarrow{\eta}_t,$$

where

$$\overleftarrow{A}_t \equiv \langle \Delta x_t \Delta x_{t+1}^\mathsf{T}\rangle \langle \Delta x_{t+1} \Delta x_{t+1}^\mathsf{T}\rangle^{-1}, \quad \overleftarrow{m}_t \equiv \langle x_t\rangle - \langle \Delta x_t \Delta x_{t+1}^\mathsf{T}\rangle \langle \Delta x_{t+1} \Delta x_{t+1}^\mathsf{T}\rangle^{-1} \langle x_{t+1}\rangle,$$

and $\overleftarrow{\eta}_t \sim \mathcal{N}(\overleftarrow{\eta}_t|0, \overleftarrow{\Sigma}_t)$. The statistics of $p(x_t|y_{1:T})$ then follow from the linear transformation

$$g_t = \overleftarrow{A}_t g_{t+1} + \overleftarrow{m}_t, \quad G_t = \overleftarrow{A}_t G_{t+1} \overleftarrow{A}_t^\mathsf{T} + \overleftarrow{\Sigma}_t.$$

The recursion is summarised in Algorithm 1.2. The cross moment, which is often required for learning, is easily obtained as follows:

$$\langle \Delta x_t \Delta x_{t+1}^\mathsf{T}|y_{1:T}\rangle = \overleftarrow{A}_t G_{t+1} \Rightarrow \langle x_t x_{t+1}^\mathsf{T}|y_{1:T}\rangle = \overleftarrow{A}_t G_{t+1} + g_t g_{t+1}^\mathsf{T}.$$

1.4.8 Non-linear latent Markov models

The HMM and LDS are the two main tractable workhorses of probabilistic time series modelling. However, they lie at opposite ends of the modelling spectrum: the HMM assumes fully discrete latent variables, whilst the LDS assumes fully continuous latent variables restricted to linear updates under Gaussian noise. In practice one often encounters more complex scenarios: models requiring both continuous and discrete latent variables, continuous non-linear transitions, hierarchical models with tied parameters, etc. For such cases exact inference is typically computationally intractable and approximations are required. This forms a rich area of research, and the topic of several chapters of this book. Below we give a brief overview of some classical deterministic and stochastic approximate inference techniques that have been used in the time series context.

1.5 Deterministic approximate inference

In many deterministic approximate inference methods, a computationally intractable distribution is approximated with a tractable one by optimising an objective function. For example, one may assume a family of tractable distributions $q(x|\theta_q)$, parameterised by θ_q, and

---

Algorithm 1.2 LDS backward pass. Compute the smoothed posteriors $p(x_t|y_{1:T})$. This requires the filtered results from Algorithm 1.1.

$G_T \leftarrow F_T, g_T \leftarrow f_T$

for $t \leftarrow T - 1, 1$ **do**

$\quad \{g_t, G_t\} = \text{LDSBACKWARD}(g_{t+1}, G_{t+1}, f_t, F_t; \theta_t)$

end for

function LDSBACKWARD $(g, G, f, F; \theta)$

$\mu_x \leftarrow Af + \bar{x}$

$\Sigma_{x'x'} \leftarrow AFA^\mathsf{T} + Q$

$\Sigma_{x'x} \leftarrow AF$ $\hfill$ statistics of $p(x_t, x_{t+1}|y_{1:t})$

$\overleftarrow{\Sigma} \leftarrow F - \Sigma_{x'x}^\mathsf{T} \Sigma_{x'x'}^{-1} \Sigma_{x'x}$ $\hfill$ dynamics reversal $p(x_t|x_{t+1}, y_{1:t})$

$\overleftarrow{A} \leftarrow \Sigma_{x'x}^\mathsf{T} \Sigma_{x'x'}^{-1}$

$\overleftarrow{m} \leftarrow f - \overleftarrow{A}\mu_x$

$g' \leftarrow \overleftarrow{A} g + \overleftarrow{m}$ $\hfill$ backward propagation

$G' \leftarrow \overleftarrow{A} G \overleftarrow{A}^\mathsf{T} + \overleftarrow{\Sigma}$

return g', G'

---

find the best approximation to an intractable distribution $p(x)$ by minimising the Kullback–Leibler (KL) divergence $\text{KL}\big(q(x|\theta_q)|p(x)\big) = \big\langle \log(q(x|\theta_q)/p(x)) \big\rangle_{q(x|\theta_q)}$ with respect to θ_q. The optimal $q(x|\theta_q)$ is then used to answer inference questions. In the Bayesian context, parameter learning is also a form of inference problem which is intractable for most models of interest. Below we describe a popular procedure for approximating the parameter posterior based on minimising a KL divergence.

1.5.1 Variational Bayes

In Bayesian procedures, one doesn't seek a 'single best' parameter estimate θ, but rather a posterior distribution over θ given by

$$p(\theta|y_{1:T}) = \frac{p(y_{1:T}|\theta)p(\theta)}{p(y_{1:T})}.$$

In latent variable models, the marginal likelihood $p(y_{1:T})$ is given by

$$p(y_{1:T}) = \int_\theta \int_{x_{1:T}} p(x_{1:T}, y_{1:T}|\theta)p(\theta).$$

In practice, computing the integral over both θ and $x_{1:T}$ can be difficult. The idea in variational Bayes (VB) (see, for example, [27]) is to seek an approximation

$$p(x_{1:T}, \theta|y_{1:T}) \approx q(x_{1:T}, \theta|y_{1:T}),$$

where the distribution q is restricted to the form

$$q(x_{1:T}, \theta|y_{1:T}) = q(x_{1:T}|y_{1:T})q(\theta|y_{1:T}).$$

The best distribution q in this class can be obtained by minimising the KL divergence[13]

$$KL(q(x_{1:T})q(\theta)|p(x_{1:T},\theta|y_{1:T})) = \langle \log q(x_{1:T}) \rangle_{q(x_{1:T})}$$
$$+ \langle \log q(\theta) \rangle_{q(\theta)} - \left\langle \log \frac{p(y_{1:T}|x_{1:T},\theta)p(x_{1:T}|\theta)p(\theta)}{p(y_{1:T})} \right\rangle_{q(x_{1:T})q(\theta)}.$$

The non-negativity of the divergence results in a lower bound on the marginal likelihood

$$\log p(y_{1:T}) \geq - \langle \log q(x_{1:T}) \rangle_{q(x_{1:T})} - \langle \log q(\theta) \rangle_{q(\theta)}$$
$$+ \langle \log p(y_{1:T}|x_{1:T},\theta)p(x_{1:T}|\theta)p(\theta) \rangle_{q(x_{1:T})q(\theta)}.$$

In many cases of interest, this lower bound is computationally tractable. Minimising the KL divergence with respect to $q(x_{1:T})$ and $q(\theta)$ is equivalent to maximising the lower bound, which can be achieved by iterating the following numerical updates to convergence

1. $q(x_{1:T})^{new} \propto \exp \langle \log p(y_{1:T}|x_{1:T},\theta)p(x_{1:T}|\theta) \rangle_{q(\theta)}$

2. $q(\theta)^{new} \propto p(\theta) \exp \langle \log p(y_{1:T}|x_{1:T},\theta) \rangle_{q(x_{1:T})}$.

If we seek a point approximation $q(\theta) = \delta(\theta - \theta^*)$, the above simplifies to

1. $q(x_{1:T})^{new} \propto p(y_{1:T}|x_{1:T},\theta)p(x_{1:T}|\theta)$

2. $\theta^{new} = \underset{\theta}{\text{argmax}} \left\{ \langle \log p(y_{1:T}|x_{1:T},\theta) \rangle_{q(x_{1:T})} + \log p(\theta) \right\}$,

giving the penalised expectation maximisation (EM) algorithm [5]. For latent Markov models,

$$\langle \log p(y_{1:T}|x_{1:T},\theta) \rangle_{q(x_{1:T})} = \sum_t \langle \log p(y_t|x_t,\theta) \rangle_{q(x_t)} + \sum_t \langle \log p(x_t|x_{t-1},\theta) \rangle_{q(x_{t-1},x_t)}$$

so that the EM algorithm requires smoothed single and pairwise expectations [23].

1.5.2 Assumed density filtering

For more complex latent Markov models than the ones described in the previous sections, the filtering recursion (1.9) is in general numerically intractable. For continuous x_t and non-linear-Gaussian transition $p(x_t|x_{t-1})$ the integral over x_{t-1} may be difficult, or give rise to a distribution that is not in the same distributional family as $p(x_{t-1}|y_{1:t-1})$. In such cases, a useful approximation can be obtained with the assumed density filtering (ADF) method, in which the distribution obtained from the filtering recursion is projected back to a chosen family [1].

More specifically, assume that we are given an approximation $q(x_{t-1}|y_{1:t-1})$ to $p(x_{t-1}|y_{1:t-1})$, where $q(x_{t-1}|y_{1:t-1})$ is a distribution chosen for its numerical tractability (a Gaussian for example). Using the filtering recursion (1.9), we obtain an approximation for the filtered distribution at t

$$\tilde{q}(x_t|y_{1:t}) \propto \int_{x_{t-1}} p(y_t|x_t)p(x_t|x_{t-1})q(x_{t-1}|y_{1:t-1}).$$

---

[13]To simplify the subsequent expressions, we omit conditioning on the observations in the approximating distribution.

However, in general, $\tilde{q}(x_t|y_{1:t})$ will not be in the same family as $q(x_{t-1}|y_{1:t-1})$. To deal with this we project $\tilde{q}$ to the family q using

$$q(x_t|y_{1:t}) = \underset{q(x_t|y_{1:t})}{\operatorname{argmin}} \operatorname{KL}(\tilde{q}(x_t|y_{1:t})|q(x_t|y_{1:t})).$$

For q in the exponential family, this corresponds to matching the moments of $q(x_t|y_{1:t})$ to those of $\tilde{q}(x_t|y_{1:t})$. Assumed density filtering is a widely employed approximation method and also forms part of other methods, such as approximate smoothing methods. For example, ADF is employed as part of the expectation correction method for approximate smoothing in the switching LDS (see Chapter 8 of this book). Furthermore, many approximation methods are based on ADF-style approaches. Below, we provide one example of an ADF-style approximation method for a Poisson model.

Example   In this example, we discuss a model for tracking the number of objects in a given region based on noisy observations. Similar types of models appear in applications such as population dynamics (immigration) and multi-object tracking (see Chapters 3 and 11).

Suppose that, over time, objects of a specific type appear and disappear in a given region. At time step $t-1$, there are s_{t-1} objects in the region. At the next time step t, each of the s_{t-1} objects survives in the region independently of other objects with probability π_{sur}. We denote with $\bar{s}_t$ the number of surviving objects. Additionally, v_t new objects arrive with rate b, independent of existing objects, so that the number of objects present in the region at time step t becomes $s_t = \bar{s}_t + v_t$. By indicating with $\mathcal{BI}$ and $\mathcal{PO}$ the Binomial and Poisson distribution respectively, the specific survive–birth process is given by

Survive $\qquad \bar{s}_t|s_{t-1} \sim \mathcal{BI}(\bar{s}_t|s_{t-1}, \pi_{sur}) = \binom{s_{t-1}}{\bar{s}_t}\pi_{sur}^{\bar{s}_t}(1 - \pi_{sur})^{s_{t-1}-\bar{s}_t},$

Birth $\qquad s_t = \bar{s}_t + v_t, \qquad v_t \sim \mathcal{PO}(v_t|b) = \dfrac{b^{v_t}}{v_t!}e^{-b}.$

Due to errors, each of the s_t objects is detected only with probability π_{det}, meaning that some objects remain possibly undetected. We denote with $\hat{s}_t$ the number of detected objects among the s_t objects. On the other hand, there is a number e_t of spurious objects that are detected (with rate c), so that we actually observe $y_t = \hat{s}_t + e_t$ objects. The specific detect–observe process is given by

Detect $\qquad \hat{s}_t|s_t \sim \mathcal{BI}(\hat{s}_t|s_t, \pi_{det}),$

Observe in clutter $\qquad y_t = \hat{s}_t + e_t, \qquad e_t \sim \mathcal{PO}(e_t|c).$

The belief network representation of this model is given in Fig. 1.8.

The inferential goal is to estimate the true number of objects s_t from the filtered posterior $p(s_t|y_{1:t})$. Unfortunately, the filtered posterior is not a distribution in any standard form and becomes increasingly difficult to represent as we proceed in time. To deal with this, we make use of an ADF-style approach to obtain a Poisson approximation to the filtered posterior at each time step.

If we assume that $p(s_{t-1}|y_{1:t-1})$ is Poisson, then a natural way to compute $p(s_t|y_{1:t})$ would be to use

$$p(s_t|y_{1:t}) \propto p(y_t|s_t)p(s_t|y_{1:t-1}).$$

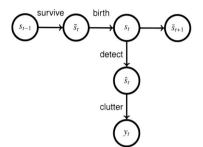

Figure 1.8 Belief network representation of the counting model. The goal is to compute the filtering density $p(s_t|y_{1:t})$. Nodes $\hat{s}_{t-1}$, y_{t-1} are omitted for clarity.

The first term $p(y_t|s_t)$ is obtained as the sum of a Binomial and a Poisson random variable. The second term $p(s_t|y_{1:t-1})$ may be computed recursively from $p(s_{t-1}|y_{1:t-1})$ and is Poisson distributed (see below). Performing ADF moment matching of the non-standard $p(s_t|y_{1:t})$ to a Poisson distribution is however not straightforward.

A simpler alternative approach (and not generally equivalent to fitting the best Poisson distribution to $p(s_t|y_{1:t})$ in the minimal KL divergence sense) is to project $p(\hat{s}_t|y_{1:t})$ to a Poisson distribution using moment matching and then form

$$p(s_t|y_{1:t}) = \sum_{\hat{s}_t} p(s_t|\hat{s}_t, y_{1:t-1})p(\hat{s}_t|y_{1:t}) = \sum_{\hat{s}_t} \frac{p(s_t, \hat{s}_t, y_{1:t-1})}{p(\hat{s}_t, y_{1:t-1})}p(\hat{s}_t|y_{1:t})$$
$$= p(s_t|y_{1:t-1})\sum_{\hat{s}_t}\frac{p(\hat{s}_t|s_t)}{p(\hat{s}_t|y_{1:t-1})}p(\hat{s}_t|y_{1:t}), \qquad (1.12)$$

which, as we will see, is also Poisson distributed. Before proceeding with explaining the recursion, we state two useful results for Poisson random variables. Let s and e be Poisson random variables with respective intensities λ and ν. Then

Superposition The sum $y = s + e$ is Poisson distributed with intensity $\lambda + \nu$.

Conditioning The distribution of s conditioned on e is given by $p(s|e) = \mathcal{BI}(s|e, \lambda/\nu)$.

Using these results we can derive a recursion as follows. At time $t - 1$ we assume $p(s_{t-1}|y_{1:t-1}) = \mathcal{PO}(s_{t-1}|\lambda_{t-1|t-1})$. This gives

$$p(\bar{s}_t|y_{1:t-1}) = \sum_{s_{t-1}} p(\bar{s}_t|s_{t-1})p(s_{t-1}|y_{1:t-1}) = \mathcal{PO}(\bar{s}_t|\pi_{sur}\lambda_{t-1|t-1}),$$

where we have used the following general result derived from the conditioning property:

$$\sum_n \mathcal{BI}(m|n, \pi)\mathcal{PO}(n|\lambda) = \mathcal{PO}(m|\pi\lambda).$$

From the birth process and using the superposition property we obtain

$$p(s_t|y_{1:t-1}) = \mathcal{PO}(s_t|\lambda_{t|t-1}), \qquad \lambda_{t|t-1} = b + \pi_{sur}\lambda_{t-1|t-1}.$$

This gives

$$p(\hat{s}_t|y_{1:t-1}) = \sum_{s_t} p(\hat{s}_t|s_t)p(s_t|y_{1:t-1}) = \mathcal{PO}(\hat{s}_t|\pi_{det}\lambda_{t|t-1}).$$

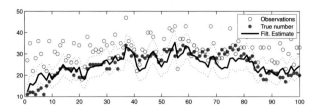

Figure 1.9 Assumed density filtering for object tracking. The horizontal axis denotes the time index and the vertical axis the number of objects. The dotted lines represent one standard deviation of the filtered posterior.

From the observe in clutter process and using the superposition property we obtain the predictive distribution

$$p(y_t|y_{1:t-1}) = \mathcal{PO}(y_t|\lambda_{t|t-1}\pi_{det} + c).$$

The posterior distribution of the number of detected objects is therefore

$$p(\hat{s}_t|y_{1:t}) = \mathcal{BI}(\hat{s}_t|y_t, \lambda_{t|t-1}\pi_{det}/(\lambda_{t|t-1}\pi_{det} + c)).$$

A well-known Poisson approximation to the Binomial distribution based on moment matching has intensity

$$\lambda^* = \underset{\lambda}{\text{argmin}} \, \text{KL}(\mathcal{BI}(s|y, \pi)|\mathcal{PO}(s|\lambda)) = y\pi,$$

so that

$$p(\hat{s}_t|y_{1:t}) \approx \mathcal{PO}(\hat{s}_t|\gamma), \qquad \gamma \equiv y_t\lambda_{t|t-1}\pi_{det}/(\lambda_{t|t-1}\pi_{det} + c).$$

Using Eq. (1.12) with the Poisson approximation to $p(\hat{s}_t|y_{1:t})$, we obtain

$$p(s_t|y_{1:t}) \approx \mathcal{PO}(s_t|\lambda_{t|t-1}) \sum_{\hat{s}_t} \frac{\mathcal{BI}(\hat{s}_t|s_t, \pi_{det})}{\mathcal{PO}(\hat{s}_t|\pi_{det}\lambda_{t|t-1})} \mathcal{PO}(\hat{s}_t|\gamma)$$

$$\propto \frac{(\lambda_{t|t-1}(1 - \pi_{det}))^{s_t}}{s_t!} \underbrace{\sum_{\hat{s}_t} \binom{s_t}{\hat{s}_t} \left(\frac{\gamma}{\lambda_{t|t-1}(1 - \pi_{det})} \right)^{\hat{s}_t}}_{\left(1 + \frac{\gamma}{\lambda_{t|t-1}(1-\pi_{det})}\right)^{s_t}},$$

so that

$$p(s_t|y_{1:t}) \approx \mathcal{PO}(s_t|\lambda_{t|t}), \qquad \lambda_{t|t} = (1 - \pi_{det})\lambda_{t|t-1} + y_t \frac{\pi_{det}\lambda_{t|t-1}}{c + \pi_{det}\lambda_{t|t-1}}.$$

Intuitively, the first term in $\lambda_{t|t}$ corresponds to the undetected objects, whilst the second term is the Poisson approximation to the Binomial posterior that results from observing the sum of two Poisson random variables with intensities c and $\pi_{det}\lambda_{t|t-1}$. At time $t = 1$, we initialise the intensity $\lambda_{1|0}$ to the birth intensity.

In Fig. 1.9, we show the results of the filtering recursion on data generated from the model. As we can see, the tracking performance is good even though the filter involves an approximation.

This technique is closely related to the *Poissonisation* method used heavily in probabilistic analysis of algorithms [20]. In Chapters 3 and 11, an extension called the probability hypothesis density (PHD) filter to multi-object tracking is considered. Instead of tracking a scalar intensity, an intensity function over the whole space is approximated. The PHD filter combines ADF with approximate inference methods such as sequential Monte Carlo (see Section 1.6).

1.5.3 Expectation propagation

In this section, we review another powerful deterministic approximation technique called expectation propagation (EP) [19]. We present here EP in the context of approximating the posterior $p(x_t|y_{1:T})$ of a continuous latent Markov model $p(x_{1:T}, y_{1:T})$, see also Chapter 7. According to Eqs. (1.4) and (1.7), the exact single and pairwise marginals have the form

$$p(x_t|y_{1:T}) \propto \alpha(x_t)\beta(x_t),$$
$$p(x_t, x_{t+1}|y_{1:T}) \propto \alpha(x_t)p(y_{t+1}|x_{t+1})p(x_{t+1}|, x_t)\beta(x_{t+1}).$$

Starting from these equations, we can retrieve the recursions (1.3)–(1.5) for α and β by requiring that the single marginal is consistent with the pairwise marginal, that is

$$p(x_{t+1}|y_{1:T}) = \int_{x_t} p(x_t, x_{t+1}|y_{1:T}),$$
$$\alpha(x_{t+1})\beta(x_{t+1}) \propto \int_{x_t} \alpha(x_t)p(y_{t+1}|x_{t+1})p(x_{t+1}|, x_t)\beta(x_{t+1}).$$

Cancelling $\beta(x_{t+1})$ from both sides we immediately retrieve the standard α recursion. One may derive the β recursion similarly by integrating the pairwise marginal over x_{t+1}. For complex situations, the resulting $\alpha(x_{t+1})$ is not in the same family as $\alpha(x_t)$, giving rise to representational difficulties. As in ADF, we therefore project $\alpha(x_{t+1})$ back to a chosen family. Whilst this is reasonably well defined, since $\alpha(x_{t+1})$ represents a filtered distribution, it is unclear how to project $\beta(x_t)$ to a chosen family since $\beta(x_t)$ is not a distribution in x_t. In EP, this problem is resolved by first defining

$$\tilde{q}(x_{t+1}) \propto \int_{x_t} \alpha(x_t)p(y_{t+1}|x_{t+1})p(x_{t+1}|, x_t)\beta(x_{t+1}),$$

and then iterating the following updates to convergence

$$\alpha(x_{t+1}) = \underset{\alpha(x_{t+1})}{\operatorname{argmin}} \operatorname{KL}\left(\tilde{q}(x_{t+1})|\frac{1}{Z_{t+1}}\alpha(x_{t+1})\beta(x_{t+1})\right),$$
$$\beta(x_t) = \underset{\beta(x_t)}{\operatorname{argmin}} \operatorname{KL}\left(\tilde{q}(x_t)|\frac{1}{Z_t}\alpha(x_t)\beta(x_t)\right),$$

where Z_t and Z_{t+1} are normalisation constants. In exponential family approximations, these updates correspond to matching the moments of $\tilde{q}$ to the moments of $\alpha(x)\beta(x)$.

1.6 Monte Carlo inference

Many inference problems such as filtering and smoothing can be considered as computing expectations with respect to a (posterior) distribution. A general numerical method for approximating the expectation $\mathrm{E}_\pi[\varphi(x)] = \int_x \varphi(x)\pi(x)$ of a function φ of a random variable x is given by sampling. Consider a procedure that draws samples from a multivariate distribution $\hat{\pi}(x^1, \ldots, x^N)$. For $X = \{x^1, \ldots, x^N\}$, the random variable

$$\bar{E}_{X,N} \equiv \frac{\varphi(x^1) + \cdots + \varphi(x^N)}{N}$$

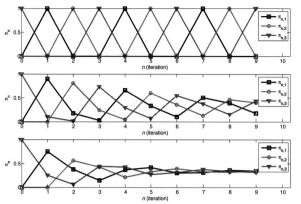

$\epsilon = 0$: Periodic chain that fails to converge to a stationary distribution.

$\epsilon = 0.1$: Chain that converges to the stationary (uniform) distribution.

$\epsilon = 0.25$: Chain that converges to the stationary (uniform) distribution more quickly than for $\epsilon = 0.1$.

Figure 1.10 Convergence to the stationary distribution. For $\epsilon = 0$, the state transition diagram would be disconnected, hence the chain fails to be irreducible and therefore to converge.

has expectation

$$\mathsf{E}_{\hat{\pi}}\left[\bar{E}_{X,N}\right] = \frac{1}{N} \sum_n \mathsf{E}_{\hat{\pi}}\left[\phi(x^n)\right].$$

If the marginal distribution of each x^n is equal to the target distribution

$$\hat{\pi}(x^n) = \pi(x^n), \qquad n = 1, \ldots, N$$

then

$$\mathsf{E}_{\hat{\pi}}\left[\bar{E}_{X,N}\right] = \mathsf{E}_\pi\left[\varphi(x)\right],$$

that is $\bar{E}_{X,N}$ is an unbiased estimator of $\mathsf{E}_\pi\left[\varphi(x)\right]$. If, in addition, the samples are generated independently,

$$\hat{\pi}(x^1, \ldots, x^N) = \prod_{n=1}^{N} \hat{\pi}(x^n),$$

and $\mathsf{E}_\pi\left[\varphi(x)\right]$ and $\mathsf{V}_\pi[\varphi(x)]$ are finite, the central limit theorem guarantees that, for sufficiently large N, $\bar{E}_{X,N}$ is Gaussian distributed with mean and covariance

$$\mathsf{E}_\pi\left[\varphi(x)\right], \qquad \frac{\mathsf{V}_\pi[\varphi(x)]}{N}.$$

That is the variance of the estimator drops with increasing N. These results have important practical consequences: If we have a procedure that draws *iid* samples $x^1, \ldots, x^N$ from π, then the sample average $\bar{E}_{X,N}$ converges rapidly to the exact expectation $\mathsf{E}_\pi\left[\varphi(x)\right]$ as N increases and provides a 'noisy' but unbiased estimator for any finite N. For large N the error behaves as $N^{-1/2}$ and is independent of the dimensionality of x. The key difficulty, however, is in generating independent samples from the target distribution π. Below we discuss various Monte Carlo methods that asymptotically provide samples from the target distribution, varying in the degree to which they generate independent samples.

1.6.1 Markov chain Monte Carlo

In Markov chain Monte Carlo (MCMC) methods, samples from a desired complex distribution $\pi(x)$ are approximated with samples from a simpler distribution defined by a specially constructed time-homogeneous Markov chain. Given an initial state x^1, a set of samples $x^2, \ldots, x^N$ from the chain are obtained by iteratively drawing from the transition distribution ('kernel') $K(x^n|x^{n-1})$.[14] The distribution $\pi_n(x^n)$ satisfies

$$\pi_n(x^n) = \int_{x^{n-1}} K(x^n|x^{n-1})\pi_{n-1}(x^{n-1}),$$

which we compactly write as $\pi_n = K\pi_{n-1}$. The theory of Markov chains characterises the convergence of the sequence $\pi_1, \pi_2, \ldots$ If the sequence converges to a distribution π, then π (called the stationary distribution) satisfies $\pi = K\pi$. For an ergodic chain, namely irreducible and aperiodic,[15] there exists a unique stationary distribution to which the sequence converges, irrespective of the initial state x^1. To illustrate the idea, consider the Markov chain of Section 1.3.1 in which the robot moves freely under the transition model defined in Eq. (1.1), repeated here for convenience

$$K = \epsilon \begin{pmatrix} 1 & 0 & 0 \\ 0 & 1 & 0 \\ 0 & 0 & 1 \end{pmatrix} + (1-\epsilon) \begin{pmatrix} 0 & 0 & 1 \\ 1 & 0 & 0 \\ 0 & 1 & 0 \end{pmatrix}.$$

The robot starts at cell 3, i.e., $\pi_1 = (\pi_{11}, \pi_{12}, \pi_{13}) = (0, 0, 1)^\top$. In Fig. 1.10, we plot the cell probabilities of $\pi_n = K^{n-1}\pi_1$ as n increases for various choices of ϵ. Provided $0 < \epsilon \leq 1$, all chains converge to the uniform distribution $\pi = (1/3, 1/3, 1/3)$, however, with differing convergence rates.

   This discussion suggests that, if we can design a transition kernel K such that the associated Markov chain is ergodic and has the target distribution π as its stationary distribution, at least in principle we can generate samples from the Markov chain that eventually will tend to be from π. After ignoring the initial 'burn in' part of the generated path as the sequence moves to the stationary distribution, the subsequent part can be used to estimate expectations under π. Notice, however, that the samples generated will typically be dependent and therefore the variance of the estimate may not scale inversely with the number of samples from the chain.

Metropolis–Hastings

Designing a transition kernel K for a given target π is straightforward via the approach proposed by Metropolis [18] and later generalised by Hastings [12]. Suppose that we are given a target density $\pi = \phi/Z$, where Z is a (possibly unknown) normalisation constant. The Metropolis–Hastings (MH) algorithm uses a proposal density $q(x|x')$ for generating a candidate sample x, which is accepted with probability $0 \leq \alpha(x|x') \leq 1$ defined as

$$\alpha(x|x') = \min\left\{1, \frac{q(x'|x)\pi(x)}{q(x|x')\pi(x')}\right\}.$$

The MH transition kernel K has the following form

$$K(x|x') = q(x|x')\alpha(x|x') + \delta(x - x')\rho(x'),$$

---

[14]Note that the sample index is conceptually different from the time index in a time series model; here n is the iteration number of the sampling algorithm.

[15]For finite state Markov chains, irreducibility means that each state can be visited starting from any other, while aperiodicity means that each state can be visited at any iteration n larger than some fixed number.

Algorithm 1.3 Metropolis–Hastings

1: Initialise x^1 arbitrarily.
2: **for** $n = 2, 3 \ldots$ **do**
3:        Propose a candidate: $x^{\text{cand}} \sim q(x^{\text{cand}}|x^{n-1})$.
4:        Compute acceptance probability:

$$\alpha(x^{\text{cand}}|x^{n-1}) = \min\left\{1, \frac{q(x^{n-1}|x^{\text{cand}})\pi(x^{\text{cand}})}{q(x^{\text{cand}}|x^{n-1})\pi(x^{n-1})}\right\}.$$

5:        Sample from uniform distribution: $u \sim \mathcal{U}(u|[0, 1])$.
6:        **if** $u < \alpha$ **then**
7:              Accept candidate: $x^n \leftarrow x^{\text{cand}}$.
8:        **else**
9:              Reject candidate: $x^n \leftarrow x^{n-1}$.
10:      **end if**
11: **end for**

---

where $0 \leq \rho(x') \leq 1$ is defined as

$$\rho(x') = \int (1 - \alpha(x|x'))q(x|x')\mathrm{d}x.$$

This kernel satisfies the *detailed balance* property

$$
\begin{aligned}
K(x|x')\pi(x') &= (q(x|x')\alpha(x|x') + \delta(x - x')\rho(x'))\pi(x') \\
&= q(x|x')\min\left\{1, \frac{q(x'|x)\pi(x)}{q(x|x')\pi(x')}\right\}\pi(x') + \delta(x - x')\rho(x')\pi(x') \\
&= \min\{q(x|x')\pi(x'), q(x'|x)\pi(x)\} + \delta(x - x')\rho(x')\pi(x') \\
&= q(x'|x)\min\left\{\frac{q(x|x')\pi(x')}{q(x'|x)\pi(x)}, 1\right\}\pi(x) + \delta(x' - x)\rho(x)\pi(x) \\
&= K(x'|x)\pi(x).
\end{aligned}
$$

By integrating both sides over x', we obtain

$$\pi(x) = \int K(x|x')\pi(x')\mathrm{d}x',$$

and therefore π is a stationary distribution of K. Note that to compute the acceptance probability α we only need to evaluate ϕ, since the normalisation constant Z cancels out. For a given target π and proposal $q(x'|x)$ we now have a procedure for sampling from a Markov chain with stationary distribution π. The procedure is detailed in Algorithm 1.3.

Gibbs sampling

The Gibbs sampler [10, 17] is a MCMC method which is suitable for sampling a multivariate random variable $x = (x_1, \ldots, x_D)$ with joint distribution $p(x)$. Gibbs sampling proceeds by partitioning the set of variables x into a chosen variable x_i and the rest $x = (x_i, x_{-i})$. The assumption is that the conditional distributions $p(x_i|x_{-i})$ are tractable. One then proceeds coordinate-wise by sampling from the conditionals as in Algorithm 1.4.

Gibbs sampling can be viewed as MH sampling with the proposal

$$q(x|x') = p(x_i|x'_{-i})\delta(x_{-i} - x'_{-i}).$$

Algorithm 1.4 Gibbs sampler

1: Initialise $x^1 = (x_1^1, \ldots, x_D^1)$ arbitrarily.
2: **for** $n = 2, 3 \ldots$ **do**
3:      $x_1^n \sim p(x_1^n | x_2^{n-1}, x_3^{n-1}, \ldots, x_D^{n-1})$.
4:      $x_2^n \sim p(x_2^n | x_1^n, x_3^{n-1}, \ldots, x_D^{n-1})$.
     $\vdots$
5:      $x_D^n \sim p(x_D^n | x_1^n, x_2^n, \ldots, x_{D-1}^n)$.
6: **end for**

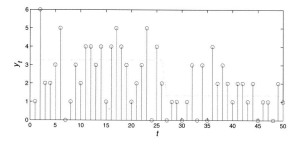

Figure 1.11 A typical realisation from the changepoint model. The time index is indicated by t and the number of counts by y_t. The true intensities are shown with a dotted line: at time step $\tau = 26$, the intensity drops from $\lambda_1 = 3.2$ to $\lambda_2 = 1.2$.

Using this proposal results in a MH acceptance probability of 1, so that every candidate sample is accepted. Dealing with evidence (variables in known states) is straightforward – one sets the evidential variables into their states and samples from the remaining variables.

Example: Gibbs sampling for a changepoint model

We illustrate the Gibbs sampler on a changepoint model for count data [13]. In this model, at each time t we observe the count of an event y_t. All the counts up to an unknown time τ are *iid* realisations from a Poisson distribution with intensity λ_1. From time $\tau + 1$ to T, the counts come from a Poisson distribution with intensity λ_2. We assume that the changepoint τ is uniformly distributed over $1, \ldots, T$ and that the intensities λ_1, λ_2 are Gamma distributed

$$\mathcal{G}(\lambda_i | a, b) = \frac{1}{\Gamma(a)} b^a \lambda_i^{a-1} e^{-b\lambda_i}, \qquad i = 1, 2.$$

This leads to the following generative model

$$\tau \;\sim\; \mathcal{U}(\tau | 1, \ldots, T), \quad \lambda_i \sim \mathcal{G}(\lambda_i | a, b), \qquad i = 1, 2,$$

$$y_t \;\sim\; \begin{cases} \mathcal{PO}(y_t | \lambda_1) & 1 \leq t \leq \tau, \\ \mathcal{PO}(y_t | \lambda_2) & \tau < t \leq T. \end{cases}$$

A typical draw from this model is shown in Fig. 1.11. The inferential goal is to compute the posterior distribution $p(\lambda_1, \lambda_2, \tau | y_{1:T})$ of the intensities and changepoint given the count data. In this problem this posterior is actually tractable and serves to assess the quality of the Gibbs sampling approximation.

    To implement Gibbs sampling we need to compute the distribution of each variable, conditioned on the rest. These conditionals can be conveniently derived by writing the log

---

Algorithm 1.5 A Gibbs sampler for the changepoint model

1: Initialise λ_2^1, τ^1.
2: **for** $n = 2, 3 \ldots$ **do**
3:     $\lambda_1^n \sim p(\lambda_1^n|\tau^{n-1}, y_{1:T}) = \mathcal{G}(a + \sum_{t=1}^{\tau^{n-1}} y_t, \tau^{n-1} + b)$.
4:     $\lambda_2^n \sim p(\lambda_2^n|\tau^{n-1}, y_{1:T}) = \mathcal{G}(a + \sum_{t=\tau^{n-1}+1}^{T} y_t, T - \tau^{n-1} + b)$.
5:     $\tau^n \sim p(\tau^n|\lambda_1^n, \lambda_2^n, y_{1:T})$.
6: **end for**

---

of the joint distribution of all variables and collecting terms that depend only on the free variable. The log of the joint distribution is given by

$$\log p(y_{1:T}, \lambda_1, \lambda_2, \tau) = \log \left(p(\lambda_1)p(\lambda_2)p(\tau) \prod_{t=1}^{\tau} p(y_t|\lambda_1) \prod_{t=\tau+1}^{T} p(y_t|\lambda_2) \right).$$

This gives

$$\log p(\lambda_1|\tau, \lambda_2, y_{1:T}) = \left(a + \sum_{t=1}^{\tau} y_t - 1 \right) \log \lambda_1 - (\tau + b)\lambda_1 + \text{const.},$$

$$\log p(\tau|\lambda_1, \lambda_2, y_{1:T}) = \sum_{t=1}^{\tau} y_t \log \lambda_1 + \sum_{t=\tau+1}^{T} y_t \log \lambda_2 + \tau(\lambda_2 - \lambda_1) + \text{const.},$$

and a similar form for $\log p(\lambda_1|\tau, y_{1:T})$, so that both $p(\lambda_1|\tau, y_{1:T})$ and $p(\lambda_2|\tau, y_{1:T})$ are Gamma distributions. The resulting Gibbs sampler is given in Algorithm 1.5. Samples from the obtained posterior distribution are plotted in Fig. 1.12. For this particularly simple problem, Gibbs sampling works well, with the estimated sample marginal estimates of λ and τ close to the values we expect based on the known parameters used to generate the data.

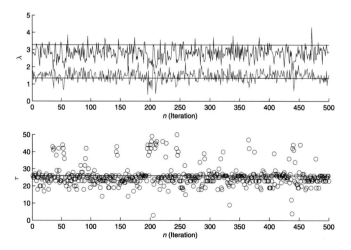

Figure 1.12 Gibbs samples from the posterior of the changepoint model vs. sample iteration. True values are shown with a horizontal line. (top) Intensities λ_1 and λ_2. (bottom) Changepoint index τ.

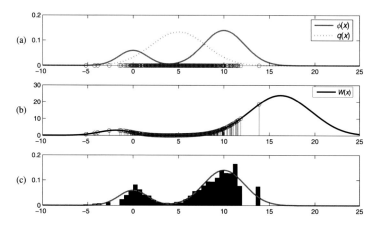

Figure 1.13 Importance sampling. (a) The solid curve denotes the unnormalised target distribution $\phi(x)$ and the dashed curve the tractable IS distribution $q(x)$. Samples from $q(x)$ are assumed straightforward to generate and are plotted on the axis. (b) To account for the fact that the samples are from q and not from the target p, we need to reweight the samples. The IS distribution q generates too many samples where p has low mass, and too few where p has high mass. The samples in these regions are reweighted accordingly. (c) Binning the weighted samples from q, we obtain an approximation to p such that averages with respect to this approximation will be close to averages with respect to p.

1.6.2 Sequential Monte Carlo

The MCMC techniques described above are batch algorithms that require the availability of all data records. These techniques are therefore unsuitable when the data needs to be processed sequentially and can be prohibitive for long time series. In such cases, it is desirable to use alternative methods which process the data sequentially and take a constant time per observation. In this context, sequential Monte Carlo (SMC) techniques [6, 8] have proved useful in many applications. These methods are based on importance sampling/resampling which we review below.

Importance sampling

Suppose that we are interested in computing the expectation $\mathsf{E}_p\left[\varphi(x)\right]$ with respect to a distribution $p(x) = \phi(x)/Z$, where the non-negative function $\phi(x)$ is known but the overall normalisation constant Z is assumed to be computationally intractable. In importance sampling (IS), instead of sampling from the target distribution $p(x)$, we sample from a tractable distribution $q(x)$ and reweight the obtained samples to form an unbiased estimator of $\mathsf{E}_p\left[\varphi(x)\right]$. IS is based on the realisation that we can write the expectation with respect to p as a ratio of expectations with respect to q, that is

$$\mathsf{E}_p\left[\varphi(x)\right] = \frac{1}{Z}\int \varphi(x)\frac{\phi(x)}{q(x)}q(x) = \frac{\mathsf{E}_q\left[\varphi(x)W(x)\right]}{Z} = \frac{\mathsf{E}_q\left[\varphi(x)W(x)\right]}{\mathsf{E}_q\left[W(x)\right]},$$

where $W(x) \equiv \phi(x)/q(x)$ is called the *weight function*. Thus $\mathsf{E}_p\left[\varphi(x)\right]$ can be approximated using samples $x^1,\ldots,x^N$ from q as

$$\frac{\sum_{i=1}^{N}W^i\varphi(x^i)/N}{\sum_{i=1}^{N}W^i/N},$$

where $W^i \equiv W(x^i)$. The samples $x^1, \ldots, x^N$ are also known as 'particles'. Using normalised weights $w^i \equiv W^i / \sum_{i'=1}^{N} W^{i'}$, we can write the approximation as

$$\sum_{i=1}^{N} w^i \varphi(x^i).$$

An example for a bimodal distribution $p(x)$ and unimodal distribution $q(x)$ is given in Fig. 1.13, showing how the weights compensate for the mismatch between q and p.

1.6.3   Resampling

Unless the IS distribution $q(x)$ is close to the target distribution $p(x)$, the normalised weights will typically have significant mass in only a single component. This issue can be partially addressed using resampling. Given a weighted particle system $\sum_{i=1}^{N} w^i \delta(x - x^i)$, resampling is the term for a set of methods for generating randomly a reweighted particle system of the form $\frac{1}{M} \sum_{i=1}^{N} n_i \delta(x - x^i)$. Specifically, a resampling algorithm returns an occupancy vector $n_1, \ldots, n_N$ which satisfies $n_i \in \{0, 1, 2, \ldots, M\}$, $\sum_i n_i = M$. For the resampling algorithm to produce an unbiased estimator of the original system $\sum_{i=1}^{N} w^i \delta(x - x^i)$ we require

$$\mathsf{E}\Big[\frac{1}{M} \sum_{i=1}^{N} n_i \delta(x - x^i)\Big] = \sum_{i=1}^{N} \frac{1}{M} \mathsf{E}[n_i] \delta(x - x^i).$$

Hence, provided $\mathsf{E}[n_i] = M w^i$, expectations carried out using the resampled particles will be unbiased. It is typical (though not necessary) to set $M = N$. Intuitively, resampling is a randomised pruning algorithm in which we discard particles with low weight. Unlike a deterministic pruning algorithm, the random but unbiased nature of resampling ensures an asymptotically consistent algorithm. For a discussion and comparison of resampling schemes in the context of SMC see [3, 8].

1.6.4   Sequential importance sampling

We now apply IS to the latent Markov models of Section 1.3. The resulting sequential IS methods are also known as particle filters. The goal is to estimate the posterior

$$p(x_{1:t}|y_{1:t}) = \underbrace{p(y_{1:t}|x_{1:t})p(x_{1:t})}_{\phi(x_{1:t})} / \underbrace{p(y_{1:t})}_{Z_t},$$

where we assume that the normalisation term Z_t is intractable. At each time t, we have an importance distribution $q_t(x_{1:t})$, from which we draw samples $x_{1:t}^i$ with corresponding importance weights

$$W_t^i = \phi(x_{1:t}^i)/q_t(x_{1:t}^i).$$

Without loss of generality, we can construct q sequentially

$$q_t(x_{1:t}) = q_t(x_t|x_{1:t-1})q_t(x_{1:t-1}).$$

In particle filtering, one chooses a distribution q that only updates the current x_t and leaves previous samples unaffected. This is achieved using

$$q_t(x_{1:t}) = q_t(x_t|x_{1:t-1})q_{t-1}(x_{1:t-1}).$$

The weight function $W_t(x_{1:t})$ then admits a recursive formulation

$$W_t(x_{1:t}) = \frac{\phi(x_{1:t})}{q_t(x_{1:t})} = \frac{p(y_t|x_t)p(x_t|x_{t-1})\prod_{\tau=1}^{t-1} p(y_\tau|x_\tau)p(x_\tau|x_{\tau-1})}{q_t(x_t|x_{1:t-1})\prod_{\tau=1}^{t-1} q_\tau(x_\tau|x_{1:\tau-1})}$$

$$= \underbrace{\frac{p(y_t|x_t)p(x_t|x_{t-1})}{q_t(x_t|x_{1:t-1})}}_{v_t} W_{t-1}(x_{1:t-1}),$$

where v_t is called the incremental weight. Particle filtering algorithms differ in their choices for $q_t(x_t|x_{1:t-1})$. The optimal choice (in terms of reducing the variance of the weights) is the one step filtering distribution [7]

$$q_t(x_t|x_{1:t-1}) = p(x_t|x_{t-1}, y_t).$$

However, sampling from this distribution is difficult in practice, and simpler distributions are therefore employed. The *bootstrap* filter uses the transition

$$q_t(x_t|x_{1:t-1}) = p(x_t|x_{t-1}),$$

for which the incremental weight becomes $v_t = p(y_t|x_t)$. In this case, the IS distribution does not make any use of the recent observation and therefore has the tendency to lose track of the high probability regions of the posterior. Indeed, it can be shown that the variance of the importance weights for the bootstrap filter increases in an unbounded fashion [7, 17] so that, after a few time steps, the particle set typically loses track of the exact posterior mode. A crucial extra step to make the algorithm work is resampling, which prunes branches with low weights and keeps the particle set located in high probability regions. It can be shown that, although the particles become dependent due to resampling, the estimations are still consistent and converge to the true values as the number of particles increases to infinity.

A generic particle filter is given in Algorithm 1.6 and in Fig. 1.14 we illustrate the dynamics of the algorithm in a tracking scenario. At time step $t - 1$ each 'parent' particle generates offspring candidates x_t from the IS distribution. The complete set of offspring is then weighted and resampled to generate a set of particles at time t. In the figure parent particles are linked to their surviving offspring.

1.7 Discussion and summary

Probabilistic time series models enable us to reason in a consistent way about temporal events under uncertainty. The probabilistic framework is particularly appealing for its conceptual clarity, and the use of a graphical model representation simplifies the development of the models and associated inference algorithms. The Markov independence assumption, which states that only a limited memory of the past is needed for understanding the present, plays an important role in time series models. This assumption reduces the burden in model specification and simplifies the computation of quantities of interest.

We reviewed several classical probabilistic Markovian models such AR models, hidden Markov models and linear dynamical systems, for which inference is tractable. We then discussed some of the main approximate approaches for the case of intractable inference, namely deterministic methods such as variational techniques and assumed density filtering and stochastic methods such as Monte Carlo sampling.

Many real-world time series problems are highly specialised and require novel models. The probabilistic approach, coupled with a graphical representation, facilitates the

---

Algorithm 1.6 Particle filter

---

for $i = 1, \ldots, N$ **do**

    Compute the IS distribution: $q_t(x_t | x^i_{1:t-1})$.

    Generate offsprings: $\hat{x}^i_t \sim q_t(x_t | x^i_{1:t-1})$.

    Evaluate importance weights

$$v^i_t = \frac{p(y_t | \hat{x}^i_t) p(\hat{x}^i_t | x^i_{t-1})}{q_t(\hat{x}^i_t | x^i_{1:t-1})}, \qquad W^i_t = v^i_t W^i_{t-1}.$$

end for

if Not Resample **then**

    Extend particles: $x^i_{1:t} = (x^i_{1:t-1}, \hat{x}^i_t)$, $i = 1, \ldots, N$.

else

    Normalise importance weights: $\tilde{Z}_t \leftarrow \sum_j W^j_t$, $\tilde{\mathbf{w}}_t \leftarrow (W^1_t, \ldots, W^N_t)/\tilde{Z}_t$.

    Generate associations: $(a(1), \ldots, a(N)) \leftarrow \text{Resample}(\tilde{\mathbf{w}}_t)$.

    Discard or keep particles and reset weights

$$x^i_{0:t} \leftarrow (x^{a(i)}_{0:t-1}, \hat{x}^{a(i)}_t), \qquad W^i_t \leftarrow \tilde{Z}_t/N, \qquad i = 1, \ldots, N.$$

end if

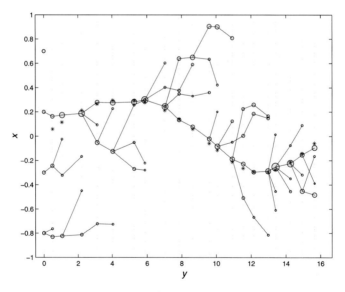

Figure 1.14 Illustration of the dynamics of a particle filter with $N = 4$ particles. The underlying latent Markov model corresponds to an object moving with positive velocity on the real line. The vertical axis corresponds to the latent log-velocities x and the horizontal axis to the observed noisy positions y: the underlying velocities of the process are shown as '*', while the observed positions are shown by dotted vertical lines. The nodes of the tree correspond to the particle positions and the sizes are proportional to normalised weights $\tilde{w}^{(i)}$.

development of tailored models and helps to reason about the computational complexity of their implementation. The field is currently very active, with many novel developments in modelling and inference, several of which are discussed in the remainder of this book.

Acknowledgments Silvia Chiappa would like to thank the European Commission for supporting her research through a Marie Curie Intra–European Fellowship.

Bibliography

[1] B. D. Anderson and J. B. Moore. *Optimal Filtering*. Prentice-Hall, 1979.

[2] G. Box, G. M. Jenkins and G. Reinsel. *Time Series Analysis: Forecasting and Control*. Prentice Hall, 1994.

[3] O. Cappé, R. Douc and E. Moulines. Comparison of resampling schemes for particle filtering. In *4th International Symposium on Image and Signal Processing and Analysis*, pages 64–69, 2005.

[4] O. Cappé, E. Moulines and T. Rydén. *Inference in Hidden Markov Models*. Springer-Verlag, 2005.

[5] A. Dempster, N. Laird and D. Rubin. Maximum likelihood from incomplete data via the EM algorithm. *Journal of the Royal Statistical Society, Series B*, **39**(1):1–38, 1977.

[6] A. Doucet, N. de Freitas and N. J. Gordon, editors. *Sequential Monte Carlo Methods in Practice*. Springer-Verlag, 2001.

[7] A. Doucet, S. Godsill and C. Andrieu. On sequential Monte Carlo sampling methods for Bayesian filtering. *Statistics and Computing*, **10**(3):197–208, 2000.

[8] A. Doucet and A. M. Johansen. A tutorial on particle filtering and smoothing: fifteen years later. *Handbook of Nonlinear Filtering*. Oxford University Press, 2010.

[9] J. Durbin. The fitting of time series models. *Rev. Inst. Int. Stat.*, 28, pages 233–243, 1960.

[10] S. Geman and D. Geman. Stochastic relaxation, Gibbs distributions and the Bayesian restoration of images. In M. A. Fischland and O. Firschein, editors, *Readings in Computer Vision: Issues, Problems, Principles, and Paradigms*, pages 564–584. Kaufmann, 1987.

[11] F. Gustafsson. *Adaptive filtering and change detection*. John Wiley & Sons, 2000.

[12] W. K. Hastings. Monte Carlo sampling methods using Markov chains and their applications. *Biometrika*, **57**:97–109, 1970.

[13] A. M. Johansen, L. Evers and N. Whiteley. *Monte Carlo Methods*, Lecture Notes, Department of Mathematics, Bristol University, 2008.

[14] R. E. Kalman. A new approach to linear filtering and prediction problems. *Transaction of the ASME-Journal of Basic Engineering*, 35–45, 1960.

[15] S. Kotz, N. Balakrishnan and N. L. Johnson. *Continuous Multivariate Distributions*, volume 1, Models and Applications. John Wiley & Sons, 2000.

[16] S. L. Lauritzen. *Thiele: Pioneer in Statistics*. Oxford University Press, 2002.

[17] J. S. Liu. *Monte Carlo Strategies in Scientific Computing*. Springer, 2004.

[18] N. Metropolis and S. Ulam. The Monte Carlo method. *Journal of the American Statistical Association*, **44**(247):335–341, 1949.

[19] T. Minka. Expectation Propagation for approximate Bayesian inference. PhD thesis, MIT, 2001.

[20] M. Mitzenmacher and E. Upfal. *Probability and Computing: Randomized Algorithms and Probabilistic Analysis*. Cambridge University Press, 2005.

[21] J. R. Norris. *Markov Chains*. Cambridge University Press, 1997.

[22] P. Park and T. Kailath. New square-root smoothing algorithms. *IEEE Transactions on Automatic Control*, **41**:727–732, 1996.

[23] L. R. Rabiner. A tutorial on hidden Markov models and selected applications in speech recognition. *Proceedings of the IEEE*, **77**(2):257–286, 1989.

[24] H. Rauch, F. Tung and C. Striebel. Maximum likelihood estimates of linear dynamic systems. *American Institute of Aeronautics and Astronautics Journal*, **3**(8):1445–1450, 1965.

[25] R. L. Stratonovich. Application of the Markov processes theory to optimal filtering. *Radio Engineering and Electronic Physics*, **5**(11):1–19, 1960. Translated from Russian.

[26] M. Verhaegen and P. Van Dooren. Numerical Aspects of Different Implementations. *IEEE Transactions On Automatic Control*, **31**(10):907–917, 1986.

[27] M. Wainwright and M. I. Jordan. Graphical models, exponential families, and variational inference. *Foundations and Trends in Machine Learning*, **1**:1–305, 2008.

Contributors

David Barber, Department of Computer Science, University College London

A. Taylan Cemgil, Department of Computer Engineering, Boğaziçi University, Istanbul, Turkey

Silvia Chiappa, Statistical Laboratory, Centre for Mathematical Sciences, University of Cambridge

2

Adaptive Markov chain Monte Carlo: theory and methods

Yves Atchadé, Gersende Fort, Eric Moulines and Pierre Priouret

2.1 Introduction

Markov chain Monte Carlo (MCMC) methods allow us to generate samples from an arbitrary distribution π known up to a scaling factor; see [46]. The algorithm consists in sampling a Markov chain $\{X_k, k \geq 0\}$ on a state space X with transition probability P admitting π as its unique *invariant* distribution.

In most MCMC algorithms known so far, the transition probability P of the Markov chain depends on some tuning parameter θ defined on some space Θ which can be either finite dimensional or infinite dimensional. The success of the MCMC procedure depends crucially upon a proper choice of θ.

To illustrate, consider the standard Metropolis–Hastings (MH) algorithm. For simplicity, we assume that π has a density also denoted by π with respect to the Lebesgue measure on $X = \mathbb{R}^d$ endowed with its Borel σ-field X. Given that the chain is at x, a candidate y is sampled from a *proposal transition density* $q(x, \cdot)$ and is accepted with probability $\alpha(x, y)$ defined as

$$\alpha(x, y) = 1 \wedge \frac{\pi(y)}{\pi(x)} \frac{q(y, x)}{q(x, y)},$$

where $a \wedge b \stackrel{\text{def}}{=} \min(a, b)$. Otherwise, the move is rejected and the Markov chain stays at its current location x.

A commonly used choice for the proposal kernel is the symmetric increment random walk leading to the random walk MH algorithm (hereafter SRWM), in which $q(x, y) = q(y - x)$ for all $(x, y) \in X \times X$, for some symmetric proposal density function q on X. A possible choice of the increment distribution q is the multivariate normal with zero-mean and covariance matrix Γ, $\mathcal{N}(0, \Gamma)$, leading to the N-SRWM algorithm. As illustrated in Fig. 2.1 in the one-dimensional case $d = 1$, if the variance is either too small or too large, then the convergence rate of the N-SRWM algorithm will be slow and any inference from values drawn from the chain is likely to be unreliable.[1]

Intuitively, this may be understood as follows. If the variance is too small, then almost all the proposed values are accepted, and the algorithm behaves almost as a random walk. Because the difference between two successive values is small, the algorithm visits the state space very slowly. On the contrary, if the variance is too large, most of the proposed moves fall far out in the tails of the target distribution. These proposals are often rejected and the algorithm stays at the same place. Finding a proper scale is thus

---

[1] After J. Rosenthal, this effect is referred to as the *Goldilocks* principle.

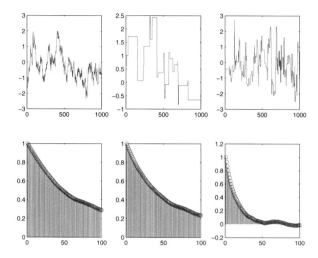

Figure 2.1 The N-SRWM in one dimension.

mandatory. In [23] the authors have shown that if the target and the proposal distributions are both Gaussian, then an appropriate choice for covariance matrix for the N-SRWM is $\Gamma = (2.38^2/d)\Gamma_\pi$, where Γ_π is the covariance matrix of the target distribution. This scaling was proven to be optimal in a large-dimensional context ($d \to \infty$); see [23], [48] and [49, Theorem 5].

In practice this covariance matrix Γ is determined by trial and error. This hand-tuning requires some expertise and can be time-consuming. In order to circumvent this problem, [30] (see also [31]) have proposed a novel algorithm, referred to as *adaptive Metropolis*, to update continuously Γ during the run, according to the past values of the simulations. This algorithm can be summarised as follows. At iteration k, we estimate the sample mean and the covariance of the draws

$$\mu_{k+1} = \mu_k + \frac{1}{k+1}(X_{k+1} - \mu_k), \tag{2.1}$$

$$\Gamma_{k+1} = \Gamma_k + \frac{1}{k+1}((X_{k+1} - \mu_k)(X_{k+1} - \mu_k)^T - \Gamma_k), \qquad k \geq 0, \tag{2.2}$$

X_{k+1} being simulated from the Metropolis kernel with Gaussian proposal distribution $\mathcal{N}(0, (2.38^2/d)\Gamma_k)$. This algorithm (and its variants) proved to be very successful in performing Bayesian inference of high-dimensional time series occurring in remote sensing and ecology; see for example [28, 29, 39].

It was recognised by [4] in an influential report that such a scheme can be cast into the more general framework of *controlled MCMC*. Controlled MCMC is a specific example of an *internal* adaptation setting where the θ is updated from the past history of the chain. Other examples of internal adaptation algorithms, which do not necessarily rely on a stochastic approximation step, are given in Section 2.2.1; see also [5] and [52].

When attempting to simulate from probability measures with multiple modes or when the dimension of the state space is large, the Markov kernels might mix so slowly that an *internal* adaptation strategy cannot always be expected to work. Other forms of adaptation can then be considered, using one or several *auxiliary* processes, which are run in parallel to the chain $\{X_k, k \geq 0\}$ targeting π. Because the target chain is adapted using some auxiliary processes, we refer to this adaptation framework as *external*.

The idea of running several MCMC in parallel and making them interact has been suggested by many authors; see for example [15, 16, 34]. This simple construction has been shown to improve the overall mixing of the chain, by allowing the badly mixing chain to explore the state more efficiently with the help of the auxiliary chain.

It is possible to extend significantly this simple idea by allowing more general interactions between the auxiliary chains. In particular [36] suggested to make the auxiliary chains interact with the whole set of past simulations. Instead of allowing us to swap only the current states of the auxiliary chains, the current state of the target chain may be replaced with one of the states visited by an auxiliary chain in the past. The selection of this state can be guided by sampling in the past of the auxiliary chains, with weights depending on the current value of the state. This class of methods is referred to as *interacting MCMC*. These chains can be cast into the framework outlined above, by allowing the parameter θ to take its value in an infinite-dimensional space.

The purpose of this chapter is to review adaptive MCMC methods, emphasising the links between internal (controlled MCMC) and external (interacting MCMC) algorithms. The emphasis of this review is to evidence general methodology to construct convergent adaptive MCMC algorithms and to sketch some of the results required to prove their convergence. This chapter complements two recent surveys on this topic by [5] and [52] which put more emphasis on the design of internal algorithms.

The chapter is organised as follows. In Section 2.2 the general framework of adaptive MCMC is presented and several examples are given. In Section 2.3 we establish the convergence of the marginal distribution of $\{X_k, k \geq 0\}$, and in Section 2.4 we establish a strong law of large numbers for additive functionals. Finally, in Section 2.5, we show how to apply these results to the equi-energy sampler of [36].

Notation

In the sequel, we consider Markov chains taking values in a general state space X, equipped with a countably generated σ-field $\mathcal{X}$. For any measure ζ on $(X, \mathcal{X})$ and any ζ-integrable function f, we set $\zeta(f) \stackrel{\text{def}}{=} \int_X f(x)\,\zeta(\mathrm{d}x)$. A Markov kernel P on $(X, \mathcal{X})$ is a mapping from $X \times \mathcal{X}$ into $[0, 1]$ such that, for each $A \in \mathcal{X}$, $x \mapsto P(x, A)$ is a non-negative, bounded and measurable function on X, and, for each $x \in X$, $A \mapsto P(x, A)$ is a probability on $\mathcal{X}$. For any bounded measurable function $f : X \to \mathbb{R}$, we denote by $Pf : X \to \mathbb{R}$ the function $x \mapsto Pf(x) \stackrel{\text{def}}{=} \int P(x, \mathrm{d}x')\, f(x')$. For a measure ν on $(X, \mathcal{X})$, we denote by νP the measure on $(X, \mathcal{X})$ defined by, for any $A \in \mathcal{X}$, $\nu P(A) \stackrel{\text{def}}{=} \int P(x, A)\, \nu(\mathrm{d}x)$. For a bounded function f the supremum norm is denoted by $|f|_\infty$. For a signed measure μ on $(X, \mathcal{X})$, the total variation norm is given by $\|\mu\|_{TV} \stackrel{\text{def}}{=} \sup_{f, |f|_\infty \leq 1} |\mu(f)|$.

2.2 Adaptive MCMC algorithms

We let $\{P_\theta, \theta \in \Theta\}$ be a parametric family of Markov kernels on $(X, \mathcal{X})$. We consider a process $(\Omega, \mathcal{A}, \mathbb{P}, \{(X_k, \theta_k), k \geq 0\})$ and a filtration $\{\mathcal{F}_k, k \geq 0\}$ (an increasing sequence of σ-fields summarising the history of the process). It is assumed that **(i)** $\{(X_k, \theta_k), k \geq 0\}$ is adapted (in the sense that for each $n \geq 0$, (X_k, θ_k) is $\mathcal{F}_k$-measurable) and **(ii)** for any non-negative function f,

$$\mathbb{E}\left[f(X_{k+1})\,|\,\mathcal{F}_k\right] = P_{\theta_k} f(X_k) = \int P_{\theta_k}(X_k, \mathrm{d}y)f(y) \quad \mathbb{P} - \text{a.s.}$$

In words, the latter relation means that at each time instant $k \geq 0$ the next value X_{k+1} is drawn from the transition kernel $P_{\theta_k}(X_k, \cdot)$. As seen in the introduction, an adaptive MCMC algorithm is said to be *internal* if the next value of the parameter θ_{k+1} is computed from the past value of the simulations $X_0, \ldots, X_{k+1}$ and of the parameters $\theta_0, \ldots, \theta_k$. It is said to be *external* if the next value θ_{k+1} is computed using an auxiliary process $\{Y_k, k \geq 0\}$ run independently from the process $\{X_k, k \geq 0\}$. More precisely, it is assumed that the process $\{\theta_k, k \geq 0\}$ is adapted to the natural filtration of the process $\{Y_k, k \geq 0\}$, meaning that for each k, θ_k is a function of the history $Y_{0:k} \stackrel{\text{def}}{=} (Y_0, Y_1, \ldots, Y_k)$ of the auxiliary process. In the latter case, conditioned on the auxiliary process $\{Y_k, k \geq 0\}$, $\{X_k, k \geq 0\}$ is an inhomogeneous Markov chain such that for any bounded measurable function f

$$\mathbb{E}\left[f(X_{k+1}) \mid X_{0:k}, Y_{0:k}\right] = P_{\theta_k} f(X_k).$$

Below we give several examples of internal and external adaptive MCMC algorithms.

2.2.1 Internal adaptive algorithms

Controlled MCMC

In the controlled MCMC case, for any $\theta \in \Theta$, the kernel P_θ has an invariant distribution π. The parameter θ_k is updated according to a single step of a stochastic approximation procedure,

$$\theta_{k+1} = \theta_k + \gamma_{k+1} H(\theta_k, X_k, X_{k+1}), \quad k \geq 0, \tag{2.3}$$

where X_{k+1} is sampled from $P_{\theta_k}(X_k, \cdot)$. In most cases, the function H is chosen so that the adaptation is easy to implement, requiring only moderate amounts of extra computer programming, and not adding a large computational overhead; see [51] and [38] for implementation details. For reasons that will become obvious below, the rate of adaptation tends to zero as the number k of iterations goes to infinity, i.e. $\lim_{k \to \infty} \gamma_k = 0$. On the other hand, $\sum_{k=0}^{\infty} \gamma_k = \infty$, meaning that the sum of the parameter moves can still be infinite, i.e. the sequence $\{\theta_k, k \geq 0\}$ may move at an infinite distance from the initial value θ_0. It is not necessarily required that the parameters $\{\theta_k, k \geq 0\}$ converge to some fixed value. An in-depth description of controlled MCMC algorithms is given in [5], illustrated with many examples (some of which are given below).

Under appropriate conditions, the recursions (2.3) converge to the set of solutions of the equation $h(\theta) = 0$ where $\theta \mapsto h(\theta)$ is the *mean-field* associated to H defined as

$$h(\theta) \stackrel{\text{def}}{=} \int_X H(\theta, x, x') \pi(\mathrm{d}x) P_\theta(x, \mathrm{d}x').$$

The convergence of Eq. (2.3) is discussed in numerous monographs: see for example [11, 20, 37, 17, 3].

The adaptive Metropolis algorithm

Returning to the adaptive Metropolis example in the introduction, the parameter θ is equal to the mean and the covariance matrix of the multivariate distribution, $\theta = (\mu, \Gamma) \in \Theta = (\mathbb{R}^d, C_+^d)$, where C_+^d is the cone of symmetric non-negative $d \times d$ matrices. The expression of H is explicitly given in Eqs. (2.1) and (2.2). Assuming that $\int_X |x|^2 \pi(\mathrm{d}x) < \infty$, one can easily check that the associated mean-field function is given by

$$h(\theta) = \int_X H(\theta, x) \pi(\mathrm{d}x) = \left[\mu_\pi - \mu, (\mu_\pi - \mu)(\mu_\pi - \mu)^T + \Gamma_\pi - \Gamma\right],$$

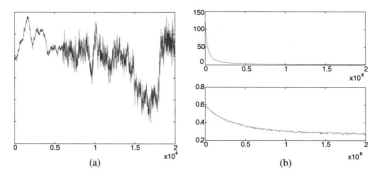

Figure 2.2 (a) Trace plot of the 20000 first iterations of the AM algorithm. (b) Top: suboptimality factor as a function of the number of iterations. Bottom: mean acceptance rate as a function of the number of iterations (obtained by averaging the number of accepted moves on a sliding window of size 6000).

where μ_π and Γ_π denote the mean and covariance of the target distribution,

$$\mu_\pi \stackrel{\text{def}}{=} \int_X x\,\pi(\mathrm{d}x) \quad \text{and} \quad \Gamma_\pi \stackrel{\text{def}}{=} \int_X (x-\mu_\pi)(x-\mu_\pi)^T \pi(\mathrm{d}x).$$

It is easily seen that this algorithm has a unique stationary point $\theta_\star = (\mu_\pi, \Gamma_\pi)$. Provided that the step-size is appropriately chosen, a stochastic approximation procedure will typically converge toward that stationary point; see for example [3, 2].

The behavior of the adaptive metropolis (AM) algorithm is illustrated in Fig. 2.2. The target distribution is a multivariate Gaussian distribution $\mathcal{N}(0, \Sigma)$ with dimension $d = 200$. The eigenvalues of the covariance of the target distribution are regularly spaced in the interval $[10^{-2}, 10^3]$. This is a challenging simulation task because the dispersion of the eigenvalues of the target covariance is large. The proposal distribution at step $k \geq 2d$ is

$$P_{\theta_k}(x, \cdot) = (1 - \beta)\mathcal{N}(x, (2.38)^2\Gamma_k/d) + \beta\mathcal{N}(x, 0.1\,\mathrm{Id}/d),$$

where Γ_k is the current estimate of the covariance matrix given in Eq. (2.2) and β is a positive constant (we take $\beta = 0.05$, as suggested in [47]). The initial value for Γ_0 is Id. The rationale of using such β is to avoid the algorithm being stuck with a singular covariance matrix (in the original AM algorithm, [31] suggested to regularise the covariance matrix by loading the diagonal; another more sophisticated solution based on projections onto compact sets is considered in [2]).

Figure 2.2 displays the trace plot of the first coordinate of the chain for dimension $d = 200$ together with the suboptimality criterion introduced in [49], defined as

$$b_k \stackrel{\text{def}}{=} d\frac{\sum_{i=1}^d \lambda_{i,k}^{-2}}{\left(\sum_{i=1}^d \lambda_{i,k}^{-1}\right)^2},$$

where $\lambda_{i,k}$ are the eigenvalues of the matrix $\Gamma_k^{1/2}\Gamma_\pi^{-1/2}$. Usually we will have $b_k > 1$, and the closer b_k is to 1, the better. The criterion being optimised in AM is therefore b_k^{-1}. Since the seminal papers by [30], there have been numerous successful applications of this scheme, in particular to some Bayesian inverse problems in atmospheric chemistry. Some interesting variants have been considered, the most promising one being the DRAM adaptation [29], which adds a new component to the AM method that is called Delayed Rejection (DR) [45]. In the DR method, instead of one proposal distribution, several proposals can be used. These propositions are used in turn, until a new value is accepted or a full sweep is done. The DR acceptance probability formulation ensures that the chain is reversible with respect to the target distribution. In the DRAM method the DR algorithm is used together with several different adaptive Gaussian proposals. This helps the algorithm in two ways. First, it enhances the adaptation by providing accepted values that make the adaptation start earlier. Second, it allows the sampler to work better for non-Gaussian targets and with non-linear correlations between the components; see [29].

The coerced acceptance rate algorithm

For a Metropolis algorithm, a mean acceptance rate close to zero typically reflects that the scale is too large (the moves are rejected). On the contrary, a mean acceptance rate close to 1 typically occurs when the scale is too small (the moves are almost all accepted; see Fig. 2.1). The choice of a proper scale can be automated by controlling the expected acceptance probability. For simplicity, we consider only the one-dimensional SRWM, where θ is the scale. In this case, we choose

$$H(x, x') \stackrel{\text{def}}{=} \{\alpha(x, x') - \alpha_\star\}$$

which is associated to the mean-field

$$h(\theta) = \int \pi(\mathrm{d}x) P_\theta(x, \mathrm{d}x') \alpha(x, x') - \alpha_\star,$$

where the acceptance ratio is $\alpha(x, x') = 1 \wedge \pi(x')/\pi(x)$. The value of $\alpha_\star$ can be set to 0.4 or 0.5 (the 'optimal' value in this context is 0.44).

The same idea applies in large-dimensional context. We may for example couple this approach with the AM algorithm: instead of using the asymptotic $(2.38)^2/d$ factor, we might let the algorithm determine automatically a proper scaling by controlling both the covariance matrix of the proposal distribution and the mean acceptance rate.

To illustrate the behaviour of the algorithm, we learn simultaneously the covariance and the scaling. The target distribution is zero-mean Gaussian with covariance drawn at random as above in dimension $d = 100$. The results are displayed in Fig. 2.3.

Regional adaptation algorithms

More sophisticated adaptation techniques may be used. An obvious idea is to try to make the adaptation 'local', i.e. to adapt to the local behaviour of the target density. Such techniques have been introduced to alleviate the main weakness of the adaptive Metropolis algorithm when applied to a spatially non-homogeneous target which is due to the use of a single global covariance distribution for the proposal. Consider for example the case where the target density is a mixture of Gaussian distributions, $\pi = \sum_{j=1}^{p} a_j \mathcal{N}(\mu_j, \Sigma_j)$. Provided that the overlap between the components is weak, and the covariances Σ_j are widely different, then there does not exist a common proposal distribution which is well-fitted to sample in the regions surrounding each mode. This example suggests to tune the empirical covariance matrices by learning the *history* of the past simulations in different regions of the state space. To be more specific, assume that there exists a partition $\mathsf{X} = \bigcup_{j=1}^{p} \mathsf{X}_j$. Then, according to the discussion above, it is beneficial to use different proposal distributions in each set of the partition. We might for example use the proposal

$$q_\theta(x; x') = \sum_{j=1}^{p} \mathbb{1}_{\mathsf{X}_j}(x) \phi(x'; x, \Gamma_j),$$

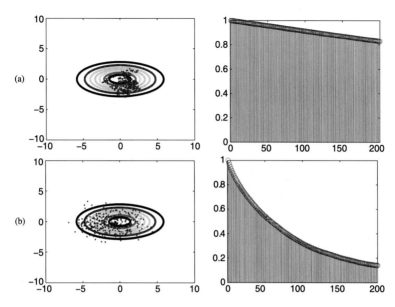

Figure 2.3 (a) SRWM algorithm with identity covariance matrix with optimal scaling; (b) Adaptive Metropolis with adapted scaling; the targeted value of the mean acceptance rate is $\alpha_\star = 0.234$.

where $\mathbb{1}_A(x)$ is the indicator of the set A, and $\phi(x; \mu, \Gamma)$ is the density of a d-dimensional Gaussian distribution with mean μ and covariance Γ. Here, the parameter θ collects the covariances of the individual proposal distributions within each region. With such a proposal, the acceptance ratio of the MH algorithm becomes

$$\alpha_\theta(x; x') = 1 \wedge \sum_{i,j=1}^{p} \frac{\pi(x')}{\pi(x)} \frac{\phi(x; x', \Gamma_j)}{\phi(x'; x, \Gamma_i)} \mathbb{1}_{X_i}(x) \mathbb{1}_{X_j}(x').$$

To adapt the covariance matrices $\{\Gamma_i, i = 1, \ldots, p\}$ we can for example use the updates (2.1) and (2.2) within each region. To ensure a proper communication between the regions, it is recommended to mix the adaptive kernel with a fixed kernel. This technique is investigated in [18].

There are many other possible forms of adaptive MCMC and many of these are presented in the recent surveys by [47, 5, 52].

Adaptive independence sampler

Another interesting direction of research is to adapt the proposal distribution of an independence sampler. In this algorithm, the proposed moves do not depend on the current state, i.e. $q(x, x') = q(x')$ where q is some probability density on X. In such a case the acceptance ratio can be written as $\alpha(x, x') = 1 \wedge (\pi(x')q(x)/\pi(x)q(x'))$. When the proposal q is equal to the target π, the acceptance ratio is one and the correlation between adjacent elements of the chain is zero. Thus it is desirable to choose the proposal distribution q to be as close as possible to the target π. In an adaptive MCMC framework, a natural strategy is to adjust a trial proposal to obtain a new proposal that is closer to π.

A natural idea is to choose a parametric family of distributions $\{q_\theta, \theta \in \Theta\}$, and to adapt the parameter θ from the history of the draws. This technique is of course closely related to the adaptive importance sampling idea; see for example [53].

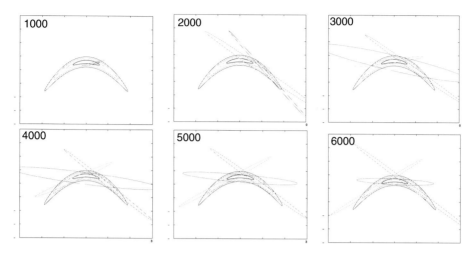

Figure 2.4 Adaptive fit of a mixture of three Gaussian distributions with arbitrary means and covariance using the maximum likelihood approach developed in [2]. See plate section for colour version.

Because of its flexibility and tractability, a finite mixture of Gaussian distributions is an appealing proposal family. Recall that any continuous distribution can be approximated arbitrarily well by a finite mixture of normal Gaussians with common covariance matrix; in addition, a discrete mixture of Gaussians is fast to sample from, and its likelihood is easy to calculate. In this case, the parameters θ are the mixing proportions, means and common covariance of the component densities. Several approaches have been considered to fit these parameters. Other mixtures from the exponential family can also be considered, such as a discrete/continuous mixture of Student's t-distribution (see [5] for details).

In [2], the authors suggest to fit these parameters using a maximum likelihood approach or, equivalently, by maximising the cross-entropy between the proposal distribution and the target. This algorithm shares some similarities with the so-called adaptive independence sampler developed in [35]. In this framework, the parameters are fitted using a sequential version of the expectation maximisation (EM) algorithm [13] (several improvements on this basic scheme are presented in [5]).

In [27], the authors proposed a principled version replacing the EM by the k-harmonic mean, an extension of the k-means algorithm that allows for soft membership. This algorithm happens to be less sensitive to convergence to local minima than the recursive EM algorithm; in addition degeneracies of the covariance matrices of the components can be easily prevented. An example of fit is given in Fig. 2.4.

Adaptive Gibbs sampler and Metropolis-within-Gibbs sampler

Gibbs samplers are commonly used MCMC algorithms for sampling from complicated high-dimensional probability distributions π in cases where the full conditional distributions of π are easy to sample from. To introduce these algorithms, some additional notations are required. Let $(\mathsf{X}, \mathcal{X})$ be a d-dimensional state space, $\mathsf{X} = \mathsf{X}_1 \times \cdots \times \mathsf{X}_d$ and write $X_k \in \mathsf{X}$ as $X_k = (X_{k,1}, \ldots, X_{k,d})$. We shall use the shorthand notation $X_{k,-i} \overset{\text{def}}{=} (X_{k,1}, \ldots, X_{k,i-1}, X_{k,i+1}, \ldots, X_{k,d})$, and similarly $\mathsf{X}_{-i} = \mathsf{X}_1 \times \cdots \times \mathsf{X}_{i-1} \times \mathsf{X}_{i+1} \times \cdots \times \mathsf{X}_d$. We denote by $\pi_i(x, \cdot) = \pi(\cdot | x_{-i})$ the conditional distribution of X_i given $X_{-i} = x_{-i}$ when $X \sim \pi$. The set $\{\pi_i\}_{i=1}^d$ of transition density functions is referred to as the set of full conditional distributions.

The random scan Gibbs sampler draws X_k given X_{k-1} iteratively by first choosing one coordinate at random according to some selection probabilities $\theta \overset{\text{def}}{=} (\theta_1, \ldots, \theta_d)$ and then updating that coordinate by sampling from the associated full conditional distributions. This random scan strategy was in fact the routine suggested by [24] in their seminal Gibbs sampling paper. Of course, alternatives to the random scan strategies are available. The transition kernel of this MCMC is a mixture of the full conditional distributions, the mixing weights being equal to $(\theta_1, \ldots, \theta_d)$. The key condition is that the chain induced by the Gibbs sampling scheme is ergodic and, in particular, each coordinate of X is visited infinitely often in the limit.

The random scan provides much flexibility in the choice of sampling strategy. Most implementations use equal selection probabilities. While this updating scheme may seem fair, it is counter the intuition of visiting coordinates of X which are more variable and thus more difficult to sample more often. Some recent work has suggested that the use of non-uniform selection probabilities may significantly improve the sampling performance; see for example [40, 42, 41, 19].

Therefore, for random scan Gibbs samplers, a design decision is choosing the selection probabilities which will be used to select which coordinate to update next. An adaptive random scan Gibbs sampler will typically adapt at each iteration the selection probabilities θ_k (according to the past values of the simulations $X_0, \ldots, X_k$ and of the selection probabilities $\theta_0, \ldots, \theta_{k-1}$), then select a new component $I_{k+1} \in \{1, \ldots, d\}$ to update with a probability equal to the current fit of the selection probability θ_k, draw $X_{k+1,I_{k+1}}$ from the corresponding conditional distribution $\pi(\cdot|X_{k,-I_{k+1}})$, and finally update the state vector by setting $X_{k+1,-I_{k+1}} = X_{k,-I_{k+1}}$ for the remaining components. Several possible ways of adapting the selection probabilities are introduced in [41].

Another possibility consists in using a Metropolis-within-Gibbs algorithm, where the i-th component is updated not using the full conditional distribution π_i but using a Metropolis–Hastings step with the usual MH acceptance probability for π_i (see [47, 52]). In this setting both the selection probability and the proposal distributions associated to each individual component sampler can be adapted simultaneously. The first attempt to adapt a Metropolis-within-Gibbs algorithm is the Single-Component Adaptive Metropolis introduced in [32]. In this algorithm, the selection probabilities are kept constant and only the scale of the individual component proposals are adapted. Refined Metropolis-within-Gibbs involving simultaneous adaptation of the selection probabilities and of the proposal distributions has been introduced in [54] where this methodology has been applied successfully to high-dimensional inference for statistical genetics.

2.2.2   External adaptive algorithm

We now turn to the description of external adaptive algorithms. This class of algorithm is currently less popular than internal adaptive algorithms since samples from an auxiliary process are required. This increases significantly the computational burden of the algorithm. Nevertheless, the improvements in convergence speed can be so large that sampling an auxiliary process to help the original sampler might be, in certain difficult simulation tasks, an attractive solution.

The use of an auxiliary process to learn the proposal distribution in an independent MH algorithm has been considered in [15] and [16]. In this setting, the parameter θ_k is a distribution obtained using a histogram. This approach works best in situations where the dimension of the state space d is small, otherwise the histogram estimation becomes very unreliable (in [16] only one- and two-dimensional examples are considered).

Another form of interaction has been introduced in [36]: instead of trying to learn a well fitted proposal distribution, these authors suggest to 'swap' the current state of the Markov chain with a state sampled from the history of the auxiliary processes. A similar idea has been advocated in [6]. In this setting, the 'parameter' θ_k is infinite dimensional, and these algorithms may be seen as a kind of *nonparametric* extension of the controlled MCMC procedures.

All these new ideas originate from *parallel tempering* and *simulated tempering*, two influential algorithms developed in the early 1990s to speed up the convergence of MCMC algorithms; see [25, 43, 26]. In these approaches, the sampling algorithm moves progressively to the target distribution π through a sequence of distributions which are deemed to be easier to sample than the target distribution itself. The idea behind *parallel tempering* algorithm by [25] is to perform parallel Metropolis sampling at different *temperatures*. Occasionally, a *swap* between the states of two neighbouring chains (two chains running at adjacent temperature levels) is proposed. The acceptance probability for the swap is computed to ensure that the joint states of all the parallel chains evolve according to the Metropolis–Hastings rule targeting the product distribution. The objective of the parallel tempering is to use the faster mixing of the high temperature chains to improve the mixing of the low temperature chains. The *simulated tempering algorithm* introduced in [43] exploits a similar idea but using a markedly different approach. Instead of using multiple parallel chains, this algorithm runs a single chain but augments the state of this chain by an auxiliary variable, the temperature, that is dynamically moved up or down the temperature ladder. We discuss now more precisely the equi-energy sampler, which is the most emblematic example of external adaptive algorithm.

The equi-energy sampler

The equi-energy (EE) sampler exploits the parallel tempering idea, in the sense that the algorithm runs several chains at different temperatures, but allows for more general interactions between states of the neighbouring chains. The idea is to replace an instantaneous swap by a so-called *equi-energy* move. To avoid cumbersome notations, we assume here that there is a single auxiliary process, but it should be stressed that the EE sampler has been reported to work better by using multiple auxiliary processes covering a wide range of temperatures.

Let π be the target density distribution on $(\mathsf{X}, \mathcal{X})$. For $\beta \in (0, 1)$ define the tempered density $\tilde{\pi} \propto \pi^{1-\beta}$. The auxiliary process $\{Y_n, n \geq 0\}$ is X-valued and such that its marginal distribution converges to $\tilde{\pi}$ as n goes to infinity. Let P be a transition kernel on $(\mathsf{X}, \mathcal{X})$ with unique invariant distribution π (in most cases, P is a MH kernel).

Let $\epsilon \in (0, 1)$ be the probability of proposing a swap between the states of two neighbouring chains. Define a partition $\mathsf{X} = \bigcup_{\ell=1}^K \mathsf{X}_\ell$, where X_ℓ are the so-called *rings* (a term linked with the particular choice of the partition in [36], which is defined as the level set of the logarithm of the target distribution).

At iteration n of the algorithm, two actions may be taken:

1. With probability $(1 - \epsilon)$, we move the current state X_n according to the Markov kernel P.

2. With probability ϵ, we propose to swap the current state X_n with a state Z drawn from the past of the auxiliary process with weights proportional to $\{g(X_n, Y_i), i \leq n\}$, where

$$g(x, y) \overset{\text{def}}{=} \sum_{\ell=1}^{K} \mathbb{1}_{\mathsf{X}_\ell \times \mathsf{X}_\ell}(x, y).$$

More precisely, we propose a move Z at random within the same ring as X_n. This move is accepted with probability $\alpha(X_n, Z)$, where the acceptance probability α is defined by $\alpha : \mathsf{X} \times \mathsf{X} \to [0, 1]$ defined by

$$\alpha(x, y) \overset{\text{def}}{=} 1 \wedge \left(\frac{\pi(y)}{\tilde{\pi}(y)} \left[\frac{\pi(x)}{\tilde{\pi}(x)} \right]^{-1} \right) = 1 \wedge \frac{\pi^\beta(y)}{\pi^\beta(x)}. \tag{2.4}$$

More formally, let Θ be the set of the probability measures on $(\mathsf{X}, \mathcal{X})$. For any distribution $\theta \in \Theta$, define the Markov transition kernel

$$P_\theta(x, \cdot) \overset{\text{def}}{=} (1 - \epsilon_\theta(x))P(x, A) + \epsilon_\theta(x)K_\theta(x, A)$$

with

$$K_\theta(x, A) \overset{\text{def}}{=} \int_A \alpha(x, y) \frac{g(x, y)\theta(dy)}{\theta[g(x, \cdot)]} + \mathbb{1}_A(x) \int \{1 - \alpha(x, y)\} \frac{g(x, y)\theta(dy)}{\theta[g(x, \cdot)]},$$

where $\theta[g(x, \cdot)] \overset{\text{def}}{=} \int g(x, y)\theta(dy)$ and

$$\epsilon_\theta(x) = \epsilon \mathbb{1}_{\theta[g(x, \cdot)] > 0}.$$

The kernel $K_{\tilde{\pi}}$ can be seen as a Hastings–Metropolis kernel with proposal kernel $g(x, y)\tilde{\pi}(y) / \int g(x, y)\tilde{\pi}(dy)$ and target distribution π. Hence, $\pi P_{\tilde{\pi}} = \pi$.

Using the samples drawn from this process, a family of weighted empirical probability distributions $\{\theta_n, n \geq 0\}$ is recursively constructed as follows:

$$\theta_n \overset{\text{def}}{=} \frac{1}{n+1} \sum_{j=0}^{n} \delta_{Y_j} = \left(1 - \frac{1}{n+1}\right)\theta_{n-1} + \frac{1}{n+1}\delta_{Y_n},$$

where δ_y is the Dirac mass at y and, by convention, $\theta_{-1} = 0$. Given the current value X_n and the sequence $\{\theta_k, k \leq n\}$, X_{n+1} is obtained by sampling the kernel $P_{\theta_n}(X_n, \cdot)$.

Figure 2.5 illustrates the effectiveness of the EE sampler. In this example the target distribution is the two-dimensional Gaussian mixture introduced in [36, p. 1591–1592]. Figure 2.5(a) represents independent sample points from the target distribution. This distribution has 20 well separated modes (most local modes are more than 15 standard deviations away from the nearest ones) and poses a serious challenge for sampling algorithms. We test a plain SRWM, parallel tempering and the EE sampler on this problem. For parallel tempering and the EE sampler, we use 5 parallel chains with $\beta = 0$, 0.64, 0.87, 0.95, 0.98. For the equi-energy sampling, we define 5 equi-energy rings $\mathsf{X}_1 = \{x \in \mathbb{R}^2 : -\log \pi(x) < 2\}$, $\mathsf{X}_2 = \{x \in \mathbb{R}^2 : 2 \leq -\log \pi(x) < 6.3\}$, $\mathsf{X}_3 = \{x \in \mathbb{R}^2 : 6.3 \leq -\log \pi(x) < 20\}$, $\mathsf{X}_4 = \{x \in \mathbb{R}^2 : 20 \leq -\log \pi(x) < 63.2\}$ and $\mathsf{X}_5 = \{x \in \mathbb{R}^2 : -\log \pi(x) \geq 63.2\}$. Figure 2.5(b) plots the first 2000 iterations from the EE sampler; Fig. 2.5(c) plots the first 2000 iterations from parallel tempering, and Fig. 2.5(d) plots the first 2000 iterations from a plain SRWM algorithm. The plain SRWM exhibits very poor mixing for this example. Parallel tempering mixes better but the EE sampler mixes even faster.

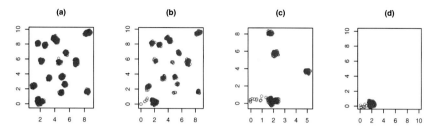

Figure 2.5 Comparison of (b) equi-energy sampler, (c) parallel tempering and (d) a plain SRWM. (a) Target distribution.

2.3 Convergence of the marginal distribution

There is a difficulty with both the internal and external adaptation procedures: as the parameter estimate θ_k depends on the whole past either of the process or the auxiliary process, the process $\{X_k, k \geq 0\}$ is no longer a Markov chain and classical convergence results do not hold. This may cause serious problems, as illustrated in this naive example. Let $X = \{1, 2\}$ and consider, for $\theta, t_1, t_2 \in \Theta = (0, 1)$ with $t_1 \neq t_2$, the following Markov transition probability matrices

$$P_\theta = \begin{bmatrix} 1 - \theta & \theta \\ \theta & 1 - \theta \end{bmatrix}, \qquad \tilde{P} = \begin{bmatrix} 1 - t_1 & t_1 \\ t_2 & 1 - t_2 \end{bmatrix}.$$

For any $\theta \in \Theta$, $\pi = (1/2, 1/2)$ satisfies $\pi P_\theta = \pi$. However if we let θ_k be a given function $\Xi : X \to (0, 1)$ of the current state, i.e. $\theta_k = \Xi(X_k)$ with $\Xi(i) = t_i$, $i \in \{1, 2\}$, one defines a new Markov chain with transition probability $\tilde{P}$. Now $\tilde{P}$ has $[t_2/(t_1 + t_2), t_1/(t_1 + t_2)]$ as invariant distribution. Instead of improving the mixing, the adaptation has in such a case destroyed the convergence to π.

The first requirement for an MCMC algorithm to be well-behaved is that the distribution of X_n converges weakly to the target distribution π as $n \to \infty$, i.e. for any measurable bounded function $f : X \to \mathbb{R}$, $\lim_{n \to \infty} \mathbb{E}[f(X_n)] = \pi(f)$. When this limit holds uniformly for any bounded function $f : X \to \mathbb{R}$, this convergence of the marginal $\{X_n, n \geq 0\}$ is also referred to in the literature as the *ergodicity of the marginal* of the adaptive MCMC $\{X_n, n \geq 0\}$ (see e.g. [50]).

Ergodicity of the marginal distributions for internal adaptive algorithms has been studied, under various assumptions, by [50, 2, 7]. The analysis of external adaptive MCMC algorithms began more recently and the theory is still less developed; see [1] and [12].

2.3.1 Main result

For any $\theta, \theta' \in \Theta$, define

$$D_{TV}(\theta, \theta') \stackrel{\text{def}}{=} \sup_{x \in X} \|P_\theta(x, \cdot) - P_{\theta'}(x, \cdot)\|_{TV}.$$

For $x \in X$, $\theta \in \Theta$ and for any $\epsilon > 0$, define

$$M_\epsilon(x, \theta) \stackrel{\text{def}}{=} \inf\{n \geq 0, \|P_\theta^n(x, \cdot) - \pi_\theta\|_{TV} \leq \epsilon\}.$$

Consider the following assumptions

A1 For any $\theta \in \Theta$, P_θ is a transition kernel on $(\mathsf{X}, \mathcal{X})$ that possesses a unique invariant probability measure π_θ.

A2 *(Diminishing adaptation)* The sequence $\{D_{\mathrm{TV}}(\theta_n, \theta_{n-1}), n \geq 1\}$ converges to zero in probability.

A3 *(Containment condition)* For any $\epsilon > 0$, the sequence $\{M_\epsilon(X_n, \theta_n), n \geq 0\}$ is bounded in probability, i.e. $\lim_{M \to \infty} \lim \sup_{n \to \infty} \mathbb{P}(M_\epsilon(X_n, \theta_n) \geq M) = 0$.

The diminishing adaptation condition requires that the amount of change (expressed in terms of the supremum of the total variation distance between the two successive kernels P_{θ_n} and $P_{\theta_{n+1}}$) at the nth iteration vanishes as $n \to \infty$. This does not necessarily imply however that the parameter sequence $\{\theta_n, n \geq 0\}$ converges to some fixed value. Since the user controls the updating scheme, assumption A2 can be ensured by controlling the amount of change of the parameter value θ_n.

If the function H in the stochastic approximation procedure (2.3) is bounded, then the amount of change in the parameter at the nth iteration is just $O(\gamma_n)$ and hence goes to 0 provided that $\lim_{n \to \infty} \gamma_n = 0$.

The containment condition is most easily established by checking a uniform in $\theta \in \Theta$ ergodicity; see for example Section 2.5 and [50, 7, 10].

The central result of this section is Theorem 2.1, which allows us to compare the marginal distribution of X_n and the distribution $\pi_{\theta_{n-N}}$ for some appropriately chosen integer N:

Theorem 2.1 *Assume A1, A2 and A3. Then, for any $\epsilon > 0$, there exists N such that*

$$\lim \sup_{n \to \infty} \sup_{|f|_\infty \leq 1} \left| \mathbb{E}\left[f(X_n)\right] - \pi_{\theta_{n-N}}(f) \right] \right| \leq \epsilon.$$

When $\pi_\theta = \pi_\star$ for any $\theta \in \Theta$, this result shows the convergence of the marginal distribution to $\pi_\star$; see also [50, Theorem 13]. The fact that some of the conditions A1, A2 and A3 are also necessary has been discussed in this case; see [9].

If the sequence $\{\pi_{\theta_n}, n \geq 0\}$ is known to converge to $\pi_\star$, then Theorem 2.1 implies the following corollary.

Corollary 2.2 *Assume A1, A2 and A3. Assume in addition that for some bounded measurable function f*

$$\lim_{n \to \infty} \pi_{\theta_n}(f) = \pi_\star(f), \quad \mathbb{P} - a.s.$$

Then, $\lim_{n \to \infty} \mathbb{E}\left[f(X_n)\right] = \pi_\star(f)$.

2.4 Strong law of large numbers

In this section, we establish a strong law of large numbers (LLN) for adaptive MCMC. The authors in [31] were the first to prove the consistency of Monte Carlo averages for the algorithm described by Eqs. (2.1) and (2.2) for bounded functions, using mixingales techniques; these results have later been extended by [8] to unbounded functions. In [2] the authors have established the consistency and the asymptotic normality of $n^{-1} \sum_{k=1}^n f(X_k)$ for bounded and unbounded functions for controlled MCMC algorithms associated to a stochastic approximation procedure (see [7] for extensions). The authors in [50] prove a weak law of large numbers for bounded functions for general adaptive MCMC samplers. Finally, [6] provides a consistency result for an external adaptive sampler.

The proof is based on the so-called martingale technique (see [44, Chapter 17]). We consider first this approach in the simple case of a homogeneous Markov chain, i.e. $P_\theta = P$. In this context, this technique amounts to decomposing $n^{-1} \sum_{k=1}^n f(X_k) - \pi_\star(f)$ as $n^{-1} M_n(f) + R_n(f)$, where $\{M_n(f), n \geq 0\}$ is a $\mathbb{P}$-martingale (w.r.t. the natural filtration) and $R_n(f)$ is a remainder term. The martingale is shown to converge a.s. using standard results and the remainder term is shown to converge to 0. This decomposition is not unique and different choices can be found in the literature. The most usual is based on the *Poisson equation* with forcing function f, namely $\hat{f} - P\hat{f} = f - \pi_\star(f)$. Sufficient conditions for the existence of a solution to the Poisson equation can be found in [44, Chapter 17]. In terms of $\hat{f}$, the martingale and the remainder terms may be expressed as

$$M_n(f) \overset{\text{def}}{=} \sum_{k=1}^n \left\{ \hat{f}(X_k) - P\hat{f}(X_{k-1}) \right\}, \qquad R_n(f) \overset{\text{def}}{=} n^{-1} \left[P\hat{f}(X_0) - P\hat{f}(X_n) \right].$$

Proposition 2.3, which follows directly from [33, Theorem 2.18], provides sufficient conditions for the almost-sure convergence of $n^{-1} \sum_{k=1}^n f(X_k)$ to $\pi_\star(f)$.

Proposition 2.3 *Let $\{X_k, k \geq 0\}$ be a Markov chain with transition kernel P and invariant distribution $\pi_\star$. Let $f : X \to \mathbb{R}$ be a measurable function; assume that the Poisson equation $g - Pg = f - \pi_\star(f)$ with forcing function f possesses a solution denoted by $\hat{f}$. Assume in addition that (i) $|P\hat{f}(X_0)| < \infty$, $\mathbb{P}$-p.s. (ii) $\limsup_{n \to \infty} n^{-1} |P\hat{f}(X_n)| = 0$ $\mathbb{P}$-a.s. and (iii) there exists $p \in [1, 2]$ such that $\sum_k k^{-p} \mathbb{E}\left[|\hat{f}(X_k) - P\hat{f}(X_{k-1})|^p \,\middle|\, \mathcal{F}_{k-1} \right] < +\infty$ $\mathbb{P}$-a.s. , then*

$$\lim_{n \to \infty} n^{-1} \sum_{k=1}^n f(X_k) = \pi_\star(f), \qquad \mathbb{P} - a.s.$$

The method based on martingales has been successfully used to prove the strong LLN (and central limit theorems) for different adaptive chains (see e.g. [2, 7, 6]). A weak law of large numbers for bounded functions is also established in [50] using a different approach.

We develop below a general scheme of proof for the strong LLN, based on the martingale approach. Let $f : X \to \mathbb{R}$ be a measurable function. For any $\theta \in \Theta$, let $\hat{f}_\theta$ denote a solution to the Poisson equation $g - P_\theta g = f - \pi_\theta(f)$ with forcing function f. Consider the following decomposition

$$n^{-1} \sum_{k=1}^n \{ f(X_k) - \pi_{\theta_{k-1}}(f) \} = n^{-1} M_n(f) + \sum_{i=1}^2 R_{n,i}(f),$$

where

$$M_n(f) \overset{\text{def}}{=} \sum_{k=1}^n \{ \hat{f}_{\theta_{k-1}}(X_k) - P_{\theta_{k-1}} \hat{f}_{\theta_{k-1}}(X_{k-1}) \}, \quad R_{n,1}(f) \overset{\text{def}}{=} n^{-1} \left(P_{\theta_0} \hat{f}_{\theta_0}(X_0) - P_{\theta_{n-1}} \hat{f}_{\theta_{n-1}}(X_n) \right),$$

$$R_{n,2}(f) \overset{\text{def}}{=} n^{-1} \sum_{k=1}^{n-1} \{ P_{\theta_k} \hat{f}_{\theta_k}(X_k) - P_{\theta_{k-1}} \hat{f}_{\theta_{k-1}}(X_k) \}.$$

$\{M_n(f), n \geq 0\}$ is a $\mathbb{P}$-martingale and $R_{n,i}(f)$, $i = 1, 2$ are remainder terms. Conditions for the almost-sure convergence to zero of $\{n^{-1} M_n(f), n \geq 0\}$ and of the residual term

$\{R_{n,1}(f), n \geq 1\}$ are similar to those of Proposition 2.3. The remaining term $R_{n,2}(f)$ requires additional attention.

All the ingredients to establish the LLN are summarised in the following theorem.

Theorem 2.4 *Assume A1. Let f be a measurable function such that, for any $\theta \in \Theta$, a solution $\hat{f}_\theta$ to the Poisson equation $g - P_\theta g = f - \pi_\theta(f)$ with forcing function f exists. If*

(i) $|P_{\theta_0} \hat{f}_{\theta_0}(X_0)| < \infty$, $\mathbb{P}$-a.s.

(ii) $\limsup_{n \to \infty} n^{-1} |P_{\theta_{n-1}} \hat{f}_{\theta_{n-1}}(X_n)| = 0$, $\mathbb{P}$-a.s.

(iii) there exists $p \in [1, 2]$ such that

$$\sum_k k^{-p} \mathbb{E}\left[|\hat{f}_{\theta_{k-1}}(X_k) - P_{\theta_{k-1}} \hat{f}_{\theta_{k-1}}(X_{k-1})|^p \,\big|\, \mathcal{F}_{k-1} \right] < \infty, \quad \mathbb{P} - a.s.$$

(iv) the series $\sum_k k^{-1} |P_{\theta_k} \hat{f}_{\theta_k}(X_k) - P_{\theta_{k-1}} \hat{f}_{\theta_{k-1}}(X_k)|$ is finite $\mathbb{P}$-a.s.

then $\lim_{n \to \infty} n^{-1} \sum_{k=1}^n \{f(X_k) - \pi_{\theta_{k-1}}(f)\} = 0$, $\mathbb{P}$-a.s.

If $\pi_\theta = \pi_\star$ for any $\theta \in \Theta$, Theorem 2.4 implies the strong LLN for the function f. When $\pi_\theta \neq \pi_\star$, we have to prove the a.s. convergence of $n^{-1} \sum_{k=1}^n \pi_{\theta_{k-1}}(f)$ to $\pi_\star(f)$, which can be deduced from the a.s. convergence of $\{\pi_{\theta_n}(f), n \geq 0\}$ to $\pi_\star(f)$. Sufficient conditions for unbounded functions f are considered in [22].

2.5   Convergence of the equi-energy sampler

We study the convergence of the EE sampler described in Section 2.2.2 in the case $K = 1$. The case $K > 1$ is studied in [22, 21]. We prove the convergence of the marginals and a strong LLN for bounded continuous functions. Extensions of the strong LLN to unbounded functions can be found in [6] and [22].

If $\{Y_n, n \geq 0\}$ is such that $n^{-1} \sum_{k=1}^n f(Y_k) \to \tilde{\pi}(f)$ a.s. for any bounded function f, the empirical distributions $\{\theta_n, n \geq 0\}$ converge weakly to $\tilde{\pi}$ so that, asymptotically, the dynamic of X_n is given by $P_{\tilde{\pi}}$. Since $\pi P_{\tilde{\pi}} = \pi$, it is expected that π governs the distribution of $\{X_n, n \geq 0\}$ asymptotically. By application of the results of Sections 2.3 and 2.4 this intuition can now be formalised.

The following conditions are assumed:

EES1 π is a bounded positive density distribution on X.

Proposition 2.5 *(a) Assume EES1. For any $\theta \in \Theta$, the transition kernel P_θ possesses a unique probability invariant distribution π_θ. Furthermore, for all $x \in$ X, $k \geq 0$,*

$$\|P_\theta^k(x, \cdot) - \pi_\theta\|_{TV} \leq \rho^k(\theta) \, \|\delta_x - \pi_\theta\|_{TV}, \qquad \rho(\theta) \stackrel{\text{def}}{=} 1 - \epsilon \int \frac{\pi^\beta(x)}{\sup_X \pi^\beta} \theta(dx).$$

(b) The condition A2 holds.

EES2 For any bounded function $f :$ X $\to \mathbb{R}$, $\lim_n \theta_n(f) = \tilde{\pi}(f)$ $\mathbb{P}$-a.s.

Condition EES2 holds whenever $\{Y_n, n \geq 0\}$ is an ergodic Markov chain with stationary distribution $\tilde{\pi}$. A sufficient condition for ergodicity is the phi-irreducibility, the aperiodicity and the existence of a unique invariant distribution $\tilde{\pi}$ for the transition kernel of the chain $\{Y_n, n \geq 0\}$. For example, such a Markov chain $\{Y_n, n \geq 0\}$ can be obtained by running a HM sampler with invariant distribution $\tilde{\pi}$, with proposal distribution chosen in such a way that the sampler is ergodic (see e.g. [46]).

Proposition 2.6 *Assume EES1 and EES2. Then condition A3 holds.*

The convergence of $\pi_{\theta_n}(f)$ to $\pi(f)$ for some bounded function f is difficult; such convergence is established (under weak additional conditions) for *continuous* functions in [22].

Theorem 2.7 *Assume EES1, EES2 and $\lim_n \pi_{\theta_n}(f) = \pi(f)$ for some function f. Then,*

$$\lim_n \left| \mathbb{E}\left[f(X_n) \right] - \pi(f) \right| = 0.$$

Similarly, by checking the conditions of Theorem 2.4, we may establish the following theorem.

Theorem 2.8 *Assume EES1, EES2 and $\lim_n \pi_{\theta_n}(f) = \pi(f)$ for some bounded function f. Then $\lim_n n^{-1} \sum_{k=1}^n f(X_k) = \pi(f) = 0$ a.s.*

2.6 Conclusion

The adaptive MCMC framework provides a wide class of simulation methods, allowing the efficiency of the sampler to be improved, in some situations significantly. The theory of internal adaptive algorithms is now quite well understood and the key design constraints to develop a successful procedure are known. Some useful applications of this method have already been proposed for Bayesian inference for difficult large-scale problems, in particular in inverse problems for remote sensing applications and in bioinformatics. There are still a lot of open problems. Most of the adaptation techniques known so far are global, whereas in most problems it happens to be more sensible to adopt state-dependent (or at least regional) adaptation. The use of the internal adaptive algorithm for hybrid Monte Carlo is yet in its infancy; even the choice of a sensible adaptation criterion in this case is not obvious. Here again, it is likely that the proposal should ideally be state- or regional-dependent.

The external adaptive algorithms are very promising. The theory is less mature, the first complete convergence proofs (under some restrictive assumptions) have been obtained only very recently. The potential of these methods in applications is important and yet largely unexplored. Using the previous experiences of tempered MCMC algorithms, it is likely that these algorithms have the potential of offering significant gains, and some encouraging results have already been reported. The optimisation of the simulation structure is still far from being well understood: the number of subprocesses, the amount of interactions between the subprocesses, the choice of the target distributions for the subprocesses have to be investigated both from the methodological and the theoretical sides.

2.A Appendix: Proof of Section 2.5

Since $K = 1$, the transition kernel P_θ is given by

$$P_\theta(x, A) = (1 - \epsilon)P(x, A) + \epsilon \left\{ \int_A \alpha(x, y)\theta(dy) + \delta_x(A) \int (1 - \alpha(x, y)) \theta(dy) \right\}.$$

2.A.1   Proof of Proposition 2.5

(a) It is sufficient to prove that the Dobrushin coefficient of the transition kernel P_θ is upper bounded by $\rho(\theta)$ (see e.g. [14, Theorem 4.3.16.]). Denote by $\delta(P_\theta)$ the Dobrushin coefficient. By definition, (see e.g. [14, Definition 4.3.7. and Lemma 4.3.5.])

$$\delta(P_\theta) \leq 1 - \inf \sum_{i=1}^{N} \{P_\theta(x, A_i) \wedge P_\theta(y, A_i)\},$$

where the infimum is taken over all $(x, y) \in X^2$ and all finite measurable partitions $A_1, \ldots, A_N$ of X. By definition of P_θ and $\alpha(x, y)$ (see Eq. (2.4))

$$P_\theta(x, A) \geq \epsilon \int_A \left\{ 1 \wedge \frac{\pi^\beta(y)}{\pi^\beta(x)} \right\} \theta(dy) \geq \epsilon \int_A \pi^\beta(y) \left\{ \frac{1}{\pi^\beta(y)} \wedge \frac{1}{\pi^\beta(x)} \right\} \theta(dy)$$

$$\geq [\sup_X \pi^\beta]^{-1} \epsilon \int_A \pi^\beta(y) \, \theta(dy) = (1 - \rho(\theta)) \, \nu_\theta(A),$$

where $\nu_\theta(A) \propto \int_A \pi^\beta(y) \, \theta(dy)$ is a probability distribution. This implies that $\delta(\theta) \leq \rho(\theta)$ and concludes the proof.

(b) By definition of the transition kernel, for any bounded function f,

$$P_\theta f(x) - P_{\theta'} f(x) = \epsilon \int \alpha(x, y) \{f(y) - f(x)\} (\theta(dy) - \theta'(dy)).$$

Since $|\alpha(x, y)| \leq 1$, $\sup_{|f|_\infty \leq 1} |P_\theta f(x) - P_{\theta'} f(x)| \leq 2\epsilon \sup_{|f|_\infty \leq 1} |\theta(f) - \theta'(f)|$. Therefore, we have to prove that $\{\|\theta_n - \theta_{n-1}\|_{TV}, n \geq 1\}$ converges to zero in probability. This holds since

$$|\theta_n(f) - \theta_{n-1}(f)| \leq \frac{|f(Y_n)|}{n+1} + \frac{1}{n(n+1)} \sum_{k=0}^{n-1} |f(Y_k)| \leq \frac{2}{n+1} |f|_\infty.$$

2.A.2   Proof of Proposition 2.6

Let $\eta > 0$, and set $\gamma \overset{\text{def}}{=} \sup_X \pi^\beta$. Under EES1, $\rho(\theta) \in (0, 1)$ for any $\theta \in \Theta$. By Proposition 2.5, $M_\eta(x, \theta) \leq \log \eta / \log \rho(\theta)$ thus proving that the sequence $\{M_\eta(X_n, \theta_n), n \geq 0\}$ is bounded in probability if

$$\lim_{M \to +\infty} \limsup_n \mathbb{P} \left(K(\theta_n) \leq \frac{1 - \eta^{1/M}}{\epsilon \gamma} \right) = 0, \qquad K(\theta) \overset{\text{def}}{=} \int \pi^\beta(x) \theta(dx).$$

Since $K(\theta_n) = (n+1)^{-1} \sum_{k=0}^{n} \pi^\beta(Y_k)$ and under EES1 $\sup_X \pi^\beta = \gamma^{-1} < +\infty$; then, under EES2, $\lim_n K(\theta_n) = \int \pi^\beta(x) \tilde{\pi}(dx) = C_\beta$ almost-surely, where C_β is such that $\tilde{\pi} = C_\beta \pi^{1-\beta}$. We have $C_\beta \geq 1$ and it can be assumed without loss of generality that M is large enough so that $(1 - \eta^{1/M})/(\epsilon\gamma) < C_\beta/2$. We then have

$$\mathbb{P} \left(K(\theta_n) \leq \frac{1 - \eta^{1/M}}{\epsilon\gamma} \right) \leq \mathbb{P} \left(K(\theta_n) - C_\beta \leq -C_\beta/2 \right) \leq \mathbb{P} \left(|K(\theta_n) - C_\beta| \geq C_\beta/2 \right).$$

Since $\{K(\theta_n) - C_\beta, n \geq 0\}$ converges a.s. to zero, the rhs converges to zero as $n \to \infty$, thus concluding the proof.

2.A.3 Proof of Theorem 2.8

Let f such that $|f|_\infty \leq 1$. By Proposition 2.5, for any θ, the function $\hat{f}_\theta$ exists on X and $|\hat{f}_\theta|_\infty \leq 2[1 - \rho(\theta)]^{-1}$.

Condition (i) is satisfied since $|P_{\theta_0}\hat{f}_{\theta_0}(X_0)| \leq |\hat{f}_{\theta_0}|_\infty \leq 2[1 - \rho(\theta_0)]^{-1}$, and $\rho(\theta_0) \in (0,1)$.

Condition (ii) follows from $|P_{\theta_{n-1}}\hat{f}_{\theta_{n-1}}(X_n)| \leq 2[1 - \rho(\theta_{n-1})]^{-1}$ and the fact that $\lim_{n\to\infty}\rho(\theta_n) = \rho(\tilde{\pi}) \in (0,1)$ $\mathbb{P}$-a.s. (which holds under EES2).

For $p \in (1,2]$

$$\left|\hat{f}_{\theta_{k-1}}(X_k) - P_{\theta_{k-1}}\hat{f}_{\theta_{k-1}}(X_{k-1})\right|^p \leq 2^p |\hat{f}_{\theta_{k-1}}|_\infty^p \leq 2^{p+1}[1 - \rho(\theta_{k-1})]^{-p}.$$

Under EES2, $\lim_{n\to\infty}\rho(\theta_n) = \rho(\tilde{\pi}) \in (0,1)$ $\mathbb{P}$-a.s. showing (iii).

Finally, we have (see [22])

$$P_\theta \hat{f}_\theta - P_{\theta'} \hat{f}_{\theta'} = \sum_{n\geq 1}\sum_{j=0}^{n-1}\left(P_\theta^j - \pi_\theta\right)(P_\theta - P_{\theta'})\left(P_{\theta'}^{n-j-1}f - \pi_{\theta'}(f)\right) + (\pi_{\theta'} - \pi_\theta)P_{\theta'}\hat{f}_{\theta'}.$$

For the first term, by Proposition 2.5, there exists a constant C such that for any θ, θ'

$$\left|\sum_{n\geq 1}\sum_{j=0}^{n-1}\left(P_\theta^j - \pi_\theta\right)(P_\theta - P_{\theta'})\left(P_{\theta'}^{n-j-1}f - \pi_{\theta'}(f)\right)\right|$$

$$\leq C\sum_{n\geq 1}\sum_{j=0}^{n-1}\|P_\theta - P_{\theta'}\|_{\mathrm{TV}}\,\rho(\theta)^j\,\rho(\theta')^{n-1-j}$$

$$\leq 2C\epsilon\,\|\theta - \theta'\|_{\mathrm{TV}}\,[1 - \rho(\theta)]^{-1}[1 - \rho(\theta')]^{-1}.$$

By definition of θ_k, $\|\theta_k - \theta_{k-1}\|_{\mathrm{TV}} = O(1/k)$ (see the proof of Proposition 2.5); and under EES2, $\lim_k \rho(\theta_k) = \rho(\tilde{\pi}) \in (0,1)$ a.s. This implies that the series

$$\sum_k \frac{1}{k}\left|\sum_{n\geq 1}\sum_{j=0}^{n-1}\left(P_{\theta_k}^j - \pi_{\theta_k}\right)(P_{\theta_k} - P_{\theta_{k-1}})\left(P_{\theta_{k-1}}^{n-j-1}f - \pi_{\theta_{k-1}}(f)\right)\right|$$

is finite $\mathbb{P}$-a.s. For the second term,

$$\left|(\pi_{\theta'} - \pi_\theta)P_{\theta'}\hat{f}_{\theta'}\right| \leq \|\pi_\theta - \pi_{\theta'}\|_{\mathrm{TV}}\,|\hat{f}_{\theta'}|_\infty \leq 2[1 - \rho(\theta')]^{-1}\,\|\pi_\theta - \pi_{\theta'}\|_{\mathrm{TV}}.$$

Combining the decomposition

$$\pi_\theta(f) - \pi_{\theta'}(f) = \left(P_{\theta'}^l f(x) - \pi_{\theta'}(f)\right) + \left(\pi_\theta(f) - P_\theta^l f(x)\right) + \left(P_\theta^l f(x) - P_{\theta'}^l f(x)\right),$$

and Proposition 2.5, we have for any $l \geq 1$, $x \in$ X and θ, θ'

$$\|\pi_\theta - \pi_{\theta'}\|_{\mathrm{TV}} \leq 2\left\{\rho^l(\theta) + \rho^l(\theta')\right\} + \sup_{h, |h|_\infty \leq 1}\sum_{j=0}^{l-1}\left|P_\theta^j(P_\theta - P_{\theta'})\left(P_{\theta'}^{l-j-1}h(x) - \pi_{\theta'}(h)\right)\right|.$$

Since $\rho(\theta) \in (0,1)$ for all θ, this yields by Proposition 2.5

$$\|\pi_\theta - \pi_{\theta'}\|_{\mathrm{TV}} \leq \frac{2}{1 - \rho(\theta)}\|P_\theta - P_{\theta'}\|_{\mathrm{TV}} \leq \frac{4\epsilon}{1 - \rho(\theta)}\|\theta - \theta'\|_{\mathrm{TV}}.$$

Using again EES2 and the property $\|\theta_k - \theta_{k-1}\|_{\mathrm{TV}} = O(1/k)$, the series

$$\sum_k \frac{1}{k}\left|(\pi_{\theta_{k-1}} - \pi_{\theta_k})P_{\theta_{k-1}}\hat{f}_{\theta_{k-1}}\right|$$

converges $\mathbb{P}$-a.s. The proof is concluded.

Bibliography

[1] C. Andrieu, A. Jasra, A. Doucet and P. Del Moral. On non-linear Markov chain Monte Carlo via self-interacting approximations. To appear, Bernoulli 2011.

[2] C. Andrieu and E. Moulines. On the ergodicity property of some adaptive MCMC algorithms. *Annals of Applied Probability*, **16**(3):1462–1505, August 2006.

[3] C. Andrieu, E. Moulines and P. Priouret. Stability of stochastic approximation under verifiable conditions. *SIAM Journal on Control and Optimization*, **44**(1):283–312 (electronic), 2005.

[4] C. Andrieu and C. Robert. Controlled Markov chain Monte Carlo methods for optimal sampling. Technical Report 125, Cahiers du Ceremade, 2001.

[5] C. Andrieu and J. Thoms. A tutorial on adaptive MCMC. *Statistics and Computing*, **18**(4):343–373, 2008.

[6] Y. Atchadé. A cautionary tale on the efficiency of some adaptive Monte Carlo schemes. Technical report, ArXiv:0901:1378v1, 2009.

[7] Y. Atchadé and G. Fort. Limit theorems for some adaptive MCMC algorithms with subgeometric kernels. *Bernoulli*, **16**(1): 116–154, 2010.

[8] Y. F. Atchadé and J. S. Rosenthal. On adaptive Markov chain Monte Carlo algorithms. *Bernoulli*, **11**(5):815–828, 2005.

[9] Y. Bai. Simultaneous drift conditions for adaptive Markov chain Monte Carlo algorithms. Technical report, University of Toronto, available at www.probability.ca/jeff/ftpdir/yanbai2.pdf, 2009.

[10] Y. Bai, G. O. Roberts and J. S. Rosenthal. On the containment condition for adaptive Markov chain Monte Carlo algorithms. Technical report, University of Toronto, available at www.probability.ca/jeff/, 2009.

[11] A. Benveniste, M. Métivier and P. Priouret. *Adaptive Algorithms and Stochastic Approximations*, volume 22. Springer, 1990. Translated from the French by Stephen S. S. Wilson.

[12] B. Bercu, P. Del Moral and A. Doucet. A functional central limit theorem for a class of interacting Markov chain Monte Carlo methods. *Electronic Journal of Probability*, **14**(73):2130–2155, 2009.

[13] O. Cappé and E. Moulines. On-line expectation-maximization algorithm for latent data models. *Journal of the Royal Statistical Society B*, **71**(3):593–613, 2009.

[14] O. Cappé, E. Moulines and T. Rydén. *Inference in Hidden Markov Models*. Springer, 2005.

[15] D. Chauveau and P. Vandekerkhove. Un algorithme de Hastings-Metropolis avec apprentissage séquentiel. *Comptes cendus de l'Academie des Sciences Paris Séries I Mathematique*, **329**(2):173–176, 1999.

[16] D. Chauveau and P. Vandekerkhove. Improving convergence of the Hastings-Metropolis algorithm with an adaptive proposal. *Scandinavian Journal of Statistics*, **29**(1):13–29, 2002.

[17] H-F. Chen. *Stochastic Approximation and Its Applications*, volume 64 of *Nonconvex Optimization and Its Applications*. Kluwer Academic Publishers, 2002.

[18] R. V. Craiu, J. S. Rosenthal and C. Yang. Learn from thy neighbor: Parallel-chain adaptive MCMC. *Journal of the American Statistical Association*, **104**(488):1454–1466, 2009.

[19] P. Diaconis, K. Khare and L. Saloff-Coste. Gibbs sampling, exponential families and orthogonal polynomials (with discussion and rejoinder). *Statistical Science*, **23**(2):151–178, 2008.

[20] M. Duflo. *Random Iterative Models*, volume 34. Springer, 1997. Translated from the 1990 French original by S. S. Wilson and revised by the author.

[21] G. Fort, E. Moulines and P. Priouret. Convergence of interacting MCMC: central limit theorem. Technical report, Institut Telecom/Telecom ParisTech; CNRS/UMR 5181, 2010.

[22] G. Fort, E. Moulines and P. Priouret. Convergence of adaptive and interacting Markov chain Monte Carlo algorithms. Technical report, Institut Telecom/Telecom ParisTech; CNRS/UMR 5141, 2010.

[23] A. Gelman, G. O. Roberts and W. R. Gilks. Efficient Metropolis jumping rules. In *Bayesian Statistics, 5 (Alicante, 1994)*, pages 599–607, Oxford University Press 1996.

[24] S. Geman and D. Geman. Stochastic relaxation, Gibbs distributions and the Bayesian restoration of images. *IEEE Transactions on Pattern Analysis and Machine Intelligence*, **6**:721–741, 1984.

[25] C. J. Geyer. Markov chain Monte Carlo maximum likelihood. *Computing Science and Statistics: Proc. 23rd Symposium on the Interface, Interface Foundation, Fairfax Station, VA*, pages 156–163, 1991.

[26] C. J. Geyer and E. A. Thompson. Annealing Markov chain Monte Carlo with applications to ancestral inference. *Journal of the American Statistical Association*, **90**:909–920, 1995.

[27] P. Giordani and R. Kohn. Adaptive independent Metropolis-Hastings by fast estimation of mixtures of normals, 2008.

[28] H. Haario, M. Laine, M. Lehtinen, E. Saksman and J. Tamminen. Markov chain Monte Carlo

methods for high dimensional inversion in remote sensing. *Journal of the Royal Statistical Society B*, **66**(3):591–607, 2004.

[29] H. Haario, M. Laine, A. Mira and E. Saksman. DRAM: efficient adaptive MCMC. *Statistics and Computing*, **16**:339–354, 2006.

[30] H. Haario, E. Saksman and J. Tamminen. Adaptive proposal distribution for random walk Metropolis algorithm. *Computational Statistics*, **14**:375–395, 1999.

[31] H. Haario, E. Saksman and J. Tamminen. An adaptive Metropolis algorithm. *Bernoulli*, 7:223–242, 2001.

[32] H. Haario, E. Saksman and J. Tamminen. Componentwise adaptation for high dimensional MCMC. *Computational Statistics*, **20**(2):265–273, 2005.

[33] P. Hall and C. C. Heyde. *Martingale Limit Theory and its Application*. Academic Press, New York, London, 1980.

[34] A. Jasra, D. A. Stephens and C. C. Holmes. On population-based simulation for static inference. *Statistics and Computing*, **17**(3):263–279, 2007.

[35] J. Keith, D. Kroese and G. Sofronov. Adaptive independence samplers. *Statistics and Computing*, **18**:409–420, 2008.

[36] S. C. Kou, Q. Zhou and W. H. Wong. Equi-energy sampler with applications in statistical inference and statistical mechanics. *Annals of Statistics*, **34**(4):1581–1619, 2006.

[37] H. J. Kushner and G. G. Yin. *Stochastic Approximation and Recursive Algorithms and Applications*, volume 35. Springer, 2nd edition, 2003.

[38] M. Laine. MCMC toolbox for Matlab, 2008. www.helsinki.fi/ mjlaine/mcmc/.

[39] M. Laine and J. Tamminen. Aerosol model selection and uncertainty modelling by adaptive mcmc technique. *Atmospheric and Chemistry Physics*, **8**:7697–7707, 2008.

[40] R. Levine. A note on markov chain Monte-Carlo sweep strategies. *Journal of Statistical Computation and Simulation*, **75**(4):253–262, 2005.

[41] R. Levine and G. Casella. Optimizing random scan Gibbs samplers. *Journal of Multivariate Analysis*, **97**:2071–2100, 2006.

[42] R. A. Levine, Z. Yu, W. G. Hanley and J. A. Nitao. Implementing Random Scan Gibbs Samplers. *Computational Statistics*, **20**:177–196, 2005.

[43] E. Marinari and G. Parisi. Simulated tempering: A new Monte Carlo scheme. *Europhysics Letters*, **19**:451–458, 1992.

[44] S. P. Meyn and R. L. Tweedie. *Markov Chains and Stochastic Stability*. Cambridge University Press, 2009.

[45] A. Mira. On Metropolis-Hastings algorithms with delayed rejection. *Metron*, **LIX**(3-4):231–241, 2001.

[46] C. P. Robert and G. Casella. *Monte Carlo Statistical Methods*. Springer, 2nd edition, 2004.

[47] G. Roberts and J. Rosenthal. Examples of adaptive MCMC. *Journal of Computational and Graphical Statistics* **18**(2):349–367, 2009.

[48] G. O. Roberts, A. Gelman and W. R. Gilks. Weak convergence and optimal scaling of random walk Metropolis algorithms. *Annals of Applied Probability*, **7**(1):110–120, 1997.

[49] G. O. Roberts and J. S. Rosenthal. Optimal scaling for various Metropolis-Hastings algorithms. *Statistical Science*, **16**(4):351–367, 2001.

[50] G. O. Roberts and J. S. Rosenthal. Coupling and ergodicity of adaptive Markov chain Monte Carlo algorithms. *Journal of Applied Probability*, **44**(2):458–475, 2007.

[51] J. S. Rosenthal. AMCMC: An R interface for adaptive MCMC. *Computational Statistics and Data Analysis*, **51**(12):5467–5470, 2007.

[52] J. S. Rosenthal. Optimal proposal distributions and adaptive MCMC. In *MCMC Handbook*. Chapman & Hall/CRC Press, 2009.

[53] R. Y. Rubinstein and D. P. Kroese. *The Cross-Entropy Method*. Springer, 2004.

[54] E. Turro, N. Bochkina, A-M. Hein and S. Richardson. Bgx: a Bioconductor package for the Bayesian integrated analysis of Affymetrix Genechips. *BMC Bioinformatics*, **8**(1):439, 2007.

Contributors

Yves Atchadé, University of Michigan, 1085 South University, Ann Arbor, 48109, MI, USA
Gersende Fort, LTCI, CNRS–Telecom ParisTech, 46 rue Barrault, 75634 Paris Cedex 13, France
Eric Moulines, LTCI, CNRS–Telecom ParisTech, 46 rue Barrault, 75634 Paris Cedex 13, France
Pierre Priouret, LPMA, Université P. & M. Curie, Boîte courrier 188, 75252 Paris Cedex 05, France

3

Auxiliary particle filtering: recent developments

Nick Whiteley and Adam M. Johansen

3.1 Background

3.1.1 State space models

State space models (SSMs) are very popular statistical models for time series. Such models describe the trajectory of some system of interest as an unobserved E-valued Markov chain, known as the *signal process*. Let $X_1 \sim \nu$ and $X_n|(X_{n-1} = x_{n-1}) \sim f(\cdot|x_{n-1})$ denote this process. Indirect observations are available via an *observation* process, $\{Y_n\}_{n \in \mathbb{N}}$. Conditional upon X_n, Y_n is independent of the remainder of the observation and signal processes, with $Y_n|(X_n = x_n) \sim g(\cdot|x_n)$.

For any sequence $\{z_n\}_{n \in \mathbb{N}}$, we write $z_{i:j} = (z_i, z_{i+1}, ..., z_j)$. In numerous applications, we are interested in estimating, recursively in time, an analytically intractable sequence of posterior distributions $\{p(x_{1:n}|y_{1:n})\}_{n \in \mathbb{N}}$, of the form

$$p(x_{1:n}|y_{1:n}) \propto \nu(x_1)g(y_1|x_1) \prod_{k=2}^{n} f(x_k|x_{k-1})g(y_k|x_k). \tag{3.1}$$

A great deal has been written about inference for SSMs – see [4, 20, 22] for example – and their counterparts in continuous time [2]. *Filtering*, which corresponds to computing $p(x_n|y_{1:n})$ for each n, is a task of particular interest. Estimation problems in a variety of scientific disciplines can naturally be cast as filtering tasks. A canonical example arises in engineering, where the signal process describes the location and intrinsic parameters of a physical object, observations arise from a noisy sensor and the task is to reconstruct the state of the object as accurately as possible, as observations arrive. Other examples arise from the processing of biological, chemical, seismic, audio, video and financial data. In all these cases the SSM provides a flexible and simple framework in which to describe the relationship between a physically interpretable or abstract hidden process and observed data. Further background information on this and related classes of models can be found in Chapter 1 of this book.

This chapter is concerned with a class of Monte Carlo algorithms which address the problem of filtering in SSMs by approximating the distributions of interest with a set of weighted random samples. Attention is focused on an algorithm known as the auxiliary particle filter (APF). The APF has seen widespread use in several application areas and a number of algorithms employing the same underlying mechanism have been developed. Existing applications include filtering in object tracking and stochastic volatility models, [44] (in which the APF was introduced), [6]; time-varying autoregressive models for audio processing, [1]; exact filtering for diffusions, [24]; multi-object tracking, [54] and belief propagation in graphical models [3].

The remainder of this section introduces a standard approach to the filtering problem, sequential importance resampling (SIR) and describes the APF. Section 3.2 illustrates the strong connection between these algorithms, and provides some guidance upon implementation of the APF. Section 3.3 illustrates a number of extensions which are suggested by these connections. Section 3.4 describes an elementary technique for variance reduction when applying the APF to SSMs. Termed the stratified APF (sAPF), this algorithm uses low variance sampling mechanisms to assign particles to strata of the state space. The performance of the method is demonstrated in the context of a switching stochastic volatility model using stock index returns data.

3.1.2 Particle filtering

As described above, a common objective when performing inference in SSMs is the recursive approximation of a sequence of posterior distributions (Eq. (3.1)). There are a small number of situations in which these distributions can be obtained in closed form (notably the linear-Gaussian case, which leads to the Kalman filter). However, in general it is necessary to employ approximations. One of the most versatile approaches is to use sequential Monte Carlo (SMC) methods. Whilst typically more computationally demanding than alternative deterministic techniques (for example see Part II of this volume), SMC methods are very flexible and have attractive theoretical properties, some of which are discussed below.

The term *particle filtering* is often used to describe the approximation of the optimal filtering equations using SMC techniques. Two common implementations of such algorithms are described in the next two sections. The objective with all such methods is to approximate, sequentially in time, the distribution of X_n given that $Y_{1:n} = y_{1:n}$.

The unnormalised posterior distribution $p(x_{1:n}, y_{1:n})$ given in Eq. (3.1) satisfies

$$p(x_{1:n}, y_{1:n}) = p(x_{1:n-1}, y_{1:n-1})f(x_n|x_{n-1})g(y_n|x_n).$$

Consequently, the posterior $p(x_{1:n}|y_{1:n})$ satisfies the following recursion

$$p(x_{1:n}|y_{1:n}) = p(x_{1:n-1}|y_{1:n-1})\frac{f(x_n|x_{n-1})g(y_n|x_n)}{p(y_n|y_{1:n-1})}, \tag{3.2}$$

where

$$p(y_n|y_{1:n-1}) = \int p(x_{n-1}|y_{1:n-1})f(x_n|x_{n-1})g(y_n|x_n)dx_{n-1:n}.$$

In the literature, the recursion satisfied by the marginal distribution $p(x_n|y_{1:n})$ is often presented. It is straightforward to check (by integrating out $x_{1:n-1}$ in Eq. (3.2)) that

$$p(x_n|y_{1:n}) = \frac{g(y_n|x_n)p(x_n|y_{1:n-1})}{p(y_n|y_{1:n-1})}, \tag{3.3}$$

where

$$p(x_n|y_{1:n-1}) = \int f(x_n|x_{n-1})p(x_{n-1}|y_{1:n-1})dx_{n-1}. \tag{3.4}$$

Recursion (3.4) is known as the prediction step and recursion (3.3) is known as the update step. However, most particle filtering methods rely on a numerical approximation of recursion (3.2) and not of (3.3)–(3.4). This is the case for the majority of the algorithms described in this chapter. One exception, which is described in more detail in Section 3.3.1, is the marginal particle filter [38] which allows the use of an auxiliary variable technique admitting a similar interpretation to that discussed in the context of the standard APF below.

Sequential Monte Carlo techniques propagate a collection of weighted samples, termed *particles*, from one iteration to the next in such a way that they provide an approximation of the filtering distribution at each iteration. These collections of particles are used both to approximate integrals with respect to the distributions of interest (and hence to provide estimates of statistics of interest) and to approximate those distributions themselves, thereby allowing inference at the next time step. For a more detailed explanation of these algorithms and an illustration of how most SMC methods may be interpreted as SIR, see [22].

3.1.3 Sequential importance resampling

Sequential importance resampling is one of the simplest SMC approaches to the filtering problem. In fact, as illustrated in Algorithm 3.1, this technique can be used to sample from essentially any sequence of distributions defined on a sequence of spaces of strictly increasing dimension. At its nth iteration, Algorithm 3.1 provides an approximation of $\pi_n(x_{1:n})$. A crucial step in this algorithm is resampling. This involves duplicating particles with high weights, discarding particles with low weights and reweighting to preserve the distribution targeted by the weighted sample. This step prevents a large amount of computational power being wasted on samples with weights close to zero whilst retaining the consistency of associated estimators. The simplest scheme, multinomial resampling, achieves this by drawing N times from the empirical distribution of the weighted particle set (lower variance alternatives are summarised in [20] and compared in [17]).

Algorithm 3.1 The generic SIR algorithm

At time 1
    for $i = 1$ to N **do**
        Sample $X_1^{(i)} \sim q_1(\cdot)$.
        Set $W_1^{(i)} \propto \frac{\pi_1(X_1^{(i)})}{q_1(X_1^{(i)})}$.
    end for
    Resample $\left\{X_1^{(i)}, W_1^{(i)}\right\}$ to obtain $\left\{X_1^{\prime(i)}, \frac{1}{N}\right\}$.
At time $n \geq 2$
    for $i = 1$ to N **do**
        Set $X_{1:n-1}^{(i)} = X_{1:n-1}^{\prime(i)}$.
        Sample $X_n^{(i)} \sim q_n(\cdot | X_{n-1}^{(i)})$.
        Set $W_n^{(i)} \propto \frac{\pi_n(X_{1:n}^{(i)})}{q_n(X_n^{(i)} | X_{n-1}^{(i)}) \pi_{n-1}(X_{1:n-1}^{(i)})}$.
    end for
    Resample $\left\{X_{1:n}^{(i)}, W_n^{(i)}\right\}$ to obtain $\left\{X_{1:n}^{\prime(i)}, \frac{1}{N}\right\}$.

In a filtering context, $\pi_n(x_{1:n}) = p(x_{1:n}|y_{1:n})$ and the expectation of some test function φ_n with respect to the filtering distribution $\overline{\varphi}_n = \int \varphi_n(x_n) p(x_n|y_{1:n}) dx_n$ can be estimated using

$$\widehat{\varphi}_{n,SIR}^N = \sum_{i=1}^{N} W_n^{(i)} \varphi_n(X_n^{(i)}),$$

where $W_n^{(i)} = w_n(X_{n-1:n}^{(i)}) / \sum_{j=1}^{N} w_n(X_{n-1:n}^{(j)})$ and

$$w_n(x_{n-1:n}) = \frac{\pi_n(x_{1:n})}{q_n(x_n|x_{n-1})\pi_{n-1}(x_{1:n-1})} \propto \frac{g(y_n|x_n)f(x_n|x_{n-1})}{q_n(x_n|x_{n-1})}. \tag{3.5}$$

Note that Eq. (3.5) depends upon only the two most recent components of the particle trajectory, and thus Algorithm 3.1 can be implemented with storage requirements which do not increase over time and is suitable for online applications. In fact, SIR can be regarded as a selection-mutation (genetic-type) algorithm constructed with a precise probabilistic interpretation. Viewing SIR as a particle approximation of a Feynman–Kac flow [13] allows many theoretical results to be established.

This simple SIR algorithm involves resampling at every iteration. In general, this may not be necessary. Whilst resampling permits stability of the algorithm in the long run, each act of resampling leads to a short-term increase in estimator variance. A common strategy, dating back at least to [39], is to resample only when the degeneracy of the importance weights, as measured for example by the coefficient of variation, exceeds some threshold. Theoretical analyses of algorithms which resample in this manner have been presented in [16] and [18].

It is commonly accepted that, when designing algorithms for particle filtering, one should endeavour to ensure that the variance of the importance weights is made as small as possible. In pursuit of this objective, it is usual to attempt to employ proposal distributions which are as close as possible to the so-called optimal form, $q_n(x_n|x_{n-1}) \propto f(x_n|x_{n-1})g(y_n|x_n)$ which makes the incremental importance weight independent of x_n. In practice, it is rarely possible to sample from a distribution of the optimal form, although a number of techniques for obtaining good approximations have been developed.

3.1.4 Auxiliary particle filters

The use of a well-chosen proposal distribution ensures that knowledge of the current observation is incorporated into the proposal mechanism and so particles are not moved blindly into regions of the state space which are extremely unlikely in light of that observation. However it seems wasteful to resample particles at the end of iteration $n-1$ prior to looking at y_n. That is, it is natural to ask whether it is possible to employ knowledge about the next observation *before* resampling to ensure that particles which are likely to be compatible with that observation have a good chance of surviving – is it possible to preserve diversity in the particle set by taking into account the immediate future as well as the present when carrying out selection? The APF first proposed by [44, 45] invoked an auxiliary variable construction in answer to this question.

The essence of this APF was that the sampling step could be modified to sample, for each particle, an auxiliary variable, corresponding to a particle index, according to a distribution which weights each particle in terms of its compatibility with the coming observation. A suitable weighting is provided by some $\widehat{p}(y_n|x_{n-1})$, an approximation of $p(y_n|x_{n-1}) = \int g(y_n|x_n)f(x_n|x_{n-1})dx_n$ (if the latter is not available analytically). Then the new state value is sampled as the offspring of the particle indicated by this auxiliary variable. It is straightforward to see that this is equivalent to resampling according to those weights before carrying out a standard sampling and resampling iteration. In the terminology of [44], an APF which employs the exact $p(y_n|x_{n-1})$ and proposes according to $q_n(x_n|x_{n-1}) \propto f(x_n|x_{n-1})g(y_n|x_n)$ is called 'fully adapted'.

A similar approach in which the auxiliary weights are combined with those of the standard weighting was proposed in [5], which involved a single resampling during each iteration of the algorithm (see Algorithm 3.2).

Algorithm 3.2 Auxiliary particle filter

At time 1
    for $i = 1$ to N **do**
        Sample $X_1^{(i)} \sim q_1(\cdot)$.
        Set $\widetilde{W}_1^{(i)} \propto \frac{g(y_1|X_1^{(i)})\nu(X_1^{(i)})}{q_1(X_1^{(i)})}$.
    end for
At time $n \geq 2$
    for $i = 1$ to N **do**
        Set $W_{n-1}^{(i)} \propto \widetilde{W}_{n-1}^{(i)} \times \widehat{p}(y_n|X_{n-1}^{(i)})$.
    end for
    Resample $\left\{X_{n-1}^{(i)}, W_{n-1}^{(i)}\right\}$ to obtain $\left\{X_{n-1}'^{(i)}, \frac{1}{N}\right\}$.
    for $i = 1$ to N **do**
        Set $X_{n-1}^{(i)} = X_{n-1}'^{(i)}$.
        Sample $X_n^{(i)} \sim q_n(\cdot|X_{n-1}^{(i)})$.
        Set $\widetilde{W}_n^{(i)} \propto \frac{g(y_n|X_n^{(i)})f(X_n^{(i)}|X_{n-1}^{(i)})}{\widehat{p}(y_n|X_{n-1}^{(i)})q_n(X_n^{(i)}|X_{n-1}^{(i)})}$.
    end for

3.2 Interpretation and implementation

Whilst the APF has seen widespread use, remarkably the first asymptotic analyses of the algorithm have appeared very recently. These analyses provide some significant insights into the performance of the algorithm and emphasise some requirements that a successful implementation must meet.

3.2.1 The APF as SIR

When one considers the APF as a sequence of weighting and sampling operations it becomes apparent that it also has an interpretation as a mutation-selection algorithm. In fact, with a little consideration it is possible to identify the APF as an example of an SIR algorithm.

It was noted in [33] that the APF described in [5] corresponds to the SIR algorithm which is obtained by setting

$$\pi_n(x_{1:n}) = \widehat{p}(x_{1:n}|y_{1:n+1}) \propto p(x_{1:n}|y_{1:n})\widehat{p}(y_{n+1}|x_n).$$

In the SIR interpretation of the APF $p(x_{1:n}|y_{1:n})$ is not approximated directly, but rather importance sampling is used to estimate $\bar{\varphi}_n$, with (weighted) samples which target the importance distribution $\pi_{n-1}(x_{1:n-1})q_n(x_n|x_{n-1})$ provided by an SIR algorithm. The resulting estimate is given by

$$\widetilde{\varphi}_{n,APF}^{N} = \sum_{i=1}^{N} \widetilde{W}_{n}^{(i)} \varphi_n(X_n^{(i)}),$$

where $\widetilde{W}_n^{(i)} = \widetilde{w}_n(X_{n-1:n}^{(i)})/\sum_{j=1}^{N} \widetilde{w}_n(X_{n-1:n}^{(j)})$ and

$$\widetilde{w}_n(x_{n-1:n}) = \frac{p(x_{1:n}|y_{1:n})}{\pi_{n-1}(x_{1:n-1})q_n(x_n|x_{n-1})} \propto \frac{g(y_n|x_n)f(x_n|x_{n-1})}{\widehat{p}(y_n|x_{n-1})q_n(x_n|x_{n-1})}. \tag{3.6}$$

Note that for a fully adapted APF, the importance weights by which estimation are made are uniform. Only the case in which resampling is carried out once per iteration has been considered here. Empirically this case has been preferred for many years and one would intuitively expect it to lead to lower variance estimates. However, it would be straightforward to apply the same reasoning to the scenario in which resampling is carried out both before and after auxiliary weighting as in the original implementations (doing this leads to an SIR algorithm with twice as many distributions as previously but there is no difficulty in constructing such an algorithm).

Theoretical consequences

One of the principal advantages of identifying the APF as a particular type of SIR algorithm is that many detailed theoretical results are available for the latter class of algorithm. Indeed, many of the results provided in [13], for example, can be applied directly to the APF via this interpretation. Thus formal convergence results can be obtained without any additional analysis. Via this route, a central limit theorem (CLT), for example, was shown to hold in the case of the APF by [33]. In [19] the authors independently established a CLT for the APF by other means. For both the APF and SIR filter, the asymptotic variance for the CLT can be derived, as presented in the following proposition.

Proposition Under the regularity conditions given in [8, Theorem 1] or [13, Section 9.4, pp. 300–306], which prove this result for SIR algorithms (analysis of SIR and other algorithms can also be found in [18]), we have

$$\sqrt{N}\left(\widetilde{\varphi}_{n,SIR}^{N} - \overline{\varphi}_n\right) \Rightarrow N\left(0, \sigma_{SIR}^2(\varphi_n)\right), \quad \sqrt{N}\left(\widetilde{\varphi}_{n,APF}^{N} - \overline{\varphi}_n\right) \Rightarrow N\left(0, \sigma_{APF}^2(\varphi_n)\right),$$

where '$\Rightarrow$' denotes convergence in distribution and $N\left(0, \sigma^2\right)$ is the zero-mean normal of variance σ^2. Moreover, at time $n = 1$ we have

$$\sigma_{SIR}^2(\varphi_1) = \sigma_{APF}^2(\varphi_1) = \int \frac{p(x_1|y_1)^2}{q_1(x_1)}(\varphi_1(x_1) - \overline{\varphi}_1)^2 \, dx_1,$$

whereas for $n > 1$

$$\sigma_{SIR}^2(\varphi_n) = \int \frac{p(x_1|y_{1:n})^2}{q_1(x_1)} \Delta\varphi_{1,n}(x_1)^2 dx_1$$

$$+ \sum_{k=2}^{n-1} \int \frac{p(x_{1:k}|y_{1:n})^2}{p(x_{1:k-1}|y_{1:k-1})q_k(x_k|x_{k-1})} \Delta\varphi_{k,n}(x_{1:k})^2 dx_{1:k}$$

$$+ \int \frac{p(x_{1:n}|y_{1:n})^2}{p(x_{1:n-1}|y_{1:n-1})q_n(x_n|x_{n-1})}(\varphi_n(x_{1:n}) - \overline{\varphi}_n)^2 \, dx_{1:n}, \tag{3.7}$$

where

$$\Delta\varphi_{k,n}(x_{1:k}) = \int \varphi_n(x_{1:n})p(x_{k+1:n}|y_{k+1:n}, x_k) dx_{k+1:n} - \overline{\varphi}_n$$

and

$$\sigma_{APF}^2(\varphi_n) = \int \frac{p(x_1|y_{1:n})^2}{q_1(x_1)} \Delta\varphi_{1,n}(x_1)^2 \mathrm{d}x_1$$
$$+ \sum_{k=2}^{n-1} \int \frac{p(x_{1:k}|y_{1:n})^2}{\widehat{p}(x_{1:k-1}|y_{1:k})q_k(x_k|x_{k-1})} \Delta\varphi_{k,n}(x_{1:k})^2 \mathrm{d}x_{1:k}$$
$$+ \int \frac{p(x_{1:n}|y_{1:n})^2}{\widehat{p}(x_{1:n-1}|y_{1:n})q_n(x_n|x_{n-1})} (\varphi_n(x_{1:n}) - \bar{\varphi}_n)^2 \mathrm{d}x_{1:n}. \qquad (3.8)$$

Obtaining asymptotic variance expressions in the same form for SIR and the APF allows their comparison on a term-by-term basis. This permits some insight into their relative performance in simple scenarios such as that considered in the following section.

It should, of course, be noted that with a slight change to the conditions (in using the APF one must correct estimates relative to those provided by the SIR algorithm which it corresponds to – that is, one integrates a function $\widetilde{w}_n \times \varphi_n$ with respect to an SIR algorithm targeting the auxiliary distributions in order to approximate the expectation of φ_n) essentially any of the results obtained for SIR algorithms can be applied to auxiliary particle filters in the same way. Lastly, we note that by choosing $\widehat{p}(y_n|x_{n-1}) = 1$, one recovers from the APF the SIR algorithm.

3.2.2   Implications for implementation

It is immediately apparent that, as SIR and the APF are essentially the same algorithm with a different choice of importance weights (in that the only difference in their implementation is which importance weights are used for resampling and which for estimation), very little additional implementation effort is required to develop both variants of an algorithm. Implementation can be simplified further by employing a generic SMC library such as [31].

In real-world settings this may be worthwhile as it may not be straightforward to assess, theoretically, which will provide better estimates at a given computational cost (even when the APF does allow significant reductions in variance to be obtained, it may incur a considerable per-sample cost in the evaluation of a complicated approximation to the predictive likelihood).

From an implementation point of view, perhaps the most significant feature of this interpretation is that it makes clear the criticality of choosing a $\widehat{p}(y_n|x_{n-1})$ which is *more* diffuse than $p(y_n|x_{n-1})$ (as a function of x_{n-1}). For importance sampling schemes in general, it is well known that a proposal distribution with lighter tails than the target distribution can lead to an estimator with infinite variance. In the case of the APF the proposal distribution is defined in terms of $\widehat{p}(y_n|x_{n-1})$, with the importance weight according to which estimates are made being Eq. (3.6). It is therefore clear that the popular choice of approximating the predictive likelihood by the likelihood evaluated at the mode of the transition density is a dangerous strategy. This is likely to explain the poor performance of APF algorithms based on this idea which have appeared in the literature.

A number of other generic approaches lead to more conservative implementations. Each of these techniques may be applicable in some circumstances:

- One simple option is to take

$$\widehat{p}(y_n|x_{n-1}) \propto \int \widehat{g}(y_n|x_n)\widehat{f}(x_n|x_{n-1})\mathrm{d}x_n,$$

with the approximations to the likelihood and transition densities being chosen to have heavier tails than the true densities and to permit this integral to be evaluated. For some models it is possible to compute the moments of $p(x_n, y_n|x_{n-1}) = g(y_n|x_n)f(x_n|x_{n-1})$ up to second order, conditional on x_{n-1} [48]. These can then be used to form a Gaussian approximation of $p(x_n, y_n|x_{n-1})$ and thus to $p(y_n|x_{n-1})$, with the variance adjusted to ensure Eq. (3.6) is bounded.

- The multivariate t distribution provides a flexible family of approximating distributions: approximating $p(y_n|x_{n-1})$ with a t distribution centred at the mode but with heavier tails than the true predictive likelihood provides a safeguard against excessive concentration whilst remaining similar in spirit to the simple point-approximation approach.

- In cases in which the underlying dynamic model is ergodic, the tractability of the multivariate t distribution provides another strategy. If one approximates the joint distribution of (X_{n-1}, X_n, Y_n) at stationarity with a multivariate t distribution of approximately the correct mean and correlation with tails at least as heavy as those of the true distribution, then one can obtain the marginal distribution of (X_{n-1}, Y_n) under this approximation analytically – it, too, is a multivariate t distribution. Given a multivariate t distribution for (X_{n-1}, Y_n), the conditional density (again, under this approximation) of y_n given x_{n-1} is available in closed form [43].

- In the multimodal case, the situation is more complicated. It may be possible to employ a mixture of multivariate t distributions in order to approximate complicated distributions. In very complex settings it may not be practical to approximate the predictive likelihood accurately.

Whilst it remains sensible to attempt to approximate the optimal (in the sense of minimising the variance of the importance weights) transition density

$$q_n(x_n|x_{n-1}) \propto g(y_n|x_n)f(x_n|x_{n-1})$$

and the true predictive likelihood, it is not the case that the APF necessarily out-performs the SIR algorithm using the same proposal even in this setting. This phenomenon is related to the fact that the mechanism by which samples are proposed at the current iteration of the algorithm impacts the variance of estimates made at subsequent time steps.

There are two issues to consider when assessing the asymptotic variance of estimators provided by SIR or APF-type algorithms. Firstly, as the operation performed in both cases is essentially importance sampling, there are likely to be particular functions which are more accurately estimated by each of the algorithms (especially if only a few time steps are considered). An illustrative example was provided in [33], which we discuss in more detail below. The other issue is that the APF can only be expected to provide better estimates in general if, for $k < n$, $p(x_{1:k}|y_{1:k+1})$ is closer to $p(x_{1:k}|y_{1:n})$ than $p(x_{1:k}|y_{1:k})$ is (consider the 'importance-weight' terms in the variance decompositions (3.7) and (3.8) in the case where the true predictive likelihood is used). This seems likely to be true for the vast majority of SSMs encountered in practice and so the APF is likely to yield more stable estimates provided that a good approximation of the predictive likelihood is available.

Analysis of binary state space model

In this section we consider the application of SIR and the APF to a very simple SSM. The performance of the two algorithms is then compared in terms of asymptotic variance. The

simplicity of the model is such that the asymptotic variances can be evaluated easily in
terms of the model parameters, which in this case directly specify the forgetting properties
of the signal process and the amount of information provided by the observations. The
hope is that, by considering such a simple model, it is possible to gain some insight into the
relative performance of SIR and the APF.

The SSM is specified as follows:

$$E = \{0, 1\}, \qquad\qquad p(x_1 = 0) = 0.5, \qquad\qquad p(x_n = x_{n-1}) = 1 - \delta,$$
$$y_n \in E, \qquad\qquad p(y_n = x_n) = 1 - \varepsilon.$$

The test function $\varphi(x_{1:2}) := x_2$ was used, in the 'full adaptation' setting, with $y_{1:2} = (0, 1)$

$$q_1(x_1) := p(x_1|y_1), \qquad\qquad q_n(x_n|x_{n-1}) := p(x_n|x_{n-1}, y_n),$$
$$\widehat{p}(y_n|x_n) := \int g(y_n|x_n)f(x_n|x_{n-1})dx_n.$$

Figure 3.1(a) illustrates the difference in variance of these two methods as obtained in
[33]. In order to understand this, it's useful to consider the asymptotic variance of the two
estimators (which follow directly from Eqs. (3.7) and (3.8)):

$$\sigma^2_{SIR}(\varphi) = \int \frac{p(x_1|y_{1:2})^2}{q_1(x_1)} \left(\int \varphi(x_{1:2})\, p(x_2|y_2, x_1)\, dx_2 - \overline{\varphi} \right)^2 dx_1$$
$$+ \int \frac{p(x_{1:2}|y_{1:2})^2}{p(x_1|y_1)q_2(x_2|x_1)} (\varphi(x_{1:2}) - \overline{\varphi})^2\, dx_{1:2},$$

$$\sigma^2_{APF}(\varphi) = \int \frac{p(x_1|y_{1:2})^2}{q_1(x_1)} \left(\int \varphi(x_{1:2})p(x_2|y_2, x_1)dx_2 - \overline{\varphi} \right)^2 dx_1$$
$$+ \int \frac{p(x_{1:2}|y_{1:2})^2}{\widehat{p}(x_1|y_{1:2})q_2(x_2|x_1)} (\varphi(x_{1:2}) - \overline{\varphi})^2\, dx_{1:2}.$$

The first terms of these expansions are identical; the difference between the two algorithms is due entirely to the second term. The SIR term corresponds to the variance of an
importance sampling estimate of $\overline{\varphi}$ using $p(x_1|y_1)p(x_2|x_1, y_2)$ as an importance distribution
and self-normalised weights:

$$\int \frac{p(x_{1:2}|y_{1:2})^2}{p(x_1|y_1)\, p(x_2|x_1, y_2)} (\varphi(x_{1:2}) - \overline{\varphi})^2\, dx_{1:2}.$$

The APF term corresponds to the variance of φ under the filtering distribution

$$\int \frac{p(x_{1:2}|y_{1:2})^2}{p(x_1|y_{1:2})p(x_2|x_1, y_2)} (\varphi(x_{1:2}) - \overline{\varphi})^2\, dx_{1:2} = \int p(x_{1:2}|y_{1:2}) (\varphi(x_{1:2}) - \overline{\varphi})^2\, dx_{1:2}.$$

The latter can be treated equivalently as the variance of a self-normalised importance
sampling estimate using the target distribution as a proposal. Therefore we can appeal to
existing results on self-normalised importance sampling estimators in order to compare the
two algorithms.

It is well known [25, Theorem 3] that the optimal proposal distribution (in the sense
of minimising the variance) for self-normalised importance sampling is $\propto |\varphi(x) - \overline{\varphi}|\pi(x)$

$\downarrow X_1 \vert X_2 \rightarrow$	0	1
0	$\dfrac{(1-\delta)(1-\epsilon)\epsilon}{2(1-\delta)\epsilon(1-\epsilon)+\delta((1-\epsilon^2)+\epsilon^2)}$	$\dfrac{\delta(1-\epsilon)^2}{2(1-\delta)\epsilon(1-\epsilon)+\delta((1-\epsilon^2)+\epsilon^2)}$
1	$\dfrac{\delta\epsilon^2}{2(1-\delta)\epsilon(1-\epsilon)+\delta((1-\epsilon^2)+\epsilon^2)}$	$\dfrac{(1-\delta)(1-\epsilon)\epsilon}{2(1-\delta)\epsilon(1-\epsilon)+\delta((1-\epsilon^2)+\epsilon^2)}$

Table 3.1 Target distribution (and APF proposal).

$\downarrow X_1 \vert X_2 \rightarrow$	0	1
0	$\dfrac{(1-\delta)\epsilon(1-\epsilon)}{\epsilon(1-\delta)+\delta(1-\epsilon)}$	$\dfrac{\delta(1-\epsilon)^2}{\epsilon(1-\delta)+\delta(1-\epsilon)}$
1	$\dfrac{\delta\epsilon^2}{\delta\epsilon+(1-\delta)(1-\epsilon)}$	$\dfrac{(1-\delta)\epsilon(1-\epsilon)}{\delta\epsilon+(1-\delta)(1-\epsilon)}$

Table 3.2 SIR proposal.

where φ is the function of interest and π is the target distribution. It is immediately apparent that the marginal distribution of X_1 under the APF proposal distribution is optimal for *any* function which depends only upon X_2. Thus the distribution of X_1 in the SIR expression would definitely *increase* the variance of any estimate *if* the distribution of X_2 was the same in both cases. However, the marginal distribution of X_2 in the two proposal distributions is different and there do exist functions for which that provided by the SIR filter leads to a lower variance.

In the case of interest here, i.e. $\varphi(x_{1:2}) = x_2$, we know that the APF has the optimal marginal distribution for X_1 and that the SIR algorithm produces samples with an inferior distribution for X_1. Therefore, any instances in which the SIR algorithm produces lower variance estimates are due to the distribution of X_2. For simplicity, we consider the marginal distribution of this variable in what follows, noting that in the real scenario the distribution of X_1 will improve the APF's performance.

The joint distribution of X_1, X_2 in the target (and APF proposal) is given in Table 3.1 and that for SIR in Table 3.2.

It aids interpretation to notice that $\bar{\varphi} = \sum_{x_2} x_2 p(x_2 \vert y_{1:2}) = p(x_2 = 1 \vert y_{1:2})$. Consequently, the optimal proposal distribution, $q_{opt}(x_2) \propto p(x_2 \vert y_{1:2}) \vert \varphi(x_2) - \bar{\varphi} \vert$ is uniform over x_2

$$q_{opt}(0) \propto p(x_2 = 0 \vert y_{1:2}) \vert \varphi(0) - \bar{\varphi} \vert = (1 - \bar{\varphi})\bar{\varphi},$$
$$q_{opt}(1) \propto p(x_2 = 1 \vert y_{1:2}) \vert \varphi(1) - \bar{\varphi} \vert = \bar{\varphi}(1 - \bar{\varphi}).$$

This tells us that the marginal distribution for x_2 which minimises the variance of the estimate of *this particular integral* is uniform over its possible values. The APF generally places more mass on the state supported by the observation than the SIR filter. Consequently, the APF only produces a marginal distribution for X_2 closer to this optimal form when the prior would place the majority of its mass on the state which is not supported by the observation. Even in this setting, the APF can improve things when we obtain unlikely observations, but may increase the variance when the observation agrees with the prior.

Figure 3.1 illustrates that this mechanism is consistent with what is observed. Figure 3.1(a) shows the difference in estimator variance over a range of values of (δ, ϵ); Fig. 3.1(b) and Fig. 3.1(c) respectively show the marginal probability that $X_2 = 1$ under the proposal distribution associated with the APF and SIR algorithm, and Fig. 3.1(d) shows the difference in $\mathcal{L}_1$ distance to the optimal value for the two approaches. It is clear that the regions in which the SIR algorithm performs well are those in which it provides a much closer to uniform distribution over X_2. Careful inspection reveals that the APF outperforms

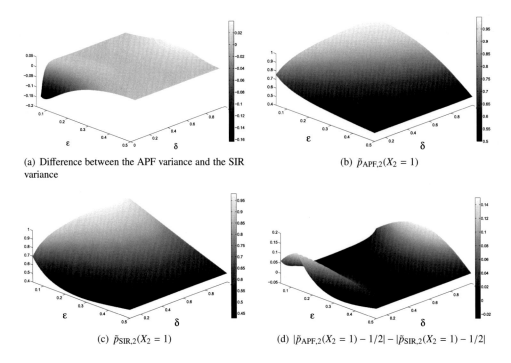

(a) Difference between the APF variance and the SIR variance

(b) $\tilde{p}_{\mathrm{APF},2}(X_2 = 1)$

(c) $\tilde{p}_{\mathrm{SIR},2}(X_2 = 1)$

(d) $|\tilde{p}_{\mathrm{APF},2}(X_2 = 1) - 1/2| - |\tilde{p}_{\mathrm{SIR},2}(X_2 = 1) - 1/2|$

Figure 3.1 Properties of the APF and SIR in the binary, perfect-adaptation setting.

SIR slightly outside of the regions in which it more closely approximates the uniform distribution over X_2. This is due to the distribution of X_1 (which influences the importance weight) as noted earlier. It should also be noted that it is when δ and ϵ are both small that one would expect the sub-optimal nature of the SIR distribution over X_1 to have the greatest effect and this is, indeed, where the APF performance is most obviously better.

More generally, one would expect much of the intuition obtained from this simple scenario to apply reasonably directly in more general settings. The APF leads to samples distributed in a way which is closer to the target distribution; it is possible that for some test functions the final step of the APF does not lead to an optimal marginal distribution but this distribution is not intended to operate solely as a device for estimating an integral: it is also used to obtain subsequent distributions and as such, tracking the sequence of target distributions is of vital importance.

For this reason, minimising incremental variance and otherwise attempting to track these distributions as faithfully as possible remains our preferred method for designing APF algorithms. We also feel that, on average (with respect to observation sequences generated with respect to the true filter, say), the APF is likely to outperform SIR whenever a good approximation to the predictive likelihood is available – especially if a broad class of functions are to be integrated. Note, in particular, the form of the general variance decomposition: it shows that asymptotically the APF uses distributions of the form $\hat{p}(x_{1:k-1}|y_{1:k})$ to approximate $p(x_{1:k-1}|y_{1:n})$ where the SIR algorithm uses $p(x_{1:k-1}|y_{1:k-1})$. It's approximating the distribution well that minimises the additional variance which results from these terms, and the APF does this better than SIR (assuming that, at least on average, $p(x_{k-1,k}|y_{1:k})$ is a better proxy for $p(x_{k-1:k}|y_{1:n})$ than $p(x_{k-1}|y_{1:k-1})p(x_k|x_{k-1}, y_k)$, which is the case for any reasonable situation).

3.2.3 Other interpretations and developments

Much has been written about the APF in the decade since it was first proposed. Some work based upon the similarity between it and other algorithms precedes that described above. One of the first works to discuss the connections between SIR and the APF was [27]. Closer in spirit to the unified view presented above was [30], which showed how a number of algorithms could be interpreted within a common framework. This framework differs slightly from that presented above, and one of the principal motivations of that approach was the elimination of an explicit resampling step (which is often viewed as being a rather unnatural operation in the discrete-time setting). This seems to be the first paper to observe that 'the APF can be considered as an alternative formulation of the general SIR algorithm or vice versa'. However, the slightly less standard formulation employed prevents the easy transferral of results from SIR to the APF which was the primary purpose of [33].

A direct analysis of the particle system underlying the APF was performed recently [19] using results obtained in [18]. This confirmed the intuitive and empirical results that resampling once per iteration leads to a lower variance estimate than resampling twice. One principal component of this work was the determination of the auxiliary weighting function which minimises the variance of estimates of a particular test function obtained *one step ahead* of the current iterations. The 'second stage weights' of [19] specify the auxiliary sequence of distributions associated with the auxiliary particle filter. The form which they suggest is optimal for these weights is the following replacement for $\hat{p}(y_{n+1}|x_n)$

$$\hat{t}_\varphi(x_n, y_{n+1}) = \sqrt{\int \frac{f(x_{n+1}|x_n)^2 g(y_{n+1}|x_{n+1})^2}{q(x_{n+1}|x_n)} (\varphi_{n+1}(x_{n+1}) - \overline{\varphi}_{n+1})^2 dx_{n+1}}.$$

Whilst this is of theoretical interest, it requires the computation of a predictive integral which is likely to be even more difficult than that required to obtain the predictive likelihood. In addition to the practical difficulties, it is not clear that it will always be wise to employ the proposed strategy. When performing any Monte Carlo filtering, the particle set is used for two purposes at each time instant: to approximate integrals of interest and the distribution required at the next time step. Using this form of weighting is intended to optimise the estimate of the integral at the next time step. However, it need not lead to a good approximation of the distribution itself. Consequently, when this weighting function is used one may be left with a poorer approximation to the filtering distribution than with simpler approaches based upon matching only the distribution and not particular test functions. In such cases, use of this approach may lead to poorer estimation in the future. It is for precisely the same reason that customised proposal distributions tuned for a specific test function are not generally used in particle filtering, and thus a more conservative approach with less adaptation in the proposal mechanism remains sensible.

In subsequent work [10], a criterion independent of the functions of interest was employed to develop methods for designing adaptive algorithms based upon the auxiliary particle filter. This strategy seeks to minimise the Kullback–Liebler divergence or χ^2-distance between the proposal and target distributions in an adaptive manner (and is similar in spirit to attempting to get as close to the optimal proposal as possible).

3.3 Applications and extensions

We argue that the innovation of the APF is essentially that, in sampling from a sequence of distributions using an SIR strategy, it can be advantageous to take account of one-step-ahead knowledge about the distributions of interest (more general information could, in principle, be used but it is not easy to envisage realistic scenarios in which this will be practical). This section summarises some other applications of this principle outside of the standard particle filtering domain in which it has previously been applied.

3.3.1 Marginal particle filters

As noted above, most particle filtering methods rely on a numerical approximation of Eq. (3.2) and not of Eqs. (3.3) and (3.4) even when only the final time marginal is of interest. This is due to the difficulty associated with evaluating the integral which appears in Eq. (3.4) explicitly. One possible solution to this approach, proposed in [38], is to approximate these integrals using the particle set itself. Doing this increases the computational cost considerably, but allows the algorithm to be defined directly on a smaller space than would otherwise be the case. This is of importance when approximating the derivative of the optimal filter in online parameter estimation and optimal control applications [46, 35].

It is also possible to implement an auxiliary particle filter variant of the marginal particle filter, taking the following form (the standard marginal particle filter is obtained by setting the auxiliary weighting function $\hat{p}(y_{n+1}|x_n)$ to a constant function):

Algorithm 3.3 Auxiliary Marginal Particle Filter

At time 1
  for $i = 1$ to N **do**
    Sample $X_1^{(i)} \sim q(\cdot)$.
    Set $\widetilde{W}_1^{(i)} \propto \dfrac{\nu(X_1^{(i)})g(y_1|X_1^{(i)})}{q(X_1^{(i)})}$.
  end for
At time $n \geq 2$
  for $i = 1$ to N **do**
    Set $W_{n-1}^{(i)} \propto \widetilde{W}_{n-1}^{(i)} \widehat{p}(y_n|X_{n-1}^{(i)})$.
  end for
  Resample $\left\{X_{n-1}^{(i)}, W_{n-1}^{(i)}\right\}$ to obtain $\left\{X_{n-1}'^{(i)}, \frac{1}{N}\right\}$.
  for $i = 1$ to N **do**

    Sample $X_n^{(i)} \sim q(x_n|y_n, X_{n-1}'^{(i)})$.
    Set $\widetilde{W}_n^{(i)} \propto \dfrac{g(y_n|X_n^{(i)})\sum_{j=1}^{N} W_{n-1}^{(j)} f\left(X_n^{(i)}|X_{n-1}^{(j)}\right)}{\sum_{j=1}^{N} W_{n-1}^{(j)} q\left(X_n^{(i)}|y_n, X_{n-1}^{(j)}\right)\widehat{p}(y_n|X_{n-1}^{(j)})}$.
  end for

We have presented this algorithm in a form as close as possible to that of the other algorithms described here. It differs in some details from the original formulation. In particular, we do not assume that the predictive likelihood is obtained by approximating the predictive distribution with an atom at its mode – it is not necessary to do this and as discussed in the context of the APF there are some difficulties which may arise as a result of such an approach. As with the APF, it is necessary to use an importance correction when using this filter to approximate the filtering distributions.

This approach leads to algorithms with a computational complexity which is $O(N^2)$ in contrast to most particle filters, which are $O(N)$ algorithms. This would ordinarily be prohibitive, but it was noted in [38] that techniques widely used for the approximate solution of N-body problems in computational physics and recently applied to statistical learning [29] can be applied to this problem for a broad class of likelihood functions, thereby reducing the complexity to $O(N \log N)$ at the cost of a small (and controllable) approximation.

3.3.2 Sequential Monte Carlo samplers

Sequential Monte Carlo samplers are a class of algorithms for sampling iteratively from a sequence of distributions, denoted by $\{\pi_n(x_n)\}_{n \in \mathbb{N}}$, defined upon a sequence of potentially arbitrary spaces, $\{E_n\}_{n \in \mathbb{N}}$, [14, 15]. The approach involves the application of SIR to a cleverly constructed sequence of synthetic distributions which admit the distributions of interest as marginals. It is consequently straightforward to employ the same strategy as that used by the APF – see [32] which also illustrates that convergence results for this class of algorithms follow directly. In this context it is not always clear that there is a good choice of auxiliary distributions, although it is relatively natural in some settings.

The synthetic distributions, $\{\widetilde{\pi}_n(x_{1:n})\}_{n \in \mathbb{N}}$, employed by standard SMC samplers are defined to be

$$\widetilde{\pi}_n(x_{1:n}) = \pi_n(x_n) \prod_{p=1}^{n-1} L_p\left(x_{p+1}, x_p\right),$$

where $\{L_n\}_{n \in \mathbb{N}}$ is a sequence of 'backward' Markov kernels *from* E_n *into* E_{n-1}. With this structure, an importance sample from $\widetilde{\pi}_n$ is obtained by taking the path $x_{1:n-1}$, a sample from $\widetilde{\pi}_{n-1}$, and extending it with a Markov kernel, K_n, which acts from E_{n-1} into E_n, providing samples from $\widetilde{\pi}_{n-1} \times K_n$ and leading to the importance weight

$$w_n(x_{n-1:n}) = \frac{\widetilde{\pi}_n(x_{1:n})}{\widetilde{\pi}_{n-1}(x_{1:n-1})K_n(x_{n-1}, x_n)} = \frac{\pi_n(x_n)L_{n-1}(x_n, x_{n-1})}{\pi_{n-1}(x_{n-1})K_n(x_{n-1}, x_n)}. \tag{3.9}$$

In many applications, each $\pi_n(x_n)$ can only be evaluated pointwise up to a normalising constant and the importance weights defined by Eq. (3.9) are normalised in the same manner as in the SIR algorithm. Resampling may then be performed.

The optimal (in the sense of minimising the variance of the asymptotic importance weights if resampling is performed at each iteration) choice of L_{n-1} is

$$L_{n-1}(x_n, x_{n-1}) = \frac{\pi_{n-1}(x_{n-1})K(x_{n-1}, x_n)}{\int \pi_{n-1}(x'_{n-1})K(x'_{n-1}, x_n)\mathrm{d}x'_{n-1}},$$

which produces a sampler equivalent to one defined only on the marginal spaces of interest. In practice, it is not generally possible to use the optimal auxiliary kernels and good approximations to this optimal form are required in order to obtain samplers with good variance properties.

If one wishes to sample from a sequence of distributions $\{\pi_n\}_{n \in \mathbb{N}}$ then an alternative to directly implementing an SMC sampler which targets this sequence of distributions, is to employ an auxiliary sequence of distributions, $\{\mu_n\}_{n \in \mathbb{N}}$, and an importance sampling correction (with weights $\widetilde{w}_n(x_n) = \pi_n(x_n)/\mu_n(x_n)$) to provide estimates. This is very much in the spirit of the APF. Such a strategy was termed auxiliary SMC (ASMC) in [32]. Like the APF, the objective is to maintain a more diverse particle set by using as much information as possible before, rather than after, resampling.

Resample-move: inverting sampling and resampling

As has been previously noted [15], in a setting in which every iteration shares a common state space, $E_n = E$, and in which an MCMC kernel of invariant distribution π_n is employed as the proposal, making use of the auxiliary kernel

$$L_{n-1}(x_n, x_{n-1}) = \frac{\pi_n(x_{n-1})K_n(x_{n-1}, x_n)}{\pi_n(x_n)},$$

the importance weights are simply $w_n(x_{n-1}, x_n) = \pi_n(x_{n-1})/\pi_{n-1}(x_{n-1})$. In addition to its simplicity, this expression has the interesting property that the weight is independent of the proposed state, x_n.

It is possible to interpret this approach as correcting for the discrepancy between the previous and present distributions entirely by importance weighting with the application of an MCMC kernel of the appropriate distribution simply serving to improve the diversity of the sample. It is intuitively clear that one should apply the importance weighting and resample *before* proposing new states in the interests of maximising sample diversity. This has been observed previously. Indeed doing so leads to algorithms with the same structure as the resample-move (RM) particle filtering algorithm [26]. By making the following identifications

$$\mu_n(x_n) = \pi_{n+1}(x_n),$$

$$L_{n-1}(x_n, x_{n-1}) = \frac{\mu_{n-1}(x_{n-1})K_n(x_{n-1}, x_n)}{\mu_{n-1}(x_n)} = \frac{\pi_n(x_{n-1})K_n(x_{n-1}, x_n)}{\pi_n(x_n)},$$

$$w_n(x_{n-1:n}) = \frac{\mu_n(x_n)}{\mu_{n-1}(x_n)} = \frac{\pi_{n+1}(x_n)}{\pi_n(x_n)},$$

$$\widetilde{w}_n(x_n) = \mu_{n-1}(x_n)/\mu_n(x_n) = \pi_n(x_n)/\pi_{n+1}(x_n),$$

it is possible to cast this approach into the form of an ASMC sampler. This formal representation allows existing theoretical results to be applied to both RM and its generalisations.

Filtering piecewise-deterministic processes

The SMC samplers framework was employed by [53] to provide filtering estimates for a class of continuous-time processes. In addition to providing an example of the class of algorithms which are described above, this approach also illustrates that SMC samplers and their auxiliary counterparts can provide useful extensions of SIR-type algorithms in time series analysis.

Piecewise-deterministic processes (PDPs) are a class of stochastic processes whose sample paths, $\{\zeta_t\}_{t \geq 0}$ evolve deterministically in continuous time between a sequence of random times $\{\tau_j\}_{j \in \mathbb{N}}$, at which the path jumps to new, random values $\{\theta_j\}_{j \in \mathbb{N}}$. The prior law of the (τ_j, θ_j) is typically specified by a Markov kernel with density $f(\theta_{n,j}, \tau_{n,j}|\theta_{n,j-1}, \tau_{n,j-1})$.

Filtering for partially observed PDP models involves computing a sequence of posterior distributions given observations $\{Y_n\}_{n \in \mathbb{N}}$. In object-tracking applications, [28], the observations may be related to the PDP trajectory by $Y_n = H(\zeta_{t_n}, U_n)$, where U_n is a noise disturbance, H is some non-linear function and $\{t_n\}_{n \in \mathbb{N}}$ is an increasing sequence of observation times. In financial applications such as the pricing of reinsurance [12] and options [7], each Y_n is the restriction to the interval $(t_{n-1}, t_n]$ of a Cox process with conditional intensity $(\zeta_t)_{t \in (t_{n-1}, t_n]}$. In general, the observation model is specified by a likelihood function $g(y_n|\zeta_{(t_{n-1}, t_n]})$.

The nth posterior $\pi_n(k_n, \theta_{n,0:k_n}, \tau_{n,1:k_n}|y_{1:n})$, is a distribution over

$$E_n = \biguplus_{k=0}^{\infty} \{k\} \times \Theta^{k+1} \times \mathbb{T}_{n,k},$$

where $\Theta \subset \mathbb{R}^d$ is a parameter space, $\mathbb{T}_{n,k} = \{\tau_{n,1:k_n} : 0 \leq \tau_{n,1} < \ldots < \tau_{n,k_n} \leq t_n\}$ and $\uplus$ indicates disjoint union. The posterior distribution is specified by

$$\pi_n(k_n, \theta_{n,0:k_n}, \tau_{n,1:k_n}|y_{1:n}) \propto \nu(\theta_{n,0})S(t_n, \tau_{n,k_n}) \prod_{j=1}^{k_n} f(\theta_{n,j}, \tau_{n,j}|\theta_{n,j-1}, \tau_{n,j-1}) \prod_{p=1}^{n} g(y_n|\zeta_{(t_{n-1},t_n]}),$$

with the convention $\tau_{n,0} = 0$ and where $S(t_n, \tau_{n,k_n})$ is the survivor function associated with the prior distribution over inter-jump times for the interval $[0, t_n]$. The SMC samplers framework is applied to approximate the distributions of interest, using a proposal kernel consisting of a mixture of moves which extend each particle from E_{n-1} to E_n by adjusting recent jump-time/parameter pairs and adding new ones. An auxiliary scheme for filtering can be obtained by selecting the auxiliary distribution μ_n to be:

$$\mu_n(k_n, \theta_{n,0:k_n}, \tau_{n,1:k_n}) \propto V_n(\theta_{n,k_n}, \tau_{n,k_n})\pi_n(k_n, \theta_{n,0:k_n}, \tau_{n,1:k_n}|y_{1:n}),$$

where $V_n(\theta_{n,k_n}, \tau_{n,k_n})$ is a non-negative potential function which provides information about y_{n+1}. This can be done by approximating the predictive likelihood in the same manner as in the discrete-time case, although some care is required as there may be one or more jumps between observations and these must be considered when approximating that predictive likelihood. This strategy was seen to perform well in [53].

3.3.3 The probability hypothesis density filter

An unusual application of ideas from the APF can be found in the area of multiple-object tracking. This is an inference task in which one seeks to estimate, in an online manner, the time-varying number and positions of a collection of hidden objects, given a sequence of noisy observations. What makes this task especially difficult is that it is not known which (if any) of the observations arise from which hidden objects. In many applications, the hidden objects are vehicles and the observations arise from sensor measurements, but many other problems in diverse application areas such as communications engineering, biology, audio and music processing can be cast in the same framework. Some examples are noted in [54]. See also Part IV of this volume.

In this scenario, one option is to represent the collection of hidden objects at a single time step as a spatial Poisson process with some inhomogeneous intensity measure. The intensity measure determines the expected number of objects within any region of the state space. Given this representation, the problem of tracking a large collection of objects is reduced to the problem of approximating, sequentially in time, this intensity measure. The use of SMC methods to approximate this measure has been suggested several times and an auxiliary-particle-filter-type implementation has recently been developed.

In principle, filtering for a multi-object tracking model involves computing a sequence of distributions with essentially the same form as Eq. (3.1). Here, E is $E = \uplus_{k=0}^{\infty} X^k$, where $X \subset \mathbb{R}^d$ is the state space of an individual object: each $X_n = X_{n,1:k_n}$ comprises a random number, k_n, of points, each in X, and can be regarded as a *spatial point process* (see [42, 50, 11] for background theory). We refer the reader to Chapter 10 of this volume for further information, but essential to the discussion below is the following concept. The first moment of the distribution of a point process may be specified in terms of an *intensity function*, $\alpha : E \to \mathbb{R}_+$, so that

$$\mathsf{E}[N(A)] = \int_A \alpha_n(x)\mathrm{d}x, \quad A \in \mathcal{B}(X),$$

where $N(A)$ is the number of points of X which are in the set A and $\mathcal{B}(X)$ is the Borel σ-algebra on X.

A simple multi-object model has the following structure. The hidden objects present at time $n-1$ each survive to time n with location dependent probability $p_S(x_{n-1})$. Each of the surviving objects evolves independently according to a Markov kernel with density $f(x_n|x_{n-1})$. New objects appear according to a Poisson process with intensity function $\gamma(x_n)$. Each of the surviving and new objects produces an observation with distribution $g(y|x)$. In addition to these detections, spurious observations, termed 'clutter', arise from an independent Poisson process with intensity $\kappa(y)$. The observation set at time n therefore consists of a random number of points, $Y_n = Y_{n,1:M_n}$. Crucially, it is not known which of the points of Y_n arise from hidden objects and which are clutter.

Performing filtering when $E = \biguplus_{k=0}^{\infty} X^k$ is practically very difficult due to the high and variable dimensionality of this space. The probability hypothesis density (PHD) filter, [41], approximates the optimal filter for this problem by assuming that the state process is a-posteriori Poisson (and hence fully characterized by its first moment) and characterising the intensity of that process.

For the model described above, the PHD filtering scheme yields the following prediction/update recursion for intensity functions

$$\alpha_n(x_n) = \int_X f(x_n|x_{n-1})p_S(x_{n-1})\breve{\alpha}_{n-1}(x_{n-1})dx_{n-1} + \gamma(x_n), \tag{3.10}$$

$$\breve{\alpha}_n(x_n) = \sum_{r=1}^{m_n} \frac{g(y_{n,r}|x_n)}{Z_{n,r}}\alpha_n(x_n), \tag{3.11}$$

where for $r = 1, 2, ..., m_n$, $Z_{n,r} = \int_E g(y_{n,r}|x)\alpha_n(x)dx + \kappa(y_{n,r})$. In this notation, $\alpha_n(x)$ and $\breve{\alpha}_n(x)$ are respectively termed the predicted and updated intensities at time n. The problem is then to compute the recursion (3.10)–(3.11) for a given observation sequence, with estimates of k_n and $x_{n,1:k_n}$ made from characteristics of $\breve{\alpha}_n$. For many models this is intractable, due to the integrals involved and because $\breve{\alpha}_n$ is typically of mixture form with a number of components which is increasing in n. Some degree of approximation is therefore required.

Sequential Monte Carlo methods may be employed to approximate the sequence of intensity functions $\{\breve{\alpha}_n(x_n)\}_{n \in \mathbb{N}}$, [55, 49, 52, 34, 9]. In contrast to the case of particle filters which approximate probability distributions, it is necessary for the collection of weighted samples used here to characterise the total mass of the intensity function in addition to its form. Akin to the APF, an auxiliary SMC implementation has recently been proposed in [54]. Empirical results demonstrate that the PHD recursion is particularly well suited to an auxiliary SMC approach. As in the APF, this involves resampling from a particle set which has been re-weighted by a potential function.

In outline, this approach introduces an extended state space $X' = X \cup \{s\}$, where s is an isolated 'source' point which does not belong to X, then defines an intensity function denoted $\beta_n(x_{n-1:n}, r)$ on $X' \times X \times \{1, ..., m_n\}$ as follows:

$$\beta_n(x_{n-1:n}, r) = \frac{g(y_{n,r}|x_n)}{Z_{n,r}}\left[f(x_n|x_{n-1})p_S(x_{n-1})\breve{\alpha}_{n-1}(x_{n-1})\mathbb{I}_X(x_{n-1}) + \gamma(x_n)\delta_s(x_{n-1})\right]. \tag{3.12}$$

Note that

$$\breve{\alpha}_n(x_n) = \sum_{r=1}^{m_n} \int_{X'} \beta_n(x_{n-1:n}, r)dx_{n-1}. \tag{3.13}$$

The algorithm of [54] uses IS to target Eq. (3.12) and thus yields a particle approximation of $\check{\alpha}_n(x_n)$ due to Eq. (3.13).

Assume that there is available a particle approximation of $\check{\alpha}_{n-1}(x_{n-1})$, denoted by $\check{\alpha}_{n-1}^N(x_{n-1})$. N samples are drawn from some distribution $q_n(r)$ over $\{1, 2, ..., m_n\}$, yielding $\{R_n^{(i)}\}_{i=1}^N$. For each i, $X_{n-1}^{(i)}$ is then drawn from

$$\pi_{n-1,R^{(i)}}^N(x_{n-1}) \propto \widehat{p}(y_{n,R^{(i)}}|x_{n-1}) \left[\check{\alpha}_{n-1}^N(x_{n-1})\mathbb{I}_X(x_{n-1}) + \delta_s(x_{n-1}) \right], \qquad (3.14)$$

$\widehat{p}(y_{n,r}|x_{n-1})$ being an approximation of $p(y_{n,r}|x_{n-1})$, which is itself defined by

$$p(y_{n,r}|x_{n-1}) = \mathbb{I}_X(x_{n-1})p_S(x_{n-1}) \int_X g(y_{n,r}|x_n)f(x_n|x_{n-1})\mathrm{d}x_n + \mathbb{I}_{\{s\}}(x_{n-1}) \int_X g(y_{n,r}|x_n)\gamma(x_n)\mathrm{d}x_n.$$

For each i, $X_n^{(i)}$ is then drawn from a kernel $q_n(\cdot|X_{n-1}^{(i)}, R_n^{(i)})$. The importance weight which targets Eq. (3.12) is given by

$$\widetilde{w}_n(x_{n-1:n}, r) \propto \frac{g(y_{n,r}|x_n)[f(x_n|x_{n-1})p_S(x_{n-1})\mathbb{I}_X(x_{n-1}) + \gamma(x_n)\mathbb{I}_{\{s\}}(x_{n-1})]}{q_{n,r}(x_n|x_{n-1})\pi_{n-1,r}(x_{n-1})q_n(r)},$$

with each normalising constant $\mathcal{Z}_{n,r}$ also estimated by IS, much as in SMC algorithms for SSMs. The result is a particle approximation of $\check{\alpha}_n(x_n)$. Reference [54] also shows how to choose $q_n(r)$ in an optimal fashion.

The connection with the APF is evident from the form of Eq. (3.14): drawing from this auxiliary distribution involves resampling from the existing particle set re-weighted by a potential function incorporating knowledge of the next observation. As demonstrated empirically in [54], compared to non-auxiliary SMC implementations, this method can result in importance weights of lower variance and more reliable estimates.

3.4 Further stratifying the APF

It is common knowledge that the use of multinomial resampling in a particle filter unnecessarily increases the Monte Carlo variance of the associated estimators and that the use of residual, systematic or stratified approaches can significantly reduce that variance [17]. This is also true in the case of the APF and one should always employ minimum variance resampling strategies. Under some circumstances it may be possible to achieve a further variance reduction in the APF.

Consider again the SSM from Section 3.1.1. Let $(E_j)_{j=1}^M$ denote a partition of E. Introducing an auxiliary stratum-indicator variable, $s_n = \sum_{j=1}^M j\mathbb{I}_{E_j}(x_n)$, we redefine the SSM on a higher-dimensional space, with the signal process being $E \times \{1, 2, ..., M\}$-valued, with transition kernel

$$r(x_n, s_n|x_{n-1}, s_{n-1}) = r(x_n|s_n, x_{n-1})r(s_n|x_{n-1}),$$

where

$$r(x_n|s_n, x_{n-1}) \propto \mathbb{I}_{E_{s_n}}(x_n)f(x_n|x_{n-1}), \qquad r(s_n|x_{n-1}) = \int_{E_{s_n}} f(x_n|x_{n-1})\mathrm{d}x_n.$$

The initial distribution of the extended chain is defined in a similar manner and the likelihood function remains unchanged. The posterior distributions for the extended model then obey the recursion

$$p(x_{1:n}, s_{1:n}|y_{1:n}) \propto g(y_n|x_n)r(x_n|s_n, x_{n-1})r(s_n|x_{n-1})p(x_{1:n-1}, s_{1:n-1}|y_{1:n-1}). \qquad (3.15)$$

Note that the marginal distribution of $x_{1:n}$ in Eq. (3.15) coincides with the original model.

As in the SIR interpretation of the APF, we then construct an auxiliary sequence of distributions, $\{\pi(x_{1:n-1}, s_{1:n})\}_{n\in\mathbb{N}}$, which will be targeted with an SIR algorithm, where

$$\pi(x_{1:n-1}, s_{1:n}) \propto \widehat{p}(y_n|s_n, x_{n-1})\widehat{r}(s_n|x_{n-1})p(x_{1:n-1}, s_{1:n-1}|y_{1:n-1}). \tag{3.16}$$

The key feature of Eq. (3.16) is that the resampling step of the corresponding SIR algorithm will select pairs of previous state values x_{n-1} and current strata s_n. This assignment can be performed with a low variance resampling mechanism. The corresponding algorithm, which we refer to as the stratified auxiliary particle filter (sAPF) is given below.

Algorithm 3.4 Stratified auxiliary particle filter

At time 1
  for $i = 1$ to N **do**
    Sample $X_1^{(i)} \sim q_1(\cdot)$.
    Set $\widetilde{W}_1^{(i)} \propto \frac{g(y_1|X_1^{(i)})\nu(X_1^{(i)})}{q_1(X_1^{(i)})}$.
  end for
At time $n \geq 2$
  for $i = 1$ to N **do**
    for $j = 1$ to M **do**
      Set $W_{n-1}^{(i,j)} \propto \widetilde{W}_{n-1}^{(i)} \times \widehat{p}(y_n|X_{n-1}^{(i)}, s_n = j)\widehat{r}(s_n = j|X_{n-1}^{(i)})$.
    end for
  end for
  Resample $\left\{X_{n-1}^{(i)}, j, W_{n-1}^{(i,j)}\right\}_{(i,j)\in\{1,...,N\}\times\{1,...,M\}}$ to obtain $\left\{X_{n-1}'^{(i)}, S_n^{(i)}, \frac{1}{N}\right\}$.
  for $i = 1$ to N **do**
    Set $X_{n-1}^{(i)} = X_{n-1}'^{(i)}$.
    Sample $X_n^{(i)} \sim q_n(\cdot|X_{n-1}^{(i)}, S_n^{(i)})$.
    Set $\widetilde{W}_n^{(i)} \propto \frac{g(y_n|X_n^{(i)})f(X_n^{(i)}|X_{n-1}^{(i)})}{\widehat{p}(y_n|X_{n-1}^{(i)}, S_n^{(i)})\widehat{r}(S_n^{(i)}|X_{n-1}^{(i)})q_n(X_n^{(i)}|X_{n-1}^{(i)}, S_n^{(i)})}$.
  end for

For each i, we first draw each $X_n^{(i)}|x_{n-1}^{(i)}, s_n^{(i)} \sim q_n(\cdot|x_{n-1}^{(i)}, s_n^{(i)})$. Then, instead of randomly sampling a value $s_{n+1}^{(i)}$, we evaluate one importance weight for every possible value of s_{n+1}, resulting in a collection of $N \times M$ weighted sample points. The resampling step of the SIR algorithm then draws N times from the resulting distribution on $\{1, 2, ..., N\} \times \{1, 2, ..., M\}$. The method of [36], proposed in the context of a particular class of tracking problems can be viewed as a special case of the proposed algorithm. However, [36] did not employ low-variance resampling schemes, which is, as will be shown below, the key to obtaining both a variance reduction and a decrease in computational cost.

The importance weight which targets $p(x_{1:n}, s_{1:n}|y_{1:n})$ (i.e. the analogue of Eq. (3.6)) is then:

$$\widetilde{w}_n(x_{n-1:n}, s_n) \propto \frac{g(y_n|x_n)f(x_n|x_{n-1})}{\widehat{p}(y_n|s_n, x_{n-1})\widehat{r}(s_n|x_{n-1})q_n(x_n|s_n, x_{n-1})}.$$

This effectively assigns both a parent particle *and* a stratum to each offspring. Crucially, this assignment can be performed with a low-variance resampling mechanism. This approach is especially of interest in the context of *switching* SSMs, where the state space has a natural partition structure by definition. We consider the application to such models below. First, we consider the effect of the above sampling scheme on the conditional variance of the resulting estimates.

3.4.1 Reduction in conditional variance

The following section illustrates the principal benefit of the proposed approach: a significant reduction in computational cost in those situations in which a natural stratification exists. This section illustrates that incorporating this additional stratification cannot make things worse in the sense that the variance of resulting estimators will be at most the same as those obtained with a non-stratified variant of those estimators. For simplicity we compare the performance of the sAPF to that of the APF in terms of the conditional variance arising from a single act of resampling and assigning particles to strata.

There are several ways in which one might go about using a low-variance mechanism in the resampling step of Algorithm 3.4. All the methods described in [17] are applicable and in this section we consider one way of using the *stratified* resampling mechanism, see [37, 23]. This method uses a form of inversion sampling to draw N samples from the distribution defined by the particle set. Inversion sampling itself involves generating $\mathcal{U}[0, 1]$ random variates and passing them through the generalised inverse of the target distribution function [47]. The stratified resampling scheme is so-named because it involves partitioning $[0, 1]$ into N strata of length $1/N$. A single uniform variate is then drawn on each sub-interval and passed through the inverse of the CDF, see [17] for further details.

We next consider how the stratified resampling mechanism could be used in the sAPF and how it would be used in the regular APF. It should be noted that the scheme described below is not the *only* way in which stratified resampling can be applied within the sAPF. Indeed there are alternatives which may be of even lower variance. However, the scheme described below is simple enough to permit direct analysis, providing some insight into how variance reduction can be achieved.

As part of the discussion which follows, we need some notation to indicate when the stratified resampling scheme is used and to specify the resulting random variables.

For a collection of random variables $\{X^{(i)}\}_{i=1}^{N}$, and a suitable probability distribution μ, we use the notation $\{X^{(i)}\}_{i=1}^{N} \overset{ss}{\sim} \mu$ to indicate that the samples $\{X^{(i)}\}_{i=1}^{N}$ are generated using the stratified resampling mechanism targeting μ. Consider a collection of weighted samples $\{X^{(i)}, W^{(i)}\}_{i=1}^{N}$ such that $\sum_{i=1}^{N} W^{(i)} = 1$ and the associated empirical probability distribution

$$\sum_{i=1}^{N} W^{(i)} \delta_{X^{(i)}}(\mathrm{d}x).$$

Resampling N times from this distribution can be interpreted as generating, via some mechanism, a set of N ancestors, with $A^{(i)}$ denoting the ancestor of the ith particle so that the resulting empirical distribution can be written as

$$\frac{1}{N} \sum_{i=1}^{N} \delta_{X^{(A^{(i)})}}(\mathrm{d}x),$$

i.e. in relation to the notation of Algorithm 3.4, $X'^{(i)} \equiv X^{(A^{(i)})}$. It will also be convenient to specify the number of replicates of each existing sample and a cumulative count of these

APF	sAPF
$\{A^{(i)}\}_{i=1}^{N} \overset{ss}{\sim} \sum_{i=1}^{N} W^{(i)} \delta_i(da).$	$\{A^{(i)}\}_{i=1}^{N} \overset{ss}{\sim} \sum_{i=1}^{N} W^{(i)} \delta_i(da).$
for $i = 1$ to N $\quad S^{(i)} \sim \sum_{j=1}^{M} W^{(j|A^{(i)})} \delta_j(ds).$ **end for**	**for** $i = 1$ to N $\quad$ **if** $N_i > 0$ $\quad\quad \{S^{(j)}\}_{j=N_{i-1}^*+1}^{N_i^*} \overset{ss}{\sim} \sum_{j=1}^{M} W^{(j|i)} \delta_j(ds).$ $\quad$ **end if** **end for**

Table 3.3 Resampling and assignment to strata for the APF and sAPF algorithms, both employing stratified sampling. Here, the APF uses the low-variance sampling mechanism in assigning ancestors. By contrast, the sAPF uses the low-variance mechanism in both assigning ancestors and strata.

replicates, so for $i \in \{1, ..., N\}$ we define

$$N_i = \sum_{j=1}^{N} \mathbb{I}_{[A^{(j)}=i]}, \qquad N_i^* = \sum_{j=1}^{i} N_j.$$

Finally, to connect with the notation of Algorithm 3.4 we also set

$$W^{(i)} = \sum_{j=1}^{M} W^{(i,j)}, \qquad W^{(j|i)} = \frac{W^{(i,j)}}{\sum_{j=1}^{M} W^{(i,j)}},$$

where the time index has been suppressed (as it is throughout this section) for clarity.

With these conventions in hand, we consider a set, $\{X^{(i)}, W^{(i)}\}_{i=1}^{N}$, of weighted samples resulting from some iteration of an SMC algorithm and conditional upon this weighted sample set, analyse the variance arising from resampling the particles and assigning particles to strata.

Table 3.3 shows how an algorithm which employs the stratified sampling mechanism in both the resampling and strata-selection steps can be compared with the standard algorithm. Figure 3.2 shows a graphical representation of the procedures.

Given the weighted sample set $\{X^{(i)}, W^{(i)}\}_{i=1}^{N}$, procedures of Table 3.3 both result in a set of ancestor and strata indicators. For a function $\varphi : \{1, ..., M\} \times E \to \mathbb{R}$ we write $\widehat{\varphi}_{\text{sAPF}}^{N}$ and $\widehat{\varphi}_{\text{APF}}^{N}$ for the estimators of the form

$$\frac{1}{N} \sum_{i=1}^{N} \varphi(S^{(i)}, X^{(A^{(i)})})$$

which arise from the sAPF and the APF, respectively. The following proposition establishes that the sAPF scheme of Table 3.3 does indeed yield a reduction in conditional variance over the APF scheme.

Proposition 3.1 *For an integrable function* $\varphi : \{1, ..., M\} \times E \to \mathbb{R}$ *and for all N,*

$$\text{Var}\{\widehat{\varphi}_{\text{sAPF}}^{N} | \mathcal{F}\} \leq \text{Var}\{\widehat{\varphi}_{\text{APF}}^{N} | \mathcal{F}\},$$

where $\mathcal{F} = \sigma(\{X^{(i)}, W^{(i)}\}_{i=1}^{N}).$

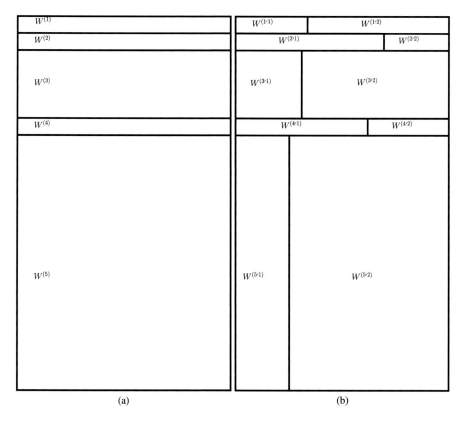

$$W^{(1)} \quad W^{(1\cdot1)} \quad W^{(1\cdot2)}$$

(a) (b)

Figure 3.2 An illustration of stratified resampling within the APF (a) and the sAPF (b) with $N = 5$ particles and $M = 2$ strata. For the APF, each box corresponds to an existing particle; for the sAPF, each box corresponds to an existing particle/stratum pair. In both cases, the area of each box is proportional to the corresponding weight and a number of particles proportional to the area of each box is sampled with the appropriate parameters. In the case of the APF the boxes have heights proportional to the weights of the particles and constant width: only the parent particle is assigned by the low-variance sampling mechanism. In the case of the sAPF the height of the boxes remains proportional to the weight of the particle, $W^{(i)} = \sum_j W^{(i,j)}$, but the assignment of both parent and stratum is performed using the low-variance sampling mechanism.

Proof The variances are first decomposed in the following manner

$$\mathrm{Var}\{\widehat{\varphi}^N_{\mathrm{sAPF}}|\mathcal{F}\} = \mathsf{E}[\mathrm{Var}\{\widehat{\varphi}^N_{\mathrm{sAPF}}|\mathcal{G}\}|\mathcal{F}] + \mathrm{Var}\{\mathsf{E}[\widehat{\varphi}^N_{\mathrm{sAPF}}|\mathcal{G}]|\mathcal{F}\}, \qquad (3.17)$$

$$\mathrm{Var}\{\widehat{\varphi}^N_{\mathrm{APF}}|\mathcal{F}\} = \mathsf{E}[\mathrm{Var}\{\widehat{\varphi}^N_{\mathrm{APF}}|\mathcal{G}\}|\mathcal{F}] + \mathrm{Var}\{\mathsf{E}[\widehat{\varphi}^N_{\mathrm{APF}}|\mathcal{G}]|\mathcal{F}\}, \qquad (3.18)$$

where $\mathcal{G} = \mathcal{F} \vee \sigma(\{A^{(i)}\}^N_{i=1})$. Comparison is then performed term-by-term. First consider the conditional expectations

$$\mathsf{E}[\widehat{\varphi}^N_{\mathrm{sAPF}}|\mathcal{G}] = \frac{1}{N} \sum_{\{i:N_i>0\}} \sum_{j=1}^{N_i} \int_{\frac{j-1}{N_i}}^{\frac{j}{N_i}} N_i \varphi(D_i^{\mathrm{inv}}(u), X^{(i)}) \mathrm{d}u$$

$$= \frac{1}{N} \sum_{\{i:N_i>0\}}^{N} N_i \int_0^1 \varphi(D_i^{\mathrm{inv}}(u), X^{(i)}) \mathrm{d}u = \mathsf{E}[\widehat{\varphi}^N_{\mathrm{APF}}|\mathcal{G}], \qquad (3.19)$$

where D_i^{inv} is the generalised inverse CDF associated with $\sum_{j=1}^M W^{(j|i)} \delta_j$.

Next consider the conditional variances. First note that for both the sAPF and APF the $\{S^{(i)}\}_{i=1}^N$ are conditionally independent given $\{A^{(i)}\}_{i=1}^N$. Hence

$$\mathrm{Var}\{\widehat{\varphi}_{\mathrm{sAPF}}^N|\mathcal{G}\} = \frac{1}{N^2} \sum_{i=1}^N \mathsf{E}[[\varphi(S^{(i)}, X^{(A^{(i)})})]^2|\mathcal{G}] - \frac{1}{N^2} \sum_{i=1}^N [\mathsf{E}[\varphi(S^{(i)}, X^{(A^{(i)})})|\mathcal{G}]]^2$$

$$= \frac{1}{N^2} \sum_{i=1}^N N_i \int_0^1 [\varphi(D_i^{\mathrm{inv}}(u), X^{(i)})]^2 du - \frac{1}{N^2} \sum_{\{i:N_i>0\}} \sum_{j=1}^{N_i} \left[\int_{\frac{j-1}{N_i}}^{\frac{j}{N_i}} N_i \varphi(D_i^{\mathrm{inv}}(u), X^{(i)}) du \right]^2,$$

$$(3.20)$$

whereas for the APF

$$\mathrm{Var}\{\widehat{\varphi}_{\mathrm{APF}}^N|\mathcal{G}\} = \frac{1}{N^2} \sum_{i=1}^N N_i \int_0^1 [\varphi(D_i^{\mathrm{inv}}(u), X^{(i)})]^2 du - \frac{1}{N^2} \sum_{i=1}^N N_i \left[\int_0^1 \varphi(D_i^{\mathrm{inv}}(u), X^{(i)}) du \right]^2.$$

$$(3.21)$$

Applying Jensen's inequality to the second term in Eqs. (3.20) and (3.21) shows that

$$\mathrm{Var}\{\widehat{\varphi}_{\mathrm{sAPF}}^N|\mathcal{G}\} \le \mathrm{Var}\{\widehat{\varphi}_{\mathrm{APF}}^N|\mathcal{G}\}. \tag{3.22}$$

The result follows upon combining Eqs. (3.17), (3.18), (3.19) and (3.22).   □

It is stressed that Proposition 3.1 deals with the *conditional* variance, given $\{X^{(i)}, W^{(i)}\}_{i=1}^N$. This gives some insight into the performance of the algorithm, but ideally one would like to confirm a reduction in the unconditional variance. In the case that residual resampling is used, it may be possible to apply similar techniques to those used in [8] in order to establish a reduction in unconditional asymptotic variance.

3.4.2 Application to switching state space models

Switching SSMs are a particular class of models in which the state of the unobserved process can be expressed in terms of two components, $X_n = (S_n, \theta_n)$, with s_n valued in $\{1, 2, ..., M\}$ and θ_n valued in some space Θ, typically a subset of $\mathbb{R}^d$. The corresponding state space is of the form

$$E = \{1, \ldots, M\} \times \Theta = \biguplus_{j=1}^M \{j\} \times \Theta,$$

so the state space has a natural partition structure. Note that $E_j = \{j\} \times \Theta$ so automatically we have $s_n = \sum_{j=1}^M j \mathbb{I}_{E_j}(x_n)$ as before.

We will focus on models of the form

$$p(\theta_{1:n}, s_{1:n}|y_{1:n}) \propto g(y_n|\theta_n)r(\theta_n|\theta_{n-1}, s_n)r(s_n|s_{n-1})p(\theta_{1:n-1}, s_{1:n-1}|y_{1:n-1}),$$

which arise in a wide variety of applications, including target tracking, [21]; audio signal processing, [1]; and econometrics, [6]. Note that due to the structure of the model we have $r(s_n|x_{n-1}) = r(s_n|s_{n-1})$.

In this model s_n is a latent state, which is not observed. The model of the hidden process $(\theta_n)_{n \in \mathbb{N}}$ can be interpreted as *switching* between M distinct dynamic regimes, with transitions between these regimes governed a priori by the transition kernel $r(s_n|s_{n-1})$. This allows a larger degree of flexibility than in standard SSMs and is especially useful for modelling time series which exhibit temporal heterogeneity.

In the conditionally linear-Gaussian case, given a trajectory $s_{1:n}$ it is possible to compute $p(\theta_{1:n}|y_{1:n}, s_{1:n})$ using the Kalman filter and thus SMC algorithms for filtering can be devised in which the θ components of the state are integrated out analytically, see [21]. We do not assume such a structure, although the methods described above are applicable in that case. The sAPF algorithm for the specific case of switching state space models is given below.

Algorithm 3.5 sAPF for switching state space models

At time 1
  for $i = 1$ to N **do**
    Sample $(\theta_1^{(i)}, S_1^{(i)}) \sim q_1(\cdot)$.
    Set $\widetilde{W}_1^{(i)} \propto \frac{g(y_1|\theta_1^{(i)})\nu(\theta_1^{(i)}, S_1^{(i)})}{q_1(\theta_1^{(i)}, S_1^{(i)})}$.
  end for
At time $n \geq 2$
  for $i = 1$ to N **do**
    for $j = 1$ to M **do**
      Set $W_{n-1}^{(i,j)} \propto \widetilde{W}_{n-1}^{(i)} \times \widehat{p}(y_n|\theta_{n-1}^{(i)}, s_n = j)r(s_n = j|S_{n-1}^{(i)})$.
    end for
  end for
  Resample $\left\{\theta_{n-1}^{(i)}, j, W_{n-1}^{(i,j)}\right\}_{(i,j)\in\{1,...,N\}\times\{1,...,M\}}$ to obtain $\left\{\theta_{n-1}'^{(i)}, S_n^{(i)}, \frac{1}{N}\right\}$.
  for $i = 1$ to N **do**
    Set $\theta_{n-1}^{(i)} = \theta_{n-1}'^{(i)}$.
    Sample $\theta_n^{(i)} \sim q_n(\cdot|\theta_{n-1}^{(i)}, S_n^{(i)})$.
    Set $\widetilde{W}_n^{(i)} \propto \frac{g(y_n|\theta_n^{(i)})r(\theta_n^{(i)}|\theta_{n-1}^{(i)}, S_n^{(i)})}{\widehat{p}(y_n|\theta_{n-1}^{(i)}, S_n^{(i)})q_n(\theta_n^{(i)}|\theta_{n-1}^{(i)}, S_n^{(i)})}$.
  end for

We next consider application of the sAPF to a Markov-switching stochastic volatility (SV) model, as studied in [6]. Stochastic volatility models with switching regime allow occasional discrete shifts in the parameter determining the level of the log volatility of financial returns. They have been advocated as a means by which to avoid overestimation of volatility persistence, see [51] and references therein.

The log-volatility process $\{\theta_n\}_{n\in\mathbb{N}}$ and observations $\{Y_n\}_{n\in\mathbb{N}}$ obey the following equations

$$\theta_n = \phi\theta_{n-1} + \alpha_{s_n} + \zeta_n, \quad Y_n = \epsilon_n \exp(\theta_n/2),$$

where ζ_n is an independent $\mathcal{N}(0, \sigma_\theta^2)$ random variable and ϵ_n is an independent $\mathcal{N}(0, 1)$ random variable. The parameter ϕ is the persistence of volatility shocks, $\{\alpha_j\}_{j=1}^M$ are the log-volatility levels and s_n is the latent regime indicator, so that

$$\alpha_{s_n} = \gamma_1 + \sum_{j=2}^M \gamma_j \mathbf{I}_{[s_n \geq j]},$$

where $\{\gamma_j\}_{j=1}^M$ are log-volatility increments. The prior transition kernel $r(s_n|s_{n-1})$ is specified by a stochastic matrix with entry p_{kl} being the probability of a transition from state k to state l.

In order to construct the potential function $\widehat{p}(y_n|\theta_{n-1}, s_n)$ and the proposal distribution $q_n(\theta_n|\theta_{n-1}, s_n)$ we employ a slight modification of the technique proposed in [44] for standard SV models. The idea is to exploit the log-concavity of the likelihood function and form an approximation of $g(y_n|\theta_n)$ by taking a first-order Taylor expansion of the log-likelihood about the conditional mean of θ_n. With an abuse of notation we write $\bar{\theta}_n := \phi\theta_{n-1} + \alpha_{s_n}$. The approximation of the likelihood is then specified by

$$\log \widehat{g}(y_n|\theta_n; \theta_{n-1}, s_n) = \log g(y_n|\bar{\theta}_n) + (\theta_n - \bar{\theta}_n) \cdot \frac{\partial}{\partial\theta} \log g(y_n|\theta)\Big|_{\bar{\theta}_n}. \qquad (3.23)$$

We then choose

$$q_n(\theta_n|s_n, \theta_{n-1}) \propto \widehat{g}(y_n|\theta_n; \theta_{n-1}, s_n)r(\theta_n|\theta_{n-1}, s_n),$$

which is a Gaussian density, $\mathcal{N}(\mu_{q_n}, \sigma^2_{q_n})$, with parameters

$$\mu_{q_n} = \phi\theta_{n-1} + \alpha_{s_n} + \frac{\sigma^2_\theta}{2}\left[y_n^2 \exp(-\phi\theta_{n-1} - \alpha_{s_n}) - 1\right],$$
$$\sigma^2_{q_n} = \sigma^2_\theta.$$

Furthermore, we employ the following approximation of the predictive likelihood

$$\widehat{p}(y_n|\theta_{n-1}, s_n) \propto \int \widehat{g}(y_n|\theta_n; \theta_{n-1}, s_n)r(\theta_n|\theta_{n-1}, s_n)\mathrm{d}\theta_n$$

$$\propto \exp\left(\frac{1}{2\sigma^2_\theta}(\mu^2_{q_n} - (\phi\theta_{n-1} + \alpha_{s_n})^2)\right)$$

$$\times \exp\left(-\frac{y_n^2}{2}\exp(-\phi\theta_{n-1} - \alpha_{s_n})(1 + \phi\theta_{n-1} + \alpha_{s_n})\right).$$

The importance weight is given by

$$\widetilde{w}_n(\theta_{n-1:n}, s_n) \propto \frac{g(y_n|\theta_n)}{\widehat{g}(y_n|\theta_n; \theta_{n-1}, s_n)}$$

$$\propto \exp\left\{-\frac{y_n^2}{2}\left[\exp(-\theta_n) - \exp(-\bar{\theta}_n)[1 - (\theta_n - \bar{\theta}_n)]\right]\right\}.$$

Due to the fact that $\log g(y_n|\theta)$ is concave as a function of θ and from the definition (3.23), the importance weight $\widetilde{w}_n(\theta_{n-1:n}, s_n)$ is bounded above.

The Bovespa Index (IBOVESPA) is an index of approximately 50 stocks traded on the São Paulo Stock Exchange. Figure 3.3 shows weekday returns on the IBOVESPA index for the period 1/2/97–1/15/01. As highlighted in [6], during this period there occurred several international currency events which affected Latin American markets, generating higher levels of uncertainty and consequently higher levels of volatility. These events are listed in Table 3.4 and are indicated by the vertical dotted lines in Fig. 3.3. This dataset was analysed in [40], where an SMC algorithm was used to perform filtering whilst simultaneously estimating static parameters. We concentrate on the filtering problem and set static parameters to pre-determined values.

07/02/1997	Thailand devalues the Baht by as much as 20%
08/11/1997	IMF and Thailand set a rescue agreement
10/23/1997	Hong Kong's stock index falls 10.4%
	South Korean Won starts to weaken
12/02/1997	IMF and South Korea set a bailout agreement
06/01/1998	Russia's stock market crashes
06/20/1998	IMF gives final approval to a loan package to Russia
08/19/1998	Russia officially falls into default
10/09/1998	IMF and World Bank joint meeting to discuss the economic crisis
	The Federal Reserve cuts interest rates
01/15/1999	The Brazilian government allows its currency, the Real,
	to float freely by lifting exchange controls
02/02/1999	Arminio Fraga is named President of Brazil's Central Bank

Table 3.4 Events which impacted Latin American markets [6].

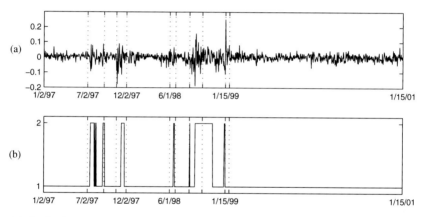

Figure 3.3 Stochastic volatility model. (a) Daily returns on the IBOVESPA index from February 1997 to January 2001. (b) MAP one-step-ahead prediction of the switching state s_n. State 2 is the high-volatility regime.

The sAPF was compared to a standard APF for this model, with the latter employing the same approximation of the likelihood in the proposal distributions, i.e.

$$q_n(\theta_n, s_n | \theta_{n-1}, s_{n-1}) \propto \widehat{g}(y_n | \theta_n; \theta_{n-1}, s_n) r(\theta_n | \theta_{n-1}, s_n) r(s_n | s_{n-1}),$$

$$\widehat{p}(y_n | \theta_{n-1}, s_{n-1}) \propto \sum_{j=1}^{M} \left\{ r(s_n = j | s_{n-1}) \int \widehat{g}(y_n | \theta_n; \theta_{n-1}, s_n = j) r(\theta_n | \theta_{n-1}, s_n = j) d\theta_n \right\}.$$

Systematic resampling was used in both algorithms.[1] Based on the parameter estimates made in [6], we set $M = 2$, $p_{11} = 0.993$, $p_{22} = 0.973$, $\alpha_1 = -1.2$, $\alpha_2 = -0.9$, $\phi = 0.85$, $\sigma_\theta^2 = 0.1$.

For each algorithm, the variance of the minimum means square error (MMSE) filtering estimate of the log volatility was computed at each iteration, over 500 independent runs.

---

[1] Although systematic resampling does not uniformly outperform other approaches it is extremely widely used in the applied filtering literature. Although it is computationally attractive, care is required when using this approach for the reasons documented in [17].

	APF		sAPF	
N	$\bar{\sigma}^2$	CPU / s	$\bar{\sigma}^2$	CPU / s
10	0.0906	0.8394	0.0850	0.2526
20	0.0544	1.5397	0.0492	0.3558
50	0.0325	3.6665	0.0290	0.6648
100	0.0274	10.7095	0.0230	1.1801
200	0.0195	17.7621	0.0189	2.7231
500	0.0195	35.4686	0.0185	5.3206

Table 3.5 Stochastic volatility model: variance of filtering estimate and average CPU time per run over 500 runs for the IBOVESPA data.

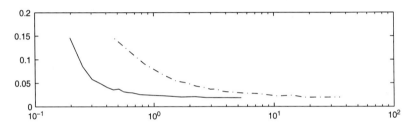

Figure 3.4 Stochastic volatility model: variance of filtering estimate vs. average CPU time in secs. over 500 runs for the IBOVESPA data. Solid: sAPF, dash-dot: APF.

These variances were then summarised by taking their arithmetic mean and are shown in Table 3.5.

This shows how the variance of filtering estimates of the log-volatility and mean CPU time per run for the two algorithms relate to the number of particles used. For the same number of particles, the sAPF algorithm exhibits lower variance of filtering estimates. The results also show that, for the same number of particles, the sAPF can be computationally cheaper than the APF. This can be explained as follows. The algorithms involve precisely the same arithmetic operations in order to compute both the auxiliary importance weights and the importance weights by which estimation is performed. However, in terms of random number generation, the APF is more expensive: it uses one random variate to perform systematic resampling, then for each particle draws $S_n^{(i)}$ from a distribution on $\{1, ..., M\}$ and samples $\theta_n^{(i)}$ from $q_n(\cdot|\theta_{n-1}, s_n)$. By contrast, the sAPF uses one random variate to perform systematic resampling (which assigns values of both $X_{n-1}^{(i)}$ and $S_n^{(i)}$) and then for each particle samples $\theta_n^{(i)}$ from $q_n(\cdot|\theta_{n-1}, s_n)$.

Although the cost-saving will be dependent on the programming language employed, the results indicate that the savings can be significant. In this case both algorithms were implemented in MatLab, and the code was made common to both algorithms in all places possible. The performance benefit in terms of estimator variance versus CPU time is illustrated in Fig. 3.4.

Figure 3.5 shows boxplots of the number of particles in the high-volatility regime over 100 independent runs of each algorithm. The pairs of boxplots correspond to the dates 3/1/99 (left), 14/1/99 (middle) and 15/1/99 (right). During this period, it can be seen from Fig. 3.3 that an increase in volatility occurs; $N = 100$ particles were used in both algorithms. The count of number of particles in the high-volatility regime was

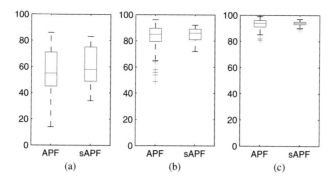

Figure 3.5 Stochastic volatility model. Boxplots, over 100 runs of each algorithm, of the number of particles in the high-volatility regime at iterations corresponding to the dates 13/1/99 (a), 14/1/99 (b) and 15/1/99 (c). $N = 100$.

made immediately after resampling in the case of the sAPF and immediately after making proposals in the case of the APF, i.e. at equivalent steps of the algorithms. Across the three dates the sAPF exhibits lower variability than the APF and the mean number of particles in the high-volatility regime is lower for the APF. That is, the sAPF shows less variability in its approximation of the distribution over strata: this improved distributional approximation is the underlying mechanism which leads to improved variance properties.

Figure 3.3 shows the one-step-ahead MAP prediction of the switching state s_n, using the sAPF algorithm with $N = 500$ particles. Recall that $s_n = 2$ is the high-volatility regime. The results show that the model is able to recognise changes in the level of volatility and these changes roughly coincide with the currency crisis events listed in Table 3.4. The results are very similar to those obtained in [6].

3.5 Conclusions

This article has attempted to summarise the state of the art of the auxiliary particle filter. Our intention is to provide some insight into the behaviour of the APF and its relationship with other particle-filtering algorithms, in addition to summarising a number of recent methodological extensions. One of the most significant points is perhaps this: the APF is simply an example of a sequential estimation procedure in which one can benefit from the early introduction of information about subsequent distributions, combined with an importance sampling correction. In the context of time series analysis, this approach is useful when performing filtering in SSMs and the same approach can be exploited elsewhere.

Bibliography

[1] C. Andrieu, M. Davy and A. Doucet. Efficient particle filtering for jump Markov systems. Application to time-varying autoregressions. *IEEE Transactions on Signal Processing*, **51**(7):1762–1770, 2003.

[2] A. Bain and D. Crisan. *Fundamentals of Stochastic Filtering*. Stochastic Modelling and Applied Probability. Springer Verlag, 2009.

[3] M. Briers, A Doucet and S. S. Singh. Sequential auxiliary particle belief propagation. In *Proceedings of International Conference on Information Fusion*, 2005.

[4] O. Cappé, E. Moulines and T. Ryden. *Inference in Hidden Markov Models*. Springer Verlag, 2005.

[5] J. Carpenter, P. Clifford and P. Fearnhead. An improved particle filter for non-linear problems. *IEEE Proceedings on Radar, Sonar and Navigation*, **146**(1):2–7, 1999.

[6] C. M. Carvalho and H. F. Lopes. Simulation-based sequential analysis of Markov switching stochastic volatility models. *Computational Statistics and Data Analysis*, **51**:4526–4542, 2007.

[7] S. Centanni and M. Minozzo. Estimation and filtering by reversible jump MCMC for a doubly stochastic Poisson model for ultra-high-frequency financial data. *Statistical Modelling*, **6**(2):97–118, 2006.

[8] N. Chopin. Central limit theorem for sequential Monte Carlo methods and its applications to Bayesian inference. *Annals of Statistics*, **32**(6):2385–2411, 2004.

[9] D. E. Clark and J. Bell. Convergence results for the particle PHD filter. *IEEE Transactions on Signal Processing*, **54**(7):2652–2661, July 2006.

[10] J. Cornebise, E. Moulines and J. Olsson. Adaptive methods for sequential importance sampling with application to state space models. *Statistics and Computing*, **18**:461–480, 2008.

[11] D. J. Daley and D. Vere-Jones. *An Introduction to the Theory of Point Processes*, volume I: Elementary Theory and Methods of *Probability and Its Applications*. Springer, second edition, 2003.

[12] A. Dassios and J. Jang. Kalman-Bucy filtering for linear system driven by the Cox process with shot noise intensity and its application to the pricing of reinsurance contracts. *Journal of Applied Probability*, **42**(1):93–107, 2005.

[13] P. Del Moral. *Feynman-Kac Formulae: Genealogical and Interacting Particle Systems with applications*. Probability and Its Applications. Springer Verlag, New York, 2004.

[14] P. Del Moral, A. Doucet and A. Jasra. Sequential Monte Carlo methods for Bayesian Computation. In *Bayesian Statistics 8*. Oxford University Press, 2006.

[15] P. Del Moral, A. Doucet and A. Jasra. Sequential Monte Carlo samplers. *Journal of the Royal Statistical Society Series B*, **63**(3):411–436, 2006.

[16] P. Del Moral, A. Doucet and A. Jasra. On adaptive resampling procedures for sequential Monte Carlo methods. Technical Report HAL-INRIA RR-6700, INRIA, 2008.

[17] R. Douc, O. Cappé and E. Moulines. Comparison of resampling schemes for particle filters. In *Proceedings of the 4th International Symposium on Image and Signal Processing and Analysis*, volume I, pages 64–69, 2005.

[18] R. Douc and E. Moulines. Limit theorems for weighted samples with applications to sequential Monte Carlo methods. *Annals of Statistics*, **36**(5):2344–2376, 2008.

[19] R. Douc, E. Moulines and J. Olsson. Optimality of the auxiliary particle filter. *Probability and Mathematical Statistics*, **29**(1):1–28, 2009.

[20] A. Doucet, N. de Freitas and N. Gordon, editors. *Sequential Monte Carlo Methods in Practice*. Statistics for Engineering and Information Science. Springer Verlag, 2001.

[21] A. Doucet, N. Gordon and V. Krishnamurthy. Particle filters for state estimation of jump Markov linear systems. *IEEE Transactions on Signal Processing*, **49**(3):613–624, 2001.

[22] A. Doucet and A. M. Johansen. A tutorial on particle filtering and smoothing: Fifteen years later. In D. Crisan and B. Rozovsky, editors, *The Oxford Handbook of Nonlinear Filtering*. Oxford University Press, 2011. To appear.

[23] P. Fearnhead. Sequential Monte Carlo methods in filter theory. PhD thesis, University of Oxford, 1998.

[24] P. Fearnhead, O. Papaspiliopoulos and G. O. Roberts. Particle filters for partially observed diffusions. *Journal of the Royal Statistical Society B*, **70**:755–777, 2008.

[25] J. Geweke. Bayesian inference in econometric models using Monte Carlo integration. *Econometrica*, **57**(6):1317–1339, 1989.

[26] W. R. Gilks and Carlo Berzuini. RESAMPLE-MOVE filtering with Cross-Model jumps. In Doucet *et al.* [20], pages 117–138.

[27] S. Godsill and T. Clapp. Improvement strategies for Monte Carlo particle filters. In Doucet *et al.* [20], pages 139–158.

[28] S. J. Godsill, J. Vermaak, K-F. Ng and J-F. Li. Models and algorithms for tracking of manoeuvring objects using variable rate particle filters. *Proc. IEEE*, April 2007.

[29] A. G. Gray and A. W. Moore. N-body problems in statistical learning. In *Advances in Neural Information Processing Systems 13*, pages 521–527. MIT Press, 2000.

[30] K. Heine. Unified framework for sampling/importance resampling algorithms. In *Proceedings of Fusion 2005, July 25–29, 2005, Philadelphia*. 2005.

[31] A. M. Johansen. SMCTC: Sequential Monte Carlo in C++. *Journal of Statistical Software*, **30**(6):1–41, 2009.

[32] A. M. Johansen and A. Doucet. Auxiliary variable sequential Monte Carlo methods. Research Report 07:09, University of Bristol, Department of Mathematics – Statistics Group, University Walk, Bristol, BS8 1TW, UK, 2007.

[33] A. M. Johansen and A. Doucet. A note on the auxiliary particle filter. *Statistics and Probability Letters*, **78**(12):1498–1504, 2008.

[34] A. M. Johansen, S. Singh, A. Doucet and B. Vo. Convergence of the SMC implementation of the PHD filter. *Methodology and Computing in Applied Probability*, **8**(2):265–291, 2006.

[35] N. Kantas. Sequential Decision Making in General State Space Models. PhD thesis, University of Cambridge, 2009.

[36] R. Karlsson and N. Bergman. Auxiliary particle filters for tracking a maneuvering target. In *Proceedings of the 39th IEEE Conference on Decision and Control*, pages 3891–3895, 2000.

[37] G. Kitagawa. Monte Carlo filter and smoother for non-Gaussian nonlinear state space models. *Journal of Computational and Graphical Statistics*, **5**(1):1–25, March 1996.

[38] M. Klass, N. de Freitas and A. Doucet. Towards practical n^2 Monte Carlo: The marginal particle filter. In *Proceedings of Uncertainty in Artificial Intelligence*, 2005.

[39] J. S. Liu and R. Chen. Sequential Monte Carlo methods for dynamic systems. *Journal of the American Statistical Association*, **93**(443):1032–1044, 1998.

[40] H. F. Lopes and C. M. Carvalho. Factor stochastic volatility with time varying loadings and Markov switching regimes. *Journal of Statistical Planning and Inference*, **137**:3082–3091, 2007.

[41] R. P. S. Mahler. Multitarget Bayes filtering via first-order multitarget moments. *IEEE Transactions on Aerospace and Electronic Systems*, pages 1152–1178, October 2003.

[42] R. P. S. Mahler. *Statistical Multisource-Multitarget Information Fusion*. Artech House, 2007.

[43] S. Nadarajah and S. Kotz. Mathematical properties of the multivariate *t* distribution. *Acta Applicandae Mathematicae*, **89**:53–84, 2005.

[44] M. K. Pitt and N. Shephard. Filtering via simulation: Auxiliary particle filters. *Journal of the American Statistical Association*, **94**(446):590–599, 1999.

[45] M. K. Pitt and N. Shephard. Auxiliary variable based particle filters. In Doucet *et al.* [20], chapter 13, pages 273–293.

[46] G. Poyiadjis, A. Doucet and S.S. Singh. Particle methods for optimal filter derivative: application to parameter estimation. In *Proceedings of IEEE International Conference on Acoustics, Speech and Signal Processing (ICASSP)*, volume 5, pages 925–928, 2005.

[47] C. P. Robert and G. Casella. *Monte Carlo Statistical Methods*. Springer Texts in Statistics. Springer, 2004.

[48] S. Saha, P. K. Mandal, Y. Boers, H. Driessen, and A. Bagchi. Gaussian proposal density using moment matching in SMC methods. *Statistics and Computing*, **19**:203–208, 2009.

[49] H. Sidenbladh. Multi-target particle filtering for the probability hypothesis density. In *Proceedings of the International Conference on Information Fusion, Cairns, Australia*, pages 800–806, 2003.

[50] S. S. Singh, B.-N. Vo, A. Baddeley and S. Zuyev. Filters for spatial point processes. *Siam Journal on Control and Optimization*, **48**(4):2275–2295, 2008.

[51] M. K. P. So, K. Lam and W. K. Li. A stochastic volatility model with Markov switching. *Journal of Business and Economic Statistics*, **16**(2):244–253, 1998.

[52] B. Vo, S. Singh and A. Doucet. Sequential Monte Carlo methods for multitarget filtering with random finite sets. *IEEE Transactions on Aerospace and Electronic Systems*, **41**(4):1224–1245, 2005.

[53] N. Whiteley, A. M. Johansen and S. Godsill. Monte Carlo filtering of piecewise-deterministic processes. *Journal of Computational and Graphical Statistics*, 2011. To appear.

[54] N. Whiteley, S. Singh and S. Godsill. Auxiliary particle implementation of the probability hypothesis density filter. *IEEE Transactions on Aerospace and Electronic Systems*, **46**(3):1437–1454, 2010.

[55] T. Zajic and R. P. S. Mahler. Particle-systems implementation of the PHD multitarget tracking filter. In *Proceedings of SPIE*, pages 291–299, 2003.

Contributors

Nick Whiteley, Statistics Group, Department of Mathematics, University of Bristol
Adam M. Johansen, Department of Statistics, University of Warwick

4

Monte Carlo probabilistic inference for diffusion processes: a methodological framework

Omiros Papaspiliopoulos

4.1 Introduction

We consider statistical inference for models specified by stochastic differential equations (SDEs). Stochastic differential equations provide a natural model for processes which at least conceptually evolve continuously in time and have continuous sample paths. From a more pragmatic point of view they offer a flexible framework for modelling irregularly spaced time series data. As a result they are used as statistical models throughout science; for example in finance [48, 20, 2], biology [26], molecular kinetics [29, 31]. They are increasingly used in more mainstream statistical applications, e.g. longitudinal data analysis [49], space-time models [8] and functional data analysis, see for example [45] and discussion therein. Specifically, an SDE for a d-dimensional process $V \in R^d$ is specified as follows:

$$dV_s = b(s, V_s)\,ds + \sigma(s, V_s)\,dB_s, \quad s \in [0, T], \tag{4.1}$$

where B is an m-dimensional standard Brownian motion, $b(\cdot, \cdot) : R_+ \times R^d \to R^d$ is called the *drift*, and $\sigma(\cdot, \cdot) : R_+ \times R^d \to R^{d \times m}$ is called the *diffusion coefficient*. Boundary conditions are needed to complete the model specification. Certain assumptions are required on b and σ to ensure that Eq. (4.1) has a unique weak solution, see for example Theorem 5.2.1 of [38]. The unique solution is known as a diffusion process. It can be shown that it is a strong Markov process, thus it shares the Markov semigroup property with the solutions of ordinary differential equations, which are obtained in the no-noise limit $\sigma = 0$. Note that the dimension of the driving Brownian motion can differ from that of the state process. In statistical applications an interesting possibility is to take $d > m$. For example, we can model a process with differentiable sample paths by specifying an SDE on the process and its time-derivatives. This gives rise to the so-called hypo-elliptic diffusion processes [44]. A simple popular hypo-elliptic model is the integrated Brownian motion which is often used in target tracking applications, see for example [27], and it relates to inference for unknown regression functions [53].

The diffusion process can be used to model directly observed data, or it can be used to model latent processes which relate to the observable via likelihood functions. Statistical inference in such contexts consists of estimating unknown parameters involved in the specification of the drift and the diffusion coefficient, and estimating the process itself when it is unobserved. We are interested in likelihood-based inference for the unknown parameters, i.e. maximum likelihood and Bayesian methods; and in probabilistic inference for the unobserved processes, i.e. inference according to the conditional law of the process given the observed data, where the prior law is given by the SDE specification (4.1). To simplify the presentation we will refer to such estimation procedures as *probabilistic inference*.

A major difficulty with probabilistic inference for diffusion processes is the intractability of the transition density

$$p_{s,t}(v, w) = \Pr[V_t \in dw \,|\, V_s = v] / dw; \quad t > s; \quad w, v \in R^d. \tag{4.2}$$

This is due to the fact that only in very few cases can the SDE be analytically solved. At infinitely small time increments, i.e for $t - s \approx 0$, Eq. (4.2) can be satisfactorily approximated by a Gaussian. However, this approximation is very poor for arbitrary time increments. Intuitively, the transition distribution for longer time increments is a non-linear convolution of Gaussian distributions, hence it is intractable. It is known that for fixed observation frequency, quasi-maximum likelihood estimators of parameters based on a first-order Gaussian approximation to Eq. (4.2) are in general inconsistent [24]. On the other hand, this difficulty has motivated exciting research for analytic and Monte Carlo (MC) approximations of Eq. (4.2), see for example [1, 30, 40] and references therein. Typically, these approaches involve systematic bias due to time and/or space discretisations.

The methodological framework developed and reviewed in this chapter concerns the *unbiased* MC estimation of the transition density, and the *exact* simulation of diffusion processes. The former relates to auxiliary variable methods, and it builds on a rich generic MC machinery of unbiased estimation and simulation of infinite series expansions. This machinery is employed in diverse application areas such as population genetics and operational research. The latter is a recent significant advance in the numerics for diffusions and it is based on the so-called Wiener–Poisson factorisation of the diffusion measure. It has interesting connections to exact simulation of killing times for the Brownian motion and interacting particle systems, which are uncovered in this chapter.

The methodological framework we develop leads to unbiased probabilistic inference for diffusion processes. Our focus is more on the methodology than on its specific application to inference. Nevertheless, for clarity we consider the so-called continuous–discrete non-linear filtering problem, see for example [14]. An overview of how to combine this framework with standard computational algorithms such as the expectation maximisation (EM) and Markov chain Monte Carlo (MCMC) to perform likelihood-based inference for diffusions is given in [7].

The rest of the chapter is organised as follows. Section 4.2 introduces the continuous–discrete non-linear filtering problem, which serves as a motivating example. The section introduces the idea of replacing unknown densities by positive unbiased estimators and its interpretation as an auxiliary variable technique. Section 4.3 gives a representation of the transition density for a class of diffusion processes, which is key to our framework. Section 4.4 shows how to use this representation to achieve exact simulation of diffusion processes. Section 4.5 provides further insights to the exact simulation by linking it to the simulation of killing times of Brownian motion exploiting the connection between the exponential distribution and the Poisson process. It also relates the construction to interacting particle systems. Section 4.6 gives a detailed account of the machinery involved in deriving unbiased estimators of the diffusion transition density. This machinery is interesting outside the context of SDEs and links to the literature are provided. Section 4.7 closes with a discussion.

4.2 Random weight continuous–discrete particle filtering

The development in this section follows to some extent [21]. We consider that Eq. (4.1) is unobserved, but partial information is available at discrete times $0 < t_1 < t_2 < \cdots < t_n$ in terms of observations $y_1, y_2, \ldots, y_n$ which are linked to the diffusion via a likelihood function, $f(y_i|V_{t_i})$. We also elicit a prior distribution on the diffusion initial state, say $p_0(V_0)$. Hence, we have a continuously evolving *signal* modelled as a diffusion process, and discrete-time observations. We are interested in the recursive calculation of the so-called filtering distributions, i.e. the sequence of posterior distributions $p(V_{t_i}|y_{1:i})$ which will be denoted by $\pi_i(V_{t_i})$, where by standard convention $y_{1:i} = (y_1, \ldots, y_i)$. This is known as the continuous–discrete filtering problem, see for example [14]. To simplify notation in this section we will subscribe the discrete skeleton of V by i rather than t_i, i.e $V_i := V_{t_i}$. Hence, we actually deal with a discrete-time Markov chain V_i, $i = 0, \ldots, n$, observed with noise. Hence the problem of interest can be coined as a discrete-time filtering problem, as follows.

Using marginalisation, the Bayes' theorem and the Markov property, we obtain the following fundamental filtering recursion:

$$\pi_{i+1}(V_{i+1}) \propto \int f(y_{i+1}|V_{i+1}) p_{t_i, t_{i+1}}(V_i, V_{i+1}) \pi_i(V_i) \mathrm{d}V_i. \tag{4.3}$$

Only in very specific cases can the filtering distributions be characterised by a finite number of parameters which can recursively be computed. A model amenable to this type of analysis is obtained when V is the solution of a linear SDE (e.g. the integrated Brownian) observed with additive Gaussian error. In this case we can use the Kalman filter to do the computations.

For non-linear models, however, the state of the art is to approximate the filtering distributions using MC. The corresponding algorithms, known as *particle filters* (PFs) [17], are characterised by two main steps. First, an approximation of π_i by a discrete distribution, denoted by π_i^N, whose support is a set of N particles, $\{V_i^{(j)}\}_{j=1}^N$, with associated (un-normalised probability) weights $\{w_i^{(j)}\}_{j=1}^N$. Substituting π_i^N for π_i in Eq. (4.3), yields a (continuous density) approximation to π_{i+1}

$$\tilde{\pi}_{i+1}(V_{i+1}) \propto \sum_{j=1}^N w_i^{(j)} f(y_{i+1}|V_{i+1}) p_{t_i, t_{i+1}}(V_i^{(j)}, V_{i+1}). \tag{4.4}$$

The aim of one iteration of the PF is to construct a further particle (discrete distribution) approximation to $\tilde{\pi}_{i+1}$. The second main step of the PF is to use importance sampling to sample from Eq. (4.4), thus obtaining a particle approximation for $\tilde{\pi}_{i+1}$. A general framework for achieving this is given by the auxiliary particle filter of [43]. We choose a proposal density of the form

$$\sum_{j=1}^N \beta_i^{(j)} q_{i+1}(V_{i+1}|V_i^{(j)}, y_{i+1}),$$

where the β_is are probabilities, and the q_is are probability density functions. These steps are summarised in Algorithm 4.1. Step PF2 of the algorithm includes a decision to *resample* among existing particles when the variance of the proposal weights β exceeds a certain threshold. The decision is taken using the effective sample size, see for example Chapter 2 of [33]. Note that, when taking $C < N$ and $\beta_i^{(k)} = 1/N$, resampling is never performed and the approach reduces to a direct importance sampling with target π_{i+1} and proposals generated *independently* from $\prod_{k=0}^{i+1} q_k$. The (at least occasional) resampling, however, which introduces *dependence* among the particles, is crucial to break the curse of dimensionality inherent in an importance sampling algorithm. The resulting particle filter has good theoretical properties including consistency [12] and central limit theorems for estimates of posterior moments [14, 10, 32], as $N \to \infty$. Under conditions relating to exponential forgetting of initial conditions for the signal, PF errors stabilise as $n \to \infty$ [13, 32]. Additionally, the filtering distributions are obtained at computational cost $O(N)$, and unbiased estimators of the normalising constants (important in parameter estimation and model comparisons) are readily available. Improvements on independent sampling in PF1 can be made: see inter alia the stratified sampling ideas of [9].

Algorithm 4.1 Auxiliary PF for state space models.

PF0 Simulate $V_0^{(j)} \sim p_0(V_0)$, and set $w_0^{(j)} = 1/N$, for $j = 1, \ldots, N$.
for $i = 0, \ldots, n-1, j = 1, \ldots, N$ **do**
  PF1 Calculate the effective sample size of the $\{\beta_i^{(k)}\}$, $ESS = (\sum_{k=1}^N (\beta_i^{(k)})^2)^{-1}$.
  If $ESS < C$, for some fixed constant C, simulate k_{i+1}^j from $p(k) = \beta_i^{(k)}$, $k = 1, \ldots, N$
  and set $\delta_{i+1}^{(j)} = 1$; otherwise set $k_{i+1}^j = j$ and $\delta_{i+1}^{(j)} = \beta_i^{(j)}$.
  PF2 Simulate $V_{i+1}^{(j)}$ from $q_{i+1}(\cdot | V_i^{k_{i+1}^j}, y_{i+1})$.
  PF3 Assign particle $V_{i+1}^{(j)}$ a weight

$$w_{i+1}^{(j)} = w_i^{(k_{i+1}^j)} \frac{\delta_{i+1}^{(j)} f(y_{i+1}|V_{i+1}^{(j)}) p_{t_i,t_{i+1}}(V_i^{(k_{i+1}^j)}, V_{i+1}^{(j)})}{\beta_i^{(k_{i+1}^j)} q_{i+1}(V_{i+1}^{(j)}|V_i^{(k_{i+1}^j)}, y_{i+1})}. \tag{4.5}$$

end for

Algorithm 4.1 applies generally to state space time series models. However, when the signal is a discretely sampled diffusion process, the PF cannot be applied due to the intractability of the system transition density, which is necessary in the calculation of the weights. One way to bypass this problem is to simulate the particles V_{i+1} according to the diffusion dynamics; then the transition density cancels out from Eq. (4.5). This requires the *exact simulation* of diffusions, which is discussed in Section 4.4. Another possibility is to try to obtain *unbiased estimators* for the transition density $p_{s,t}(u, v)$ for arbitrary s, t, u, v. The unbiasedness is needed to ensure that the particles are *properly weighted*, see for example Section 2.5.4 of [33].

Section 4.6 shows how for each pair (u, v) and times (s, t), with $s < t$, to simulate *auxiliary* variables Ψ according to a distribution $Q(\cdot; s, t, u, v)$, and to specify a computable function $r(\Psi, s, t, u, v)$, with the property that $\mathbb{E}[r(\Psi, s, t, u, v)] = p_{s,t}(u, v)$. Then, the so-called *random weight PF* (RWPF) inserts a further step between PF2 and PF3: simulate $\Psi_{i+1}^{(j)}$ from

$Q(\cdot; t_i, t_{i+1}, V_i^{(k_{i+1}^j)}, V_{i+1}^{(j)})$ and compute $r(\Psi_{i+1}^{(j)}, t_i, t_{i+1}, V_i^{(k_{i+1}^j)}, V_{i+1}^{(j)})$. This quantity replaces the intractable transition density in Eq. (4.5). The RWPF is introduced in [46] and [21].

When r is positive this formulation has an interpretation as an expansion of the state space using auxiliary variables. According to our construction, conditionally on V_i and V_{i+1}, Ψ_{i+1} is independent of Ψ_j and V_j for any j different from $i, i + 1$. Additionally, it follows easily from the unbiasedness and positivity of r that, for any u, $r(\psi, t_i, t_{i+1}, u, v)$ is a probability density function as a function of (ψ, v) with respect to the product measure $Leb(dv) \times Q(d\psi; , t_i, t_{i+1}, u, v)$, where Leb denotes the Lebesgue measure. Consider now an alternative discrete-time Markov model with unobserved states $(V_i, \Psi_i), i = 1, \ldots, n$, transition density r and observed data y_i with observation density $f(y_i|V_i)$. By construction the marginal filtering distributions of V_i in this model are precisely π_i. Consider an auxiliary PF applied to this model where we choose with probabilities $\beta_i^{(j)}$ each of the existing particles $(V_i^{(j)}, \Psi_i^{(j)})$, and generate new particles in the following way: V_{i+1} is proposed from q_{i+1} as described before, and conditionally on this value, Ψ_{i+1} is simulated according to Q. Then, it can be checked that the weight assigned to each particle is precisely that in the RWPF. Therefore, the RWPF is equivalent to an auxiliary PF on this discrete-time model whose latent structure has been augmented with the auxiliary variables Ψ_i. It is worth mentioning that the potential of using unbiased estimators of intractable densities while retaining the 'exactness' of MC algorithms is being increasingly recognised. The idea already appears in a disguised form in the auxiliary PF of [43] and explicitly in the rejection control algorithm, see for example Section 2.6.1 of [33]. The authors in [7] elaborate on this idea to design approximation-free MCMC algorithms for probabilistic inference for diffusions, [34, 35] devise novel MCMC algorithms for parameter estimation for models with intractable normalising constants (which are functions of the parameters), [4] develop and analyse theoretically a general class of MCMC algorithms where the target density is replaced by an importance sampling estimator, and [3] show how to obtain exact MCMC algorithms for state space models when the likelihood is estimated by the PF. Additionally, [41] show that the MCEM algorithm can be adjusted using these ideas to increase monotonically an objective function. The random weight idea appears also within the variance reduction approach of [25] in the context of option pricing.

Clearly, the replacement of an importance sampling weight, say w, with an unbiased estimator, say r, increases the variance: $\text{Var}\{r\} = \text{Var}\{w\} + E[\text{Var}\{r|w\}]$, since $E[r|w] = w$, provided all variances exist. The expression suggests that the random weight importance sampler will be most efficient when $E[\text{Var}\{r|w\}]$ is relatively small compared to $\text{Var}\{w\}$.

In the auxiliary PF formulation given in Algorithm 4.1 the positivity of the estimators is not necessary, since the resampling probabilities are controlled by β_i. Therefore, even if the actual weights w_i are negative, the algorithm in principle can still be carried out and yield consistent estimates of expectations over the filtering distributions. Clearly, in this case the w_is lose their interpretation as un-normalised probabilities; this is further discussed in Section 4.7. On the other hand, the generic Algorithm 4.2, proposed originally in [22], can be applied to ensure the positivity of the unbiased estimators. Suppose that we have N particles with true but unknown weights $w^{(j)}$ and for each j, let $r^{(i,j)} i = 1, 2, \ldots$, be a sequence of conditionally independent unbiased estimators of $w^{(j)}$. The procedure yields a random weight $r^{(j)} = \sum_{i=1}^{\tau} r^{(i,j)}$, where τ is a stopping time which depends on the sign of all weights. If $E[\tau] < \infty$, then $E[r^{(j)}|w^{(j)}] = E[\tau]w^{(j)}$; this follows from Wald's identity, see Theorem 2 of [22]. The intractable normalising constant $E[\tau]$ in the weights creates no problems, since it is common to all particles and will be cancelled out when the particle weights are re-normalised.

Algorithm 4.2 Creating positive unbiased importance weights exploiting Wald's identity.

Set $i = 1$, simulate $r^{(1,j)}$ and set $r^{(j)} = r^{(1,j)}$, for all $j = 1, \dots, N$.
If $\min_j\{r^{(j)}\} > 0$ then STOP.
$i := i + 1$, simulate $r^{(i,j)}$ and set $r^{(j)} = r^{(j)} + r^{(i,j)}$, for all $j = 1, \dots, N$.

4.3 Transition density representation for a class of diffusions

The exact simulation and unbiased estimation methods developed in the chapter critically rely on a representation of the diffusion transition density. The representation relies on certain assumptions. To simplify exposition, we will assume from now on that Eq. (4.1) is time-homogeneous.

(A1) In the SDE (4.1), $d = m$, $\sigma = I$, and b is of *gradient form*, i.e. there exists a function $U : R^d \to R$ (known as the potential) such that $b = \nabla U$.

The assumptions in (A1) are easily satisfied when $d = 1$. In that case, the assumption on b reduces to a differentiability condition. Additionally, when $\sigma(v)$ is a differentiable function of v, V can be transformed to a process with unit diffusion coefficient, by applying the transformation $v \to x = \int^v 1/\sigma(u)du$. Therefore, (A1) is restrictive only in multi-dimensional settings. Hence, in the rest of the chapter we will consider a d-dimensional diffusion process X which solves the following SDE:

$$dX_s = \nabla U(X_s)\,ds + dB_s, \quad s \in [0, T], \tag{4.6}$$

where B is a d-dimensional Brownian motion, and $X_0 = x$. In the sequel X will also be used to denote an arbitrary continuous path, whose meaning will be clear from the context.

Let $\mathbb{P}_0$ denote the law of the Brownian motion on the space of continuous paths, and let $\mathbb{P}_b$ denote the probability law of X implied by Eq. (4.6). We can appeal to the Cameron–Martin–Girsanov theorem for Itô processes, see for example Theorem 8.6.6 of [38], to obtain the likelihood ratio between the two measures on the time increment $[0, t]$. Applying also integration by parts facilitated by the gradient form of the drift, we obtain

$$\frac{d\mathbb{P}_b}{d\mathbb{P}_0}\Big|_t(X) = \exp\left\{U(X_t) - U(x) - \int_0^t \phi(X_s)ds\right\}, \tag{4.7}$$

where $\phi(u) := (\|b(u)\|^2 + \Delta U(u))/2$, Δ is the Laplacian operator and $\|\cdot\|$ the Euclidean norm. Let $\mathbb{P}^*_{b;t,y}$ and $\mathbb{P}^*_{0;t,y}$ denote the laws on $[0, t]$ of X and B respectively, conditioned to hit at time t the value $y \in R^d$. A diffusion process conditioned to start and finish at specific values is known as a *diffusion bridge*.

Consider the decomposition of the laws $\mathbb{P}_b$ and $\mathbb{P}_0$ into the marginal distributions at time t and the diffusion bridge laws conditioned on X_t

$$\frac{d\mathbb{P}_b}{d\mathbb{P}_0}\Big|_t(X) = \frac{p_{0,t}(x, y)}{\mathcal{G}_{0,t}(x, y)}\frac{d\mathbb{P}^*_{b;t,y}}{d\mathbb{P}^*_{0;t,y}}(X),$$

where $\mathcal{G}_{0,t}(x, y)$ is the Gaussian transition density of the dominating Brownian motion. Then, re-arranging, we have the fundamental identity which underpins the methodological framework we develop here

$$\frac{d\mathbb{P}^*_{b;t,y}}{d\mathbb{P}^*_{0;t,y}}(X) = \frac{\mathcal{G}_{0,t}(x, y)}{p_{0,t}(x, y)}\exp\left\{U(y) - U(x) - \int_0^t \phi(X_s)ds\right\}. \tag{4.8}$$

Re-arranging Eq. (4.8) and taking expectations on both sides with respect to $\mathbb{P}^*_{0;t,y}$, we obtain the following representation for the transition density:

$$p_{0,t}(x,y) = \mathcal{G}_{0,t}(x,y)\exp\{U(y) - U(x)\}\mathbb{E}_{\mathbb{P}^*_{0;t,y}}\left[\exp\left\{-\int_0^t \phi(X_s)ds\right\}\right]. \tag{4.9}$$

Therefore, we obtain the transition density as an expectation of an exponential transformation of a path integral, where the expectation is taken over the *Brownian bridge* measure.

The derivation of the likelihood ratio for diffusion bridge measures (4.8) can be made formal, see for example Theorem 2 of [15]. On a more general level, Eq. (4.9) follows from the basic principles of conditional expectation. In particular let $(\Omega, \mathcal{F})$ be a measurable space, $\mathbb{P}$ and $\mathbb{Q}$ be two probability measures on the space with Radon–Nikodym derivative $\xi = d\mathbb{P}/d\mathbb{Q}$, and let $\mathcal{G} \subseteq \mathcal{F}$ be a sub-σ-algebra. Then, the derivative $d\mathbb{P}/d\mathbb{Q}$ restricted to $\mathcal{G}$ is $\mathbb{E}[\xi|\mathcal{G}]$. This is a very classical result which can be used to establish the existence of conditional expectation. On the other hand, assuming the existence of conditional expectation (using the projection approach, see for example [54]), the result follows from the definition of conditional expectation and the tower property of iterated conditional expectations. This basic result is instrumental in the statistical analysis of partially observed stochastic processes; for example in [16] it is used to define an EM algorithm for partially observed continuous-time Markov processes. To obtain Eq. (4.9) we specify $\mathcal{G}$ as the σ-algebra generated by X_t and use the result in conjunction with Eq. (4.7).

For a thorough presentation of MC identities for transition densities of diffusions, treatment of the general time-inhomogeneous and multivariate case and the historical development of these results see Sections 3 and 4 of [40].

4.4   Exact simulation of diffusions

The authors in [5] and [6] recognised that Eq. (4.7) suggests an algorithm for the exact simulation of diffusion sample paths using rejection sampling. The algorithm is known generally as the *exact algorithm (EA)* and appeared in the literature in three generations corresponding to successive relaxations on the conditions which it requires, namely EA1 and EA2 presented in [5], and EA3 presented in [6].

For the development of the EA two further (relatively mild) assumptions are needed.

(A2) The function ϕ in Eq. (4.9) is lower bounded; let $\ell := \inf_u \phi(u) > -\infty$.

(A3) The function $\rho(y) := \exp\{U(y) - \|y - x\|^2/(2t)\}$ is integrable in y for some t and for all x.

To avoid unnecessary notation, let us redefine ϕ as

$$\phi(u) = (\|b(u)\|^2 + \Delta U(u))/2 - \ell \geq 0. \tag{4.10}$$

We fix a time horizon t, such that (A3) holds, and consider the problem of simulating X_t according to the solution of Eq. (4.6) given $X_0 = x$, or equivalently according to the transition distribution $p_{0,t}(x,y)dy$. Assumption (A3) allows us to define the so-called biased Wiener measure on the space of continuous paths on $[0, t]$ by its Radon–Nikodym derivative with respect to $\mathbb{P}_0$,

$$\frac{dZ}{dP_0}\Big|_t(X) = \exp\{U(X_t)\},$$

that is Z is obtained from P_0 by biasing the marginal distribution of the latter at time t using the potential function U. Conditionally on the end-point, the two measures are identical. Then, by piecing everything together we have that

$$\frac{dP_b}{dZ}\Big|_t(X) \propto \exp\left\{-\int_0^t \phi(X_s)ds\right\} \leq 1. \tag{4.11}$$

Therefore, there exists a rejection sampling algorithm on the path space for simulating diffusion sample paths $(X_s, 0 \leq s \leq t)$ according to P_b using proposals from Z and accepting them with probability (4.11). Nevertheless, it is far from obvious how to carry out such an algorithm on the computer, i.e. using a finite number of steps. This can be achieved by benefiting from a seemingly remarkable connection between the Brownian motion and the Poisson process, contained in the following theorem [6].

Theorem 4.1. *(Wiener–Poisson factorisation) Let $\mathbb{L}$ denote the law of a unit rate Poisson process on $[0, t] \times [0, \infty)$ and define the extended law $Z \otimes \mathbb{L}$ with typical realisation (X, Φ), with $\Phi = \{(\chi_j, \psi_j)\}_{j\geq1}$ and $\{\psi_j\}$ non-decreasing. Define the event*

$$\Gamma := \bigcap_{j\geq1}\{\phi(X_{\chi_j}) < \psi_j\}. \tag{4.12}$$

Then, P_b on $[0, t]$ is the marginal distribution of X when $(X, \Phi) \sim Z \otimes \mathbb{L}|\Gamma$.

Effectively, the theorem formalises the observation that the exponential term in Eq. (4.11) can be identified as the probability that an independent Poisson process on $[0, t]\times[0, \infty)$ has no points under the epigraph of $s \to \phi(X_s)$ for a given path X. The connection between the Poisson process and the diffusion measure is investigated and motivated further in Section 4.5.

Given knowledge of the range of ϕ, we can appeal to the principle of *retrospective sampling* [39] to provide an algorithm for the exact simulation of X_t which can be carried out using a finite amount of computation. Suppose for instance that ϕ is also upper bounded, that is

$$\text{there exists an } r < \infty \text{ such that } \sup_u \phi(u) < r. \tag{4.13}$$

Then, the condition posed by Eq. (4.12) is trivially satisfied by all points of the Poisson process with $\psi_j > r$, and only a finite number of comparisons have to be made to check the condition. Additionally, since Φ is independent of X, we can first simulate the Poisson process on $[0, t]\times[0, r]$ and unveil X at the times χ_j specified by the Poisson process. When Eq. (4.12) is satisfied the simulated skeleton of X (which contains X_t) is retained, otherwise it is rejected and the procedure is repeated. This amounts to generating pairs (X, Φ) according to $Z \otimes \mathbb{L}$ and accepting them when $(X, \Phi) \in \Gamma$, where we have used the upper bound of ϕ and retrospective sampling to check the condition using finite computation. The algorithm is given in Algorithm 4.3, and each accepted draw X_t is a sample from the target diffusion at time t. For convenience, the χ_js are now ordered whereas the ψ_js are not. Note also that Step 2 simulates from the finite-dimensional distributions of Z.

When ϕ is unbounded, the joint simulation according to Z of X and a random box which contains it is required. This is the EA3 which is described in detail in [6]. The extra

---

Algorithm 4.3 (EA1) The exact algorithm for the simulation of X_t according to the SDE (4.6) when Eq. (4.13) holds.

---

1. Generate a Poisson process $0 < \chi_1 < \chi_2 < \cdots$ of rate r on $[0, t]$. Let κ be the number of points. Generate a sequence of uniform random variables $\psi_j \sim \text{Uni}[0, r]$, $j = 1, \ldots, \kappa$.
2. Simulate $X_t \sim \rho$ given in (A3). Simulate $\{X_{\chi_1}, \ldots, X_{\chi_\kappa}\}$, according to the Brownian bridge started at $X_0 = x$ and finishing at X_t.
3. If $\psi_j > \phi(X_{\chi_j})$ for all $j \le \kappa$ then accept X_t; otherwise return to 2.

---

effort needed in EA3 comes at an increased computational cost: the careful and extensive numerical investigation in [42] suggests as a rule of thumb that EA3 is about 10 times slower than EA1. Since EA is based on rejection sampling, when applied directly to $[0, t]$ the computational effort necessary to yield a draw grows exponentially with t. However, this is not the true complexity of the algorithm. The Markov property permits an implementation of the algorithm which has $O(t)$ complexity, since the time increment $[0, t]$ can be split and the EA be applied sequentially. A further interesting property is that the acceptance probability of the EA is roughly constant when applied to intervals t/d as d increases; this is a by-product of the gradient structure of the drift and the form of Eq. (4.11). This argument is supported empirically in [42], who find that EA1 has complexity $O(d)$ in the dimension of the target diffusion. On the other hand, the complexity of EA3 as a function of d is worse than linear due to maximisations needed in the implementation of the algorithm.

4.5   Exact simulation of killed Brownian motion

The Wiener–Poisson factorisation in Theorem 4.1 appears at first striking since it connects the law of a diffusion process to that of the Brownian motion and an independent Poisson process. However, this result is less surprising given a representation of the class of diffusions (4.6) as killed Brownian motion; see for example Section 8.2 of [38] where also the connections to the Feynman–Kac formula are discussed. In particular, consider an exponentially distributed random variable $E \sim \text{Exp}(1)$ independent of X, and define the killing time T as the following function of E and X:

$$T = \inf\left\{s : \int_0^s \phi(X_s)\mathrm{d}s = E\right\},$$

where ϕ is given in Eq. (4.10). Thus,

$$\Pr\left[T > t | X\right] = \exp\left\{-\int_0^t \phi(X_s)\mathrm{d}s\right\}. \tag{4.14}$$

Then, it is easy to see that the scheme described in Algorithm 4.4 yields an importance sampling approximation of the law of X_t induced by the SDE (4.6). The resulting weighted sample $\{(X_t^{(j)}, w_t^{(j)})\}_{j=1}^N$ is a particle approximation of the law of X_t. The killing step (Step 4 in Algorithm 4.4) ensures that the law of the path conditioned to be alive has a density with respect to the Wiener measure given by the right-hand side of Eq. (4.14), and the weighting (Step 5) is necessary to ensure that the path has density proportional to Eq. (4.7). However, the scheme of Algorithm 4.4 is not practically implementable, since it involves an infinite amount of simulation in Step 3.

Algorithm 4.4 Importance sampling approximation of the law of X_t by killed Brownian motion.

---
1. Set $j = 0$.
2. **while** $j < N$ **do**
3.   Generate $E \sim \text{Exp}(1)$.
4.   Generate a Brownian path X started from x, and keep track of $\int_0^s \phi(X_s)ds$. Stop when
    $s = t$.
5.   Rejection: If $\int_0^s \phi(X_s)ds > E$ reject the path, goto 1.
6.   Weighting: If $\int_0^s \phi(X_s)ds < E$ then $j := j + 1$, set $X_t^{(j)} = X_t$, $w_t^{(j)} = e^{U(X_t)}$. Goto 2.
7. **end while**

Note that for a given X, T is the first arrival time of a time-inhomogeneous Poisson process with intensity $\phi(X_s)$. Assume now that Eq. (4.13) holds. Then, we can simulate T *exactly* by thinning a dominating Poisson process with intensity r. Let $0 < \chi_1 < \chi_2 < \cdots$, be the time-ordered arrival times of the dominating Poisson process. Then, if each arrival χ_j is accepted with probability $\phi(X_{\chi_j})/r$, T is the first accepted arrival time. Algorithm 4.5 is a modification of Algorithm 4.4; we call it the exact killing (EK) algorithm. The result-

---

Algorithm 4.5 Exact killing: Exact simulation of a killed Brownian motion using thinning.

---
1. Set $j = 0$.
2. **while** $j < N$ **do**
3.   Set $\chi_0 = 0$, $i = 0$
4.   Set $i := i + 1$, simulate χ_i.
5.   Simulate X_{χ_i} given $X_{\chi_{i-1}}$ according to the Brownian motion dynamics. If $\chi_i > t$
    then simulate X_t given X_{χ_i} and $X_{\chi_{i-1}}$ according to the Brownian bridge dynamics, set
    $j := j + 1$ and $X_t^{(j)} = X_t$, $w_t^{(j)} = e^{U(X_t)}$. Goto 2.
6.   If $\chi_i < t$, simulate $\psi_i \sim \text{Uni}(0, r)$. If $\psi_i > \phi(X_{\chi_i})$, then goto 3, else goto 2.
7. **end while**

---

ing weighted sample $\{(X_t^{(j)}, w_t^{(j)})\}_{j=1}^N$ is again a particle approximation of the law of X_t obtained by rejection (killing) and weighting, but now the procedure can be carried out exactly using a finite number of uniform and Gaussian random variables. This is made feasible precisely by the thinning of a Poisson super-process with rate r and it relies on the assumption (4.13).

Algorithm 4.5 has intriguing connections to other exact simulation schemes for Markov processes. For example, the thinning of a Poisson super-process is a main ingredient of the algorithm of [23] for the exact simulation of discrete state space continuous-time Markov chains conditioned to start and finish at specific states. Most relevant to this article, is its direct connection with EA1 given in Algorithm 4.3. In fact, the two algorithms share exactly the same rejection step; EK needs to weight the accepted draws, whereas EA1 by fixing the final time t a priori, includes this bias in the dynamics of the proposal process which are according to $\mathbb{Z}$.

On the other hand, EK gives a particle approximation to the flow of distributions $t \rightarrow \mathbb{P}_{b|t}$. Since EK also relies on rejection sampling, the computational effort to yield a particle at time t increases exponentially with t. The Markov property can be exploited here as well, by defining time increments of size, δ say. If a particle is alive at time $i\delta$ but dies before $(i + 1)\delta$, a new path is restarted from the value it has at time $i\delta$ rather than re-starting from time 0. Provided that the variance of the weights w_t does not increase with t (note that they depend only on X_t rather than the whole history) the complexity of the algorithm is $O(t)$.

One can avoid the rejections involved in EK at the expense of introducing dependence among the simulated particles. Let N be a population of particles which move freely according to the Brownian dynamics. To each particle j, we assign a death time T_j, as before. Once a particle dies, then a randomly chosen particle of the remaining ones duplicates and each branch evolves conditionally independently. Again, it is easy to see that we can construct a super-process with intensity $r \times N$ which will contain all possible death times of all particles. We simulate iteratively these arrivals, at each arrival time χ_i, we pick at random one of the existing particles, j say, and propose to kill it. To do that, we realise its value at that time, we simulate $\psi_i \sim \text{Uni}[0, r]$, and check if $\psi_i < \phi(X_{\chi_i}^{(j)})$. If this is so we kill it and duplicate a randomly chosen one among the rest of the particles. If not, the particle remains alive. It is clear from the lack of memory of the underlying super-process, that at each arrival time, and after checking for killing and possibly adjusting the population, we can forget everything that has happened and start again from the current population of particles. To obtain an importance sample approximation for $\mathbb{P}_b|_t$ we weight each alive particle $X_t^{(j)}$ time t with $w_t^{(j)} = e^{U(X_t)}$ weight. Hence, we can simulate exactly the genealogy of this interacting particle system which tracks the law of the diffusion process.

4.6 Unbiased estimation of the transition density using series expansions

The machinery required for producing unbiased estimators of diffusion transition densities is very broad in its scope and it is only mildly linked to the structure of diffusion processes. The techniques we present here are intrinsically linked to the MC solution to fixed-point problems, see for example [28] for applications in population genetics, [52] in the context of solutions of partial differential equations (PDEs), [18] for a recent contribution in the literature and references, and Section 2.5.6 of [33] for a gentle introduction to the idea. The purpose in this section is to develop all components separately, emphasising their generic purpose, and then piece them all together to solve the problem of interest in this chapter. The decoupling of the techniques greatly simplifies the understanding of the final method but also suggests possibilities for improvements. The main components of the methodology can be identified as follows. (i) Expansion of functions into power series. This allows the unbiased estimation of the function given unbiased estimators of its argument. The expansion of the exponential function and the so-called Poisson estimator are treated in Section 4.6.1. Some optimality issues for the estimator are discussed and biased alternatives mentioned. (ii) Unbiased truncation of infinite series. There are various techniques for the unbiased estimation of an infinite sum, based either on importance sampling or on integration by parts (effectively application of Fubini's theorem) followed by importance sampling. This is treated in Section 4.6.2. (iii) Further structure is available when the unbiased estimator of the exponential of a path integral of a Markov process is required. Compared to (i) the added feature is the explicit dependence of the unbiased estimators of the argument of the function. This is explored in Section 4.6.3, which couples this material with (ii) to yield a general class of unbiased estimators. The richer structure allows a more insightful mathematical formulation of the problem, as one of importance sampling in a countable union of product spaces. This point of view leads to the fourth component of the methodology. (iv) Simulation from certain probability measures defined on a countable union of product spaces. This is treated in Section 4.6.4, and provides the optimal importance sampling estimator for the problem posed in Section 4.6.3. This formalism links directly with the so-called MC method for solving integral equation and fixed-point problems. This is outlined in Section 4.6.4. There, we argue that the power expansion idea and the technique for solving integral equations, although related, are not equivalent. An illustration of the estimation of the transition density of the Cox–Ingersoll–Ross diffusion process, considering the unbiased estimator and various biased estimators, is presented in Section 4.6.6.

4.6.1 Power series expansions: the exponential function and the Poisson estimator

We consider two related problems. Let X be an unknown quantity, and let $\tilde{X}_j$ be independent (conditionally on X) unbiased estimators of X, i.e. $\mathsf{E}[\tilde{X}|X] = X$, where $\tilde{X}$ denotes a generic element of the sequence. We assume that the $\tilde{X}_j$s have a common finite absolute moment, $\mathsf{E}[|\tilde{X}||X] < \infty$. In many examples the $\tilde{X}_j$s have the same distribution conditionally on X. Let f be a non-linear function. Then, we are interested in estimating (a) $f(X)$ or (b) $\mathsf{E}[f(X)]$ when X is a random variable. In fact, we are typically interested in (b), however the argument is the same for both cases, hence we consider the two problems jointly. When f is linear the problem is trivial. However, when f is a real analytic function there is still the possibility of getting unbiased estimators via series expansions. We concentrate on the case where $f(x) = e^x$. Then, for any fixed c, we have

$$e^X = e^c \sum_{i=0}^{\infty} (X - c)^i / i! = e^c \sum_{i=0}^{\infty} \mathsf{E}\left[\prod_{j=1}^{i}(\tilde{X}_i - c)|X\right] / i! = e^c \mathsf{E}\left[\sum_{i=0}^{\infty} \prod_{j=1}^{i}(\tilde{X}_i - c)/i!\right], \quad (4.15)$$

where the product $\prod_{j=1}^{0}$ is defined to be equal to 1. The role of c will be discussed later. Note that the absolute moment assumption on the $\tilde{X}$ justifies the third step in the above argument by dominated convergence. Hence, the infinite sum is an unbiased estimator of e^X. Still, this is not a realisable estimator. The topic of truncating unbiasedly infinite sums becomes of pivotal importance and it is discussed in the following section. At a more elementary level, one way to yield a feasible estimator is to recognise the similarity of the expression to an expectation of a Poisson random variable. In fact, it is easy to check directly that for any $\lambda > 0$

$$e^{\lambda + c} \prod_{i=1}^{\kappa} \frac{\tilde{X}_j - c}{\lambda}, \quad \kappa \sim Po(\lambda) \quad (4.16)$$

is a realisable unbiased estimator of e^X. We term Eq. (4.16) the *Poisson estimator*. Its second moment is easy to work out provided that the $\tilde{X}_j$s have a common second moment, $\mathsf{E}[\tilde{X}^2|X] < \infty$:

$$\exp\left\{\lambda + 2c + \frac{1}{\lambda}\mathsf{E}\left[(\tilde{X} - c)^2|X\right]\right\}. \quad (4.17)$$

The two constants c and λ are user-specified and relate to the sign and the variance of the estimator. For example, if $\tilde{X}$ is lower bounded, c can be chosen to make the Poisson estimator positive, if this is desired (see for example Section 4.2). However, with two degrees of freedom the question of optimality in terms of variance is ill-posed, as shown in the following proposition whose proof is straightforward.

Proposition 4.1. *Optimal implementation of the Poisson estimator for estimating e^X: Taking $c = -\lambda$, and $\lambda \to \infty$, the variance of the estimator converges monotonically to 0 and the estimator converges to e^X in mean square sense.*

Working directly from Eq. (4.17) we have that, for fixed c, the optimal choice for λ is $E[(\tilde{X} - c)^2|X]^{1/2}$, whereas for a given computational budget λ the optimal choice for c is $X - \lambda$. These are not feasible estimators, but can guide good choices.

Note that a biased plug-in alternative estimator is available in this context, which is given by $\exp\{\sum_{j=1}^{N} \tilde{X}_j/N\}$, where N plays the role of λ in the Poisson estimator. Even in this simple context the comparison of the two estimators in mean square error is not obvious. We will see these two possibilities in the context of diffusions in Sections 4.6.3 and 4.6.6.

In most cases of interest X is a random variable and we are actually interested in estimating $E[e^X]$ with respect to the law of X. The argument presented earlier can be repeated to show that Eq. (4.16) is unbiased for this quantity, however we need the stronger condition

$$E[\exp\{E[|\tilde{X}||X]\}] < \infty$$

as a sufficient condition to justify the third step in the development. For given λ and c a sufficient condition to ensure a finite second moment is

$$E\left[\exp\left\{\frac{1}{\lambda}(E[\tilde{X}^2|X] - 2cX)\right\}\right] < \infty.$$

The expected value of Eq. (4.17) gives the second moment. In this case we need to average, say M, independent realisations of the estimator. Hence the computational cost is on average λM and the choice of optimal allocation in terms of λ and M is non-trivial.

Furthermore, c and λ can be chosen to depend on X. In [21] the authors proposed such generalised Poisson estimators to ensure positivity of the estimators. The estimator and its variance have the forms specified above, the conditions however which ensure their existence have to be modified appropriately.

4.6.2   Unbiased truncation of infinite series

In the previous section an estimator was given in terms of an infinite sum in Eq. (4.15). To avoid the impossible computation, we extracted an unbiased estimator of the sum by expressing it as an expectation of a Poisson random variable. It turns out that this is just one instance of a generic methodology for unbiased estimation of infinite sums. Abstracting, let us consider the problem of finding an unbiased estimator of

$$S = \sum_{k=1}^{\infty} \alpha_k, \tag{4.18}$$

where we assume that the sum is finite a.s. As in the previous section, we might be interested in $E[S]$ when the α_ks are random variables, but the argument follows in a similar way. There are (at least) three ways to obtain an unbiased estimator of Eq. (4.18), two of which turn out to be equivalent.

Firstly, we can use importance sampling. Let $\beta_k > 0$ be probabilities, i.e. $\sum_k \beta_k = 1$. Then α_K/β_K is an unbiased estimator of S, where K is simulated according to $\Pr[K = k] = \beta_k$. If

$$S_a = \sum_{k=1}^{\infty} |\alpha_k| < \infty, \tag{4.19}$$

then Jensen's inequality shows that it is optimal to take $\beta_k = |\alpha_k|/S_a$.

An alternative argument to yield effectively the same estimator, but useful when using this machinery in more elaborate contexts (see for example Section 4.6.3), is to define a sequence of 'killing' probabilities $0 < p_k < 1$, for $k = 1, 2 \ldots$. Then, consider a discrete-time survival process where death happens at each time k with probability p_k. Let K be the death time. Then

$$\frac{\alpha_K}{\prod_{i=1}^{K-1}(1 - p_i)p_K}$$

is an unbiased estimator of S. Note that $\Pr[K = k] = \prod_{i=1}^{k-1}(1 - p_i)p_k$. It is easy to check that $\sum_k \prod_{i=1}^{k-1}(1 - p_i)p_k \leq 1$. If the sum is strictly less than 1 then $K = \infty$ has a positive probability, which then yields an infeasible estimator. If the sum is 1, then the two estimators we have discussed are equivalent and correspond to the representation of a distribution in terms of the probabilities or the hazard function. The importance sampling estimator is obtained by taking $\beta_k = \prod_{i=1}^{k-1}(1 - p_i)p_k$. On the other hand, for given probabilities β_k, let G be the survival function, $G(k) = \sum_{i=k}^{\infty} \beta_i$. Then, taking $p_k = 1 - G(k)/G(k - 1)$ yields the second estimator.

The third estimator is based on an application of Fubini's theorem, which can be applied in this context under Eq. (4.19). Let again β_k be probabilities with survival function G. Then

$$\sum_k \alpha_k = \sum_k \frac{\alpha_k}{G(k)}G(k) = \sum_k \frac{\alpha_k}{G(k)} \sum_{i=k}^{\infty} \beta_i = \sum_{k=1}^{\infty} \sum_{i=k}^{\infty} \frac{\alpha_k}{G(k)}\beta_i = \sum_{i=1}^{\infty} \sum_{k=1}^{i} \frac{\alpha_k}{G(k)}\beta_i,$$

which suggests the following unbiased estimator of S:

$$\sum_{k=i}^{K} \alpha_i/G(i) = \sum_{i=1}^{K} \alpha_i / \prod_{i=1}^{K-1}(1 - p_i),$$

where K is simulated according to $\Pr[K = k] = \beta_k$, and the equality follows from the equivalent representation in terms of killing probabilities.

It should be clear that the Poisson estimator (4.16) corresponds to a very specific setting where we use the importance sampling estimator with Poisson proposal probabilities for estimating the infinite expansion. It should also be clear that the other schemes we have discussed in this section can be used to provide unbiased estimators of e^X and its expected value. These alternative estimators start with Eq. (4.15) and apply a technique for the unbiased estimation of the infinite sum.

4.6.3 Unbiased estimation of the expected value of exponential functions of Markov process path integrals

A very interesting instance of the generic context of Section 4.6.1 is when X is a path integral of a Markov process. With a slight abuse of notation, suppose that we are interested in estimating

$$I(x, t) := E\left[\exp\left\{\int_t^1 g(s, X_s)ds\right\}\right], \quad t \leq 1, \tag{4.20}$$

where X is a Markov process in R^d, with explicit transition density $p_{s,t}(x, y)$, such that $X_t = x$. The upper limit of the integration can be arbitrary; here it is taken to be 1 for notational simplicity. This problem was considered by [51] and solved with an approach which combines the power expansions with the unbiased estimation of infinite series, as described below. Notice that the estimation problem in Eq. (4.20) is raised when considering the estimation of the transition density for the class of diffusion processes considered in Section 4.3; see Eq. (4.9) where X is the Brownian bridge. The use of the estimators for the estimation of diffusion transition densities was considered in [7], see also Section 4.6.6.

By the standard MC integration trick, we have that $(1-t)g(\chi, X_\chi)$, where $\chi \sim \text{Uni}(t, 1)$ is conditionally on X an unbiased estimator of the exponent in Eq. (4.20). Working precisely as in Section 4.6.1, under the sufficient condition

$$I_a(x, t) := \mathsf{E}\left[\exp\left\{\int_t^1 |g(s, X_s)|ds\right\}\right] < \infty, \quad \text{for all } t \le 1,$$

we get the following infinite-series unbiased estimator of Eq. (4.20):

$$\sum_{k=0}^{\infty} \int_t^1 \cdots \int_{u_{n-1}}^1 \int_{R^d} \cdots \int_{R^d} \prod_{i=1}^{n} g(u_i, x_i) p_{u_{i-1}, u_i}(x_{i-1}, x_i) dx_n \cdots dx_1 du_n \cdots du_1, \quad (4.21)$$

with the convention that $x_0 = x, u_0 = t$. This infinite expansion can be treated with the machinery of Section 4.6.2 to yield feasible unbiased estimators of Eq. (4.20). For example, an importance sampling estimator based on $Po(\lambda(1 - t))$ probabilities and simulation of X according to its transition density yields the Poisson estimator

$$e^{(\lambda+c)(1-t)} \prod_{j=1}^{\kappa} \frac{g(\chi_j, X_{\chi_j}) - c}{\lambda}, \quad \kappa \sim Po(\lambda(1 - t)), \chi_j \sim \text{Uni}(t, 1). \quad (4.22)$$

Note however that with the same variables we can consider the alternative estimator based on the application of Fubini's theorem discussed in Section 4.6.2, or indeed use a different proposal distribution for the index K (e.g. the negative binomial).

The specific structure of the exponent in Eq. (4.20) (as opposed to the generic one in Section 4.6.1) permits a mathematically richer formulation of the estimation problem. This is done in [51] (see in particular Propositions 1, 2 and 4 of the article). This formulation casts the estimation of Eq. (4.20) as a familiar problem in MC. Specifically, let us define the following union of product spaces, $\mathcal{Y} := \bigcup_{k=0}^{\infty} \mathcal{Y}_k$ where $\mathcal{Y}_k = \{k\} \times \mathcal{X}^{k+1}$, and in our context $\mathcal{X}$ is the space $[t, 1] \times R^d$. Let us now define the following signed measure φ on $\mathcal{Y}$ indexed by (x, t), and given by the formulae

$$\varphi(k, d(t_0, x_0) \times \cdots \times d(t_k, x_k) ; x, t) = \delta_{(t,x)}(d(t_0, x_0)) \prod_{i=1}^{k} 1_{t_i}[t_{i-1}, 1]g(t_i, x_i)p_{t_{i-1}, t_i}(x_{i-1}, x_i)dt_i dx_i,$$

where δ denotes the Dirac delta function, and $1_x[A]$ is 1 if $x \in A$ and 0 otherwise. In this formulation, Eq. (4.21) shows that Eq. (4.20) is the normalising constant of φ: $I(x, t) = \varphi(\mathcal{Y}; x, t)$, hence we can reformulate the original problem as one of estimating a normalising constant. Importance sampling is one possibility to do this by constructing measures on $\mathcal{Y}$ and computing the Radon–Nikodym derivative between the two measures for the generated samples. Provided that the normalising constant of the proposal distribution is known, the weight assigned to each generated sample is an unbiased estimator of $\varphi(\mathcal{Y}; x, t)$. Summarising, the expansion in a power series and the explicit structure of the exponent allow the re-formulation of estimation of Eq. (4.20) as the computation of a normalising constant of a signed measure. The material of Section 4.6.2 together with standard MC techniques effectively gives methods for constructing proposal distributions on $\mathcal{Y}$ to be used in the importance sampling. Reference [51] gives the following generic estimator where $p_0(s, x) > 0$ is a killing probability and $q_{s,t}(x, y)$ is an alternative tractable transition density

$$\prod_{i=1}^{K} \frac{g(\chi_i, X_{\chi_i}) p_{\chi_{i-1}, \chi_i}(X_{\chi_{i-1}}, X_{\chi_i})}{(1 - p_0(\chi_{i-1}, X_{\chi_{i-1}})) q_{\chi_{i-1}, \chi_i}(X_{\chi_{i-1}}, X_{\chi_i})} \frac{1}{p_0(\chi_K, X_{\chi_K})},$$

where the χ_is are ordered uniforms on $[t, 1]$ and the X_{χ_i} are generated according to the transitions q. Let $|\varphi|$ be the total variation of φ, thus it is obtained by replacing g with its absolute value in the definition given above. Then, by Jensen's inequality (as in Section 4.6.2) it follows that the optimal proposal distribution in terms of minimising the variance of the estimator, is $|\varphi|/I_a(x, t)$. Simulation from probability measures in $\mathcal{Y}$ is treated in the next section.

We close with the remark that alternative biased plug-in estimators (as discussed in Section 4.6.1) are available. For example, one may consider

$$\exp\left\{\frac{1-t}{N} \sum_{j=1}^{N} g(\chi_j, X_{\chi_j})\right\}$$

with the random elements as in Eq. (4.22). Alternative numerical approximation of the integral in the exponent of Eq. (4.20) can also be considered. A comparison among different schemes is carried out in Section 4.6.6.

4.6.4 Simulation from probability measures on unions of spaces

The fourth main ingredient of the methodological framework for unbiased estimation is linked with the simulation from the following series of measures. Consider the following abstract problem: let $\gamma(x)$ be a positive function on X; $p(x, y)$ a transition density (i.e. probability density in y and measurable in x), where $x, y \in X$; and $\delta_x(dy)$ the Dirac measure centred at x. Consider the product space $\mathcal{Y} := \bigcup_{k=0}^{\infty} \{k\} \times X^{k+1}$ with typical element $(k, x_0, x_1, \ldots, x_k)$ with the convention $x_0 = x$. We have already seen this context in Section 4.6.3, where $X = [t, 1] \times R^d$.

We define the following positive measure on $\mathcal{Y}$ indexed by $x \in X$:

$$v(k, dx_1 \times \cdots \times dx_{k+1} ; x) := \delta_x(dx_0) \prod_{i=1}^{k} p(x_{i-1}, x_i) \gamma(x_i) dx_1 \cdots dx_{k+1}.$$

We assume that $I(x) := v(\mathcal{Y}; x) < \infty$, and define $\tilde{v}(\cdot; x) := v(\cdot; x)/I(x)$ to be the corresponding probability measure on $\mathcal{Y}$. Note that by definition $I(x) > 1$. The aim of this section is to simulate draws from $\tilde{v}$ and to show that distributions of this form provide the optimal importance sampling distributions in the context of Section 4.6.3. The construction is theoretical, since it will typically not be feasible to carry out the simulation. Nevertheless, it provides insights on the optimal implementation of the unbiased estimators we consider in this chapter.

To start with note the fundamental recursion implied by the definition of the measures and the normalising constants

$$I(x) = 1 + \int_{\mathcal{Y}} I(x_1)p(x, x_1)\gamma(x_1)dx_1. \tag{4.23}$$

Using the same argument that led to Eq. (4.23) we can obtain the following marginal-conditional distributions under $\tilde{\nu}$: $\tilde{\nu}(k = 0; x) = 1/I(x)$, $\tilde{\nu}(dx_1, k > 0; x) \propto p(x, x_1)\gamma(x_1)I(x_1)dx_1$. In the same way we obtain the general expressions

$$\tilde{\nu}(k > i - 1, dx_1, \ldots, dx_i; x) = I(x_i) \prod_{j=1}^{i} p(x_{j-1}, x_j)\gamma(x_j),$$

$$\tilde{\nu}(dx_i | x, x_1, \ldots, x_i, k > i - 1) = p(x_{i-1}, x_i)\gamma(x_i)I(x_i)dx_1/(I(x_{i-1}) - 1),$$

$$\tilde{\nu}(k = i | x, x_1, \ldots, x_i, k > i) = 1/I(x_i).$$

The last two equations give the necessary structure for the simulation from $\tilde{\nu}$ using a Markov chain, by sequentially at each stage i first simulating a new value x_i and then deciding on whether to stop the simulation. The procedure results with a string $(k, x_0, x_1, \ldots, x : k)$. The problem of simulation from probability measures on $\mathcal{Y}$ with structure as $\tilde{\nu}$ was recently considered in [18] using trans-dimensional MCMC; see also the article for further references. This problem, together with the corresponding task of estimating the normalising constant, comes up in a large number of scientific contexts. This is due to the fact that it is intrinsically related to the numerical solution of fixed-point problems. This is described in the following section.

4.6.5   Monte Carlo for integral equations

Suppose that we are interested in the solution of the following integral equation:

$$I(x) = h(x) + \int_{X} p(x, y)I(y)dy, \tag{4.24}$$

where h is explicitly known for all x. This type of equation (and its discrete-valued counterparts) appear in a variety of problems. We have already seen an instance; $I(x, t)$ in Eq. (4.20) satisfies such an equation with $h = 1$. By successive substitution of I in the equation we obtain the infinite expansion

$$I(x) = h(x) + \sum_{k=1}^{\infty} \int_{X^k} \prod_{i=1}^{k} p(x_{i-1}, x_i)h(x_k)dx_1 \times \cdots dx_k,$$

with the convention $x_0 = x$. The analogy with the problems treated in Sections 4.6.2 and 4.6.4 is direct. This is the reason why the same machinery which is used in the solution of the fixed-point problems becomes useful in the unbiased estimation of the diffusion transition density. Nevertheless, the power expansions discussed in Section 4.6.1 do not necessarily lead to a fixed-point problem. However, the techniques of Section 4.6.2 still apply to yield unbiased estimators even in these cases.

4.6.6   Illustrating example: the CIR density

We close the section with an illustration of the methodology on the estimation of the transition density of the so-called Cox–Ingersoll–Ross (CIR) diffusion [11]. This is a one-dimensional diffusion with b and σ in Eq. (4.1) given by $-\rho(x - \mu)$ and $\sigma\sqrt{x}$ respectively, where $\rho > 0, \sigma > 0, \mu$ are parameters and $x \in R_+$. This diffusion is not in the form (4.6) but it can be transformed as described in Section 4.3. When the transformation is applied, the transition density of the original process is linked by a change of variables to the transition density of the unit-diffusion-coefficient process; see [7]. However, in this model, when the process is transformed, its measure is absolutely continuous with respect to the law of the Brownian motion conditioned to remain positive, which is known as the *Bessel process*. Therefore, Eq. (4.9) holds but the expectation is taken with respect to the law of the Bessel bridge. In our numerical results it turns out that it does not really make a difference whether one works with the Brownian or the Bessel bridge. We consider four estimators. First, the unbiased estimator obtained by using the Poisson estimator (4.22) to estimate the expectation in Eq. (4.9) (using the Bessel bridge dominating measure). Second, a biased estimator based on Riemmann approximation of the exponent in Eq. (4.9). This is in the spirit of the plug-in estimators discussed in Section 4.6.3 but where the times to evaluate the path are chosen deterministically. This estimator in the context of diffusions was considered in [37]. Finally, we consider two estimators obtained using the discrete-time approach of [19]. We use their estimator on the original CIR process and on the transformed to unit-diffusion-coefficient process. The estimator of [19] applied to the transformed process is closely related to the estimator of [37]: the only difference is that the latter applies numerical integration to a Cameron–Martin–Girsanov formula with the stochastic integral eliminated using integration by parts, whereas the former applies numerical integration on the expression which contains the stochastic integral.

The transition density of the CIR is explicitly known, hence it can be used to assess the root mean square error of the estimators. Our simulation setup is as follows. We consider the parameter values used in the simulation study in [19]: $(\rho, \mu, \sigma) = (0.5, 0.06, 0.15)$ and starting point for the diffusion $X_0 = 0.1$. We consider two final times, a small one $t = 1/252$ and a large one $t = 1/2$, and we estimate the transition density for three different ending points which correspond to the 10, 50 and 90 percent quantiles of the transition distribution. For the biased estimators we consider various values for N, the number of evaluations on a given path, $N = 2^i, i = 2, 3, \ldots, 8$. For the Poisson estimator we choose the average computational cost to be the same as that of the biased estimators and we take $c = \lambda$. In each case we average M independent realisations of the estimator, where we take $M = N^2$ following the asymptotic result of [47]. For the estimation of the root mean square error of each estimator we average 120 independent replicates.

Figure 4.1 contains the results of the simulation, where we plot the logarithm of the root mean square error against the logarithm of the number of evaluations per path. The study shows the variance reduction effectuated by the expression of the transition density in Eq. (4.9). Moreover, the unbiased estimator works very well in this setup. In this chapter we have pursued unbiasedness due to its connection with auxiliary variable methods. Nevertheless, the results show that the estimator has comparable or better performance than biased alternatives.

4.7 Discussion and directions

We have reviewed and developed a rich methodological framework for the MC assisted probabilistic inference for diffusion processes. On one hand, the framework is based on representations of the diffusion process which can be exploited for its exact simulation. On the other hand, the framework relies on a generic importance sampling machinery which has been used in various other contexts. The exact algorithm and the Poisson estimator build

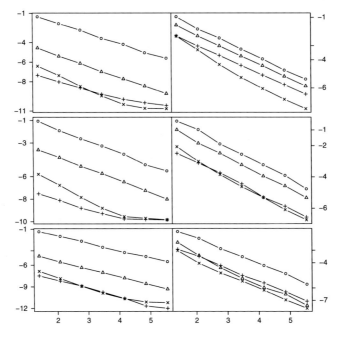

Figure 4.1 Logarithm of the root mean square error of the estimators against the logarithm of the number of imputed points per simulated path. The transition of the CIR process is estimated for three ending points corresponding to the 10 (top), 50 (middle) and 90 (bottom) quantiles of the transition distribution. The time increment is $t = 1/252$ (left) and $t = 1/2$ (right). (∘) Durham and Gallant without variance transformation, (△) Durham and Gallant with variance transformation, (+) Nicolau, (×) Poisson estimator.

bridges between these two aspects, see for example the discussion in [7]. It is interesting to understand deeper the connections; this might lead to new exact simulation algorithms outside the framework described in Section 4.4. A different instance of this interplay appears in the exact simulation from the stationary distribution of a Markov chain. There, a uniform ergodicity condition leads to an infinite-series expansion for the stationary distribution which can then be used for exact simulation.

The methodology for diffusions is based on the convenient representation of the transition density in Section 4.3, which relies on certain assumptions about the drift and the diffusion coefficient of the process. The conditions are strong when $d > 1$. On the other hand, Theorem 3.1 of [52] establishes that the transition density of a generic diffusion process solves an integral equation of the type (4.24) with h and p explicitly given. This representation relies on different conditions which relate to smoothness and boundedness of the drift and diffusion coefficients. Additionally, p might not be a positive kernel. Nevertheless, this alternative representation is amenable to the type of unbiased MC estimation using the tools of Section 4.6, and this has been pursued in [52] and [50]. In current work we are exploring the possibilities of using this representation to achieve exact simulation of the diffusion at fixed times, and evaluating the practical usefulness of this alternative.

The chapter has given little attention to the important question of choosing between unbiased and biased estimators of the transition density and other diffusion functionals. This question has not been seriously addressed since the primary purpose of the chapter is to present in a unified manner a collection of ideas central to the construction of unbiased MC schemes. Biased estimators of diffusion functionals can be easily obtained using the Euler or other type of approximations; see the discussion in Sections 4.6.3 and 4.6.6. It is difficult to give very general statements about which type of estimator should be preferred, particularly since exact calculation of mean square error is complicated even in simple examples. Research in obtaining some simple general rules is underway. In Section 4.6.6 we provide a simple comparison for the estimation of the CIR transition density, and a much broader evaluation of competing biased and unbiased MC schemes is in progress. On the other hand, a certain amount of empirical comparisons has been published, see for example Sections 4.1 and 5.1 of [21] and Section 4 of [50]. Wagner finds significant reduction in mean square error via the application of variance reduction techniques and recommends a combination of unbiased estimators with such techniques. Closing this discussion, a generic argument in favour of unbiased estimation of unknown quantities within an MC scheme is that of 'consistency'. The RWPF of Section 4.2 provides consistent estimates of the filtering distributions as $N \to \infty$. Working with biased estimates requires that the bias is eliminated at a specific rate hence consistency is achieved by letting both N and the amount of imputation go to infinity at appropriate rates. Similarly, an MCEM algorithm will typically give consistent parameter estimates as the number of data go to infinity even with fixed MC effort. This is not so when the MC contains bias. The (appropriate) replacement of intractable densities by positive unbiased estimators within an MCMC algorithm [4, 3] does not perturb the limiting distribution; this is crucial since it is typically difficult to quantify the amount of bias that would be introduced otherwise.

Finally, as pointed out earlier, variance reduction techniques can be very effective in estimation of diffusion functionals. The biased Wiener measure proposal of Section 4.4 can be used for this purpose; see for example [50] for implementation of such ideas. Variance reduction methods for diffusions are studied for example in [36]. These possibilities within the exact simulation framework are being currently investigated.

Acknowledgments   The author would like to acknowledge financial support by the Spanish government through a 'Ramon y Cajal' fellowship and the grants MTM2008-06660 and MTM2009-09063, the Berlin Mathematical School for hosting him as a visiting Professor while preparing this manuscript, Giorgos Sermaidis for useful suggestions and Christian Robert and Randal Douc for motivating discussions on the unbiased estimation techniques.

Bibliography

[1] Y. Aït-Sahalia. Likelihood inference for diffusions: a survey. In *Frontiers in Statistics*, pages 369–405. Imperial College Press, 2006.

[2] Y. Ait-Sahalia and R. Kimmel. Maximum likelihood estimation of stochastic volatility models. *Journal of Financial Economics*, **83**(2):413–452, 2007.

[3] C. Andrieu, A. Doucet and R. Holenstein. Particle Markov chain Monte Carlo. *Journal of the Royal Statistical Society Series B, Statistical Methodology*, **72**(3):269–342, 2010.

[4] C. Andrieu and G. O. Roberts. The pseudo-marginal approach for efficient Monte Carlo computations. *Annals of Statistics*, **37**(2):697–725, 2009.

[5] A. Beskos, O. Papaspiliopoulos and G. O. Roberts. Retrospective exact simulation of diffusion sample paths with applications. *Bernoulli*, **12**(6):1077–1098, 2006.

[6] A. Beskos, O. Papaspiliopoulos and G. O. Roberts. A factorisation of diffusion measure and finite sample path constructions. *Methodology and Computing in Applied Probability*, **10**(1):85–104, 2008.

[7] A. Beskos, O. Papaspiliopoulos, G. O. Roberts and P. Fearnhead. Exact and computationally efficient likelihood-based estimation for discretely observed diffusion processes. *Journal of the Royal Statistical Society B*, **68**(part 3):333–382, 2006.

[8] P. E. Brown, K. F. Kåresen, G. O. Roberts, and S. Tonellato. Blur-generated non-separable space-time models. *Journal of the Royal*

Statistical Society Series B Statistical Methodology, **62**(4):847–860, 2000.

[9] J. Carpenter, P. Clifford and P. Fearnhead. Improved particle filter for nonlinear problems. *IEE Proceedings Radar, Sonar and Navigation*, **146**(1):2–7, 1999.

[10] N. Chopin. Central limit theorem for sequential Monte Carlo methods and its application to Bayesian inference. *Annals of Statistics*, **32**(6):2385–2411, 2004.

[11] J. C. Cox, J. E. Ingersoll Jr and S. A. Ross. A theory of the term structure of interest rates. *Econometrica: Journal of the Econometric Society*, pages 385–407, 1985.

[12] D. Crisan. Particle filters – a theoretical perspective. In A. Doucet, N. de Freitas, and N. Gordon, editors, *Sequential Monte Carlo Methods in Practice*, pages 17–41. Springer–Verlag, 2001.

[13] P. Del Moral and A. Guionnet. On the stability of interacting processes with applications to filtering and genetic algorithms. *Annales de l'Institut Henri Poincaré Probabilités et Statistiques*, **37**:155–194, 2001.

[14] P. Del Moral and L. Miclo. *Branching and Interacting Particle Systems. Approximations of Feymann-Kac Formulae with Application to Non-linear Filtering*, volume 1729. Springer, 2000.

[15] B. Delyon and Y. Hu. Simulation of conditioned diffusion and application to parameter estimation. *Stochastic Processes and their Applications*, **116**(11): 1660–1675, 2006.

[16] A. Dembo and O. Zeitouni. Parameter estimation of partially observed continuous time stochastic processes via the EM algorithm. *Stochastic Processes and their Applications*, **23**(1):91–113, 1986.

[17] A. Doucet, N. De Freitas and N. Gordon. *Sequential Monte Carlo Methods in Practice*. Springer Verlag, 2001.

[18] A. Doucet, A. M. Johansen and V. B. Tadic. On solving integral equations using Markov Chain Monte Carlo. Available from www.cs.ubc.ca/ arnaud/TR.html, 2008.

[19] G. B. Durham and A. R. Gallant. Numerical techniques for maximum likelihood estimation of continuous-time diffusion processes. *Journal of Business and Economic Statistics*, **20**(3):297–338, 2002. With comments and a reply by the authors.

[20] B. Eraker, M. Johannes and N. Polson. The impact of jumps in volatility and returns. *Journal of Finance*, **58**(3):1269–1300, 2003.

[21] P. Fearnhead, O. Papaspiliopoulos and G. O. Roberts. Particle filters for partially observed diffusions. *Journal of the Royal Statistical Society B*, **70**:755–777, 2008.

[22] P. Fearnhead, O. Papaspiliopoulos, G. O. Roberts and A. Stuart. Random weight particle filtering of continuous time processes. *Journal of the Royal Statistical Society Series B, Statistical Methodology*, **72**(4):497–512, 2010.

[23] P. Fearnhead and C. Sherlock. An exact Gibbs sampler for the Markov-modulated Poisson process. *Journal of the Royal Statistical Society B*, **68**(5):767–784, 2006.

[24] D. Florens-Zmirou. Approximate discrete-time schemes for statistics of diffusion processes. *Statistics*, **20**(4):547–557, 1989.

[25] P. Glasserman and J. Staum. Conditioning on one-step survival for barrier options. *Operations Research*, **49**:923–937, 2001.

[26] A. Golightly and D. J. Wilkinson. Bayesian sequential inference for stochastic kinetic biochemical network models. *Journal of Computational Biology*, **13**:838–851, 2006.

[27] N. J. Gordon, D. J. Salmond and A. F. M. Smith. Novel approach to nonlinear/non-Gaussian Bayesian state estimation. *IEE Proceedings F Radar and Signal Processing*, **140**:107–113, 1993.

[28] R. C. Griffiths and S. Tavaré. Simulating probability distributions in the coalescent. *Theoretical Population Biology*, **46**:131–158, 1994.

[29] I. Horenko and C. Schütte. Likelihood-based estimation of multidimensional Langevin models and its application to biomolecular dynamics. *Multiscale Modeling and Simulation*, **7**(2):731–773, 2008.

[30] A. S. Hurn, Jeisman, J. I. and K. A. Lindsay. Seeing the wood for the trees: A critical evaluation of methods to estimate the parameters of stochastic differential equations. *Journal of Financial Econometrics*, **5**(3):390–455, 2007.

[31] S. C. Kou, X. S. Xie and J. S. Liu. Bayesian analysis of single-molecule experimental data. *Journal of the Royal Statistical Society Series C*, **54**(3):469–506, 2005.

[32] H. R. Künsch. Recursive Monte Carlo filters: Algorithms and theoretical analysis. *Annals of Statistics*, pages 1983–2021, 2005.

[33] Jun S. Liu. *Monte Carlo Strategies in Scientific Computing*. Springer Series in Statistics. Springer, 2008.

[34] J. Møller, A. N. Pettitt, R. Reeves and K. K. Berthelsen. An efficient Markov chain Monte Carlo method for distributions with intractable normalising constants. *Biometrika*, **93**(2):451–458, 2006.

[35] I. A. Murray, Z. Ghahramani and D. J. C MacKay. MCMC for doubly-intractable distributions. *In Proceedings of the 14th Annual Conference on Uncertainty in Artificial Intelligence pages 359–366*, 2006.

[36] N. J. Newton. Variance reduction for simulated diffusions. *SIAM Journal on Applied Mathematics*, **54**(6):1780–1805, 1994.

[37] J. Nicolau. A new technique for simulating the likelihood of stochastic differential equations. *Economic Journal*, **5**(1):91–103, 2002.

[38] B. K. Øksendal. *Stochastic Differential Equations: An Introduction With Applications*. Springer-Verlag, 1998.

[39] O. Papaspiliopoulos and G. O. Roberts. Retrospective Markov chain Monte Carlo for Dirichlet process hierarchical models. *Biometrika*, **95**:169–186, 2008.

[40] O. Papaspiliopoulos and G. O. Roberts. Importance sampling techniques for estimation of diffusion models. In *SEMSTAT*. Chapman and Hall, 2009.

[41] O. Papaspiliopoulos and G. Sermaidis. Monotonicity properties of the Monte Carlo EM algorithm and connections with simulated likelihood. Available from www2. warwick.ac.uk/fac/sci/statistics/crism/ research/2007/paper07-24, 2007.

[42] S. Pelucchetti and G. O. Roberts. An empirical study of the efficiency of EA for diffusion simulation. CRiSM Technical report 08-14, available from www2. warwick.ac.uk/fac/sci/statistics/crism/ research/2008/paper08-14, 2008.

[43] M. K. Pitt and N. Shephard. Filtering via simulation: auxiliary particle filters. *Journal of the American Statistical Association*, **94**(446):590–599, 1999.

[44] Y. Pokern, A. M. Stuart and P. Wiberg. Parameter estimation for partially observed hypoelliptic diffusions. *Journal of the Royal Statistical Society Series B Statistical Methodology*, **71**(1):49–73, 2009.

[45] J. O. Ramsay, G. Hooker, D. Campbell and J. Cao. Parameter estimation for differential equations: a generalized smoothing approach.

Journal of the Royal Statistical Society Series B Statistical Methodology, **69**(5):741–796, 2007. With discussions and a reply by the authors.

[46] M. Rousset and A. Doucet. Discussion of Beskos et al. *Journal of the Royal Statistical Society B*, **68**:374–375, 2006.

[47] O. Stramer and J. Yan. Asymptotics of an efficient Monte Carlo estimation for the transition density of diffusion processes. *Methodology and Computing Applied Probability*, **9**(4):483–496, 2007.

[48] S. M. Sundaresan. Continuous-time methods in finance: A review and an assessment. *Journal of Finance*, **55**:1569–1622, 2000.

[49] J. M. G. Taylor, W. G. Cumberland and J. P. Sy. A stochastic model for analysis of longitudinal AIDS data. *Journal of the American Statistical Association*, **89**(427):727–736, 1994.

[50] W. Wagner. Monte Carlo evaluation of functionals of solutions of stochastic differential equations. Variance reduction and numerical examples. *Stochastic Analysis and Applications*, **6**(4):447–468, 1988.

[51] W. Wagner. Unbiased multi-step estimators for the Monte Carlo evaluation of certain functional integrals. *Journal of Computational Physics*, **79**(2):336–352, 1988.

[52] W. Wagner. Unbiased Monte Carlo estimators for functionals of weak solutions of stochastic differential equations. *Stochastics and Stochastics Reports*, **28**(1):1–20, 1989.

[53] G. Wahba. Bayesian 'confidence intervals' for the cross-validated smoothing spline. *Journal of the Royal Statistical Society Series B*, **45**(1):133–150, 1983.

[54] D. Williams. *Probability with Martingales*. Cambridge Mathematical Textbooks. Cambridge University Press, 1991.

Contributor

Omiros Papaspiliopoulos, Department of Economics, Universitat Pompeu Fabra, Barcelona, Spain

5

Two problems with variational expectation maximisation for time series models

Richard Eric Turner and Maneesh Sahani

5.1   Introduction

Variational methods are a key component of the approximate inference and learning toolbox. These methods fill an important middle ground, retaining distributional information about uncertainty in latent variables, unlike maximum a posteriori methods, and yet generally requiring less computational time than Markov chain Monte Carlo methods. In particular the variational expectation maximisation (vEM) and variational Bayes algorithms, both involving variational optimisation of a free-energy, are widely used in time series modelling. Here, we investigate the success of vEM in simple probabilistic time series models. First we consider the inference step of vEM, and show that a consequence of the well-known compactness property of variational inference is a failure to propagate uncertainty in time, thus limiting the usefulness of the retained distributional information. In particular, the uncertainty may appear to be smallest precisely when the approximation is poorest. Second, we consider parameter learning and analytically reveal systematic biases in the parameters found by vEM. Surprisingly, simpler variational approximations (such as mean-field) can lead to less bias than more complicated structured approximations.

5.2   The variational approach

We begin this chapter with a brief theoretical review of the variational expectation maximisation algorithm, before illustrating the important concepts with a simple example in the next section. The vEM algorithm is an approximate version of the expectation maximisation (EM) algorithm [4]. Expectation maximisation is a standard approach to finding maximum likelihood (ML) parameters for latent variable models, including hidden Markov models and linear or non-linear state space models (SSMs) for time series. The relationship between EM and vEM is revealed when EM is formulated as a variational optimisation of a free-energy [5, 11]. Consider observations collected into a set Y, that depend on latent variables X and parameters θ. We seek to maximise the likelihood of the parameters, $\log p(Y|\theta)$. By introducing a new distribution over the latent variables, $q(X)$, we can form a lower bound on the log-likelihood using Jensen's inequality,

$$\log p(Y|\theta) = \log \int dX \, p(Y, X|\theta) = \log \int dX \, p(Y, X|\theta) \frac{q(X)}{q(X)}$$

$$\geq \int dX \, q(X) \log \frac{p(Y, X|\theta)}{q(X)} = \mathcal{F}(q(X), \theta).$$

The lower bound is called the free-energy. The free-energy is smaller than the log-likelihood by an amount equal to the Kullback–Leibler (KL) divergence between $q(X)$ and the posterior distribution of the latent variables, $p(X|Y, \theta)$,

$$\mathcal{F}(q(X), \theta) = \int dX \, q(X) \log \frac{p(X|Y, \theta) p(Y|\theta)}{q(X)}$$

$$= \log p(Y|\theta) - \int dX \, q(X) \log \frac{q(X)}{p(X|Y, \theta)}$$

$$= \log p(Y|\theta) - KL(q(X)\|p(X|Y, \theta)).$$

This expression shows that, for fixed θ, the optimum value for q is equal to $p(X|Y, \theta)$, at which point the KL divergence vanishes and the free-energy equals the log-likelihood. Thus, alternate maximisation of $\mathcal{F}(q, \theta)$ with respect to q (the E-step) and θ (the M-step) will eventually find parameters that maximise the likelihood locally.

The EM algorithm is widely used to find ML parameter estimates. However, in many models calculation of this posterior is intractable. For example, it is often impossible to find an analytic form for $p(X|Y)$ because the normalising constant involves an intractable integral. Another common source of intractability arises in models in which the number of latent variables is very large. For instance, a model with K binary latent variables generally requires a posterior distribution over all 2^K possible states of those variables. For even moderately large K this results in a computational intractability.

One possible method of side-stepping these intractabilities is to use the vEM approach [8] which is to instead optimise q restricted to a class of distributions Q, within which the minimum of the KL divergence can tractably be found[1]

$$q_{vEM}(X) = \arg\min_{q(X) \in Q} KL(q(X)\|p(X|Y, \theta)) = \arg\min_{q(X) \in Q} \int dX \, q(X) \log \frac{q(X)}{p(X|Y, \theta)}. \quad (5.1)$$

The optimal q is called the variational approximation to the posterior. Constrained optimisation of q now alternates with optimisation of θ to find a maximum of the free-energy, though not necessarily the likelihood. The optimal parameters are taken to approximate the ML values.

There are two main ways in which q can be restricted to a class of tractable distributions Q. The first method is to specify a parametric form for the approximating distribution, $q(X) = q_\gamma(X)$. A common choice is a Gaussian in which case the variational parameters, γ, are the mean and the covariance. The E-Step of vEM then amounts to minimising the KL divergence with respect to the parameters of the approximating distribution,

$$q_{vEM} = \arg\min_{\gamma} KL(q_\gamma(X)\|p(X|Y, \theta)).$$

---

[1] Other variational bounds may also be used in learning (see e.g. [6]). However the term variational EM is generally reserved for the free-energy bound that we discuss in this chapter.

The second method is to define the class Q to contain all distributions that factor over disjoint sets C_i of the latent variables in the problem,

$$q(X) = \prod_{i=1}^{I} q_i(x_{C_i}).$$

For example, if each latent variable appears in a factor of its own, the approximation is called *mean-field*,

$$q_{MF}(X) = \prod_{i=1}^{I} q_i(x_i).$$

Partial factorisations, which keep some of the dependencies between variables are called *structured approximations*. Generally, these methods which rely on factored classes may be more powerful than using a pre-specified parametric form, as the optimal analytic form of the factors may often be obtained by direct optimisation of the free-energy. To find this form we solve for the stationary points of a Lagrangian that combines the free-energy with the constraint that each factor is normalised. With respect to a factor $q_i(x_{C_i})$ we have

$$\frac{\delta}{\delta q_i(x_{C_i})} \left[\mathcal{F}(q(X), \theta) - \sum_{i=1}^{I} \lambda_i \left(\int dx_{C_i} q_i(x_{C_i}) - 1 \right) \right] = 0,$$

where the λ_i are Lagrange multipliers. Taking the functional derivative, and solving, we obtain

$$q_i(x_{C_i}) \propto \exp\left(\langle \log p(Y, X|\theta) \rangle_{\prod_{j \neq i} q_j(x_{C_j})} \right). \tag{5.2}$$

This set of equations, one for each factor, may be applied iteratively to increase the free-energy. The procedure is guaranteed to converge, as the free-energy is convex in each of the factors $q_i(x_{C_i})$ [3].

5.2.1 A motivating example

Let us illustrate the EM and vEM algorithms described above by applying them to a simple model. The same example will also serve to motivate the problems which are addressed later in this chapter. In the model a one-dimensional observation, y, is generated by adding a zero-mean Gaussian noise variable with variance σ_y^2 to a latent variable, x, itself drawn from a zero-mean Gaussian, but with unit variance, that is

$$p(x) = \text{Norm}(x; 0, 1), \quad p(y|x, \sigma_y^2) = \text{Norm}(y; x, \sigma_y^2).$$

The model may be viewed as a very simple form of factor analysis with a one-dimensional observation and one factor. There is only one parameter to learn: the observation noise, σ_y^2. For tutorial purposes, we consider exact maximum-likelihood learning of this parameterfrom a single data-point. In fact, it is a simple matter to calculate the likelihood of the observation noise, $p(y|\sigma_y^2) = \text{Norm}(y; 0, \sigma_y^2 + 1)$, and therefore this quantity could be optimised directly to find the maximum-likelihood estimate. However, an alternative approach is to use the EM algorithm. The EM algorithm begins by initialising the observation noise. Next, in the E-Step, the approximating distribution q is updated to the posterior distribution over the latent variables given the current value of the parameters, that is,

$$q(x) = p(x|y, \sigma_y^2) = \text{Norm}\left(x; \frac{y}{1 + \sigma_y^2}, \frac{\sigma_y^2}{1 + \sigma_y^2} \right).$$

Then, in the M-Step, the observation noise is updated by maximising the free-energy with respect to the parameter, which has a closed-form solution, $\sigma_y^2 = y^2 - 2y\langle x\rangle_q + \langle x^2\rangle_q$. The E- and M-Step updates are then iterated, and this amounts to coordinate ascent of the free-energy (with respect to the distribution and then to the parameter) as illustrated in the upper left panel of Fig. 5.1(a). Moreover, as the free-energy is equal to the log-likelihood after each E-Step has been performed (see Fig. 5.1(b)), the algorithm converges to a local optimum of the likelihood.

An alternative to exact ML learning is to use the vEM algorithm to return approximate ML estimates. This requires the q distribution to be restricted to a particular class. As factored approximations are not an option for this one-dimensional model, a parametric restriction is considered. An instructive constraint is that the approximating distribution is a Gaussian with a flexible mean, but with a fixed variance. In the E-Step of vEM, the mean is set to minimise the KL divergence, which occurs when it is equal to the posterior mean. Therefore,

$$q_{\mu_q}(x) = \text{Norm}(x;\mu_q,\sigma_q^2) \quad \text{where} \quad \mu_q = \frac{y}{1 + \sigma_y^2} \quad \text{and} \quad \sigma_q^2 = \text{const.}$$

The M-Step of vEM is identical to the M-Step of EM, but the expectations are taken with respect to the new distribution. As a result the free-energy is no longer pinned to the log-likelihood after an E-Step and therefore vEM is not guaranteed to converge to a local optimum of the likelihood. In fact, for the model considered here, the vEM estimate is biased away from the maximum in the likelihood, towards regions of parameter space where the variational bound is tightest (see Fig. 5.1). One of the main questions considered in this chapter is to what extent such biases are a general feature of vEM.

5.2.2 Chapter organisation

The motivating example described above is a simple one, but it indicates that parameter estimates from EM and vEM can be quite different. However, it is unclear whether similar biases would arise for more realistic models, and in particular in those for time series. Moreover, the example involved estimating one parameter from one observation. A complete analysis should also compare EM and vEM on large datasets. After all, it is well known that maximum-likelihood estimators can perform poorly when a large number of parameters have to be estimated from a small dataset, thus the discrepancy between EM and vEM noted above is not necessarily concerning. Of particular interest is the behaviour of vEM in the limit of infinite data. Maximum-likelihood estimators are often consistent, meaning that they converge to the true parameters in this limit. Do vEM estimators inherit this property? The motivating example indicates that a key determinant is the parameter dependence of the tightness of the free-energy bound, given by $\text{KL}(q(x)|p(y|x,\theta))$, and whether this is significant in comparison to the peak in the likelihood. The size of this contribution to the free-energy is studied in a simple setting in Section 5.4. One intriguing possibility is that the best approximations for learning are not necessarily those that yield the tightest bounds, but rather those in which the tightness of the bounds depends least on the parameters. Evidence that such an effect exists is provided in Section 5.4.4 and further investigation, in Section 5.4.6, reveals that it is fairly common.

Before analysing the biases in parameters learned using vEM, we consider the E-Step of vEM in isolation. It is well known that variational approximations, like those derived in the vEM E-Step, tend to be compact [10]. That is, variational approximations tend to have a smaller entropy than the true distribution. The evidence for this folk-theorem is reviewed

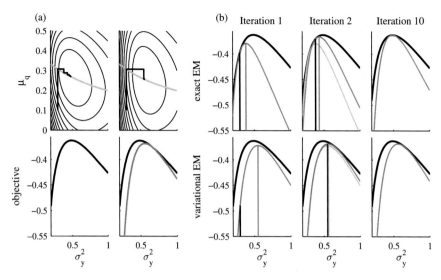

Figure 5.1 Schematics of EM and vEM using the model described in the text where the observation takes the value y = 0.4. **(a) Top Left**: Thin black curves are the contours of the free-energy, $\mathcal{F}_{EM}(q, \sigma_y^2)$, for exact EM as a function of the observation noise (σ_y^2, abscissa) and the mean of the posterior distribution (μ_q, ordinate). The variance of the approximating distribution, σ_q^2, is set to the optimal value at each point. The thick grey line indicates the optimal choice for μ_q i.e. the mean of the posterior distribution $p(x|y, \sigma_y^2)$. Ten updates using the EM algorithm are shown (thick black lines). Each update consists of an E-Step, which moves vertically to the optimal setting of μ_q (thick grey line), and an M-Step, which moves horizontally to the optimal setting of σ_y^2. By iterating these steps the algorithm converges via coordinate ascent to the optimum of the free-energy, which is also the optimum of the likelihood. **Bottom Left**: Log-likelihood of the observation noise. The value of the log-likelihood corresponds to the contour values along the thick grey line in the plot above. **Top Right**: Contours of the free-energy, $\mathcal{F}_{vEM}(q, \sigma_y^2)$, for vEM (black lines) in which the variance of the approximating distribution is fixed to the value $\sigma_q^2 = 0.4$. The position of the optimum has shifted to a larger value of the observation noise and the vEM algorithm converges onto this optimum (thick black lines). **Bottom Right**: The optimal free-energy (thick grey line) is a lower bound on the log-likelihood of the observation noise (thick black line). The value of the free-energy corresponds to the contour values along the thick grey line in the plot above. **(b) Top Left**: Schematic showing the first M-Step for exact EM. After an initial E-Step the free-energy, $\mathcal{F}_{EM}(q_1, \sigma_y^2)$, (thick grey line) is tight to the log-likelihood (thick black curved line) at the current value of the parameters (indicated by the vertical black line). In the M-Step q is fixed, and the optimal parameters are found (thick vertical grey line). This corresponds to the first horizontal line in the top left subplot of A. **Top Middle**: Schematic showing the second M-Step of exact EM. After the second E-Step, the updated free-energy, $\mathcal{F}_{EM}(q_2, \sigma_y^2)$, (thick, dark grey line) is tight to the log-likelihood (thick black line) at the current value of the parameters (indicated by the thick black vertical line). The old free-energy is shown for reference (thick, light grey line). The result of the second M-Step is indicated by the thick vertical grey line. **Top Right**: Schematic showing the free-energy, $\mathcal{F}_{EM}(q_{10}, \sigma_y^2)$, (thick grey line) after 10 iterations. The optimum is clearly close to that of the log-likelihood (thick black line). **Bottom Left**: Schematic showing the first M-Step for vEM. As compared with the panel above, the free-energy, $\mathcal{F}_{vEM}(q(\mu_{q1}, \sigma_{q1}^2), \sigma_y^2)$, (thick grey line) is not tight to the log-likelihood (thick black line). **Bottom Middle**: Schematic showing the second M-Step for vEM. **Bottom Right**: Schematic showing the free-energy after 10 iterations, $\mathcal{F}_{vEM}(q(\mu_{q10}, \sigma_{q10}^2), \sigma_y^2)$, (thick grey line). The optimum clearly lies to the right of the optimum of the log-likelihood (thick black line). It is biased to where the variational approximation is tightest.

in the next section with particular emphasis on the relevance to time series modelling. In Section 5.3.3, we show that a consequence of compactness in mean-field approximations is a complete failure to propagate uncertainty between time steps, this makes the popular mean-field approximations most over-confident exactly when they are poorest.

Both the compactness and parameter learning biases are exemplified using very simple time series models, although the conclusions are likely to apply more generally.

5.3 Compactness of variational approximations

In this section we consider approximating a known distribution, $p(\mathrm{x})$, with a simpler one, $q(\mathrm{x})$, by minimising the variational KL divergence, $\mathrm{KL}(q(\mathrm{x})\|p(\mathrm{x}))$. This operation forms the E-Step of vEM (see Eq. (5.1)) and so its behaviour has implications on how the full algorithm behaves. Before considering a number of instructive examples, it is immediately clear from the form of the variational KL that at any point where the true density is zero, the approximation must also be zero (otherwise the KL divergence will be infinity). A consequence of this fact is that when a distribution which has two modes that are separated by a region of zero density is approximated by a unimodal distribution, then the approximation will model just one of the modes, rather than averaging across them. This is one example of a general tendency for variational approximations to have a smaller entropy than the target distribution. This section explores this so-called compactness property of variational approximations, before considering the implications for time series modelling.

5.3.1 Approximating mixtures of Gaussians with a single Gaussian

As explained above, when the true distribution contains two modes which are separated by an intermediate region of zero density, the approximation will be compact. However, it is unclear what happens when the intermediate region does not dip to zero. In order to investigate this situation, consider approximating a one-dimensional mixture of Gaussians with a single Gaussian, where

$$p(\mathrm{x}|\theta) = \sum_{k=1}^{K} \pi_k \mathrm{Norm}(\mathrm{x}; \mu_k, \sigma_k^2), \quad q(\mathrm{x}) = \mathrm{Norm}(\mathrm{x}; \mu_q, \sigma_q^2).$$

In Fig. 5.2 a number of examples are shown for a range of different parameter choices for the mixture. As expected, for mixtures with two clearly defined modes (right-hand column of Fig. 5.2), the approximation matches the mode with the largest variance, rather than averaging across both of them [2]. In these cases the entropy of the approximation is less than that of the true distribution. However, for intermediate distributions, in which the modes are joined by a significant bridge of probability-density, the variational approximation does average across the modes and in some cases the entropy of the approximation is larger than the true distribution. The conclusion is that the compactness property is a useful guide to the behaviour of variational methods when applied to highly multimodal distributions, but that there are examples when variational methods are not compact (as measured by their entropy relative to that of the true distribution). Variational approximations commonly used in clustering are an example of the former [2], but variational approximations to independent component analysis can result in the latter [12].

5.3.2 Approximating a correlated Gaussian with a factored Gaussian

The examples above indicate how compactness operates for univariate distributions, when the approximating distribution is restricted to a particular parametric form. Next, we consider approximating a bivariate distribution using the mean-field approximation. The true distribution is a zero-mean, correlated Gaussian distribution with principal axes oriented in the directions $\mathbf{e}_1 = \frac{1}{\sqrt{2}}[1, 1]^T$ and $\mathbf{e}_2 = \frac{1}{\sqrt{2}}[1, -1]^T$ with variances σ_1^2 and σ_2^2 respectively [10], that is

$$p(\mathrm{x}_1, \mathrm{x}_2|\Sigma) = \mathrm{Norm}(\mathrm{x}_1, \mathrm{x}_2; 0, \Sigma), \quad \Sigma = \sigma_1^2 \mathbf{e}_1 \mathbf{e}_1^T + \sigma_2^2 \mathbf{e}_2 \mathbf{e}_1^T.$$

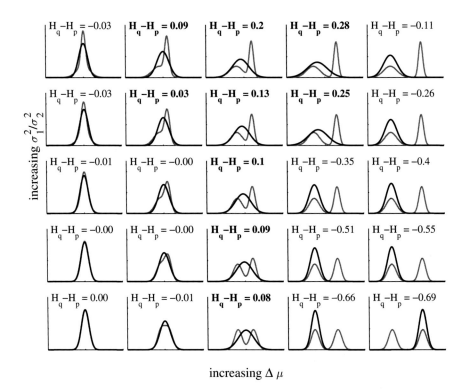

increasing $\Delta \mu$

Figure 5.2 Each panel shows a variational approximation to a true distribution. The true distribution is a mixture of two Gaussians (grey line) and the approximating family is a Gaussian (black line). The parameters of the mixture were set so that each component has equal weight ($\pi_1 = \pi_2 = \frac{1}{2}$). The difference between the means of the mixture components increases from the left column of panels (where $\mu_1 - \mu_2 = 0$) to the right column of panels (where $\mu_1 - \mu_2 = 10$). The ratio of the variances increases from the bottom row of panels (where $\sigma_1^2/\sigma_2^2 = 1$) to the top row of panels (where $\sigma_1^2/\sigma_2^2 = 10$). The smaller of the two variances is fixed, $\sigma_2^2 = 1$. The bottom left is therefore a mixture of two Gaussians with the same mean and variance, and this is another Gaussian. The approximation is therefore exact and the entropy difference, shown at the top of each panel, is zero. In general the entropy of the approximation can be less than (normal font) or greater than (bold font) the true entropy.

This correlated Gaussian is approximated in the mean-field approach by a factorised distribution, $q(x_1, x_2) = q(x_1)q(x_2)$. By considering the fixed points of Eq. (5.2) the optimal updates are found to be

$$q(x_i) = \text{Norm}\left(x_i; 0, \frac{1}{2}\frac{\sigma_1^2\sigma_2^2}{\sigma_1^2 + \sigma_2^2}\right).$$

That is, the optimal factored approximating distribution is a spherical Gaussian that has a precision which is equal to the diagonal elements of the precision matrix of the original Gaussian (that is, $(\Sigma^{-1})_{i,i}$). This is an example of the more general result that variational approximations between two Gaussians match precisions, which will be seen again later in the chapter. Consider now the behaviour of the variational approximation in the case where the variance of the two components is very different (e.g. $\sigma_1^2 > \sigma_2^2$). The width of the approximating distribution becomes $\sigma_2^2/2$, and therefore independent of the longer lengthscale. In this sense the approximation is becoming compact; it matches the smallest lengthscale in the posterior. In the next subsection, this result will be rediscovered from the contrasting perspective of mean-field inference in time series models.

5.3.3   Variational approximations do not propagate uncertainty

Fully factored variational approximations (so called mean-field approximations) have been used for inference in time series models as they are fast and yet still return estimates of uncertainty in the latent variables [1]. Here, we show that in a simple model, the variational iterations fail to propagate uncertainty between the factors, rendering these estimates of uncertainty particularly inaccurate in time series models [14].

We consider a time series model with a single latent variable x_t at each time step drawn from a first-order autoregressive prior with coefficient λ and innovations variance σ^2,

$$p(x_t|x_{t-1}) = \text{Norm}(x_t; \lambda x_{t-1}, \sigma^2). \tag{5.3}$$

The marginal mean of this distribution is zero and the marginal variance is $\sigma_\infty^2 = \frac{\sigma^2}{1-\lambda^2}$. As the time series of greatest interest tend to be those which exhibit strong temporal structure, we consider models in which the autoregressive parameter λ is close to unity.[2] The observed variables y_t depend only on the latent variable at the corresponding time step. The precise form of $p(y_t|x_t)$ is not important here.

If we choose a mean-field approximating distribution which factorises over time, $q(x_{1:T}) = \prod_{t=1}^{T} q(x_t)$, the update for the latent variable at time t follows from Eq. (5.2)

$$
\begin{aligned}
q(x_t) &= \frac{1}{Z} p(y_t|x_t) \exp(\langle \log p(x_t|x_{t-1}) p(x_{t+1}|x_t) \rangle_{q(x_{t-1})q(x_{t+1})}) \\
&= \frac{1}{Z'} p(y_t|x_t) \text{Norm}\left(x_t; \frac{\lambda}{1+\lambda^2}(\langle x_{t-1} \rangle + \langle x_{t+1} \rangle), \frac{\sigma^2}{1+\lambda^2}\right) \\
&= \frac{1}{Z'} p(y_t|x_t) q_{\text{prior}}(x_t).
\end{aligned}
$$

That is, the variational update is formed by combining the likelihood with a variational prior-predictive $q_{\text{prior}}(x_t)$ that contains the contributions from the latent variables at the adjacent time step. This variational prior-predictive is interesting because it is identical to the true prior-predictive when there is no uncertainty in the adjacent variables. As such, *none* of the (potentially large) uncertainty in the value of the adjacent latent variables is propagated to $q(x_t)$, and the width of the variational predictive is consequently narrower than the width of state-conditional distribution $p(x_t|x_{t-1})$ (compare to Eq. (5.3)).[3]

Temporally factored variational methods for time series models will thus generally recover an approximation to the posterior which is narrower than the state-conditional distribution. As the whole point of time series models is that there are meaningful dependencies in the latents, and therefore the state-conditional often has a small width, the variational uncertainties may be tiny compared to the true marginal probabilities (see Fig. 5.3). Thus, the mean-field approach is not all that different from the 'zero-temperature EM' or maximum a posteriori (MAP)-based approach (in which the joint probability of observed data and latent variables is optimised alternately with respect to the latent variables – with no distributional information – and the parameters), except that we find the mean of the posterior rather than a mode. In the next section, it will be shown that this

---

[2]In fact the effective time scale of Eq. (5.3) is $\tau_{eff} = -1/\log(\lambda)$ and so a change in λ from 0.9 to 0.99 is roughly equivalent to a change from 0.99 to 0.999. This is important when the size of the biases in the estimation of λ are considered (Section 5.4.3).

[3]This problem only gets worse if the prior dynamics have longer dependencies, e.g. if $p(x_t|x_{t-1:t-\tau}) = \text{Norm}(\sum_{t'=1}^{\tau} \lambda_{t'} x_{t-t'}, \sigma^2)$, in which case the variational prior-predictive has a variance $\frac{\sigma^2}{1+\sum_{t'=1}^{\tau} \lambda_{t'}^2}$.

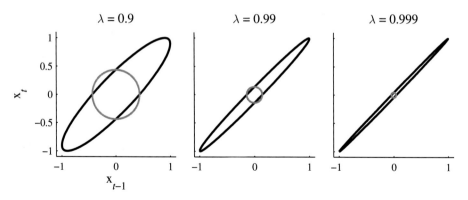

Figure 5.3 Compactness in mean-field approximations for time series. The average true prior-predictive (black ellipses, showing the probability density contour at one standard deviation) is shown together with the mean-field approximations (grey circles, also showing the probability density contour at one standard deviation), for three settings of λ. The marginal variance of the true prior-predictive is 1. The marginal variance of the mean-field approximation is $(1 - \lambda^2)/(1 + \lambda^2)$ which is tiny for typical values of λ in time series models. Notice that this example is equivalent to the previous example in Section 5.3.2 involving a bivariate Gaussian when, $\sigma_1^2 = \frac{\sigma^2}{1-\lambda}$ and $\sigma_2^2 = \frac{\sigma^2}{1+\lambda}$.

does have some advantages over the MAP approach, notably that pathological spikes in the likelihood can be avoided.

In conclusion, although variational methods appear to retain some information about uncertainty, they fail to propagate this information between factors. In particular, in time series with strong correlations between latents at adjacent times, the mean-field variational posterior becomes extremely concentrated, even though it is least accurate in this regime. An ideal distributional approximation would perhaps behave in the opposite fashion, returning larger uncertainty when it is likely to be more inaccurate.

5.4 Variational approximations are biased

In the last section we showed that variational approximations under-estimate the uncertainties in inference. We will now investigate how these inaccuracies affect the parameter estimates returned by vEM. This question is important in many contexts. For example, scientific enquiry is often concerned with the values of a parameter, to substantiate claims like 'natural scenes vary slowly' or 'natural sounds are sparse'.

What makes for a good variational approximation in this case? The instant reaction is that the free-energy should be as tight to the log-likelihood as possible. That is, the optimal KL divergence at each parameter setting,

$$KL^*(\theta) = \arg\max_{q(x)} KL(q(X)\|p(X|Y,\theta)),$$

should be as small as possible for all θ. However, the conclusion from the motivating example in Section 5.2.1, is that from the perspective of learning it is more important to be *equally tight everywhere*. In other words it is more important for the KL-term to be as parameter-independent as possible: If $KL^*(\theta)$ varies strongly as a function of the parameters, this can shift the peaks in the free-energy away from the peaks in the likelihood, toward the regions where the bound is tighter. This perspective explains a previous observation whereby variational Bayes typically prunes out too many components of a mixture model [9].

We now illustrate this effect in a linear SSM and show that consequences can include mis-estimation of the time constant with which the latent variables evolve, under-estimation of the overlap of emission weights, and unwanted pruning of emission weights. Moreover, we show that the mean-field approximation can actually have less severe parameter-dependent biases than two structural approximations, and can therefore lead to better vEM parameter estimates, even though it is less tight everywhere. We also show that the biases in parameter estimates increase considerably with the number of parameters.

5.4.1 Deriving the learning algorithms

In the following we first introduce an elementary SSM, for which we can find the exact log-likelihood, $\log p(y|\theta)$. We then examine the properties of a set of different variational learning algorithms. This set comprises a mean-field approximation, two different structural approximations and zero-temperature EM. This final approximation can be thought of as vEM where the approximating distributions are delta functions centred at the MAP estimates [11]. The analysis of these schemes proceeds as follows: First the optimal E-Step updates for these approximations are derived. Second, it is shown that, as the SSM is a simple one, the free-energies and the zero-temperature EM objective function can be written purely in terms of the parameters. That is, $\max_{q(x)} \mathcal{F}(\theta, q(x))$ and $\max_X \log p(Y, X|\theta)$ have closed-form solutions, and do not require iterative updates to be computed as is usually the case. Thus, we can study the relationship between the peaks in the log-likelihood and the peaks in the free-energies and zero-temperature EM objective function, for any dataset. This is analogous to the lower right-hand panel of Fig. 5.1(a) for the motivating example.

Consider an SSM which has two latent variables per time step, two time steps and two-dimensional observations. We take the priors on the latent variables to be linear-Gaussian, and the observations are given by summing the weighted latents at the corresponding time step and adding Gaussian noise, that is

$$p(x_{k,1}) = \text{Norm}\left(x_{k,1}; 0, \frac{\sigma_x^2}{1 - \lambda^2}\right), \qquad p(x_{k,2}|x_{k,1}) = \text{Norm}\left(x_{k,2}; \lambda x_{k,1}, \sigma_x^2\right),$$

$$p(y_{d,t}|x_{1,t}, x_{2,t}) = \text{Norm}\left(y_{d,t}; \sum_{k=1}^{2} w_{d,k} x_{k,t}, \sigma_y^2\right).$$

This defines a joint Gaussian over the observations and latent variables. From this we can compute the likelihood exactly by marginalisation. Defining the vector of observations, $\mathbf{y} = [y_{11}, y_{21}, y_{12}, y_{22}]^T$, and the matrix $M_{d,d'} = \sum_{k=1}^{2} w_{d,k} w_{d',k}$, the likelihood is given by

$$p(y_{1:2,1:2}|\theta) = \text{Norm}(\mathbf{y}; 0, \Sigma_y), \quad \Sigma_y = I\sigma_y^2 + \frac{\sigma_x^2}{1 - \lambda^2}\begin{bmatrix} M & \lambda M \\ \lambda M & M \end{bmatrix}.$$

The posterior distribution over the latent variables is also Gaussian, and is given by $p(\mathbf{x}|\mathbf{y}) = \text{Norm}(\mu_{\mathbf{x}|\mathbf{y}}, \Sigma_{\mathbf{x}|\mathbf{y}})$, where the vector of latent variables is $\mathbf{x} = [x_{11}, x_{21}, x_{12}, x_{22}]^T$.

In order to ease notation, we define weight vectors and matrices

$$\mathbf{w}_1 = \begin{bmatrix} w_{11} \\ w_{21} \end{bmatrix} = |\mathbf{w}_1| \begin{bmatrix} \cos(\phi_1) \\ \sin(\phi_1) \end{bmatrix}, \qquad \mathbf{w}_2 = \begin{bmatrix} w_{12} \\ w_{22} \end{bmatrix} = |\mathbf{w}_2| \begin{bmatrix} \cos(\phi_2) \\ \sin(\phi_2) \end{bmatrix}, \qquad W = \begin{bmatrix} w_{11} & w_{12} \\ w_{21} & w_{22} \end{bmatrix}.$$

Then, the covariance and mean of the posterior distribution are given by

$$\Sigma^{-1}_{\mathbf{x}|\mathbf{y}} = \begin{bmatrix} \frac{|\mathbf{w}_1|^2}{\sigma_y^2} + \frac{1}{\sigma_x^2} & \frac{\mathbf{w}_1^T \mathbf{w}_2}{\sigma_y^2} & -\frac{\lambda}{\sigma_x^2} & 0 \\ \frac{\mathbf{w}_1^T \mathbf{w}_2}{\sigma_y^2} & \frac{|\mathbf{w}_2|^2}{\sigma_y^2} + \frac{1}{\sigma_x^2} & 0 & -\frac{\lambda}{\sigma_x^2} \\ -\frac{\lambda}{\sigma_x^2} & 0 & \frac{|\mathbf{w}_1|^2}{\sigma_y^2} + \frac{1}{\sigma_x^2} & \frac{\mathbf{w}_1^T \mathbf{w}_2}{\sigma_y^2} \\ 0 & -\frac{\lambda}{\sigma_x^2} & \frac{\mathbf{w}_1^T \mathbf{w}_2}{\sigma_y^2} & \frac{|\mathbf{w}_2|^2}{\sigma_y^2} + \frac{1}{\sigma_x^2} \end{bmatrix}, \qquad \mu_{\mathbf{x}|\mathbf{y}} = \frac{1}{\sigma_y^2}\Sigma_{\mathbf{x}|\mathbf{y}} \begin{bmatrix} W & 0 \\ 0 & W \end{bmatrix} \mathbf{y}.$$

The posterior is correlated through time because of the linear-Gaussian prior, and correlated across chains because of explaining away.[4] The correlations through time increase as the prior becomes 'slower' ($|\lambda|$ increases) and less noisy (σ_x^2 decreases). The correlations across chains increase as the magnitude of the weights increases ($|\mathbf{w}_d|^2$), and the angle between the weights ($\phi_1 - \phi_2$) or the observation noise (σ_y^2) decreases.

We now derive the optimal E-Step for four different approximations. The first three approximations, which provide uncertainty estimates, are the fully factored mean-field approximation (q_{MF}), the approximation with factorisation over chains but not time (q_{FC}), and the approximation with factorisation over time but not chains (q_{FT}), as shown in the following table:

	factored over time	unfactored over time
chains factored	$q_{MF}(\mathbf{x})$	$q_{FC}(\mathbf{x})$
chains unfactored	$q_{FT}(\mathbf{x})$	$p(\mathbf{x}|\mathbf{y}) = q(\mathbf{x})$

The factorisations are therefore

$$q_{MF}(\mathbf{x}) = q^{(1)}_{MF}(x_{11}) q^{(2)}_{MF}(x_{12}) q^{(3)}_{MF}(x_{21}) q^{(4)}_{MF}(x_{22}),$$
$$q_{FC}(\mathbf{x}) = q^{(1)}_{FC}(x_{11}, x_{12}) q^{(2)}_{FC}(x_{21}, x_{22}),$$
$$q_{FT}(\mathbf{x}) = q^{(1)}_{FT}(x_{11}, x_{21}) q^{(2)}_{FT}(x_{12}, x_{22}).$$

The optimal E-Step updates for these three distributions are found by minimising the variational KL. Each factor is found to be Gaussian, with mean and precision that match the corresponding elements in $\mu_{\mathbf{x}|\mathbf{y}}$ and $\Sigma^{-1}_{\mathbf{x}|\mathbf{y}}$. The fourth and final approximation is zero-temperature EM (q_{MAP}), for which the E-Step is given by the MAP estimate for the latent variables for the current parameter setting. As the posterior is Gaussian, the mode and the mean are identical and so the MAP estimates are identical to the variational values for the means.

The next step is to compute the free-energies. In the first three cases, the Gaussianity of the posterior and the uncertainty-preserving variational approximations enables the KL

---

[4]Explaining away is the name given to the phenomenon in probabilistic modelling where the observation of an effect of two possible independent causes, leads to (anti-)correlation in the posterior distribution over those two causal latent variables. Suppose that either latent may take on a value that could account for the observation. Then if one does so, it 'explains away' the observed effect, and the observed data no longer constrains the other. Thus, conditioned on the observation, the distribution over each latent depends on the value of the other, even if there was no such dependence in the prior.

divergences to be calculated analytically as

$$\mathrm{KL}_i\left(\prod_{a=1}^A q_i^{(a)}(\mathbf{x}_a)\|p(\mathbf{x}|\mathbf{y})\right) = \frac{1}{2}\log\frac{\prod_{a=1}^A \det\left(\Sigma_i^{(a)}\right)}{\det\left(\Sigma_{\mathbf{x}|\mathbf{y}}\right)}.$$

That is, the KL divergence is the log-ratio of the volume of the approximation (as measured by the matrix determinants) to the volume of the true posterior. It should be noted that the whole point of variational methods is that this quantity is usually intractable to compute, and that it is only because the example is very simple that it is not the case here. Using this expression we find

$$\mathrm{KL}^*_{\mathrm{MF}} = \frac{1}{2}\log\left(\sigma_y^2 + |\mathbf{w}_1|^2\sigma_x^2\right)^2\left(\sigma_y^2 + |\mathbf{w}_2|^2\sigma_x^2\right)^2/\gamma,$$

$$\mathrm{KL}^*_{\mathrm{FC}} = \frac{1}{2}\log\left(\left(\sigma_y^2 + |\mathbf{w}_1|^2\sigma_x^2\right)^2 - \lambda^2\sigma_y^4\right)\left(\left(\sigma_y^2 + |\mathbf{w}_2|^2\sigma_x^2\right)^2 - \lambda^2\sigma_y^4\right)/\gamma,$$

$$\mathrm{KL}^*_{\mathrm{FT}} = \frac{1}{2}\log\left(\sigma_x^4|\mathbf{w}_1|^2|\mathbf{w}_2|^2\sin^2(\phi_1-\phi_2) + \left(|\mathbf{w}_1|^2 + |\mathbf{w}_2|^2\right)\sigma_x^2\sigma_y^2 + \sigma_y^4\right)^2/\gamma, \qquad (5.4)$$

where

$$\gamma = \left(\left(|\mathbf{w}_1|^2 + |\mathbf{w}_2|^2\right)\sigma_x^2\sigma_y^2 + \sigma_x^4|\mathbf{w}_1|^2|\mathbf{w}_2|^2\sin^2(\phi_1-\phi_2) + (1+\lambda^2)\sigma_y^4\right)^2$$
$$- \left(\lambda\sigma_y^2\sigma_x^2\left(|\mathbf{w}_1|^2 + |\mathbf{w}_2|^2\right) + 2\lambda\sigma_y^4\right)^2.$$

In the zero-temperature EM approximation, since the KL divergence between a Gaussian and a delta function is infinite, the KL term is discarded and the log-joint is used as a pseudo free-energy. To ease notation, in what follows $\mathrm{KL}_i = \mathrm{KL}^*_i$.

5.4.2 General properties of the bounds: a sanity check

We now verify that these results match our intuitions. For example, as the mean-field approximation is a subclass of the other approximations, it is *always* the loosest of the bounds, $\mathrm{KL}_{\mathrm{MF}} > \mathrm{KL}_{\mathrm{FC}}, \mathrm{KL}_{\mathrm{FT}} > 0$, which is borne out by the expressions. Furthermore, q_{FT} becomes looser than q_{FC} when temporal correlations dominate over the correlations-between chains. For instance, if the weights have identical magnitude, $|\mathbf{w}_1| = |\mathbf{w}_2| = |\mathbf{w}|$, then $\mathrm{KL}_{\mathrm{FT}} > \mathrm{KL}_{\mathrm{FC}}$ when explaining away (EA) becomes more important than temporal correlation (TC) in the posterior,

$$\frac{\mathrm{EA}}{\mathrm{TC}} < 1, \quad \text{where } \mathrm{EA} = \frac{|\cos(\phi_1-\phi_2)||\mathbf{w}|^2}{\sigma_y^2} \quad \text{and } \mathrm{TC} = \frac{|\lambda|}{\sigma_x^2}.$$

Moreover, q_{FC} is equivalent to the mean-field approximation, $\mathrm{KL}_{\mathrm{MF}} = \mathrm{KL}_{\mathrm{FC}}$, when there are no temporal correlations, $\lambda = 0$ or $\sigma_x^2 = \infty$, and in this case the true posterior matches q_{FT}, $\mathrm{KL}_{\mathrm{FT}} = 0$. Similarly, q_{FT} is equivalent to the mean-field approximation when the observation noise is infinity $\sigma_y^2 = \infty$, and here q_{FC} is exact ($\mathrm{KL}_{\mathrm{FC}} = 0$). Finally we note that, as q_{FT} is the only approximation which captures cross-chain correlations due to explaining away, it is the only approximation which is dependent on the relative angle between the weights.

Having verified that the expressions for the KL divergences appear reasonable, we can now consider how the maxima in the log-likelihood relate to the maxima in the free-energies. Unfortunately, there is no closed-form solution for the location of these maxima,

but in the simple examples which follow, the free-energies and likelihoods can be visualised. In general, we will be concerned with the consistency of the variational estimators,
which means the behaviour when we have a large number of observations from the same
time series. In this case the average likelihood becomes

$$\lim_{N \to \infty} \frac{1}{N} \log p(\mathbf{y}_{1:N} | \Sigma_{\mathbf{y}}) = -\frac{1}{2} \log \det \Sigma_{\mathbf{y}} - \frac{1}{2} \Sigma_{\mathbf{y}}^{-1} \lim_{N \to \infty} \frac{1}{N} \sum_{n=1}^{N} \mathbf{y}_n \mathbf{y}_n^T$$

$$= -\frac{1}{2} \log \det \Sigma_{\mathbf{y}} - \frac{1}{2} \Sigma_{\mathbf{y}}^{-1} \left\langle \mathbf{y} \mathbf{y}^T \right\rangle.$$

When the data are drawn from the forward model, $\left\langle \mathbf{y} \mathbf{y}^T \right\rangle$ can be computed analytically.
In all cases the ML estimators are found to be consistent, and therefore equal to the true
parameters in the limit of infinite data.

Although the model is simple, it has seven parameters and this means there is a great
number of possible learning scenarios, ranging from learning one parameter with the others
fixed to learning all parameters at once. In the following we highlight several illustrative
examples in order to elucidate the general properties of the variational approach. First we
consider learning a single parameter (the dynamical parameter, the observation noise, the
innovations noise, the orientation of one of the weights and the magnitude of one of the
weights) with the other parameters set to their true values. This will allow us to develop
some intuition about the ways in which different approximations lead to different biases
in the parameter estimates. In this case, the log-likelihood and free-energies are easy to
visualise; some typical examples are shown in Fig. 5.4 and Fig. 5.5. We then consider how
the bias changes as a function of the true parameters, and observe that there is no universally preferred approximation, but instead the least biased approximation depends on the
parameter that is being learned and on the value of the true parameters. Next we will study
the bias when learning the dynamic parameter and the observation noise simultaneously,
as this provides a typical example of how the variational approach performs when multiple parameters are learned. The conclusion is that the biases become significantly larger as
more parameters are estimated.

5.4.3   Learning the dynamical parameter, λ

We begin by considering learning the dynamical parameter λ, with the other parameters
fixed to their true values. In order to ensure that the effects of explaining away are properly
considered the weights are set to be identical with unit magnitude ($\mathbf{w}_1 = \mathbf{w}_2$ and $|\mathbf{w}_k|^2 = 1$).

As the magnitude of the dynamical parameter increases, so does the correlation in the
posterior between successive latent variables in the same chain ($x_{k,1}$ and $x_{k,2}$). This means
that q_{FT}, which factorises over time, results in a looser variational bound as the magnitude of λ increases (KL$_{FT}$ increases, Eq. (5.4)). Furthermore, as the correlation between
latents in the same chain increases, ($x_{k,1}$ and $x_{k,2}$), so does the correlation between x_{11} and
x_{22} (because explaining away is propagated through time by the dynamics). This means,
somewhat surprisingly, that q_{FC} which does not factorise over time, but over chains, also
becomes looser as the magnitude of λ increases. That is, KL$_{FC}$ also increases with the magnitude of λ. In both cases, this λ-dependence in the tightness of the bound means that the
corresponding variational free-energies peak at lower values of λ than the likelihood, and
therefore both approximations yield under-estimates (see [13] for a similar result).

The mean-field approximation suffers from both of the aforementioned effects, and it
is therefore looser than both. However, with regard to their *dependence* on λ, KL$_{MF}$ and

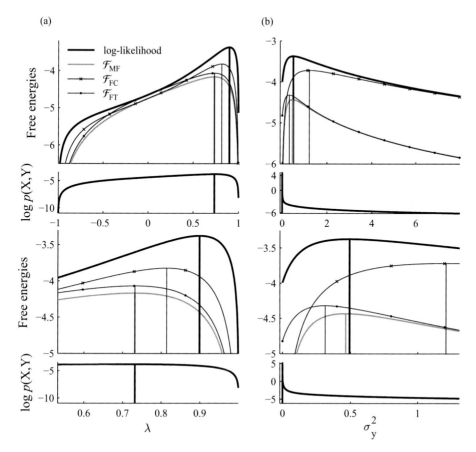

Figure 5.4 Biases in the free-energies for learning the dynamical parameter, λ, and the observation noise, σ_y^2, of a simple linear dynamical system. The true parameters were $\lambda = 0.9$, $\sigma_x^2 = 1 - \lambda^2 = 0.19$, $\mathbf{w}_1^T = [1,0]$, $\mathbf{w}_2^T = [1,0]$ and $\sigma_y^2 = 0.43$. In both columns (a) and (b), one parameter is learned and the others are set to their true values. Column (a) shows the results of learning λ, and column (b) shows the results of learning σ_y^2. Large panels show the log-likelihood (thick black line) and the free-energies of the uncertainty preserving methods ($\mathcal{F}_{\text{MF}}$ by a thick grey line, $\mathcal{F}_{\text{FC}}$ by the crosses, and $\mathcal{F}_{\text{FT}}$ by the circles). Small panels show the zero-temperature EM approach (q_{MAP}). The maxima of these functions are indicated by the vertical lines. The maximum of the log-likelihood lies at the true value of the parameters. The bottom two panels show a zoomed in region of the top two panels.

KL$_{\text{FT}}$ are equivalent. Consequently q_{MF} and q_{FT} recover identical values for the dynamical parameter, even though the former is looser. Curiously, the solution from zero-temperature EM (q_{MAP}) is also identical to those solutions. One of the conclusions from this is that most severe approximation need not necessarily yield the most biased parameter estimates.

5.4.4   Learning the observation noise, σ_y^2, and the dynamical noise, σ_x^2

Next we consider learning the observation noise σ_y^2, with the other parameters fixed to their true values. Once again, in order to ensure that the effects of explaining away are properly considered we set $\mathbf{w}_1 = \mathbf{w}_2$ and $|\mathbf{w}_k|^2 = 1$.

Decreasing the observation noise increases the correlation between variables at the same time step, i.e., between x_{1t} and x_{2t}. This means that q_{FC}, which factors over chains, becomes worse as σ_y^2 decreases, and therefore KL$_{\text{FC}}$ is an increasing function of σ_y^2.

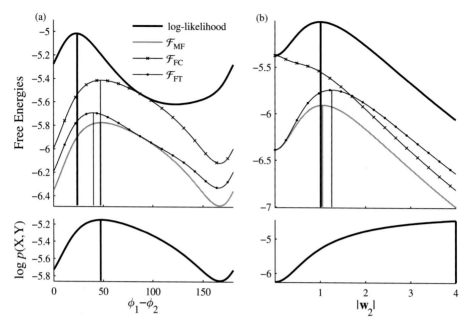

Figure 5.5 Biases in the free-energies for learning the weights of a simple linear dynamical system. The true parameters are $\lambda = 0.9$, $\sigma_x^2 = 1 - \lambda^2 = 0.19$, $\mathbf{w}_1^T = [1, 0]$, $\mathbf{w}_2^T = [\cos(\pi/8), \sin(\pi/8)]$ and $\sigma_y^2 = 0.3$. In both columns, (a) and (b), one parameter is learned and the others are set to their true values. (a) Learning the orientation (ϕ_2) of the second weight, $\mathbf{w}_2^T = [\cos(\phi_2), \sin(\phi_2)]$. (b) Learning the magnitude of the second weight, $\mathbf{w}_2^T = |\mathbf{w}_2|[\cos(\pi/8), \sin(\pi/8)]$. Large panels show the log-likelihood (thick black line) and the free-energies of the uncertainty preserving methods ($\mathcal{F}_{MF}$ by a thick grey line, $\mathcal{F}_{FC}$ by the crosses, and $\mathcal{F}_{FT}$ by the circles). Small panels show the zero-temperature EM approach (q_{MAP}). The maxima of these functions are indicated by the vertical lines. The maximum of the log-likelihood lies at the true value of the parameters.

On the other hand, as the observation process becomes less noisy the hidden states are more precisely determined by local information, and so correlations between them in the prior become less important. Thus q_{FT}, which factorises over time but not over chains, becomes tighter as σ_y^2 decreases, i.e. KL_{FT} is a decreasing function of σ_y^2. We have therefore established that KL_{FC} and KL_{FT} have opposite dependencies on σ_y^2. As the mean-field approximation shares both of these effects its maximum lies somewhere between the two, depending on the settings of the parameters. This means that whilst q_{FT} under-estimates the observation noise, and q_{FC} over-estimates it, the loosest approximation of the three, the mean-field approximation, can actually provide the best estimate, as its peak lies in between the two. In the next section we will characterise the parameter regime over which this occurs.

The final approximation scheme, zero-temperature EM, behaves catastrophically when it is used to learn the observation noise, σ_y^2. This is caused by a narrow spike in the likelihood-surface at $\sigma_y^2 = 0$. At this point the latent variables arrange themselves to explain the data perfectly, and so there is no likelihood penalty (of the sort $-\frac{1}{2\sigma_y^2}(y_{1,t} - x_{1,t} - x_{2,t})^2$). In turn, this means the noise variance can be shrunk to zero which maximises the remaining terms ($\propto -\log \sigma_y^2$). The small cost picked up from violating the prior-dynamics is no match for this infinity. This is not a very useful solution from either the perspective of learning or inference. It is a pathological example of overfitting:[5] there is an infinitesimal region of the likelihood-posterior surface with an infinite peak. By integrating over the latent variables, even if only approximately in a variational method for example, such peaks are discounted, as they are associated with negligible probability mass and so make only a small contribution to the integral. Thus, although variational methods often do not preserve as much uncertainty information as we would like, and are often biased, by recovering means and not modes they may still provide better parameter estimates than the catastrophic zero-temperature EM approach.

Finally we note that learning the dynamical noise σ_x^2 with the other parameters fixed at their true values results in a very similar situation: q_{FC} under-estimates σ_x^2, and q_{FT} over-estimates it, while the mean-field approximation returns a value in between. Once again the MAP solution suffers from an overfitting problem whereby the inferred value of σ_x^2 is driven to zero. The fact that learning σ_y^2 and σ_x^2 results in similar effects indicates that the conclusions drawn from these examples are quite general.

5.4.5 Learning the magnitude and direction of one emission weight

Finally we consider learning the emission weights. In order to explicate the various factors at work it is useful to separately consider learning the orientation of the weight vector and its magnitude. Consider first learning the orientation of one of the weights whilst its magnitude, and the value of the other parameters in the model, are known and fixed to their true values (shown in Fig. 5.5). The relative orientation of the pair of weights is the critical quantity, because this determines the amount of explaining away. If the weights are orthogonal ($\phi_1 - \phi_2 = \pi(n+1/2)$), there is no explaining away ($\langle x_{1t} x_{2t} \rangle_{p(x|y)} = 0$), and so q_{FC} is exact and q_{MF} and q_{FT} are equivalent. In contrast, if the weights are parallel ($\phi_1 - \phi_2 = n\pi$), explaining away is maximised and q_{MF} and q_{FC} are at their loosest because they do not model the dependencies between the chains. In this region q_{FT} is also at its loosest (because it does not capture the 'diagonal' correlations $\langle x_{11} x_{22} \rangle_{p(x|y)}$ and $\langle x_{21} x_{12} \rangle_{p(x|y)}$ which are strongest here). The result is that all the approximations are biased toward settings of the weights which are more orthogonal than the true setting. The bias in q_{MF}, q_{FC} and q_{MAP} are equal and can be substantial (see Fig. 5.5 and Fig. 5.6). The bias in q_{FT} is somewhat less as it captures the correlations induced by explaining away.

Finally, we consider learning the magnitude of the second weight when all other parameters are set to their true values (this includes the direction of the second weight). For low magnitudes, q_{FC} is tightest as the temporal correlations dominate over explaining away, but for high magnitudes the situation is reversed and q_{FT} is tightest. Consequently, q_{FC} under-estimates the magnitudes (often severely thereby pruning the weight entirely, see Fig. 5.5(b)), whilst q_{FT} over-estimates the magnitudes. As the mean-field approximation suffers from both effects, its estimates lie between the two and can therefore be less biased. Once again the MAP solution suffers from an over-fitting problem, where the estimated weight magnitudes blow up to infinity.

5.4.6 Characterising the space of solutions

In the previous section we found examples where the mean-field approximation was the most unbiased (see Fig. 5.4(b) and Fig. 5.5(b)). How typical is this scenario? To answer this question we look at the extent of the bias in parameter values returned by the four approximate learning schemes, over a wide range of different datasets with different true parameter values. As the likelihood or free-energy surfaces may be multimodal – and we are

---

[5]This is the SSM analogue to Mackay's (2003) so-called KABOOM! problem in soft K-means.

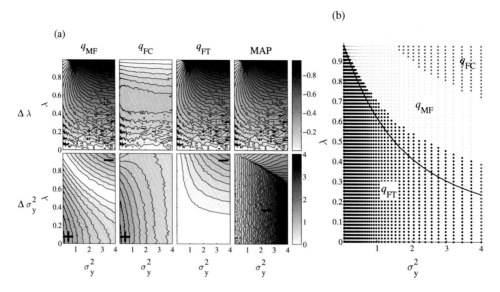

Figure 5.6 (a) Biases in inferring a single parameter as a function of σ_y^2 and λ. Lighter colours indicate a bias of smaller magnitude. The bias is defined as $\Delta\Theta = \Theta_{INF} - \Theta_{ML}$ so that over-estimation results in a positive bias. For all points, $\sigma_x^2 = 1 - \lambda^2$. The columns correspond to the four approximations. Top Row: Bias in estimating λ. All the schemes return underestimates and so the biases are always negative. Bottom Row: Bias in estimating σ_y^2. The sign of the bias is indicated by the '+' and '−' symbols. (b) The best approximation for finding σ_y^2 indicated by marker-type (q_{MF} grey filled-circles, q_{FC} black crosses and q_{FT} black open-circles). The black solid line is $r = \sigma_x^2/|\lambda|\sigma_y^2 = 1$. Below r q_{FT} is tightest, while above r q_{FC} is tightest.

not interested here in failures of learning due to local optima – the optimal parameters were found using three different optimisation schemes: grid-based search; direct gradient ascent on the free-energy; and coordinate ascent of the free-energy (or vEM). For the examples of this section, all three methods returned identical results up to experimental error.

One typical example – the bias in inferring λ for many different maximum-likelihood settings of σ_y^2 and λ – appears in Fig. 5.6(a,top row). In each case σ_x^2 was set to its true value, $1 - \lambda^2$. The parameter λ is under-estimated in all cases, often substantially (e.g. for q_{MF}, q_{FT} and q_{MAP}, at high σ_y^2 and λ values, the bias is almost one). The bias of q_{FC} is always smaller than that of the other approximations, and thus in this case it is to be preferred everywhere. However, this simple situation where one of the approximation schemes is universally superior does not generalise when learning other parameters. For example, the bias in inferring σ_y^2 is shown in Fig. 5.6(a, bottom row). As noted in the previous section, q_{FC} over-estimates the observation noise, whilst q_{FT} and q_{MAP} under-estimate it. The mean-field approximation combines the behaviours of q_{FC} and q_{FT} and therefore under-estimates in regions where λ and σ_y^2 are small, and over-estimates in regions where λ and σ_y^2 are large. In the intermediate region, these effects cancel and this is the region in which the mean-field approximation is the best approximation. This is shown in Fig. 5.6(b) which indicates the best approximation to use for inferring the observation noise in different parts of the space. The figure shows that the mean-field solution is to be preferred over a fairly large part of the space.

Next we consider biases in estimating the weight vectors (see Fig. 5.7). When learning the vector orientations, q_{MF}, q_{FC} and q_{MAP} turn out to exhibit identical biases. (Indeed, it is generally true that if the MAP solution does not suffer from over-fitting, then it is equal

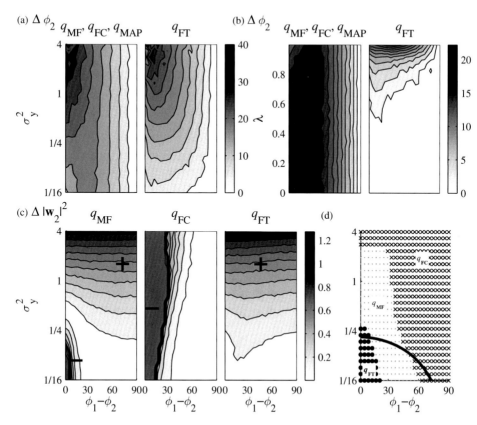

Figure 5.7 Parameter dependence of the biases in learning the weights. (a) Biases in learning the relative orientation ($\Delta\phi$) of the weights as a function of the true relative orientation ($\phi_1 - \phi_2$) and the observation noise σ_y^2. The magnitude of the weights is unity, $|\mathbf{w}_k| = 1$, and the dynamical parameters are set to $\lambda = 0.9$ and $\sigma_x^2 = 1 - \lambda^2$. All of the approximations over-estimate the angular separation of the weights, but q_{FT} is less or equally biased everywhere. (b) Biases in learning the relative orientation of the weights as a function of the true orientation ($\phi_1 - \phi_2$) and the dynamical parameter, λ. The observation noise is fixed to $\sigma_y^2 = 0.1$ and the state-noise to $\sigma_x^2 = 1 - \lambda^2$. In this case too q_{FT} is less or equally biased everywhere. (c) Biases in learning the magnitude of the second weight as a function of the true relative orientation ($\phi_1 - \phi_2$) and the observation noise. The other parameters are set to, $\lambda = 0.9$ and $\sigma_x^2 = 1 - \lambda^2$. The MAP estimate q_{MAP} returns an infinite value for the weights everywhere and is therefore not shown. (d) The least biased approximation for finding the magnitude of the weight (indicated by marker-type; q_{MF} grey filled-circles, q_{FC} black crosses and q_{FT} black open-circles) as a function of the relative orientation of the weights and the observation noise. Above the solid line q_{FC} is the tighter approximation, whilst below it q_{FT} is the tighter approximation.

to the mean-field approximation in these Gaussian models.) These approximations do not model explaining away and thus they are most biased in regions where the true weights are approximately parallel ($\phi_1 \approx \phi_2$). On the other hand, q_{FT} does capture inter-chain correlations, and thus is superior for any setting of the true parameters.[6] When learning the weight vector magnitudes, q_{FT} is superior in regions where explaining away is large compared to the temporal correlations, whilst q_{FC} is superior in regions where temporal correlations

---

[6]It is common practice to use zero-temperature EM (q_{MAP}) to learn weights in sparse-coding models and then to make a detailed statistical comparison of the learned weights to biological analogues derived from experiments in visual cortex. The result here – that zero-temperature EM recovers weights which are significantly more orthogonal than the true weights – raises concerns that this practice is seriously affected by biases in the learned weights.

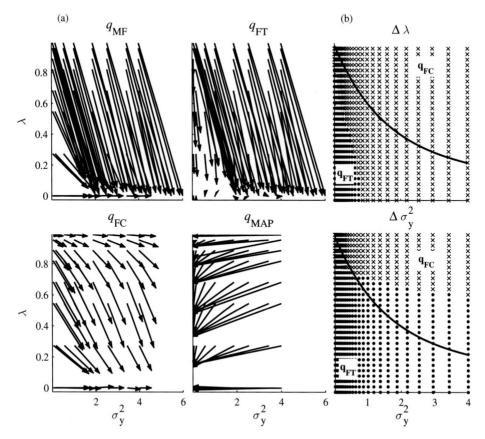

Figure 5.8 Simultaneous inference of λ and σ_y^2 with biases shown as a function of the true settings of the parameters. (a) For each approximation a number of simulations are run and each is represented by an arrow. The arrow begins at the true setting of the parameters and the tip ends at the inferred value. Ideally the arrows would be very short, but in fact they are often very large. (b) The best uncertainty preserving approximation ($\{q_{MF}, q_{FC}, q_{FT}\}$) for finding λ (top) and σ_y^2 (bottom) indicated by marker-type (q_{MF} is never superior, q_{FC} black crosses and q_{FT} black open-circles). The black solid line is $r = \sigma_x^2/|\lambda|\sigma_y^2 = 1$ and below it q_{FT} is tightest, and above it q_{FC} is tightest.

dominate over explaining away. However, there is a large intermediate region where the mean-field approximation is the least biased. Once again, the tightness of the free-energy approximations is a poor indicator of which is the least biased.

The main conclusions from this section are that the biases in variational methods are often severe. The examples above indicate that factorisations across time can ignore strong temporal correlations in the data, and factorisations across chains can erroneously prune out emission weights. Furthermore, which is the best approximation depends not only on which parameter has to be learned, but also on the true value of the parameters. Surprisingly, mean-field approximations are often superior to structured methods when a single parameter is estimated.

5.4.7   Simultaneous learning of pairs of parameters

So far we have considered estimating a single parameter keeping the others at their true values. What happens when we infer pairs of parameters at once? Consider, for instance, inferring the dynamical parameter λ and the observation noise σ_y^2 with σ_x^2 held at its true value (see Fig. 5.8). As before, three methods are used to find the optimal parameter settings (gridding, gradient ascent and vEM). In this case, a small minority of the objective functions is multimodal, thus the agreement between the methods depends on the initialisation. To avoid this ambiguity, the gradient-based methods were initialised at the values returned from the method of gridding the space. This procedure located the global optima.

The most striking feature of Fig. 5.8(a) is that the biases are often very large (even in regimes where the structural approximations are at their tightest). In principle, if the mapping between the inferred parameters and true parameters were known, it might be possible to correct for the biases in the variational estimates. However, multiple different settings of the true parameters result in the same inferred parameters. Therefore it is impossible to correct the variational estimates in this way.

Fig. 5.8(b) shows that, in contrast to the case where only one parameter is inferred at a time, the mean-field solution is no longer superior to the structural approximations. It also indicates that whilst tightness is a guide for choosing the best approximation, it is not very accurate. It is also notable that, when all three parameters are inferred together (data not shown), the biases become even larger.

5.4.8 Discussion of the scope of the results

The examples considered in this chapter were chosen to be simple so that exact results could be computed and visualised. It is necessary, however to analyse how the effects described here generalise to longer time series ($T > 2$) with more hidden variables ($K > 2$). Unfortunately, it is generally not tractable to analyse these, more complex, scenarios. However, increasing the length of the time series and the number of latent chains results in a posterior distribution that has a richer correlational structure. That is, the posterior covariance matrix has a greater number of off-diagonal terms. The variational approximations considered here would therefore ignore larger parts of this structure, and so one might expect the KL terms and the associated biases to be correspondingly larger.

There are many ways of assessing the performance of vEM. This chapter has focused exclusively on the consistency of the methods and the biases in the learned parameters. However, another relevant set of criteria come from tasks which require prediction of some kind, for instance, to fill in missing data or to denoise. How does vEM fare in this new scenario? In order to answer this question it is necessary to specify the task more accurately. Consider a task in which the first stage involves learning the model parameters from a training set, and the second involves filling in a section of missing data in a test set using the mean of the approximate posterior. Given the same set of parameters, all four approximations will make identical predictions for the missing section (the mean of the true posterior). The differences between the approximations are therefore entirely dependent on the quality of the parameters learned during the first stage of the experiments. As the task requires accurate learning of both the temporal dynamics (to predict the missing latent variables) and the emission weights (to predict the missing data from the missing latent variables), all the approximation schemes will perform poorly compared to the optimal prediction.

5.5 Conclusion

We have discussed two problems in the application of vEM to time series models. First, the compactness property of variational inference leads to a failure in propagating posterior uncertainty through time. Second, the dependence of the tightness of the variational lower bound on the model parameters often leads to strong biases in parameter estimates. We found that the relative bias of different approximations depends not only on which parameter is sought, but also on its true value. Moreover, the tightest bound does not always yield the smallest bias: in some cases, structured approximations are more biased than the mean-field approach. Variational methods, however, avoid the over-fitting problem which plagues MAP estimation. Despite the shortcomings, variational methods remain a valid, efficient alternative to computationally expensive Markov chain Monte Carlo methods. However, the choice of the variational distribution should be complemented with an analysis of the dependency of the variational bound on the model parameters. Hopefully, these examples will inspire new algorithms that pool different variational approximations in order to achieve better performance [7].

Acknowledgments We thank David Mackay for inspiration. This research was supported by the Gatsby Charitable Foundation.

Bibliography

[1] M. J. Beal. Variational Algorithms for approximate Bayesian Inference. PhD thesis, University College London, May 1998.

[2] C. Bishop. *Pattern Recognition and Machine Learning*. Springer, 2006.

[3] S. Boyd and L. Vandenberghe. *Convex Optimization*. Cambridge University Press, March 2004.

[4] A. P. Dempster. Maximum-likelihood from incomplete data via the EM algorithm. *Journal of the Royal Statistical Society*, **39**(1):1–38, 1977.

[5] R. Hathaway. Another interpretation of the EM algorithm for mixture distributions. *Statistics and Probability Letters*, **4**:53–56, 1986.

[6] T. Jaakkola and M. Jordan. Bayesian parameter estimation via variational methods. *Statistics and Computing*, **10**(1): 25–37, January 2000.

[7] T. S. Jaakkola and M. I. Jordan. Improving the mean field approximation via the use of mixture distributions. In *Learning in Graphical Models*, pages 163–173. MIT Press, 1999.

[8] M. I. Jordan, Z. Ghahramani, T. S. Jaakkola and L. K. Saul. An introduction to variational methods for graphical models. *Machine Learning*, **37**(2):183–233, 1999.

[9] D. J. C. MacKay. A problem with variational free energy minimization. 2001.

[10] D. J. C. MacKay. *Information Theory, Inference, and Learning Algorithms*. Cambridge University Press, 2003. available from www.inference.phy.cam.ac.uk/mackay/itila/.

[11] R. Neal and G. E. Hinton. A view of the EM algorithm that justifies incremental, sparse, and other variants. In *Learning in Graphical Models*, pages 355–368. Kluwer Academic Publishers, 1998.

[12] R. E. Turner, P. Berkes, M. Sahani and D. J. C. MacKay. Counter-examples to variational free-energy compactness folk theorems. Technical report, University College London, 2008.

[13] B. Wang and D. M. Titterington. Lack of consistency of mean field and variational Bayes approximations for state space models. *Neural Processing Letters*, **20**(3):151–170, 2004.

[14] J. Winn and T. Minka. Expectation propagation and variational message passing: a comparison with infer.net. In *Neural Information Processing Systems Workshop: Inference in continuous and hybrid models*, 2007.

Contributors

Richard Eric Turner, Gatsby Computational Neuroscience Unit, Alexandra House, 17 Queen Square, London WCIN 3A

Maneesh Sahani, Gatsby Computational Neuroscience Unit, Alexandra House, 17 Queen Square, London WCIN 3A

6

Approximate inference for continuous-time Markov processes

Cédric Archambeau and Manfred Opper

6.1   Introduction

Markov processes are probabilistic models for describing data with a sequential structure. Probably the most common example is a dynamical system, of which the state evolves over time. For modelling purposes it is often convenient to assume that the system states are not directly observed: each observation is a possibly incomplete, non-linear and noisy measurement (or transformation) of the underlying hidden state. In general, observations of the system occur only at discrete times, while the underlying system is inherently continuous in time. Continuous-time Markov processes arise in a variety of scientific areas such as physics, environmental modelling, finance, engineering and systems biology.

The continuous-time evolution of the system imposes strong constraints on the model dynamics. For example, the individual trajectories of a diffusion process are rough, but the mean trajectory is a smooth function of time. Unfortunately, this information is often under- or unexploited when devising practical systems. The main reason is that inferring the state trajectories and the model parameters is a difficult problem as trajectories are infinite-dimensional objects. Hence, a practical approach usually requires some sort of approximation. For example, Markov chain Monte Carlo (MCMC) methods usually discretise time [41, 16, 34, 2, 20], while particle filters approximate continuous densities by a finite number of point masses [13, 14, 15]. More recently, approaches using perfect simulation have been proposed [7, 8, 18]. The main advantage of these MCMC techniques is that they do not require approximations of the transition density using time discretisations. Finally, a variety of approaches like extensions to the Kalman filter/smoother [38] and moment closure methods [17] express the statistics of state variables by a finite set of moments, for example based on Gaussian assumptions.

In this chapter we discuss a promising variational approach to the inference problem for continuous-time Markov processes, which was introduced by [3, 4]. We will focus on diffusion processes, where the system state is a continuous variable subject to a deterministic forcing, called *drift*, and a stochastic noise process, called *diffusion*. However, the approach can also be applied to other processes, such as Markov jump processes (MJPs) [31, 11, 37]. In MJPs the state trajectories are still continuous-time functions, but the system state can only take discrete values. For diffusions, the approach is based on a Gaussian approximation, but as in perfect simulation MCMC, it is not based on a discrete-time approximation of the transition density. The approximate statistics are made not ad hoc as in the case of the

Kalman filter/smoother, but introduced in such a way that the true intractable probability measure is optimally approximated.

This chapter is organised as follows. In Section 6.2 we define partly observed diffusion processes and state the inference problem. In Section 6.3 we characterise the probability measure over state trajectories given the data and show that the resulting posterior process is a non-stationary Markov process. In Section 6.4 we introduce the variational approximation and show how this approach can be applied to Markov processes and in particular to diffusions. Note, however, that unlike in most variational approaches we do not assume any form of factorised approximation. In Section 6.5, we consider a practical smoothing algorithm based on the Gaussian variational approximation and discuss the form of the solution in more detail. Finally, we draw conclusions in Section 6.8.

6.2 Partly observed diffusion processes

We will be concerned with (Itô) stochastic differential equations (SDEs), where the dynamics of a state variable $x(t) \in R^d$ is given by

$$\mathrm{d}x(t) = f(x(t))\mathrm{d}t + D^{1/2}(x(t)) \, \mathrm{d}W(t). \tag{6.1}$$

The vector function f is called the drift. The second term describes a (in general state-dependent) white noise process defined through a positive semi-definite matrix D, called diffusion matrix, and a Wiener process $W(t)$. We can think of this process as the limit of the discrete-time process

$$x(t + \Delta t) - x(t) = f(x(t))\Delta t + D^{1/2}(x(t)) \sqrt{\Delta t} \, \epsilon_t, \tag{6.2}$$

where ϵ_t is now a vector of iid Gaussian random variables. The specific scaling of the white noise with $\sqrt{\Delta t}$ gives rise to the nondifferentiable trajectories of *sample paths* characteristic for a diffusion process [23, 25, 29]. Equation (6.2) is known as the Euler–Maruyama approximation of Eq. (6.1).

We assume the diffusion process is stationary, i.e. f and D are not explicit functions of time, although this is not required. We have only access to a finite set of noisy observations $Y \equiv \{y_i\}_{i=1}^N$ of the unobserved process $x(t)$ at times t_i for $i = 1, \ldots, N$. Conditioned on the state x we assume that observations are independent with an observation likelihood $p(y|x)$. We are interested in the problem where f and D are known only up to some unknown parameters θ. It is usually necessary to add the unknown initial state $x(0) = x_0$ to the parameters.

Our goals are then to learn as much as possible from the observations in order to infer the system parameters θ, the initial state x_0 and to estimate the unknown sample path $x(t)$ over some interval $0 \leq t \leq T$. The latter task (when all observations during this time are used) is called *smoothing*.

In a maximum likelihood approach (or more precisely type II maximum likelihood [6] or evidence maximisation [28, 9]) one would solve the first two problems by integrating out the latent process $x(t)$ and then maximising the marginal likelihood $p(Y|x_0, \theta)$ with respect to θ and x_0. In a fully Bayesian approach, one would encode prior knowledge in a prior density $p(x_0, \theta)$ and would obtain the information about the unknowns in the posterior density $p(x_0, \theta|Y) \propto p(Y|x_0, \theta) \, p(x_0, \theta)$. In both cases, the computation of $p(Y|x_0, \theta)$ is essential, but in general analytically intractable.

6.3 Hidden Markov characterisation

Let us first assume the parameters are known. To deal with the reconstruction of a sample path we compute $p_t(x|Y, x_0, \theta)$, which is the marginal posterior of the state at time t, i.e. $x(t) = x$. This marginal can be computed in the same way as the marginals of standard discrete-time hidden Markov models [33]. The only difference is that we have to deal with continuous-time and continuous states.

Using the Markov nature of the process[1] and Bayes' rule it is not hard to show that we can represent this posterior as a product of two factors

$$p_t(x|Y, x_0, \theta) \propto \underbrace{p(x(t)|Y_{<t}, x_0, \theta)}_{\doteq p_t^{(F)}(x)} \underbrace{p(Y_{\geq t}|x(t))}_{\doteq \psi_t(x)},$$

where $p_t^{(F)}(x)$ is the posterior density of $x(t) = x$ based on the observations $Y_{<t} \equiv \{y_i\}_{t_i < t}$ before time t and $\psi_t(x)$ is the likelihood of the future observations $Y_{\geq t} = \{y_i\}_{t_i \geq t}$ conditioned on $x(t) = x$.

For times smaller than the next observation time $p_t^{(F)}(x)$ fulfils the *Fokker–Planck* (or *Kolmogorov forward*) *equation* [23] corresponding to the SDE defined in Eq. (6.1)

$$\left\{ \frac{\partial}{\partial t} + \nabla^{\top} f - \frac{1}{2} \text{Tr}(\nabla \nabla^{\top}) D \right\} p_t^{(F)}(x) = 0, \tag{6.3}$$

where ∇ is the vector differential operator. The Fokker–Planck equation describes the time evolution of the density $p_t^{(F)}(x)$ given some earlier density, e.g. at the most recent observation time.

The second factor is found to obey the *Kolmogorov backward equation* corresponding to the SDE defined in Eq. (6.1), that is

$$\left\{ \frac{\partial}{\partial t} + f^{\top} \nabla + \frac{1}{2} \text{Tr}(D \nabla \nabla^{\top}) \right\} \psi_t(x) = 0. \tag{6.4}$$

This equation describes the time evolution of $\psi_t(x)$, i.e. the likelihood of future observations. The knowledge of $\psi_t(x)$ also gives us the desired marginal likelihood as

$$p(Y|x_0, \theta) = \psi_0(x).$$

Equations (6.3) and (6.4) hold for times between observations. The information about the observations enters the formalism through a set of jump conditions for $p_t^{(F)}$ and $\psi_t(x)$ at the observation times. This result is known as the so-called *KSP equations* [26, 42, 32].

Intuitively, the occurrence of jumps can be understood as follows. Assume we are moving forward in time up to time t, where we encounter the observation $y(t)$. The information associated to y_t is removed from $\psi_t(x)$ and incorporated into $p_t^{(F)}(x)$. Mathematically, the

---

[1] More specifically, we need the *Chapman–Kolmogorov equation* to compute $p_t(x|Y_{<t}, x_0, \theta)$. By the Markov property we have $p(x(t)|x(s), x(r)) = p(x(t)|x(s))$, such that

$$\int dx(s) \, p(x(t), x(s)|x(r)) = \int dx(s) \, p(x(t)|x(s)) \, p(x(s)|x(r)) = p(x(t)|x(r)),$$

for all $r \leq s \leq t$. Hence, using this result recursively and then applying Bayes' rule leads to

$$p(x(t)|Y_{<t}, x_0, \theta) \propto p(x(t)|x_0, \theta) \, p(Y_{<t}|x(t)).$$

'prior' $p_t^{(F)}(x)$ is updated using the likelihood factor $p(y(t)|x(t))$ causing jumps in $p_t^{(F)}(x)$ and $\psi_t(x)$ at time t

$$p_t^{(F)}(x) \leftarrow \frac{1}{Z} p_t^{(F)}(x) \, p(y(t)|x(t)), \tag{6.5}$$

$$\psi_t(x) \leftarrow \frac{\psi_t(x)}{p(y(t)|x(t))}, \tag{6.6}$$

where Z is a normalising constant. Moreover, by direct differentiation of $p_t(x|Y, x_0, \theta)$ with respect to time and using Eqs. (6.3) and (6.4), we find after some calculations that the posterior also fulfils the Fokker–Planck equation

$$\left\{ \frac{\partial}{\partial t} + \nabla^\top g - \frac{1}{2} \mathrm{Tr}(\nabla\nabla^\top)D \right\} p_t(x|Y, x_0, \theta) = 0, \tag{6.7}$$

with a new drift defined as

$$g(x, t) = f(x) + D(x)\nabla \ln \psi_t(x). \tag{6.8}$$

This shouldn't be too surprising because conditioning on the observations does not change the causal structure of the process $x(t)$. It is still a Markov process, but a non-stationary one due to the observations. Note that there are no jumps for $p_t(x|Y, x_0, \theta)$ as it is equal to the product of Eqs. (6.5) and (6.6).

Hence, the process of exact inference boils down to solving the linear partial differential equation (PDE) (6.4) backwards in time starting with the final condition $\psi_T(x)$ and taking the jumps $\psi_{t_i^-}(x) = \psi_{t_i}(x)p(y_i|x_i)$ into account to get the function $\psi_t(x)$ from which both the likelihood $p(Y|x_0, \theta)$ and the posterior drift (6.8) are obtained. Finally, the posterior marginals are computed by solving the linear PDE (6.7) forwards in time for some initial condition $p_0^{(F)}(x)$.

6.3.1 Example

As an analytically tractable one-dimensional example we consider the simple Wiener process $dx(t) = dW(t)$ starting at $x(0) = 0$ together with a single, noise-free observation at $t = T$, i.e. $x(T) = y$. The forward equation

$$\frac{\partial p_t^{(F)}(x)}{\partial t} - \frac{1}{2} \frac{\partial^2 p_t^{(F)}(x)}{\partial x^2} = 0$$

with initial condition $p_0^{(F)}(x) = \delta(x)$ is solved by $p_t^{(F)}(x) = \mathcal{N}(0, t)$, while the backward equation

$$\frac{\partial \psi_t(x)}{\partial t} + \frac{1}{2} \frac{\partial^2 \psi_t(x)}{\partial x^2} = 0$$

with end condition $\psi_T(x) = \delta(x - y)$ is solved by $\psi_t(x) = \mathcal{N}(y, T - t)$. The posterior density and the posterior drift are then respectively given by

$$p_t(x|x(T) = y, x(0) = 0) \propto p_t^{(F)}(x) \, \psi_t(x) = \mathcal{N}(ty/T, t(T - t)/T), \tag{6.9}$$

$$g(x, t) = \frac{\partial \ln \psi_t(x)}{\partial x} = \frac{y - x}{T - t}, \tag{6.10}$$

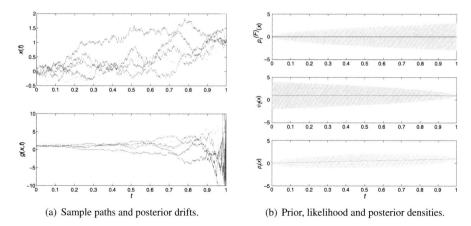

(a) Sample paths and posterior drifts.   (b) Prior, likelihood and posterior densities.

Figure 6.1 Illustration of a one-dimensional diffusion process without drift and unit diffusion coefficient, starting at the origin and with a noise free observation $y = 1$ at $t = 1$. The posterior process is a Brownian bridge. Note how the drift increases drastically when getting close to the final time. (a) shows five sample paths with their corresponding posterior drift functions. (b) shows the mean and variance (shaded region) of the prior, the likelihood and the posterior marginals. Observe how the variance of the posterior $p_t(x)$ is largest in the middle of the time interval and eventually decreases to 0 at $t = 1$. See plate section for colour version.

for $0 < t < T$. A process with drift (6.10) is known as a *Brownian bridge* (see Fig. 6.1). Inspection of Eq. (6.9) shows that any path of the process starting at the origin and diffusing away will eventually go to the noise-free observation y at time T.

In general, especially in higher dimensions, the solution of the PDEs will not be analytically tractable. Also numerical methods for PDE solving [25] might become too time consuming. Hence, we may have to consider other types of approximations. One such possibility will be discussed next.

6.4 The variational approximation

A different idea for solving the inference problem might be to attempt a direct computation of the marginal likelihood or *partition function* $Z(x_0, \theta) \doteq p(Y|x_0, \theta)$. Using the Markov property of the process $x(t)$ we obtain

$$Z(x_0, \theta) = \int \prod_{i=1}^{N} \{ \mathrm{d}x_i \, p\,(x_i|x_{i-1}, \theta) \, p(y_i|x_i)\},$$

where x_i is a shorthand notation for $x(t_i)$ and x_0 is fixed. Unfortunately, except for simple linear SDEs, the transition density $p(x_i|x_{i-1}, \theta)$ is not known analytically. In fact it would have to be computed by solving the Fokker–Planck equation (6.3).

Nevertheless, at least formally we can write Z as an *infinite-dimensional* or functional integral over paths $x(t)$ starting at x_0 using a proper weighting of the paths. Using the Girsanov change of measure formula from stochastic calculus [29] one could write such a path integral as

$$Z = \int \mathrm{d}\mu \exp\left(-\frac{1}{2}\int_0^T \{f^\top D^{-1} f \mathrm{d}t - 2f^\top D^{-1} \mathrm{d}x\}\right) \prod_{i=1}^{N} p(y_i|x_i),$$

where $\mathrm{d}\mu$ denotes a Gaussian measure over paths starting at $x(0) = x_0$ induced by the simple *linear* SDE $\mathrm{d}x(t) = D^{1/2}(x(t)) \, \mathrm{d}W(t)$ without drift. Note that, in the case of a diagonal diffusion matrix and a drift derived from a potential, the Itô integral $\int f^\top D^{-1} dx$ can be transformed into an ordinary integral. These types of functional integrals play an important role in quantum statistical physics (usually written in a slightly different notation). Most functional integrals cannot be solved exactly, but the variational approach of statistical physics pioneered by Feynman, Peierls, Bogolubov and Kleinert [19, 24] gives us an idea on how to approximate Z.

Consider some configuration χ of the system of interest. In our application χ is identified with the path $x(t)$ in the time window $[0, T]$. We can represent the probabilities over configurations in the form $dp(\chi) = \frac{1}{Z} d\mu(\chi) e^{-H(\chi)}$, where $H(\chi) = \frac{1}{2} \int_0^T \{ f^\top D^{-1} f dt - 2 f^\top D^{-1} dx \} - \sum_{i=1}^N \ln p(y_i | x_i)$ is the *Hamiltonian*, which in statistical physics corresponds to the energy associated to the configuration. To compute an approximation to the partition function $Z = \int d\mu(\chi) \, e^{-H(\chi)}$, we first approximate $dp(\chi)$ by a simpler distribution $dq(\chi) = \frac{1}{Z_0} d\mu(\chi) \, e^{-H_0(\chi)}$, which is defined by a simpler Hamiltonian $H_0(\chi)$ and for which Z_0 is tractable. Using a simple convexity argument and *Jensen's inequality*, we get an approximation to the log partition function or *free-energy* by the bound

$$-\ln Z \le -\ln Z_0 + \langle H \rangle - \langle H_0 \rangle, \tag{6.11}$$

where the brackets denote expectations with respect to the measure q. Usually H_0 contains free parameters, which can be adjusted in such a way that the inequality becomes as tight as possible by minimising the upper bound on the right-hand side.

To define a tractable variational approximation (6.11) for our inference problem, we would use an H_0 which is quadratic functional in the process $x(t)$. This would lead to a Gaussian measure over paths. While this is indeed possible we prefer a different, but equivalent formulation of the variational method, which neither needs the definition of a Hamiltonian, nor the application of stochastic calculus. The variational method in this formulation has been extensively applied in recent years in machine learning to problems involving finite-dimensional latent variables [22, 30, 10].

6.4.1 The variational approximation in machine learning

Let us denote the observations by Y and assume a finite-dimensional latent variable X. Consider some prior distribution $p(X|\theta)$ parameterised by θ and some likelihood function $p(Y|X)$. To approximate the intractable posterior $p(X|Y, \theta) \propto p(Y|X) \, p(X|\theta)$ we directly choose a simpler trial distribution $q(X)$. The optimal q is chosen to minimise the *Kullback–Leibler* (KL) *divergence* or relative entropy [12]

$$\mathrm{KL}[q \| p] = \left\langle \ln \frac{q(X)}{p(X|Y, \theta)} \right\rangle \ge 0.$$

This inequality directly leads to the bound

$$-\ln Z(\theta) \le -\langle \ln p(Y|X) \rangle + \mathrm{KL}[q(X) \| p(X|\theta)] \doteq \mathcal{F}(q, \theta). \tag{6.12}$$

The right-hand side of Eq. (6.12) defines the so-called *variational free-energy* which is an upper bound to the marginal likelihood of the data. Hence, minimising such a bound with respect to the parameters θ can be viewed as an approximation to the (type II) maximum likelihood method.

One can also apply the variational method in a Bayesian setting, where we have a prior distribution $p(\theta)$ over model parameters [27]. To approximate the posterior $p(\theta|Y)$, we set

$p(X, \theta|Y) \approx q(X|\theta)q(\theta)$ and apply the variational method to the joint space of variables X and θ. Let $q(X|\theta)$ be the distribution which minimises the variational free-energy $\mathcal{F}(q, \theta)$ of Eq. (6.12). We then get

$$q(\theta) = \frac{e^{-\mathcal{F}(q,\theta)} \, p(\theta)}{\int e^{-\mathcal{F}(q,\theta)} \, p(\theta) \, d\theta}$$

as the best variational approximation to $p(\theta|Y)$.

6.4.2 The variational approximation for Markov processes

In the case of partly observed diffusion processes we are interested in the posterior measure over latent paths, which are infinite-dimensional objects. The prior measure $p(\chi|x_0, \theta)$ is derived from an SDE of the form (6.1) and the posterior measure $p(\chi|Y, x_0, \theta)$ is computed from Bayes' rule

$$\frac{p(\chi|Y, x_0, \theta)}{p(\chi|x_0, \theta)} = \frac{\prod_{i=1}^{N} p(y_i|x_i)}{Z(x_0, \theta)}, \qquad 0 \le t \le T.$$

When the exact posterior is analytically intractable, we consider a trial posterior $q(\chi)$ that we would like to match to the true posterior by applying the variational principle. All we need is an expression for the KL divergence. From Section 6.3, we know that the posterior process is Markovian and obeys an SDE with the time-dependent drift (6.8), that is

$$dx(t) = g(x(t), t)dt + D^{1/2}(x(t)) \, dW(t). \tag{6.13}$$

Consider two continuous-time diffusion processes having the same diffusion matrix $D(x)$,[2] but different drift functions $f(x)$ and $g(x)$. We call the probability measures induced over the corresponding sample paths respectively $p(\chi)$ and $q(\chi)$. Although we could prove the following rigorously using Girsanov's change of measure theorem [23, 29], we will use a simpler, more intuitive heuristic in this chapter which can also be applied to Markov jump processes.

Let us discretise time into small intervals of length Δt and consider discretised sample paths $X = \{x_k = x(t_k = k\Delta t)\}_{k=1}^{K}$ with their corresponding multivariate probabilities $p(X|x_0)$ and $q(X|x_0)$. We aim to compute the KL divergence between the measures dp and dq over some interval $[0, T]$ as the limit of

$$KL\,[q(X)\|p(X)] = \int dX \, q(X|x_0) \ln \frac{q(X|x_0)}{p(X|x_0)}$$

$$= \sum_{k=1}^{K} \int dx_{k-1} \, q(x_{k-1}) \int dx_k \, q(x_k|x_{k-1}) \ln \frac{q(x_k|x_{k-1})}{p(x_k|x_{k-1})},$$

where we have used the Markov property to represent $p(X|x_0)$ and $q(X|x_0)$ respectively as $\prod_k p(x_k|x_{k-1})$ and $\prod_k q(x_k|x_{k-1})$. By plugging in the specific short term behaviour (i.e. $\Delta t \to 0$) of the transition probabilities, since we are dealing with diffusions, we obtain the Gaussian forms

$$p(x_k|x_{k-1}) \propto \exp\left(-\frac{1}{2\Delta t} \|x_k - x_{k-1} - f(x_{k-1})\Delta t\|^2_{D(x_{k-1})}\right),$$

$$q(x_k|x_{k-1}) \propto \exp\left(-\frac{1}{2\Delta t} \|x_k - x_{k-1} - g(x_{k-1})\Delta t\|^2_{D(x_{k-1})}\right),$$

---

[2] It can be shown that the KL divergence diverges for different diffusions matrices.

where $\|f\|_D^2 = f^\top D^{-1} f$. Following [4], a direct computation taking the limit $\Delta t \to 0$ yields

$$\mathrm{KL}\left[q(X)\|p(X)\right] = \frac{1}{2}\int_0^T dt \left\{\int dq_t(x) \; \|g(x) - f(x)\|_{D(x)}^2\right\},$$

where $q_t(x)$ is the posterior marginal at time t. Note that this result is still valid if the drift function and the diffusion matrix are time dependent.

Hence, the variational free-energy in the context of diffusion processes can be written as

$$\mathcal{F}(q,\theta) = \mathrm{KL}[q(\chi)\|p(\chi|\theta)] - \sum_i \langle \ln p(y_i|x_i)\rangle_{q_{t_i}}, \qquad (6.14)$$

where χ is a continuous sample path in the interval $[0, T]$. The bound (6.11) is equivalent to the bound (6.14) for appropriate definitions of Hamiltonians $H(\chi)$ and $H_0(\chi)$. The advantage of the bound (6.14) is that we can directly compute the KL divergence for Markov processes, without defining $H(\chi)$ and $H_0(\chi)$ explicitly. The results can also be applied to MJPs as proposed by [31].

6.4.3 The variational problem revisited

Before discussing approximations, we will show that total minimisation of the free-energy yields our previous result (Eq. (6.8)). For the corresponding derivation in the case of MJPs see [36]. The free-energy can be written as

$$\mathcal{F}(q,\theta) = \int_0^T dt \int dx \, q_t(x) \left\{\frac{1}{2}\|g(x,t) - f(x)\|_{D(x)}^2 + u(x,t)\right\},$$

where the observations are included in the term

$$u(x,t) = -\sum_i \ln p(y_i|x)\, \delta(t - t_i).$$

The drift g and the marginal q_t are connected by the Fokker–Planck equation

$$\frac{\partial q_t}{\partial t} = \left\{-\nabla^\top g + \frac{1}{2}\mathrm{Tr}(\nabla\nabla^\top)D\right\} q_t \doteq L_g q_t$$

as a constraint in the optimisation of q_t. We can deal with this constraint by introducing a Lagrange multiplier function $\lambda(x,t)$ to obtain the following *Lagrange functional*:

$$\mathcal{L} \doteq \mathcal{F}(q,\theta) - \int_0^T dt \int dx \, \lambda(x,t)\left(\frac{\partial q_t(x)}{\partial t} - (L_g q_t)(x)\right).$$

Performing independent variations of q_t and g leads respectively to the following *Euler–Lagrange* equations:

$$\frac{1}{2}\|g - f\|_D^2 + u + \left\{g^\top\nabla + \frac{1}{2}\mathrm{Tr}(D\nabla\nabla^\top)\right\}\lambda + \frac{\partial\lambda}{\partial t} = 0,$$

$$D^{-1}(g - f) + \nabla\lambda = 0,$$

where we have used integration by parts when appropriate. Defining the logarithmic transformation $\lambda(x,t) = -\ln\psi_t(x)$ and rearranging yields then the conditions

$$\left\{\frac{\partial}{\partial t} - u(x,t)\right\}\psi_t(x) = \left\{-f^\top(x)\nabla - \frac{1}{2}\mathrm{Tr}(D(x)\nabla\nabla^\top)\right\}\psi_t(x),$$

$$g(x,t) = f(x) + D(x)\nabla\ln\psi_t(x), \qquad (6.15)$$

for all $t \in [0, T]$. By noting that $u(x, t) = 0$ except at the observation times, we find that these results are equivalent to Eqs. (6.4) and (6.8); the Dirac δ functions yield the proper jump conditions when there are observations. Note that this derivation still holds if f and D are time dependent.

6.5 The Gaussian variational approximation

In practice, rather than assuming the correct functional form (6.15), we will view g as a variational function with a simplified form. The function g can then be optimised to minimise the free-energy.

Gaussian distributions are a natural choice for approximations. For example, they have been used frequently in statistical physics applications. For previous (finite-dimensional) applications in machine learning see [5, 39, 21]. In the present inference case, a Gaussian approximating measure over paths, that is a Gaussian process, is considered. In this case the drift must be a *linear* function of the state x. We consider a drift of the form $g(x, t) = -A(t)x + b(t)$, where $A(t)$ and $b(t)$ are functions to be optimised. In addition, we limit ourselves to the special case of a *constant* diffusion matrix D [3, 4]. The approximation equally holds in the case of time-dependent diffusions. The more general case of multiplicative noise processes, that is with state-dependent diffusion matrices, will be discussed in Section 6.6.

Since we are dealing with a Gaussian process, the marginals $q_t(x)$ are Gaussian densities. This result represents a significant simplification of the calculations. First, $q_t(x)$ are fully specified by their marginal means $m(t)$ and their marginal covariances $S(t)$. Second, we don't need to solve PDEs, but are left with simpler ordinary differential equations (ODEs). Since SDE (6.13) is linear, we have

$$dm \doteq \langle dx \rangle = (-Am + b)dt ,$$
$$dS \doteq \langle d((x - m)(x - m)^\top) \rangle = (-AS - SA^\top)dt + Ddt + O(dt^2),$$

where the term Ddt is obtained by applying the stochastic chain rule.[3] Hence, the evolution of $m(t)$ and of $S(t)$ is described by the following set of ODEs:

$$\frac{dm(t)}{dt} = -A(t)m(t) + b(t), \tag{6.16}$$

$$\frac{dS(t)}{dt} = -A(t)S(t) - S(t)A^\top(t) + D. \tag{6.17}$$

We can follow a similar approach as in Section 6.4.3 to optimise the Gaussian variational approximation. More specifically, we use these ODEs as a constraint during the optimisation. Let us define $e(x, t) = \frac{1}{2}\|g(x, t) - f(x)\|_D^2$. The Lagrangian functional is now defined as

$$\mathcal{L} = \int_0^T dt \, \langle e(x, t) + u(x, t) \rangle_{q_t} - \int_0^T dt \, \lambda^\top(t) \left(\frac{dm(t)}{dt} + A(t)m(t) - b(t) \right)$$
$$- \int_0^T dt \, \text{Tr} \left(\Psi(t) \left(\frac{dS(t)}{dt} + A(t)S(t) + S(t)A^\top(t) - D \right) \right), \tag{6.18}$$

---

[3]This result can also be obtained by an informal derivation not relying on stochastic calculus but only using properties of the Wiener process [3].

where $\lambda(t)$ and $\Psi(t)$ are vector and matrix Lagrange parameter functions which depend on time only. Performing independent variations of $m(t)$ and $S(t)$ (which is equivalent to performing an independent variation of q_t) yields an additional set of ODEs

$$\frac{d\lambda(t)}{dt} = -\nabla_m \langle e(x,t)\rangle_{q_t} + A^\top(t)\lambda(t), \tag{6.19}$$

$$\frac{d\Psi(t)}{dt} = -\nabla_S \langle e(x,t)\rangle_{q_t} + \Psi(t)A(t) + A^\top(t)\Psi(t), \tag{6.20}$$

along with jump conditions at observation times

$$\lambda_i = \lambda_i^- - \nabla_m \langle u(x,t)\rangle_{q_t}\big|_{t=t_i}, \qquad \lambda_i^- = \lim_{t\uparrow t_i}\lambda(t), \tag{6.21}$$

$$\Psi_i = \Psi_i^- - \nabla_S \langle u(x,t)\rangle_{q_t}\big|_{t=t_i}, \qquad \Psi_i^- = \lim_{t\uparrow t_i}\Psi(t). \tag{6.22}$$

Hence, the Fokker–Planck equation is replaced by Eqs. (6.16) and (6.17) in the Gaussian variational approximation, while the Kolmogorov backward equation is replaced by Eqs. (6.19) and (6.20). Based on Eqs. (6.19)–(6.22) we can devise a smoothing algorithm as described in [3, 4]. Also, a procedure to infer θ (which parameterises f and D) is discussed in detail in [4].

One important advantage of the Gaussian variational approach is that representations can be based on a discretisation of ODEs instead of a direct discretisation of the SDE. The loss of accuracy is expected to be less severe because of the smoothness of the paths [25]. Also, the approximation holds in continuous-time and is thus independent of the chosen representations unlike most MCMC schemes [2, 20]. In contrast to these discrete-time MCMC schemes, perfect simulation MCMC for continuous-time systems was recently proposed [7, 8, 18]. This method is so far restricted to problems where drift terms are derived as gradients of a potential function, which is not required in the Gaussian variational approximation. The main similarity between the Gaussian variational approximation and these advanced MCMC approaches is that they do not depend on a discrete-time approximation of the transition density. However, the Gaussian variational approximation differs from perfect simulation in its approximation of the non-Gaussian transition density by a (time-dependent) Gaussian one.

Thorough experimental comparisons are still required to assess the advantages and disadvantages of the different methods, but the Gaussian variational approximation is likely to be computationally faster as it is not based on sampling; it only cares about the marginal means and covariances, which can be computed efficiently by forward integration (Eqs. (6.16) and (6.17)). On the other hand, perfect MCMC sampling captures the posterior measure more accurately if run for a sufficiently long period of time.

6.5.1   Interpretation of the solution

In this subsection we discuss the form of the Gaussian variational solution in more detail. We perform the independent variation of $A(t)$ and $b(t)$, which can be viewed as performing the independent variation of g as in Section 6.4.3. This leads to the following conditions

$$A(t) = -\left\langle \nabla(f^\top)(x,t)\right\rangle_{q_t} + 2D\Psi(t), \tag{6.23}$$

$$b(t) = \langle f(x,t)\rangle_{q_t} + A(t)m(t) - D\lambda(t), \tag{6.24}$$

for all t. In order to obtain Eq. (6.23) we used the identity $\langle f(x-m)^\top\rangle = \langle\nabla(f^\top)\rangle S$, which holds for any non-linear function $f(\cdot)$ applied to a Gaussian random variable x. The solution (6.23)–(6.24) is closely related to a solution known as *statistical linearisation* [35].

Consider a non-linear function f applied to a continuous random variable x with density q. We are interested in the best linear approximation $-Ax + b$ to f. Instead of directly truncating the Taylor series of f to obtain a linear approximation, we would like to take into account the fact that x is a random variable. Statistical linearisation takes this information into account by taking A and b such that the linear approximation is optimal in the mean squared sense:

$$A, b \leftarrow \min_{A,b} \left\langle \|f(x) + Ax - b\|^2 \right\rangle_q .$$

When x is a Gaussian random variable it is easy to show that the solution to this problem is given by $A = -\langle \nabla(f^\top)(x) \rangle_q$ and $b = \langle f(x) \rangle_q + Am$. Comparing these expressions to Eqs. (6.23) and (6.24), it can be observed that the variational solution reduces to the statistical linearisation solution when the Lagrange multipliers are zero. Recalling that the Lagrange multipliers account for the constraints and the observations, one can see that the solution (6.23)–(6.24) is biased compared to the standard statistical linearisation solution. This bias corresponds to a correction based on future information and it is weighted by the diffusion matrix. The weighting by D makes sense as the magnitude of the correction should depend on the amount of stochasticity in the system.

6.5.2 Example

Applications of the Gaussian variational approximation to statistical inference for non-linear SDEs can be found in [3, 4]. We illustrate the basic idea of the calculation only for the simple, analytically tractable case of Section 6.3.1. For later use, we introduce an extra parameter σ in the model which controls the diffusion coefficient, i.e. we set $dx(t) = \sigma dW(t)$.

We have $g(x, t) = -a(t)x(t) + b(t)$. The evolution of the mean $m(t)$ and variance $s(t)$ simplify to

$$\frac{dm}{dt} = -a(t)m(t) + b(t), \tag{6.25}$$

$$\frac{ds}{dt} = -2a(t)s(t) + \sigma^2. \tag{6.26}$$

We model the noise free observation as the limit of a Gaussian observation centred at y and with variance $\sigma_0^2 \rightarrow 0$. Hence, we have

$$
\begin{aligned}
\mathcal{L} = &\int_0^T dt \left\{ \frac{1}{2\sigma^2}a^2(s + m^2) + \frac{1}{2\sigma^2}b^2 - \frac{1}{\sigma^2}amb \right\} \\
&+ \int_0^T dt \, \frac{1}{2\sigma_0^2}(y^2 + s + m^2 - 2my)\delta(t - T) \\
&- \int_0^T dt \, \lambda\left(\frac{dm}{dt} + am - b\right) - \int_0^T dt \, \psi\left(\frac{ds}{dt} + 2as - \sigma^2\right).
\end{aligned}
\tag{6.27}
$$

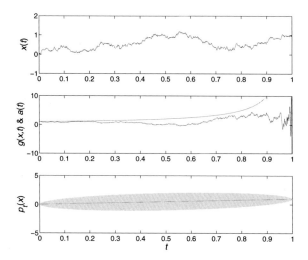

Figure 6.2 Illustration of a one-dimensional diffusion process without drift and unit diffusion coefficient, starting at the origin and with a noise-free observation $y = 1$ at $t = 1$. The top panel shows a sample path, whilst the middle panel shows the corresponding drift $g(x, t) = -a(t)x(t) + b(t)$ and the variational parameter $a(t)$. The bottom panel shows the posterior process, which corresponds to the one obtained in Fig. 6.1.

The Euler–Lagrange equations (6.19–6.24) are then given by

$$\frac{d\lambda(t)}{dt} = -\frac{a^2(t)m(t)}{\sigma^2} + \frac{a(t)b(t)}{\sigma^2} + a(t)\lambda(t), \tag{6.28}$$

$$\frac{d\psi(t)}{dt} = -\frac{a^2(t)}{2\sigma^2} + 2\psi(t)a(t), \tag{6.29}$$

$$a(t) = 2\sigma^2\psi(t), \tag{6.30}$$

$$b(t) = a(t)m(t) - \sigma^2\lambda(t), \tag{6.31}$$

along with the jump conditions

$$\lambda(T) = \lambda(T^-) - \frac{m(T) - y}{\sigma_0^2}, \qquad \psi(T) = \psi(T^-) - \frac{1}{2\sigma_0^2}.$$

Substitution of Eq. (6.30) into Eq. (6.29) leads to $\frac{d\psi}{dt} = 2\sigma^2\psi^2$ with the end condition $\frac{1}{2\sigma_0^2}$. It follows that the solution to this ODE is given by $\psi(t) = \frac{1}{2\sigma^2(T-t)+2\sigma_0^2}$. Second, substitution of Eq. (6.31) into Eq. (6.28) implies λ is a constant. The end condition yields $\lambda = \frac{m(T)-y}{\sigma_0^2}$. Next, substitution of Eq. (6.31) into Eq. (6.25) leads to $m(t) = -\sigma^2\lambda t + c$ with $c = 0$ as $m(0) = 0$, such that $m(T) = \frac{yT}{\sigma_0^2/\sigma^2+T}$. Hence, we obtain

$$a(t) = \frac{\sigma^2}{\sigma^2(T-t)+\sigma_0^2}, \qquad b(t) = \frac{\sigma^2 y}{\sigma^2(T-t)+\sigma_0^2}.$$

This leads to the same result for $g(x, t)$ as Eq. (6.10) when $\sigma_0^2 \to 0$. The solution is illustrated in Fig. 6.2.

6.6 Diffusions with multiplicative noise

In Section 6.5 we discussed the Gaussian variational approximation of diffusion processes with a constant or a time-dependent diffusion matrix. However, the methodology can still be applied to diffusion processes with multiplicative noise.

In some cases one can apply an explicit transformation to transform the original diffusion process with multiplicative noise into a diffusion process with a unit diffusion matrix [1]. The resulting drift is then expressed in terms of f and D via Itô's formula. Although this ad hoc approach is always possible when the state space is one dimensional, such a transformation typically does not exist in the multivariate case.

In the general case of a state-dependent diffusion, the ODEs describing the evolution of the mean $m(t)$ and the covariance $S(t)$ are defined by

$$\frac{dm(t)}{dt} = -A(t)m(t) + b(t), \tag{6.32}$$

$$\frac{dS(t)}{dt} = -A(t)S(t) - S(t)A^\top(t) + \langle D(x(t), t) \rangle_{q_t}. \tag{6.33}$$

The only difference with Eqs. (6.16) and (6.17) is that in Eq. (6.33) the expectation of the diffusion matrix appears. Hence, we can construct a Gaussian process approximation of the posterior process using the moments of the marginals (6.32) and (6.33) as constraints. Note, however, that $A(t)$ and $b(t)$ are no longer given by Eqs. (6.23) and (6.24), but have a more complicated form.

6.7 Parameter inference

The formulation of the variational approach in terms of Eq. (6.18) is especially useful when we would like to estimate model parameters by an approximate type II maximum likelihood method. In this approximation, we use the free-energy $\mathcal{F}(q^*, \theta)$ evaluated at the optimal variational Gaussian measure q^* for given parameters θ as a proxy for the negative log-marginal likelihood $-\ln Z(\theta)$.

The optimal parameters θ^* are obtained by minimising $\mathcal{F}$, which requires the computation of the gradients $\nabla_\theta \mathcal{F}(q^*, \theta)$. Although q^* is a function of θ, this optimisation problem is facilitated by the following argument. For each θ, we have $\mathcal{L} = \mathcal{F}(q^*, \theta)$ at the stationary solution, which is also stationary with respect to marginal moments, variational parameters and Lagrange parameters. Hence, to compute the gradients $\nabla_\theta \mathcal{F}(q^*, \theta)$, we just have to take the *explicit* gradients of $\mathcal{L}$ with respect to θ, while keeping all other quantities fixed.

6.7.1 Example

This idea is illustrated for the simple diffusion example of Section 6.3.1, where we have introduced a parameter σ to control the diffusion variance: $dx(t) = \sigma dW(t)$. We are interested in computing the derivative of the negative log-marginal likelihood of the single observation y (at time T) with respect to σ^2.

For a direct computation, let us first note that $p_t^{(F)}(x) = \mathcal{N}(0, \sigma^2 t)$. The marginal likelihood for y is given by

$$p(y|, \sigma^2) = \int \delta(y - x(T)) p_T^{(F)}(x) dx(T) = \mathcal{N}(0, \sigma^2 T),$$

which yields

$$-\frac{\partial \ln p(y|\sigma^2)}{\partial \sigma^2} = \frac{1}{2\sigma^2} - \frac{y^2}{2\sigma^4 T}.$$

On the other hand, differentiating Eq. (6.27) with respect to σ^2 leads to

$$\frac{\partial \mathcal{L}}{\partial \sigma^2} = -\frac{1}{2\sigma^4} \int_0^T dt \left(a^2 s + \sigma^4 \lambda^2 \right) + \int_0^T dt \, \psi(t) = \frac{1}{2\sigma^2} - \frac{y^2}{2\sigma^4 T}.$$

The first equality is obtained by differentiating Eq. (6.27) and using Eq. (6.31). To get the final result we inserted the explicit results for $a(t)$, $\lambda(t)$ and $\psi(t)$ obtained in Section 6.5.2 for $\sigma_0^2 \to 0$, as well as the corresponding solution to Eq. (6.26): $s(t) = \frac{\sigma^2 t}{T}(T - t)$.

6.8   Discussion and outlook

Continuous-time Markov processes, such as diffusion processes and Markov jump processes, play an important role in the modelling of dynamical systems. In a variety of applications, the state of the system is a (time-dependent) random variable of which the realisation is not directly observed. One has only access to noisy observations taken at a discrete set of times. The problem is then to infer from data the unknown state trajectory and the model parameters, which define the dynamics. While it is fairly straightforward to present a theoretical solution to these estimation problems, a practical solution in terms of PDEs or by MCMC sampling can be time consuming. One is thus interested in efficient approximations.

In this work we described a method to fit a Gaussian process to a non-Gaussian process induced by a SDE. The method is based on the variational principle originally developed in statistical physics and now extensively used in machine learning. It provides a practical alternative to exact methods and MCMC. Unlike previous variational approaches [43] it is not required to discretise the sample paths, nor to factorise the posterior across time. Although this might lead to good results when the number of observations is large compared to the speed of the dynamics, this approach leads in general to poor results. For a systematic discussion of the effect of factorisation in discrete-time dynamical systems we refer the interested reader to Chapter 5. By contrast our approximation does not assume any form of factorisation of the posterior. Rather, we choose a posterior process within a tractable family, namely the Gaussian family, which explicitly preserves the time dependency. Moreover, the approximation holds in continuous-time such that discretisation is only required for representation purposes.

The Gaussian variational approximation is attractive as it replaces the problem of directly solving a SDE (or equivalently a set of PDEs) by the simpler problem of solving a set of ODEs. The variational parameters are optimised to obtain the best possible approximation. This optimisation is done concurrently with the estimation of the model parameters, which enable us to learn the dynamics of the system. However, the proposed approach might be too time consuming in high-dimensional applications, such as numerical weather prediction. The main reason is that the dynamics of the marginal covariance S scales with d^2, d being the state space dimension. Hence, one could envisage suboptimal schemes in which the variational parameters are reparameterised by a small number of auxiliary quantities. Another potential issue is the estimation of the multivariate Gaussian expectations, which appear in the computation of A and b, as well as the computation of free-energy $\mathcal{F}$. In low-dimensional state spaces they can be estimated naively using sampling. Alternatively, one can use quadrature methods, but most existing approaches break down or are too slow in higher-dimensional spaces and/or for highly non-linear dynamics.

As mentioned earlier there are ongoing efforts to develop computationally efficient algorithms for fully Bayesian inference in diffusion processes. A very promising direction is to combine the Gaussian variational method and MCMC. One could for example develop an MCMC algorithm which uses the variational approximating process as a proposal process [40]. Sample paths could then be simulated using the optimal non-stationary linear diffusion and flexible blocking strategies would be used to further improve the mixing.

Acknowledgments This work was partly funded by the EPSRC VISDEM project (EP/C005848/1), as well as by the PASCAL 2 European network of excellence.

Bibliography

[1] Y. Ait-Sahalia. Closed-form likelihood expansions for multivariate diffusions. *Annals of Statistics*, **36**:906–937, 2008.

[2] F. J. Alexander, G. L. Eyink and J. M. Restrepo. Accelerated Monte Carlo for optimal estimation of time series. *Journal of Statistical Physics*, **119**:1331–1345, 2005.

[3] C. Archambeau, D. Cornford, M. Opper and J. Shawe-Taylor. Gaussian process approximation of stochastic differential equations. *Journal of Machine Learning Research: Workshop and Conference Proceedings*, **1**:1–16, 2007.

[4] C. Archambeau, M. Opper, Y. Shen, D. Cornford and J. Shawe-Taylor. Variational inference for diffusion processes. In J. C. Platt, D. Koller, Y. Singer, and S. Roweis, editors, *Advances in Neural Information Processing Systems 20*, pages 17–24. MIT Press, 2008.

[5] D. Barber and C. M. Bishop. Ensemble learning for multi-layer networks. In M. I. Jordan, M. J. Kearns, and S. A. Solla, editors, *Advances in Neural Information Processing Systems 10*, pages 395–401. MIT Press, 1998.

[6] James O. Berger. *Statistical Decision Theory and Bayesian Analysis*. Springer, 1985.

[7] A. Beskos, O. Papaspiliopoulos, G. Roberts and P. Fearnhead. Exact and computationally efficient likelihood-based estimation for discretely observed diffusion processes (with discussion). *Journal of the Royal Statistical Society B*, **68**(3):333–382, 2006.

[8] A. Beskos, G. Roberts, A. Stuart and J. Voss. MCMC methods for diffusion bridges. *Stochastics and Dynamics*, **8**(3): 319–350, 2008.

[9] C. M. Bishop. *Neural Networks for Pattern Recognition*. Oxford University Press, 1995.

[10] C. M. Bishop. *Pattern Recognition and Machine Learning*. Springer, 2006.

[11] I. Cohn, T. El-hay, N. Friedman and R. Kupferman. Mean field variational approximation for continuous-time Bayesian networks. In *25th International Conference on Uncertainty in Artificial Intelligence*, pages 91–100, 2009.

[12] T. M. Cover and J. A. Thomas. *Elements of Information Theory*. John Wiley & Sons, 1991.

[13] D. Crisan and T. Lyons. A particle approximation of the solution of the Kushner-Stratonovitch equation. *Probability Theory and Related Fields*, **115**(4):549–578, 1999.

[14] P. Del Moral and J. Jacod. Interacting particle filtering with discrete observations. In A. Doucet, N. de Freitas and N. Gordon, editors, *Sequential Monte Carlo Methods in Practice*, pages 43–76. MIT Press, 2001.

[15] P. Del Moral, J. Jacod and P. Protter. The Monte Carlo method for filtering with discrete-time observations. *Probability Theory and Related Fields*, **120**:346–368, 2002.

[16] B. Eraker. MCMC analysis of diffusion models with application to finance. *Journal of Business and Economic Statistics*, **19**:177–191, 2001.

[17] G. L. Eyink, J. L. Restrepo and F. J. Alexander. A mean field approximation in data assimilation for nonlinear dynamics. *Physica D*, **194**:347–368, 2004.

[18] P. Fearnhead, O. Papaspiliopoulos and G. O. Roberts. Particle filters for partially-observed diffusions. *Journal of the Royal Statistical Society B*, **70**:755–777, 2008.

[19] R. P. Feynman and A. R. Hibbs. *Quantum Mechanics and Path integrals*. McGraw-Hill Book Company, 1965.

[20] A. Golightly and D. J. Wilkinson. Bayesian sequential inference for nonlinear multivariate diffusions. *Statistics and Computing*, **16**:323–338, 2006.

[21] A. Honkela and H. Valpola. Unsupervised variational Bayesian learning of nonlinear models. In L. Saul, Y. Weiss, and L. Bottou, editors, *Advances in Neural Information Processing Systems 17*, pages 593–600. MIT Press, 2005.

[22] M. I. Jordan, editor. *Learning in Graphical Models*. MIT Press, 1998.

[23] I. Karatzas and S. E. Schreve. *Brownian Motion and Stochastic Calculus*. Springer, 1998.

[24] H. Kleinert. *Path Integrals in Quantum Mechanics, Statistics, Polymer Physics, and Financial Markets*. World Scientific, 2006.

[25] P. E. Kloeden and E. Platen. *Numerical Solution of Stochastic Differential Equations*. Springer, 1999.

[26] H. J. Kushner. On the differential equations satisfied by conditional probability densities of Markov processes with applications. *Journal of SIAM, Series A: Control*, 2:106–119, 1962.

[27] H. Lappalainen and J. W. Miskin. Ensemble learning. In M. Girolami, editor, *Advances in Independent Component Analysis*, pages 76–92. Springer-Verlag, 2000.

[28] D. J. C. MacKay. Bayesian interpolation. *Neural Computation*, 4(3):415–447, 1992.

[29] B. Øksendal. *Stochastic Differential Equations*. Springer-Verlag, 2005.

[30] M. Opper and D. Saad, editors. *Advanced Mean Field Methods: Theory and Practice*. MIT Press, 2001.

[31] M. Opper and G. Sanguinetti. Variational inference for Markov jump processes. In J. C. Platt, D. Koller, Y. Singer, and S. Roweis, editors, *Advances in Neural Information Processing Systems 20*, pages 1105–1112 MIT Press, 2008.

[32] E. Pardoux. Equations du filtrage non linéaire, de la prédiction et du lissage. *Stochastics*, 6:193–231, 1982.

[33] L. Rabiner. A tutorial on hidden Markov models and selected applications in speech recognition. *Proceedings of the IEEE*, 2(77):257–286, 1989.

[34] G. Roberts and O. Stramer. On inference for partially observed non-linear diffusion models using the Metropolis-Hastings algorithm. *Biometrika*, 88(3): 603–621, 2001.

[35] J. B. Roberts and P. D. Spanos. *Random Vibration and Statistical Linearization*. Dover Publications, 2003.

[36] A. Ruttor, G. Sanguinetti and M. Opper. Approximate inference for stochastic reaction processes. In M. Rattray, N. D. Lawrence, M. Girolami and G. Sanguinetti, editors, *Learning and Inference in Computational Systems Biology*, pages 189–205. MIT Press, 2009.

[37] G. Sanguinetti, A. Ruttor, M. Opper and C. Archambeau. Switching regulatory models of cellular stress response. *Bioinformatics*, 25(10):1280–1286, 2009.

[38] S. Särkkä. Recursive Bayesian Inference on Stochastic Differential Equations. PhD thesis, Helsinki University of Technology, Finland, 2006.

[39] M. Seeger. Bayesian model selection for support vector machines, Gaussian processes and other kernel classifiers. In T. G. Dietterich, S. Becker and Z. Ghahramani, editors, *Advances in Neural Information Processing Systems 12*, pages 603–609. MIT Press, 2000.

[40] Y. Shen, C. Archambeau, D. Cornford and M. Opper. Markov Chain Monte Carlo for inference in partially observed nonlinear diffusions. In *Proceedings Newton Institute for Mathematical Sciences workshop on Inference and Estimation in Probabilistic Time-Series Models*, pages 67–78, 2008.

[41] O. Elerian, S. Chiband and N. Shephard. Likelihood inference for discretely observed nonlinear diffusions. *Econometrika*, 69(4):959–993, 2001.

[42] R. L. Stratonovich. Conditional Markov processes. *Theory of Probability and its Applications*, 5:156–178, 1960.

[43] B. Wang and D. M. Titterington. Lack of consistency of mean field and variational Bayes approximations for state space models. *Neural Processing Letters*, 20(3):151–170, 2004.

Contributors

Cédric Archambeau, Department of Computer Science, University College London, Gower Street, London WCIE 6BT

Manfred Opper, Technische Universität Berlin, Fakultät IV – Elektrotechnik und Informatik, Franklinstr. 28/29, D-10587 Berlin, Germany

7

Expectation propagation and generalised EP methods for inference in switching linear dynamical systems

Onno Zoeter and Tom Heskes

7.1 Introduction

Many real-world problems can be described by models that extend the classical linear Gaussian dynamical system with (unobserved) discrete regime indicators. In such extended models the discrete indicators dictate what transition and observation model the process follows at a particular time. The problems of tracking and estimation in models with manoeuvring targets [1], multiple targets [25], non-Gaussian disturbances [15], unknown model parameters [9], failing sensors [20] and different trends [8] are all examples of problems that have been formulated in a conditionally Gaussian state space model framework. Since the extended model is so general it has been invented and re-invented many times in multiple fields, and is known by many different names, such as switching linear dynamical system, conditionally Gaussian state space model, switching Kalman filter model and hybrid model.

Although the extended model has a lot of expressive power, it is notorious for the fact that exact estimation of posteriors is intractable. In general, exact filtered, smoothed or predicted posteriors have a complexity exponential in the number of observations. Even when only marginals on the indicator variables are required the problem remains NP-hard [19].

In this chapter we introduce a deterministic approximation scheme that is particularly suited to find smoothed one and two time slice posteriors. It can be seen as a symmetric backward pass and iteration scheme for previously proposed assumed density filtering approaches [9].

The chapter is organised as follows. In Section 7.2 we present the general model; variants where only the transition or only the observation model switch, or where states or observations are multi- or univariate can be treated as special cases. In Section 7.3 we describe the assumed density filtering approach that forms the basis for our approximation scheme. In Section 7.4 we introduce the symmetric backward pass. Since both the forward and the backward pass consist of local, greedy projections it makes sense to iterate them. In Section 7.5 we introduce the objective that is minimised by such an iteration scheme and give an intuition how we should interpret fixed points. In Section 7.6 we provide an extension of the basic method based on generalised expectation propagation. In Section 7.7 we describe two earlier approximate smoothing passes that are often used for conditionally Gaussian state space models, but that in contrast to the approach presented in this chapter

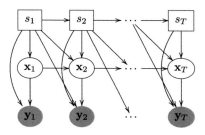

Figure 7.1 The belief network that encodes the conditional independencies in the SLDS. Ellipses denote Gaussian distributed variables and rectangles denote multinomial distributed variables. Shading emphasises the fact that a particular variable is observed.

make additional approximations in the smoothing phase. In Section 7.8 we describe experiments that test the validity of the proposed method and compare it with the alternative backward pass and state-of-the-art sampling techniques.

7.2 Notation and problem description

In a *switching linear dynamical system (SLDS)* it is assumed that an observed sequence $\mathbf{y}_{1:T}$ of T, d-dimensional observations is generated as noisy observations from a first-order Markov process. The latent space consists of a q-dimensional continuous state $\mathbf{x}_t$ and a discrete state s_t that can take on M values. Conditioned on s_{t-1} and s_t, $\mathbf{x}_t$ is a linear function of $\mathbf{x}_{t-1}$ subjected to Gaussian white noise, that is

$$p(\mathbf{x}_t|\mathbf{x}_{t-1}, s_{t-1}, s_t, \boldsymbol{\theta}) \sim \mathcal{N}(\mathbf{x}_t; A_{s_{t-1}, s_t}\mathbf{x}_t, Q_{s_{t-1}, s_t}). \tag{7.1}$$

In the above we have used $\boldsymbol{\theta}$ to denote the set of model parameters and $\mathcal{N}(.;.,.)$ to denote the Gaussian probability density function. The observation model is also linear-Gaussian and may differ between settings of s_{t-1} and s_t, that is

$$p(\mathbf{y}_t|\mathbf{x}_t, s_{t-1}, s_t, \boldsymbol{\theta}) \sim \mathcal{N}(\mathbf{y}_t; C_{s_{t-1}, s_t}\mathbf{x}_t, R_{s_{t-1}, s_t}). \tag{7.2}$$

The discrete state follows a first-order Markov chain in the discrete space

$$p(s_t|s_{t-1}, \boldsymbol{\theta}) = \Pi_{s_{t-1} \to s_t}. \tag{7.3}$$

At $t = 1$ we have $p(s_1|\boldsymbol{\theta}) = \pi_{s_1}$ and $p(\mathbf{x}_1|s_1, \boldsymbol{\theta})$ is a Gaussian with known parameters. The belief network that encodes the conditional independencies implied by these equations is presented in Fig. 7.1.

Throughout this chapter the parameters $\boldsymbol{\theta}$ are assumed to be known. The interest is in estimating the filtered and smoothed one- and two-slice posteriors. If we treat $\mathbf{z}_t \equiv \{s_t, \mathbf{x}_t\}$ as a single *conditionally Gaussian (CG)* distributed random variable, we obtain an independence structure identical to the basic linear dynamical system. (Appendix 7.A introduces the CG distribution and defines standard operations.) This might lead us to assume that inference is easy. However, this is not the case. One way to see this is by looking at the posterior

$$p(s_t, \mathbf{x}_t | \mathbf{y}_{1:T}, \boldsymbol{\theta}) = \sum_{s_{1:T \backslash t}} p(\mathbf{x}_t | s_{1:T}, \mathbf{y}_{1:T}, \boldsymbol{\theta}) p(s_{1:T} | \mathbf{y}_{1:T}, \boldsymbol{\theta}). \qquad (7.4)$$

Since the history of regime changes is unknown, we have to take into account all possible sequences of indicator variables $s_{1:T}$. The CG family is not closed under marginalisation, so the result of summing over all possible sequences in Eq. (7.4) is of a more complex form than a simple CG distribution: conditioned on s_t the posterior is a Gaussian mixture with M^{T-1} components.

A second way of interpreting the exponential growth is by inspecting a recursive filtering algorithm. At every time step the number of components in the exact posterior increases by a factor M, since all the components considered in the previous slice are propagated to and updated in the next slice by M possible models. In the next section we describe an approximate inference algorithm where this growth is avoided by a projection at every time step.

7.3 Assumed density filtering

7.3.1 Local approximations

In the previous section we have seen that the number of components in the exact filtered posteriors increases M-fold with every new observation. An obvious, and in practice very powerful, approximation is to first incorporate evidence $\mathbf{y}_t$ and then to approximate the resulting posterior over $\mathbf{z}_t$ by a 'best fitting' conditional Gaussian distribution. Here 'best fitting' is defined as the CG distribution that minimises the *Kullback–Leibler (KL) divergence* [17] between the original and approximate distribution. The KL-divergence between distributions $\hat{p}(\mathbf{z}_t)$ and $q(\mathbf{z}_t)$ is defined as

$$\mathrm{KL}\left(\hat{p}(\mathbf{z}_t) \| q(\mathbf{z}_t)\right) \equiv \sum_{\mathbf{z}_t} \hat{p}(\mathbf{z}_t) \log \frac{\hat{p}(\mathbf{z}_t)}{q(\mathbf{z}_t)} \qquad (7.5)$$

and is not symmetric in $\hat{p}$ and q. In Eq. (7.5) we have used the shorthand notation of $\sum_{\mathbf{z}_t}$ for denoting the operation of integrating over $\mathbf{x}_t$ and summing over s_t, a shorthand that we will use in the remainder of this chapter. The CG distribution $\hat{q}(\mathbf{z}_t)$ closest to $\hat{p}(\mathbf{z}_t)$ in the sense of KL-divergence is the CG distribution that has the same moments as $\hat{p}$ (see e.g. [27]). That is, for each value of s_t, the mixture $\hat{p}(\mathbf{x}_t|s_t)$ is approximated in $\hat{q}(\mathbf{x}_t|s_t)$ by a single Gaussian with the same mean and covariance as $\hat{p}(\mathbf{x}_t|s_t)$. Motivated by these 'collapses' of mixtures into single Gaussians, we introduce the notation

$$\hat{q}(\mathbf{z}_t) = \mathrm{Collapse}\left(\hat{p}(\mathbf{z}_t)\right) \equiv \underset{q \in CG}{\mathrm{argmin}}\, \mathrm{KL}\left(\hat{p}(\mathbf{z}_t) \| q(\mathbf{z}_t)\right).$$

A precise definition is given in Appendix 7.A.

7.3.2 The sum-product algorithm

If the growth of complexity is avoided by a local projection in every recursion step, the computational requirements of an approximate filter are linear in the number of observations instead of exponential. This resulting approximate forward pass is referred to as *assumed density filtering*, or *generalised pseudo Bayes 2 (GPB 2)* [1], amongst others, and has been proposed independently many times. The oldest reference we are aware of is in [9].

Algorithm 7.1 Assumed density filtering

$\hat{q}_1(\mathbf{z}_1) = \alpha_1(\mathbf{z}_1) \propto \psi_1(\mathbf{z}_1)$. For $t = 2, 3, \ldots T$, compute approximate filtered posteriors $\hat{q}_t(\mathbf{z}_t)$ as follows:

1. Construct a two-slice joint $\hat{p}_t(\mathbf{z}_{t-1}, \mathbf{z}_t) \propto \alpha_{t-1}(\mathbf{z}_{t-1})\psi_t(\mathbf{z}_{t-1}, \mathbf{z}_t)$.

2. Marginalise to obtain a one-slice filtered marginal $\hat{p}_t(\mathbf{z}_t) = \sum_{\mathbf{z}_{t-1}} \hat{p}_t(\mathbf{z}_{t-1}, \mathbf{z}_t)$.

3. Approximate $\hat{p}_t(\mathbf{z}_t)$ by $\hat{q}_t(\mathbf{z}_t)$, the CG distribution closest to $\hat{p}_t(\mathbf{z}_t)$ in KL-sense $\hat{q}_t(\mathbf{z}_t) = \text{Collapse}\,(\hat{p}_t(\mathbf{z}_t))$.

4. Set $\alpha_t(\mathbf{z}_t) = \hat{q}_t(\mathbf{z}_t)$.

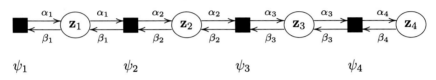

Figure 7.2 The factor graph corresponding to a SLDS with four observations and with factors ψ_t defined by Eqs. (7.6) and (7.7).

In Algorithm 7.1 assumed density filtering is presented in the spirit of the *sum-product algorithm* [16]. The model equations (7.1), (7.2) and (7.3) enter as *factors* ψ_t, which are potentials defined as

$$\psi_t(\mathbf{z}_{t-1}, \mathbf{z}_t) \equiv p(\mathbf{y}_t, \mathbf{z}_t | \mathbf{z}_{t-1}, \boldsymbol{\theta}) = p(\mathbf{y}_t | \mathbf{x}_t, s_{t-1}, s_t, \boldsymbol{\theta})p(\mathbf{x}_t | \mathbf{x}_{t-1}, s_{t-1}, s_t, \boldsymbol{\theta})p(s_t | s_{t-1}, \boldsymbol{\theta}), \quad (7.6)$$
$$\psi_1(\mathbf{z}_0, \mathbf{z}_1) \equiv p(\mathbf{y}_1, \mathbf{z}_1 | \boldsymbol{\theta}) = p(\mathbf{y}_1 | \mathbf{x}_1, s_1, \boldsymbol{\theta})p(\mathbf{x}_1 | s_1, \boldsymbol{\theta})p(s_1 | \boldsymbol{\theta}). \quad (7.7)$$

To make the similarity between the filtering and smoothing pass clearer we introduce a distinct notation for approximate one-slice marginals, $\hat{q}_t(\mathbf{z}_t) \approx p(\mathbf{z}_t | \mathbf{y}_{1:T}, \boldsymbol{\theta})$, and *forward messages*, $\alpha_t(\mathbf{z}_t)$. The messages fulfil a similar role as in the regular Kalman filter. In an exact filter, the forward messages would satisfy $\alpha_t(\mathbf{z}_t) \propto p(\mathbf{z}_t | \mathbf{y}_{1:t}, \boldsymbol{\theta})$, here they are approximations of these quantities.

Figure 7.2 represents the *factor graph* [16] that corresponds to Algorithms 7.1 and 7.2 presented in Section 7.4. Variables are represented by ovals, factors by solid squares and messages by arcs. Note that the variables $\mathbf{y}_{1:T}$ are not depicted, they are always observed and part of the factors.

The assumed density filter starts at $t = 1$. The term $\hat{q}_1(\mathbf{z}_1)$ is obtained by normalizing ψ_1

$$\hat{q}_1(\mathbf{z}_1) \propto \psi_1(\mathbf{z}_1).$$

The posterior $\hat{q}_1(\mathbf{z}_1)$ is a CG distribution with $\hat{q}_1(\mathbf{x}_1 | s_1 = m)$ corresponding to the prior $p(\mathbf{x}_1 | s_1 = m, \boldsymbol{\theta})$ updated in the light of observation $\mathbf{y}_1$ and observation model m. Similarly $\hat{q}_1(s_1 = m)$ is the prior probability that the system starts in regime m appropriately weighted by the likelihood that $\mathbf{y}_1$ was generated by model m. Since $\hat{q}_1(\mathbf{z}_1)$ is still CG, there is no need for an approximation at this point. Since the current approximation of the belief state of $\mathbf{z}_1$ is only based on $\mathbf{y}_1$ we set $\alpha_1(\mathbf{z}_1) = \hat{q}_1(\mathbf{z}_1)$. The need for messages will become clear in the next sections.

A recursive filtering step is done by making a prediction and measurement update step. The message α_{t-1} is multiplied by ψ_t and normalised to get a belief over the states $\mathbf{z}_{t-1,t}$

$$\hat{p}_t(\mathbf{z}_{t-1,t}) \propto \alpha_{t-1}(\mathbf{z}_{t-1})\psi_t(\mathbf{z}_{t-1,t}).$$

At the start of the recursion, $\alpha_{t-1}(\mathbf{z}_{t-1})$ is a conditional Gaussian potential with M modes. The belief $\hat{p}_t(\mathbf{z}_{t-1,t})$ is a conditional Gaussian distribution with M^2 components: the M components from $\alpha_{t-1}(\mathbf{z}_{t-1})$ propagated and updated according to M different models.

The marginal $\hat{p}_t(\mathbf{z}_t) = \sum_{\mathbf{z}_{t-1}} \hat{p}_t(\mathbf{z}_{t-1}, \mathbf{z}_t)$ is not CG. Instead $\hat{p}_t(\mathbf{x}_t|s_t)$ is a *mixture* of Gaussians with M components. If we were to use $\hat{p}_t(\mathbf{z}_t)$ as the new forward message, the filtering pass would give exact results, but, at the next step in the recursion in Step 1 in Algorithm 7.1, the number of components in the joint would increase by a factor M, implying a number of components that is exponential in t.

To avoid this growth $\hat{p}_t(\mathbf{z}_t)$ is approximated by the CG distribution closest to $\hat{p}_t(\mathbf{z}_t)$ in KL-sense

$$\hat{q}_t(\mathbf{z}_t) = \text{Collapse}\,(\hat{p}_t(\mathbf{z}_t))\,.$$

As for $\hat{q}_1(\mathbf{z}_1)$, if we only perform a single forward pass, the approximate beliefs $\hat{q}_t(\mathbf{z}_t)$ are only based on $\mathbf{y}_{1:t}$. Therefore, we set $\alpha_t(\mathbf{z}_t) = \hat{q}_t(\mathbf{z}_t)$.

Since the growth of complexity is prevented by the projection in Step 3 of Algorithm 7.1 the running time of assumed density filtering is linear in T, the number of observations.

7.4   Expectation propagation

In this section we introduce the expectation propagation (EP) approximate smoothing algorithm that is based on the same projection principles as the assumed density filter. The smoother that is symmetric to the assumed density filter (i.e. does not introduce any further approximations apart from the projection onto the conditional Gaussians) can be understood as an expectation propagation algorithm [21].

7.4.1   Backward pass

After establishing a deterministic approximation for the forward pass in Section 7.3, it is natural to look for an analogous backward, or smoothing, pass. Several attempts have been made in the literature [14, 25]. These have all included extra approximations beyond the projections onto the conditional Gaussian family; we will briefly review these in Section 7.7. Other approximations such as [10] are restricted to models with invertible dynamics.

The smoothing pass depends on *backward messages* $\beta_t(\mathbf{z}_t)$, with $t = 1, 2, \ldots, T$. These messages are analogous to the backward messages in the *hidden Markov model (HMM)* smoother or the smoother from the two-filter algorithm for the *linear dynamical system (LDS)*. In the exact case we have

$$\beta_t(\mathbf{z}_t) \propto p(\mathbf{y}_{t+1:T}|\mathbf{z}_t, \boldsymbol{\theta}), \tag{7.8}$$

such that $\alpha_t(\mathbf{z}_t)\beta_t(\mathbf{z}_t) \propto p(\mathbf{z}_t|\mathbf{y}_{1:T}, \boldsymbol{\theta})$, which is of the form (7.4). In the current approximation scheme we have

$$\alpha_t(\mathbf{z}_t)\beta_t(\mathbf{z}_t) \propto \hat{q}_t(\mathbf{z}_t) \approx p(\mathbf{z}_t|\mathbf{y}_{1:T}, \boldsymbol{\theta}), \tag{7.9}$$

where $\hat{q}_t(\mathbf{z}_t)$ is CG. In the factor graph in Fig. 7.2 this definition is depicted as follows: an approximate posterior belief over a variable can be constructed by multiplying all messages coming into that variable node.

A potential problem with an approximate backward pass based on β_t's is that, whereas forward messages α_t can always be normalised, the backward messages β_t in general cannot. The fact that β_t messages cannot always be normalised can be understood from Eq. (7.8); it is a correction term for $\mathbf{z}_t$ (i.e. has $\mathbf{z}_t$ as a conditioning term) and hence integrating over $\mathbf{z}_t$ does not necessarily yield a finite value.

The KL-divergence is only defined on proper distributions. We therefore cannot define a backward pass by projecting backward messages directly.

We propose to use an approximation which can be viewed as a special case of expectation propagation [21]. A key difference with the previous approaches mentioned above is that instead of approximating messages, first *beliefs* are constructed which are then approximated. The new messages are then deduced from the approximated beliefs.

The message passing scheme is symmetric in the forward and backward pass. As in the previous section the presentation in Algorithm 7.2 is in the spirit of the sum-product algorithm.

It suffices to describe the backward recursion. The recursion starts by introducing a message $\beta_T = 1$. Then, for $t \leq T$, the backward message β_{t-1} is computed as a function of β_t, the local potential ψ_t and the forward message α_{t-1}. Given α_{t-1}, ψ_t and β_t an approximated two-slice posterior belief $\hat{p}_t(\mathbf{z}_{t-1,t})$ can be computed as

$$\hat{p}_t(\mathbf{z}_{t-1}, \mathbf{z}_t) \propto \alpha_{t-1}(\mathbf{z}_{t-1})\psi_t(\mathbf{z}_{t-1}, \mathbf{z}_t)\beta_t(\mathbf{z}_t).$$

In the factor graph in Fig. 7.2 this operation should be interpreted as follows: an approximate posterior belief over the domain of the factor t can be obtained by multiplying all incoming messages with factor ψ_t itself and normalising.

As in the forward pass the marginal $\hat{p}_t(\mathbf{z}_{t-1})$ is a conditional mixture of Gaussians instead of CG. However since $\hat{p}_t(\mathbf{z}_{t-1})$ constitutes a proper distribution, the approximation

$$\hat{q}_{t-1}(\mathbf{z}_{t-1}) = \text{Collapse}\,(\hat{p}_t(\mathbf{z}_{t-1}))$$

is now well defined. From the definition in Eq. (7.9), we have

$$\hat{q}_{t-1}(\mathbf{z}_{t-1}) = \alpha_{t-1}(\mathbf{z}_{t-1})\beta_{t-1}(\mathbf{z}_{t-1}).$$

The message $\alpha_{t-1}(\mathbf{z}_{t-1})$ is kept fixed in this recursion step, so the new $\beta_{t-1}(\mathbf{z}_{t-1})$ follows by a division as in Step 4 in Algorithm 7.2.

In the forward pass a new forward message α_t is computed analogously as a function of the old forward message α_{t-1}, the local potential ψ_t and the backward message β_t, by constructing $\hat{q}_t(\mathbf{z}_t)$ and dividing by $\beta_t(\mathbf{z}_t)$. If we initialise all messages with 1, on the first forward pass the scheme is identical to the assumed density filtering algorithm discussed in Section 7.3.

A new two-slice marginal implies two new one-slice beliefs, so in Step 4 we could compute two new messages instead of one. However, computing new backward (β_{t-1}) messages on a forward pass is redundant since these messages will be replaced on a backward pass before they would be used. A similar reasoning goes for the computation of new forward messages on a backward pass.

Algorithm 7.2 Expectation propagation for the SLDS

Compute a forward pass by performing the following steps for $t = 1, 2, \ldots, T$, with $t' \equiv t$, and a backward pass by performing the same steps for $t = T - 1, T - 2, \ldots, 1$, with $t' \equiv t - 1$. Possibly iterate forward-backward passes until convergence. At the boundaries keep $\alpha_0 = \beta_T = 1$.

1. Construct a two-slice belief $\hat{p}_t(\mathbf{z}_{t-1}, \mathbf{z}_t) \propto \alpha_{t-1}(\mathbf{z}_{t-1}) \psi_t(\mathbf{z}_{t-1}, \mathbf{z}_t) \beta_t(\mathbf{z}_t)$.

2. Marginalise to obtain a one-slice marginal $\hat{p}_t(\mathbf{z}_{t'}) = \sum_{\mathbf{z}_{t''}} \hat{p}_t(\mathbf{z}_{t-1}, \mathbf{z}_t)$, with $t'' \equiv \{t - 1, t\} \backslash t'$.

3. Find $\hat{q}_{t'}(\mathbf{z}_{t'})$ that approximates $\hat{p}_t(\mathbf{z}_{t'})$ best in the Kullback–Leibler sense $\hat{q}_{t'}(\mathbf{z}_{t'}) = \text{Collapse}\,(\hat{p}_t(\mathbf{z}_{t'}))$.

4. Infer the new message by division $\alpha_t(\mathbf{z}_t) = \frac{\hat{q}_t(\mathbf{z}_t)}{\beta_t(\mathbf{z}_t)}$, $\beta_{t-1}(\mathbf{z}_{t-1}) = \frac{\hat{q}_{t-1}(\mathbf{z}_{t-1})}{\alpha_{t-1}(\mathbf{z}_{t-1})}$.

7.4.2 Iteration

If in Step 3 of Algorithm 7.2 the new one-slice marginal is not approximated, i.e. if exact marginalisation is performed, one forward, and one backward pass would suffice. This can easily be seen from the fact that the forward and backward messages can be computed independently: since the (exact) summation is a linear operation multiplying with $\beta_t(\mathbf{z}_t)$ in Step 1 and dividing again in Step 4 is redundant. In fact, the above scheme is identical to the two-filter approach of finding smoothed estimates in a linear dynamical system if these redundant multiplication and division operations are left out. In the current setting however, with a 'collapse' operation in Step 3 that is not linear in α_{t-1} nor in β_t (see Appendix 7.A), the forward and backward messages do interfere. Different backward messages β_t result in different forward messages α_t and vice versa.

Thus instead of performing one forward and backward pass, Steps 1 to 4 in Algorithm 7.2 can be iterated to find local approximations that are as consistent as possible. In Section 7.5 we introduce an objective that can be said to be associated to such an iterative scheme: minima of the objective correspond to fixed points of the iteration.

7.4.3 Supportiveness

One issue that is not discussed in Algorithm 7.2 is *supportiveness*. We say that Step 4 in Algorithm 7.2 is supported, if all the beliefs that change because of the construction of the new messages remain normalisable. On the first forward pass this is automatically satisfied. Since α_1 is a proper distribution and $\beta_t = 1$ for all t and all ψ_t are proper conditional distributions, by induction, all α_t are proper distributions as well. A new message $\alpha_t^{\text{new}}(\mathbf{z}_t)$ changes belief $\hat{p}_{t+1}^{\text{new}}(\mathbf{z}_{t,t+1}) \propto \alpha_t^{\text{new}}(\mathbf{z}_t) \psi_t(\mathbf{z}_{t,t+1}) \beta_{t+1}(\mathbf{z}_{t+1})$, which is normalisable by construction since $\beta_{t+1}(\mathbf{z}_{t+1})$ is 1 on the first forward pass. However, in general, due to the division in Step 4, after a message is updated neighbouring two-slice potentials are not guaranteed to be normalisable. For example on a backward pass, after replacing β_t with β_t^{new} (based on the two-slice belief $\hat{p}_{t+1}^{\text{new}}(\mathbf{z}_{t,t+1})$), the neighboring belief

$$\hat{p}_t^{\text{new}}(\mathbf{z}_{t-1,t}) \propto \alpha_{t-1}(\mathbf{z}_{t-1}) \psi_t(\mathbf{z}_{t-1,t}) \beta_t^{\text{new}}(\mathbf{z}_t)$$

may not be normalisable. The requirement is that the sum of the respective inverse covariance matrices is positive definite. If a normalisability problem is detected, messages α_t^{new}

and $\beta_{t-1}^{\mathrm{new}}$ can be computed as *damped* versions of the messages α_t^* and β_{t-1}^* suggested by Step 4. We define damping as a convex combination of old and suggested messages in *canonical space* (see Appendix 7.A), e.g. for a damped forward message

$$\alpha_t^{\mathrm{new}} = \epsilon \alpha_t^* + (1 - \epsilon)\alpha_t^{\mathrm{old}}. \tag{7.10}$$

In Eq. (7.10), α_t^{new}, α_t^*, and α_t^{old} (in boldface) are the canonical parameter vectors of their corresponding potentials. If a regular update ($\epsilon = 1$) results in a non-normalisable potential, a damping parameter ϵ with $0 \le \epsilon < 1$ is chosen such that the resulting precision matrices for the neighboring two-slice belief are positive definite.

7.5   Free-energy minimisation

In this section we discuss the objective that is minimised when the steps in Algorithm 7.2 are iterated. We first show that in the exact case, the task of finding smoothed one- and two-slice posteriors can be formulated as a minimisation problem. Although this minimisation problem remains intractable, it forms the basis for an approximate objective discussed in the second part of this section.

A variational distribution $p(\mathbf{z}_{1:T})$ can be introduced to get an objective $\mathcal{F}$ that is sometimes referred to as a *free-energy* [28]

$$-\log Z = \min_p \mathcal{F}(p) \equiv \min_p \mathrm{KL}\,(p\|p^*) - \log Z. \tag{7.11}$$

In the above p^* is a shorthand for the exact posterior $p(\mathbf{z}_{1:T}|\mathbf{y}_{1:T}, \boldsymbol{\theta})$, and the minimisation is over all proper distributions over the same domain as p^*. Since the KL-divergence is never negative and 0 if and only if $p = p^*$, $\mathcal{F}$ has a unique minimum at which the equality in Eq. (7.11) holds. In particular, if p forms a minimum of $\mathcal{F}$ its one- and two-slice marginals will be equal to those of p^*.

In terms of the potentials ψ_t, the exact posterior is written as

$$p^*(\mathbf{z}_{1:T}|\mathbf{y}_{1:T}, \boldsymbol{\theta}) = \frac{1}{Z} \prod_{t=1}^{T} \psi_t(\mathbf{z}_{t-1}, \mathbf{z}_t),$$

with $Z \equiv p^*(\mathbf{y}_{1:T}|\boldsymbol{\theta})$ the normalisation constant. If we plug this into $\mathcal{F}$ we obtain

$$\mathcal{F}(p) = E(p) - S(p),$$

$$E(p) \equiv -\sum_{t=1}^{T} \sum_{\mathbf{z}_{t-1,t}} p(\mathbf{z}_{t-1}, \mathbf{z}_t) \log \psi_t(\mathbf{z}_{t-1}, \mathbf{z}_t),$$

$$S(p) \equiv -\sum_{\mathbf{z}_{1:T}} p(\mathbf{z}_{1:T}) \log p(\mathbf{z}_{1:T}). \tag{7.12}$$

We see that the first term $E(p)$, the *energy*, factors automatically since the posterior is a product of two-slice potentials ψ_t. For arbitrary $p(\mathbf{z}_{1:T})$ the second term $S(p)$, the *entropy*, does not factorise. However we can use the fact that the exact joint posterior on a chain is of the form (see e.g. [27])

$$p^*(\mathbf{z}_{1:T}) = \frac{\prod_{t=2}^{T} p^*(\mathbf{z}_{t-1}, \mathbf{z}_t)}{\prod_{t=2}^{T-1} p^*(\mathbf{z}_t)}.$$

We can therefore restrict the minimisation problem to range over all possible *chains* parameterised by their one- and two-slice marginals

$$p(\mathbf{z}_{1:T}) = \frac{\prod_{t=2}^{T} p_t(\mathbf{z}_{t-1}, \mathbf{z}_t)}{\prod_{t=2}^{T-1} q_t(\mathbf{z}_t)}. \tag{7.13}$$

In Eq. (7.13) the one- and two-slice marginals $q_t(\mathbf{z}_t)$ and $p_t(\mathbf{z}_{t-1}, \mathbf{z}_t)$ should be properly normalised distributions and such that they agree on their overlap

$$\sum_{\mathbf{z}_{t-1}} p_t(\mathbf{z}_{t-1}, \mathbf{z}_t) = q_t(\mathbf{z}_t) = \sum_{\mathbf{z}_{t+1}} p_{t+1}(\mathbf{z}_t, \mathbf{z}_{t+1}). \tag{7.14}$$

Plugging Eq. (7.13) into Eq. (7.12) we get a minimisation problem over a collection of one- and two-slice marginals

$$-\log Z = \min_{\{p_t, q_t\}} \mathcal{F}(\{p_t, q_t\}) \tag{7.15}$$

$$\equiv \min_{\{p_t, q_t\}} \left\{ \sum_{t=1}^{T} \sum_{\mathbf{z}_{t-1,t}} p_t(\mathbf{z}_{t-1}, \mathbf{z}_t) \log \frac{p_t(\mathbf{z}_{t-1}, \mathbf{z}_t)}{\psi_t(\mathbf{z}_{t-1}, \mathbf{z}_t)} - \sum_{t=2}^{T-1} \sum_{\mathbf{z}_t} q_t(\mathbf{z}_t) \log q_t(\mathbf{z}_t) \right\},$$

under the constraints that the marginals are proper distributions and consistent (Eq. (7.14)). Thus the exact posteriors can be found by a minimisation procedure in terms of (constrained) one- and two-slice marginals.

A problem remains of course that, as described in Section 7.2, the exact one- and two-slice posteriors p_t and q_t are very complex, and in general will have exponentially many modes. Therefore, even if we find a scheme that could minimise $\mathcal{F}(\{p_t, q_t\})$, the results could not be computed nor stored efficiently. So we will approximate Eq. (7.15) by restricting the one-slice $q_t(\mathbf{z}_t)$ marginals to be conditionally Gaussian, i.e. the conditional posteriors $p(\mathbf{x}_t|s_t, \mathbf{y}_{1:T}, \boldsymbol{\theta})$ are approximated by a single Gaussian. The approximated, or 'pseudo' marginals are denoted by $\hat{p}_t$ and $\hat{q}_t$. The resulting free-energy is given by

$$\mathcal{F}_{\text{EP}}(\hat{p}, \hat{q}) \equiv \sum_{t=1}^{T} \sum_{\mathbf{z}_{t-1,t}} \hat{p}_t(\mathbf{z}_{t-1}, \mathbf{z}_t) \log \frac{\hat{p}_t(\mathbf{z}_{t-1}, \mathbf{z}_t)}{\psi_t(\mathbf{z}_{t-1}, \mathbf{z}_t)} - \sum_{t=2}^{T-1} \sum_{\mathbf{z}_t} \hat{q}_t(\mathbf{z}_t) \log \hat{q}_t(\mathbf{z}_t). \tag{7.16}$$

Restricting the marginals makes exact agreement on overlaps possible only in trivial solutions. Instead the consistency requirements are weakened: overlapping two-slice marginals only need to agree on their expectations. That is, apart from being properly normalised, the marginals are required to have the same moments after a collapse

$$\langle f(\mathbf{z}_t) \rangle_{\hat{p}_t} = \langle f(\mathbf{z}_t) \rangle_{\hat{q}_t} = \langle f(\mathbf{z}_t) \rangle_{\hat{p}_{t+1}}. \tag{7.17}$$

In the above, $f(\mathbf{z}_t)$ is the vector of sufficient statistics of the conditional Gaussian family over $\mathbf{z}_t$ (as defined in Appendix 7.A) and $\langle \cdot \rangle_p$ denotes expectation with respect to p.

The intuition and motivation behind this approximate free-energy is similar to the assumed density filtering approach. It is hoped that the collection of marginals $\hat{p}_t(\mathbf{z}_{t-1,t})$ and $\hat{q}_t(\mathbf{z}_t)$ are reasonable approximations to the exact marginals $p(\mathbf{z}_{t-1,t}|\mathbf{y}_{1:T}, \boldsymbol{\theta})$ and $p(\mathbf{z}_t|\mathbf{y}_{1:T}, \boldsymbol{\theta})$. The weak consistency constraints ensure that the two possible ways of computing the one-slice marginal $\hat{q}_t$ (based on $\hat{p}_t$ or $\hat{p}_{t+1}$) are identical after a collapse.

Iterating the forward and backward pass as described in Section 7.4 can be interpreted as a heuristic to find a minimum of $\mathcal{F}_{\text{EP}}$ under constraints (7.17). The following theorem describes this relationship.

Theorem 7.1 *The collection of beliefs $\hat{p}_t(\mathbf{z}_{t-1,t})$ and $\hat{q}_t(\mathbf{z}_t)$ form fixed points of Algorithm 7.2 if and only if they are zero gradient points of $\mathcal{F}_{EP}$ under the appropriate constraints.*

The proof is presented in Appendix 7.B.

The relationship between the algorithm and the objective $\mathcal{F}_{EP}$ is in fact somewhat stronger. It can be shown that if the algorithm converges, the collection of beliefs correspond to a local minimum of $\mathcal{F}_{EP}$ under the constraints. The proof is somewhat more involved and is given in [11].

It must be stressed that Theorem 7.1 does not claim that the algorithm always converges. In hard problems the algorithm might get trapped in cycles or diverge. For such hard problems it often helps to make smaller or *damped* updates (Eq. (7.10)). In practice we observe that Algorithm 7.2 nearly always converges to a very reasonable approximation and for most 'harder' problems damping resolves convergence problems. However in a thorough implementation direct minimisation of $\mathcal{F}_{EP}$ may be used when Algorithm 7.2 fails to converge. A direct minimisation procedure is presented in [11]. This procedure is a lot slower than Algorithm 7.2, so therefore the latter remains the method of choice for a practical application.

7.6   Generalised expectation propagation

The objective (7.16) is closely related to the Bethe free-energy [28]. The Bethe free-energy has the same form, but does not restrict the parametric family of the pseudo marginals, and keeps strong consistency constraints. The Bethe free-energy and the associated loopy belief propagation algorithm are used for problems where the parametric families pose no problems (are closed under product and summation), but where the conditional independence structure contains cycles. In such cases the tree-form in Eq. (7.13) yields an approximation.

The introduction of EP as an approximation of the Bethe free-energy motivates a *generalised expectation propagation* algorithm [12] that is analogous to the Kikuchi's extension of the Bethe free-energy [29]. For the SLDS this will allow us to maintain more components in the approximate marginals and update local greedy approximations in the filter by refining them in a backward pass and iteration scheme.

In the basic EP free-energy (7.16) the minimisation is w.r.t. beliefs over two-slice marginals, $\tilde{p}_t(\mathbf{z}_{t-1,t})$, which we refer to as *outer clusters*, and the *overlaps* of these outer clusters, the one-slice marginals $\tilde{q}_t(\mathbf{z}_{t-1,t})$. In the so-called *negative entropy*,

$$\sum_{t=2}^{T}\sum_{\mathbf{z}_{t-1,t}} \tilde{p}_t(\mathbf{z}_{t-1,t})\log \tilde{p}_t(\mathbf{z}_{t-1,t}) - \sum_{t=2}^{T-1}\sum_{\mathbf{z}_t} \tilde{q}_t(\mathbf{z}_t)\log \tilde{q}_t(\mathbf{z}_t),$$

from Eq. (7.16), the outer clusters enter with a plus, the overlaps with a minus sign. These 1 and -1 powers can be interpreted as *counting numbers* that ensure that every variable effectively is counted once in the (approximate) entropy in Eq. (7.16). If the free-energy is exact (i.e. no parametric choice for the beliefs, and strong consistency constraints), the local beliefs are exact marginals, and as in Eq. (7.13), the counting numbers can be interpreted as powers that dictate how to construct a global distribution from the pseudo marginals.

In the Kikuchi's extension the outer clusters are taken larger. The minimisation is then w.r.t. beliefs over outer clusters, their direct overlaps, the overlaps of the overlaps, etc. With each belief again proper counting numbers are associated. One way to construct a valid Kikuchi based approximation is as follows [29]. Choose outer clusters $\mathbf{z}_{outer(i)}$ and associate with them the counting number $c_{outer(i)} = 1$. The outer clusters should be such that all

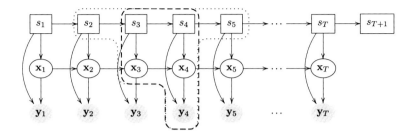

Figure 7.3 Cluster definitions for $\kappa = 0$ (dashed) and $\kappa = 1$ (dotted).

domains $\mathbf{z}_{t-1,t}$ of the model potentials $\Psi_t(\mathbf{z}_{t-1,t})$ are fully contained in at least one outer cluster. Then recursively define the overlaps of the outer clusters $\mathbf{z}_{over(i)}$, the overlaps of the overlaps, etc. The counting number associated with cluster γ is given by the Möbius recursion

$$c_\gamma = 1 - \sum_{\mathbf{z}_{\gamma'} \supset \mathbf{z}_\gamma} c_{\gamma'}. \tag{7.18}$$

A crucial observation for the SLDS is that it makes sense to take outer clusters larger than the cliques of a *(weak) junction tree*. If we do not restrict the parametric form of $\tilde{q}_t(\mathbf{z}_t)$ and keep exact constraints, the cluster choice in Eq. (7.13) gives exact results. However, the restriction that $\tilde{q}_t(\mathbf{z}_t)$ must be conditional Gaussian, and the weak consistency constraints imply an approximation: only part of the information from the past can be passed on to the future and vice versa. With weak constraints it is beneficial to take larger outer clusters and larger overlaps, since the weak consistency constraints are then over a larger set of sufficient statistics and hence 'stronger'.

We define symmetric extensions of the outer clusters as depicted in Fig. 7.3. The size of the clusters is indicated by $0 \leq \kappa \leq \left\lceil \frac{T-2}{2} \right\rceil$

$$\mathbf{z}_{outer(i)} = \{s_{i:i+2(\kappa+1)-1}, x_{i+\kappa, i+\kappa+1}\}, \quad i = 1, \ldots, T - \kappa - 1, \tag{7.19}$$
$$\mathbf{z}_{over(i)} = \mathbf{z}_{outer(i)} \cap \mathbf{z}_{outer(i+1)}, \quad i = 1, \ldots, T - \kappa - 2.$$

In the outer clusters only the discrete space is extended because the continuous part can be integrated out analytically and the result stays in the conditional Gaussian family. The first and the last outer cluster have a slightly larger set. In addition to the set (7.19) the first cluster also contains $x_{1:i+\kappa-1}$ and the last also $x_{i+\kappa+2:T}$. This implies a choice where the number of outer clusters is as small as possible at the cost of a larger continuous part in the first and the last cluster. A slightly different choice would have more clusters, but only two continuous variables in every outer cluster.

To demonstrate the construction of clusters and the computation of their associated counting numbers we will look at the case of $\kappa = 1$. Below the clusters are shown schematically, with outer clusters on the top row, and recursively the overlaps of overlaps, etc.

$s_{1,2,3,4}$		$s_{2,3,4,5}$		$s_{3,4,5,6}$		$s_{4,5,6,7}$
$x_{1,2,3}$		$x_{3,4}$		$x_{4,5}$		$x_{5,6,7}$
	$s_{2,3,4}$		$s_{3,4,5}$		$s_{4,5,6}$	
	x_3		x_4		x_5	
		$s_{3,4}$		$s_{4,5}$		
		x_4				
			s_4			

The outer clusters all have counting number 1. The direct overlaps each have two larger clusters in which they are contained. Their associated counting numbers follow from Eq. (7.18) as $1 - 2 = -1$. The overlaps of overlaps have five clusters in which they are contained, their counting numbers are $1 - (3 - 2) = 0$. The clusters on the lowest level have nine parents, which results in a counting number $1 - (4 - 3 + 0) = 0$. It is easily verified that with $\kappa = 0$ we obtain the cluster and counting number choice of Section 7.4.

A second crucial observation for the SLDS is that the choice of outer clusters (7.19) implies that we only have to consider outer clusters and direct overlaps, i.e. the phenomenon that all clusters beyond the direct overlaps get an associated counting number of 0 in the example above extends to all κ. This is a direct result of the fact that the clusters from Eq. (7.19) form the cliques and separators in a (weak) junction tree. That is, another way to motivate a generalisation with the cluster choice (7.19) is to replace Eq. (7.13) with

$$p(\mathbf{z}_{1:T}|\mathbf{y}_{1:T}, \boldsymbol{\theta}) = \frac{\prod_{i=1}^{N} p(\mathbf{z}_{outer(i)}|\mathbf{y}_{1:T}, \boldsymbol{\theta})}{\prod_{j=1}^{N-1} p(\mathbf{z}_{over(j)}|\mathbf{y}_{1:T}, \boldsymbol{\theta})}, \tag{7.20}$$

and use this choice in Eq. (7.16) to obtain an extension. In Eq. (7.20), $N = T - \kappa - 1$ denotes the number of outer clusters in the approximation. The aim then becomes to minimise

$$\mathcal{F}_{GEP} = -\sum_{i=1}^{N} \sum_{\mathbf{z}_{outer(i)}} \tilde{p}_i(\mathbf{z}_{outer(i)}) \log \Psi^{(i)}(\mathbf{z}_{outer(i)})$$

$$+ \sum_{i=1}^{N} \sum_{\mathbf{z}_{outer(i)}} \tilde{p}_i(\mathbf{z}_{outer(i)}) \log \tilde{p}_i(\mathbf{z}_{outer(i)})$$

$$- \sum_{i=1}^{N-1} \sum_{\mathbf{z}_{over(i)}} \tilde{q}_i(\mathbf{z}_{over(i)}) \log \tilde{q}_i(\mathbf{z}_{over(i)}), \tag{7.21}$$

w.r.t. the potentials $\tilde{p}_i(\mathbf{z}_{outer(i)})$, and $\tilde{q}_i(\mathbf{z}_{over(i)})$. For $i = 2, 3, \ldots N - 1$, the potentials $\Psi^{(i)}(\mathbf{z}_{over(i)})$ are identical to the potentials $\psi_{i+\kappa+1}(\mathbf{z}_{i+\kappa,i+\kappa+1})$ from Eq. (7.6). At the boundaries they are a product of potentials that are 'left over'

$$\Psi^{(1)} = \prod_{j=1}^{\kappa+2} \psi_j(\mathbf{z}_{j-1,j}), \quad \Psi^{(N)} = \prod_{j=T-\kappa}^{T} \psi_j(\mathbf{z}_{j-1,j}),$$

with $\Psi^{(1)} = \prod_{j=1}^{T} \psi_j(\mathbf{z}_{j-1,j})$ if $N = 1$.

The approximation in the *generalised EP free-energy*, $\mathcal{F}_{GEP}$, arises from the restriction that $\tilde{q}_i(\mathbf{z}_{over(i)})$ is conditional Gaussian and from the fact that overlapping potentials are only required to be weakly consistent

$$\langle f(\mathbf{z}_{over(i)}) \rangle_{\tilde{p}_i} = \langle f(\mathbf{z}_{over(i)}) \rangle_{\tilde{q}_i} = \langle f(\mathbf{z}_{over(i)}) \rangle_{\tilde{p}_{i+1}}.$$

The benefit of the (weak) junction tree choice of outer clusters and overlaps is that we can employ the same algorithm for the $\kappa = 0$ as for the $\kappa > 0$ case. Algorithm 7.3 can be seen as a single-loop minimisation heuristic. Using a proof analogous to the proof for Theorem 7.1 one can show that the algorithm can be interpreted as fixed-point iteration in the space of Lagrange multipliers that are added to Eq. (7.21) to enforce the weak consistency constraints [30]. Just as for EP itself, convergence of Algorithm 7.3 is not guaranteed.

In Algorithm 7.3 the messages are initialised as conditional Gaussian potentials, such that $\tilde{q}_i(\mathbf{z}_{over(i)}) = \alpha_i(\mathbf{z}_{over(i)})\beta_i(\mathbf{z}_{over(i)})$ are normalised. A straightforward initialisation would

---

Algorithm 7.3 Generalised EP for the SLDS.

Compute a forward pass by performing the following steps for $i = 1, 2, \ldots, N - 1$, with $i' \equiv i$, and a backward pass by performing the same steps for $i = N, N - 1, \ldots, 2$, with $i' \equiv i - 1$. Iterate forward-backward passes until convergence. At the boundaries keep $\alpha_0 = \beta_N = 1$.

1. Construct an outer-cluster belief

$$\tilde{p}_i(\mathbf{z}_{outer(i)}) = \frac{\alpha_{i-1}(\mathbf{z}_{over(i-1)})\Psi^{(i)}(\mathbf{z}_{outer(i)})\beta_i(\mathbf{z}_{over(i)})}{Z_i},$$

 with $Z_i = \sum_{\mathbf{z}_{outer(i)}} \alpha_{i-1}(\mathbf{z}_{over(i-1)})\Psi^{(i)}(\mathbf{z}_{outer(i)})\beta_i(\mathbf{z}_{over(i)})$.

2. Compute one-slice marginal $\tilde{p}_i(\mathbf{z}_{over(i')}) = \sum_{\mathbf{z}_{outer(i)} \setminus \mathbf{z}_{over(i')}} \tilde{p}_i(\mathbf{z}_{outer(i)})$.

3. Find $\tilde{q}_{i'}(\mathbf{z}_{over(i')})$ that approximates $\tilde{p}_i(\mathbf{z}_{over(i')})$ best in Kullback–Leibler (KL) sense $\tilde{q}_{i'}(\mathbf{z}_{over(i')}) = \text{Collapse}\left(\tilde{p}_i(\mathbf{z}_{over(i')})\right)$.

4. Infer the new message by division

$$\alpha_i(\mathbf{z}_{over(i)}) = \frac{\tilde{q}_i(\mathbf{z}_{over(i)})}{\beta_i(\mathbf{z}_{over(i)})}, \quad \beta_{i-1}(\mathbf{z}_{over(i-1)}) = \frac{\tilde{q}_{t-1}(\mathbf{z}_{over(i-1)})}{\alpha_{i-1}(\mathbf{z}_{over(i-1)})}.$$

---

be to initialise all messages proportional to 1. If at the start all products of matching messages are normalised, we can interpret the product of local normalisations $\prod_{i=1}^{N} Z_i$ as an approximation of the normalisation constant Z.

The choice of $0 \leq \kappa \leq \lceil \frac{T-2}{2} \rceil$ allows a trade off between computational complexity and degrees of freedom in the approximation. With $\kappa = 0$, we obtain the EP/Bethe free-energy equivalent from Section 7.4. With $\kappa = \lceil \frac{T-2}{2} \rceil$ there is only one cluster and we obtain a strong junction tree, and the found posteriors are exact.

To conclude the introduction of the generalised expectation propagation algorithm it is instructive to describe the link with tree-EP [22]. In tree-EP the approximating family p forms a tree. The original introduction in [22] was as an extension of belief propagation, i.e. with strong consistency constraints, without projection steps. The preceding discussion should make it clear that all objectives with strong consistency constraints are suitable candidates to explore for finding approximations in more general models where only weak consistency constraints can be worked with. Thus tree-EP can be seen as describing a large subset of the possible GEP approximations. Since the cluster choices one obtains by choosing p a tree perform quite well in practice [26] it is worthy of further study. We refer the interested reader to [26] who, apart from experiments, also provide equivalence classes for energies (for the strong consistency constraints case) and give further rules of thumb on how to best pick outer clusters and counting numbers.

7.7 Alternative backward passes

7.7.1 Approximated backward messages

The smoothing pass in Algorithm 7.2 is the first that is symmetric in the sense that no additional approximations are introduced in the smoothing pass. This section describes two previous approaches and shows how they differ from the method proposed in Algorithm 7.2.

The forward pass in [14] is identical to the assumed density filtering discussed in Section 7.3. The backward pass differs from the one proposed in Algorithm 7.2. We refer to it as *alternative backward pass (ABP)* in the remainder of this chapter. The ABP is based on the traditional Kalman smoother form (as opposed to the two-filter approach to smoothing in EP). Instead of $\beta_t(\mathbf{z}_t) \approx p(\mathbf{y}_{t+1:T}|\mathbf{z}_t)$ messages, approximations to the smoothed posteriors $p(\mathbf{x}_t|s_t, \mathbf{y}_{1:T})$ and $p(s_t|\mathbf{y}_{1:T})$ form the basis for recursion. The smoother treats the discrete and continuous latent states separately and differently. This forces us to adapt our notation slightly. In this section we use $p(.)$ for (uncollapsed) distributions over two slices, $\psi(.)$ for the model equations (to emphasise the similarities with the factors from Section 7.3), and $q(.)$ for (collapsed) one-slice marginals. For compactness we do not explicitly write down the dependence on θ.

As in the forward pass M^2 modes are computed ($p(\mathbf{x}_t, s_t, s_{t+1}|\mathbf{y}_{1:T})$ for all instantiations of s_t and s_{t+1}) and subsequently collapsed

$$q(\mathbf{x}_t, s_t|\mathbf{y}_{1:T}) = \text{Collapse}\left(\sum_{s_{t+1},\mathbf{x}_{t+1}} p(\mathbf{x}_t, \mathbf{x}_{t+1}, s_t, s_{t+1}|\mathbf{y}_{1:T})\right).$$

The ABP differs from Algorithm 7.2 in the construction of $p(\mathbf{x}_t, \mathbf{x}_{t+1}, s_t, s_{t+1}|\mathbf{y}_{1:T})$. The conditional posterior over $\mathbf{x}_t$ is computed as follows [14]:

$$
\begin{aligned}
p(\mathbf{x}_t, \mathbf{x}_{t+1}|s_t, s_{t+1}, \mathbf{y}_{1:T}) &= p(\mathbf{x}_t|\mathbf{x}_{t+1}, s_t, s_{t+1}, \mathbf{y}_{1:t})p(\mathbf{x}_{t+1}|s_t, s_{t+1}, \mathbf{y}_{1:T}) \\
&\approx p(\mathbf{x}_t|\mathbf{x}_{t+1}, s_t, s_{t+1}, \mathbf{y}_{1:t})q(\mathbf{x}_{t+1}|s_{t+1}, \mathbf{y}_{1:T}) \qquad (7.22)\\
&= \frac{p(\mathbf{x}_t, \mathbf{x}_{t+1}|s_t, s_{t+1}, \mathbf{y}_{1:t})}{p(\mathbf{x}_{t+1}|s_t, s_{t+1}, \mathbf{y}_{1:t})}q(\mathbf{x}_{t+1}|s_{t+1}, \mathbf{y}_{1:T}) \\
&= \frac{q(\mathbf{x}_t|s_t, \mathbf{y}_{1:t})\psi(\mathbf{x}_{t+1}|\mathbf{x}_t, s_t, s_{t+1})}{p(\mathbf{x}_{t+1}|s_t, s_{t+1}, \mathbf{y}_{1:t})}q(\mathbf{x}_{t+1}|s_{t+1}, \mathbf{y}_{1:T}),
\end{aligned}
$$

where the approximation is due to the fact that if we condition on $\mathbf{y}_\tau$, with $\tau \leq t$, $\mathbf{x}_{t+1}$ is not independent of s_t.

The required posterior over the discrete latent state, $p(s_t = j, s_{t+1} = k|\mathbf{y}_{1:T})$, is computed as

$$
\begin{aligned}
p(s_t, s_{t+1}|\mathbf{y}_{1:T}) &= q(s_{t+1}|\mathbf{y}_{1:T})p(s_t|s_{t+1}, \mathbf{y}_{1:T}) \\
&\approx q(s_{t+1}|\mathbf{y}_{1:T})p(s_t|s_{t+1}, \mathbf{y}_{1:t}) \qquad\qquad\qquad (7.23)\\
&= \frac{q(s_{t+1}|\mathbf{y}_{1:T})p(s_t, s_{t+1}|\mathbf{y}_{1:t})}{q(s_{t+1}|\mathbf{y}_{1:t})} \\
&= \frac{q(s_{t+1}|\mathbf{y}_{1:T})\psi(s_{t+1}|s_t)q(s_t|\mathbf{y}_{1:t})}{q(s_{t+1}|\mathbf{y}_{1:t})}.
\end{aligned}
$$

Note that the need for the extra approximations in Eqs. (7.22) and (7.23) comes from the fact that the posteriors for discrete and continuous latent states are treated separately. The posteriors are computed by conditioning on either the discrete or the continuous latent state, i.e. only half of $\mathbf{z}_t$. A property of a Markov chain is that conditioning on the entire latent state at t renders past, future and observation independent. This property is exploited in the regular Kalman smoother and EP, but is not used in the ABP. Summarising, the ABP smoother from [14] requires two additional approximations beyond the projection onto the CG family. In contrast, EP requires no additional approximations.

7.7.2 Partial smoothing

The filter in [25] is related to the filter in Section 7.3. However, instead of approximating filtered and smoothed estimates with a CG distribution it approximates them with a single mode. The scheme computes

$$p(\mathbf{x}_{t-1,t}, s_t|\mathbf{y}_{1:t}) \propto \psi(\mathbf{y}_t, \mathbf{x}_t, s_t|\mathbf{x}_{t-1})q(\mathbf{x}_{t-1}|\mathbf{y}_{1:t}), \qquad (7.24)$$

$$q(\mathbf{x}_t|\mathbf{y}_{1:t}) = \text{Collapse}\left(\sum_{s_t, \mathbf{x}_{t-1}} p(\mathbf{x}_{t-1,t}, s_t|\mathbf{y}_{1:t})\right),$$

with $q(\mathbf{x}_t|\mathbf{y}_{1:t})$ a Gaussian distribution (compared to a mixture with M modes in the ABP and in Algorithm 7.2). This forward pass is also known as *generalised pseudo Bayes 1 (GPB 1)* [2]. The filtering recursion is treated in [25] as if it were exact if the switches only govern the observation model (no links from s_t to $\mathbf{x}_t$ in Fig. 7.1). However, even with such restrictions the greedy local projections result in an approximation of the exact one- and two-slice marginals. Following the argumentations in [18] it can be seen that the combinatoric explosion described in Section 7.2 is a property of all conditionally Gaussian dynamic models. It is essentially caused by the unobserved continuous chain $\mathbf{x}_{1:T}$ which couples all discrete states $s_{1:T}$.

In the smoothing pass of [25] the probabilities over discrete states s_t are not smoothed (only approximations of filtered regime posteriors are available by integrating $\mathbf{x}_{t-1,t}$ in Eq. (7.24)). The posterior over continuous states $\mathbf{x}_t$ are computed using the standard Kalman smoother recursion as if there are no switches.

7.8 Experiments

In this section we compare the behaviour of EP, the ABP and state-of-the-art sampling techniques. Other interesting approximation methods include the structured mean-field approach from [7] and other variants of Gibbs sampling such as [24]. However, previous studies [7, 4] have shown that these approaches are less likely to outperform the methods we discuss here. Hence we did not include them in the description and the experiments.

In the first part the methods are evaluated using artificially generated models and short data sequences. For these sequences all approximations can be compared with the exact results. In the second part we study the quality of the proposed approximation on longer sequences. Since for these longer sequences exact results are unattainable we compare the proposed method with Gibbs sampling.

7.8.1 Comparisons with exact posteriors

We generate models by drawing parameters from conjugate priors. The regime prior at $t = 1$ is multinomial. Its parameters are drawn from a uniform distribution and subsequently normalised. The parameters in the rows of $\Pi_{s_{t-1} \to s_t}$, the regime transition probabilities, are treated similarly. The elements of the initial state mean and the observation matrices C are drawn from a standard normal distribution. The state transition matrices A, are also constructed based on draws from the standard normal distribution. The covariances for the white Gaussian noise in the transition and observation models and for the initial state, are drawn from an inverse Wishart distribution with 10 degrees of freedom and scale matrix $0.01I$.

We drew 100 models with $\mathbf{x}_t \in R^3$, $\mathbf{y}_t \in R^2$ and 2 regimes, and generated a sequence of length 8 for each of these models. Using Eq. (7.4) we computed the exact posteriors.

For each task we computed approximate one-slice smoothed posteriors using the following methods.

EP1 Algorithm 7.2 with one forward-backward pass. The computational complexity[1] of this algorithm is $O(M^2T)$, with M the number of regimes and T the number of time slices.

EP Algorithm 7.2 until convergence or at most 20 iterations. The computational complexity is $O(M^2TI)$, with I the number of iterations.

ABP Using the approach from [14] described in Section 7.7, the associated complexity is $O(M^2T)$.

Gibbs 1000 samples generated using the efficient Gibbs sampler from [4]. In this sampler the continuous latent states $x_{1:T}$ are integrated out analytically. The computational cost is $O(KMT)$, with K the number of samples. The first 20 samples of the MCMC chain are discarded. Note that with $K = 1020$ the computational complexity of this approach for the current setting with $T = 8$ and $M = 2$ is higher than that of exact computation which has associated complexity $O(M^T)$.

RBPS-M Using Rao–Blackwellised particle smoothing [6, 5]. As in the Gibbs sampler, the performance of the particle smoother is significantly improved by analytically integrating out $x_{1:T}$. The number of particles is set to be identical to the number of regimes. The computational complexity is $O(KMT)$, thus choosing the number of particles, K, equal to M results in computational costs identical to EP1. Since the sequences are short, relatively few resampling steps are performed, and as a result the diversity at the start of the drawn sequences $s_{1:T}$ is still acceptable. Therefore we did not implement extra 'rejuvenation' methods [6] to increase variance on the smoothing pass.

RBPS-10M Using the Rao–Blackwellised particle smoother with the number of particles 10 times the number of regimes.

Ideally we would compute statistics such as $\mathrm{KL}\left(p_{\mathrm{exact}}(z_t)\|p_{\mathrm{approx}}(z_t)\right)$ for every time slice and every approximation method. However this often leads to an infinite KL divergence for sampling approaches, since it is not uncommon that for a particular time slice one of the regimes is not represented by at least one sample. Instead we compute the mean squared error for the posterior state mean, and the mean KL after collapsing both the exact and approximated posteriors onto a single Gaussian per state x_t

$$\frac{1}{T}\sum_{t=1}^{T}\mathrm{KL}\left(\mathrm{Collapse}(p(x_t|y_{1:T},\theta))\|\mathrm{Collapse}(p_{\mathrm{approx}}(x_t))\right),$$

i.e. a KL divergence that gives an indication of how well the mean and covariances of the exact and approximated posteriors match. Figure 7.4 gives the MSE based ranks of the algorithms we compared, an analogous figure with KL based ranks looks indistinguishable for this set of experiments and is not shown. Figure 7.5(a) gives a typical result.

---

[1]The 'big O' notation gives the order of the computation time disregarding constant factors which depend on the particular implementation. The complexities of operations on Gaussian potentials depend on the dimensions of the observations and the states, but are equal for all methods. We therefore treat these operations as constants in the complexity description.

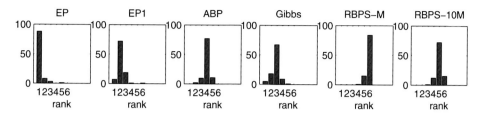

Figure 7.4 Histogram of ranks of the tested algorithms on 100 artificially generated problems. Rank 1 indicates smallest distance with exact state posterior in the MSE sense, rank 6 indicates largest distance.

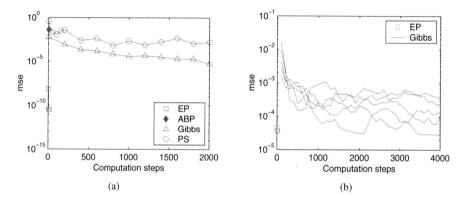

Figure 7.5 (a) Results from a 'typical' task from the experiments represented in Fig. 7.4. Mean squared error is shown versus 'computation steps'. One iteration of EP is equivalent to M^2 such computation steps, drawing K samples for the Gibbs sampler or working with K particles in the particle smoother is equivalent to KM steps. This makes the x-axis roughly proportional to CPU time. For the particle smoother, 14 different runs with different values for K were used, a line connects these for clarity. (b) Results from an experiment with a long observation sequence. Mean squared errors in the posterior state means for five independent Gibbs runs and EP are shown. The estimate based on samples from the combined five Gibbs runs is taken as ground truth. Observe that the distance of the deterministic approximation to the ground truth is of the same order as the individual Gibbs runs.

From Fig. 7.4 we see that Algorithm 7.2 nearly always outperforms traditional methods. The results from Fig. 7.5(a) show that all methods give reasonable results (although Fig. 7.5(a) only shows results for a single task, the results for the others are comparable). Although both the particle smoother and the Gibbs sampler would give exact results in the limit of infinite K, the rate at which this is attained is slow. If we stop after a finite, but considerable time, we see that for the models studied here Algorithm 7.2 gives more accurate results, and does so in a fraction of the computation time. Comparing the results between the first iteration for EP with the forward-backward pass in ABP from [14], we see that the extra approximations in the backward pass in [14] indeed have a negative effect.

The results presented in this section represent properties of the set of SLDS models associated with the generating parameters as described above. It would be worthwhile to more carefully explore the space of SLDS models. The work by [23] gives some support for generality. In their paper expectation propagation for the SLDS is derived as well and experiments compare the performance of EP and a Rao–Blackwellised particle filter on a signal detection problem. The results are similar to the ones presented here: for the sampler to achieve results similar in quality to the EP iteration significantly more CPU cycles are needed.

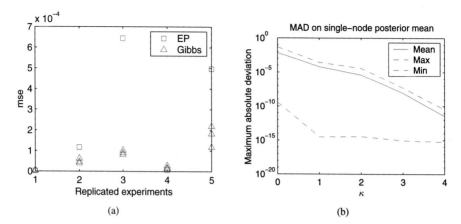

(a)   (b)

Figure 7.6 (a) Results from five experiments similar to the experiment from Fig. 7.5(b) based on three instead of five individual chains. For every replication the mean squared distance in the posterior state means between EP and the ground truth, and three individual Gibbs chains and the ground truth are plotted. The ground truth is taken to be the state means based on the combined three Gibbs chains. (b) Maximum absolute deviation between exact and approximate single-slice posterior state mean as a function of κ. Shown are the mean, maximum and minimum over ten replications. In all replications $T = 10$, so $\kappa = 4$ gives exact results. The small differences between the mean, maximum and minimum deviations that are observed in the plot for $\kappa = 4$ are caused by different round-off errors in the generalised EP and the original strong junction tree implementations.

7.8.2   Comparisons with Gibbs sampling

In this section we study the quality of the approximations on sequences with 100 observations. In our experiments we compare the deterministic approximation with five independent runs of the Gibbs sampler, drawing 2000 samples each. This corresponds roughly to a minute computation time for the deterministic approach and a weekend for the five runs.

Figure 7.5(b) shows a comparison of the posterior means based on the individual Gibbs runs and the deterministic approximation and the posterior means computed from the combined samples of all the five runs. As can be seen all approximations lie relatively close, which probably indicates that all approximations give reasonably correct results.

Since for any three vectors a, b and c

$$(a - c)^\mathsf{T}(a - c) = 2\left((a - b)^\mathsf{T}(a - b) + (b - c)^\mathsf{T}(b - c)\right) - (a + c - 2b)^\mathsf{T}(a + c - 2b)$$
$$\leq 2\left((a - b)^\mathsf{T}(a - b) + (b - c)^\mathsf{T}(b - c)\right),$$

we have an effective bound on the mean squared error of EP. Taking a, b and c to be the EP, Gibbs and exact posterior state means respectively, we get that the EP MSE is bounded by two times the sum of the Gibbs MSE and the Gibbs-EP mean squared distance, that is

$$E_{\text{EP}} \leq 2\left(E_{\text{Gibbs}} + D_{\text{Gibbs,EP}}\right). \tag{7.25}$$

Thus from Eq. (7.25), and the analogous bound for the Gibbs error, we see that the difference in error between the Gibbs and EP approximation is of the order $D_{\text{Gibbs,EP}}$. This Gibbs–EP mean squared distance can be read off from Fig. 7.5(b) and is relatively small. Figure 7.5(b) shows results from a single experiment. In Fig. 7.6(a) the results of five replications of this experiment (based on three instead of five individual Gibbs chains) are shown. In the five replications the mean squared distance between EP and Gibbs is consistently small.

The experiments in this section give empirical evidence that our proposed approxima-tion does not break down on longer sequences. For the analogous approximate filter in a fully discrete network (where the projection is onto a factorised distribution) Boyen and Koller [3] show that the errors incurred by the approximation disappear at a geometric rate due to the stochastic nature of the transition model. Intuitively, as exact and approximate estimates are propagated through the transition model some of the 'information' in both is forgotten, resulting in a smearing effect which makes both predicted distributions closer. Although the experiments in this section support a conjecture that such a proof can be extended to the conditional Gaussian case, the required technical conditions on the model and the proof itself remain work for future research.

7.8.3   Effect of larger outer clusters

To explore the effect of κ in Algorithm 7.3, we ran an experiment where a sequence of length 10 was generated from a model drawn from the same distribution as in Section 7.8.1. For every sequence, approximate single node posteriors $\tilde{q}(\mathbf{x}_t|\mathbf{y}_{1:T},\boldsymbol{\theta})$ were computed using Algorithm 7.3 with $\kappa = 0, 1, 2, 3, 4$. Since the sequence is of length 10, it is also possible to compute the exact posterior. Figure 7.6(b) shows the maximum absolute error in the single node posterior means as a function of κ. The lines show the average over 10 replications, the maximum encountered and the minimum.

For sequences with length 10, $\kappa = 4$ is guaranteed to give exact results. So in theory, the lines in Fig. 7.6(b) should meet at $\kappa = 4$. The discrepancies in Fig. 7.6(b) are explained by different round-off errors in our implementations of Algorithm 7.3 and the strong junction tree algorithm.

In all our experiments we have observed that, with the inference problem fixed, the accuracy in the posterior mean systematically increases when κ is increased. It should be noted however that due to the local nature of the approximations such increases are not guaranteed. This is completely analogous to the fact that a generalised belief propaga-tion algorithm need not yield results that are better than the regular belief propagation approximation on which they are based. In fact in certain applications of generalised belief propagation where loops are ignored significant decreases in accuracy have been observed (see e.g. [13]). However in the generalised expectation propagation algorithm, and particularly in its use here for the SLDS where no loops are disregarded, we would actually expect the results we see here: keeping more components in the approximation in general will increase the accuracy of the approximation.

7.9   Discussion

This chapter has discussed a deterministic approximation scheme for the well-known infer-ence problem in conditionally Gaussian state space models. Whereas the complexity of exact inference scales exponentially with the number of observations, the new approximate method requires computation time linear in the number of observations.

The approach can be seen as a symmetric backward pass to previously proposed assumed density filtering methods and is based on the expectation propagation algorithm. In the literature several alternative backward passes have been introduced. An important benefit of the method described in this chapter is that the underlying philosophy for the for-ward and backward passes are the same and that, unlike the previously known methods, no additional approximations need to be made in the backward pass. Numerical experiments suggest that removing these additional approximations leads to a significant increase in accuracy.

The approximation method works for the general switching linear dynamical system. No specific assumptions such as invertibility of transition or observation models are needed. Since both the forward and the backward passes perform greedy and local approximations it makes sense to iterate passes to find a 'best' approximation. Section 7.5 described a variant of the Bethe free-energy that is related to such a scheme. Fixed points of iterations of forward-backward passes correspond to extrema of this energy. The fixed points have a natural interpretation closely related to properties of the exact posterior.

An extension of the basic algorithm can be obtained based on generalised expectation propagation. Such an extension keeps more components in the approximation. It does so in such a way that these extended approximations from the filtering pass can be improved in a principled way in the smoothing pass. In our experiments we see that increasing the size of the outer clusters in the approximation, and hence increasing the number of components that are retained in the approximation, systematically increases the accuracy of the approximation.

The main benefit of the more involved approximation is expected to be for 'difficult' models where the ambiguity in the discrete states can only be resolved based on observations from several consecutive time steps. However a formal characterisation of 'easy' and 'difficult' problems currently does not exist and a systematic empirical study remains work for future research.

In general we feel that expectation propagation and generalised expectation propagation based approximations form a promising foundation for fast and accurate inference algorithms for the switching linear dynamical system. But several open issues remain.

The first point is that the iteration schemes in Algorithms 7.2 and 7.3 are not guaranteed to converge. More elaborate double-loop techniques exist [11], but these are significantly slower, so an appropriate adaptation of the message-passing algorithm is highly desirable. Furthermore, the double-loop schemes do not prevent problems with supportiveness and may even make things worse.

A second more technical point is that in the algorithm CG potentials are multiplied and marginalised. For the multiplication canonical parameters are necessary, the marginalisation requires moments. The conversion from one form to the other implies the inversion of covariance and precision matrices. This can result in numerical problems in a basic implementation. There currently does not exist an implementation that is guaranteed to be numerically stable yet avoids additional approximation in the backward pass. Chapter 8 discusses these problems in more detail and introduces an alternative.

Perhaps the most ambitious direction of future research, is that of a guarantee of the approximation quality. The authors in [19] show that for the general switching linear dynamical system constant factor approximations remain NP-hard. But one might hope that either for a specific subclass of models or after observing a specific sequence of observations a guarantee can be given.

7.A Appendix: Operations on conditional Gaussian potentials

To allow for simple notation in the main text this appendix introduces the conditional Gaussian (CG) distribution. A discrete variable s and a continuous variable $\mathbf{x}$ are jointly CG distributed if the marginal of s is multinomial distributed and, conditioned on s, $\mathbf{x}$ is

Gaussian distributed. Let $\mathbf{x}$ be d-dimensional and let S be the set of values s can take. In the moment form the joint distribution reads

$$p(s, \mathbf{x}) = \pi_s (2\pi)^{-d/2} |\Sigma_s|^{-1/2} \exp\left[-\frac{1}{2}(\mathbf{x} - \mu_s)^{\mathsf{T}} \Sigma_s^{-1}(\mathbf{x} - \mu_s)\right],$$

with moment parameters $\{\pi_s, \mu_s, \Sigma_s + \mu_s \mu_s^{\mathsf{T}}\}$, where π_s is positive for all s and satisfies $\sum_s \pi_s = 1$, and Σ_s is a positive definite matrix. The definition of $\Sigma_s + \mu_s \mu_s^{\mathsf{T}}$ instead of Σ_s is motivated by Eq. (7.28) below. For compact notation sets with elements dependent on s will implicitly range over $s \in S$. In canonical form the CG distribution is given by

$$p(s, \mathbf{x}) = \exp\left[g_s + \mathbf{x}^{\mathsf{T}} \mathbf{h}_s - \frac{1}{2} \mathbf{x}^{\mathsf{T}} K_s \mathbf{x}\right], \tag{7.26}$$

with canonical parameters $\{g_s, \mathbf{h}_s, K_s\}$.

The so-called *link function* $g(\cdot)$ maps canonical parameters to moment parameters

$$g(\{g_s, \mathbf{h}_s, K_s\}) = \{\pi_s, \mu_s, \Sigma_s + \mu_s \mu_s^{\mathsf{T}}\}$$
$$\pi_s = \exp(g_s - \bar{g}_s)$$
$$\mu_s = K_s^{-1} \mathbf{h}_s$$
$$\Sigma_s = K_s^{-1},$$

with $\bar{g}_s \equiv \frac{1}{2}\log|\frac{K_s}{2\pi}| - \frac{1}{2}\mathbf{h}_s^{\mathsf{T}} K_s \mathbf{h}_s$, the part of g_s that depends on $\mathbf{h}_s$ and K_s. The link function is unique and invertible

$$g^{-1}(\{\pi_s, \mu_s, \Sigma_s + \mu_s \mu_s^{\mathsf{T}}\}) = \{g_s, \mathbf{h}_s, K_s\}$$
$$g_s = \log \pi_s - \frac{1}{2}\log|2\pi\Sigma_s| - \frac{1}{2}\mu_s^{\mathsf{T}}\Sigma_s^{-1}\mu_s$$
$$\mathbf{h}_s = \Sigma_s^{-1}\mu_s$$
$$K_s = \Sigma_s^{-1}.$$

A conditional Gaussian *potential* is a generalisation of the above distribution in the sense that it has the same form as in Eq. (7.26) but need not integrate to 1; K_s is restricted to be symmetric, but need not be positive definite. If K_s is positive definite the moment parameters are determined by $g(.)$. In this section we will use $\phi(s, \mathbf{x}; \{g_s, \mathbf{h}_s, K_s\})$ to denote a CG potential over s and $\mathbf{x}$ with canonical parameters $\{g_s, \mathbf{h}_s, K_s\}$.

Multiplication and division of CG potentials are the straightforward extensions of the analogous operations for multinomial and Gaussian potentials. In canonical form

$$\phi(s, \mathbf{x}; \{g_s, \mathbf{h}_s, K_s\})\phi(s, \mathbf{x}; \{g_s', \mathbf{h}_s', K_s'\}) = \phi(s, \mathbf{x}; \{g_s + g_s', \mathbf{h}_s + \mathbf{h}_s', K_s + K_s'\}),$$
$$\phi(s, \mathbf{x}; \{g_s, \mathbf{h}_s, K_s\})/\phi(s, \mathbf{x}; \{g_s', \mathbf{h}_s', K_s'\}) = \phi(s, \mathbf{x}; \{g_s - g_s', \mathbf{h}_s - \mathbf{h}_s', K_s - K_s'\}).$$

With the above definition of multiplication we can define a unit potential

$$1(s, \mathbf{x}) \equiv \phi(s, \mathbf{x}; \{0, \mathbf{0}, 0\}),$$

which satisfies $1(s, \mathbf{x})p(s, \mathbf{x}) = p(s, \mathbf{x})$ for all CG potentials $p(s, \mathbf{x})$. We will sometimes use the shorthand 1 for the unit potential when its domain is clear from the text.

In a similar spirit we can define multiplication and division of potentials with different domains. If the domain of one of the potentials (the denominator in case of division) forms a subset of the domain of the other we can *extend* the smaller to match the larger and perform a regular multiplication or division as defined above. The continuous domain of the small potential is extended by adding zeros in $\mathbf{h}_s$ and K_s at the corresponding positions. The discrete domain is extended by replicating parameters, e.g. extending s to $[s\ t]^\mathsf{T}$ we use parameters $g_{st} = g_s$, $\mathbf{h}_{st} = \mathbf{h}_s$, and $K_{st} = K_s$.

Marginalisation is less straightforward for CG potentials. Integrating out continuous dimensions is analogous to marginalisation in Gaussian potentials and is only defined if the corresponding moment parameters are defined. Marginalisation is then defined as converting to moment form, 'selecting' the appropriate rows and columns from $\boldsymbol{\mu}_s$ and Σ_s, and converting back to canonical form. More problematic is the marginalisation over discrete dimensions of the CG potential. Summing out s results in a distribution $p(\mathbf{x})$ which is a mixture of Gaussians with mixing weights $p(s)$, i.e. the CG family is not closed under summation.

We define *weak marginalisation* [18] as exact marginalisation followed by a *collapse*: a projection of the exact marginal onto the CG family. The projection minimises the Kullback–Leibler divergence $KL(p\|q)$ between p, the exact (strong) marginal and q, the weak marginal

$$q(s, \mathbf{x}) = \underset{q \in CG}{\operatorname{argmin}}\ \mathrm{KL}\,(p\|q) \equiv \underset{q \in CG}{\operatorname{argmin}} \sum_{s,\mathbf{x}} p(s, \mathbf{x}) \log \frac{p(s, \mathbf{x})}{q(s, \mathbf{x})}.$$

This projection is only defined for properly normalised distributions p and has the property that, conditioned on s the weak marginal has the same mean and covariance as the exact marginal. The weak marginal can be computed by *moment matching* (see e.g. [27]). If $p(\mathbf{x}|s)$ is a mixture of Gaussians for every s with mixture weights $\pi_{r|s}$, means $\boldsymbol{\mu}_{sr}$, and covariances Σ_{sr} (e.g. the exact marginal $\sum_r p(s, r, \mathbf{x})$ of CG distribution $p(s, r, \mathbf{x})$), the moment matching procedure is defined as

$$\text{Collapse}\,(p(s, \mathbf{x})) \equiv p(s)\mathcal{N}(\mathbf{x}; \boldsymbol{\mu}_s, \Sigma_s)$$

$$\boldsymbol{\mu}_s \equiv \sum_r \pi_{r|s}\boldsymbol{\mu}_{sr}$$

$$\Sigma_s \equiv \sum_r \pi_{r|s}\left(\Sigma_{sr} + (\boldsymbol{\mu}_{sr} - \boldsymbol{\mu}_s)(\boldsymbol{\mu}_{sr} - \boldsymbol{\mu}_s)^\mathsf{T}\right).$$

Contrary to exact marginalisation, this projection is not linear, and hence in general:

$$\text{Collapse}\,(p(s, \mathbf{x})q(\mathbf{x})) \neq \text{Collapse}\,(p(s, \mathbf{x}))\,q(\mathbf{x}).$$

In even more compact notation, denoting with $\delta_{s,m}$ the Kronecker delta function, we can write a CG potential as

$$p(s, \mathbf{x}) = \exp[v^\mathsf{T} f(s, \mathbf{x})], \tag{7.27}$$

with

$$f(s, \mathbf{x}) \equiv [\delta_{s,m}\ \delta_{s,m}\mathbf{x}^\mathsf{T}\delta_{s,m}\text{vec}(\mathbf{x}\mathbf{x}^\mathsf{T})^\mathsf{T}|m \in S]^\mathsf{T}, \qquad v \equiv [g_s\ \mathbf{h}_s^\mathsf{T}\ -\frac{1}{2}\text{vec}(K_s)^\mathsf{T}|s \in S]^\mathsf{T}$$

the sufficient statistics and the canonical parameters respectively. In this notation the moment parameters follow from the canonical parameters as

$$g(v) = \langle f(s, \mathbf{x})\rangle_{\exp[v^\mathsf{T} f(s,\mathbf{x})]} \equiv \sum_s \int d\mathbf{x} f(s, \mathbf{x}) \exp[v^\mathsf{T} f(s, \mathbf{x})]. \tag{7.28}$$

7.B Appendix: Proof of Theorem 7.1

In this section we present the proof of Theorem 7.1. The proof and intuition are analogous to the result that fixed points of loopy belief propagation can be mapped to extrema of the Bethe free-energy [28].

Theorem 7.1 *The collection of beliefs $\hat{p}_t(\mathbf{z}_{t-1,t})$ and $\hat{q}_t(\mathbf{z}_t)$ form fixed points of Algorithm 7.2 if and only if they are zero gradient points of $\mathcal{F}_{EP}$ under the appropriate constraints.*

Proof. The properties of the fixed points of message passing follow from the description of Algorithm 7.2. We get the CG form (7.27) of messages α_t and β_t and their relationship with one- and two-slice marginals

$$\hat{p}_t(\mathbf{z}_{t-1,t}) \propto \alpha_{t-1}(\mathbf{z}_{t-1})\psi_t(\mathbf{z}_{t-1,t})\beta_t(\mathbf{z}_t), \qquad \hat{q}_t(\mathbf{z}_t) \propto \alpha_t(\mathbf{z}_t)\beta_t(\mathbf{z}_t)$$

by construction, and consistency after a collapse

$$\langle f(\mathbf{z}_t)\rangle_{\hat{p}_t} = \langle f(\mathbf{z}_t)\rangle_{\hat{q}_t} = \langle f(\mathbf{z}_t)\rangle_{\hat{p}_{t+1}} , \tag{7.29}$$

as a property of a fixed point.

To identify the nature of stationary points of $\mathcal{F}_{EP}$ we first construct the Lagrangian by adding Lagrange multipliers $\alpha_t(\mathbf{z}_t)$ and $\beta_t(\mathbf{z}_t)$ for the forward and backward consistency constraints and $\gamma_{t-1,t}$ and γ_t for the normalisation constraints.

$$
\begin{aligned}
\mathcal{L}_{EP}(\hat{p},\hat{q},\alpha,\beta,\gamma) = &\sum_{t=1}^{T}\sum_{\mathbf{z}_{t-1,t}} \hat{p}_t(\mathbf{z}_{t-1,t})\log\frac{\hat{p}_t(\mathbf{z}_{t-1,t})}{\psi_t(\mathbf{z}_{t-1,t})} - \sum_{t=2}^{T-1}\sum_{\mathbf{z}_t}\hat{q}_t(\mathbf{z}_t)\log\hat{q}_t(\mathbf{z}_t) \\
&- \sum_{t=2}^{T-1}\alpha_{t-1}(\mathbf{z}_{t-1})^{\mathsf{T}}\left[\sum_{\mathbf{z}_{t-1,t}}f_{t-1}(\mathbf{z}_{t-1})\hat{p}_t(\mathbf{z}_{t-1,t}) - \sum_{\mathbf{z}_{t-1}}f_{t-1}(\mathbf{z}_{t-1})\hat{q}_{t-1}(\mathbf{z}_{t-1})\right] \\
&- \sum_{t=2}^{T-1}\beta_t(\mathbf{z}_t)^{\mathsf{T}}\left[\sum_{\mathbf{z}_{t-1,t}}f_t(\mathbf{z}_t)\hat{p}_t(\mathbf{z}_{t-1,t}) - \sum_{\mathbf{z}_t}f_t(\mathbf{z}_t)\hat{q}_t(\mathbf{z}_t)\right] \\
&- \sum_{t=1}^{T}\gamma_{t-1,t}\left[\sum_{\mathbf{z}_{t-1,t}}\hat{p}_t(\mathbf{z}_{t-1,t}) - 1\right] - \sum_{t=2}^{T-1}\gamma_t\left[\sum_{\mathbf{z}_t}\hat{q}_t(\mathbf{z}_t) - 1\right].
\end{aligned}
$$

Note that $\alpha_t(\mathbf{z}_t)$ and $\beta_t(\mathbf{z}_t)$ (in boldface to distinguish them from messages and to emphasise that they are vectors) are vectors of canonical parameters as defined in Appendix 7.A.

The stationarity conditions follow by setting the partial derivatives to 0. Taking derivatives w.r.t. $\hat{p}_t(\mathbf{z}_{t-1,t})$ and $\hat{q}_t(\mathbf{z}_t)$ gives

$$\frac{\partial\mathcal{L}_{EP}}{\partial\hat{p}_t(\mathbf{z}_{t-1,t})} = \log\hat{p}_t(\mathbf{z}_{t-1,t}) + 1 - \log\psi_t(\mathbf{z}_{t-1,t}) - \alpha_{t-1}(\mathbf{z}_{t-1})^{\mathsf{T}}f_{t-1}(\mathbf{z}_{t-1}) - \beta_t(\mathbf{z}_t)^{\mathsf{T}}f_t(\mathbf{z}_t) - \gamma_{t-1,t},$$

$$\frac{\partial\mathcal{L}_{EP}}{\partial\hat{q}_t(\mathbf{z}_t)} = -\log\hat{q}_t(\mathbf{z}_t) - 1 + \alpha_t(\mathbf{z}_t)^{\mathsf{T}}f_t(\mathbf{z}_t) + \beta_t(\mathbf{z}_t)^{\mathsf{T}}f_t(\mathbf{z}_t) - \gamma_t.$$

Setting above derivatives to 0 and filling in the solutions for $\gamma_{t-1,t}$ and γ_t (which simply form the log of the normalisation constants) results in

$$\hat{p}_t(\mathbf{z}_{t-1,t}) \propto e^{\alpha_{t-1}(\mathbf{z}_{t-1})^{\mathsf{T}}f_{t-1}(\mathbf{z}_{t-1})}\psi_t(\mathbf{z}_{t-1,t})e^{\beta_t(\mathbf{z}_t)^{\mathsf{T}}f_t(\mathbf{z}_t)}, \qquad \hat{q}_t(\mathbf{z}_t) \propto e^{\alpha_t(\mathbf{z}_t)^{\mathsf{T}}f_t(\mathbf{z}_t) + \beta_t(\mathbf{z}_t)^{\mathsf{T}}f_t(\mathbf{z}_t)}.$$

The conditions $\frac{\partial \mathcal{L}_{EP}}{\partial \alpha_t(\mathbf{z}_t)} = 0$ and $\frac{\partial \mathcal{L}_{EP}}{\partial \beta_t(\mathbf{z}_t)} = 0$ retrieve the forward-equals-backward constraints (7.29).

So if we identify α_t as the vector of the canonical parameters of the message α_t and β_t as the vector of the canonical parameters of the message β_t, we see that the conditions for stationarity of $\mathcal{F}_{EP}$ and fixed points of Algorithm 7.2 are the same. $\square$

As can be seen from the above proof, iteration of the forward-backward passes can be interpreted as fixed-point iteration in terms of Lagrange multipliers.

Bibliography

[1] Y. Bar-Shalom and X.-R. Li. *Estimation and Tracking: Principles, Techniques, and Software.* Artech House, 1993.

[2] Y. Bar-Shalom and T. Fortmann. *Tracking and Data Association.* Academic Press, 1988.

[3] X. Boyen and D. Koller. Tractable inference for complex stochastic processes. In *Proceedings of the 14th Annual Conference on Uncertainty in Artificial Intelligence,* pages 33-42 Morgan Kaufmann Publishers, 1998.

[4] C. Carter and R. Kohn. Markov chain Monte Carlo in conditionally Gaussian state space models. *Biometrika,* **83**(3):589–601, 1996.

[5] R. Chen and J. S. Liu. Mixture Kalman filters. *Journal of the Royal Statistical Society, Series B,* **62**:493–508, 2000.

[6] A. Doucet, N. de Freitas, K. Murphy and S. Russel. Rao-Blackwellized particle filtering for dynamic Bayesian networks. In *Proceedings of the 17th Annual Conference on Uncertainty in Artificial Intelligence* pages 176–183. Morgan Kaufmann Publishers, 2001.

[7] Z. Ghahramani and G. E. Hinton. Variational learning for switching state-space models. *Neural Computation,* **12**(4):963–996, 1998.

[8] J. Hamilton. A new approach to the economic analysis of nonstationary time series and the business cycle. *Econometrica,* **57**(2):357–384, 1989.

[9] P. J. Harrison and C. F. Stevens. Bayesian forecasting. *Journal of the Royal Statistical Society Society B,* **38**:205–247, 1976.

[10] R. E. Helmick, W. D. Blair and S. A. Hoffman. Fixed-interval smoothing for Markovian switching systems. *IEEE Transactions on Information Theory,* **41**:1845–1855, 1995.

[11] T. Heskes and O. Zoeter. Expectation propagation for approximate inference in dynamic Bayesian networks. In *Proceedings of the 18th Annual Conference on Uncertainty in Artificial Intelligence,* pages 216–223. Morgan Kaufmann Publishers, 2002.

[12] T. Heskes and O. Zoeter. Generalized belief propagation for approximate inference in hybrid Bayesian networks. In C. Bishop and B. Frey, editors, *Proceedings of the Ninth International Workshop on Artificial Intelligence and Statistics,* 2003.

[13] H. J. Kappen and W. Wiegerinck. Novel iteration schemes for the cluster variation method. In *Advances in Neural Information Processing Systems 14,* pages 415–422. MIT Press, 2002.

[14] C.-J. Kim and C. R. Nelson. *State-Space Models with Regime Switching.* MIT Press, 1999.

[15] G. Kitagawa. Monte Carlo filter and smoother for non-Gaussian nonlinear state space models. *Journal of Computational and Graphical Statistics,* **5**(1):1–25, 1996.

[16] F. R. Kschischang, B. J. Frey and H.-A. Loeliger. Factor graphs and the sum-product algorithm. *IEEE Transactions on Information Theory,* **47**(2):498–519, 2001.

[17] S. Kullback and R. A. Leibler. On information and sufficiency. *Annals of Mathematical Statistics,* **22**(1):76–86, 1951.

[18] S. L. Lauritzen. Propagation of probabilities, means, and variances in mixed graphical association models. *Journal of the American Statistical Association,* **87**:1098–1108, 1992.

[19] U. Lerner and R. Parr. Inference in hybrid networks: Theoretical limits and practical algorithms. In *Proceedings of the 17th Annual Conference on Uncertainty in Artificial Intelligence,* pages 310–318. Morgan Kaufmann Publishers, 2001.

[20] U. Lerner, R. Parr, D. Koller and G. Biswas. Bayesian fault detection and diagnosis in dynamic systems. In *Proceedings of the 17th National Conference on Artificial Intelligence,* pages 531–537, 2000.

[21] T. Minka. Expectation propagation for approximate Bayesian inference. In *Proceedings of the 17th Annual Conference on Uncertainty in Artificial Intelligence (UAI 2001).* Morgan Kaufmann Publishers, 2001.

[22] T. Minka and Y. Qi. Tree-structured approximations by expectation propagation. In *Advances in Neural Information Processing Systems,* pages 193–200. MIT Press, 2004.

[23] Y. Qi and T. Minka. Expectation propagation for signal detection in flat-fading channels. *IEEE transactions on Wireless Communications,* **6**:348–355, 2007.

[24] N. Shephard. Partial non-Gaussian state space models. *Biometrika,* **81**:115–131, 1994.

[25] R. H. Shumway and D. S. Stoffer. Dynamic linear models with switching. *Journal of the American Statistical Association*, **86**:763–769, 1991.

[26] M. Welling, T. Minka and Y. W. Teh. Structured region graphs: Morphing EP into GBP. In *Proceedings of the Twenty-First Conference Annual Conference on Uncertainty in Artificial Intelligence*, pages 609–614. AUAI Press, 2005.

[27] J. Whittaker. *Graphical Models in Applied Multivariate Statistics*. John Wiley and Sons, 1989.

[28] J. Yedidia, W. Freeman and Y. Weiss. Generalized belief propagation. In *Advances in Neural Information Processing Systems 13*, pages 689–695, MIR Press, 2001.

[29] J. Yedidia, W. Freeman and Y. Weiss. Constructing free energy approximations and generalized belief propagation algorithms. Technical report, MERL, 2004.

[30] O. Zoeter and T. Heskes. Change point problems in linear dynamical systems. *Journal of Machine Learning Research*, **6**:1999–2026, 2005.

Contributors

Onno Zoeter, Xerox Research Centre Europe, 6 Chemin de Maupertuis, 36240 Meylan, France

Tom Heskes, Institute for Computing and Information Sciences, Radboud University Nijmegen, Heyendaalseweg 135, 6525 AJ Nijmegen, The Netherlands

8

Approximate inference in switching linear dynamical systems using Gaussian mixtures

David Barber

8.1 Introduction

The linear dynamical system (LDS) (see Section 1.3.2) is a standard time series model in which a latent linear process generates the observations. Complex time series which are not well described globally by a single LDS may be divided into segments, each modelled by a potentially different LDS. Such models can handle situations in which the underlying model 'jumps' from one parameter setting to another. For example a single LDS might well represent the normal flows in a chemical plant. However, if there is a break in a pipeline, the dynamics of the system changes from one set of linear flow equations to another. This scenario could be modelled by two sets of linear systems, each with different parameters, with a discrete latent variable at each time $s_t \in \{\text{normal, pipe broken}\}$ indicating which of the LDSs is most appropriate at the current time. This is called a switching LDS (SLDS) and used in many disciplines, from econometrics to machine learning [2, 9, 15, 13, 12, 6, 5, 19, 21, 16].

8.2 The switching linear dynamical system

At each time t, a switch variable $s_t \in \{1, \dots, S\}$ describes which of a set of LDSs is to be used. The observation (or 'visible') variable $\mathbf{v}_t \in \mathcal{R}^V$ is linearly related to the hidden state $\mathbf{h}_t \in \mathcal{R}^H$ by

$$\mathbf{v}_t = \mathbf{B}(s_t)\mathbf{h}_t + \boldsymbol{\eta}^v(s_t), \qquad \boldsymbol{\eta}^v(s_t) \sim \mathcal{N}\left(\boldsymbol{\eta}^v(s_t)|\bar{\mathbf{v}}(s_t), \boldsymbol{\Sigma}^v(s_t)\right). \tag{8.1}$$

Here s_t describes which of the set of emission matrices $\mathbf{B}(1), \dots, \mathbf{B}(S)$ is active at time t. The observation noise $\boldsymbol{\eta}^v(s_t)$ is drawn from one of a set of Gaussians with different means $\bar{\mathbf{v}}(s_t)$ and covariances $\boldsymbol{\Sigma}^v(s_t)$. The transition of the continuous hidden state $\mathbf{h}_t$ is linear,

$$\mathbf{h}_t = \mathbf{A}(s_t)\mathbf{h}_{t-1} + \boldsymbol{\eta}^h(s_t), \qquad \boldsymbol{\eta}^h(s_t) \sim \mathcal{N}\left(\boldsymbol{\eta}^h(s_t)|\bar{\mathbf{h}}(s_t), \boldsymbol{\Sigma}^h(s_t)\right), \tag{8.2}$$

and the switch variable s_t selects a single transition matrix from the available set $\mathbf{A}(1), \dots, \mathbf{A}(S)$. The Gaussian transition noise $\boldsymbol{\eta}^h(s_t)$ also depends on the switch variables. The dynamics of s_t itself is Markovian, with transition $p(s_t|s_{t-1})$. For the more general 'augmented' (aSLDS) model the switch s_t is dependent on both the previous s_{t-1}

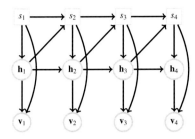

Figure 8.1 The independence structure of the aSLDS. Square nodes s_t denote discrete switch variables; $\mathbf{h}_t$ are continuous latent/hidden variables, and $\mathbf{v}_t$ continuous observed/visible variables. The discrete state s_t determines which linear dynamical system from a finite set of linear dynamical systems is operational at time t. In the SLDS links from h to s are not normally considered.

and $\mathbf{h}_{t-1}$. The probabilistic model defines a joint distribution, see Fig. 8.1,

$$p(\mathbf{v}_{1:T}, \mathbf{h}_{1:T}, s_{1:T}) = \prod_{t=1}^{T} p(\mathbf{v}_t|\mathbf{h}_t, s_t)p(\mathbf{h}_t|\mathbf{h}_{t-1}, s_t)p(s_t|\mathbf{h}_{t-1}, s_{t-1}),$$

$$p(\mathbf{v}_t|\mathbf{h}_t, s_t) = \mathcal{N}\left(\mathbf{v}_t | \bar{\mathbf{v}}(s_t) + \mathbf{B}(s_t)\mathbf{h}_t, \Sigma^v(s_t)\right),$$

$$p(\mathbf{h}_t|\mathbf{h}_{t-1}, s_t) = \mathcal{N}\left(\mathbf{h}_t | \bar{\mathbf{h}}(s_t) + \mathbf{A}(s_t)\mathbf{h}_{t-1}, \Sigma^h(s_t)\right).$$

At time $t = 1$, $p(s_1|\mathbf{h}_0, s_0)$ denotes the prior $p(s_1)$, and $p(\mathbf{h}_1|\mathbf{h}_0, s_1)$ denotes $p(\mathbf{h}_1|s_1)$. The SLDS can be thought of as a marriage between a hidden Markov model and an LDS. The SLDS is also called a jump Markov model/process, switching Kalman filter, switching linear Gaussian state space model, conditional linear Gaussian model.

8.2.1 Exact inference is computationally intractable

Performing exact filtered and smoothed inference in the SLDS is intractable, scaling exponentially with time, see for example [16]. As an informal explanation, consider filtered posterior inference, for which, by analogy with Section 1.4.1 the forward pass is

$$p(s_{t+1}, \mathbf{h}_{t+1}|\mathbf{v}_{1:t+1}) = \sum_{s_t} \int_{\mathbf{h}_t} p(s_{t+1}, \mathbf{h}_{t+1}|s_t, \mathbf{h}_t, \mathbf{v}_{t+1})p(s_t, \mathbf{h}_t|\mathbf{v}_{1:t}). \tag{8.3}$$

At time step 1, $p(s_1, \mathbf{h}_1|\mathbf{v}_1) = p(\mathbf{h}_1|s_1, \mathbf{v}_1)p(s_1|\mathbf{v}_1)$ is an indexed Gaussian. At time step 2, due to the summation over the states s_1, $p(s_2, \mathbf{h}_2|\mathbf{v}_{1:2})$ is an indexed set of S Gaussians. In general, at time t, $p(s_t, \mathbf{h}_t|\mathbf{v}_{1:t})$ is an indexed set of S^{t-1} Gaussians. Even for small t, the number of components required to exactly represent the filtered distribution is computationally intractable. Analogously, smoothing is also intractable.

The origin of the intractability of the SLDS therefore differs from 'structural intractability' since, in terms of the cluster variables $x_{1:T}$ with $x_t \equiv (s_t, \mathbf{h}_t)$ and visible variables $\mathbf{v}_{1:T}$, the graph of the distribution is singly connected. From a purely graph-theoretic viewpoint, one would therefore envisage no difficulty in carrying out inference. Indeed, as we saw above, the derivation of the filtering algorithm is straightforward since the graph of $p(x_{1:T}, \mathbf{v}_{1:T})$ is singly connected. However, the numerical representation of the messages requires an exponentially increasing number of terms.

In order to deal with this intractability, several approximation schemes have been introduced, [8, 9, 15, 13, 12]. Here we focus on techniques which approximate the switch conditional posteriors using a limited mixture of Gaussians. Since the exact posterior distributions are mixtures of Gaussians, but with an exponentially large number of components, the aim is to drop low-weight components such that the resulting limited number of Gaussians still accurately represents the posterior.

8.3 Gaussian sum filtering

Equation (8.3) describes the exact filtering recursion. Whilst the number of mixture components increases exponentially with time, intuitively one would expect that there is an effective time scale over which the previous visible information is relevant. In general, the influence of ancient observations will be much less relevant than that of recent observations. This suggests that a limited number of components in the Gaussian mixture should suffice to accurately represent the filtered posterior [1].

Our aim is to form a recursion for $p(s_t, \mathbf{h}_t|\mathbf{v}_{1:t})$ using a Gaussian mixture approximation of $p(\mathbf{h}_t|s_t, \mathbf{v}_{1:t})$. Given an approximation of the filtered distribution $p(s_t, \mathbf{h}_t|\mathbf{v}_{1:t}) \approx q(s_t, \mathbf{h}_t|\mathbf{v}_{1:t})$, the exact recursion (8.3) is approximated by

$$q(s_{t+1}, \mathbf{h}_{t+1}|\mathbf{v}_{1:t+1}) = \sum_{s_t} \int_{\mathbf{h}_t} p(s_{t+1}, \mathbf{h}_{t+1}|s_t, \mathbf{h}_t, \mathbf{v}_{t+1}) q(s_t, \mathbf{h}_t|\mathbf{v}_{1:t}). \tag{8.4}$$

This approximation to the filtered posterior at the next time step will contain S times more components than at the previous time step. Therefore to prevent an exponential explosion in mixture components we need to collapse this mixture in a suitable way. We will deal with this once the new mixture representation for the filtered posterior has been computed.

To derive the updates it is useful to break the filtered approximation from Eq. (8.4) into continuous and discrete parts

$$q(\mathbf{h}_t, s_t|\mathbf{v}_{1:t}) = q(\mathbf{h}_t|s_t, \mathbf{v}_{1:t}) q(s_t|\mathbf{v}_{1:t}), \tag{8.5}$$

and derive separate filtered update formulae, as described below. An important remark is that many techniques approximate $p(\mathbf{h}_t|s_t, \mathbf{v}_{1:t})$ using a *single* Gaussian. Naturally, this gives rise to a mixture of Gaussians for $p(\mathbf{h}_t|\mathbf{v}_{1:t})$. However, in making a single Gaussian approximation to $p(\mathbf{h}_t|s_t, \mathbf{v}_{1:t})$ the representation of the posterior may be poor. Our aim here is to maintain an accurate approximation to $p(\mathbf{h}_t|s_t, \mathbf{v}_{1:t})$ by using a *mixture* of Gaussians.

8.3.1 Continuous filtering

The exact representation of $p(\mathbf{h}_t|s_t, \mathbf{v}_{1:t})$ is a mixture with S^{t-1} components. To retain computational feasibility we approximate this with a limited I-component mixture

$$q(\mathbf{h}_t|s_t, \mathbf{v}_{1:t}) = \sum_{i_t=1}^{I} q(\mathbf{h}_t|i_t, s_t, \mathbf{v}_{1:t}) q(i_t|s_t, \mathbf{v}_{1:t}),$$

where $q(\mathbf{h}_t|i_t, s_t, \mathbf{v}_{1:t})$ is a Gaussian parameterised with mean $\mathbf{f}(i_t, s_t)$ and covariance $\mathbf{F}(i_t, s_t)$. Strictly speaking, we should use the notation $\mathbf{f}_t(i_t, s_t)$ since, for each time t, we have a set of means indexed by i_t, s_t, but we drop these dependencies in the notation used here.

To find a recursion for the approximating distribution, we first assume that we know the filtered approximation $q(\mathbf{h}_t, s_t|\mathbf{v}_{1:t})$ and then propagate this forwards using the exact dynamics. To do so consider first the exact relation

$$q(\mathbf{h}_{t+1}|s_{t+1}, \mathbf{v}_{1:t+1}) = \sum_{s_t,i_t} q(\mathbf{h}_{t+1}, s_t, i_t|s_{t+1}, \mathbf{v}_{1:t+1})$$

$$= \sum_{s_t,i_t} q(\mathbf{h}_{t+1}|s_t, i_t, s_{t+1}, \mathbf{v}_{1:t+1}) q(s_t, i_t|s_{t+1}, \mathbf{v}_{1:t+1}). \tag{8.6}$$

Wherever possible we substitute the exact dynamics and evaluate each of the two factors above. By decomposing the update in this way the new filtered approximation is of the form of a Gaussian mixture, where $q(\mathbf{h}_{t+1}|s_t, i_t, s_{t+1}, \mathbf{v}_{1:t+1})$ is Gaussian and $q(s_t, i_t|s_{t+1}, \mathbf{v}_{1:t+1})$ are the weights or mixing proportions of the components. We describe below how to compute these terms explicitly. Equation (8.6) produces a new Gaussian mixture with $I \times S$ components which we collapse back to I components at the end of the computation.

Evaluating $q(\mathbf{h}_{t+1}|s_t, i_t, s_{t+1}, \mathbf{v}_{1:t+1})$

We aim to find a filtering recursion for $q(\mathbf{h}_{t+1}|s_t, i_t, s_{t+1}, \mathbf{v}_{1:t+1})$. Since this is conditional on switch states and components, this corresponds to a single LDS forward step, which can be evaluated by considering first the joint distribution

$$q(\mathbf{h}_{t+1}, \mathbf{v}_{t+1}|s_t, i_t, s_{t+1}, \mathbf{v}_{1:t}) = \int_{\mathbf{h}_t} p(\mathbf{h}_{t+1}, \mathbf{v}_{t+1}|\mathbf{h}_t, \cancel{s_t}, \cancel{i_t}, s_{t+1}, \mathbf{v}_{1:t})q(\mathbf{h}_t|s_t, i_t, \cancel{s_{t+1}}, \mathbf{v}_{1:t}),$$

and subsequently conditioning on $\mathbf{v}_{t+1}$. To ease the burden on notation we assume $\bar{\mathbf{h}}_t, \bar{\mathbf{v}}_t \equiv 0$ for all t. By propagating

$$q(\mathbf{h}_t|\mathbf{v}_{1:t}, i_t, s_t) = \mathcal{N}\left(\mathbf{h}_t|\mathbf{f}(i_t, s_t), \mathbf{F}(i_t, s_t)\right)$$

with the dynamics (8.1) and (8.2), we obtain that $q(\mathbf{h}_{t+1}, \mathbf{v}_{t+1}|s_t, i_t, s_{t+1}, \mathbf{v}_{1:t})$ is a Gaussian with covariance and mean elements

$$\Sigma_{hh} = \mathbf{A}(s_{t+1})\mathbf{F}(i_t, s_t)\mathbf{A}^{\mathsf{T}}(s_{t+1}) + \Sigma^h(s_{t+1}),$$

$$\Sigma_{vv} = \mathbf{B}(s_{t+1})\Sigma_{hh}\mathbf{B}^{\mathsf{T}}(s_{t+1}) + \Sigma^v(s_{t+1}),$$

$$\Sigma_{vh} = \mathbf{B}(s_{t+1})\Sigma_{hh} = \Sigma_{hv}^{\mathsf{T}},$$

$$\boldsymbol{\mu}_v = \mathbf{B}(s_{t+1})\mathbf{A}(s_{t+1})\mathbf{f}(i_t, s_t), \quad \boldsymbol{\mu}_h = \mathbf{A}(s_{t+1})\mathbf{f}(i_t, s_t). \tag{8.7}$$

These results are obtained from integrating the exact dynamics over $\mathbf{h}_t$, using the results in Section 1.4.7.

To find $q(\mathbf{h}_{t+1}|s_t, i_t, s_{t+1}, \mathbf{v}_{1:t+1})$ we condition $q(\mathbf{h}_{t+1}, \mathbf{v}_{t+1}|s_t, i_t, s_{t+1}, \mathbf{v}_{1:t})$ on $\mathbf{v}_{t+1}$ using the standard Gaussian conditioning formula, Section 1.4.7, to obtain

$$q(\mathbf{h}_{t+1}|s_t, i_t, s_{t+1}, \mathbf{v}_{1:t+1}) = \mathcal{N}\left(\mathbf{h}_{t+1}|\boldsymbol{\mu}_{h|v}, \Sigma_{h|v}\right)$$

with

$$\boldsymbol{\mu}_{h|v} = \boldsymbol{\mu}_h + \Sigma_{hv}\Sigma_{vv}^{-1}\left(\mathbf{v}_{t+1} - \boldsymbol{\mu}_v\right), \qquad \Sigma_{h|v} = \Sigma_{hh} - \Sigma_{hv}\Sigma_{vv}^{-1}\Sigma_{vh}.$$

Evaluating the mixture weights $q(s_t, i_t|s_{t+1}, \mathbf{v}_{1:t+1})$

The mixture weight in Eq. (8.6) can be found from

$$q(s_t, i_t|s_{t+1}, \mathbf{v}_{1:t+1}) \propto q(\mathbf{v}_{t+1}|i_t, s_t, s_{t+1}, \mathbf{v}_{1:t})q(s_{t+1}|i_t, s_t, \mathbf{v}_{1:t})q(i_t|s_t, \mathbf{v}_{1:t})q(s_t|\mathbf{v}_{1:t}).$$

The factor $q(\mathbf{v}_{t+1}|i_t, s_t, s_{t+1}, \mathbf{v}_{1:t})$ is Gaussian with mean $\boldsymbol{\mu}_v$ and covariance Σ_{vv}, as given in Eq. (8.7). The factors $q(i_t|s_t, \mathbf{v}_{1:t})$ and $q(s_t|\mathbf{v}_{1:t})$ are given from the previous filtered iteration. Finally, $q(s_{t+1}|i_t, s_t, \mathbf{v}_{1:t})$ is found from (where angled brackets denote expectation)

$$q(s_{t+1}|i_t, s_t, \mathbf{v}_{1:t}) = \begin{cases} \langle p(s_{t+1}|\mathbf{h}_t, s_t)\rangle_{q(\mathbf{h}_t|i_t, s_t, \mathbf{v}_{1:t})} & \text{augmented SLDS,} \\ p(s_{t+1}|s_t) & \text{standard SLDS,} \end{cases} \tag{8.8}$$

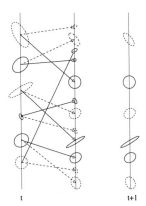

Figure 8.2 Gaussian sum filtering. The leftmost column depicts the pre-
vious Gaussian mixture approximation $q(\mathbf{h}_t, s_t|\mathbf{v}_{1:t})$ for two states $S = 2$
(dashed and solid) and three mixture components $I = 3$. The area of the
oval indicates the weight of the component. There are $S = 2$ different linear systems which take each of the components of the mixture into a new
filtered state, the arrow indicating which dynamic system is used. After
one time step each mixture component branches into a further S com-
ponents so that the joint approximation $q(\mathbf{h}_{t+1}, s_{t+1}|\mathbf{v}_{1:t+1})$ contains S^2I
components (middle column). To keep the representation computationally
tractable the mixture of Gaussians for each state s_{t+1} is collapsed back
to I components. This means that each state needs to be approximated
by a smaller I component mixture of Gaussians. There are many ways to
achieve this. A naive but computationally efficient approach is to simply
ignore the lowest weight components, as depicted on the right column.

where the result above for the standard SLDS follows from the independence assumptions
present in the standard SLDS. In the aSLDS, the term in Eq. (8.8) will generally need to be
computed numerically. A simple approximation is to evaluate Eq. (8.8) at the mean value of
the distribution $q(\mathbf{h}_t|i_t, s_t, \mathbf{v}_{1:t})$. To take covariance information into account an alternative
would be to draw samples from the Gaussian $q(\mathbf{h}_t|i_t, s_t, \mathbf{v}_{1:t})$ and thus approximate the aver-
age of $p(s_{t+1}|\mathbf{h}_t, s_t)$ by sampling. Note that this does not equate Gaussian sum filtering with
a sequential sampling procedure, such as particle filtering, Section 1.6.4. The sampling here
is exact, for which no convergence issues arise.

Closing the recursion

We are now in a position to calculate Eq. (8.6). For each setting of the variable s_{t+1}, we
have a mixture of $I \times S$ Gaussians. To prevent the number of components increasing
exponentially, we numerically collapse $q(\mathbf{h}_{t+1}|s_{t+1}, \mathbf{v}_{1:t+1})$ back to I Gaussians to form

$$q(\mathbf{h}_{t+1}|s_{t+1}, \mathbf{v}_{1:t+1}) \rightarrow \sum_{i_{t+1}=1}^{I} q(\mathbf{h}_{t+1}|i_{t+1}, s_{t+1}, \mathbf{v}_{1:t+1})q(i_{t+1}|s_{t+1}, \mathbf{v}_{1:t+1}).$$

Any method of choice may be supplied to collapse a mixture to a smaller mixture. A
straightforward approach is to repeatedly merge low-weight components, as explained in
Section 8.3.4. In this way the new mixture coefficients $q(i_{t+1}|s_{t+1}, \mathbf{v}_{1:t+1})$, $i_{t+1} \in 1, \ldots, I$,
are defined. This completes the description of how to form a recursion for the continuous
filtered posterior approximation $q(\mathbf{h}_{t+1}|s_{t+1}, \mathbf{v}_{1:t+1})$ in Eq. (8.5).

8.3.2   Discrete filtering

A recursion for the switch variable distribution in Eq. (8.5) is given by

$$q(s_{t+1}|\mathbf{v}_{1:t+1}) \propto \sum_{i_t, s_t} q(s_{t+1}, i_t, s_t, \mathbf{v}_{t+1}, \mathbf{v}_{1:t}).$$

The right-hand side of the above equation is proportional to

$$\sum_{s_t, i_t} q(\mathbf{v}_{t+1}|s_{t+1}, i_t, s_t, \mathbf{v}_{1:t})q(s_{t+1}|i_t, s_t, \mathbf{v}_{1:t})q(i_t|s_t, \mathbf{v}_{1:t})q(s_t|\mathbf{v}_{1:t}),$$

for which all terms have been computed during the recursion for $q(\mathbf{h}_{t+1}|s_{t+1}, \mathbf{v}_{1:t+1})$. We now
have all the quantities required to compute the Gaussian sum approximation of the filtering

---

Algorithm 8.1 aSLDS forward pass. Approximate the filtered posterior $p(s_t|\mathbf{v}_{1:t})$ ≡ α_t, $p(\mathbf{h}_t|s_t, \mathbf{v}_{1:t})$ ≡ $\sum_{i_t} w_t(i_t, s_t) \mathcal{N}(\mathbf{h}_t|\mathbf{f}_t(i_t, s_t), \mathbf{F}_t(i_t, s_t))$. Also return the approximate log-likelihood L ≡ $\log p(\mathbf{v}_{1:T})$. I_t are the number of components in each Gaussian mixture approximation. We require $I_1 = 1, I_2 \leq S, I_t \leq S \times I_{t-1}$. $\theta(s) = \mathbf{A}(s), \mathbf{B}(s), \mathbf{\Sigma}^h(s), \mathbf{\Sigma}^v(s), \bar{\mathbf{h}}(s), \bar{\mathbf{v}}(s)$. See also Algorithm 1.1.

---

for $s_1 \leftarrow 1$ **to** S **do**
  $\{\mathbf{f}_1(1, s_1), \mathbf{F}_1(1, s_1), \hat{p}\}$ = LDSFORWARD$(0, 0, \mathbf{v}_1; \theta(s_1))$
  $\alpha_1 \leftarrow p(s_1)\hat{p}$
end for

for $t \leftarrow 2$ **to** T **do**
  for $s_t \leftarrow 1$ **to** S **do**
    for $i \leftarrow 1$ **to** I_{t-1}, **and** $s \leftarrow 1$ **to** S **do**
      $\{\boldsymbol{\mu}_{x|y}(i, s), \mathbf{\Sigma}_{x|y}(i, s), \hat{p}\}$ = LDSFORWARD$(\mathbf{f}_{t-1}(i, s), \mathbf{F}_{t-1}(i, s), \mathbf{v}_t; \theta(s_t))$
      $p^*(s_t|i, s)$ ≡ $\langle p(s_t|\mathbf{h}_{t-1}, s_{t-1} = s)\rangle_{p(\mathbf{h}_{t-1}|i_{t-1}=i, s_{t-1}=s, \mathbf{v}_{1:t-1})}$
      $p'(s_t, i, s) \leftarrow w_{t-1}(i, s)p^*(s_t|i, s)\alpha_{t-1}(s)\hat{p}$
    end for
    Collapse the $I_{t-1} \times S$ mixture of Gaussians defined by $\boldsymbol{\mu}_{x|y}, \mathbf{\Sigma}_{x|y}$, and weights $p(i, s|s_t) \propto p'(s_t, i, s)$ to a Gaussian with I_t components, $p(\mathbf{h}_t|s_t, \mathbf{v}_{1:t}) \approx \sum_{i_t=1}^{I_t} p(i_t|s_t, \mathbf{v}_{1:t})p(\mathbf{h}_t|s_t, i_t, \mathbf{v}_{1:t})$. This defines the new means $\mathbf{f}_t(i_t, s_t)$, covariances $\mathbf{F}_t(i_t, s_t)$ and mixture weights $w_t(i_t, s_t)$ ≡ $p(i_t|s_t, \mathbf{v}_{1:t})$.
    Compute $\alpha_t(s_t) \propto \sum_{i,s} p'(s_t, i, s)$
  end for
  normalise α_t
  $L \leftarrow L + \log \sum_{s_t, i, s} p'(s_t, i, s)$
end for

---

forward pass. A schematic representation of Gaussian sum filtering is given in Fig. 8.2 and the pseudo-code is presented in Algorithm 8.1.

8.3.3 The likelihood $p(\mathbf{v}_{1:T})$

The likelihood $p(\mathbf{v}_{1:T})$ may be found from

$$p(\mathbf{v}_{1:T}) = \prod_{t=0}^{T-1} p(\mathbf{v}_{t+1}|\mathbf{v}_{1:t}),$$

$$p(\mathbf{v}_{t+1}|\mathbf{v}_{1:t}) \approx \sum_{i_t, s_t, s_{t+1}} q(\mathbf{v}_{t+1}|i_t, s_t, s_{t+1}, \mathbf{v}_{1:t})q(s_{t+1}|i_t, s_t, \mathbf{v}_{1:t})q(i_t|s_t, \mathbf{v}_{1:t})q(s_t|\mathbf{v}_{1:t}).$$

In the above expression, all terms have been computed when forming the recursion for the filtered posterior $q(\mathbf{h}_{t+1}, s_{t+1}|\mathbf{v}_{1:t+1})$.

8.3.4 Collapsing Gaussians

We wish to collapse a mixture of N Gaussians

$$p(\mathbf{x}) = \sum_{i=1}^{N} p_i \mathcal{N}(\mathbf{x}|\boldsymbol{\mu}_i, \mathbf{\Sigma}_i) \tag{8.9}$$

to a mixture of $K < N$ Gaussians. We present a simple method which has the advantage of computational efficiency, but the disadvantage that no spatial information about the mixture is used [20]. First we describe how to collapse a mixture to a single Gaussian $\mathcal{N}(\mathbf{x}|\boldsymbol{\mu}, \boldsymbol{\Sigma})$. This can be achieved by setting $\boldsymbol{\mu}$ and $\boldsymbol{\Sigma}$ to be the mean and covariance of the mixture distribution (8.9), that is

$$\boldsymbol{\mu} = \sum_i p_i \boldsymbol{\mu}_i, \qquad \boldsymbol{\Sigma} = \sum_i p_i \left(\boldsymbol{\Sigma}_i + \boldsymbol{\mu}_i \boldsymbol{\mu}_i^\mathsf{T}\right) - \boldsymbol{\mu}\boldsymbol{\mu}^\mathsf{T}.$$

To collapse to a K-component mixture we may retain the $K - 1$ Gaussians with the largest mixture weights and merge the remaining $N - K - 1$ Gaussians to a single Gaussian using the above method. Alternative heuristics such as recursively merging the two Gaussians with the lowest mixture weights are also reasonable. More sophisticated methods which retain some spatial information would clearly be potentially useful. The method presented in [15] is a suitable approach which considers removing Gaussians which are spatially similar, thereby retaining a sense of diversity over the possible solutions.

8.3.5 Relation to other methods

Gaussian sum filtering can be considered a form of 'analytical particle filtering' in which instead of point distributions (delta functions) being propagated, Gaussians are propagated. The collapse operation to a smaller number of Gaussians is analogous to resampling in particle filtering. Since a Gaussian is more expressive than a delta function, the Gaussian sum filter is generally an improved approximation technique over using point particles. See [3] for a numerical comparison. This Gaussian sum filtering method is an instance of assumed density filtering, see Section 1.5.2.

8.4 Expectation correction

Approximating the smoothed posterior $p(\mathbf{h}_t, s_t|\mathbf{v}_{1:T})$ is more involved than filtering and requires additional approximations. For this reason smoothing is more prone to failure since there are more assumptions that need to be satisfied for the approximations to hold. The route we take here is to assume that a Gaussian sum filtered approximation has been carried out, and then approximate the γ backward pass, analogous to that of Section 1.4.3. The exact backward pass for the SLDS reads

$$p(\mathbf{h}_t, s_t|\mathbf{v}_{1:T}) = \sum_{s_{t+1}} \int_{\mathbf{h}_{t+1}} p(\mathbf{h}_t, s_t|\mathbf{h}_{t+1}, s_{t+1}, \mathbf{v}_{1:t}) p(\mathbf{h}_{t+1}, s_{t+1}|\mathbf{v}_{1:T}), \qquad (8.10)$$

where $p(s_{t+1}|\mathbf{v}_{1:T})$ and $p(\mathbf{h}_{t+1}|s_{t+1}, \mathbf{v}_{1:T})$ are the discrete and continuous components of the smoothed posterior at the next time step. The recursion runs backwards in time, beginning with the initialisation $p(\mathbf{h}_T, s_T|\mathbf{v}_{1:T})$ set by the filtered result (at time $t = T$, the filtered and smoothed posteriors coincide). Apart from the fact that the number of mixture components will increase at each step, computing the integral over $\mathbf{h}_{t+1}$ in Eq. (8.10) is problematic since the conditional distribution term is non-Gaussian in $\mathbf{h}_{t+1}$. For this reason it is more useful in deriving an approximate recursion to begin with the exact relation

$$p(s_t, \mathbf{h}_t|\mathbf{v}_{1:T}) = \sum_{s_{t+1}} p(s_{t+1}|\mathbf{v}_{1:T}) p(\mathbf{h}_t|s_t, s_{t+1}, \mathbf{v}_{1:T}) p(s_t|s_{t+1}, \mathbf{v}_{1:T}),$$

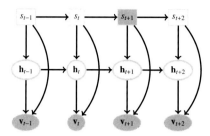

Figure 8.3 The EC backpass approximates $p(\mathbf{h}_{t+1}|s_{t+1}, s_t, \mathbf{v}_{1:T})$ by $p(\mathbf{h}_{t+1}|s_{t+1}, \mathbf{v}_{1:T})$. The motivation for this is that s_t influences $\mathbf{h}_{t+1}$ only indirectly through $\mathbf{h}_t$. However, $\mathbf{h}_t$ will most likely be heavily influenced by $\mathbf{v}_{1:t}$, so that not knowing the state of s_t is likely to be of secondary importance. The light shaded node is the variable we wish to find the posterior for. The values of the dark shaded nodes are known, and the dashed node indicates a known variable which is assumed unknown in forming the approximation.

which can be expressed more directly in terms of the SLDS dynamics as

$$p(s_t, \mathbf{h}_t|\mathbf{v}_{1:T}) = \sum_{s_{t+1}} p(s_{t+1}|\mathbf{v}_{1:T}) \left\langle p(\mathbf{h}_t|\mathbf{h}_{t+1}, s_t, s_{t+1}, \mathbf{v}_{1:t}, \cancel{\mathbf{v}_{t+1:T}}) \right\rangle_{p(\mathbf{h}_{t+1}|s_t,s_{t+1},\mathbf{v}_{1:T})}$$

$$\times \left\langle p(s_t|\mathbf{h}_{t+1}, s_{t+1}, \mathbf{v}_{1:T}) \right\rangle_{p(\mathbf{h}_{t+1}|s_{t+1},\mathbf{v}_{1:T})}.$$

In forming the recursion we assume access to the distribution $p(s_{t+1}, \mathbf{h}_{t+1}|\mathbf{v}_{1:T})$ from the future time step. However, we also require the distribution $p(\mathbf{h}_{t+1}|s_t, s_{t+1}, \mathbf{v}_{1:T})$ which is not directly known and needs to be inferred – a computationally challenging task. In the expectation correction (EC) approach [3] one assumes the approximation (see Fig. 8.3)

$$p(\mathbf{h}_{t+1}|s_t, s_{t+1}, \mathbf{v}_{1:T}) \approx p(\mathbf{h}_{t+1}|s_{t+1}, \mathbf{v}_{1:T}), \qquad (8.11)$$

resulting in an approximate recursion for the smoothed posterior

$$p(s_t, \mathbf{h}_t|\mathbf{v}_{1:T}) \approx \sum_{s_{t+1}} p(s_{t+1}|\mathbf{v}_{1:T}) \left\langle p(\mathbf{h}_t|\mathbf{h}_{t+1}, s_t, s_{t+1}, \mathbf{v}_{1:t}) \right\rangle_{\mathbf{h}_{t+1}} \left\langle p(s_t|\mathbf{h}_{t+1}, s_{t+1}, \mathbf{v}_{1:T}) \right\rangle_{\mathbf{h}_{t+1}},$$

where $\langle \cdot \rangle_{\mathbf{h}_{t+1}}$ represents averaging with respect to the distribution $p(\mathbf{h}_{t+1}|s_{t+1}, \mathbf{v}_{1:T})$. In carrying out the above approximate recursion, we will end up with a mixture of Gaussians that grows at each time step. To avoid the exponential explosion problem, we use a finite mixture approximation

$$p(\mathbf{h}_{t+1}, s_{t+1}|\mathbf{v}_{1:T}) \approx q(\mathbf{h}_{t+1}, s_{t+1}|\mathbf{v}_{1:T}) = q(\mathbf{h}_{t+1}|s_{t+1}, \mathbf{v}_{1:T})q(s_{t+1}|\mathbf{v}_{1:T}),$$

and plug this into the recursion above. A recursion for the approximation is given by

$$q(\mathbf{h}_t, s_t|\mathbf{v}_{1:T}) = \sum_{s_{t+1}} q(s_{t+1}|\mathbf{v}_{1:T}) \left\langle q(\mathbf{h}_t|\mathbf{h}_{t+1}, s_t, s_{t+1}, \mathbf{v}_{1:t}) \right\rangle_{q(\mathbf{h}_{t+1}|s_{t+1},\mathbf{v}_{1:T})}$$

$$\times \left\langle q(s_t|\mathbf{h}_{t+1}, s_{t+1}, \mathbf{v}_{1:t}) \right\rangle_{q(\mathbf{h}_{t+1}|s_{t+1},\mathbf{v}_{1:T})}. \qquad (8.12)$$

As for filtering, wherever possible, we replace approximate terms by their exact counterparts and parameterise the posterior using

$$q(\mathbf{h}_{t+1}, s_{t+1}|\mathbf{v}_{1:T}) = q(\mathbf{h}_{t+1}|s_{t+1}, \mathbf{v}_{1:T})q(s_{t+1}|\mathbf{v}_{1:T}). \qquad (8.13)$$

To reduce the notational burden here we outline the method only for the case of using a single component approximation in both the forward and backward passes. The extension to using a mixture to approximate each $p(\mathbf{h}_{t+1}|s_{t+1}, \mathbf{v}_{1:T})$ is conceptually straightforward and deferred to Section 8.4.5. In the single Gaussian case we assume we have a Gaussian approximation available for

$$q(\mathbf{h}_{t+1}|s_{t+1}, \mathbf{v}_{1:T}) = \mathcal{N}\left(\mathbf{h}_{t+1}|\mathbf{g}(s_{t+1}), \mathbf{G}(s_{t+1})\right),$$

which below is 'propagated' backwards in time using the smoothing recursion.

8.4.1 Continuous smoothing

For given s_t, s_{t+1}, a recursion for the smoothed continuous variable is obtained using

$$q(\mathbf{h}_t|s_t, s_{t+1}, \mathbf{v}_{1:T}) = \int_{\mathbf{h}_{t+1}} p(\mathbf{h}_t|\mathbf{h}_{t+1}, s_t, s_{t+1}, \mathbf{v}_{1:t})q(\mathbf{h}_{t+1}|s_{t+1}, \mathbf{v}_{1:T}). \tag{8.14}$$

In forming the recursion, we assume that we know the distribution

$$q(\mathbf{h}_{t+1}|s_{t+1}, \mathbf{v}_{1:T}) = \mathcal{N}\left(\mathbf{h}_{t+1}|\mathbf{g}(s_{t+1}), \mathbf{G}(s_{t+1})\right).$$

To compute Eq. (8.14) we then perform a single update of the LDS backward recursion, Algorithm 1.2.

8.4.2 Discrete smoothing

The second average in Eq. (8.12) corresponds to a recursion for the discrete variable and is given by

$$\langle q(s_t|\mathbf{h}_{t+1}, s_{t+1}, \mathbf{v}_{1:t})\rangle_{q(\mathbf{h}_{t+1}|s_{t+1}, \mathbf{v}_{1:T})} \equiv q(s_t|s_{t+1}, \mathbf{v}_{1:T}).$$

This average cannot be computed in closed form. The simplest approach is to approximate it by evaluation at the mean, that is[1]

$$\langle q(s_t|\mathbf{h}_{t+1}, s_{t+1}\mathbf{v}_{1:t})\rangle_{q(\mathbf{h}_{t+1}|s_{t+1}, \mathbf{v}_{1:T})} \approx q(s_t|\mathbf{h}_{t+1}, s_{t+1}, \mathbf{v}_{1:t})\big|_{\mathbf{h}_{t+1}=\langle\mathbf{h}_{t+1}|s_{t+1}, \mathbf{v}_{1:T}\rangle},$$

where $\langle\mathbf{h}_{t+1}|s_{t+1}, \mathbf{v}_{1:T}\rangle$ is the mean of $\mathbf{h}_{t+1}$ with respect to $q(\mathbf{h}_{t+1}|s_{t+1}, \mathbf{v}_{1:T})$. This gives the approximation

$$\langle q(s_t|\mathbf{h}_{t+1}, s_{t+1}, \mathbf{v}_{1:t})\rangle_{q(\mathbf{h}_{t+1}|s_{t+1}, \mathbf{v}_{1:T})} \approx \frac{1}{Z} \frac{e^{-\frac{1}{2}\mathbf{z}_{t+1}^{\mathsf{T}}(s_t, s_{t+1})\Sigma^{-1}(s_t, s_{t+1}|\mathbf{v}_{1:t})\mathbf{z}_{t+1}(s_t, s_{t+1})}}{\sqrt{\det\left(\Sigma(s_t, s_{t+1}|\mathbf{v}_{1:t})\right)}} q(s_t|s_{t+1}, \mathbf{v}_{1:t}),$$

where

$$\mathbf{z}_{t+1}(s_t, s_{t+1}) \equiv \langle\mathbf{h}_{t+1}|s_{t+1}, \mathbf{v}_{1:T}\rangle - \langle\mathbf{h}_{t+1}|s_t, s_{t+1}, \mathbf{v}_{1:t}\rangle,$$

and Z ensures normalisation over s_t; $\Sigma(s_t, s_{t+1}|\mathbf{v}_{1:t})$ is the filtered covariance of $\mathbf{h}_{t+1}$ given s_t, s_{t+1} and the observations $\mathbf{v}_{1:t}$, which may be taken from Σ_{hh} in Eq. (8.7). Approximations which take covariance information into account can also be considered, although the above method may suffice in practice [3, 17].

8.4.3 Collapsing the mixture

From Sections 8.4.1 and 8.4.2 we now have all the terms to compute the approximation to Eq. (8.12). As for the filtering, however, the number of mixture components is multiplied by S at each iteration. To prevent an exponential explosion of components, the mixture is then collapsed to a single Gaussian

$$q(\mathbf{h}_t, s_t|\mathbf{v}_{1:T}) = q(\mathbf{h}_t|s_t, \mathbf{v}_{1:T})q(s_t|\mathbf{v}_{1:T}).$$

The collapse to a mixture is discussed in Section 8.4.5.

---

[1] In general this approximation has the form $\langle f(x)\rangle_{p(x)} \approx f(\langle x\rangle_{p(x)})$.

8.4.4 Relation to other methods

A classical smoothing approximation for the SLDS is generalised pseudo Bayes (GPB) [2, 12, 11]. GPB makes the following approximation

$$p(s_t|s_{t+1}, \mathbf{v}_{1:T}) \approx p(s_t|s_{t+1}, \mathbf{v}_{1:t}),$$

which depends only on the filtered posterior for s_t and does not include any information passing through the variable $\mathbf{h}_{t+1}$. Since

$$p(s_t|s_{t+1}, \mathbf{v}_{1:t}) \propto p(s_{t+1}|s_t)p(s_t|\mathbf{v}_{1:t}),$$

computing the smoothed recursion for the switch states in GPB is equivalent to running the RTS backward pass on a hidden Markov model, independently of the backward recursion for the continuous variables:

$$p(s_t|\mathbf{v}_{1:T}) = \sum_{s_{t+1}} p(s_t, s_{t+1}|\mathbf{v}_{1:T}) = \sum_{s_{t+1}} p(s_t|s_{t+1}, \mathbf{v}_{1:T})p(s_{t+1}|\mathbf{v}_{1:T})$$

$$\approx \sum_{s_{t+1}} p(s_t|s_{t+1}, \mathbf{v}_{1:t})p(s_{t+1}|\mathbf{v}_{1:T})$$

$$= \sum_{s_{t+1}} \frac{p(s_{t+1}|s_t)p(s_t|\mathbf{v}_{1:t})}{\sum_{s_t} p(s_{t+1}|s_t)p(s_t|\mathbf{v}_{1:t})} p(s_{t+1}|\mathbf{v}_{1:T}).$$

The only information the GPB method uses to form the smoothed distribution $p(s_t|\mathbf{v}_{1:T})$ from the filtered distribution $p(s_t|\mathbf{v}_{1:t})$ is the Markov switch transition $p(s_{t+1}|s_t)$. This approximation discounts some information from the future since information passed via the continuous variables is not taken into account. In contrast to GPB, EC preserves future information passing through the continuous variables.

8.4.5 Using mixtures in the expectation correction backward pass

The extension to the mixture case is straightforward, based on the representation

$$p(\mathbf{h}_t|s_t, \mathbf{v}_{1:T}) \approx \sum_{j_t=1}^{J} q(j_t|s_t, \mathbf{v}_{1:T})q(\mathbf{h}_t|j_t, s_t, \mathbf{v}_{1:T}).$$

Analogously to the case with a single component,

$$q(\mathbf{h}_t, s_t|\mathbf{v}_{1:T}) = \sum_{i_t, j_{t+1}, s_{t+1}} p(s_{t+1}|\mathbf{v}_{1:T})p(j_{t+1}|s_{t+1}, \mathbf{v}_{1:T})q(\mathbf{h}_t|j_{t+1}, s_{t+1}, i_t, s_t, \mathbf{v}_{1:T})$$

$$\times \langle q(i_t, s_t|\mathbf{h}_{t+1}, j_{t+1}, s_{t+1}, \mathbf{v}_{1:t}) \rangle_{q(\mathbf{h}_{t+1}|j_{t+1}, s_{t+1}, \mathbf{v}_{1:T})}.$$

The average in the last line of the above equation can be tackled using the same techniques as outlined in the single Gaussian case. To approximate $q(\mathbf{h}_t|j_{t+1}, s_{t+1}, i_t, s_t, \mathbf{v}_{1:T})$ we consider this as the marginal of the joint distribution

$$q(\mathbf{h}_t, \mathbf{h}_{t+1}|i_t, s_t, j_{t+1}, s_{t+1}, \mathbf{v}_{1:T}) = q(\mathbf{h}_t|\mathbf{h}_{t+1}, i_t, s_t, j_{t+1}, s_{t+1}, \mathbf{v}_{1:t})q(\mathbf{h}_{t+1}|i_t, s_t, j_{t+1}, s_{t+1}, \mathbf{v}_{1:T}).$$

As in the case of a single mixture, the problematic term is $q(\mathbf{h}_{t+1}|i_t, s_t, j_{t+1}, s_{t+1}, \mathbf{v}_{1:T})$. Analogously to Eq. (8.11), we make the assumption

$$q(\mathbf{h}_{t+1}|i_t, s_t, j_{t+1}, s_{t+1}, \mathbf{v}_{1:T}) \approx q(\mathbf{h}_{t+1}|j_{t+1}, s_{t+1}, \mathbf{v}_{1:T}),$$

Algorithm 8.2 aSLDS: EC backward pass. Approximates $p(s_t|\mathbf{v}_{1:T})$ and $p(\mathbf{h}_t|s_t, \mathbf{v}_{1:T}) \equiv \sum_{j_t=1}^{J_t} u_t(j_t, s_t)\mathcal{N}(\mathbf{g}_t(j_t, s_t), \mathbf{G}_t(j_t, s_t))$ using a mixture of Gaussians. $J_T = I_T, J_t \leq S \times I_t \times J_{t+1}$. This routine needs the results from Algorithm 8.1.

$\mathbf{G}_T \leftarrow \mathbf{F}_T, \mathbf{g}_T \leftarrow \mathbf{f}_T, u_T \leftarrow w_T$
for $t \leftarrow T - 1$ **to** 1 **do**
    for $s \leftarrow 1$ **to** S, $s' \leftarrow 1$ **to** S, $i \leftarrow 1$ **to** I_t, $j' \leftarrow 1$ **to** J_{t+1} **do**
      $(\mu, \Sigma)(i, s, j', s') = $ LDSBACKWARD$(\mathbf{g}_{t+1}(j', s'), \mathbf{G}_{t+1}(j', s'), \mathbf{f}_t(i, s), \mathbf{F}_t(i, s), \theta(s'))$

      $p(i_t, s_t|j_{t+1}, s_{t+1}, \mathbf{v}_{1:T})$
           $= \langle p(s_t = s, i_t = i|\mathbf{h}_{t+1}, s_{t+1} = s', j_{t+1} = j', \mathbf{v}_{1:t}) \rangle_{p(\mathbf{h}_{t+1}|s_{t+1}=s', j_{t+1}=j', \mathbf{v}_{1:T})}$

      $p(i, s, j', s'|\mathbf{v}_{1:T}) \leftarrow p(s_{t+1} = s'|\mathbf{v}_{1:T})u_{t+1}(j', s')p(i_t, s_t|j_{t+1}, s_{t+1}, \mathbf{v}_{1:T})$
    end for
    for $s_t \leftarrow 1$ **to** S **do**
      Collapse the mixture defined by weights $p(i_t = i, s_{t+1} = s', j_{t+1} = j'|s_t, \mathbf{v}_{1_t}) \propto$ $p(i, s_t, j', s'|\mathbf{v}_{1:T})$, means $\mu(i_t, s_t, j_{t+1}, s_{t+1})$ and covariances $\Sigma(i_t, s_t, j_{t+1}, s_{t+1})$ to a mixture with J_t components. This defines the new means $\mathbf{g}_t(j_t, s_t)$, covariances $\mathbf{G}_t(j_t, s_t)$ and mixture weights $u_t(j_t, s_t)$.
      $p(s_t|\mathbf{v}_{1:T}) \leftarrow \sum_{i_t, j', s'} p(i_t, s_t, j', s'|\mathbf{v}_{1:T})$
    end for
end for

---

meaning that information about the current switch state s_t, i_t is ignored. We can then form

$$p(\mathbf{h}_t|s_t, \mathbf{v}_{1:T}) = \sum_{i_t, j_{t+1}, s_{t+1}} p(i_t, j_{t+1}, s_{t+1}|s_t, \mathbf{v}_{1:T})p(\mathbf{h}_t|i_t, s_t, j_{t+1}, s_{t+1}, \mathbf{v}_{1:T}).$$

This mixture can then be collapsed to a smaller mixture to give

$$p(\mathbf{h}_t|s_t, \mathbf{v}_{1:T}) \approx \sum_{j_t} q(j_t|s_t, \mathbf{v}_{1:T})q(\mathbf{h}_t|j_t, \mathbf{v}_{1:T}).$$

The resulting procedure is sketched in Algorithm 8.2, including using mixtures in both forward and backward passes.

8.5 Demonstration: traffic flow

An illustration of modelling and inference with an SLDS is given in the network of traffic flow problem, Fig. 8.4. Here there are four junctions a, b, c, d, and traffic flows along theroads in the direction indicated. Traffic flows into the junction and then goes via different routes to d. Flow out of a junction must match the flow in to a junction (up to noise). There are traffic light switches at junctions a and b which, depending on their state, route traffic differently along the roads. Using ϕ to denote flow, we model the flows using the switching linear system

$$\begin{pmatrix} \phi_a(t) \\ \phi_{a \to d}(t) \\ \phi_{a \to b}(t) \\ \phi_{b \to d}(t) \\ \phi_{b \to c}(t) \\ \phi_{c \to d}(t) \end{pmatrix} = \begin{cases} \phi_a(t-1) \\ \phi_a(t-1)\,(0.75 \times \mathbb{I}[s_a(t) = 1] + 1 \times \mathbb{I}[s_a(t) = 2]) \\ \phi_a(t-1)\,(0.25 \times \mathbb{I}[s_a(t) = 1] + 1 \times \mathbb{I}[s_a(t) = 3]) \\ \phi_{a \to b}(t-1)0.5 \times \mathbb{I}[s_b(t) = 1] \\ \phi_{a \to b}(t-1)\,(0.5 \times \mathbb{I}[s_b(t) = 1] + 1 \times \mathbb{I}[s_b(t) = 2]) \\ \phi_{b \to c}(t-1) \end{cases}$$

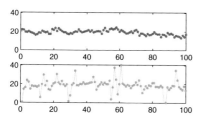

Figure 8.4 A representation of the traffic flow between junctions at a, b, c, d, with traffic lights at a and b. If $s_a = 1$ $a \rightarrow d$ and $a \rightarrow b$ carry 0.75 and 0.25 of the flow out of a respectively. If $s_a = 2$ all the flow from a goes through $a \rightarrow d$; for $s_a = 3$, all the flow goes through $a \rightarrow b$. For $s_b = 1$ the flow out of b is split equally between $b \rightarrow d$ and $b \rightarrow c$. For $s_b = 2$ all flow out of b goes along $b \rightarrow c$.

Figure 8.5 Time evolution of the traffic flow measured at two points in the network. Sensors measure the total flow into the network $\phi_a(t)$ and the total flow out of the network, $\phi_d(t) = \phi_{a \rightarrow d}(t) + \phi_{b \rightarrow d}(t) + \phi_{c \rightarrow d}(t)$. The total inflow at a undergoes a random walk. Note that the flow measured at d can momentarily drop to zero if all traffic is routed through $a \rightarrow b \rightarrow c$ for two time steps.

By identifying the flows at time t with a six-dimensional vector hidden variable $\mathbf{h}_t$, we can write the above flow equations as

$$\mathbf{h}_t = \mathbf{A}(s_t)\mathbf{h}_{t-1} + \boldsymbol{\eta}_t^h$$

for a set of suitably defined matrices $\mathbf{A}(s)$ indexed by the switch variable $s = s_a \otimes s_b$, which takes $3 \times 2 = 6$ states. We additionally include noise terms to model cars parking or de-parking during a single time frame. The covariance Σ^h is diagonal with a larger variance at the inflow point a to model that the total volume of traffic entering the system can vary. Noisy measurements of the flow into the network are taken at a

$$v_{1,t} = \phi_a(t) + \eta_1^v(t),$$

along with a noisy measurement of the total flow out of the system at d

$$v_{2,t} = \phi_d(t) = \phi_{a \rightarrow d}(t) + \phi_{b \rightarrow d}(t) + \phi_{c \rightarrow d}(t) + \eta_2^v(t).$$

The observation model can be represented by $\mathbf{v}_t = \mathbf{Bh}_t + \boldsymbol{\eta}_t^v$ using a constant 2×6 projection matrix $\mathbf{B}$. This is clearly a very crude model of traffic flows since in a real system one cannot have negative flows. Nevertheless it serves to demonstrate the principles of modelling and inference using switching models. The switch variables follow a simple Markov transition $p(s_t|s_{t-1})$ which biases the switches to remain in the same state in preference to jumping to another state. Given the above system and a prior which initialises all flow at a, we draw samples from the model using forward (ancestral) sampling and form the observations $\mathbf{v}_{1:100}$, Fig. 8.5. Using only the observations and the known model structure we then attempt to infer the latent switch variables and traffic flows using Gaussian sum filtering with $I = 2$ and EC with $J = 1$ mixture components per switch state, Fig. 8.6.

8.6 Comparison of smoothing techniques

In order to demonstrate the potential advantages of Gaussian sum approximate inference we chose a problem that, from the viewpoint of classical signal processing, is difficult, with changes in the switches not identifiable by simply eyeballing a short-time Fourier transform of the signal. The setup, as described in Fig. 8.7, is such that the latent trajectory $\mathbf{h}$

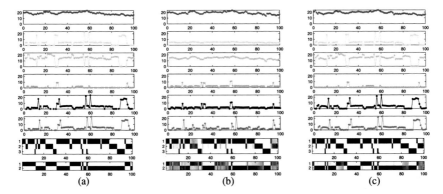

Figure 8.6 Given the observations from Fig. 8.5 we infer the flows and switch states of all the latent variables. (a) The correct latent flows through time along with the switch variable state used to generate the data. (b) Filtered flows based on a $I = 2$ Gaussian sum forward pass approximation. Plotted are the six components of the vector $\langle \mathbf{h}_t | \mathbf{v}_{1:t} \rangle$ with the posterior distribution of the s_a and s_b traffic light states $p(s_t^a | \mathbf{v}_{1:t}), p(s_t^b | \mathbf{v}_{1:t})$ plotted below. (c) Smoothed flows $\langle \mathbf{h}_t | \mathbf{v}_{1:T} \rangle$ and corresponding smoothed switch states $p(s_t | \mathbf{v}_{1:T})$ using EC with $J = 1$.

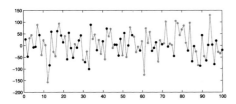

Figure 8.7 A sample from the inference problem for comparison of smoothing techniques. This scalar observation data $(V = 1)$ of $T = 100$ time steps is generated from an LDS with two switch states, $S = 2$: $A(s) = 0.9999 * \text{orth}(\text{randn}(H, H))$, $B(s) = \text{randn}(V, H)$, $\bar{v}_t \equiv 0$, $\bar{h}_1 = 10 * \text{randn}(H, 1)$, $\bar{h}_{t>1} = 0$, $\Sigma_1^h = I_H$, $p_1 = \text{uniform}$. The output bias is zero. The hidden space has dimension $H = 30$, with low transition noise, $\Sigma^h(s) = 0.01I_H$, $p(s_{t+1}|s_t) \propto 1_{S \times S}$. The output noise is relatively high, $\Sigma^v(s) = 30I_V$.

$(H = 30)$ is near deterministic; however, the noise in the observations $(V = 1)$ produces high uncertainty as to where this trajectory is, needing to track multiple hypotheses until there is sufficient data to reliably reveal which of the likely hypotheses is correct. For this reason, the filtered distribution is typically strongly multimodal and methods that do not address this perform poorly. The transition and emission matrices were sampled at random (see Fig. 8.7 for details); each random sampling of parameters generated a problem instance on which the rival algorithms were evaluated. We sequentially generated hidden states h_t, s_t and observations v_t from the known SLDS and then, given only the model and the observations, the task was to infer $p(h_t, s_t | v_{1:T})$. Since the exact computation is exponential in T, a formal evaluation of the method is infeasible. A simple alternative is to assume that the original sample states $s_{1:T}$ are the 'correct' inferred states, and compare the most probable posterior smoothed estimates $\arg\max_{s_t} p(s_t | v_{1:T})$ with the assumed correct sample s_t. Performance over a set of problem instances can then be assesed. All deterministic algorithms were initialised using the corresponding filtered results, as was Gibbs sampling. The running time of all algorithms was set to be roughly equal to that of EC using $I = J = 4$ mixture components per switch state.

8.6.1 Filtering as approximate smoothing

In Fig. 8.8 we present the accuracy of techniques that use filtering $p(s_t | \mathbf{v}_{1:t})$ as an approximation of the smoothed posterior $p(s_t | \mathbf{v}_{1:T})$. Many of the smoothing approaches we

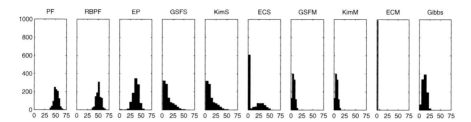

Figure 8.8 The number of errors in estimating a binary switch $p(s_t|v_{1:T})$ over a time series of length $T = 100$, for the problem described in Fig. 8.7. Hence 50 errors corresponds to random guessing. Plotted are histograms of the errors over 1000 experiments. (PF) Particle filter. (RBPF) Rao–Blackwellised PF. (EP) Expectation propagation. (GSFS) Gaussian sum filtering using a single Gaussian. (KimS) Kim's smoother, *i.e.* GPB, using the results from GSFS. (ECS) Expectation correction using a single Gaussian ($I = J = 1$). (GSFM) GSF using a mixture of $I = 4$ Gaussians. (KimM) Kim's smoother using the results from GSFM. (ECM) Expectation correction using a mixture with $I = J = 4$ components. In Gibbs sampling, we use the initialisation from GSFM.

examined are initialised with filtered approximations and it is therefore interesting to see the potential improvement that each smoothing algorithm makes over the filtered estimates. In each case the histogram of errors in estimating the switch variable s_t for t from 1 to 50 is presented, based on a set of 1000 realisations of the observed sequence.

Particle filter   We included the particle filter (PF) for comparison with Gaussian sum filtering (GSF) and to demonstrate the baseline performance of using filtering to approximate the smoothed posterior. For the PF, 1000 particles were used, with Kitagawa resampling, [14]. In this case the PF performs poorly due to the difficulty of representing continuous high-dimensional posterior distributions ($H = 30$) using a limited number of point particles and the underlying use of importance sampling in generating the samples. The Rao–Blackwellised particle filter (RBPF) [7] attempts to alleviate the difficulty of sampling in high-dimensional spaces by approximate integration over the continuous hidden variable. For the RBPF, 500 particles were used, with Kitagawa resampling. We were unable to improve on the standard PF results using this technique, most likely due to the fact that the available RBPF implementation assumed a single Gaussian per switch state.

Gaussian sum filtering   Whilst our interest is primarily in smoothing, for EC and GPB we need to initialise the smoothing algorithm with filtered estimates. Using a single Gaussian (GSFS) gives reasonable results, though using a mixture with $I = 4$ components per switch state (GSFM) improves on the single component case considerably, indicating the multimodal nature of the filtered posterior. Not surprisingly, the best filtered results are given using GSF, since this is better able to represent the variance in the filtered posterior than the PF sampling methods.

8.6.2 Approximate smoothing

Generalised pseudo Bayes   For this problem, Kim's GPB method does not improve on the Gaussian sum filtered results, using either a mixture $I = 4$ (KimM) or a single component $I = 1$ (KimS). In this case the GPB approximation of ignoring all future observations, provided only the future switch state s_{t+1} is known, is too severe.

Expectation correction For EC we use the mean approximation for the numerical integration of Eq. (8.13). In ECS a single Gaussian per switch state is used $I = J = 1$, with the backward recursion initialised with the filtered posterior. The method improves on GSFS, though the performance is still limited due to only using a single component. When using multiple components, $I = J = 4$, ECM has excellent performance, with a near perfect estimation of the most likely smoothed posterior class. One should bear in mind that EC, GPB, Gibbs and EP are initialised with the same GSF filtered distributions.

Gibbs sampling Gibbs sampling provides an alternative non-deterministic procedure [4]. For a fixed state sequence $s_{1:T}$, $p(v_{1:T} \mid s_{1:T})$ is easily computable since this is just the likelihood of an LDS with transitions and emissions specified by the assumed given switch states. We therefore attempt to sample from the posterior $p(s_{1:T} \mid v_{1:T}) \propto p(v_{1:T} \mid s_{1:T}) p(s_{1:T})$ directly. We implemented a standard single-site Gibbs sampler in which all switch variables are fixed, except s_t, and then a sample from $p(s_t \mid s_{\backslash t}, v_{1:T})$ drawn, with the 100 update sweeps forwards from the start to the end time and then in the reverse direction. The average of the final 80 forward-backward sweeps was used to estimate the smoothed posterior. Such a procedure may work well provided that the initial setting of $s_{1:T}$ is in a region of high probability – otherwise sampling by such individual coordinate updates may be extremely inefficient. For this case, even if the Gibbs sampler is initialised in a reasonable way (using the results from GSFM) the sampler is unable to deal with the strong temporal correlations in the posterior and on average degrades the filtering results.

Expectation propagation Expectation propagation (EP) [18] has had considerable success in approximate inference in graphical models, and has been ported to approximate inference in the SLDS (see Chapter 7). For our particular problem, we found EP to be numerically unstable, often struggling to converge.[2] To encourage convergence, we used the damping method in [10], performing 20 iterations with a damping factor of 0.5. Nevertheless, the disappointing performance of EP is most likely due to conflicts resulting from numerical instabilities introduced by the frequent conversions between moment and canonical representations. In addition, the current implementation of EP assumes that the posterior is well represented by a single Gaussian per switch state, and the inherent multimodality of the posterior in this experiment may render this assumption invalid.

8.7 Summary

Exact inference in the class of switching linear dynamical systems is computationally difficult. Whilst deriving exact filtering and smoothing recursions is straightforward, representing the filtered and smoothed posterior for time step t requires a mixture of Gaussians with a number of components scaling exponentially with t. This suggests the Gaussian sum class of approximations in which a limited number of Gaussian components is retained. We discussed how both filtering and smoothing recursions can be derived for approximations in which multiple Gaussians are assumed per switch state, extending on previous approximations which assume a single Gaussian per switch state. In extreme cases we showed how using such mixture approximations of the switch conditional posterior can improve the accuracy of the approximation considerably. Our Gaussian sum smoothing approach, expectation correction, can be viewed as a form of analytic particle smoothing. Rather than

---

[2] Generalised EP [21], which groups variables together improves on the results, but is still far inferior to the EC results presented here – Onno Zoeter personal communication.

propagating point distributions (delta-functions), as in the particle approaches, EC propagates Gaussians, which are more able to represent the variability of the distribution, particularly in high dimensions. An important consideration in time series models is numerical stability. Expectation correction uses standard forward and backward linear dynamical system message updates and is therefore able to take advantage of well-studied methods for numerically stable inference. Our smoothing technique has been successfully applied to time series of length $O\left(10^5\right)$ without numerical difficulty [17]. Code for implementing EC is available from the author's website and is part of the BRMLTOOLBOX.

Bibliography

[1] D. L. Alspach and H. W. Sorenson. Nonlinear Bayesian estimation using Gaussian sum approximations. *IEEE Transactions on Automatic Control*, **17**(4):439–448, 1972.

[2] Y. Bar-Shalom and Xiao-Rong Li. *Estimation and Tracking : Principles, Techniques and Software*. Artech House, 1998.

[3] D. Barber. Expectation correction for smoothing in switching linear Gaussian state space models. *Journal of Machine Learning Research*, 7:2515–2540, 2006.

[4] C. Carter and R. Kohn. Markov chain Monte Carlo in conditionally Gaussian state space models. *Biometrika*, **83**:589–601, 1996.

[5] A. T. Cemgil, B. Kappen and D. Barber. A generative model for music transcription. *IEEE Transactions on Audio, Speech and Language Processing*, **14**(2):679 – 694, 2006.

[6] S. Chib and M. Dueker. Non-Markovian regime switching with endogenous states and time-varying state strengths. Econometric Society 2004 North American Summer Meetings 600, Econometric Society, August 2004.

[7] A. Doucet, N. de Freitas, K. Murphy and S. Russell. Rao-Blackwellised particle filtering for dynamic Bayesian networks. *Uncertainty in Artificial Intelligence*, 2000.

[8] S. Frühwirth-Schnatter. *Finite Mixture and Markov Switching Models*. Springer, 2006.

[9] Z. Ghahramani and G. E. Hinton. Variational learning for switching state-space models. *Neural Computation*, **12**(4):963–996, 1998.

[10] T. Heskes and O. Zoeter. Expectation propagation for approximate inference in dynamic Bayesian networks. In A. Darwiche and N. Friedman, editors, *Uncertainty in Artificial Intelligence*, pages 216–223, 2002.

[11] C.-J. Kim. Dynamic linear models with Markov-switching. *Journal of Econometrics*, **60**:1–22, 1994.

[12] C.-J. Kim and C. R. Nelson. *State-Space Models with Regime Switching*. MIT Press, 1999.

[13] G. Kitagawa. The two-filter formula for smoothing and an implementation of the Gaussian-sum smoother. *Annals of the Institute of Statistical Mathematics*, **46**(4):605–623, 1994.

[14] G. Kitagawa. Monte Carlo filter and smoother for non-Gaussian nonlinear state space models. *Journal of Computational and Graphical Statistics*, **5**(1):1–25, 1996.

[15] U. Lerner, R. Parr, D. Koller and G. Biswas. Bayesian fault detection and diagnosis in dynamic systems. In *Proceedings of the Seventeenth National Conference on Artificial Intelligence (AIII-00)*, pages 531–537, 2000.

[16] U. N. Lerner. Hybrid Bayesian networks for reasoning about complex systems. PhD thesis, Stanford University, 2002.

[17] B. Mesot and D. Barber. Switching linear dynamical systems for noise robust speech recognition. *IEEE Transactions of Audio, Speech and Language Processing*, **15**(6):1850–1858, 2007.

[18] T. Minka. A family of algorithms for approximate Bayesian inference. PhD thesis, MIT Media Lab, 2001.

[19] V. Pavlovic, J. M. Rehg and J. MacCormick. Learning switching linear models of human motion. In *Advances in Neural Information Processing Systems (NIPS)*, number 13, pages 981–987, 2001. MIT Press.

[20] D. M. Titterington, A. F. M. Smith and U. E. Makov. *Statistical Analysis of Finite Mixture Distributions*. John Wiley & Sons, 1985.

[21] O. Zoeter. Monitoring non-linear and switching dynamical systems. PhD thesis, Radboud University Nijmegen, 2005.

Contributor

David Barber, Department of Computer Science, University College London

9

Physiological monitoring with factorial switching linear dynamical systems

John A. Quinn and Christopher K. I. Williams

9.1 Introduction

A common way to handle non-linearity in complex time series data is to try splitting the data up into a number of simpler segments. Sometimes we have domain knowledge to support this piecewise modelling approach, for example in condition monitoring applications. In such problems, the evolution of some observed data is governed by a number of hidden factors that switch between different modes of operation. In real-world data, e.g. from medicine, robotic control or finance, we might be interested in factors which represent pathologies, mechanical failure modes, or economic conditions respectively. Given just the monitoring data, we are interested in recovering the state of the factors that gave rise to it.

A good model for this type of problem is the switching linear dynamical system (SLDS), which has been discussed in previous chapters. A latent 'switch' variable in this type of model selects between different linear-Gaussian state spaces. In this chapter we consider a generalisation, the factorial switching linear dynamical system (FSLDS), where instead of a single switch setting there are multiple discrete factors that collectively determine the dynamics. In practice there may be a very large number of possible factors, and we may only have explicit knowledge of commonly occurring ones.

We illustrate how the FSLDS can be used in the physiological monitoring of premature babies in intensive care. This application is a useful introduction because it has complex observed data, a diverse range of factors affecting the observations, and the challenge of many 'unknown' factors. It also provides an opportunity to demonstrate the ways in which domain knowledge can be incorporated into the FSLDS model. Many of the specific modelling details here are also directly applicable to physiological monitoring of adults, in intensive care and other settings.

Observations and factors

Babies born three or four months prematurely are kept, in their first days or weeks *post partum*, in a closely regulated environment, with a number of probes continuously collecting physiological data such as heart rate, blood pressure, temperature and concentrations of gases in the blood. These vital signs (literally 'signs of life') are used in neonatal intensive care to help diagnose the condition of a baby in a critical state. The state of health

Channel name	Label
Core body temperature (°C)	Core temp.
Diastolic blood pressure (mmHg)	Dia. Bp
Heart rate (bpm)	HR
Peripheral body temperature (°C)	Periph. temp.
Saturation of oxygen in pulse (%)	SpO_2
Systolic blood pressure (mmHg)	Sys. Bp
Transcutaneous partial pressure of CO_2 (kPa)	$TcPCO_2$
Transcutaneous partial pressure of O_2 (kPa)	$TcPO_2$
Incubator temperature (°C)	Incu Temp.
Incubator humidity (%)	Incu Humidity.

Table 9.1 Physiological (upper) and environmental (lower) measurement channels in this application, with labels used to denote them later in the chapter.

of a baby cannot be observed directly, but different states of health are associated with particular patterns of measurements. Given observations of the heart rate, body temperature and so on, inferences can therefore be made about the operation of the underlying physiological systems – e.g. whether they are functioning normally, or whether there seems to be evidence of some pathology. This task is complicated by the fact that the observations depend not just on the state of a baby's physiology but also on the operation of the monitoring equipment. There is observation noise due to inaccuracies in the probes, and some operations can cause the measurements to become corrupted with artefacts. The specific data channels we consider here are listed in Table 9.1, each sampled once per second.

Types of known, common factors which affect these observations fall into two categories: artefactual and physiological. The known factors we concentrate on in this chapter are

- *Bradycardia* : Temporary decrease in heart rate (physiological).

- *Blood sample* : Artefactual rise in systolic and diastolic blood pressure measurements while a sample is taken (artefactual).

- *Temperature probe disconnection* : The core temperature probe cools to ambient temperature (artefactual).

- *Handling* : Opening of the incubator, leading to a drop in incubator humidity with increased physiological variation (artefactual).

In addition to these common factors there are many examples of physiological variation due to rare factors, or for which no explanation is available.

Outline of the chapter

In Section 9.2 we introduce the model and compare it to other models for condition monitoring. In Section 9.3 we explain how to handle novel dynamics, i.e. the presence of unknown factors. In Section 9.4 we describe parameter estimation of the model, showing how domain knowledge can be incorporated. Inference is discussed in Section 15.4 and we demonstrate the operation of the system in Section 9.6. The description in this chapter gives an overview of the application and model; for more specific implementation details see [11, 9]. Demonstration code is also available [10].

9.2   Model

We first recap on the SLDS before generalising to the factorial case. In such a model the observations $y_{1:T}, y_t \in \mathbb{R}^{d_y}$, are generated by hidden dynamics $x_{1:T}, x_t \in \mathbb{R}^{d_x}$, according to

$$x_t \sim \mathcal{N}\left(A^{(s_t)}x_{t-1} + d^{(s_t)}, Q^{(s_t)}\right), \quad y_t \sim \mathcal{N}\left(C^{(s_t)}x_t, R^{(s_t)}\right) \tag{9.1}$$

where $s_t \in \{1, \ldots, K\}$ is a discrete variable defining which of a set of K different dynamics is active at time t. Here $A^{(s_t)}$ is a square system matrix, $d^{(s_t)}$ is a drift vector, $C^{(s_t)}$ is the state-observations matrix, and $Q^{(s_t)}$ and $R^{(s_t)}$ are noise covariance matrices. In this formulation, all dynamical parameters can be switched between regimes. Similar models referred to in the above literature sometimes switch only the state dynamics $\{A, Q\}$, or the observation dynamics $\{C, R\}$. Conditioned on a setting of s_t, the model is equivalent to a linear dynamical system.

It is possible to factorise the switch variable, so that M factors $f_t^{(1)}, \ldots, f_t^{(M)}$ affect the observations y_t. The factor $f^{(m)}$ can take on $L^{(m)}$ different values. The state space is the cross product of the factor variables, that is

$$s_t = f_t^{(1)} \otimes f_t^{(2)} \otimes \cdots \otimes f_t^{(M)}$$

with $K = \prod_{m=1}^{M} L^{(m)}$ being the number of settings that s_t can take on. The value of $f_t^{(m)}$ depends on $f_{t-1}^{(m)}$, and the factors are a priori independent, so that

$$p(s_t \mid s_{t-1}) = \prod_{m=1}^{M} p\left(f_t^{(m)} \mid f_{t-1}^{(m)}\right). \tag{9.2}$$

The joint distribution of the model is

$$p(s_{1:T}, x_{1:T}, y_{1:T}) = p(s_1)p(x_1)p(y_1 \mid x_1, s_1) \prod_{t=2}^{T} p(s_t \mid s_{t-1})p(x_t \mid x_{t-1}, s_t)p(y_t \mid x_t, s_t),$$

where $s_{1:T}$ denotes the sequence $s_1, s_2, \ldots, s_T$ (similarly for $x_{1:T}$ and $y_{1:T}$), $p(x_t \mid x_{t-1}, s_t)$ and $p(y_t \mid x_t, s_t)$ are defined in Eq. (9.1), and $p(s_t \mid s_{t-1})$ is defined in Eq. (9.2).

By considering the factored nature of the switch setting, we have an observation term of the form $p(y_t \mid x_t, f_t^{(1)}, \ldots, f_t^{(M)})$. This can be parameterised in different ways. In this work, we specify conditional independencies between particular components of the observation y_t given the factor settings. This is explained further in Section 9.4.5. Although we make use of prior factored dynamics in Eq. (9.2) in this work, it is very simple to generalise the model so that this no longer holds. The inference algorithms described in Section 15.4 can still be applied. However, the separate factors are crucial in structuring the system dynamics and observations model.

In the physiological monitoring application, factor settings $f_t^{(1)}, \ldots, f_t^{(M)}$ represent different conditions (e.g. whether a probe has fallen off or not, whether there is a specific problem with the circulatory system or not). The state x_t can contain estimates of the 'true' values of physiological properties, based on noisy, artefact-prone observations y_t.

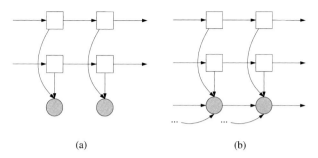

Figure 9.1 Belief network representations of different factorial models, with $M = 2$ factors. Squares indicate discrete variables, circles indicate continuous variables and shaded nodes indicate observed variables. (a) The factorial HMM. (b) The factorial AR-HMM, in which each observation depends on previous values.

9.2.1 Comparison with other switching models for condition monitoring

We have assumed the existence of a discrete switch variable which indexes different modes of operation. In our formulation, the problem of condition monitoring is essentially to infer the value of this switch variable over time from new data. We are particularly interested in the class of models in which there are first-order Markovian transitions between the switch settings at consecutive time steps. Given the switch setting it is possible to characterise the different dynamic regimes on other ways, yielding alternative models for condition monitoring. In this section, we first review the hidden Markov model (HMM) and autoregressive hidden Markov model (AR-HMM), and then discuss their advantages and disadvantages for condition monitoring with respect to the FSLDS.

A simple model for a single regime is the Gaussian distribution on y_t. When this is conditioned on a discrete, first-order Markovian switching variable, we obtain an instance of an HMM. This model can therefore be used for condition monitoring when the levels and variability of different measurement channels are significant (though note that in general the HMM can use any reasonable distribution on y_t).

Autoregressive (AR) models are a common choice for modelling stationary time series. Conditioning an AR model on a Markovian switching variable we obtain an autoregressive hidden Markov model (AR-HMM), also known as a switching AR model – see e.g. [14]. This provides a model for conditions in which observations might be expected to oscillate or decay, for example. During inference, the model can only confidently switch into a regime if the last p observations have been generated under that regime; there will be a loss of accuracy if any of the measurement channels have dropped out in that period, for example, or another artefactual process has affected any of the readings.

The general condition monitoring problem involves independent factors which affect a system. In both of these models the switch variable can be factorised, giving the factorial HMM [5] and the factorial AR-HMM respectively. The belief network representations for these two constructions are shown in Fig. 9.1.

By characterising each regime as a linear dynamical system (LDS) we obtain the FSLDS. The SLDS can be thought of as a 'hybrid' model, having both discrete switch settings as in the HMM and continuous hidden state as in a linear dynamical system. The FSLDS is similar, though with the discrete switch setting structure of the factorial HMM. Note, however, that observations in the FHMM [5] are generated through an additive process in which each factor makes a contribution. The mechanisms used to generate

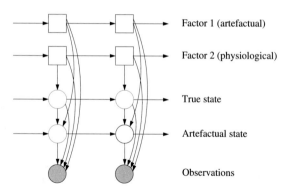

Factor 1 (artefactual)

Factor 2 (physiological)

True state

Artefactual state

Observations

Figure 9.2 Factorial switching linear dynamical system for physiological condition monitoring, with $M = 2$ factors as an example. The state is split up into two sets of variables, containing estimates of the 'true' physiology and of the levels of artefactual processes.

observations under different factor settings can in general be more complex and non-linear than this, as in the overwriting mechanism explained in Section 9.4.5.

The FSLDS models have a number of representational advantages for condition monitoring. First, we can have many dimensions of hidden state for each observed dimension. This allows us to deal with situations in which different elements affect the observations, as we will demonstrate in the examples later in this chapter.

In the physiological monitoring case we can construct detailed representations of the causes underlying the observations. For instance, as we demonstrate in Sections 9.4.1 and 9.4.2, the state can be split into two groups of continuous latent variables representing respectively the 'true' physiology and the levels associated with different artefactual processes. In this application, factors can be physiological or artefactual processes. Physiological factors can affect any state variable, whereas artefactual processes affect only artefactual state. This formulation of the model for physiological condition monitoring is illustrated in Fig. 9.2.

The FSLDS also gives us the ability to represent different sources of uncertainty in the system. We can explicitly specify the intra-class variability in the dynamics using the parameter Q and the measurement noise using the parameter R. There is no way to make this distinction in either of the other models, which have only one noise term per regime. However, this flexibility in the FSLDS is obtained at the cost of greater complexity, particularly in terms of computing inferences, as we will see in Section 9.5.

9.3 Novel conditions

So far we have assumed that the monitoring data contains a limited number of regimes, for which labelled training data is available. In real-world monitoring applications, however, there is often such a great number of potential dynamical regimes that it might be impractical to model them all, or we might never have comprehensive knowledge of them. It can therefore be useful to include a factor in the condition monitoring model which represents all 'unusual cases'.

In this section we present a method for modelling previously unseen dynamics as an extra factor in the model, referred to as the 'X-factor'. This represents all dynamics which are not normal and which also do not correspond to any of the known regimes. A sequence of data can only be said to have novelty relative to some reference, so the model is learnt taking into account the parameters of the normal regime. The inclusion of this factor in the model has two potential benefits. First, it is useful to know when novel regimes are encountered, e.g. in order to raise an alarm. Second, the X-factor provides a measure of confidence for the system. That is, when a regime is confidently classified as 'none of the above', we know that there is some structure in the data which is lacking in the model.

9.3.1 The X-factor

First consider a case in which we have independent, one-dimensional observations which normally follow a Gaussian distribution. If we expect that there will also occasionally be spurious observations which come from a different distribution, then a natural way to model them is by using a wider Gaussian with the same mean. Observations close to the mean retain a high likelihood under the original Gaussian distribution, while outliers are claimed by the new model.

The same principle can be applied when there are a number of known distributions, so that the model is conditionally Gaussian, $y \mid s \sim N\left(\mu^{(s)}, \Sigma^{(s)}\right)$. For condition monitoring we are interested in problems where we assume that the possible settings of s represent a 'normal' mode and a number of known additional modes. In physiological monitoring, for example, the normal mode corresponds to the times when the physiology is stable and there is no artefactual corruption of the observed data. Additional modes correspond e.g. to known problems with the monitoring equipment or specific pathologies. We assume here that the normal regime is indexed by $s = 1$, and the additional known modes by $s = 2, \ldots, K$. In this static case, we can construct a new model, indexed by $s = *$, for unexpected data points by inflating the covariance of the normal mode, so that

$$\Sigma^{(*)} = \xi \Sigma^{(1)}, \qquad \mu^{(*)} = \mu^{(1)}, \tag{9.3}$$

where normally $\xi > 1$. We refer to this type of construction for unexpected observations as an 'X-factor'. The parameter ξ determines how far outside the normal range new data points have to fall before they are considered 'not normal'.

The likelihood functions for a normal class and a corresponding X-factor are shown in Fig. 9.3(a). Clearly, data points that are far away from the normal range are more likely to be classified as belonging to the X-factor. For condition monitoring this can be used in conjunction with a number of known classes, as shown in Fig. 9.3(b). Here, the X-factor

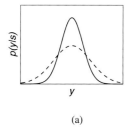
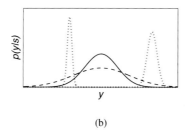
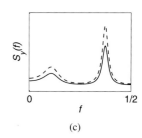

| (a) | (b) | (c) |

Figure 9.3 (a) Class conditional likelihoods in a static 1D model, for the normal class (solid) and the X-factor (dashed). (b) Likelihoods of the normal class and X-factor in conjunction with other known, abnormal regimes (shown dotted). (c) The power spectral density of a latent AR(5) process with white observation noise (solid), and that of a corresponding X-factor process (dashed).

has the highest likelihood for regions which are far away from any known modes, as well as far away from normality.

We can generalise this approach to dynamic novelty detection by adding a new factor to a trained factorial switching linear dynamical model, by inflating the system noise covariance of the normal dynamics

$$Q^{(*)} = \xi Q^{(1)}, \tag{9.4}$$

$$\left\{A^{(*)}, C^{(*)}, R^{(*)}, d^{(*)}\right\} = \left\{A^{(1)}, C^{(1)}, R^{(1)}, d^{(1)}\right\}. \tag{9.5}$$

To help understand why Eqs. (9.4) and (9.5) are a dynamic generalisation of Eq. (9.3), consider the specific case of a hidden scalar AR(p) process,

$$x_t \sim N\left(\sum_{k=1}^{p} \alpha_k x_{t-k}, \sigma_q^2\right), \qquad y_t \sim N(x_t, \sigma_r^2).$$

The power spectral density for the hidden process x_t at frequency f is given by

$$S_x(f) = \frac{\sigma_q^2}{\left|1 - \sum_{k=1}^{p} \alpha_k e^{-2\pi i f k}\right|^2},$$

where $-\frac{1}{2} \le f \le \frac{1}{2}$, assuming one observed value per unit of time. By inflating σ_q^2 (as specified in Eq. (9.4)) we observe that the power is increased at each frequency. The observed process has spectrum $S_y(f) = S_x(f) + \sigma_r^2$. As the scale of $S_y(f)$ is determined by the magnitudes of the two noise variances, inflating σ_q^2 will have the effect of increasing the power at every frequency, as illustrated in Fig. 9.3(c).

In the LDS, any sequence of x's is jointly Gaussian. Consider the case where the state is a scalar variable, the eigenfunctions are sinusoids and the eigenvalues are given by the power spectrum. As increasing the system noise has the effect of increasing the power at all frequencies in the state sequence, we have a dynamical analogue of the static construction given above.

A similar model for changes in dynamics is mentioned by [13, p. 458 and §12.4], who suggest it as the parameterisation of an extra state in the unfactorised SLDS for modelling large jumps in the x-process, and suggest setting $\xi = 100$. Their analysis in §12.4.4 shows that this is used to model single-time-step-level changes, and not (as we are doing) sustained periods of abnormality. We find a much smaller value $\xi = 1.2$ to be effective for our task (larger values of ξ mean that an observation sequence must deviate further from normal dynamics to be claimed by the X-factor). A different generative model for the X-factor in principle would be white noise, but we find in practice that this model is too dissimilar to the real signal and is not effective.

The nature of the measurement noise, and hence the value of the parameter $R^{(s)}$, is assumed to be the same for both the normal regime and for the X-factor. Care needs to be taken that the known factor dynamics do not have a very high variance compared to the normal dynamics. It is clear from Fig. 9.3(b) that the X-factor will not be effective if any of the factors are wider than normality. This can be ascertained by examining the spectra of the different model dynamics.

9.4 Parameter estimation

In a condition monitoring problem, it is assumed that we are able to interpret at least some of the regimes in the data – otherwise we would be less likely to have an interest in monitoring them. We can therefore usually expect to obtain some labelled training data $\{y_{1:T}, s_{1:T}\}$. When available, this data greatly simplifies the learning process, because knowing the switch setting in the FSLDS makes the model equivalent to an LDS. The learning process is therefore broken down into the training of a set of LDS models – one per switch setting. We might choose a particular parameterisation, such as an AR model of order p hidden by observation noise and fit parameters accordingly. Expectation maximisation (EM) can be used to improve parameter settings given an initialisation [3]. We describe particular methods used for parameter estimation in the physiological monitoring application which incorporate both of these ideas.

When labelled training data is available, estimates of the factor transition probabilities are given by $P(f_t^{(m)} = j \mid f_{t-1}^{(m)} = i) = \frac{n_{ij}+\zeta}{\sum_{k=1}^{M}(n_{ik}+\zeta)}$, where n_{ij} is the number of transitions from factor setting i to setting j in the training data. The constant terms ζ (set to $\zeta = 1$ in the experiments described later in the chapter) are added to prevent any of the transition probabilities from being zero or very small.

Some verification of the learned model is possible by clamping the switch setting to a certain value and studying the resulting LDS. One simple but effective test is to draw a sample sequence and check by eye whether it resembles the dynamics of training data which is known to follow the same regime [1, §5.7]. Some insight into the quality of the parameter settings can also be gained by considering estimation of the hidden state x in the LDS. The Kalman filter equations yield both an *innovation sequence*, $\tilde{y}_{1:T}$ (the difference between the predicted and actual observations), and a specification of the covariance of the innovations under ideal conditions. An illuminating test is therefore to compare the actual and ideal properties of the innovation sequence when applied to training data. In particular, the innovations $\tilde{y}_t$ should come from a Gaussian distribution with zero mean and a specific covariance, and should be uncorrelated in time. We find in practice that such tests are useful when training FSLDS models for condition monitoring. For more details about verification in linear dynamical systems, see [1, §5.5].

We now show examples of learning different aspects of the FSLDS in the physiological monitoring setting. We begin with system identification for the 'normal' physiological dynamics (i.e. the dynamics which are observed when the baby is stable and there is no artefactual influence) in Section 9.4.1. We then show how to model an artefactual process, the drawing of a blood sample, in Section 9.4.2. In Section 9.4.3, we introduce the training of a physiological factor associated with bradycardia, a specific heart problem. Learning the X-factor parameter ξ is covered in Section 9.4.4. Finally in Section 9.4.5 we demonstrate how to combine dynamical models into the overall factorised SLDS.

9.4.1　Learning normal dynamics: heart rate

Looking at examples of normal heart rate dynamics as in the top left and right panels of Fig. 9.4, it can be observed first of all that the measurements tend to fluctuate around a slowly drifting baseline. This motivates the use of a model with two hidden components: the signal x_t, and the baseline b_t. These components are therefore used to represent the true heart rate, without observation noise. The dynamics can be formulated using an AR process, such as an AR(p_1) signal that varies around an AR(p_2) baseline, as given by the following equations:

$$x_t - b_t \sim \mathcal{N}\left(\sum_{k=1}^{p_1} \alpha_k(x_{t-k} - b_{t-k}), \eta_1\right), \quad b_t \sim \mathcal{N}\left(\sum_{k=1}^{p_2} \beta_k b_{t-k}, \eta_2\right)$$

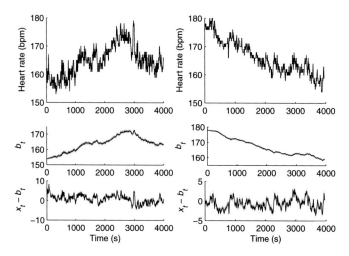

Figure 9.4 In these two examples, HR measurements (top left and top right panels) are varying quickly within normal ranges. The estimated distributions of the underlying signal (bottom left and bottom right panels) are split into a smooth baseline process and zero-mean high-frequency component, given by applying the Kalman filter equations with parameters learnt as in Section 9.4.1.

where η_1, η_2 are noise variances. For example, an AR(2) signal with AR(2) baseline has the following state space representation:

$$\mathbf{x}_t = \begin{bmatrix} x_t \\ x_{t-1} \\ b_t \\ b_{t-1} \end{bmatrix}, \quad A = \begin{bmatrix} \alpha_1 & \alpha_2 & \beta_1 - \alpha_1 & \beta_2 - \alpha_2 \\ 1 & 0 & 0 & 0 \\ 0 & 0 & \beta_1 & \beta_2 \\ 0 & 0 & 1 & 0 \end{bmatrix},$$

$$Q = \begin{bmatrix} \eta_1 + \eta_2 & 0 & 0 & 0 \\ 0 & 0 & 0 & 0 \\ 0 & 0 & \eta_2 & 0 \\ 0 & 0 & 0 & 0 \end{bmatrix}, \quad C = [1\ 0\ 0\ 0]. \tag{9.6}$$

It is straightforward to adjust this construction for different values of p_1 and p_2. The measurements are therefore generally taken to be made up of a baseline with low-frequency components and a signal with high-frequency components. We begin training this model with a heuristic initialisation, in which we take sequences of training data and remove high-frequency components by applying a symmetric 300-point moving average filter. The resulting signal is taken to be the low-frequency baseline. The residual between the original sequences and the moving-averaged sequences are taken to contain both stationary high-frequency haemodynamics as well as measurement noise. These two signals can be analysed according to standard methods and modelled as AR or integrated AR processes (specific cases of autoregressive integrated moving average (ARIMA) processes [12]) of arbitrary order. Heart rate sequences were found to be well modelled by an AR(2) signal varying around an ARIMA(1,1,0) baseline. An ARIMA model is a compelling choice for the baseline, because with a low noise term it produces a smooth drift.[1] Having found this

---

[1] The ARIMA(1,1,0) model has the form $(X_t - \beta X_{t-1}) = \alpha_1(X_{t-1} - \beta X_{t-2}) + Z_t$ where $\beta = 1$ and $Z_t \sim N(0, \sigma_Z^2)$. This can be expressed in un-differenced form as a non-stationary AR(2) model. In our implementation we set $\beta = 0.999$ and with $|\alpha_1| < 1$ we obtain a stable AR(2) process, which helps to avoid problems with numerical instability. This slight damping makes the baseline mean-reverting, so that the resulting signal is stationary. This has desirable convergence properties for dropout modelling.

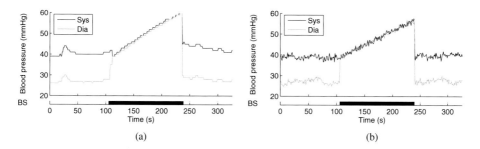

Figure 9.5 Genuine blood sample, and a sample drawn from the model with switch settings clamped to be the same; BS indicates the factor switch setting, where black denotes $f_t^{(BS)} = 1$ (blood sample dynamics) and grey denotes $f_t^{(BS)} = 0$ (normal dynamics).

initial setting of the model parameters, EM updates are then applied. These are similar to the updates given in [3], though constrained so that we retain the structure in Eq. (9.6). This has been found to be particularly useful for refining the estimates of the noise terms Q and R.

Examples of the heart rate model being applied using a Kalman filter to sequences of heart rate data are shown in Fig. 9.4, which plots the noisy observations y_t (upper panels) and estimates of the baseline b_t and high frequency components $x_t - b_t$ (middle and lower panels respectively).

9.4.2 Learning artefactual dynamics: blood sampling

An arterial blood sample might be taken every few hours from each baby. This involves diverting blood from the arterial line containing the pressure sensor, so that measurements are entirely unrelated from the baby's physiology. Throughout the operation a saline pump acts against the sensor, causing an artefactual ramp in the blood pressure measurements. The slope of the ramp is not always the same, as the rate at which saline is pumped can vary. See Fig. 9.5(a) for an example. During this process, the systolic and diastolic blood pressures of the baby evolve as normal but are unobserved.

For this artefactual rise, we specify a structural model in which the artefactual measurements a_t evolve according to a gradient which is subject to a random walk

$$a_t \sim N\left(a_{t-1} + d_a + c_{t-1}, \sigma_a^2\right), \quad c_t \sim N\left(c_{t-1}, \sigma_c^2\right).$$

Each of these terms are scalars. Parameter d_a is a positive constant specifying the average drift, which is modified by the random walk term c_t. The Gaussian noise on a_t with variance σ_a^2 models the differences in slope of blood samples taken at different times, while the noise on c_t with variance σ_c^2 models the change in slope within a single blood sample operation. During the procedure, both blood pressure readings (systolic and diastolic) are generated by the same underlying value a_t.

Using a state space form we obtain the following hidden state dynamics for a_t, c_t

$$x_t = \begin{bmatrix} a_t \\ c_t \end{bmatrix}, \quad d_{BS} = \begin{bmatrix} d_a \\ 0 \end{bmatrix}, \quad A_{BS} = \begin{bmatrix} 1 & 1 \\ 0 & 1 \end{bmatrix}, \quad Q_{BS} = \begin{bmatrix} \sigma_a^2 & 0 \\ 0 & \sigma_c^2 \end{bmatrix}.$$

The observations y_t are two-dimensional, where $y_{t,1}$ is the systolic blood pressure and $y_{t,2}$ is the diastolic blood pressure. The observation model is given by

$$C_{BS} = \begin{bmatrix} 1 & 0 \\ 1 & 0 \end{bmatrix}, \quad R_{BS} = \begin{bmatrix} r_{SysBP} & 0 \\ 0 & r_{DiaBP} \end{bmatrix}.$$

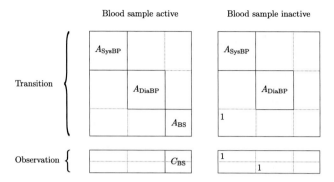

Figure 9.6 State spaces for normal dynamics and for blood sampling.

The parameters are straightforward to learn from training data. Let T denote a two-dimensional time series spanning n time steps and containing an example of the observed systolic and diastolic blood pressures during a blood sample operation, such that $T = \{y_{t,1:2} \mid 1 \leq t \leq n\}$. If we have a set of such training sequences $T_1, \ldots, T_N$ then parameter estimation proceeds as follows:

$$d_a = \frac{1}{N} \sum_{i=1}^{N} \text{slope}(T_i), \quad \sigma_a^2 = \mathsf{V}(\{\text{slope}(T_i) \mid 1 \leq i \leq N\}),$$

where the slope of the measurements can be found either by simply calculating the gradient slope $(T) = \frac{1}{2(n-1)} [(y_{1,1} + y_{1,2}) - (y_{n,1} + y_{n,2})]$ or, better, with linear regression. The variance of the noise on c_t is found using $\sigma_c^2 = \frac{1}{N} \sum_{i=1}^{N} \mathsf{V}(\text{diff}(T_i))$, where $\text{diff}(T) = \{\frac{1}{2} [(y_{i,1} + y_{i,2}) - (y_{i-1,1} + y_{i-1,2})] \mid 2 \leq i \leq n\}$. We assume that the monitoring equipment has the same observation noise whether a blood sample is being taken or not. Therefore R_{BS} is the same as for the normal dynamics, learnt as described in the previous section.

Having set the values of each of the parameters, these dynamics can be incorporated into the full switching model. Figure 9.6 shows the structure of the full transition matrix A and the observation matrix C, for blood sample dynamics ($f^{(\text{BS})} = 1$) and for normal dynamics ($f^{(\text{BS})} = 0$). During a blood sample, observations are generated only by the artefactual state variables. State variables representing the baby's actual systolic and diastolic blood pressure are evolved according to the normal dynamics, but not observed (see Fig. 9.13(a) for an illustration of hidden state inferences in this case). During normal dynamics, the physiological state variables are observed, and a_t is tied to the estimate of systolic blood pressure.

One way to check that such a model has been adequately fitted is to sample from it and verify that the results have similar characteristics to the training data. Figure 9.5(a) shows a genuine example of measurements made while a blood sample is being taken. We then draw a sample of the same length from the switching model, Fig. 9.5(b), using the same initial state at $t = 1$ and with the switch settings clamped to be the same as for the genuine sequence. Note that the observation noise appears greater on the simulated version partly because iid Gaussian noise is being used to model quantisation effects in the training observations.

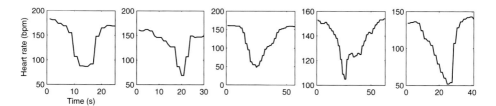

Figure 9.7 Examples of periods of bradycardia. Heart rate is measured in beats per minute (bpm).

9.4.3 Learning physiological dynamics: bradycardia

Bradycardia is a (usually temporary) reduction in the heart rate, and brief episodes are common for premature infants. It can have many causes, some benign and some serious. Examples of this phenomenon are shown in Fig. 9.7. Because there is no simple physical process governing this pattern of observations, we have less opportunity to parameterise the model based on domain knowledge. Therefore we turn to statistical principles to learn the dynamics and validate our chosen model.

There are several ways to model this pattern. For example, we could learn the dynamics of the whole sequence as a single regime, or split it up into falling and rising dynamics. In the former case, we could specify some positive second derivative, or look at the variability of the observations. In the latter case we could use drift terms to model the fall and rise, or use exponential decays towards different mean values.

Bradycardic drops and subsequent rises in heart rate were found to be adequately modelled by retraining the ARIMA(1,1,0) model for baseline heart rate dynamics. The high-frequency heart rate dynamics were kept the same as for the stable heart rate regime. As for the normal regime, this model learnt in terms of hidden ARIMA processes was used as an initial setting and updated with three iterations of EM.

9.4.4 Learning the novelty threshold

Unlike the factors for which we have an interpretation, we do not assume that labelled training data is available for learning X-factor dynamics. We therefore consider a partial labelling of the training data $y_{1:T}$, comprising of annotations for known factors and for some representative quantity of normal dynamics. The remainder of the training data is unlabelled, giving us a semi-supervised learning problem.

To apply the EM algorithm to the X-factor within a SLDS (non-factorised switch setting), the M-step update to ξ is given by

$$\tilde{\xi} = \frac{1}{\sum_{t=2}^{T} p(s_t = * \mid y_{1:T}, \theta_{\text{old}})} \tag{9.7}$$

$$\times \sum_{t=2}^{T} \left\langle (x_t - A^{(1)}x_{t-1})^\top Q^{(1)-1}(x_t - A^{(1)}x_{t-1}) \right\rangle_{x_t, x_{t-1} \mid y_{1:T}, \theta_{\text{old}}} p(s_t = * \mid y_{1:T}, \theta_{\text{old}})$$

where $s_t = *$ indexes the X-factor switch setting at time t and $\langle \cdot \rangle$ denotes expectation. We describe strategies for calculating the expectation term in Sections 9.5.1 and 9.5.2. It can be convenient to use the filtering estimate $\langle \cdot \rangle_{x_t, x_{t-1} \mid y_{1:t}, \theta_{\text{old}}}$ as an approximation.

The parameters $A^{(1)}$ and $Q^{(1)}$ are respectively the system matrix and system noise covariance matrix for the normal dynamical regime. Intuitively, this update expression calculates a Z-score, considering the covariance of novel points and the covariance of the normal regime. Every point is considered, and is weighted by the probability of having been generated by the X-factor regime. Equation (9.7) does not explicitly constrain $\tilde{\xi}$ to be greater than 1, but with appropriate initialisation it is unlikely to violate this condition.

The factorial case is a little more complicated due to the possibility that different combinations of factors can overwrite different channels. For example, if a bradycardia is occurring in conjunction with some other, unknown regime, then the heart rate dynamics are already well explained and should not be taken into account when re-estimating the X-factor parameter ξ.

An alternative to Eq. (9.7) and an extension to the factorial case is given in [9, §C.4].

9.4.5 Learning the factorial model

The previous discussion assumed that we train the model conditioned on each switch setting independently, and then combine parameters. When there are many factors this implies that a great quantity of training data is needed. In practice, however, this requirement can be mitigated.

Where there are several measurement channels it may be found that some factors 'overwrite' others. For example, if we are monitoring the physiological condition of a patient, we might have two factors: *bradycardia* and *incubator open*. If there is a period of bradycardia while the incubator is open, then we would see the same measurements as though there was only the bradycardia. It is often possible to specify an ordering of factors such that some overwrite measurement channels of others in this way. This ordering specifies conditional independencies in the factors and observations, such that

$$f^{(i)} \text{ overwrites } f^{(j)} \text{ on measurement channel } d \implies y_{t,d} \perp\!\!\!\perp f_t^{(j)} \,|\, f_t^{(i)} > 0,$$

assuming that the switch setting $f^{(j)} = 0$ means that factor j is 'inactive' and positive integers index the active dynamics of that factor. The significance of this is that examples of every combination of factors do not need to be found in order to train the factorial model. The factors can be trained independently, and then combined together by reasoning about which channels are overwritten for each combination.

9.5 Inference

Exact inference in the SLDS is intractable, thus we need to make approximations regardless of whether we are doing filtering or smoothing. We describe each case in turn in Sections 9.5.1 and 9.5.2, including its relevance to this application and the techniques which can be used to make it tractable. We then discuss modifications of the standard inference procedures to suit this application in Sections 9.5.3 and 9.5.4.

9.5.1 Filtering

During deployment of the neonatal monitoring system we are primarily interested in filtering, although fixed-lag smoothing with a small time delay would also be conceivable. We receive measurements second by second and are required to make an immediate diagnosis based only on the history.

The time taken to calculate the exact filtering distribution $p(s_t, x_t \,|\, y_{1:t})$ in the SLDS scales exponentially with t, making it intractable. This is because the probabilities of having moved between every possible combination of switch settings in times $t-1$ and t are needed to calculate the posterior at time t. Hence the number of Gaussians needed to represent the posterior exactly at each time step increases by a factor of K, the number of cross-product switch settings. The intractability of inference in this model is proved in [7], which also concentrates on a fault diagnosis setting.

Gaussian sum approximations have been reviewed in previous chapters of this book. While performing the forward pass to calculate the filtering distribution, at each time step we maintain an approximation of $p(x_t \mid s_t, y_{1:t})$ as a mixture of I Gaussians. Calculating the Kalman updates and likelihoods for every possible setting of s_{t+1} will result in the posterior $p(x_{t+1} \mid s_{t+1}, y_{1:t+1})$ having KI mixture components, which can be collapsed back into I components by matching means and variances of the distribution for each setting of s_t.

Rao–Blackwellised particle filtering (RBPF) [8] is another technique for approximate inference, which exploits the conditionally linear dynamical structure of the model to try to select particles close to the modes of the true filtering distribution. A number of particles are propagated through each time step, each with a switch state s_t and an estimate of the mean and variance of x_t. A value for the switch state s_{t+1} is obtained for each particle by sampling from the transition probabilities, after which Kalman updates are performed and a likelihood value can be calculated. Based on this likelihood, particles can be either discarded or multiplied. Because Kalman updates are not necessarily calculated for every possible setting of s_{t+1}, this method can give an increase in speed when there are many factors. The fewer particles used, the greater the trade-off of speed against accuracy, as it becomes less likely that the particles can collectively track all modes of the true posterior distribution. Rao–Blackwellised particle filtering has been shown to be successful in condition monitoring problems with switching linear dynamics, for example in fault detection in mobile robots [2].

In the factorised model, the number of switch settings may be high. There may also be some transitions with low probability. In this case, sampling from the discrete transition prior $p(s_t \mid \hat{s}_{t-1}^{(i)})$ might be problematic, as there is a chance that no particles are sampled from certain switch settings. We modify the prior so that we sample from $\hat{s}_t^{(i)} \sim q(s_t \mid \hat{s}_{t-1}^{(i)})$ where

$$q(s_t = k \mid s_{t-1} = j) = \frac{p(s_t = k \mid s_{t-1} = j) + \zeta}{\sum_{l=1}^{M} (p(s_t = l \mid s_{t-1} = j) + \zeta)},$$

which makes it more likely that particles are sampled from different switch settings. In the following experiments we use $\zeta = 0.1$. If a large setting of ζ was thought to be distorting the results, then it would be straightforward to adjust the importance weight of each particle i by a factor of $\frac{p(\hat{s}_t^{(i)} \mid \hat{s}_{t-1}^{(i)})}{q(\hat{s}_t^{(i)} \mid \hat{s}_{t-1}^{(i)})}$ at each time step to compensate.

9.5.2 Smoothing

While carrying out parameter estimation, we are interested in smoothing. Given offline training data, we can afford to exploit backwards information in order to refine estimates of the system parameters. The 'E' steps of the EM procedures cited in Section 9.4 therefore use a backwards pass of the data – though in this case we already know the switch settings s_t for all t, so we do smoothing during parameter estimation on linear dynamical systems, not on the full switching model. It can also be interesting to see how the performance on

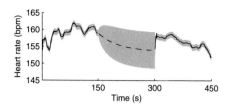

Figure 9.8 Inference of true heart rate under a dropout, with automatic handling of missing observations. The solid black line shows HR observations, where available, the dashed line shows the mean of the estimated distribution of true HR, and the shaded area shows two standard deviations of the estimated distribution.

testing data changes when calculating smoothed inferences, even though this is not realistic for deployment.

Approximate smoothed inference in the full switching model is possible with various schemes. In the previous section we described the simplifying assumption that the true filtering distribution is a mixture of Gaussians (the Gaussian sum approximation). We can make the same assumption about the smoothing distribution. Gaussian sum smoothing is possible using expectation correction (see Chapter 8). Smoothed inference can also be done with expectation propagation (see Chapter 7), or by variational approximation [3].

We now discuss some adaptations to the standard inference routines, for handling missing observations and constraining the number of possible switch transitions.

9.5.3 Handling missing observations

Zero observations in this application denote missing values, for example where a probe has been disconnected. It would be possible in principle to add an extra factor for each channel to indicate a missing observation. However each extra factor with two states slows inference down by a factor of two. To add a dropout channel for each of 10 observed channels would slow down inference by a factor of 2^{10}.

Instead we can test at each time whether there are any dimensions in y_t which are zero. Within the inference routines, for each switch setting we then use the updated observation matrix given by

$$H_{ij}^* = \begin{cases} H_{ij} & \text{where } y_j \neq 0 \\ 0 & \text{otherwise.} \end{cases}$$

The Kalman filter updates, which are incorporated in all the inference schemes we consider, have two stages: prediction (in which the variance of the estimates increases) and correction (in which the variance decreases). The effect of this modification to the observation matrix is to cancel the correction step whenever observations are unavailable. Typical inference results are shown in Fig. 9.8, where a period of heart rate measurements is missing and we show the estimated distribution of 'true' heart rate. In Section 9.4.3 we made the normal dynamics stable and mean-reverting, so that the estimates reach an equilibrium in this situation.

9.5.4 Constraining switch transitions

In this application, factors change switch settings slowly relative to the sampling rate. It is therefore unlikely that more than one factor changes its setting in any one time step. We can use this to constrain the transitions.

The discrete transition probabilities are defined by a matrix Z, where $Z_{ij} = p(s_t = j \mid s_{t-1} = i)$, given by Eq. (9.2). We can use an updated transition matrix Z^* such that

$$Z_{ij}^* = \begin{cases} Z_{ij} & \text{where } 0 \le \sum_{s=1}^{M} I\left[f^{(i)}[s] = f^{(j)}[s]\right] \le 1 \\ 0 & \text{otherwise} \end{cases}$$

where $I[\cdot]$ is the indicator function and $f^{(i)}[s]$ denotes the switch setting for factor i in the cross product switch setting s. This reduces the inference time from $O(K^2)$ to $O(K \log K)$.

9.6 Experiments

This section describes experiments used to evaluate the model for condition monitoring. Other than the X-factor, we consider here the incubator open/handling of baby factor (denoted 'IO'), the blood sample factor (denoted 'BS'), the bradycardia factor (denoted 'BR') and the temperature probe disconnection factor (denoted 'TD'). We demonstrate the operation of the transcutaneous probe recalibration factor (denoted 'TR'), but do not evaluate it quantitatively due to a scarcity of training data.

Some conventions in plotting the results of these experiments are adopted throughout this section. Horizontal bars below time series plots indicate the posterior probability of a particular factor being active, with other factors in the model marginalised out. White and black indicate probabilities of zero and one respectively.[2] In general the plots show a subset of the observation channels and posteriors from a particular model – this is indicated in the text.

Twenty-four-hour periods of monitoring data were obtained from fifteen premature infants in the intensive care unit at Edinburgh Royal Infirmary. The babies were between 24 and 29 weeks gestation (around 3–4 months premature), and all in around their first week *post partum.*

Each of the fifteen 24-hour periods was annotated by two clinical experts. At or near the start of each period, a 30-minute section of normality was marked, indicating an example of that baby's current baseline dynamics. Each of the known common physiological and artefactual patterns were also marked up.

Finally, it was noted where there were any periods of data in which there were clinically significant changes from the baseline dynamics not caused by any of the known patterns. While the previous annotations were made collaboratively, the two annotators marked up this 'abnormal (other)' category independently. The software package TSNet [6] was used to record these annotations, and the recorded intervals were then exported into Matlab. The number of intervals for each category, as well as the total and average durations, are shown in Table 9.2. The figures for the 'abnormal' category were obtained by combining the two annotations, so that the total duration is the number of points which either annotator thought to be in this category, and the number of incidences was calculated by merging overlapping intervals in the two annotations (two overlapping intervals are counted as a single incidence).

The rest of this section shows the results of performing inference on this data and comparing it to the gold standard annotations provided by the clinical experts.

---

[2]A convenient property of the models evaluated here, from the perspective of visualisation, is that the factor posteriors tend to be close to zero or one. This is partly due to the fact that the discrete transition prior $p(s_t \mid s_{t-1})$ is usually heavily weighted towards staying in the same switch setting (long dwell times).

Factor	Incidences	Total duration	Average duration
Incubator open	690	41 hours	3.5 mins
Abnormal (other)	605	32 hours	3.2 mins
Bradycardia	272	161 mins	35 secs
Blood sample	91	253 mins	2.8 mins
Temp. disconnection	87	572 mins	6.6 mins
TCP recalibration	11	69 mins	6.3 mins

Table 9.2 Number of incidences of different factors, and total time for which each factor was annotated as being active in the training data (total duration of training data $15 \times 24 = 360$ hours).

9.6.1 Evaluation of known factors

The dataset for evaluation consisted of fifteen 24-hour periods of monitoring data (one day of monitoring data for each of fifteen babies). Evaluation was done using leave-one-out cross validation, so that the 24-hour period from each baby was used for testing in turn, using data from the other fourteen babies for training.

From each 24-hour period, a 30-minute section near the start containing only normal dynamics was reserved for calibration (learning normal dynamics according to Section 9.4.3). Testing was therefore conducted on the remaining $23\frac{1}{2}$ hour periods.

The quality of the inferences made were evaluated using receiver operating characteristic (ROC) curves for the different inference methods. The ROC curve plots the rate of true positives against the rate of false negatives, such that the area under the curve (AUC) gives a balanced measure of performance even when the class sizes in the testing data are unequal. Another useful statistic which can be obtained from the ROC curve is the equal error rate (EER), which is the error rate for the threshold setting at which the false positive rate is equal to the false negative rate. We give error rates, so smaller numbers are better (some authors give $1 - EER$).

Figure 9.9 shows a plot of AUC against processing time for Gaussian sum filtering, Gaussian sum smoothing using expectation correction, and RBPF with varying numbers of particles. Figure 9.10 shows a corresponding plot for EER against processing time.

Gaussian sum filtering (forward mixture size $I = 1$) had good performance on all four factors. Gaussian sum smoothing (with a forward mixture size $I = 1$ and backward mixture size $J = 1$) with expectation correction gave improved performance in the inference of bradycardia, and similar or slightly improved performance for the other three factors.

Rao–Blackwellised particle filtering results were not so good, even with high numbers of particles, though it is interesting to note that a certain level of accuracy can be achieved with much faster inference than the other methods.

Specific examples of the operation of these models are now given. Figures 9.11–9.13 show inferences of switch settings made with the FSLDS with Gaussian sum approximation. In each case the switch settings have been accurately inferred. Figure 9.11 shows examples of transcutaneous probe recalibration, correctly classified in conjunction with a blood sample and a core temperature probe disconnection. In Fig. 9.11(b) the recalibration and disconnection begin at around the same time, as a nurse has handled the baby in order to access the transcutaneous probe, causing the temperature probe to become detached.

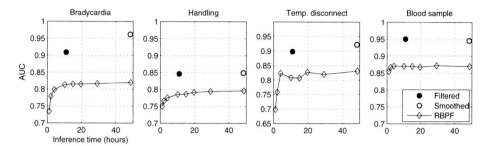

Figure 9.9 AUC for different inference methods on four known factors, for 360 hours of monitoring data. 'Filtered' and 'Smoothed' denote the performance of Gaussian sum filtering and EC smoothing respectively. RBPF inference was done with 5, 10, 20, 50, 75, 100, 150 and 250 particles.

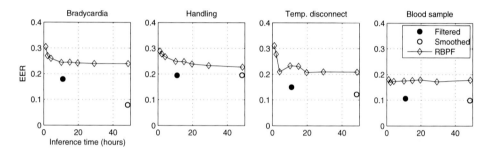

Figure 9.10 EER for different inference methods on four known factors, with data and inference methods as in Fig. 9.9.

Figure 9.12 shows inference of bradycardia, blood sampling and handling of the baby. In Fig. 9.12(a) it has been possible to recognise the disturbance of heart rate at $t = 800$ as being caused by handling of the baby, distinguished from the bradycardia earlier when there is no evidence of the incubator having been entered.

For the blood sample and temperature probe disconnection factors, the measurement data bears no relation to the actual physiology, and the model should update the estimated distribution of the true physiology in these situations accordingly. Figure 9.13 contains examples of the inferred distribution of true physiology in data periods in which these two artefacts occur. In each case, once the artefactual pattern has been detected, the physiological estimates remain constant or decay towards a mean. As time passes since the last reliable observation, the variance of the estimates increases towards a steady state.

9.6.2   Inference of novel dynamics

Examples of the operation of the X-factor are shown in Figs. 9.14–9.16. We employ two models with different sets of factors. The label '(1)' on the plots denotes the FSLDS with only one factor, the X-factor. The label '(5)' denotes the FSLDS which has five factors – the four known factors and the X-factor. Figure 9.14 shows two examples of inferred switch settings under model (5) for periods in which there are isolated physiological disturbances. Both the posteriors for the X-factor and the gold standard intervals for the 'abnormal (other)' category are shown. The physiological disturbances in both panels are cardiovascular and have clearly observable effects on the blood pressure and oxygen saturation measurements.

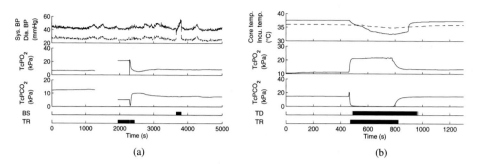

(a)   (b)

Figure 9.11 Inferred distributions of switch settings for two situations involving recalibration of the transcutaneous probe; BS denotes a blood sample, TR denotes a recalibration and TD denotes a core temperature probe disconnection. In panel (a) the recalibration is preceded by a dropout, followed by a blood sample. Diastolic BP is shown as a dashed line which lies below the systolic BP plot. Transcutaneous readings drop out at around $t = 1200$ before the recalibration. In panel (b), the solid line shows the core temperature and the dashed line shows incubator temperature. A core temperature probe disconnection is identified correctly, as well as the recalibration. Temperature measurements can occasionally drop below the incubator temperature if the probe is near to the portals; this is accounted for in the model by the system noise term Q.

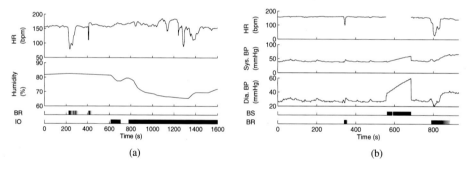

(a)   (b)

Figure 9.12 Inferred distributions of switch settings for two further situations in which there are effects due to multiple known factors. In panel (a) there are incidences of bradycardia, after which the incubator is entered. There is disturbance of heart rate during the period of handling, which is correctly taken to be associated with the handling and not an example of spontaneous bradycardia. In panel (b), bradycardia and blood samples are correctly inferred. During the blood sample, heart rate measurements (supplied by the blood pressure sensor) are interrupted.

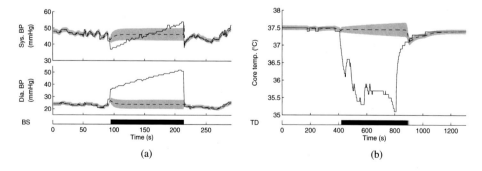

(a)   (b)

Figure 9.13 Inferred distributions of the true physiological state during artefactual corruption of measurements. Panel (a) shows correct inference of the duration of a blood sample, and panel (b) shows correct inference of a temperature probe disconnection. Measurements are plotted as a solid line, and estimates $\hat{x}_t$ relating to true physiology are plotted as a dashed line with the grey shading indicating two standard deviations. In each case, during the period in which measurements are corrupted the estimates of the true physiology are propagated with increased uncertainty.

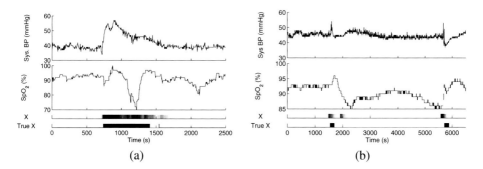

(a) (b)

Figure 9.14 Inferred switch settings for the X-factor, during periods of cardiovascular disturbance, compared to the gold standard annotations.

In Fig. 9.14(a), the X-factor is triggered by a sudden, prolonged increase in blood pressure and a desaturation, in broad agreement with the ground truth annotation. In Fig. 9.14(a) there are two spikes in BP and shifts in saturation which are picked up by the X-factor, also mainly in agreement with the annotation. A minor turning point in the two channels was also picked up at around $t = 2000$, which was not considered significant in the gold standard (a false positive).

Effects of introducing known factors to model (1) are shown in Fig. 9.15. In panel (a), there are two occurrences of spontaneous bradycardia, HR making a transient drop to around 100bpm. The X-factor alone in model (1) picks up this variation. Looking at the inferences from model (5) for the same period, it can be seen that the bradycardia factor provides a better match for the variation, and probability mass shifts correctly: the X-factor is now inactive. In panel (b), a similar effect occurs for a period in which a blood sample occurs. The X-factor picks up the change in dynamics when on its own, and when all factors are present in model (5) the probability mass shifts correctly to the blood sample factor. The blood sample factor is a superior description of the variation, incorporating the knowledge that the true physiology is not being observed, and so able to handle the discontinuity at $t = 900$ effectively.

Figure 9.16 shows examples of inferred switch settings from model (5) in which there are occurrences of both known and unknown types of variation. In Fig. 9.16(a) a bradycardia occurs in the middle of a period of elevated blood pressure and a deep drop in saturation. The bradycardia factor is active for a period which corresponds closely to the ground truth.

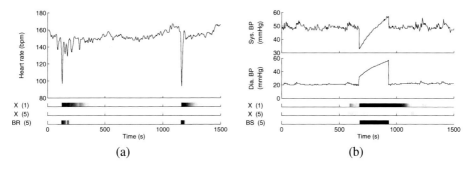

(a) (b)

Figure 9.15 Inferred switch settings for two different models, showing how known factors can explain away the X-factor. Model (1) contains the X-factor only, whereas model (5) includes the X-factor and all known factors. Panel (a) shows two instances of bradycardia, (b) shows a blood sample.

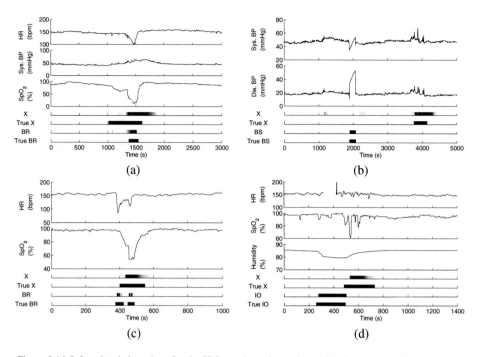

Figure 9.16 Inferred switch settings for the X-factor, in regions where other factors are active. In panel (a) a bradycardia occurs in conjunction with a rise in blood pressure and deep desaturation. The X-factor is triggered around the right region but is late compared to ground truth. In panel (b), unusual BP variation is correctly classified as being due to a blood sample, followed by variation of unknown cause. Panel (c) shows bradycardia with a desaturation picked up by the X-factor, and (d) shows the X-factor picking up disturbance after the incubator has been entered.

The X-factor picks up the presence of a change dynamics at about the right time, but its onset is delayed when compared to the ground truth interval. This again highlights a difficulty with filtered inference, since at time just over 1000 it is difficult to tell that this is the beginning of a significant change in dynamics without the benefit of hindsight. In panel (b) a blood sample is correctly picked up by the blood sample factor, while a later period of physiological disturbance on the same measurement channels is correctly picked up by the X-factor. Panel (c) shows another example of the bradycardia factor operating with the X-factor, where this time the onset of the first bradycardia is before the onset of the X-factor. The X-factor picks up a desaturation, a common pattern which is already familiar from panel (a). In panel (d), an interaction between the X-factor and the 'Incubator open' factor can be seen. From time 270 to 1000 the incubator has been opened, and all variations including the spike in HR at $t = 420$ are attributed to handling of the baby. Oncethe incubator appears to have been closed, further physiological disturbance is no longer explained as an effect of handling and is picked up by the X-factor.

Figure 9.17 shows the effect of using smoothing to infer periods of novelty. Two periods of novel dynamics are shown, with inference results for filtering (upper) and smoothing (lower). Filtered inferences of the X-factor tend to 'trail off', because without information about future observations it is difficult to tell when an unusual period of dynamics has ended. Smoothed inferences correct this, so that the inferred period of normality correspond more closely to periods of clinically significant change.

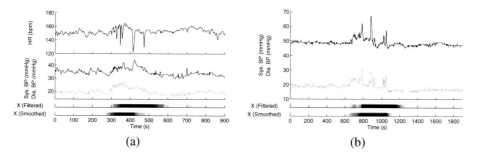

Figure 9.17 Panel (a) shows filtered inference, (b) shows smoothed inference. The grey lines show diastolic blood pressure.

9.7 Summary

This chapter has presented a general framework for inferring hidden factors from monitoring data, and has shown its successful application to the significant real-world task of monitoring the condition of a premature infant receiving intensive care. We have shown how knowledge engineering and learning can be successfully combined in this framework. Our formulation of an additional factor (the 'X-factor') allows the model to handle novel dynamics. Experimental demonstration has shown that these methods are effective when applied to genuine monitoring data.

There are a number of directions in which this work could be continued. The set of known factors presented here is limited, and more could usefully be added to the model given training data. Also, experiments with the X-factor have shown that there are a significant number of non-normal regimes in the data which have not yet been formally analysed. Future work might therefore look at learning what different regimes are claimed by the X-factor. This could be cast as an unsupervised or semi-supervised learning problem within the model. Another possible avenue would be to look at the incorporation of non-linear dynamics within the switching state space framework for physiological monitoring, using generalised linear models for state transitions or observations.

Acknowledgments   We thank Neil McIntosh for supplying annotation of the data and providing expert medical input on the experimental design. We also thank Birgit Wefers for supplying additional annotation of the data, and Jim Hunter for modifying the Time Series Workbench software for use in this research. Author JQ was funded by the premature baby charity BLISS. The work was supported in part by the IST Programme of the European Community, under the PASCAL Network of Excellence, IST-2002-506778.

Bibliography

[1] J. V. Candy, *Model-Based Signal Processing*, Wiley-IEEE Press, 2005.

[2] N. de Freitas, R. Dearden, F. Hutter, R. Morales-Menedez, J. Mutch and D. Poole. Diagnosis by a waiter and a Mars explorer. *Proceedings of the IEEE*, **92**(3), 2004.

[3] Z. Ghahramani and G. E. Hinton. Parameter estimation for linear dynamical systems. Technical report, Department of Computer Science, University of Toronto, 1996.

[4] Z. Ghahramani and G. E. Hinton. Variational learning for switching state-space models. *Neural Computation*, **12**(4):963–996, 1998.

[5] Z. Ghahramani and M. Jordan. Factorial hidden Markov models. *Machine Learning*, **29**:245–273, 1997.

[6] J. R. W. Hunter. TSNet A distributed architecture for time series analysis. In N. Peek and C. Combi, editors, *Intelligent Data Analysis in bioMedicine and Pharmacology (IDAMAP 2006)*, pages 85–92, 2006.

[7] U. Lerner and R. Parr. Inference in hybrid networks: theoretical limits and practical algorithms. In *Proceedings of the 17th Annual Conference on Uncertainty in Artificial Intelligence*, pages 310–318, 2001.

[8] K. Murphy and S. Russell. Rao-Blackwellised particle filtering for dynamic Bayesian networks. In A. Doucet, N. de Freitas, and N. Gordon, editors, *Sequential Monte Carlo in Practice*. Springer-Verlag, 2001.

[9] J. A. Quinn. Bayesian condition monitoring in neonatal intensive Care. PhD thesis, University of Edinburgh, 2007.

[10] J. A. Quinn. Neonatal condition monitoring demonstration code. www.cit.mak.ac. ug/staff/jquinn/software.html, 2007.

[11] J. A. Quinn, C. K. I. Williams and N. McIntosh. Factorial switching linear dynamical systems applied to condition monitoring in neonatal intensive care. To appear in *IEEE Transactions on Pattern Analysis and Machine Intelligence*, 2009.

[12] R. H. Shumway and D. S. Stoffer. *Time Series Analysis and Its Applications*. Springer-Verlag, 2000.

[13] M. West and J. Harrison. *Bayesian Forecasting and Dynamic Models*. Springer-Verlag, 1999.

[14] P. C. Woodland. Hidden Markov models using vector linear prediction and discriminative output functions. In *Proceedings of 1992 IEEE International Conference on Acoustics, Speech and Signal Processing*, volume 1, pages 509–512. IEEE, 1992.

Contributors

John A. Quinn, Department of Computer Science, Faculty of Computing and IT, Makerere University, Uganda

Christopher K. I. Williams, Institute for Adaptive and Neural Computation, School of Informatics, University of Edinburgh

10

Analysis of changepoint models

Idris A. Eckley, Paul Fearnhead and Rebecca Killick

10.1 Introduction

Many time series are characterised by abrupt changes in structure, such as sudden jumps in level or volatility. We consider changepoints to be those time points which divide a dataset into distinct homogeneous segments. In practice the number of changepoints will not be known. The ability to detect changepoints is important for both methodological and practical reasons including: the validation of an untested scientific hypothesis [27]; monitoring and assessment of safety critical processes [14]; and the validation of modelling assumptions [21].

The development of inference methods for changepoint problems is by no means a recent phenomenon, with early works including [39], [45] and [28]. Increasingly the ability to detect changepoints quickly and accurately is of interest to a wide range of disciplines. Recent examples of application areas include numerous bioinformatic applications [37, 15], the detection of malware within software [51], network traffic analysis [35], finance [46], climatology [32] and oceanography [34].

In this chapter we describe and compare a number of different approaches for estimating changepoints. For a more general overview of changepoint methods, we refer interested readers to [8] and [11]. The structure of this chapter is as follows. First we introduce the model we focus on. We then describe methods for detecting a single changepoint and methods for detecting multiple changepoint, which will cover both frequentist and Bayesian approaches. For multiple changepoint models the computational challenge of performing inference is to deal with the large space of possible sets of changepoint positions. We describe algorithms that, for the class of models we consider, can perform inference exactly even for large datasets. In Section 10.4 we look at practical issues of implementing these methods, and compare the different approaches through a detailed simulation study. Our study is based around the problem of detecting changes in the covariance structure of a time series, and results suggest that Bayesian methods are more suitable for detection of changepoints, particularly for multiple changepoint applications. The study also demonstrates the advantage of using exact inference methods. We end with a discussion.

10.1.1 Model and notation

Within this chapter we consider the following changepoint model. Let us assume we have time series data, $y_{1:n} = (y_1, \ldots, y_n)$. For simplicity we assume that the observation at each time t, y_t, is univariate – though extensions to multivariate data are straightforward. Our model has a number of changepoints, m, together with their positions, $\tau_{1:m} = (\tau_1, \ldots, \tau_m)$.

Each changepoint position is an integer between 1 and $n - 1$ inclusive. We define $\tau_0 = 0$ and $\tau_{m+1} = n$, and assume that the changepoints are ordered so that $\tau_i < \tau_j$ if and only if $i < j$.

The m changepoints split the data into $m + 1$ segments. The ith segment consists of data $y_{\tau_{i-1}+1:\tau_i}$ and has associated parameters θ_i. We write the likelihood function as

$$L(m, \tau_{1:m}, \theta_{1:m+1}) = p(y_{1:n}|m, \tau_{1:m}, \theta_{1:m+1}),$$

where $p(\cdot|\cdot)$ denotes a general conditional density function. Finally we assume conditional independence of data across segments, so that

$$p(y_{1:n}|m, \tau_{1:m}, \theta_{1:m+1}) = \prod_{i=1}^{m+1} p(y_{(\tau_{i-1}+1):\tau_i}|\theta_i).$$

For any segment we assume that we can calculate, either analytically or numerically, the maximum likelihood estimator for the segment parameter. We denote this estimator by $\hat{\theta}$ or $\hat{\theta}_i$ depending on the context. Thus we have

$$\max_{\theta} p(y_{(\tau_{i-1}+1):\tau_i}|\theta) = p(y_{(\tau_{i-1}+1):\tau_i}|\hat{\theta}).$$

When considering this problem within a Bayesian framework, we need to introduce priors on both the number and position of changepoints, and on the parameters for each segment. Choice for the former will be discussed below. For the latter, we assume an exchangeable prior structure. Thus we introduce a family of distributions $p(\theta|\psi)$, parameterised by hyperparameters ψ. Then, conditional on ψ, we have $p(\theta_{1:m+1}|\psi) = \prod_{i=1}^{m+1} p(\theta_i|\psi)$. Either we specify ψ, or the model is completed through an appropriate hyperprior on ψ. Note that the prior, $p(\theta|\psi)$, can be interpreted as describing the variability of the parameters across segments.

For fixed ψ, if we have a segment consisting of observations $y_{s:t}$ for $s < t$, then the segment marginal likelihood is defined as

$$Q(s, t; \psi) = \int p(y_{s:t}|\theta)p(\theta|\psi)d\theta. \qquad (10.1)$$

For the Bayesian inference algorithms that we focus on, it is important that $Q(s, t; \psi)$ can be calculated for all s, t and ψ. For many models, this can be done analytically; whilst for others it may be possible to calculate the marginal likelihoods numerically. In most cases, the assumption that we can calculate $Q(s, t; \psi)$ is equivalent to the assumption that we can calculate the posterior distribution of the parameter associated with the segment, given the start and end of the segment. Thus in this case, if we can calculate the posterior for the position and number of the changepoints, then we can easily extend this to include the segment parameters as well.

10.1.2   Example: piecewise linear regression

Assume that for each time point t we have a d-dimensional covariate $z_t = (z_t^{(1)}, \ldots, z_t^{(d)})$. Our model fits a different linear regression model within each segment. The set of parameters for the ith segment consists of the parameters of the linear regressor and the variance of the observations, $\theta_i = (\beta_i^{(1)}, \ldots, \beta_i^{(d)}, \sigma_i^2)$. We assume $p(y_{(\tau_{i-1}+1):\tau_i}|\theta_i) = \prod_{t=\tau_{i-1}+1}^{\tau_i} p(y_t|\theta_i)$, where, for $t = \tau_{i-1} + 1, \ldots, \tau_i$, $Y_t|\theta_i \sim N\left(\sum_{j=1}^{d} z_t^{(j)}\beta_i^{(j)}, \sigma_i^2\right)$, with $N(\mu, \sigma^2)$ denoting a Gaussian random variable with mean μ and variance σ^2.

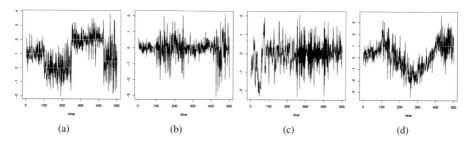

(a)   (b)   (c)   (d)

Figure 10.1 Realisations of the piecewise linear regression model. (a) Change in (constant) mean. (b) Change in variance. (c) Piecewise AR model. (d) Piecewise quadratic mean. In all cases the changepoints are at time points 100, 250 and 425. For plots (a) and (d) the underlying mean is shown.

Figure 10.1 gives example realisations from this model. Note that special cases of this model include piecewise polynomial models, where $z_t^{(j)} = t^{j-1}$; and, when $d = 0$, changepoint models for the variance of the time series. Also by letting $z_t^{(j)} = y_{t-j}$ we obtain piecewise auto-regression models. See [41, 12] for more details of these models, and their applications.

Conditional on knowing the segments, inference via maximum likelihood estimation can be performed analytically.

For a Bayesian analysis, we require a prior for θ_i. There are computational advantages in choosing the conjugate prior for this model. If we introduce hyperparameters $\psi = \{a, b, \eta, H\}$, where a and b are scalars, η is a d-dimensional vector and H is a $d \times d$ matrix, then the conjugate prior is

$$\sigma_i^2 | a, b \sim \mathcal{IG}(a, b), \quad (\beta_i^{(1)}, \dots, \beta_i^{(d)}) | \sigma^2, \eta, H \sim \mathcal{N}(\eta, \sigma^2 H).$$

Here $\mathcal{IG}$ denotes an inverse-gamma random variable. The choice of these conjugate priors means that, conditional on τ_{i-1} and τ_i, the posterior for θ_i can be calculated analytically – it is from the same inverse-gamma, multivariate normal family. Also the marginal likelihood for a segment (Eq. (10.1)) can be calculated analytically [41].

10.2 Single changepoint models

We now describe a range of methods for detecting a single changepoint. In each case we focus on the model introduced above and briefly comment on extensions to other models.

10.2.1 Likelihood-ratio-based approach

A natural approach to detecting a single changepoint is to view it as performing a hypothesis test. We define the null (H_0) and alternative (H_1) hypotheses for a change as

H_0 : No changepoint, $m = 0$.

H_1 : A single changepoint, $m = 1$.

We now introduce the general likelihood-ratio-based approach to test these hypotheses. The potential for using a likelihood-based approach to detect changepoints was first proposed by [28] who derives the asymptotic distribution of the likelihood-ratio test statistic for a change in the mean within a sequence of normally distributed observations. The

likelihood-based approach has also been extended to changes in mean related to other distributional forms including gamma [30], exponential [25] and binomial [29]; and also to
changes in variance within normally distributed observations by [24, 10].

Recalling our changepoint problem formulation above, we can construct a test statistic
which will decide whether a change has occurred. The likelihood-ratio method requires
calculating the maximum log-likelihood value under both null and alternative hypotheses.
For the null hypothesis the maximum log-likelihood value is $\log p(y_{1:n}|\hat{\theta})$.

Under the alternative hypothesis, consider a model with a changepoint at τ, with $\tau \in$
$\{1, 2, \ldots, n-1\}$. Then the maximum log-likelihood for a given τ (the profile log-likelihood
for τ) is

$$Prl(\tau) = \log p(y_{1:\tau}|\hat{\theta}_1) + \log p(y_{(\tau+1):n}|\hat{\theta}_2).$$

The maximum log-likelihood value under the alternative is $\max_\tau Prl(\tau)$. This results in the
test statistic

$$\lambda = 2\left[\max_\tau Prl(\tau) - \log p(y_{1:n}|\hat{\theta})\right].$$

The test involves choosing a threshold, c, such that we reject the null hypothesis if $\lambda > c$.
If we reject the null hypothesis, which corresponds to detecting a changepoint, then we
estimate its position as $\hat{\tau}$ the value of τ that maximises $Prl(\tau)$.

Note that changepoint problems are not regular, so the usual asymptotic results of the
likelihood-ratio statistic do not apply. Full derivations of the asymptotic distribution for the
likelihood-ratio test of univariate and multivariate normal, gamma, binomial and poisson
distributions are provided by [11]. These can be used to give an approximate threshold for
any required significance level.

The likelihood-ratio framework can naturally be extended to detecting changes in a
subset of the parameters; for example for the model in Section 10.1.2 we may be interested
in changes only in the regression parameters, or a specific subset of the regression parameters. Such problems only require a change in the calculation of the maximum likelihood
for each model, with maximisation of θ_1 and θ_2 being done over appropriate constraints for
the parameters.

10.2.2 Penalised likelihood approaches

The use of penalised likelihood approaches has been popular within the changepoint literature (see for example [23] or [54]). The popularity of this approach stems from parsimony
arguments. These methods more naturally extend to the multiple changepoint setting than
does the likelihood-ratio statistic approach. Below we outline a general approach for the
detection of changepoints using penalised likelihood.We begin by defining the general
penalised likelihood.

Definition 10.1 *Consider a model $\mathcal{M}_k$, with p_k parameters. Denote the parameters by Θ_k,
and the likelihood by $L(\Theta_k)$. The penalised likelihood is defined to be*

$$PL(\mathcal{M}_k) = -2\log \max L(\Theta_k) + p_k\phi(n),$$

*where $\phi(n)$ is the penalisation function, which is a non-decreasing function of the length of
the data, n.*

The value of M_k that minimises $PL(M_k)$ is deemed the most appropriate model. Obviously the choice of model will depend on the choice of penalty function $\phi(n)$. Various penalty functions can be considered, including Akaike's information criterion (AIC) [1], Schwarz information criterion (SIC) [42] and the Hannan–Quinn information criterion [26]. These criteria are defined as follows:

$$\text{AIC} : \phi(n) = 2$$
$$\text{SIC} : \phi(n) = \log n$$
$$\text{Hannan–Quinn} : \phi(n) = 2 \log \log n.$$

Whilst the AIC is a popular penalty term, it has been shown that it asymptotically overestimates the correct number of parameters. On the other hand, the SIC and Hannan–Quinn criteria both asymptotically estimate the correct number of parameters, and are therefore generally preferred. (See [54] for details of the SIC case.)

For the changepoint problem described in Section 10.1.1, M_k corresponds to the model with k changepoints. The associated parameter vector is $\Theta_k = (\tau_{1:k}, \theta_{1:k+1})$, which has dimension $p_k = k + (k + 1)\dim(\theta)$. For detecting a single changepoint the calculation of the two penalised likelihoods corresponding to either one or no changepoint, involves a similar likelihood maximisation step to that described in Section 10.2.1.

For estimating a single changepoint, there is a close correspondence between the penalised likelihood and the likelihood-ratio test approaches. Both involve comparing the maximum log-likelihood of the two models corresponding to one and no changepoint. A changepoint is detected if the increase in log-likelihood under the one changepoint model is greater than some threshold. The differences lie only in how this threshold is calculated.

10.2.3   Bayesian methods

To perform a Bayesian analysis we need to specify a prior probability for there being a changepoint, $\Pr(M = 1)$, and conditional on there being a changepoint, a distribution for its position $p(\tau)$. Note that $\Pr(M = 0) = 1 - \Pr(M = 1)$.

Firstly consider the case where the hyperparameters ψ are known. In this case it is straightforward to write down the posterior distribution in terms of marginal likelihoods, $Q(s, t)$, as defined in Eq. (10.1). The posterior is

$$\Pr(M = 0|y_{1:n}) \propto \Pr(M = 0)Q(1, n; \psi)$$
$$\Pr(M = 1, \tau|y_{1:n}) \propto \Pr(M = 1)p(\tau)Q(1, \tau; \psi)Q(\tau + 1, n; \psi), \text{ for } \tau = 1, \dots, n - 1.$$

In the case on which we focus, where the marginal likelihoods can be calculated analytically, this posterior is simple to calculate. It requires the above expressions to be evaluated and normalised to give the posterior probabilities. This is an $O(n)$ calculation. As mentioned above, in cases where we can calculate the marginal likelihood, we can normally calculate analytically the conditional posterior for segment parameters given the start and end of the segment. Thus we can extend the above calculation to give the joint posterior of whether there is a changepoint, its position if there is one, and the segment parameters.

If we focus on purely detecting whether there is a changepoint, then we get

$$\frac{\Pr(M = 1|y_{1:n})}{\Pr(M = 0|y_{1:n})} = \frac{\Pr(M = 1)}{\Pr(M = 0)} \left(\frac{\sum_{\tau=1}^{n-1} p(\tau)Q(1, \tau; \psi)Q(\tau + 1, n; \psi)}{Q(1, n; \psi)} \right).$$

The last term on the right-hand side is called the Bayes factor. Thus the posterior ratio of probabilities of one changepoint to no changepoint is the prior ratio multiplied by the Bayes factor. As such the Bayes factor quantifies the evidence in the data for the model with one changepoint, as opposed to the model with no changepoint.

Note that the posterior distribution depends on ψ. In particular the choice of ψ can have considerable effect on the posterior probability for a changepoint. The reason for this is linked to Bartlett's paradox [5], which shows that when comparing nested models, the use of improper priors for the parameters in the more complex model will lead to a posterior probability of one assigned to the simpler model. Even when we do not use improper priors, choices of ψ that correspond to vague priors for the segment parameters will tend to prefer the simpler model, that is inferring no changepoint. We will return to this issue in the simulation study in Section 10.4.

There are two approaches to deal with choosing ψ in the absence of prior information. The first is to introduce a prior on ψ and define the marginal likelihood for ψ as

$$\text{ML}(\psi) = \Pr(M = 0)Q(1, n; \psi) + \sum_{\tau=1}^{n-1} \Pr(M = 1)p(\tau)Q(1, \tau; \psi)Q(\tau + 1, n; \psi),$$

and let $p(\psi)$ denote the prior. Then the marginal posterior for ψ is proportional to $p(\psi)\text{ML}(\psi)$, which could be explored using Markov chain Monte Carlo (MCMC). Note that it is possible to choose an improper prior for ψ, as this is a parameter common to both the no changepoint and one changepoint models.

Computationally simpler is to adopt an empirical Bayes approach – and use the data to get a point estimate for ψ. For example, optimisation algorithms can be used to find the value of ψ that maximises $\text{ML}(\psi)$, and then inference can be made conditional on this value for ψ. This approach has the disadvantage of ignoring the effect of uncertainty in the choice of ψ.

We return to this issue when discussing Bayesian methods for multiple changepoint problems. Also, in Section 10.4 we look empirically at and compare the different approaches for dealing with no knowledge about ψ.

10.3 Multiple changepoint models

Many of the ideas for analysing single changepoint models can be adapted, at least in theory, to the analysis of multiple changepoint models. However, the analysis of multiple changepoint models is computationally much more challenging, as the number of possible positions of m changepoints increases quickly with m. For example, with 1000 data points there are just 999 possible positions of a single changepoint, but 2×10^{23} sets of possibilities for 10 changepoints. Much of the focus of the following sections is on the resulting computational challenge of detecting multiple changepoints.

We first focus on two general search methods, which can be used to extend the likelihood-ratio statistic approach to detecting multiple changepoints, and can be used to efficiently perform the maximisation required in applying penalised likelihood methods. We then introduce a new criterion for detecting changepoints, based on minimum description length, and show how the latter of these search methods can be used to find the optimal set of changepoints in this case. Finally we describe how to efficiently perform a Bayesian analysis.

10.3.1 Binary segmentation

The binary segmentation algorithm is perhaps the most established search algorithm used within the changepoint literature. Early applications of the binary segmentation search

---

Algorithm 10.1 The generic binary segmentation algorithm to find all possible changepoints.

Input:	A set of data of the form, $(y_1, y_2, \ldots, y_n)$.
	A test statistic $\Lambda(\cdot)$ dependent on the data.
	An estimator of changepoint position $\hat{\tau}(\cdot)$.
	A rejection threshold C.
Initialise:	Let $C = \emptyset$, and $S = \{[1, n]\}$.

Iterate: While $S \neq \emptyset$

  1. Choose an element of S; denote this element as $[s, t]$.

  2. If $\Lambda(y_{s:t}) < C$, remove $[s, t]$ from S.

  3. If $\Lambda(y_{s:t}) \geq C$ then:

     (a) remove $[s, t]$ from S;

     (b) calculate $r = \hat{\tau}(y_{s:t}) + s - 1$, and add r to C;

     (c) if $r \neq s$ add $[s, r]$ to S;

     (d) if $r \neq t - 1$ add $[r + 1, t]$ to S.

Output: The set of changepoints recorded, C.

---

algorithm include [43] and [44]. For details on the consistency of the binary segmentation approach for estimating the true changepoint locations, $\tau_{1:m}$, under various conditions, the reader is referred to the work of [49] and [48].

Binary segmentation can be used to extend any single changepoint method to multiple changepoints. We begin by initially applying this detection method to the whole data. If no changepoint is detected we stop, otherwise we split the data into two segments (before and after the changepoint), and apply the detection method to each segment. If a changepoint is detected in either or both segments, we split these into further segments, and apply the detection method to each new segment. This procedure is repeated until no further changepoints are detected.

Generic pseudo-code for an implementation of this procedure is given in Algorithm 10.1. This considers a general test statistic $\Lambda(\cdot)$, an estimator of changepoint position $\hat{\tau}(\cdot)$, and a rejection threshold C. The idea is that the test statistic is a function of data, such as the likelihood-ratio statistic, and we detect a changepoint in data $y_{s:t}$ if $\Lambda(y_{s:t}) > C$. If we detect a changepoint, our estimate of its position, such as the maximum likelihood estimate, is $\hat{\tau}(y_{s:t})$. Within the code, C denotes the set of detected changepoints, and S denotes a set of segments of the data that need to be tested for a changepoint. One iteration chooses a segment from S, and performs the test for a changepoint. For a negative result the segment is removed from S. Otherwise a changepoint is detected and added to C, and the segment is replaced in S by two segments defined by splitting the original segment at the changepoint. Note that in step 3(b), r is just the position of the changepoint in the original dataset, calculated from $\hat{\tau}(y_{s:t})$, the position of the changepoint in the segment $[s, t]$. In steps 3(c) and 3(d) we only add new segments to S if they contain at least two observations: otherwise the new segments can not contain further changepoints.

Binary segmentation is a fast algorithm that can be implemented with computational cost $O(n)$ where n is the length of data. However, it can be difficult to choose C appropriately – and different choices of C can lead to substantial differences in the estimate of the number of changepoints. An alternative approach to detecting multiple changepoints by recursively applying a single changepoint method is given in [31].

10.3.2   Segment neighbourhood search

References [7] and [6] consider an alternative search algorithm for changepoint detection, namely the segment neighbourhood approach (also referred to as global segmentation). The basic principle of this approach is to define some measure of data fit, $R(\cdot)$, for a segment. For inference via penalised likelihood we would set $R(y_{s:t})$ to be minus the maximum log-likelihood value for data $y_{s:t}$ given it comes from a single segment. That is

$$R(y_{s:t}) = -\log p(y_{s:t}|\hat{\theta}). \tag{10.2}$$

We then set a maximum number of segments, M, corresponding to at most $M-1$ changepoints.

The segment neighbourhood search then uses a dynamic programming algorithm to find the best partition of the data into $m+1$ segments for $m = 0, \ldots, M-1$. The best partition is found by minimising the cost function $\sum_{i=0}^{m} R(y_{\tau_i:\tau_{i+1}})$ for a partition with changepoints at positions $\tau_1, \tau_2, \ldots, \tau_m$. Thus for $R(\cdot)$ defined in Eq. (10.2), this would give the partition of the data with m changepoints that maximises the log-likelihood. The algorithm will output the best partition for $m = 0, \ldots, M-1$, and the corresponding minimum value of the cost function, which we denote $c_{1,n}^m$.

For the choice of $R(\cdot)$ given by Eq. (10.2), $2c_{1,n}^m$ will be minus twice the log-likelihood. So choosing m based on penalised likelihood is achieved by choosing m to minimise $2c_{1,n}^m + p_m\phi(n)$, where p_m is the number of parameters in the model with m changepoints, and $\phi(n)$ is the penalty function. The best partition found by the algorithm for that value of m gives the positions of the detected changepoints.

Generic pseudo-code for this approach can be seen in Algorithm 10.2, and is based on a dynamic programming approach described by [2]. The drawback of this approach is its computational cost. The segment neighbourhood search is an $O(n^2)$ computation, compared with $O(n)$ for the binary segmentation algorithm. However this cost does result in improved predictive performance in simulation studies [6].

Algorithm 10.2 The generic segment neighbourhood algorithm to find up to $R-1$ changepoints.

Input: A set of data of the form, $(y_1, y_2, \ldots, y_n)$.
A measure of fit $R(\cdot)$ dependent on the data which needs to be minimised.
An integer, $M-1$ specifying the maximum number of change points to find.

Initialise: Let n = length of data.
Calculate $q_{i,j}^1 = R(y_{i:j})$ for all $i, j \in [1, n]$ such that $i < j$.

Iterate: For $m = 2, \ldots, M$

1. Iterate step 2 for all $j \in \{1, 2, \ldots, n\}$.

2. Calculate $q_{1,j}^m = \min_{v\in[1,j)} (q_{1,v}^{m-1} + q_{v+1,j}^1)$.

3. Set $\tau_{m,1}$ to be the v that minimises $(q_{1,v}^{m-1} + q_{v+1,n}^1)$.

4. Iterate step 5 for all $i \in \{2, 3, \ldots, M\}$.

5. Let $\tau_{m,i}$ be the v that minimises $(q_{1,v}^{m-i-1} + q_{v+1,cp_{m,i-1}}^1)$.

Output: For $m = 1, \ldots, M$: the total measure of fit, $q_{1,n}^m$, for $m-1$ changepoints and the location of the changepoints for that fit, $\tau_{m,1:m}$.

10.3.3 Minimum description length

The authors in [12] propose the use of the minimum description length (MDL) principle to estimate changepoints. The basic idea is that the best-fitting model is the one which enables maximum compression of the data. For a given set of changepoints we can estimate what is called the code-length of the data. Loosely, this code-length is the amount of memory space needed to store that data. We thus estimate the number and position of the changepoints as the set of changepoints which have the minimum code-length. See [12] and references therein for further background to MDL.

Our aim here is to show how finding the best set of changepoints under MDL can be achieved using the segment neighbourhood algorithm. This guarantees finding the optimal set of changepoints according to the MDL criterion. By comparison, [12] use a complicated genetic algorithm to fit the model.

For concreteness we will focus on the model of Section 10.1.2. In this case, up to proportionality, the code-length for a set of m changepoints, $\tau_1, \ldots, \tau_m$, is defined as

$$C\mathcal{L}(m; \tau_{1:n}) = -\sum_{i=1}^{m+1} \log p(y_{(\tau_{i-1}+1):\tau_i}|\hat{\theta}_i) + \log(m+1) + (m+1)\log(n) + \sum_{i=1}^{m+1} \frac{d+1}{2} \log n_i,$$

where $n_i = \tau_i - \tau_{i-1}$ is the length of segment i, and $d+1$ is the dimension of the parameter vector associated with each segment. (See [12] for the derivation.)

Using $R(y_{s:t}) = -\log p(y_{s:t}|\hat{\theta}) + \frac{d+1}{2}\log(t-s+1)$, we can write the code-length as

$$C\mathcal{L}(m; \tau_{1:n}) = \sum_{i=1}^{m+1} R(y_{(\tau_{i-1}+1):\tau_i}) + \log(m+1) + (m+1)\log(n).$$

Thus we can use the segment neighbourhood algorithm to calculate

$$c_{1,n}^m = \min_{\tau_{1:m}} \sum_{i=1}^{m+1} R(y_{(\tau_{i-1}+1):\tau_i}),$$

for $m = 0, \ldots, M-1$. We then estimate the number of changepoints as the value m which minimises $c_{1,n}^m + \log(m+1) + (m+1)\log(n)$. The segment neighbourhood algorithm also outputs the optimal set of changepoints.

10.3.4 Bayesian methods

For a Bayesian analysis we need to specify a prior for the number and position of changepoints. There are two approaches. The first consists in specifying a prior on the number of changepoints, and then a prior for their position given the number of changepoints [22]. The second consists in specifying the prior for the number and position of changepoints indirectly through a distribution for the length of each segment. The latter has computational advantages [17] and is more natural in many applications. For example, it means that the prior does not need to be adapted based on the period of time over which the time series is observed. It is also easier to use inferences from similar datasets, which may be of different length, to construct appropriate priors. We thus focus solely on this form of prior.

Formally we introduce a probability mass function, denoted $g(\cdot; \psi)$, to be the mass function for the length of a segment. We allow there to be unknown parameters of this mass function, and these will be part of the hyperparameters of the model: hence the dependence on ψ. Associated with the mass function is a survivor function $S(\cdot; \psi)$, which satisfies

$S(t; \psi) = \sum_{i=t}^{\infty} g(i; \psi)$. With this construction, the prior probability for m changepoints at positions $\tau_1, \ldots, \tau_m$ is

$$p(m, \tau_{1:m}|\psi) = \left(\prod_{i=1}^{m} g(\tau_i - \tau_{i-1}; \psi) \right) S(\tau_{m+1} - \tau_m; \psi),$$

where as before we set $\tau_0 = 0$ and $\tau_{m+1} = n$. This prior corresponds to a product-partition model [3, 4].

A common choice for the distribution of the segment lengths is the geometric distribution with parameter p. In this case $g(t; \psi) = p(1 - p)^{t-1}$, $S(t; \psi) = (1 - p)^{t-1}$ and $p(m, \tau_{1:m}|\psi) = p^m(1-p)^{n-m-1}$. Note that this corresponds to a binomial prior on the number of changepoints, and a conditional uniform prior on their position.

We now derive the posterior conditional on a fixed value of ψ. Under the assumption that we can calculate the segment marginal likelihoods (10.1), we can integrate out the parameters associated with each segment to obtain the following marginal posterior for the number and position of changepoints

$$p(m, \tau_{1:m}|\psi, y_{1:n}) \propto S(\tau_{m+1} - \tau_m; \psi)Q(\tau_m + 1, \tau_{m+1}; \psi) \prod_{i=1}^{m} g(\tau_i - \tau_{i-1}; \psi)Q(\tau_{i-1} + 1, \tau_i; \psi).$$

$$(10.3)$$

The normalising constant is just the marginal likelihood for ψ. As mentioned above, for models where we can calculate the segment marginal likelihoods we can usually simulate from the posterior distribution of the segment parameters given the changepoint positions. Thus if we can generate samples from this posterior on the number and position of the changepoints, it is straightforward to sample from the joint posterior of the changepoints and the segment parameters. While MCMC [36] and reversible jump MCMC methods [22] can be used to generate (approximate) samples from the posterior (10.3), these methods can be computationally intensive, and lead to difficulties of diagnosing convergence of the MCMC algorithm. For example the analysis of the coal-mining disaster data in [22] is incorrect due to the MCMC algorithm not being run for long enough [17].

Instead, we describe a computationally efficient algorithm that can generate iid samples from this posterior. The algorithm has two stages. The first is a forward pass through the data; the second involves simulating the changepoints backwards in time. The algorithm is thus related to the forward-backward algorithm for hidden Markov models [18] (see Chapter 1). However the basic idea underlying this approach dates back to work by [53]; see also the methods of [3] and [38]. The version we give is suitable for online analysis of data.

For this algorithm we introduce a variable C_t to be the position of the most recent changepoint prior to time t. Thus $C_t \in \{0, 1, \ldots, t-1\}$, with $C_t = 0$ denoting no changepoint prior to t. Note that either $C_t = t - 1$, or $C_t = C_{t-1}$, depending on whether or not there is a changepoint at time $t - 1$. The forward algorithm calculates $\Pr(C_t = i|y_{1:t}, \psi)$ for $i = 0, \ldots, t - 1$. It is based on the following recursion. For $t = 2, \ldots, n$ we have

$$\Pr(C_t = i|y_{1:t}, \psi) \propto \Pr(C_{t-1} = i|y_{1:t-1}, \psi) \left(\frac{S(t - i; \psi)}{S(t - i - 1; \psi)} \right) \left(\frac{Q(i + 1, t; \psi)}{Q(i + 1, t - 1; \psi)} \right), \quad (10.4)$$

for $i = 0, \ldots, t - 2$; and

$$\Pr(C_t = t - 1|y_{1:t}, \psi) \propto Q(t, t; \psi) \sum_{j=0}^{t-2} \Pr(C_{t-1} = j|y_{1:t-1}, \psi) \left(\frac{g(t - j - 1; \psi)}{S(t - j - 1; \psi)} \right). \quad (10.5)$$

Recursion (10.4) corresponds to no changepoint at time $t-1$, $C_t = C_{t-1}$. The final two terms correspond to the prior probability of this and the likelihood of the new observation given $C_t = i$ respectively. Recursion (10.5) corresponds to a changepoint at time $t-1$. In this case $Q(t, t; \psi)$ is the likelihood of the observation and the sum is the probability of a changepoint at $t-1$ prior to observing y_t. These recursions are initiated with $\Pr(C_1 = 0|y_1) = 1$. For more details of the derivation see [19]. Details of how the output from these recursions can be used to calculate the marginal likelihood for ψ are given in [18].

The backward step generates samples from the posterior of the position and number of changepoints. It requires that the probabilities $\Pr(C_t = i|y_{1:t})$ have been stored for all $t = 1, \ldots, n$ and $i = 0, \ldots, t-1$. To generate one sample of changepoints we first simulate the last changepoint from the distribution of C_n given $y_{1:n}$. For a changepoint position $t > 0$ we can simulate the next changepoint back in time, C_t, from the conditional distribution

$$Pr(C_t = i|y_{1:n}, C_{t+1} = t, \psi) \propto Pr(C_t = i|y_{1:t}, \psi)\left(\frac{g(t-i; \psi)}{S(t-i; \psi)}\right), \text{ for } i = 1, \ldots, t-1. \quad (10.6)$$

(Note the event $C_{t+1} = t$ just corresponds to there being a changepoint at t.) The calculation of this probability mass function uses the fact that conditional on a changepoint at t, the data after this changepoint is independent of the changepoints before t. We recursively simulate changepoints backwards in time from Eq. (10.6) until we first simulate $C_t = 0$.

Full details of the forward recursion and backward simulation procedure are given in Algorithm 10.3. In this algorithm $\gamma_i^{(t)}$ denotes $\Pr(C_t = i|y_{1:t})$.

The algorithm has a computational and storage cost that is quadratic in n, the number of data points. This is because the support of C_t increases linearly with t. However, for large t, the majority of the probabilities $\Pr(C_t = i|y_{1:t})$ are negligible. Hence computational and storage savings can be made by pruning such probabilities. See [19] for a principled way of implementing such pruning, which results in an algorithm with computational and storage costs that are $O(n)$. Pruning does introduce approximation error, but empirical results [19] suggest that these approximations are negligible. The resulting algorithms can analyse large datasets efficiently, see [19] and [20] for applications to genomic data. Even in these applications, with hundreds of changepoints and n in the order of tens of thousands, generating thousands of samples from the posterior takes a matter of seconds.

Thus we have a simple, efficient and accurate method for Bayesian inference when the hyperparameters, ψ, are known. If ψ is not known we can either introduce a prior on ψ or estimate ψ from the data. The former is the fully Bayesian approach, but comes at a computational cost. Inference will require the use of MCMC or related techniques. The above algorithm can be used within MCMC to help mixing. However, this can be computationally expensive as the forward recursions need to be carried out for each proposed new value for ψ. (See [17] for suggestions on efficiently implementing an MCMC approach.) The alternative is to estimate ψ from the data – for example through maximising the marginal likelihood. Performing the maximisation is possible via a Monte Carlo expectation maximisation (EM) algorithm [50]. Results in [16] suggest that such an approach loses little in terms of statistical efficiency, but is computationally more efficient than the fully Bayesian solution of introducing a prior on ψ.

10.4 Comparison of methods

We now compare different changepoint methods for the problem of detecting a change in variance. In general detecting changes in variance is more challenging than detecting

---

Algorithm 10.3 Algorithm for simulating from the posterior distribution of changepoint positions.

Input: A set of data of the form, $(y_1, y_2, \ldots, y_n)$.
A value for the hyperparameters ψ.
Survivor functions for segment lengths $S(\cdot; \psi)$.
A weight function $W(\cdot; \psi)$, such that $W(y_{s:t}; \psi) = Q(y_{s:t}; \psi)/Q(y_{s:t-1}; \psi)$ for $t > s$,
and $W(y_s; \psi) = Q(y_s; \psi)$; where $Q(\cdot; \psi)$ is defined in (10.1).
The number of samples from the posterior, N.

Initialise: Let $t = 2$. Let $\gamma_0^{(1)} = 1$.

Iterate: For $t = 2, \ldots, n$

  1. For $i = 0, \ldots, t-2$; set

$$\gamma_i^{(t)} = \gamma_i^{(t-1)} \left(\frac{S(t-i; \psi)}{S(t-i-1; \psi)} \right) W(y_{i+1:t}; \psi).$$

  2. Set

$$\gamma_{t-1}^{(t)} = W(y_t; \psi) \sum_{j=0}^{t-2} \gamma_j^{(t-1)} \left(\frac{S(t-j-1; \psi) - S(t-j; \psi)}{S(t-j-1; \psi)} \right).$$

  3. Normalise $\gamma^{(t)}$s. Set $A = \sum_{i=0}^{t-1} \gamma_i^{(t)}$, and for $i = 0, \ldots, t-1$ set $\gamma_i^{(t)} = \gamma_i^{(t)}/A$.

Iterate: For $j = 1, \ldots, N$

  1. Simulate from the distribution with mass $\gamma_i^{(n)}$ associated with realisation i for $i = 0, \ldots, n-1$; denote the realisation by t.

  2. If $t > 0$, set $C_j = \{t\}$; otherwise $C_j = \emptyset$.

  3. While $t > 0$ repeat steps 4 and 5.

  4. Simulate from the distribution with mass proportional to

$$\gamma_i^{(t)} \left(\frac{S(t-i; \psi) - S(t-i+1; \psi)}{S(t-i; \psi)} \right),$$

  associated with realisation i for $i = 0, \ldots, t-1$; denote the realisation by t.

  5. If $t > 0$, update $C_j = \{t, C_j\}$.

Output: The N sets of changepoints, $C_1, \ldots, C_N$.

---

changes in mean, and is important in applications such as finance and environmental applications [34]. As observed in [10] the detection of changes in variance has received little attention compared to the changes in mean problem. We will look in turn at the problem of detecting a single changepoint and multiple changepoints.

10.4.1 Single changepoint model

We first present a simulation study which aims to compare the frequentist and Bayesian methods for detecting a single changepoint, and to look at how specifications of the hyperparameter ψ can affect Bayesian inference. We base our study on a specific case of the model described in Section 10.1.2. Each data point has a normal distribution with mean 0, but we allow for the possibility that the variance changes at a changepoint. Details of the analytic calculations of maximum likelihood estimates, posterior distributions and marginal likelihoods for the segments are given in the Appendix.

In particular we simulated time series consisting of 200 observations. The first 100 data points were iid from a standard normal distribution. The second 100 data points were iid from a normal distribution with mean 0 and variance σ^2. We considered six scenarios, each with different values of σ: $\sigma^2 = 1, 1.25, 1.5, 2, 3$ and 4. The first scenario corresponds to

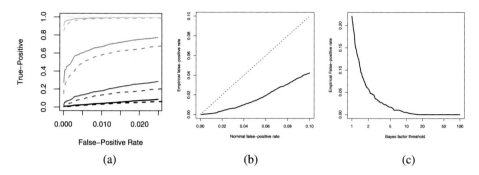

Figure 10.2 (a) ROC curves for the Bayesian (full-lines) and frequentist (dashed-lines) approaches. Each pair of lines corresponds to a different value of σ, from bottom to top: 1.25, 1.5, 2, 3 and 4. (b) Nominal false-positive rate versus empirical false-positive rate for the likelihood-ratio method. (c) Bayes factor threshold versus empirical false-positive rate for Bayesian method.

no changepoint, as the distribution of the data is identical for all 200 data points and is used to estimate false-positive rates for different methods. The remaining scenarios correspond to increasingly large changes. We simulated 10 000 independent datasets for each scenario.

Comparison of methods

We first looked at the performance of various methods to detect a changepoint within a series. For detecting a changepoint, each method is based upon comparing a statistic, such as the Bayes factor or the likelihood-ratio statistic, with a threshold value. The threshold value affects both the false-positive rate and also the proportion of true changepoints (true-positives) detected for a given value of σ^2. By varying this threshold we can plot how the latter varies with the former, and we give the results in a so-called receiver operating characteristic (ROC) curve. This enables us to calibrate the comparison of methods, so we compare the true-positive rate of different methods for a common false-positive rate.

For the Bayesian implementation, the hyperparameters ψ are the parameters of the inverse-gamma distribution for the segment variance. Initially we set the shape parameter to be 2, and the scale parameter so that the mean of the distribution was the sample variance of the data. The ROC curve results were robust to these choices; we investigate below the effect of the choice of ψ on the performance of the Bayesian approach.

Results are shown in Fig. 10.2(a). Both the likelihood-ratio and penalised likelihood methods (where we vary the penalty) give identical ROC curves, see Section 10.2.2, so we plot a single curve for both these. The results show similar performance for the Bayesian and frequentist approaches, with the Bayesian method having slightly greater power, particularly for intermediate values of σ. The intuition behind this is that for detecting change in variance there is normally substantial uncertainty about the position of the changepoint. The Bayes factor averages over this uncertainty, thus allowing for the accumulation of evidence for a changepoint; whereas frequentist methods depend only on the fit for the most likely changepoint position – and as such ignore any information from other possible changepoint locations.

Implementation of methods

The comparison above looks at the overall performance of methods via an ROC curve, examining false and true positive rates for a range of threshold values for each method. However, when implementing a method we need guidelines for choosing this threshold.

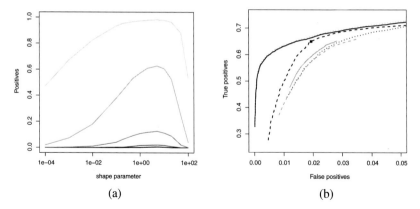

Figure 10.3 (a) Proportion of datasets with Bayes factor for no changepoint > 10, as a function of a, the shape parameter of the inverse gamma distribution. Each line corresponds to a different value of σ, bottom to top: 1.0, 1.25, 1.5, 2, 3 and 4. (b) ROC curve for multiple changepoint methods. Bayesian method (black full line); binary segmentation based on likelihood-ratio test (black dotted line); binary segmentation using Bayes factor (grey dashed line); the [31] approach for segmentation based on the likelihood-ratio test (grey full line); and penalised likelihood (black dashed line). The square dot corresponds to MDL.

For the likelihood-ratio approach, there is clear guidance on choosing the threshold based on asymptotic results which give nominal false-positive rates for different threshold values [11]. In Fig. 10.2(b) we plot empirical false-positive rates for a range of nominal false-positive rates. For the size of data we analysed, the nominal false-positive rates over-estimate the true false-positive rates, typically by a factor of around 2.

For comparison, we calculated the false-positive rates for the three penalised likelihood methods introduced in Section 10.2.2. These are AIC, SIC and Hannan–Quinn. For our data $n = 200$, so $\phi(n) = 2$, 5.3 and 3.3 respectively. The false-positive rates were 70%, 4.4% and 26% in turn. This suggests that the penalty used in AIC is too small, and results in over-detection of changepoints.

For the Bayesian approach, the test is affected by (i) the prior probability of a change-point; (ii) a threshold on the posterior probability for detecting a changepoint; and (iii) the choice of ψ. Strictly (ii) should be specified by considering the relative cost of falsely detecting a changepoint to missing one. The larger this is, the higher the threshold. How-ever, in many cases it can be difficult to specify this, and also often there is little prior information to guide (i). In these cases, it is common to use general rules of thumb for the Bayes factor [33].

In practice, the most important choice is (iii), the prior for ψ. Furthermore it can be hard to predict the effect that this choice has on the properties of the test. In particular we want to guard against choosing values of ψ that correspond to weakly informative priors which will lead to preference for the model for no changepoint.

To investigate the effect of the choice of ψ we repeated the above analysis but for a range of values for ψ, the parameters of the inverse gamma distribution for the variance. In each case we chose parameters so that the mean of the inverse gamma distribution was equal to the empirical mean and adjusted only the shape parameter, a. The choice $a \approx 0$ corresponds to a weakly informative prior. Results are given in Fig. 10.3(a). We observe that small and large values of a lead to the detection of a changepoint in fewer datasets. For the Bayesian method to accurately detect changepoints we need a value of a that leads to a prior distribution that is roughly consistent with the variation in σ across the two segments.

As discussed in Section 10.2.3, the two approaches to choosing ψ based on the data are to introduce a hyperprior on ψ or an empirical Bayes approach of estimating ψ by maximising the marginal likelihood. We tried both approaches. They provided almost identical results, so here we give the results for the empirical Bayes approach. For a threshold value of 10 for the Bayes factor for the model with no changepoints against the model with one, the false-positive rate was 0.005, with, for increasing values of σ, true-positive rates of 0.02, 0.13, 0.63, 0.98 and 1.0.

How the empirical false-positive rate varies with the threshold used for the Bayes factor is shown in Fig. 10.2(c). Note that it is difficult to predict the form of the relationship beforehand. For this example, a threshold of around 2, corresponding to twice as much evidence for one changepoint as opposed to no changepoints, corresponds to a false-positive rate of 5 per cent. Note also that a threshold of 1, which corresponds to equal evidence in the data for either one changepoint or no changepoints, has a false-positive rate much lower than 0.5, which is what we may have predicted.

10.4.2 Multiple changepoint model

We now consider the analysis of multiple changepoint models. We aim to look at the relative performance of the different methods and to quantify what affects the power to detect changepoints.

As in the single changepoint case, we simulated data under a model where the variance changes across segments. We simulated time series consisting of 2000 data points. Each dataset contained 10 changepoints, which were uniformly distributed subject to the constraint that each segment contained at least 40 observations. Within each segment, the observations were iid draws from a normal distribution with mean 0 and common variance. The distribution of the segment variances were log-normal, and the parameters of the log-normal distribution chosen so that 95 per cent of variances lay within the interval [1/10, 10]. We simulated 1000 independent datasets.

The distribution of segment variances was specifically chosen to be different from the inverse-gamma distribution used by the Bayesian method. Also, when implementing the Bayesian approach we assumed a geometric distribution of segment lengths and thus did not use the information that all segments contained at least 40 observations. This avoids any bias towards the Bayesian approach through simulating data from exactly the same class of models that the data is analysed under.

When implementing the Bayesian method we used an empirical Bayes approach, estimating hyperparameters based on maximising the marginal likelihood. The marginal likelihood was maximised using a Monte Carlo EM algorithm.

Comparison of methods

Firstly we compared different methods based on ROC curves. Making a comparison is non-trivial as the output of Bayesian and frequentist approaches differ. The former gives posterior probabilities for changepoints at each location, while the latter returns a list of inferred changepoint positions. The following approach was used, which gives comparison between false and true positive rates for both methods.

For the Bayesian approach we counted a changepoint as detected if the posterior probability of a changepoint within a distance of 20 time points either side of the true position was greater than a pre-specified threshold. For false-positives we considered non-overlapping windows of similar size that did not contain a true changepoint. A false-positive related to a window for which the posterior probability of a changepoint was above the threshold. For the frequentist methods we used a similar approach. Changepoints were considered detected if we inferred a changepoint with a distance of 20 time points of the true position. We then considered the same non-overlapping windows which did not contain a changepoint, counting a false-positive for every window in which we inferred a changepoint. The false-positive rate thus estimates the probability that we detect a changepoint within a randomly chosen window that contains no changepoint.

Results are given in Fig. 10.3(b). We compared the Bayesian approach with a number of frequentist methods. The latter included penalised likelihood and MDL using the segment neighbourhood algorithm, and binary segmentation using the likelihood-ratio test. We also implemented binary segmentation with a test based on Bayes factors [52], and the alternative segmentation strategy of [31], implemented with the likelihood-ratio test.

There are a number of features of the results that stand out. Firstly, the uniformly most powerful approach is the full-Bayesian method. This approach performs particularly well for small false-positive rates. Secondly, jointly estimating the changepoints, as in the full-Bayesian method or the penalised likelihood approach, performs better than recursively applying single changepoint detection methods using binary segmentation or the approach of [31]. This supports the results of [6].

Thirdly, of the two approaches for recursively applying single changepoint methods, that of [31] performed better than binary segmentation. This is perhaps a little surprising, as this method is used much less in the literature. Finally we notice that although the Bayesian method performed better in the single changepoint simulation study, there is very little difference between the binary segmentation approach that used likelihood ratio and the one that used Bayes factors.

While most approaches can be implemented to give ROC curves, MDL results in a single pair of false-positive and false-negative rates. This pair lies on the penalised likelihood line, and corresponds very closely to the results for penalised likelihood using SIC. Intuitively, this similarity is not surprising as the minimisation criteria for MDL and SIC are very similar (see Sections 10.2.2 and 10.3.3). We also note that using the AIC criteria performed very poorly, detecting over 50 changepoints for each dataset. This suggests that the AIC penalty is not large enough.

Factors affecting power

Finally we investigated which factors affect the ability to detect a changepoint. We considered two possible factors, firstly the change in variance and secondly the size of segments either side of the changepoint. Not surprisingly, the former has an important effect on the ability to detect changepoints. In Fig. 10.4(a) we plot, for each changepoint, the posterior probability of a changepoint against the factor by which the variance changes across the changepoint. The former was again calculated by looking for a changepoint within a window which contains all locations at a distance of 20 or less from the changepoint position. A change in variance by a factor of 2 has an average posterior probability of about 0.5, while a change by a factor of 5 or more results in posterior probabilities that are very close to 1.

We then compared power at detecting a changepoint against change in variance. To make the comparison fair, for the Bayesian approach we detected a changepoint if the posterior probability within a window was greater than a threshold. Results for the Bayesian method, MDL and binary segmentation using the likelihood-ratio test are compared in Fig. 10.4(b). The threshold for the Bayesian approach and for the likelihood-ratio test

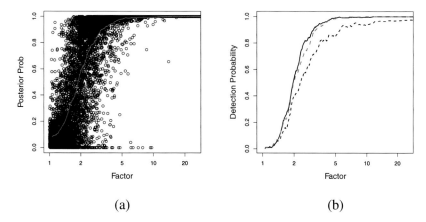

(a)   (b)

Figure 10.4 (a) Plot of posterior probability of a changepoint against the factor by which the variance changes across the changepoint for each changepoint. A smoothed estimate is given by the line. (b) Plot of power of detecting a changepoint against the factor by which variance changes: Bayesian approach (black full line); MDL (grey dashed line); and binary segmentation with likelihood-ratio test (black dashed line).

were chosen so that both methods had similar false-positive rates to MDL. The Bayesian approach and MDL have similar power curves, but the Bayesian method does better at detecting changepoints when the variance changes by a factor of between 2 and 5. The binary segmentation approach does substantially worse than the other two methods for changepoints across which the variance changes by a factor of 3 or more.

The size of segment had little effect on the probability of detection of a changepoint. Correlation of segment sizes against posterior probability of a changepoint was around 5 per cent. Similarly small correlation between segment size and detection of changepoints was found for the non-Bayesian methods.

10.5 Conclusion

We have reviewed a number of ways of detecting changepoints, comparing their performance on detecting changes in variance in a time series. Changepoint models is a large area of research and we have not been able to cover all methods for their analysis. Examples of alternative approaches include nonparametric methods [39, 40] and methods for online detection based on decision theory [47, 13].

The simulation results suggest that Bayesian methods are the most suitable for this application. One aspect of a Bayesian analysis that we have not reflected on is that the output is a distribution over the number and position of the changepoints. Thus Bayesian methods have the advantage of more easily quantifying uncertainty in changepoint positions than alternative methods. Furthermore, if interest lies in estimating the underlying segment parameters (e.g. how the variance changes over time), a Bayesian approach naturally enables the uncertainty in the changepoints to be taken into account. One disadvantage is that it is harder to summarise or represent the posterior distribution, as compared to methods which output a set of predicted changepoints. One approach is to calculate the most likely (so-called MAP) set of changepoints, which can often be calculated efficiently [9, 16]. However even here there are alternative ways of defining the MAP set of changepoints which can give different results in practice [16].

The main issue when implementing a Bayesian analysis is the choice of priors. For the models we consider here a computationally convenient, yet accurate, approach is to estimate hyperparameters of the prior distributions by maximising the marginal likelihood. This approach appears particularly suitable to multiple changepoint models where there can be substantial information about the hyperparameters due to the variation in parameters across the multiple segments.

When analysing multiple changepoint models, there are computational considerations related to searching for the best set of changepoints or exploring the posterior distribution. For the class of models we focused on, both can be done exactly using either the segment neighbourhood algorithm of Section 10.3.2 or the forward-backward algorithm of Section 10.3.4. Simulation results suggest that using these approaches results in better detection of changepoints than using approximate methods such as binary segmentation. Whilst a complicated genetic algorithm is used to detect changepoints using MDL in [12], we showed that the segment neighbourhood algorithm can be applied in this case. One disadvantage of both the segment neighbourhood algorithm and the forward-backward algorithm is that their computational cost is $O(n^2)$. Approximations to the latter have been suggested in [19], which results in an accurate algorithm whose cost is $O(n)$. One profitable area of future research would be to construct a similar approximate version of the segment neighbourhood algorithm with $O(n)$ computational cost. This is particularly important for applying this approach to analysing large datasets, such as those currently being analysed in bioinformatics.

A further disadvantage of these two algorithms is that they rely on nice properties of the model. Changepoint models which have strong dependence across segments cannot be analysed by either of these two algorithms. In this case alternatives, such as binary segmentation, MCMC or genetic algorithms would need to be used to fit models. However, our recommendation is that for models with the appropriate independence properties these two approaches should be the method of choice for fitting changepoint models.

Acknowledgments   Rebecca Killick is funded by the EPSRC and Shell Research Ltd.

10.A   Appendix: segment parameter estimation

Here we give details for estimating segment parameters, conditional on the start and end of the segment, for change in variance model used in the simulation study.

Assume throughout that the segment consists of observations $y_{s:t} = (y_s, \ldots, y_t)$, for $t > s$. There is a single segment parameter, the variance, which we denote by σ^2. The model assumes that within the segment we have conditionally independent observations with $y_i | \sigma^2 \sim N(0, \sigma^2)$, for $i = s, \ldots, t$. The maximum likelihood estimator of the parameter is $\hat{\sigma}^2 = \frac{1}{t-s+1} \sum_{i=s}^{t} y_i^2$. The resulting maximum log-likelihood value is $p(y_{s:t}|\hat{\theta}) = -\frac{n}{2} \left\{ \log(2\pi) - \log \hat{\sigma}^2 - 1 \right\}$.

For the Bayesian analysis, we have an inverse-gamma prior for σ^2 with hyperparameters $\psi = (a, b)$. The posterior distribution is

$$\sigma^2 | y_{s:t} \sim IG\left(a + \frac{(t-s+1)}{2}, b + \frac{1}{2}\sum_{i=s}^{t} y_i^2\right),$$

with marginal likelihood

$$Q(s, t; \psi) = (2\pi)^{(t-s+1)/2} \frac{\Gamma(a + (t-s+1)/2)b^a}{\Gamma(a)(b + \frac{1}{2}\sum_{i=s}^{t} y_i^2)^{a+(t-s+1)/2}}.$$

Bibliography

[1] H. Akaike. A new look at the statistical model identification. *IEEE Transactions on Automatic Control*, **19**(6):716 – 723, 1974.

[2] I. E. Auger and C. E. Lawrence. Algorithms for the optimal identification of segment neighborhoods. *Bulletin of Mathematical Biology*, **51**(1):39–54, 1989.

[3] D. Barry and J. A. Hartigan. Product partition models for change point problems. *Annals of Statistics*, **20**:260–279, 1992.

[4] D. Barry and J. A. Hartigan. A Bayesian analysis for change point problems. *Journal of the American Statistical Association*, **88**:309–319, 1993.

[5] M. S. Bartlett. A comment on D.V. Lindley's statistical paradox. *Biometrika*, **44**:533–534, 1957.

[6] J. V. Braun, R. K. Braun and H. G. Muller. Multiple changepoint fitting via quasilikelihood, with application to DNA sequence segmentation. *Biometrika*, **87**:301–314, 2000.

[7] J. V. Braun and H. G. Muller. Statistical methods for DNA sequence segmentation. *Statistical Science*, **13**(2):142–162, 1998.

[8] E. Carlstein, H. G. Muller and D. Siegmund, editors. *Change-point problems*. Institute of Mathematical Statistics Lecture Notes, 1994.

[9] T. Cemgil, H. J. Kappen and D. Barber. A generative model for music transcription. *IEEE Transactions on Audio, Speech and Language Processing*, **14**:679–694, 2006.

[10] J. Chen and A. K. Gupta. Testing and locating variance changepoints with application to stock prices. *Journal of the American Statistical Association*, **92**:739 – 747, 1997.

[11] J. Chen and A. K. Gupta. *Parametric Statistical Change Point Analysis*. Birkhauser, 2000.

[12] R. A Davis, T. C. M Lee and G. A. Rodriguez-Yam. Structural break estimation for nonstationary time series models. *Journal of the American Statistical Association*, **101**(473):223–239, 2006.

[13] S. Dayanik, C. Goulding and H. V. Poor. Bayesian sequential change diagnosis. *Mathematics of Operations Research*, **33**:475–496, 2008.

[14] J. B. Elsner, F. N. Xu and T. H. Jagger. Detecting shifts in hurricane rates using a Markov chain Monte Carlo approach. *Journal of Climate*, **17**:2652–2666, 2004.

[15] C. Erdman and J. W. Emerson. A fast Bayesian change point analysis for the segmentation of microarray data. *Bioinformatics*, **24**(19):2143–2148, 2008.

[16] P. Fearnhead. Exact Bayesian curve fitting and signal segmentation. *IEEE Transactions on Signal Processing*, **53**:2160–2166, 2005.

[17] P. Fearnhead. Exact and efficient Bayesian inference for multiple changepoint problems. *Statistics and Computing*, **16**:203–213, 2006.

[18] P. Fearnhead. Computational methods for complex stochastic systems: A review of some alternatives to MCMC. *Statistics and Computing*, **18**:151–171, 2008.

[19] P. Fearnhead and Z. Liu. Online inference for multiple changepoint problems. *Journal of the Royal Statistical Society Series B*, **69**:589–605, 2007.

[20] P. Fearnhead and D. Vasilieou. Bayesian analysis of isochores. *Journal of the American Statistical Association*, **485**:132–141, 2009.

[21] P. Fryzlewicz and S. Subba Rao. Basta: consistent multiscale multiple change-point detection for piecewise-stationary ARCH processes. *(In submission)*, 2009.

[22] P. J. Green. Reversible jump Markov chain Monte Carlo computation and Bayesian model determination. *Biometrika*, **82**:711–732, 1995.

[23] A. K. Gupta and J. Chen. Detecting changes of mean in multidimensional normal sequences with applications to literature and geology. *Computational Statistics*, **11**:211–221, 1996.

[24] A. K. Gupta and J. Tang. On testing homogeneity of variances for Gaussian models. *Journal of Statistical Computation and Simulation*, **27**:155–173, 1987.

[25] P. Haccou, E. Meelis and S. Geer. The likelihood ratio test for the change point problem for exponentially distributed random variables. *Stochastic Processes and Their Applications*, **27**:121–139, 1988.

[26] E. J. Hannan and B. G. Quinn. The determination of the order of an autoregression. *Journal of the Royal Statistical Society, Series B*, **41**(2):190–195, 1979.

[27] R. Henderson and J. N. S. Matthews. An investigation of changepoints in the annual number of cases of haemolytic uraemic syndrome. *Applied Statistics*, **42**:461–471, 1993.

[28] D. V. Hinkley. Inference about the change-point in a sequence of random variables. *Biometrika*, **57**:1–17, 1970.

[29] D. V. Hinkley and E. A. Hinkley. Inference about the change-point in a sequence of binomial random variables. *Biometrika*, **57**:477–488, 1970.

[30] D. A. Hsu. Detecting shifts of parameter in gamma sequences with applications to stock price and air traffic flow analysis. *Journal of the American Statistical Association*, **74**:31–40, 1979.

[31] C. Inclan and G. C. Tiao. Use of cumulative sums of squares for retrospective detection of changes of variance. *Journal of the American Statistical Association*, **89**(427):913–923, 1994.

[32] J. Reeves, J. Chen, X. L. Wang, R. Lund and Q. Lu. A review and comparison of changepoint detection techniques for climate data. *Journal of Applied Meteorology and Climatology*, **6**:900–915, 2007.

[33] H. Jeffreys. *The Theory of Probability*. Oxford University Press, 1961.

[34] R. Killick, I. A. Eckley, K. Ewans and P. Jonathan. Detection of changes in variance of oceanographic time-series using changepoint analysis. *Ocean Engineering*, **37**:1120–1126, 2010.

[35] D. W. Kwon, K. Ko, M. Vannucci, A. L. N. Reddy and S. Kim. Wavelet methods for the detection of anomalies and their application to network traffic analysis. *Quality and Reliability Engineering International*, **22**:953–969, 2006.

[36] M. Lavielle and E. Lebarbier. An application of MCMC methods for the multiple change-points problem. *Signal Processing*, **81**:39–53, 2001.

[37] P. Lio and M. Vannucci. Wavelet change-point prediction of transmembrane proteins. *Bioinformatics*, **16**(4):376–382, 2000.

[38] J. S. Liu and C. E. Lawrence. Bayesian inference on biopolymer models. *Bioinformatics*, **15**:38–52, 1999.

[39] E. S. Page. Continuous inspection schemes. *Biometrika*, **41**:100–115, 1954.

[40] A. N. Pettitt. A non-parametric approach to the change-point problem. *Applied Statistics*, **28**:126–135, 1979.

[41] E. Punskaya, C. Andrieu, A. Doucet and W. J. Fitzgerald. Bayesian curve fitting using MCMC with applications to signal segmentation. *IEEE Transactions on Signal Processing*, **50**:747–758, 2002.

[42] G. Schwarz. Estimating the dimension of a model. *Annals of Statistics*, **6**:461–464, 1978.

[43] A. J. Scott and M. Knott. A cluster analysis method for grouping means in the analysis of variance. *Biometrics*, **30**(3):507–512, 1974.

[44] A. Sen and M. S. Srivastava. On tests for detecting change in mean. *Annals of Statistics*, **3**(1):98–108, 1975.

[45] A. N. Shiryaev. On optimum methods in quickest detection problems. *Theory of Probability and its Applications*, **8**:26–51, 1963.

[46] V. Spokoiny. Multiscale local change point detection with applications to value-at-risk. *Annals of Statistics*, **37**:1405–1436, 2009.

[47] A. G. Tartakovsky and V. V. Veeravalli. General asymptotic Bayesian theory of quickest change detection. *Theory of Probability and Its Applications*, **49**:458–497, 2004.

[48] E. S. Venkatraman. Consistency results in multiple change-point problems. PhD thesis, Stanford University, 1993.

[49] L. J. Vostrikova. Detecting disorder in multidimensional random processes. *Soviet Mathematics Doklady*, **24**:55–59, 1981.

[50] G. C. G. Wei and M. A. Tanner. A Monte Carlo implementation of the EM algorithm and the poor man's data augmentation algorithms. *Journal of the American Statistical Association*, **85**(411):699–704, 1990.

[51] G. Yan, Z. Xiao and S. Eidenbenz. Catching instant messaging worms with change-point detection techniques. In *Proceedings of the USENIX workshop on large-scale exploits and emergent threats*, 2008.

[52] T. Y. Yang and L. Kuo. Bayesian binary segmentation procedure for a Poisson process with multiple changepoints. *Journal of Computational and Graphical Statistics*, **10**:772–785, 2001.

[53] Y. Yao. Estimation of a noisy discrete-time step function: Bayes and empirical Bayes approaches. *Annals of Statistics*, **12**:1434–1447, 1984.

[54] Y. Yao. Estimating the number of change-points via Schwarz's criterion. *Statistics and Probability Letters*, **6**:181–189, 1988.

Contributors

Idris A. Eckley, Department of Mathematics and Statistics, Lancaster University, LA1 4YF
Paul Fearnhead, Department of Mathematics and Statistics, Lancaster University, LA1 4YF
Rebecca Killick, Department of Mathematics and Statistics, Lancaster University, LA1 4YF

11

Approximate likelihood estimation of static parameters in multi-target models

Sumeetpal S. Singh, Nick Whiteley and Simon J. Godsill

11.1   Introduction

Target-tracking problems involve the online estimation of the state vector of an object under surveillance, called a target, that is changing over time. The state of the target at time n, denoted X_n, is a vector in $E_1 \subset \mathbf{R}^{d_1}$ and contains its kinematic characteristics, e.g. the target's position and velocity. Typically only noise-corrupted measurements of the state of the object under surveillance are available. Specifically, the observation at time n, denoted Y_n, is a vector in $E_2 \subset \mathbf{R}^{d_2}$ and is a noisy measurement of the target's state as acquired by a sensor, e.g. radar. The statistical model most commonly used for the sequence of random variables $\{(X_n, Y_{n+1})\}_{n \geq 0}$ is the hidden Markov model (HMM):

$$X_0 \sim \mu^\theta(\cdot), \quad X_n | (X_{n-1} = x_{n-1}) \sim f^\theta(\cdot | x_{n-1}), \quad n \geq 1, \tag{11.1}$$

$$Y_n | X_n = x_n \sim g^\theta(\cdot | x_n), \quad n \geq 1. \tag{11.2}$$

The superscript θ on these densities (as well as on all densities introduced subsequently), denotes the dependency of the model on a vector of parameters θ. We will assume a parameterisation such that $\theta \in \Theta \subset \mathbf{R}^{n_\theta}$. When the target first appears in the surveillance region, its initial state is distributed according to the probability density μ^θ on E_1. The change in its state vector from time $n - 1$ to n is determined by the Markov transition density $f^\theta(\cdot | x_{n-1})$. Furthermore, the observation generated at time n is a function of the target's state at time n and noise, or equivalently generated according to the probability density $g^\theta(\cdot | x_n)$ on E_2, and is conditionally independent of previously generated observations and state values. This model is general enough to describe the evolution of the target and the observations it generates in many applications; see [1, 13].

This chapter is concerned with the more complex and practically significant problem of tracking multiple targets simultaneously. In this case the state and observation at each time are *random finite sets* ([13]):

$$\mathbf{X}_n = \{X_{n,1}, X_{n,2}, \ldots, X_{n,K_n}\}, \quad \mathbf{Y}_n = \{Y_{n,1}, Y_{n,2}, \ldots, Y_{n,M_n}\}, \quad n \geq 1. \tag{11.3}$$

Each *element* of $\mathbf{X}_n$ is the state of an individual target. The number of targets K_n under surveillance changes over time due to targets entering and leaving the surveillance region. Some of the existing targets may not be detected by the sensor and a set of false

measurements of unknown number are also recorded due to non-target generated measurements. For example, if the sensor is radar, reflections can be generated by fixed features of
the landscape. These processes give rise to the measurement set $\mathbf{Y}_n$. (Note its cardinality
M_n changes with time.) An added complication usually encountered in applications is that
it is not known which observations arise from which targets (if any). The aim in multi-target
tracking is to estimate, at each time step, the time-varying state set from the entire history
of observation sets received until that time. The task of calibrating the multi-target tracking
model is also an important problem faced by the practitioner. In the multi-target model θ
includes both the parameters of the individual target model (11.1)–(11.2) and parameters
related to the surveillance environment. For example, θ may contain the variance of the
noise that corrupts the sensor measurements, the parameter of the distribution of false measurements, etc. In this chapter, in order to estimate the model parameters from the data,
an approximate likelihood function is devised and then maximised. Before describing this
method, it is necessary to specify the multi-target tracking problem a little more precisely.

The state $\mathbf{X}_n$ evolves to $\mathbf{X}_{n+1}$ in a Markovian fashion by a process of thinning (targets
leaving the surveillance region), displacement (Markov motion of remaining individual
targets) and augmentation of new points which correspond to new targets entering the
surveillance region. The motion of each target that has not left the surveillance region
occurs precisely according to Eq. (11.1). When a new target is introduced, its initial state is
drawn according to the probability density μ^θ in Eq. (11.1). If more than one new target is
introduced, then the initial states are sampled from μ^θ independently. The observed process
is generated from the hidden process through the same mechanisms of thinning, displacement and augmentation with false measurements. (See Section 11.2 for more details.)
Displacement here implies that the individual targets, if they generate an observation at
time n, do so in accordance with the stated model in Eq. (11.2). Mathematically $\mathbf{X}_n$ is a
spatial point process (PP) on E_1 where E_1 is the state space of a single target. Likewise,
$\mathbf{Y}_n$ is a spatial PP on E_2 where E_2 is the observation space in the single target-tracking
problem. False measurements and birth of new targets are, for example, assumed to be
independent spatial Poisson processes. Let $\mathbf{y}_{1:n} = (\mathbf{y}_1, \ldots, \mathbf{y}_n)$ denote the realisation of
observations received from time 1 to n. (Here $\mathbf{y}_i$ denotes the realisation of $\mathbf{Y}_i$.) It is possible to estimate the number of targets and their individual state values from the conditional
distribution of $\mathbf{X}_n$ given $\mathbf{Y}_{1:n} = \mathbf{y}_{1:n}$, denoted $p(\mathbf{x}_n|\mathbf{y}_{1:n})$. Due to the need to process the data
online, i.e. to update the estimates every time a new observation is received, the sequence
of marginal distributions $\{p(\mathbf{x}_n|\mathbf{y}_{1:n})\}_{n\geq0}$ is often sought after. For each n, $p(\mathbf{x}_n|\mathbf{y}_{1:n})$ has
support on the disjoint union $\uplus_{k\geq0} E_1^k$ and does not admit an analytic characterisation in
general.

Multi-target tracking has long been a focus of research in the engineering literature,
primarily driven by surveillance applications, and now a standard set of tools exists for the
analysis of such problems; see for example [2, 13]. It is possible to enlarge the model (11.3)
to include the (unobserved) associations of the observations to hidden targets. For simple
sensor and individual target motion models, the posterior distribution of the unobserved
targets and associations admits an analytic characterisation. Furthermore, this posterior
distribution can be marginalised to obtain a posterior distribution over the associations
only. Even so, the support of this marginal distribution is too large for it to be stored
in practice and approximations are made. The most frequently used approach to date (in
the surveillance literature) is to approximate the posterior by retaining only its dominant
modes. A popular sub-optimal search algorithm to locate the modes is the multiple hypothesis tracking (MHT) algorithm of [19]; see also [2, 13]. As more data are gathered over

time, which is characteristic of surveillance, the dimension of the support of the posterior distribution of associations increases and searching for the modes exhaustively is not possible. There is a large volume of work dedicated to the computational challenges of this task, i.e., how to implement the search sequentially in time and direct it towards 'good' candidates, and how to store the result efficiently; see [2]. It is fair to say that the MHT is complicated to implement, in fact, far more complicated than the algorithms in this work.

Recently, the MHT algorithm has been extended by [24] to simultaneously estimate the parameters of the multi-target model. A full Bayesian approach for estimating the model parameters using Markov chain Monte Carlo was presented in [29] for a simplified model which assumes the individual targets have linear Gaussian dynamics and similar Gaussian assumptions hold for the observations they generate. This Gaussian scenario is highly restrictive and cannot handle non-linear sensors, e.g. bearings measurements.

We now introduce the specific technique that we use to construct an approximation of the marginal likelihood of observations. When the unknown number of targets and their states at time 0 is considered to be a realisation of a Poisson PP, then it follows that for $n = 1, 2, ...$, the law of $\mathbf{X}_n$ is also Poisson (see Section 11.2 for a precise statement of this result including the modelling assumptions). The problem of estimating the number of targets and their individual state values at time n given the observations $\mathbf{Y}_{1:n}$ is then greatly simplified if $\mathbf{X}_n$ given $\mathbf{Y}_{1:n}$ can be closely approximated as a Poisson PP. In the tracking literature this problem was studied by [14]. Mahler derived an expression relating the *intensity* (or the *first moment*) of the conditional distribution of $\mathbf{X}_1$ given $\mathbf{y}_1$ to that of the prior of $\mathbf{X}_1$. The Poisson PP is completely characterised by its first moment and it can be shown that the problem of finding the best Poisson approximation to the conditional distribution of $\mathbf{X}_1$ given $\mathbf{y}_1$ is equivalent to the problem of characterising its intensity; see [14]. In addition, for the same hidden process dynamic model stated above, Mahler also derived the intensity of the conditional distribution of $\mathbf{X}_2$ given $\mathbf{y}_1$. These results were combined to yield a filter that propagates the intensity of the sequence of conditional densities $\{p(\mathbf{x}_n|\mathbf{y}_{1:n})\}_{n \geq 0}$ and is known in the tracking literature as the probability hypothesis density (PHD) filter. Detailed numerical studies using sequential Monte Carlo (SMC) approximations by [26, 27] (and references therein), as well as Gaussian approximations by [25] to the PHD filter have since demonstrated its potential as a new approach to multi-target tracking. We are not aware of any study that has specifically characterised the error incurred in approximating $\mathbf{X}_n$ given $\mathbf{y}_{1:n}$ with a Poisson PP. However, in various studies, the merit of the approximation has been confirmed by comparing the estimated intensity with the true number of targets in synthetic numerical examples. In particular, the estimates of the number of targets and their states extracted from the propagated intensity are reasonably accurate even for difficult tracking scenarios. Recent non-target tracking applications of the PHD filter include map building in robotics by [15] and tracking sinusoidal components in audio by [4].

Motivated by this, we explore the use of the same Poisson approximation technique to derive an approximation of the marginal likelihood of the observed data, i.e. $p(\mathbf{y}_{1:T})$ where T is the length of the data record. The estimate of the model parameter is then taken to be the maximising argument (with respect to the model parameters) of this approximation of the true marginal likelihood. A gradient ascent algorithm is used to find the model parameters that maximise the likelihood. Although the approximate likelihood function is not computable exactly, it and its gradient may be evaluated using SMC. The approximate likelihood function is 'characterised' by a sequence of non-negative functions on E_1, and not the space $\biguplus_{k \geq 0} E_1^k$, and even a simple SMC implementation can be reasonably efficient. (See Section 11.4 for details.) We demonstrate in numerical examples that the approximation to the true likelihood is reasonable as it allows us to learn the static parameters from the data. Even for initialisation values very far from the true model parameters, the gradient algorithm is able to converge to a vicinity of the true model parameters.

The remainder of this chapter is structured as follows. The multi-target statistical model is defined in Section 11.2. A review of the PHD filter is presented in Section 11.3 along with several results from [21] which are needed to construct the approximation of the likelihood. The approximation of the marginal likelihood of the multi-target tracking model is detailed in Section 11.4. Section 11.5 describes a SMC algorithm to evaluate this approximate likelihood and its gradient with respect to the model parameters. Section 10.6 describes model parameter estimaton. A simulation study which empirically assesses the performance of the method is presented in Section 11.7.

11.2   The multi-target model

The Poisson PP features prominently in this model and we refer the reader to [10] for an introduction to this process. To simplify the notation, only the core ingredients of the multi-target statistical model have their dependence on θ made explicit. All other derived quantities, while also dependent on θ, have θ omitted from their symbols.

Consider the process of unobserved points $\mathbf{X}_n = X_{n,1:K_n}$, where each element of $\mathbf{X}_n$ corresponds to one target and is a random point in the space E_1. $\mathbf{X}_n$ evolves to $\mathbf{X}_{n+1}$ as follows. With probability $p_S^\theta(x)$, each point of $\mathbf{X}_n$ survives and is displaced according to the Markov transition density on E_1, $f^\theta(x_{n+1}|x_n)$, introduced in Eq. (11.1). The random deletion and Markov motion happens independently for each point in $\mathbf{X}_n$. In addition to the surviving points of $\mathbf{X}_n$, new points are 'born' from a Poisson process with intensity function $\gamma^\theta(x)$. Let $\mathbf{X}_{n+1}$ denote the PP on E_1 defined by the superposition of the surviving and mutated points of $\mathbf{X}_n$ and the newly born points. At initialisation, $\mathbf{X}_0$ consists only of 'birth' points. Simulation from this Poisson model can be achieved by first sampling the cardinality according to the discrete Poisson distribution with parameter value equal to the total mass of the intensity function. The location of the points themselves are then sampled iid from the normalised intensity function. In the context of the model (11.1), the initial state of each new target is drawn from the probability density $\gamma^\theta(x)/\int \gamma^\theta(x')dx'$.

The points of $\mathbf{X}_{n+1}$ are observed through the following model. With probability $p_D^\theta(x)$, each point of $\mathbf{X}_{n+1}$, e.g. $x_{n+1,j}$, $j \in \{1, 2, ..., K_{n+1}\}$, generates a noisy observation in the observation space E_2 through the density $g^\theta(y|x_{n+1,j})$. This happens independently for each point of $\mathbf{X}_{n+1}$. Let $\widehat{\mathbf{Y}}_{n+1}$ denote the PP of observations originating from $\mathbf{X}_{n+1}$. In addition to these detected points, false measurements (or clutter points) are generated from an independent Poisson process on E_2 with intensity function $\kappa^\theta(y)$. Let $\mathbf{Y}_{n+1}$ denote the superposition of $\widehat{\mathbf{Y}}_{n+1}$ and these false measurements, and let $\mathbf{y}_{n+1} = y_{n+1,1:m_{n+1}}$ denote a realisation of $\mathbf{Y}_{n+1} = Y_{n+1,1:M_{n+1}}$.

11.3   A review of the PHD filter

This section presents an alternative derivation of the PHD filter which was proposed by [21]. The foundation of the PHD filter is a solution to a simplified inference task, which is to characterise the posterior distribution of a hidden Poisson PP $\mathbf{X}$ given observations $\mathbf{Y}$ generated as described in Section 11.2. We then introduce explicit time indexing and make connections to the PHD filtering recursions of [14].

11.3.1   Inference for partially observed Poisson processes

In this subsection we suppress dependence on the parameter θ. Let the realisation of $\mathbf{Y}$ be $\mathbf{y} = \{y_1, \dots, y_m\}$. In general it is not possible to characterise the distribution of $\mathbf{X}$ given $\mathbf{Y} = \mathbf{y}$, denoted $\mathsf{P}_{\mathbf{X}|\mathbf{y}}$, in closed form; see [12] for a similar problem solved with perfect simulation. In the case of the Poisson prior, the posterior was characterised only *indirectly* by [14] by providing the formula for its probability generating functional (p.g.fl.), obtained by differentiating the joint p.g.fl. of the observed and hidden process. The authors in [21] noted that, while this is a general proof technique, it is a technical approach that does not exploit the structure of the problem – a Poisson prior and an observed process constructed via thinning, displacement and augmentation allows for a considerably stronger result with a simpler proof by calling upon several well-known results concerning the Poisson PP. Exploiting this [21] were able to provide a closed-form expression for the posterior which is quite revealing of the 'structure' of the conditional process $\mathbf{X}$ given the observed process $\mathbf{Y}$. Corollaries of this result include the expression relating the intensity of the posterior and prior as well as the law of the association of the points of the observed process. While the result in [14] is only for a Poisson prior for $\mathbf{X}$, [21] extends the result to a Gauss-Poisson prior which covers the Poisson prior as a special case. The law $\mathsf{P}_{\mathbf{X}|\mathbf{y}}$ is the foundation of the PHD filter and its derivation presented below follows the approach of [21].

The derivation of $\mathsf{P}_{\mathbf{X}|\mathbf{y}}$ draws upon several facts concerning a Poisson PP. The first concerns marking. Let $\mathbf{X}$ be a Poisson PP on E_1 with realisation $\{x_1, \dots, x_n\}$. Let's attach to each x_i a random *mark* ζ_i, valued in $\mathcal{M}$ (the mark space) and drawn from the probability density $p(\cdot|x_i)$. Additionally, the mark of each point x_i is generated independently. Then $\{(x_1, \zeta_1), \dots, (x_n, \zeta_n)\}$ is Poisson on $E_1 \times \mathcal{M}$ with intensity $\alpha(x)p(\zeta|x)\mathrm{d}x\mathrm{d}\zeta$ ([10]). Conversely, for a Poisson PP on $E_1 \times \mathcal{M}$ with intensity $v(x, \zeta)$, given the realisation of all the first coordinates, $\{x_1, x_2, \dots, x_n\}$, then the following is known about the same PP restricted to $\mathcal{M}$. There are n points and they are jointly distributed according to the following density on $\mathcal{M}^n$

$$p(\zeta_1, \dots, \zeta_n) = \prod_{i=1}^{n} \frac{v(x_i, \zeta_i)}{\int v(x_i, \zeta)d\zeta}. \tag{11.4}$$

According to the multi-target observation model, each point x_i in the realisation of $\mathbf{X}$ generates an E_2-valued observation with probability $p_D(x_i)$. Furthermore, this happens independently for all points in the realisation of $\mathbf{X}$. At this point it is convenient to introduce the following decomposition of $\mathbf{X}$. Two point processes, $\widehat{\mathbf{X}}$ and $\widetilde{\mathbf{X}}$, are formed from $\mathbf{X}$: $\widehat{\mathbf{X}}$ comprises the points of $\mathbf{X}$ that generate observations while $\widetilde{\mathbf{X}}$ comprises the remaining unobserved points of $\mathbf{X}$. Since $\widehat{\mathbf{X}}$ is obtained from $\mathbf{X}$ by independent marking, both $\widehat{\mathbf{X}}$ and $\widetilde{\mathbf{X}}$ are independent Poisson with respective intensities $\alpha(x)p_D(x)$ and $\alpha(x)(1 - p_D(x))$ [10, p. 55]. (The superscript θ on p_D has been omitted from the notation.)

By construction, $\widetilde{\mathbf{X}}$ is unobserved while $\widehat{\mathbf{X}}$ is observed in noise through $\mathbf{Y}$, with noise here referring to the false measurements in $\mathbf{Y}$. This decomposition sheds light on the structure of the posterior: since $\widetilde{\mathbf{X}}$ is unobserved, its law is unchanged after observing $\mathbf{Y}$. As for $\widehat{\mathbf{X}}$, let its posterior be $\mathsf{P}_{\widehat{\mathbf{X}}|\mathbf{y}}$. Thus, the desired posterior $\mathsf{P}_{\mathbf{X}|\mathbf{y}}$ is

$$\mathsf{P}_{\mathbf{X}|\mathbf{y}} = \mathsf{P}_{\widetilde{\mathbf{X}}} * \mathsf{P}_{\widehat{\mathbf{X}}|\mathbf{y}},$$

where $*$ denotes convolution, which follows since $\mathbf{X}$ is the superposition of $\widetilde{\mathbf{X}}$ and $\widehat{\mathbf{X}}$. All that remains to be done is to characterise $\mathsf{P}_{\widehat{\mathbf{X}}|\mathbf{y}}$.

Let $\{\Delta\}$ be a one point set with Δ not belonging to either E_1 or E_2 and let $E_1' = E_1 \cup \{\Delta\}$. A marked PP $\mathbf{Z}$ on $E_2 \times E_1'$ is constructed as follows. Each false measurement in $\mathbf{Y}$ is assigned Δ as its mark. Each point in $\mathbf{Y}$ corresponding to a real observation is assigned as a mark the corresponding point in $\widehat{\mathbf{X}}$ that generated it. Let $\mathbf{Z}$ be this set of points formed by marking $\mathbf{Y}$. It follows that $\mathbf{Z}$ is a marked Poisson PP with intensity

$$\alpha(x)p_D(x)g(y|x)\mathbb{I}_{E_2\times E_1}(y,x)\mathrm{d}x\mathrm{d}y + \kappa(y)\mathbb{I}_{E_2\times\{\Delta\}}(y,x)\delta_\Delta(\mathrm{d}x)\mathrm{d}y,$$

where $\mathbb{I}_A$ is the indicator function of the set A and $\delta_\Delta(\mathrm{d}x)$ is the Dirac measure concentrated on Δ. Given the realisation $\mathbf{y} = \{y_1,\ldots,y_m\}$ of the first coordinate of the process then, by Eq. (11.4), the second coordinates are jointly distributed on $(E_1\cup\{\Delta\})^m$ with law

$$p(\mathrm{d}x_1,\ldots,\mathrm{d}x_m) = \prod_{i=1}^m \frac{\alpha(x_i)p_D(x_i)g(y_i|x_i)\mathbb{I}_{E_1}(x_i)\mathrm{d}x_i + \kappa(y_i)\mathbb{I}_{\{\Delta\}}(x)\delta_\Delta(\mathrm{d}x_i)}{\int_{E_1}\alpha(x)p_D(x)g(y_i|x)\mathrm{d}x + \kappa(y_i)}. \qquad (11.5)$$

Theorem 11.1 *[21, Proposition 4.1] Let $\mathbf{X}$ be a Poisson PP on E_1 with intensity $\alpha(x)$ which is observed indirectly through the PP $\mathbf{Y}$ on E_2 and $\mathbf{Y}$ is generated according to the observation model detailed in Section 11.2. The conditional distribution of $\mathbf{X}$ given the realisation $\mathbf{y} = \{y_1,\ldots,y_m\}$ of $\mathbf{Y}$, $\mathsf{P}_{\mathbf{X}|\mathbf{y}}$, coincides with the distribution of the superposition of the following two independent point processes:*
– a Poisson PP on E_1 with intensity $\alpha(x)(1 - p_D(x))\mathrm{d}x$ and
– the restriction to E_1 of an m-point PP on $E_1\cup\{\Delta\}$ with law given in Eq. (11.5).

The theorem may be alternatively interpreted as follows. To generate a realisation with distribution $\mathsf{P}_{\mathbf{X}|\mathbf{y}}$, the following procedure may be adopted. Generate a realisation of the m-point PP on $E_1\cup\{\Delta\}$ with law (11.5) by simulating the ith point according to the ith measure in the product (11.5). Discard all the points with values Δ and augment this set of remaining points with the realisation of an independent Poisson PP with intensity $\alpha(x)(1 - p_D(x))$.

Since $\mathsf{P}_{\mathbf{X}|\mathbf{y}}$ is the law of the superposition of two independent point processes, the following corollary is obvious.

Corollary 11.2 *[21, Proposition 4.1] For a bounded real-valued measurable function φ on E_1,*

$$\mathsf{E}\left[\sum_{x\in\mathbf{X}}\varphi(x)\Bigg|\mathbf{Y}=\mathbf{y}\right] = \mathsf{E}\left[\sum_{x\in\widetilde{\mathbf{X}}}\varphi(x)\right] + \mathsf{E}\left[\sum_{x\in\widehat{\mathbf{X}}}\varphi(x)\mathbb{I}_{E_1}(x)\Bigg|\mathbf{Y}=\mathbf{y}\right]$$

$$= \int_{E_1}\varphi(x)\alpha(x)(1-p_D(x))\mathrm{d}x + \sum_{i=1}^m \frac{\int_{E_1}\varphi(x)\alpha(x)p_D(x)g(y_i|x)\mathrm{d}x}{\int_{E_1}\alpha(x)p_D(x)g(y_i|x)\mathrm{d}x + \kappa(y_i)}.$$

When $\varphi(x) = \mathbb{I}_A(x)$ for some subset A of E_1 then the term on the right is precisely the expected number of points in the set A. The non-negative function (on E_1)

$$\alpha(x)(1-p_D(x)) + \sum_{i=1}^m \frac{\alpha(x)p_D(x)g(y_i|x)}{\int_{E_1}\alpha(x)p_D(x)g(y_i|x)\mathrm{d}x + \kappa(y_i)}$$

is the intensity (or first moment) of the PP with law $\mathsf{P}_{\mathbf{X}|\mathbf{y}}$. The intensity of the superposition of two independent processes is the sum of the two intensities and hence the two terms that make up the above expression. This result was first derived, using a different proof technique, in [14].

11.3.2 The PHD Filter

The foundations of the PHD filter are the following two facts.

Let $\mathbf{X}_{n-1}$ be a Poisson PP with intensity $\alpha_{n-1}(x_{n-1})$. Since $\mathbf{X}_{n-1}$ evolves to $\mathbf{X}_n$ by a process of independent thinning, displacement and augmentation with an independent Poisson birth process, it follows that marginal distribution of $\mathbf{X}_n$ is also Poisson with intensity (fact 1)

$$\alpha_n(x_n) = \int_{E_1} f^\theta(x_n|x_{n-1}) p_S^\theta(x_{n-1}) \alpha_{n-1}(x_{n-1}) \mathrm{d}x_{n-1} + \gamma^\theta(x_n)$$

$$=: (\Phi\alpha_{n-1})(x_n) + \gamma^\theta(x_n). \tag{11.6}$$

This fact may be established using the Thinning, Marking and Superposition theorems for a Poisson process; see [10]. Specifically, subjecting the realisation of the Poisson PP with intensity α_{n-1} to independent thinning and displacement results in a Poisson PP. The intensity of this PP is given by the first function on the right-hand side of Eq. (11.6). Combining the realisations of two independent Poisson point processes still results in a Poisson PP. The intensity of the resulting process is the sum of the intensities of the processes being combined. This explains the addition of the term γ^θ on the right-hand side of Eq. (11.6). Thus, it follows that if $\mathbf{X}_0$ is Poisson then so is $\mathbf{X}_n$ for all n.

It was established in Section 11.3.1 that the distribution of $\mathbf{X}_1$ conditioned on a realisation of observations $\mathbf{y}_1$ is not Poisson. However, the best Poisson approximation to $P_{\mathbf{X}_1|\mathbf{y}}$, in a Kullback–Leibler sense, is the Poisson PP which has the same intensity as $P_{\mathbf{X}_1|\mathbf{y}}$ (fact 2); see [14, 21]. (This is a general result that applies when any PP is approximated by a Poisson PP using the Kullback–Leibler criterion.) By Corollary 11.2, the intensity of the best approximating Poisson PP is

$$\alpha_{1|1}(x_1) = \left[1 - p_D^\theta(x_1) + \sum_{y \in \mathbf{y}_1} \frac{p_D^\theta(x_1) g^\theta(y|x_1)}{\int_{E_1} p_D^\theta(x) g^\theta(y|x) \alpha_{1|0}(x) \mathrm{d}x + \kappa^\theta(y)} \right] \alpha_{1|0}(x_1)$$

$$=: (\Psi_1 \alpha_{1|0})(x_1),$$

where $\alpha_{1|0}$ is the intensity of $\mathbf{X}_1$ and is given by Eq. (11.6) with $n = 1$. (Note that no observation is received at time 0.) For convenience in the following we will also write, for each n and $r = 1, 2, ..., m_n$,

$$\mathcal{Z}_{n,r} := \int_{E_n} p_D^\theta(x) g^\theta(y_{n,r}|x) \alpha_{n|n-1}(x) \mathrm{d}x.$$

The subscript on the *update* operator Ψ_1 indicates the dependence on the specific realisation of the observations received at time 1. The recursive application of the above two facts gives rise to the PHD filter. Specifically, the conditional distribution of $\mathbf{X}_n$ at each time is approximated by the best fitting Poisson distribution before the subsequent Bayes prediction step. This scheme defines a specific approximation to the optimal filtering recursions for the multi-target model whereby at each time step only the first moment of the conditional distribution is propagated

$$\alpha_{n|n-1} = (\Phi\alpha_{n-1|n-1}) + \gamma^\theta, \tag{11.7}$$

$$\alpha_{n|n} = (\Psi_n \alpha_{n|n-1}). \tag{11.8}$$

In the tracking literature these equations are referred to as the PHD filter and were first derived by [14]. The double subscripts in Eqs. (11.7) and (11.8) imply these are conditional intensities as opposed to the intensity in Eq. (11.6), which is the unconditional intensity of the hidden process.

11.4 Approximating the marginal likelihood

For a block of realised observations, $\mathbf{y}_{1:n}$, according to the model of Section 11.2, we make use of the following decomposition of the marginal likelihood:

$$p(\mathbf{y}_{1:n}) = p(\mathbf{y}_1) \prod_{k=2}^{n} p(\mathbf{y}_k|\mathbf{y}_{1:k-1})$$

$$= \int p(\mathbf{y}_1|\mathbf{x}_1)p(\mathbf{x}_1)d\mathbf{x}_1 \prod_{k=2}^{n} \int p(\mathbf{y}_k|\mathbf{x}_k)p(\mathbf{x}_k|\mathbf{y}_{1:k-1})d\mathbf{x}_k. \qquad (11.9)$$

Using the Poisson approximation of the conditional density $p(\mathbf{x}_k|\mathbf{y}_{1:k-1})$ given by the PHD filter, i.e. $\alpha_{k|k-1}$, it follows that the predictive likelihood $p(\mathbf{y}_k|\mathbf{y}_{1:k-1})$ is also Poisson and easily characterised.

Proposition 11.3 *Let $p(\mathbf{x}_{n-1}|\mathbf{y}_{1:n-1})$ be the density of a Poisson process with intensity $\alpha_{n-1|n-1}$. Then the predictive density of the observation $\mathbf{y}_n$,*

$$p(\mathbf{y}_n|\mathbf{y}_{1:n-1}) = \int p(\mathbf{y}_n|\mathbf{x}_n)p(\mathbf{x}_n|\mathbf{y}_{1:n-1})d\mathbf{x}_n,$$

is the density of a Poisson process with intensity function given by

$$\int_{E_1} g^\theta(y|x_n)p_D^\theta(x_n)\alpha_{n|n-1}(x_n)dx_n + \kappa^\theta(y). \qquad (11.10)$$

Proof Recall from the definition of the model that, given $\mathbf{x}_{n-1}$, $\mathbf{X}_n$ is formed as follows. With probability $p_S^\theta(x)$, each point of $\mathbf{x}_{n-1}$ survives and mutates according to the Markov kernel $f^\theta(\cdot|x_{n-1})$. This happens independently for each point of $\mathbf{x}_{n-1}$. Thus $\mathbf{X}_n$ consists of the surviving and mutated points of $\mathbf{x}_{n-1}$, superposed with points from an independent birth Poisson process with intensity γ^θ. From the Thinning, Marking and Superposition theorems for a Poisson process (see [10]), and under the condition of the proposition, $p(\mathbf{x}_n|\mathbf{y}_{1:n-1})$ is Poisson with intensity $\alpha_{n|n-1}$ as defined in Eq. (11.7). The observation $\mathbf{Y}_n$ is then formed as follows. With probability $p_D^\theta(x)$, each point of $\mathbf{X}_n$ is detected and generates an observation in E_2 through the probability density $g^\theta(\cdot|x_n)$. Thus $\mathbf{Y}_n$ consists of the observations originating from $\mathbf{X}_n$, superposed with an independent clutter Poisson process of intensity κ^θ. It follows once again from the Thinning, Marking and Superposition theorems that, under the condition of the proposition, $p(\mathbf{y}_n|\mathbf{y}_{1:n-1})$ is Poisson with intensity given by Eq. (11.10). □

For a realised Poisson process $\mathbf{y} = y_{1:k}$ in E_2 with intensity function $\beta(y)$, the likelihood is given by

$$p(\mathbf{y}) = \frac{1}{k!} \exp\left[-\int \beta(y)dy\right] \prod_{j=1}^{k} \beta(y_j). \qquad (11.11)$$

Combining Eq. (11.9), Proposition 11.3 and Eq. (11.11), the log-likelihood of the observed data may be approximated as follows:

$$
\ell_{\text{Po},n}(\theta) = -\sum_{k=1}^{n} \int \left[\int g^{\theta}(y_k|x_k) p_D^{\theta}(x_k) \alpha_{k|k-1}(x_k) dx_k + \kappa^{\theta}(y_k) \right] dy_k
$$
$$
+ \sum_{k=1}^{n} \sum_{r=1}^{m_k} \log \left[\int g^{\theta}(y_{k,r}|x_k) p_D^{\theta}(x_k) \alpha_{k|k-1}(x_k) dx_k + \kappa^{\theta}(y_{k,r}) \right], \quad (11.12)
$$

where the subscript Po on ℓ indicates that this is an approximation based on the Poisson approximations to $p(\mathbf{x}_n|\mathbf{y}_{1:n-1})$.

11.5 SMC approximation of the PHD filter and its gradient

In the majority of cases, the Poisson approximation (11.12) of the true log-likelihood $\log p(\mathbf{y}_{1:n})$ cannot be computed exactly and a numerical scheme to approximate the various integrals therein is needed. It was noted by [25] that under certain conditions on the multi-target model, the predicted and updated intensities are Gaussian mixtures and the recursion (11.7)–(11.8) is analytically tractable. However, the number of components in these mixtures explodes over time and so [25] employed a pruning mechanism to allow practical implementation. Extended Kalman filter and the unscented Kalman filter style deterministic approximations of the intensity recursions have also been devised to cope with a more general model. Predating these works is [27] where a SMC method to approximate the intensity functions was devised. In this section we review this original SMC algorithm and extend it to approximate the gradient of the intensity functions. The SMC approximation of the PHD likelihood and its gradient is also detailed.

Sequential Monte Carlo methods have become a standard tool for computation in non-linear optimal filtering problems and in this context have been termed particle filters. We do not give explicit details of standard particle filtering algorithms here but refer the reader to [7] and [3] for a variety of algorithms, theoretical details and applications, and [6] for a general framework. Sequential Monte Carlo algorithms may be viewed as being constructed from ideas of sequential importance sampling (SIS) and resampling. They recursively propagate a set of weighted random samples called particles, which are used to approximate a sequence of probability distributions. The algorithms are such that, as the number of particles tends to infinity and under weak assumptions, an integral with respect to the random distribution defined by the particle set converges to the integral with respect to the corresponding true distribution.

A particle implementation of the PHD filter (Eqs. (11.7) and (11.8)) was proposed simultaneously in several works; [26, 20, 30]. These implementations may be likened to the bootstrap particle filter in the sense that their 'proposal' steps ignore the new observations. An auxiliary SMC implementation that takes into account the new observations at each time was recently proposed by [28] to minimise the variance of the incremental weight. The particle algorithm of [27] will be the building block for the particle approximation of Eq. (11.12) and its gradient.

Given the particle set from the previous iteration, $\{X_{n-1}^{(i)}, W_{n-1}^{(i)}\}_{i=1}^{N}$, N samples $\{X_n^{(i)}\}_{i=1}^{N}$ are each drawn from a proposal distribution $q_n(\cdot|X_{n-1}^{(i)})$ and the predicted importance weights $\{W_{n|n-1}^{(i)}\}_{i=1}^{N}$ are computed as follows:

$$X_n^{(i)} \sim q_n(\cdot|X_{n-1}^{(i)}), \qquad W_{n|n-1}^{(i)} = \frac{f^\theta(X_n^{(i)}|X_{n-1}^{(i)})p_S^\theta(X_{n-1}^{(i)})}{q_n(X_n^{(i)}|X_{n-1}^{(i)})}W_{n-1}^{(i)}, \qquad 1 \le i \le N. \quad (11.13)$$

This proposal distribution can depend on θ, e.g. by setting q_n to be the transition density for the individual targets f^θ, as done in the numerical examples in Section 11.7. A collection of L additional samples, $\{X_n^{(i)}\}_{i=N+1}^{N+L}$, dedicated to the birth term are then drawn from a proposal distribution $p_n(\cdot)$ and the corresponding importance weights $\{W_{n|n-1}^{(i)}\}_{i=N+1}^{N+L}$ are computed:

$$X_n^{(i)} \sim p_n(\cdot), \qquad W_{n|n-1}^{(i)} = \frac{1}{L}\frac{\gamma^\theta(X_n^{(i)})}{p_n(X_n^{(i)})}, \qquad N+1 \le i \le N+L.$$

The distribution p_n can also depend on θ and the default choice would be proportional to γ^θ (provided the corresponding normalised density exists and can be sampled from easily). The approximation to the predicted intensity $\alpha_{n|n-1}$ is

$$\widehat{\alpha}_{n|n-1}(\mathrm{d}x_n) = \sum_{i=1}^{N+L} W_{n|n-1}^{(i)}\delta_{X_n^{(i)}}(\mathrm{d}x_n).$$

This may be used to approximate integrals of the form $\int_E \psi(x)\alpha_{n|n-1}(x)\mathrm{d}x$ which appear in the denominator of Eq. (11.8). For $r \in \{1, 2, ..., m_n\}$, this approximation is given by

$$\widehat{Z}_{n,r} = \sum_{i=1}^{N+L} \psi_{n,r}(X_n^{(i)})W_{n|n-1}^{(i)} + \kappa^\theta(y_{n,r}),$$

where

$$\psi_{n,r}(x) = p_D^\theta(x)g^\theta(y_{n,r}|x).$$

The particles are then re-weighted according to the update operator yielding a second collection of importance weights $\{W_n^{(i)}\}_{i=1}^{N+L}$ defined as follows:

$$W_n^{(i)} = \left[1 - p_D^\theta(X_n^{(i)}) + \sum_{r=1}^{m_n} \frac{\psi_{n,r}(X_n^{(i)})}{\widehat{Z}_{n,r}}\right]W_{n|n-1}^{(i)}.$$

The empirical measure defined by the particle set $\{X_n^{(i)}, W_n^{(i)}\}_{i=1}^{N+L}$ then approximates the updated intensity $\alpha_{n|n}$:

$$\widehat{\alpha}_{n|n}(\mathrm{d}x_n) := \sum_{i=1}^{N+L} W_n^{(i)}\delta_{X_n^{(i)}}(\mathrm{d}x_n). \qquad (11.14)$$

The importance weights, with total mass $\sum_{i=1}^{N+L} W_n^{(i)}$, are then normalised so that they sum to 1, and after resampling N times to obtain $\{X_n'^{(i)}\}_{i=1}^{N}$, the importance weights are set to the constant $(\sum_{i=1}^{N+L} W_n^{(i)})/N$. The authors in [27] also noted that the total number of particles may be varied across iterations, perhaps guided by the total mass of the updated intensity. Convergence results establishing the theoretical validity of the particle PHD filter have been obtained. Convergence of expected error was established in [27], almost sure convergence and convergence of mean-square error were established in [5] and $\mathbb{L}_p$ error bounds, almost sure convergence and a central limit theorem were established in [8].

Because of the low dimension of $\alpha_{n|n}$ (e.g. four when the state descriptor of individual targets contains position and velocity only) even a simple SMC implementation like the one outlined above may suffice. In the case when the observations are informative, and the likelihood functions are concentrated, weight degeneracy can occur with the above implementation and the auxiliary version of [28] has been shown to be more efficient.

For the gradient of the PHD filter, we will use the method proposed in [17, 18] for the closely related problem of computing the gradient of the log-likelihood for a HMM. Let $\overline{\nabla(\Phi\alpha_{n-1|n-1})}$ be a *pointwise* approximation of $\nabla(\Phi\alpha_{n-1|n-1})$, that is $\nabla(\Phi\alpha_{n-1|n-1})(x_n) \approx \overline{\nabla(\Phi\alpha_{n-1|n-1})}(x_n)$, $x_n \in E_1$. (This pointwise approximation is constructed in a sequential manner as detailed below.) One possible construction of a particle approximation to $\nabla\alpha_{n|n-1}(x_n)dx_n$ is the following:

$$\widehat{\nabla\alpha_{n|n-1}}(dx_n) = \frac{1}{N}\sum_{i=1}^{N} \frac{\overline{\nabla(\Phi\alpha_{n-1|n-1})}(X_n^{(i)})}{Q_n(X_n^{(i)})}\delta_{X_n^{(i)}}(x_n)$$

$$+ \frac{1}{L}\sum_{i=N+1}^{N+L} \frac{\nabla\gamma^{\theta}(X_n^{(i)})}{p_n(X_n^{(i)})}\delta_{X_n^{(i)}}(x_n) \qquad (11.15)$$

where

$$Q_n(x_n) = \frac{1}{\sum_{j=1}^{N+L} W_{n-1}^{(j)}} \sum_{i=1}^{N+L} q_n(x_n|X_{n-1}^{(i)})W_{n-1}^{(i)}.$$

Note that the particle set $\{X_n^{(i)}\}_{i=1}^{N}$ in Eq. (11.13) was obtained by sampling Q_n N times. (Assuming Eq. (11.14) is resampled at every time n.) Re-write the particle approximation to $\nabla\alpha_{n|n-1}$ as

$$\widehat{\nabla\alpha_{n|n-1}} = \sum_{i=1}^{N+L} \delta_{X_n^{(i)}}(x_n)A_{n|n-1}^{(i)}W_{n|n-1}^{(i)}$$

where

$$A_{n|n-1}^{(i)} = \frac{1}{N}\frac{\overline{\nabla(\Phi\alpha_{n-1|n-1})}(X_n^{(i)})}{Q_n(X_n^{(i)})}\frac{1}{W_{n|n-1}^{(i)}}, \qquad 1 \le i \le N,$$

$$A_{n|n-1}^{(i)} = \frac{\nabla\gamma^{\theta}(X_n^{(i)})}{\gamma^{\theta}(X_n^{(i)})}, \qquad N+1 \le i \le N+L.$$

The pointwise approximation to $\nabla(\Phi\alpha_{n-1|n-1})$ is

$$\overline{\nabla(\Phi\alpha_{n-1|n-1})}(x_n) = \int_{E_1} \left[\nabla\log f^{\theta}(x_n|x_{n-1})\right]f^{\theta}(x_n|x_{n-1})p_S^{\theta}(x_{n-1})\widehat{\alpha_{n-1|n-1}}(dx_{n-1})$$

$$= \int_{E_1} \left[\nabla\log p_S^{\theta}(x_{n-1})\right]f^{\theta}(x_n|x_{n-1})p_S^{\theta}(x_{n-1})\widehat{\alpha_{n-1|n-1}}(dx_{n-1})$$

$$+ \int_{E_1} f^{\theta}(x_n|x_{n-1})p_S^{\theta}(x_{n-1})\widehat{\nabla\alpha_{n-1|n-1}}(dx_{n-1}).$$

Using Eq. (11.15), the particle approximation to $\nabla \int \psi_{n,r}(x_n) \alpha_{n|n-1}(x_n) dx_n + \nabla \kappa^\theta(y_r)$, for $r = 1, 2, \ldots, m_n$, is

$$
\widehat{\nabla Z}_{n,r} = \int \nabla \psi_{n,r}(x_n) \widehat{\alpha}_{n|n-1}(dx_n) + \int \psi_{n,r}(x_n) \widehat{\nabla \alpha}_{n|n-1}(dx_n) + \nabla \kappa^\theta(y_r)
$$

$$
= \sum_{i=1}^{N+L} \left(\nabla \psi_{n,r}(X_n^{(i)}) + \psi_{n,r}(X_n^{(i)}) A_{n|n-1}^{(i)} \right) W_{n|n-1}^{(i)} + \nabla \kappa^\theta(y_r).
$$

The particle approximation of $\nabla \alpha_{n|n}$ is constructed by re-weighting the particle approximations of $\nabla \alpha_{n|n-1}$ and $\alpha_{n|n-1}$:

$$
\widehat{\nabla \alpha}_{n|n}(dx_n) = -\nabla p_D^\theta(x_n) \widehat{\alpha}_{n|n-1}(dx_n) + \left[\sum_{r=1}^{m_n} \frac{\psi_{n,r}(x_n)}{\widehat{Z}_{n,r}} \left(\nabla \log \psi_{n,r}(x_n) - \frac{\widehat{\nabla Z}_{n,r}}{\widehat{Z}_{n,r}} \right) \right] \widehat{\alpha}_{n|n-1}(dx_n)
$$

$$
+ \left[1 - p_D^\theta(x_n) + \sum_{r=1}^{m_n} \frac{\psi_{n,r}(x_n)}{\widehat{Z}_{n,r}} \right] \widehat{\nabla \alpha}_{n|n-1}(dx_n)
$$

$$
= \sum_{i=1}^{N+L} A_n^{(i)} W_n^{(i)} \delta_{X_n^{(i)}}(dx_n)
$$

where

$$
A_n^{(i)} = A_{n|n-1}^{(i)} + \left[-\nabla p_D^\theta(X_n^{(i)}) + \sum_{r=1}^{m_n} \frac{\psi_{n,r}(X_n^{(i)})}{\widehat{Z}_{n,r}} \left(\nabla \log \psi_{n,r}(X_n^{(i)}) - \frac{\widehat{\nabla Z}_{n,r}}{\widehat{Z}_{n,r}} \right) \right] \frac{W_{n|n-1}^{(i)}}{W_n^{(i)}}.
$$

The SMC estimate of ℓ_{Po} (for the same θ used in the weight calculation above and proposal distributions above) is given by

$$
\widehat{\ell}_{\mathrm{Po},n}(\theta) = - \sum_{k=1}^{n} \left[\int p_D^\theta(x_k) \widehat{\alpha}_{k|k-1}(dx_k) + \int \kappa^\theta(y_k) dy_k \right] + \sum_{k=1}^{n} \sum_{r=1}^{m_k} \log \widehat{Z}_{k,r}, \tag{11.16}
$$

and the estimate of $\nabla \ell_{\mathrm{Po},n}$ is given by

$$
\widehat{\nabla \ell}_{\mathrm{Po},n}(\theta) = - \sum_{k=1}^{n} \int \left[\sum_{i=1}^{N+L} \left(\nabla p_D^\theta(X_k^{(i)}) + p_D^\theta(X_k^{(i)}) A_{k|k-1}^{(i)} \right) W_{k|k-1}^{(i)} + \int \nabla \kappa^\theta(y_k) dy_k \right]
$$

$$
+ \sum_{k=1}^{n} \sum_{r=1}^{m_k} \frac{\widehat{\nabla Z}_{k,r}}{\widehat{Z}_{k,r}}.
$$

Algorithm 11.1 summarises the proposed SMC method for computing $\widehat{\ell}_{\mathrm{Po},n}$ and $\widehat{\nabla \ell}_{\mathrm{Po},n}$. The computational cost of this algorithm, unlike a conventional particle filter, grows quadratically in the number of particles N.

Algorithm 11.1 Particle approximation of the intensity and its gradient

---

At time 0

  for $i = 1$ to N **do**

    $X_0^{(i)} \sim q_0(\cdot), \ W_0^{(i)} = \frac{1}{N}, \ A_0^{(i)} = 0.$

  end for

  Set $\ell_{\mathrm{Po},0} = 0, \ \widehat{\nabla \ell}_{\mathrm{Po}} = [0,\ldots,0] \ (\in \mathbf{R}^d).$

At time $n \geq 1$

  Prediction step:

  for $i = 1$ to N **do**

    $X_n^{(i)} \sim q_n(\cdot | X_{n-1}^{(i)})$

    Set $W_{n|n-1}^{(i)} = \dfrac{f^\theta(X_n^{(i)} | X_{n-1}^{(i)}) p_S^\theta(X_{n-1}^{(i)})}{q_n(X_n^{(i)} | X_{n-1}^{(i)})} W_{n-1|n-1}^{(i)}.$

    Set $A_{n|n-1}^{(i)} W_{n|n-1}^{(i)} = \dfrac{1}{N} \dfrac{\overline{\nabla(\Phi \alpha_{n-1|n-1})}(X_n^{(i)})}{Q_n(X_n^{(i)})}.$

  end for

  for $i = N + 1$ to $N + L$ **do**

    $X_n^{(i)} \sim p_n(\cdot)$

    Set $W_{n|n-1}^{(i)} = \dfrac{1}{L} \dfrac{\gamma^\theta(X_n^{(i)})}{p_n(X_n^{(i)})}, \quad A_{n|n-1}^{(i)} W_{n|n-1}^{(i)} = \dfrac{\nabla \gamma^\theta(X_n^{(i)})}{p_n(X_n^{(i)})}.$

  end for

  for $r = 1$ to m_n **do**

    Set $\widehat{Z}_{n,r} = \sum_{i=1}^{N+L} \psi_{n,r}(X_n^{(i)}) W_{n|n-1}^{(i)} + \kappa^\theta(y_{n,r}).$

    Set $\widehat{\nabla Z}_{n,r} = \sum_{i=1}^{N+L} \left(\nabla \psi_{n,r}(X_n^{(i)}) + \psi_{n,r}(X_n^{(i)}) A_{n|n-1}^{(i)} \right) W_{n|n-1}^{(i)} + \nabla \kappa^\theta(y_r).$

  end for

  Weight step:

  for $i = 1$ to $N + L$ **do**

    Set $W_n^{(i)} = \left[1 - p_D^\theta(X_n^{(i)}) + \sum_{r=1}^{m_n} \dfrac{\psi_{n,r}(X_n^{(i)})}{\widehat{Z}_{n,r}} \right] W_{n|n-1}^{(i)}.$

    Set $A_n^{(i)} = A_{n|n-1}^{(i)} + \left[-\nabla p_D^\theta(X_n^{(i)}) + \sum_{r=1}^{m_n} \dfrac{\psi_{n,r}(X_n^{(i)})}{\widehat{Z}_{n,r}} \left(\nabla \log \psi_{n,r}(X_n^{(i)}) - \dfrac{\widehat{\nabla Z}_{n,r}}{\widehat{Z}_{n,r}} \right) \right] \dfrac{W_{n|n-1}^{(i)}}{W_n^{(i)}}.$

  end for

  Resample $\left\{ X_n^{(i)}, \dfrac{W_n^{(i)}}{\sum_{j=1}^{N+L} W_n^{(j)}} \right\}_{i=1}^{N+L}$ to obtain $\left\{ X_n^{(i)}, \dfrac{\sum_{j=1}^{N+L} W_n^{(j)}}{N} \right\}_{i=1}^{N}.$

  Compute likelihood and likelihood gradient:

  $\widehat{\ell}_{\mathrm{Po},n} = \widehat{\ell}_{\mathrm{Po},n-1} - \int \sum_{i=1}^{N+L} p_D^\theta(X_n^{(i)}) W_{n|n-1}^{(i)} - \int \kappa^\theta(y_n) \mathrm{d}y_n + \sum_{r=1}^{m_n} \log \widehat{Z}_{n,r}$

  $\widehat{\nabla \ell}_{\mathrm{Po},n} = \widehat{\nabla \ell}_{\mathrm{Po},n-1} - \sum_{i=1}^{N+L} \left(\nabla p_D^\theta(X_n^{(i)}) + p_D^\theta(X_n^{(i)}) A_{n|n-1}^{(i)} \right) W_{n|n-1}^{(i)} - \int \nabla \kappa^\theta(y_n) \mathrm{d}y_n + \sum_{r=1}^{m_n} \dfrac{\widehat{\nabla Z}_{n,r}}{\widehat{Z}_{n,r}}.$

11.6   Parameter estimation

11.6.1   Pointwise gradient approximation

Equipped with an approximation of the true likelihood $p(\mathbf{y}_{1:n})$ and its gradient, the parameters of the model may be estimated with a gradient ascent algorithm. This may be done in an offline fashion once a batch of observations, say $\mathbf{y}_{1:T}$, has been received, or in an online manner. This section discusses both these methods of estimation.

Let the true static parameter generating the sequence of observations, to be estimated from the observed data $\{\mathbf{y}_n\}_{n \geq 1}$, be θ^*. Given a record of observations $\{\mathbf{y}_n\}_{n=1}^T$, the log-likelihood may be maximised with the following steepest ascent algorithm. For a discrete time index, $k = 1, 2, \dots$, which does not coincide with the time index of the observation sequence,

$$\theta_{k+1} = \theta_k + a_{k+1} \left. \nabla \ell_{\mathrm{Po},T}(\theta) \right|_{\theta = \theta_k}, \qquad k \geq 1, \tag{11.17}$$

where $\{a_k\}_{k \geq 1}$ is a sequence of small positive real numbers, called the step-size sequence, that should satisfy the following constraints: $\sum_k a_k = \infty$ and $\sum_k a_k^2 < \infty$. One possible choice would be $a_k = k^{-\zeta}$, $0.5 < \zeta < 1$ (e.g. $a_k = k^{-2/3}$); see [16] for background theory on steepest ascent.

For a long observation sequence the computation of the gradient in Eq. (11.17) can be prohibitively expensive. A more attractive alternative would be a recursive procedure in which the data is run through once sequentially. For example, consider the following update scheme:

$$\theta_{n+1} = \theta_n + a_{n+1} \left. \nabla \log p_{\mathrm{Po}}(\mathbf{y}_n | \mathbf{y}_{1:n-1}) \right|_{\theta = \theta_n}.$$

Upon receiving y_n, θ_n is updated in the direction of ascent of the conditional density of this new observation. The algorithm in the present form is not suitable for online implementation due to the need to evaluate the gradient of $\log p_{\mathrm{Po}}(y_n | \mathbf{y}_{1:n-1})$ at the current parameter estimate. Doing so would require browsing through the entire history of observations. This limitation is removed by computing $\left. \nabla \log p_{\mathrm{Po}}(y_n | \mathbf{y}_{1:n-1}) \right|_{\theta = \theta_n}$ recursively using the previous values of the parameter as well. This modification is straightforward; see [18] for the closely related problem of recursive maximum likelihood estimation in HMMs.

In practice, it may be beneficial to start with a constant but small step-size, $a_n = a$ for some initial period $n < n^*$. If the step-size decreases too quickly the algorithm might get stuck at an early stage and fail to come close to a global maximum of the likelihood.

11.6.2   Simultaneous perturbation stochastic approximation (SPSA)

It is also possible to maximise ℓ_{Po} without explicit computation of the gradient using SMC. In particular, a finite difference (FD) approximation of the gradient may be constructed from the noisy evaluations of ℓ_{Po} obtained using SMC. Such approaches are often termed 'gradient-free'; see [23].

Consider the problem of maximising a real-valued function $\theta \in \Theta \to \ell(\theta)$ where Θ is an open subset of $\mathbb{R}$. The first steepest ascent algorithm based on FD approximation of the likelihood gradient is due to [9]. This involves, for example in the two-sided case, noisy evaluation of ℓ at perturbed parameter values $\theta \pm \Delta$ and the subsequent approximation of the gradient at this parameter value, $\nabla \ell(\theta)$, as follows:

$$\widehat{\nabla \ell}(\theta) = \frac{\widehat{\ell}(\theta + \Delta) - \widehat{\ell}(\theta - \Delta)}{2\Delta}.$$

The method can be generalised to the case in which $\Theta \subset \mathbb{R}^d$, $d \geq 1$, by carrying out two noisy evaluations of ℓ for each dimension of Θ, but this can become computationally expensive when the dimension is high. An alternative is the SPSA method of [22], which requires only two noisy evaluations of ℓ, regardless of the dimension of Θ. This method takes its name from the fact that it involves perturbing the multiple components of the vector θ at the same time. In the case of SPSA, the estimate of the gradient at the kth iteration of the gradient ascent algorithm (i.e. the recursion (11.17)) is

$$\widehat{\nabla_p \ell}_{\text{Po},T}(\theta_k) = \frac{\widehat{\ell}_{\text{Po},T}(\theta_k + c_k \Delta_k) - \widehat{\ell}_{\text{Po},T}(\theta_k - c_k \Delta_k)}{2 c_k \Delta_{k,p}}, \qquad p = 1, \ldots, d,$$

where $\Delta_k = [\Delta_{k,1} \; \Delta_{k,2} \; \ldots \; \Delta_{k,d}]^T$ is a random perturbation vector, $\{c_k\}_{k \geq 0}$ is a decreasing sequence of small positive numbers and $\nabla_p \ell_{\text{Po},T}$ is the partial derivative of $\ell_{\text{Po},T}$ w.r.t. the pth component of the parameter θ. The elements of Δ_k are iid, non-zero, symmetrically distributed random variables. In this case we take them to be Bernoulli ± 1 distributed, but it should be noted that some alternative distributions, such as zero-mean Gaussian distributions are theoretically invalid, see [22, Chapter 7] for further background details. The objective function $\ell_{\text{Po},T}(\theta)$ is estimated using the SMC implementation of Section 11.5. Theoretical results guaranteeing convergence of SPSA require the following conditions on the gain sequences ([23]):

$$\forall\, k,\; a_k > 0 \text{ and } c_k > 0; \quad a_k \text{ and } c_k \to 0; \quad \sum_{k=0}^{\infty} a_k = \infty; \quad \sum_{k=0}^{\infty} \frac{a_k^2}{c_k^2} < \infty.$$

Practical choices of these sequences can be based around the following expressions, advocated and related to theoretical properties of SPSA in [23]. For non-negative coefficients a, c, A, ς, τ

$$a_k = \frac{a}{(k + 1 + A)^{\varsigma}}, \qquad c_k = \frac{c}{(k + 1)^{\tau}}.$$

The recommendation is to set $\varsigma = 0.6$ and $\tau = 0.1$ and, as a rule of thumb, to choose A to be 10 per cent or less of the maximum number of allowed iterations of the steepest ascent recursion.

Throughout the simulation study in Section 11.7.3, common random numbers were used for each pair of noisy evaluations of the objective function. It has been shown by [11] that using common random numbers in this way leads to faster convergence of the steepest ascent algorithm. It should be noted that a number of other strategies, such as iterate averaging and adaptive schemes involving estimation of the Hessian matrix, can improve the performance of SPSA. These techniques are beyond the scope of this chapter and are discussed in [23].

Simultaneous perturbation stochastic approximation for maximising $\ell_{\text{Po},T}$ is summarised in Algorithm 11.2.

11.7   Simulation study

11.7.1   Model

The proposed parameter estimation methods are evaluated on a multi-target model with the following characteristics.

Algorithm 11.2 SPSA parameter estimation

At time 1

  Initialise θ_1.

At time $k \geq 1$

  Generate perturbation vector Δ_k.

  Run SMC PHD filter with $\theta = \theta_k + c_k\Delta_k$.

    Compute $\widehat{\ell}_{\mathrm{Po},T}(\theta_k + c_k\Delta_k)$ according to Eq. (11.16).

  Run SMC PHD filter with $\theta = \theta_k - c_k\Delta_k$.

    Compute $\widehat{\ell}_{\mathrm{Po},T}(\theta_k - c_k\Delta_k)$ according to Eq. (11.16).

  Set $\widehat{\nabla\ell}_{\mathrm{Po},T}(\theta_k) = \frac{\widehat{\ell}_{\mathrm{Po},T}(\theta_k+c_k\Delta_k)-\widehat{\ell}_{\mathrm{Po},T}(\theta_k-c_k\Delta_k)}{2c_k}\left[\frac{1}{\Delta_{k,1}} \quad \frac{1}{\Delta_{k,2}} \quad \cdots \quad \frac{1}{\Delta_{k,d}}\right]^T$.

  Set $\theta_{k+1} = \theta_k + a_k\widehat{\nabla\ell}_{\mathrm{Po},T}(\theta_k)$.

    A constant velocity model is assumed for individual targets. The position of a target is specified in two dimensions, restricted to the window $[0, 100] \times [0, 100]$. The state of a single target is thus specified by a four-dimensional vector $X_n = [X_n(1), X_n(2), X_n(3), X_n(4)]^T$, where the variables $(X_n(1), X_n(3))$ specify position and the variables $(X_n(2), X_n(4))$ specify velocity. The state of the single target evolves over time as follows:

$$X_n = \begin{bmatrix} 1 & 1 & 0 & 0 \\ 0 & 1 & 0 & 0 \\ 0 & 0 & 1 & 1 \\ 0 & 0 & 0 & 1 \end{bmatrix} X_{n-1} + \begin{bmatrix} V_n(1) \\ V_n(2) \\ V_n(3) \\ V_n(4) \end{bmatrix},$$

where $V_n(1)$ and $V_n(3)$ are independent Gaussian random variables with mean 0 and standard deviation $\sigma_{xs} = 0.01$; $V_n(2)$ and $V_n(4)$ are also independent Gaussian random variables with mean 0 and standard deviation $\sigma_{xv} = 0.25$. The state of individual targets is a vector in $E_1 = [0, 100] \times \mathbb{R} \times [0, 100] \times \mathbb{R}$. The birth intensity is defined as

$$\gamma^\theta(\cdot) = \Gamma\mathcal{N}(\cdot; \mu_b, \Sigma_b),$$

where $\mathcal{N}(x; \mu_b, \Sigma_b)$ denotes the multivariate normal density with mean μ_b and covariance Σ_b, evaluated at x. For the numerical example,

$$\mu_b = \begin{bmatrix} \mu_{bx} \\ 0 \\ \mu_{by} \\ 0 \end{bmatrix}, \quad \Sigma_b = \begin{bmatrix} \sigma_{bs}^2 & 0 & 0 & 0 \\ 0 & \sigma_{bv}^2 & 0 & 0 \\ 0 & 0 & \sigma_{bs}^2 & 0 \\ 0 & 0 & 0 & \sigma_{bv}^2 \end{bmatrix}.$$

    The x–y position of the target is observed in additive, isotropic Gaussian noise with standard deviation σ_y. The clutter intensity $\kappa(y)$ is uniform on $[0, 100] \times [0, 100]$:

$$\kappa(y) = \kappa\mathbb{I}_{[0,100]\times[0,100]}(y).$$

The probability of detection $p_D(x)$ and survival $p_S(x)$ is assumed constant over E_1. The measurements from individual targets and clutter are vectors in $E_2 = \mathbb{R}^2$. The parameters of the model to be inferred from the data in the numerical studies below are

$$\theta = [\sigma_y, \kappa, \Gamma, \mu_{bx}, \mu_{by}, \sigma_{bs}, \sigma_{bv}, p_D]^T$$

with $(\sigma_{xs}, \sigma_{xv}, p_S)$ assumed known.

11.7.2 Pointwise gradient approximation

The performance of gradient ascent, see Eq. (11.17) with Algorithm 11.1 to estimate the derivative of the likelihood, was evaluated using the following set of parameters: $\theta^* = [5, 4 \times 10^{-4}, 1, 50, 50, 5, 2, 0.9]^T$, i.e. the observation record was generated using these parameter values. For an observation time of length 50, these values for the model would generate, on average, 9 observations per time instant with 4 of them being false, and a total of 50 targets for all the 50 time points. The number of particles used were $N = 400$ and $L = 400$.

Figure 11.1 shows the sequence of iterates generated by Eq. (11.17) for a constant step-size sequence, i.e. $a_k = a$, and for an initial value chosen to be reasonably distant from θ^* (consult the figure for the initial values). The estimated model parameters converge to a vicinity of the true parameters but with some notable discrepancies. (Further details in the discussion to follow.) The smoothness of the traces also indicates that the estimate of the gradient with Algorithm 11.1 has low variance.

To characterise the distribution of the estimated parameters, the experiment was repeated a total of 50 times for observation records of length 15, 50 and 125. In each repetition of the experiment, the targets and observation record were generated again from the model. The distribution of the converged value for the parameters is shown in Fig. 11.2 when the gradient is approximated using Algorithm 11.1 along with their true values as horizontal lines. As can be seen from the box plots, the estimated model parameters do improve with longer observation records. The results are encouraging and are a further

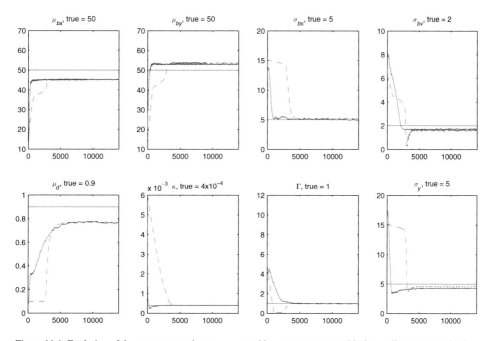

Figure 11.1 Evolution of the parameter estimates generated by steepest ascent with the gradient computed using Algorithm 11.1 (dashed) and SPSA (solid). Observation record length was 25 generated with the model outlined at the start of Section 11.7. Only the values after every 50th step are displayed. True values of parameters are indicated by the horizontal lines and the estimated values of the gradient based method are marked on the y-axis. Notable discrepancies for μ_{bx} and μ_{by} would be outliers for a longer observation record; see box plots in Fig. 11.2.

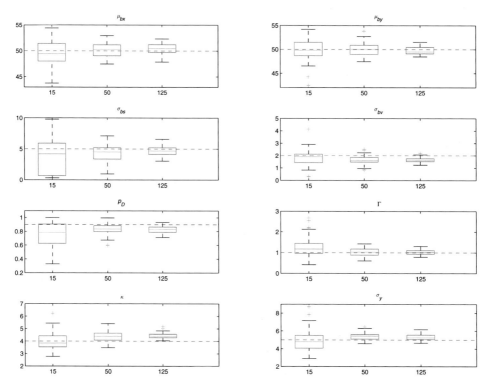

Figure 11.2 Box plots of the converged value of parameter estimates for different observation record lengths. Dashed horizontal lines indicate the true value of the parameters.

verification of the merit of the Poisson approximation of the posterior in Proposition 11.3; thus far the approximation has only been verified by comparing the estimated intensity with the true number of targets in synthetic numerical examples. It is evident from the box plots in Fig. 11.2 that there are small biases for some of the parameters. It is unclear if these are due to the insufficient number of particles used to approximate the intensity function or are inherent to the approximate likelihood itself (see Eq. (11.12)). For example, the box plots indicate a bias in the estimation of the clutter intensity; it is being over estimated. This may be explained by the small number of particles used in the simulation. On average, for an observation record of length 50, there were 9 targets at any particular time instant; 400 particles are not sufficient to follow all the modes of the intensity function (11.8) induced by these targets. Hence the observations generated by the targets are perhaps being accounted for by a higher clutter intensity estimate. We also remark that the converged values of the estimates for μ_{bx} and in μ_{by} in Fig. 11.1 would be outliers for an observation record of length 50. This can be seen from the corresponding box plots in Fig. 11.2.

11.7.3 SPSA

The SPSA scheme, Algorithm 11.2, with Algorithm 11.1 used to obtain a noisy evaluation of the Poisson likelihood, was run on the same data record as the pointwise gradient method, with the same initial conditions. A constant step-size of $a_k = a = 1 \times 10^{-5}$ and $c_k = c = 0.025$ were chosen after a few pilot runs.

A fixed step-size was chosen so as to avoid premature convergence of the algorithm. After 20 000 iterations, and having reached equilibrium, the SPSA scheme resulted in the following parameter values: $\mu_{bx} = 45.2$, $\mu_{by} = 53.6$, $\sigma_{bs} = 5.22$, $\sigma_{bv} = 1.62$, $\kappa = 3.95 \times 10^{-4}$, $p_D = 0.746$, $\Gamma = 1.01$, $\sigma_y = 4.44$. These values compare well with those obtained using the pointwise method and small discrepancies are attributable to the bias arising from the finite difference gradient approximation with c_k held constant. Algorithm 11.1 used $N = 1000$ and $L = 1000$ particles.

The SPSA scheme is simpler to implement than the pointwise gradient method, but it requires choice of both the sequences (a_n) and (c_n) and therefore may need more manual tuning in pilot runs. Also, the computational cost grows linearly with the number of particles.

11.8   Conclusion

The problem of estimating the number of targets and their states, and calibrating the multi-target statistical model is difficult and only approximate inference techniques are feasible ([13]). The focus of this work was the problem of calibrating the model. For this purpose an approximation of the true marginal likelihood of the observed data, i.e. $p(\mathbf{y}_{1:T})$ where T is the final time of the recorded data, was proposed. The estimate of the model parameters was then taken to be the maximising argument, with respect to the model parameters, of this approximation of the true marginal likelihood. A gradient ascent algorithm was used to find the model parameters that maximise the likelihood. Although the approximate likelihood function was not computable exactly, it and its gradient were estimated using SMC. The approximate likelihood function was 'characterised' by a sequence of non-negative functions on E_1, and not the space $\uplus_{k\geq0} E_1^k$, and even a simple SMC implementation can be reasonably efficient. However, compared to 'standard' SMC applications in [7], the SMC implementation was expensive. In particular the computational cost grew quadratically with the number of particles and this limited both the number of particles and the size of the data records in the numerical examples. It was demonstrated in numerical examples that the approximation to the true likelihood was reasonable as the model parameters could be inferred by maximising it. While the results are encouraging, an important issue remains to be addressed. We have not (even empirically) characterised the bias introduced by the likelihood approximation because the exact likelihood cannot be computed. A characterisation of this bias appears to be a challenging problem.

Bibliography

[1] Y. Bar-Shalom and T. E. Fortmann. *Tracking and Data Association*. Mathematics in science and engineering. Academic Press, 1964.

[2] S. Blackman and R. Popoli, editors. *Design and Analysis of Modern Tracking Systems*. Artech House radar library. Artech House, 1999.

[3] O. Cappé, S. J. Godsill and E. Moulines. An overview of existing methods and recent advances in sequential Monte Carlo. *Proceedings of the IEEE*, **96**(5):899 –924, 2007.

[4] D. Clark, A. T. Cemgil, P. Peeling and S. J. Godsill. Multi-object tracking of sinusoidal components in audio with the Gaussian mixture probability hypothesis density filter. In *Proc. of*

IEEE Workshop on Applications of Signal Processing to Audio and Acoustics, 2007.

[5] D. E. Clark and J. Bell. Convergence results for the particle PHD filter. *IEEE Transactions on Signal Processing*, **54**(7):2652–2661, 2006.

[6] P. Del Moral, A. Doucet and A. Jasra. Sequential Monte Carlo methods for Bayesian computation. In *Bayesian Statistics 8*. Oxford University Press, 2006.

[7] A. Doucet, N. de Freitas and N. Gordon, editors. *Sequential Monte Carlo Methods in Practice*. Statistics for Engineering and Information Science. Springer Verlag, 2001.

[8] A. M. Johansen, S. Singh, A. Doucet and B. Vo. Convergence of the SMC implementation of the

PHD filter. *Methodology and Computing in Applied Probability*, **8**(2):265–291, 2006.

[9] J. Kiefer and J. Wolfowitz. Stochastic estimation of the maximum of a regression function. *Annals of Mathematical Statistics*, **23**(3):462–466, 1952.

[10] J. F. C. Kingman. *Poisson Processes*. Oxford Studies in Probability. Oxford University Press, 1993.

[11] N. L. Kleinman, J. C. Spall and D. Q. Naiman. Simulation–based optimisation with stochastic approximation using common random numbers. *Management Science*, **45**(11):1571–1578, 1999.

[12] J. Lund and E. Thonnes. Perfect simulation and inference for point processes given noisy observations. *Computational Statistics*, **19**(2):317–336, 2004.

[13] R. Mahler. *Statistical Multisource-Multitarget Information Fusion*. Artech House, 2007.

[14] R. P. S. Mahler. Multitarget Bayes filtering via first-order multitarget moments. *IEEE Transactions on Aerospace and Electronic Systems*, pages 1152–1178, 2003.

[15] J. Mullane, B. Vo, M. D. Adams and W. S. Wijesoma. A PHD filtering approach to robotic mapping. In *IEEE Conf. on Control, Automation, Robotics and Vision*, 2008.

[16] G. Pflug. *Optimization of Stochastic Models: The Interface between Simulation and Optimization*. Kluwer Academic Publishers, 1996.

[17] G. Poyiadjis, A. Doucet and S. S. Singh. Maximum likelihood parameter estimation using particle methods. In *Proceedings of the Joint Statistical Meeting*, 2005.

[18] G. Poyiadjis, A. Doucet and S. S. Singh. Monte Carlo for computing the score and observed information matrix in state-space models with applications to parameter estimation. Technical Report CUED/ F-INFENG/TR.628, Signal Processing Laboratory, Department of Engineering, University of Cambridge, 2009.

[19] D. Reid. An algorithm for tracking multiple targets. *IEEE Transactions on AutomaticControl*, **24**:843854, 1979.

[20] H. Siddenblath. Multi-target particle filtering for the probability hypothesis density. In

Proceedings of the International Conference on Information Fusion, Cairns, Australia, pages 800–806, 2003.

[21] S. S. Singh, B.-N. Vo, A. Baddeley and S. Zuyev. Filters for spatial point processes. *SIAM Journal on Control and Optimization*, **48**:2275–2295, 2009.

[22] J. C. Spall. Multivariate stochastic approximation using simultaneous perturbation gradient approximation. *IEEE Transations on Automatic Control*, **37**(3):332–341, 1992.

[23] J. C. Spall. *Introduction to Stochastic Search and Optimization*. Wiley-Interscience, 1st edition, 2003.

[24] C. B. Storlie, C. M. Lee, J. Hannig and D. Nychka. Tracking of multiple merging and splitting targets: A statistical perspective (with discussion). *Statistica Sinica*, **19**(1):152, 2009.

[25] B. Vo and W.-K. Ma. The Gaussian mixture probability hypothesis density filter. *IEEE Trans. Signal Processing*, **54**(11):4091–4104, 2006.

[26] B. Vo, S. Singh and A. Doucet. Random finite sets and sequential Monte Carlo methods in multi-target tracking. In *Proceedings of the International Conference on Information Fusion, Cairns, Australia*, pages 792–799, 2003.

[27] B. Vo, S. Singh and A. Doucet. Sequential Monte Carlo methods for multitarget filtering with random finite sets. *IEEE Transactions on Aerospace and Electronic Systems*, **41**(4):1224–1245, 2005.

[28] N. Whiteley, S. Singh and S. Godsill. Auxiliary particle implementation of the probability hypothesis density filter. *IEEE Transactions on Aerospace and Electronic Systems*, **43**(3): 1437–1454, 2010.

[29] J. W. Yoon and S. S. Singh. A Bayesian approach to tracking in single molecule fluorescence microscopy. Technical Report CUED/F-INFENG/TR-612, University of Cambridge, September 2008. Working paper.

[30] T. Zajic and R. P. S. Mahler. Particle-systems implementation of the PHD multitarget tracking filter. In *Proceedings of SPIE*, pages 291–299, 2003.

Contributors

Sumeetpal S. Singh, Signal Processing Laboratory, Department of Engineering, University of Cambridge

Nick Whiteley, Statistics Group, Department of Mathematics, University of Bristol

Simon J. Godsill, Signal Processing Laboratory, Department of Engineering, University of Cambridge

12

Sequential inference for dynamically evolving groups of objects

Sze Kim Pang, Simon J. Godsill, Jack Li, François Septier and Simon Hill

12.1   Introduction

In nature there are many examples of group behaviour arising from the action of individuals without any apparent central coordinator, such as the highly coordinated movements of flocks of birds or schools of fish. These are among the most fascinating phenomena to be found in nature; where the groups seem to turn and manoeuvre as a single unit, changing direction almost instantaneously. Similarly, in man-made activities, there are many cases of group-like behaviour, such as a group of aircraft flying in formation.

There are two principal reasons why it is very helpful to model the behaviour of groups explicitly, as opposed to treating all objects independently as in most multiple target tracking approaches. The first is that the joint tracking of (*a priori*) dependent objects within a group will lead to greater detection and tracking ability in hostile environments with high noise and low detection probabilities. For example, in the radar target tracking application, if several targets are in a group formation, then some information on the positions and speeds of those targets with missing measurements (due to poor detection probability) can be inferred given those targets that are detected. Similarly, if a newly detected target appears close to an existing group, the target can be initialised using the group velocity. Secondly, if it can be determined automatically which targets are moving in formation as a group, it may then be possible to group objects according to intentionality, behaviour and friend or foe status. These are all highly desirable inference outcomes for the modern tracking application. However, little development has been reported on group tracking, with implementation problems resulting from the splitting and merging of groups hindering progress [3].

This chapter presents a new approach to group target detection and tracking by casting the problem in a general probabilistic framework, and modelling the group interactions of dynamic targets and the evolving group structure over time. This permits a unified treatment to various inference goals involving dynamic groupings, from group target detection and tracking to group structure inference. The probabilistic framework is general enough to tackle a variety of applications from target tracking in radar to group stock selection in finance. An algorithm based on Markov chain Monte Carlo (MCMC) [16, 35] will be introduced in Section 12.2 to perform inference for a sequentially evolving distribution such as the filtering distribution. The group tracking problem will be formulated in Section 12.3. Two different group tracking applications will be developed as well. The first application in

Section 12.4 is concerned with tracking groups of vehicles. The second application in Section 12.5 deals with identifying groupings of stocks over time. For each of the applications, a group dynamical model and a group structure transition model will be developed.

12.2 MCMC-particles algorithm

Many problems in engineering and science can be formulated using dynamic state space models. This involves describing the laws governing the changes of some hidden state S_t over time t, and the observations Z_t made as a result of the hidden state. The standard state space system can be specified by a stochastic process with Markovian transitions and independent observations given the state. Then the joint density of the system is given by

$$p(S_{1:t}, Z_{1:t}) = p(S_1)p(Z_1|S_1) \prod_{t'=2}^{t} p(Z_{t'}|S_{t'})p(S_{t'}|S_{t'-1}),$$

where S_t and Z_t are the system state and observation at time t, $p(S_1)$ is the initial distribution of the state, $p(S_t|S_{t-1})$ is the system dynamical model and $p(Z_t|S_t)$ is the observation model. In many modern estimation problems, the state space is almost certainly non-linear and non-Gaussian. There are different numerical methods that can provide solutions to the Bayesian estimation problems. These include adaptive grid-based solutions [9], variational methods [23] which find the best approximating distribution based on Kullback–Leibler divergence, and sequential Monte Carlo methods (also known as particle filters) [22, 10, 34, 6].

Markov chain Monte Carlo is a class of Monte Carlo algorithm which can simulate samples from a probability distribution. This essentially allows Monte Carlo integration through the use of a Markov chain. The general form of the algorithm is known as the Metropolis–Hastings (MH) algorithm (Algorithm 12.1). Here, S is the general state variable, $p(S)$ is the target density and $q(S|S^m)$ is the proposal density. The acceptance probability $\rho(S^m, S^*)$ is given by

$$\rho(S^m, S^*) = f\left(\frac{p(S^*)q(S^m|S^*)}{p(S^m)q(S^*|S^m)}\right),$$

where we defined the Metropolis–Hastings acceptance function $f(x) = \min(1, x)$.

Traditionally, MCMC is used to draw samples in a non-sequential setting. The advantages of MCMC are that it is generally more effective than particle filters in high-dimensional systems and it is easier to design for complex distributions if it can be used in a sequential fashion. This chapter will develop a sequential inference algorithm using MCMC with a particle approximation of the posterior distribution.

12.2.1 Sequential MCMC

This section provides a brief overview of existing MCMC-based algorithms which operate sequentially in time on state space problems such as those described.

Resample-move algorithm

The authors in [15] introduced the resample-move algorithm, which was one of the first methods to make use of MCMC in a sequential state estimation problem. The algorithm takes the output of a standard particle filter after resampling, and applies a MCMC move to

---

Algorithm 12.1 Metropolis–Hastings (MH) algorithm

Initialise S^0. Set $m = 0$.

while $m \leqslant N_{MCMC}$ **do**

    Sample a point $S^* \sim q(S|S^m)$ and u from a uniform distribution $\mathcal{U}(u|0, 1)$.

    if $u \leq \rho(S^m, S^*)$ **then**

        $S^{m+1} = S^*$.

    else

        $S^{m+1} = S^m$.

    end if

    Increment m.

end while

---

each particle using the posterior distribution $p(S_{1:t}|Z_{1:t})$ as the stationary distribution. The main idea is that moving each particle after resampling will improve the diversity of the particle population, and this can only improve the representation of the posterior distribution. As mentioned by [6], the resample-move algorithm does not require each MCMC chain initiated to have a burn-in period. This is because the output of the particle filter is already a reasonable approximation to the posterior filtering distribution. Given each resampled particle $S_{1:t,p}$, the target distribution of the MCMC, Algorithm 12.1, is given by

$$p(S_t|S_{1:t-1,p}, Z_{1:t}) \propto p(Z_t|S_t)p(S_t|S_{t-1,p})p(S_{1:t-1,p}|Z_{1:t-1}).$$

With a proposal function $q(S_t|S_t^m)$, then the acceptance ratio $\rho(S_t^m, S_t^*)$ is given by

$$f\left(\frac{p(S_t^*|S_{1:t-1,p}, Z_{1:t})q(S_t^m|S_t^*)}{p(S_t^m|S_{1:t-1,p}, Z_{1:t})q(S_t^*|S_t^m)}\right) = f\left(\frac{p(Z_t|S_t^*)p(S_t^*|S_{t-1,p})q(S_t^m|S_t^*)}{p(Z_t|S_t^m)p(S_t^m|S_{t-1,p})q(S_t^*|S_t^m)}\right).$$

MCMC-based particle filter

The authors in [24] provide an alternative sequential approach to using MCMC. At each time step t, a single chain is designed to obtain the filtering distribution $p(S_t|Z_{1:t})$. This is achieved by using a set of unweighted particles to represent the density $p(S_{t-1}|Z_{1:t-1})$, that is

$$p(S_{t-1}|Z_{1:t-1}) \approx \hat{p}(S_{t-1}|Z_{1:t-1}) = \sum_{p=1}^{N_p} \frac{1}{N_p}\delta(S_{t-1} - S_{t-1,p}),$$

giving

$$p(S_t|Z_{1:t}) \propto p(Z_t|S_t)\int p(S_t|S_{t-1})p(S_{t-1}|Z_{1:t-1})\mathrm{d}S_{t-1}$$

$$\approx p(Z_t|S_t)\int p(S_t|S_{t-1})\hat{p}(S_{t-1}|Z_{1:t-1})\mathrm{d}S_{t-1} = p(Z_t|S_t)\sum_{p=1}^{N_p} \frac{1}{N_p}p(S_t|S_{t-1,p}). \quad (12.1)$$

Using Eq. (12.1) as the target distribution and proposal $q(S_t|S_t^m)$, the acceptance ratio $\rho(S_t^m, S_t^*)$ is given by (Algorithm 12.1)

$$f\left(\frac{p(S_t^*|Z_{1:t})q(S_t^m|S_t^*)}{p(S_t^m|Z_{1:t})q(S_t^*|S_t^m)}\right) = f\left(\frac{p(Z_t|S_t^*)\sum_{p=1}^{N_p}\frac{1}{N_p}p(S_t^*|S_{t-1,p})q(S_t^m|S_t^*)}{p(Z_t|S_t^m)\sum_{p=1}^{N_p}\frac{1}{N_p}p(S_t^m|S_{t-1,p})q(S_t^*|S_t^m)}\right).$$

This approach is simpler in the sense that only MCMC is used, compared with the two-stage procedure of the resample-move algorithm where a resampling step is necessary. However, the computational demand of the MCMC-based particle filter can become excessive as the number of particles increases owing to the direct Monte Carlo computation of the predictive density at each time step (in general $O(N_p)$ per MCMC iteration).

Practical filter

The practical filter [33] is an algorithm which uses MCMC for sequential state inference and static parameter estimation. By assuming there is a particle approximation to the smoothing distribution $p(S_{t-k}|Z_{1:t-1})$ at time $t - k$, the practical filter runs MCMC for each of the particles to obtain the filtered state from time $t - k + 1$ to t. The practical filter makes the assumption that the lag k is large enough so that $p(S_{t-k}|Z_{1:t})$ can be approximated by $p(S_{t-k}|Z_{1:t-1})$. This is related to the approach by [8], which assumes that future observations are independent of states in the distant past. First, it is assumed that there is a particle approximation to $p(S_{t-k}|Z_{1:t-1})$, i.e.

$$p(S_{t-k}|Z_{1:t-1}) = \sum_{p=1}^{N_p} \frac{1}{N_p} \delta(S_{t-k} - S_{t-k|t-1,p}).$$

Here $S_{t-k|t-1,p}$ is used to represent the pth particle approximating the distribution $p(S_{t-k}|Z_{1:t-1})$. This is to distinguish it from the usual notation $S_{t-k,p}$ which is used to represent the pth particle from the filtering distribution $p(S_{t-k}|Z_{1:t-k})$. A typical approach to obtain $p(S_{t-k}|Z_{1:t-1})$ is to perform MCMC on the distribution $p(S_{1:t-1}|Z_{1:t-1})$. Then $p(S_{t-k}|Z_{1:t})$ can be approximated as follows:

$$p(S_{t-k}|Z_{1:t}) \approx p(S_{t-k}|Z_{1:t-1}) = \sum_{p=1}^{N_p} \frac{1}{N_p} \delta(S_{t-k} - S_{t-k|t-1,p}).$$

The lag-$(k - 1)$ smoothing distribution $p(S_{t-k+1:t}|Z_{1:t})$ is then given by

$$p(S_{t-k+1:t}|Z_{1:t}) = \int p(S_{t-k+1:t}, S_{t-k}|Z_{1:t}) dS_{t-k} = \int p(S_{t-k+1:t}|S_{t-k}, Z_{1:t}) p(S_{t-k}|Z_{1:t}) dS_{t-k}$$

$$\approx \sum_{p=1}^{N_p} \frac{1}{N_p} p(S_{t-k+1:t}|S_{t-k|t-1,p}, Z_{1:t}).$$

The practical filter runs MCMC using $p(S_{t-k+1:t}|S_{t-k|t-1,p}, Z_{1:t})$ as the target distribution for each particle. At the end of each MCMC run after N_{MCMC} iterations, the final state of the MCMC chain is $S_{t-k+1:t}^{N_{MCMC}}$. The $S_{t-k+1}^{N_{MCMC}}$ will be recorded as $S_{t-k+1|t,p}$. The particle set $\{S_{t-k+1|t,p}\}_{p=1}^{N_p}$ will then be the empirical approximation to $p(S_{t-k+1}|Z_{1:t})$. Other empirical approximations are obtained by keeping the appropriate output from the MCMC chains. For example, the filtering distribution can be obtained by keeping $S_t^{N_{MCMC}}$ for each chain.

Particle Markov chain Monte Carlo (PMCMC)

The authors in [1] introduced a class of sequential MCMC (SMC) algorithms to design efficient high-dimensional MCMC proposal distributions. In the simplest case, a MCMC algorithm is designed with the target distribution of $p(S_{1:t}|Z_{1:t})$. At each iteration of the

MCMC, the proposal $S^*_{1:t}$ is constructed by running a SMC algorithm. By considering the artificial joint density of all the random variables generated by the SMC algorithm, [1] showed that the resultant acceptance ratio $\rho(S^m_{1:t}, S^*_{1:t})$ is given by

$$\rho(S^m_{1:t}, S^*_{1:t}) = f\left(\frac{p(S^*_{1:t}|Z_{1:t})q(S^m_{1:t}|Z_{1:t})}{p(S^m_{1:t}|Z_{1:t})q(S^*_{1:t}|Z_{1:t})}\right) = f\left(\frac{\hat{p}(Z_{1:t})^*}{\hat{p}(Z_{1:t})^m}\right),$$

where $\hat{p}(Z_{1:t})^*$ and $\hat{p}(Z_{1:t})^m$ are the estimates of the marginal likelihood $p(Z_{1:t})$ of the respective runs of the SMC algorithm. This approach is computationally intensive as it attempts to draw directly from the joint density of $S_{1:t}$. For problems where $p(S_t|S_{t-1})$ does not admit an analytical expression but can be sampled from, this approach is very useful.

Further developments

In this chapter, an alternative MCMC algorithm for carrying out sequential inference will be developed. This algorithm can be considered a generalisation of some existing sequential MCMC algorithms which allows for further extensions and insights. A special case of it has been applied by [2] to a dynamical model with an expanding parameter space. It has also been applied to imputing missing data from non-linear diffusions [20].

The approach is distinct from the resample-move scheme for particle filters where MCMC is used to rejuvenate degenerate samples after resampling. In this algorithm, no resampling is required. It is less computationally intensive than the MCMC-based particle filter in [24] because it avoids numerical integration of the predictive density at every MCMC iteration. In the simplest case, the framework considered here is the MCMC implementation of the auxiliary particle filter by [32]. But the general algorithm is more flexible than that. It does not make the same approximation of the practical filter in [33], the only approximations are the empirical representation of the posterior density using particles and the assumption that the MCMC run has converged.

12.2.2 Outline of algorithm

Many applications are concerned with inferring the posterior filtering distribution $p(S_t|Z_{1:t})$ in a sequential fashion as observations arrive. Here, to develop the MCMC-particles algorithm [30, 31], we instead consider the general joint distribution of S_t and S_{t-1}

$$p(S_t, S_{t-1}|Z_{1:t}) \propto p(S_{t-1}|Z_{1:t-1})p(S_t|S_{t-1})p(Z_t|S_t). \tag{12.2}$$

In [2] the authors used a similar form where the target distribution for the MCMC is $\pi(\Phi_t, \varepsilon_{t-1}|D_{t-1}, E_{t-1}, F_t)$, this is equivalent with $S_t = \Phi_t$, $S_{t-1} = \varepsilon_{t-1}$, and $Z_{1:t} = \{D_{t-1}, E_{t-1}, F_t\}$. The authors in [20] were interested in the imputation values S_t of a discretely observed diffusion process with parameters θ. The target distribution for their MCMC is given by $p(S_t, S_{t-1}, \theta|Z_{1:t}) \propto p(S_{t-1}, \theta|Z_{1:t-1})p(S_t, Z_t|S_{t-1}, Z_{t-1}, \theta)$. A MCMC procedure will be used to draw inference from this complex distribution, i.e. (12.2) is the target distribution. Clearly, there is no closed-form representation of the posterior distribution $p(S_{t-1}|Z_{1:t-1})$ at time $t - 1$. Instead it is approximated by an empirical distribution based on the current particle set, $\hat{p}(S_{t-1}|Z_{1:t-1})$ (assumed uniformly weighted), that is

$$p(S_{t-1}|Z_{1:t-1}) \approx \hat{p}(S_{t-1}|Z_{1:t-1}) = \sum_{p=1}^{N_p} \frac{1}{N_p}\delta(S_{t-1} - S_{t-1,p}),$$

where N_p is the number of particles and p is the particle index. Then, having made many joint draws from Eq. (12.2) using an appropriate MCMC scheme, the converged MCMC output for variable S_t can be extracted to give an updated marginalised particle approximation to $p(S_t|Z_{1:t})$. In this way, sequential inference can be achieved. Instead of drawing directly from the discrete distribution, a kernel density estimate of $\hat{p}(S_{t-1}|Z_{1:t-1})$ can be used [27, 20]. This can increase the diversity of the particle samples. However, a kernel with appropriate bandwidth must be selected. In high-dimensional state spaces, it may not be easy to select a kernel which preserves the correlation structure of the various states. In general, the empirical approximation can be extended further back in time to $t - k$. This will result in a lag-k smoothing distribution

$$p(S_{t-k:t}|Z_{1:t}) \propto p(S_{t-k}|Z_{1:t-k}) \prod_{t'=t-k+1}^{t} p(S_{t'}|S_{t'-1})p(Z_{t'}|S_{t'}).$$

The above equation can be the target distribution of an MCMC implementation, in which it is possible to obtain an estimate of the smoothing distributions such as $p(S_{t-k+1}|Z_{1:t})$. In this case, at each time step t, the filtering distribution output $p(S_t|Z_{1:t})$ can be stored for use at k time steps later.

   This chapter focuses on the joint distribution (12.2) for filtering applications. At the mth MCMC iteration, a mixture sampling procedure is adopted. This involves a joint MH proposal step with probability P_J, where both S_t and S_{t-1} are updated jointly, as well as individual refinement Metropolis-within-Gibbs steps [35] with probability $1 - P_J$, where S_t and S_{t-1} are updated individually. This procedure is detailed in Algorithm 12.2 and will be referred to as the MCMC-particles algorithm. From Tierney's results [41], the resultant MCMC chain produced is irreducible and aperiodic. This follows from the fact the joint proposal step can explore the joint state space of the target distribution. As with all MCMC, the burn-in of the chain is required to ensure proper convergence. Chain thinning can be used at the expense of running the sampler longer to give the chain more time to mix. In the algorithm, the individual refinement step for S_{t-1} can have low acceptance probabilities ρ_2. This is because in high-dimensional systems the empirical predictive density

$$\hat{p}(S_t|Z_{1:t-1}) \propto \int p(S_t|S_{t-1})\hat{p}(S_{t-1}|Z_{1:t-1})dS_{t-1} \propto \sum_{p=1}^{N_p} \frac{1}{N_p} p(S_t|S_{t-1,p})$$

may be highly disjoint. In most cases, this step can be omitted with little impact on the algorithm as S_{t-1} can still be moved in the joint proposal step. This will be seen in group tracking simulations in later chapters.

   As a comparison, [2] used the individual refinement step to move the current state S_t as well as the particle representation S_{t-1}. As highlighted above, this can potentially lead to poor mixing in high-dimensional problems due to the highly disjoint predictive density of the particle representation. On the other hand, [20] used the joint draw only to move the MCMC chain. This can potentially reduce the effectiveness of the MCMC as refinement moves are not employed to explore the structured probabilistic space.

12.2.3 Toy example

To study the MCMC-particles algorithm we consider a linear Gaussian state space model:

$$S_t \sim N(S_t|FS_{t-1}, Q_W), S_1 \sim N(0, Q_W), \tag{12.4}$$
$$Z_t \sim N(Z_t|HS_t, Q_V), \tag{12.5}$$

where $F = 0.9 \times I_{20}$, $Q_W = 0.25 \times I_{20}$, $H = I_{20}$, $Q_V = 0.5 \times I_{20}$ and $N(\cdot|\mu, Q)$ is a Gaussian distribution with mean μ and covariance Q. Here, $S_t = [S_{t,1}, \ldots, S_{t,20}]$, and I_d is the

---

Algorithm 12.2 MCMC-particles algorithm

Initialise particle set $\{S_{0,p}\}_{p=1}^{N_p}$, $\hat{p}(S_0) = \sum_{p=1}^{N_p} \frac{1}{N_p}\delta(S_0 - S_{0,p})$.

for $t = 1 : T$ **do**

    for $m = 1 : N_{MCMC}$ **do**

        Draw $u \sim \mathcal{U}(u|0, 1)$.

        if $u < P_J$ **then**

            A joint proposal is made for $\{S_t^m, S_{t-1}^m\}$ using a MH step with acceptance probability

$$\rho_1 = f\left(\frac{p(S_t^*, S_{t-1}^*|Z_{1:t})q_2(S_t^{m-1}|S_t^*)q_1(S_{t-1}^{m-1}|S_{t-1}^*)}{p(S_t^{m-1}, S_{t-1}^{m-1}|Z_{1:t})q_2(S_t^*|S_t^{m-1})q_1(S_{t-1}^*|S_{t-1}^{m-1})}\right).$$

            Accept $\{S_t^m, S_{t-1}^m\} = \{S_t^*, S_{t-1}^*\}$ with probability ρ_1

        else

            S_{t-1}^m and S_t^m are refined in a series of Metropolis-within-Gibbs steps.
            The acceptance probability for the refining step of $\{S_{t-1}^*\}$ is given by

$$\rho_2 = f\left(\frac{p(S_{t-1}^*|S_t^{m-1}, Z_{1:t})q_3(S_{t-1}^{m-1}|S_{t-1}^*)}{p(S_{t-1}^{m-1}|S_t^{m-1}, Z_{1:t})q_3(S_{t-1}^*|S_{t-1}^{m-1})}\right).$$

            Accept $\{S_{t-1}^m\} = \{S_{t-1}^*\}$ with probability ρ_2.
            The acceptance probability for the refining step of $\{S_t^*\}$ is given by

$$\rho_3 = f\left(\frac{p(S_t^*|S_{t-1}^m, Z_{1:t})q_4(S_t^{m-1}|S_t^*)}{p(S_t^{m-1}|S_{t-1}^m, Z_{1:t})q_4(S_t^*|S_t^{m-1})}\right). \tag{12.3}$$

            Accept $\{S_t^m\} = \{S_t^*\}$ with probability ρ_3.

        end if

        After a burn-in period of N_{burn}, keep every N_{thin} MCMC output $S_{t,p} = S_t^m$ as the new particle set for approximating $p(S_t|Z_{1:t})$, i.e. $\hat{p}(S_t|Z_{1:t}) = \sum_{p=1}^{N_p} \frac{1}{N_p}\delta(S_t - S_{t,p})$.

    end for

end for

$d \times d$ identity matrix. Superficially, a linear Gaussian state space model does not seem to be a particularly difficult problem, since the optimal filtering distribution $p(S_t|Z_{1:t})$ can be obtained from Kalman filtering. However for simulation-based inference, the current challenge is still to be able to do accurate joint inference for high-dimensional systems. The above example is not easy for simulation-based inference precisely because of its high dimensionality of 20. Here, a comparison of simulation-based estimates with the optimal Kalman filter output can provide better insights into the effectiveness of different algorithms than just a comparison with the true states. This problem can also be treated as d independent filtering problems. Here, however, we treat it as a joint inference problem, using the d independent particle filters as a baseline for comparisons. It could be argued that correlated structures reduce the effective dimensionality and are hence easier targets for filtering.

12.2.4   Inference algorithm

The MCMC-particles algorithm is used to design the inference algorithm for the toy example. For the refinement stage of S_t in Eq. (12.3), the 20 variables $S_{t,i}$ are randomly permuted at each MCMC iteration, and updated in 5 blocks of 4 variables each. At the mth MCMC iteration, the joint proposal as well as individual refinement proposals are given below.

1. For the joint proposal $\{S_t^m, S_{t-1}^m\}$, the target distribution is $p(S_t, S_{t-1}|Z_{1:t})$. The proposal function for the joint step is given by

$$q_1(S_{t-1}|S_{t-1}^{m-1}) = \hat{p}(S_{t-1}|Z_{1:t-1}), \quad q_2(S_t|S_t^{m-1}) = p(S_t|S_{t-1}).$$

Here, $\hat{p}(S_{t-1}|Z_{1:t-1})$ is the particle approximation to the posterior distribution $p(S_{t-1}|Z_{1:t-1})$ at $t-1$; $p(S_t, |S_{t-1})$ is the state transition density given by Eq. (12.4). The acceptance probability ρ_1 is given by

$$f\left(\frac{p(S_t^*, S_{t-1}^*|Z_{1:t})q_2(S_t^{m-1}|S_t^*)q_1(S_{t-1}^{m-1}|S_{t-1}^*)}{p(S_t^{m-1}, S_{t-1}^{m-1}|Z_{1:t})q_2(S_t^*|S_t^{m-1})q_1(S_{t-1}^*|S_{t-1}^{m-1})} \right) = f\left(\frac{p(Z_t|S_t^*)}{p(Z_t|S_t^{m-1})} \right).$$

2. For the individual refinement steps, the particle state S_{t-1} is refined first, then this is followed by each of the random blocks S_{t,iB_4}. Here, $iB_4 = \{i_1, i_2, i_3, i_4\}$ represents one of the random blocks.

   (a) The target distribution for the particle refinement step is $p(S_{t-1}|S_t^{m-1}, Z_{1:t})$. The proposal function $q_3(S_{t-1}|S_{t-1}^{m-1})$ is given by

   $$q_3(S_{t-1}|S_{t-1}^{m-1}) = \hat{p}(S_{t-1}|Z_{1:t-1}).$$

   The acceptance probability ρ_2 for the particle refinement is given by

   $$f\left(\frac{p(S_{t-1}^*|S_t^{m-1}, Z_{1:t})q_3(S_{t-1}^{m-1}|S_{t-1}^{m-1})}{p(S_{t-1}^{m-1}|S_t^{m-1}, Z_{1:t})q_3(S_{t-1}^*|S_{t-1}^{m-1})} \right) = f\left(\frac{p(S_t^{m-1}|S_{t-1}^*)}{p(S_t^{m-1}|S_{t-1}^{m-1})} \right).$$

   (b) For the individual refining step for each random block S_{t,iB_4}, the target distribution is given by $p(S_{t,iB_4}|S'_{t,\backslash iB_4}, S_{t-1}^m, Z_{1:t})$. The proposal function $q_4(S_{t,iB_4}|S_{t,iB_4}^{m-1})$ is given by

   $$q_4(S_{t,iB_4}|S_{t,iB_4}^{m-1}) = p(S_{t,iB_4}|S'_{t,\backslash iB_4}, S_{t-1}^m).$$

   Here, S'_t represents all the individual state variables currently in the MCMC chain, as each random block of variables gets updated progressively. Then, $S'_{t,\backslash iB_4}$ is similar to S'_t, except it excludes the iB_4 variables; $p(S_{t,iB_4}|S'_{t,\backslash iB_4}, S_{t-1}^m)$ is a standard multivariate conditional Gaussian distribution, owing to the original Gaussian distribution of the transition density $p(S_t|S_{t-1})$ (Eq. (12.4)).

   The acceptance probability ρ_3 for the refinement of each individual random block is given by

   $$f\left(\frac{p(S_{t,iB_4}^*|S'_{t,\backslash iB_4}, S_{t-1}^m, Z_{1:t})q_4(S_{t,iB_4}^{m-1}|S_{t,iB_4}^*)}{p(S_{t,iB_4}^{m-1}|S'_{t,\backslash iB_4}, S_{t-1}^m, Z_{1:t})q_4(S_{t,iB_4}^*|S_{t,iB_4}^{m-1})} \right) = f\left(\frac{p(Z_t|S'_{t,\backslash iB_4}, S_{t,iB_4}^*)}{p(Z_t|S'_t)} \right).$$

The parameters for the inference algorithm can be found in Table 12.1.

12.2.5 Comparison with sequential importance resampling particle filter

The MCMC-particles algorithm is compared with a standard sequential importance resampling (SIR) particle filter (Algorithm 12.3) [6, 34]. The prior (12.4) is used as the importance density, i.e. $q(S_t|S_{t-1,p}, Z_t) = p(S_t|S_{t-1})$. Residual resampling is used at the

Tracking parameter	Symbol	Value
Number of particles	N_p	6000
Number of burn-in iterations	N_{burn}	600
Chain thinning	N_{thin}	2
Probability for joint proposal step	P_J	0.75

Table 12.1 Parameters for MCMC-particles algorithm for the toy example.

Algorithm 12.3 Sequential importance resampling particle filter

---

Initialise particle set $\{S_{0,p}, \frac{1}{N_p}\}_{p=1}^{N_p}$, $p(S_0) = \sum_{p=1}^{N_p} \frac{1}{N_p} \delta(S_0 - S_{0,p})$.

for $t = 1 : T$ **do**

  for $p = 1 : N_p$ **do**

    Propose $S_{t,p} \sim q(S_t | S_{t-1,p}, Z_t)$.

    Calculate

$$w_{t,p} = w_{t-1,p} \times \frac{p(Z_t | S_{t,p}) p(S_{t,p} | S_{t-1,p})}{q(S_{t,p} | S_{t-1,p}, Z_t)}.$$

  end for

  Normalise the weights by $w_{t,p} = \frac{w_{t,p}}{\sum_{p=1}^{N_p} w_{t,p}}$.

  Calculate $\hat{N}_{eff}$ [25] using

$$\hat{N}_{eff} = \frac{1}{\sum_{p=1}^{N} w_{t,p}^2}.$$

  if $\hat{N}_{eff} < N_{thr}$ **then**

    Resample the particle set $\{S_{t,p}, w_{t,p}\}_{p=1}^{N_p}$ to obtain a new approximating particle set

    $\{S_{t,p}, \frac{1}{N_p}\}_{p=1}^{N_p}$, i.e. $p(S_t | Z_{1:t}) = \sum_{p=1}^{N_p} \frac{1}{N_p} \delta(S_t - S_{t,p})$.

  end if

end for

Tracking parameter	Symbol	Value
Number of particles	N_p	22000
Effective sample size threshold	N_{thr}	$0.9N_p$

Table 12.2 Parameters for SIR particle filter for the toy example.

---

resampling stage, when the effective sample size N_{eff} [25] is lower than a threshold N_{thr}. Table 12.2 shows the parameters used for the SIR particle filter.

    Both algorithms are implemented in Matlab. The parameters for each algorithm are chosen such that the computational time is approximately equal. The initial distribution $p(X_1)$ is assumed known. A total of 20 runs of the comparison are conducted. For each run, the states and observations are generated from Eqs. (12.4) and (12.5) respectively. A Kalman filter is used to compute the optimal filtering distribution. The MCMC-particles algorithm and the SIR particle filter are used to draw samples of the joint state S_t given the observations. The estimated mean by each of the algorithms is then compared with the Kalman mean. The root mean square error (RMSE) is computed across all 20 runs, 20 dimensions and time samples from 11 to 100.

    Figures 12.1(a) and 12.1(b) show the dispersion of error of the mean estimates of the two algorithms with respect to the optimal Kalman mean over time. The MCMC-particles

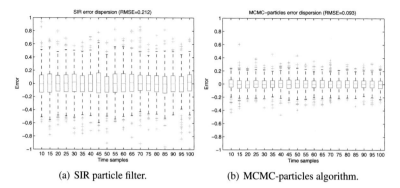

(a) SIR particle filter.   (b) MCMC-particles algorithm.

Figure 12.1 Box plots of the estimation error over time with respect to Kalman mean for SIR particle filter and MCMC-particles algorithm. It can be seen that the error dispersion is higher for SIR particle filter.

Algorithm	RMSE	Distinct particles sampled
SIR particle filter	0.212	5.07%
MCMC-particles algorithm	0.093	1.81%
SIR particle filters (independent)	0.017	65.35%

Table 12.3 This table compares the RMSE and proportion of distinct particles sampled by the SIR particle filter, the MCMC-particles algorithm and the independent SIR particle filters.

Algorithm estimates are tighter and closer to the optimal Kalman mean. This is also confirmed by Fig. 12.2 (columns 1 and 4) and Table 12.3. The better performance of the MCMC-particles algorithm in this example can probably be explained by the introduction of the individual refinement stage. This local refinement allows the output of the MCMC to better approximate the posterior distribution.

For comparison purposes, 20 independent SIR particle filters are used to track the 20 independent variables of the toy example. Each of these particle filters uses 2000 particles, which require approximately the same computational resources overall as the joint SIR particle filter. The average RMSE over 20 runs is 0.017 (Table 12.3), far better than both the MCMC-particles algorithm and the joint SIR particle filter. This clearly illustrates the challenge of doing joint inference over large dimensions. Table 12.3 also shows the average proportion of distinct particles sampled by the respective algorithm at each time step. For the SIR particle filter, it is the percentage of distinct particles that survived the resampling step. For the MCMC-particles algorithm, it is the percentage of distinct particles proposed and accepted by the algorithm. The joint SIR particle filter on average kept 5.07% distinct particles, while the MCMC-particles algorithm kept 1.81% distinct particles. This is somewhat counter-intuitive as it is generally thought that having a larger proportion of distinct particles sampled will provide better results. It seems that the MCMC-particles algorithm may be more efficient at producing better particles. For comparison, the average proportion of distinct particles sampled for the independent SIR particle filters is 65.35%.

Due to the flexible implementation of the MCMC-particles algorithm, advances in both MCMC and particle filter literature can be introduced to improve the algorithm. This can range from choosing better particles in the auxiliary particle filter [32], to using multiple interacting chains [14] or quasi Monte Carlo methods.

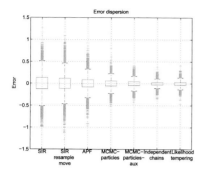

Figure 12.2 Box plot of the estimation error with respect to the Kalman mean, comparing all seven algorithms.

12.2.6 Comparison with other algorithms

Auxiliary particle filter

The auxilary particle filter (APF) was first introduced by [32]. The main idea of the APF is to perform a biased resampling procedure of the set of particles at time $t - 1$ such that more particles are obtained at places where there are observations at time t. This gives a better chance of simulating particles that might have low weights at time $t - 1$ (for example due to observation outliers), but potentially high weights at time t. The bias induced at the resampling stage is undone exactly at time t by appropriate correction of the particle weights. The auxiliary particle filter is summarised in Algorithm 12.4. From the perspective of the MCMC-particles algorithm, this 'biased' particle selection can be viewed as a special form of proposal densities $q_1(S_{t-1})$ and $q_3(S_{t-1})$ in Algorithm 12.2. The original paper on APF [32] mentioned the use of MCMC in a similar way. The equivalent proposal densities are given by

$$q_1(S_{t-1}|S_{t-1}^{m-1}) = q_3(S_{t-1}|S_{t-1}^{m-1}) = \sum_{p=1}^{N_p} \frac{L_p}{\sum_{p=1}^{N_p} L_p} \delta(S_{t-1} - S_{t-1,p}),$$

where L_p is given in Algorithm 12.4. The MCMC-particles algorithm implementation with the above proposal densities will be called the MCMC-particles-auxiliary algorithm. The summary is shown in Algorithm 12.5.

Multiple chains

In many inference problems, a single MCMC chain may exhibit slow mixing behaviour, i.e. it is slow to traverse the state space occupied by the target distribution. This is frequently due to multimodal distributions or very peaky likelihood functions. To improve mixing, one commonly used technique is to run multiple chains of MCMC, and introduce interactions between the chains. In [14] the authors introduced one of the earliest examples of multiple chain MCMC by using the product space formulation.

In this section, two further extensions are made to the MCMC-particles-auxiliary algorithm. The first extension is to run multiple independent chains of the single chain Algorithm 12.5. When a particle output is required, it is selected randomly from the state of one of the chains. There is no other interaction between the chains. This extension is summarised in Algorithm 12.6.

The second extension is to run multiple chains of Algorithm 12.5, with each of the chains having a different target distribution. For example, the target distribution $p_c(S)$ for

---

Algorithm 12.4 Auxiliary particle filter (APF)

Initialise particle set $\{S_{0,p}, \frac{1}{N_p}\}_{p=1}^{N_p}$.

for $t = 1 : T$ **do**

  for $p = 1 : N_p$ **do**

    Calculate $L_p = p(Z_t | E(S_t | S_{t-1,p}))$.

  end for

  Calculate $\forall p \; \tilde{w}_{t-1,p} = \frac{w_{t-1,p} L_p}{\sum_{p=1}^{N_p} w_{t-1,p} L_p}$.

  Resample the particle set $\{S_{t-1,p}, \tilde{w}_{t-1,p}\}_{p=1}^{N_p}$ to obtain $\{S_{t-1,p}, \frac{1}{L_p}\}_{p=1}^{N_p}$.

  for $p = 1 : N_p$ **do**

    Propose $S_{t,p} \sim q(S_t | S_{t-1,p}, Z_t)$.

    Calculate

$$w_{t,p} = \frac{1}{L_p} \frac{p(Z_t | S_{t,p}) p(S_{t,p} | S_{t-1,p})}{q(S_{t,p} | S_{t-1,p}, Z_t)}.$$

  end for

  Normalise the weights by $w_{t,p} = \frac{w_{t,p}}{\sum_{p=1}^{N_p} w_{t,p}}$.

end for

Algorithm 12.5 MCMC-particles-auxiliary algorithm

Run the MCMC-particles algorithm (Algorithm 12.2) using the proposal $q_1(S_{t-1} | S_{t-1}^{m-1}) = q_3(S_{t-1} | S_{t-1}^{m-1}) = \sum_{p=1}^{N_p} \frac{L_p}{\sum_{p=1}^{N_p} L_p} \delta(S_{t-1} - S_{t-1,p})$.

Algorithm 12.6 MCMC-particles-auxiliary algorithm with independent chains

---

Initialise and run N_c independent chains $\{S_{t-1}^c, S_t^c\}$ of the MCMC-particles-auxiliary algorithm (Algorithm 12.5).

When an output is required, select it randomly from one of the chains, i.e. $S_{t,p} = S_t^{c,m}$.

Tracking parameter	Symbol	Value
Number of particles	N_p	6000
Number of chains	N_c	4
Number of burn-in iterations	N_{burn}	600
Chain thinning	N_{thin}	2
Probability for joint proposal step	P_J	0.75

Table 12.4 Parameters for MCMC-particles-auxiliary algorithm with independent chains for the toy example.

Tracking parameter	Symbol	Value
Number of particles	N_p	6000
Number of chains	N_C	4
Number of burn-in iterations	N_{burn}	600
Chain thinning	N_{thin}	2
Probability for joint proposal step	P_J	0.75
Probability for exchange move	P_{Ex}	0.40

Table 12.5 Parameters for MCMC-particles-auxiliary algorithm with likelihood tempering for the toy example.

Tracking parameter	Symbol	Value
Number of particles	N_p	22000
Number of MCMC iterations per particle	N_R	1

Table 12.6 Parameters for SIR particle filter with resample-move step for the toy example.

chain c can be a tempered version of the original distribution $p(S)$, $p_c(S) \propto (p(S))^{\upsilon_c}$, for $\upsilon_c \in (0, 1]$.

The product space formulation of multiple chain MCMC is very flexible. Instead of tempering the entire distribution, one can choose to temper only the likelihood function (see Eq. (12.7)). For the toy example, for chain c, the observation covariance is flattened by multiplying by $c^{\frac{1}{2}}$ in Eq. (12.6). The joint distribution of the entire MCMC (12.8) is then given by the product of the individual tempered distributions (12.7). An exchange move is introduced to provide mixing and information exchange across the different chains. Algorithm 12.7 summarises the MCMC-particles-auxiliary algorithm with likelihood tempering.

Algorithm 12.7 MCMC-particles-auxiliary algorithm with likelihood tempering

---

Initialise and run N_c chains $\{S^c_{t-1}, S^c_t\}$ of the MCMC-particles-auxiliary algorithm (Algorithm 12.5), each having a target distribution given by Eq. (12.7).

After each MCMC iteration of all the chains, an exchange move is proposed randomly with probability P_{Ex}. Select c_1 and c_2 from the N_c chains randomly. The acceptance probability for the exchange move is given by

$$\rho_4 = f\left(\frac{p_{c_1}(Z_t|S^{c_2,m}_t)p_{c_2}(Z_t|S^{c_1,m}_t)}{p_{c_1}(Z_t|S^{c_1,m}_t)p_{c_2}(Z_t|S^{c_2,m}_t)}\right).$$

Exchange $\{S^{c_1,m}_t, S^{c_1,m}_{t-1}\}$ and $\{S^{c_2,m}_t, S^{c_2,m}_{t-1}\}$ with probability ρ_4.

When an output is required from the algorithm, it is selected from chain 1, i.e. $S_{t,p} = S^{1,m}_t$.

$$p_c(Z_t|S^c_t) = \text{N}(S^c_t, 0.5c^{\frac{1}{2}}I_{20}), \tag{12.6}$$

$$p_c(S^c_t, S^c_{t-1}|Z_{1:t}) \propto p(S^c_{t-1}|Z_{1:t-1})p(S^c_t|S^c_{t-1})p_c(Z_t|S^c_t), \tag{12.7}$$

$$p(S^1_t, S^1_{t-1}, \cdots, S^{N_c}_t, S^{N_c}_{t-1}|Z_{1:t}) \propto \prod_{c=1}^{N_c} p_c(S^c_t, S^c_{t-1}|Z_{1:t}). \tag{12.8}$$

Resample-move particle filter

For comparison, we also use the standard SIR particle filter with a resample-move step to improve the diversity of the particles. This is summarised in Algorithm 12.8. Table 12.6 shows the parameters used for the SIR particle filter.

Algorithm 12.8 Sequential importance resampling particle filter with resample-move step

---

Initialise and run a standard SIR particle filter algorithm (Algorithm 12.3).

After the resampling step, for each particle, initialise and run N_R iterations of the MCMC refinement Step 2(b) (page 252).

Comparison of results

The results from the previous seven algorithms are summarised in Table 12.7 and the error dispersion in Fig. 12.2. In general, the MCMC-particles algorithm and its various extensions perform well compared to SIR and APF on this high-dimensional toy example. The best performance is given by the MCMC-particles-auxiliary algorithm with independent chains, though at the expense of approximately four times the computational resources of the single chain MCMC-particles algorithm. The SIR particle filter with resample-move step also uses approximately five times the computational resources, but only provided small improvement to the result.

12.3 Group tracking

In many applications, especially military ones, targets tend to travel in groups or formations. This information can be exploited to provide better detection and tracking estimates. However, it is not easy to obtain a complete set of probabilistic models which can describe the group dynamics and group structure changes over time. As a result, [3] stated that despite the potential advantages of the group tracking approach, implementation problems such as recognising groups, incorporating new members into the groups, and splitting and merging of groups have discouraged the further development of group tracking methods. Nevertheless, [3] also mentioned that some form of group tracking is the best approach for the tracking environment with many closely spaced targets. Closely spaced targets frequently result in merged measurements. A complete probabilistic tracking model needs to be able to deal with this as well.

In dynamic group tracking, first, the targets themselves are dynamic, i.e. they have some probabilistic models specifying their evolving motion. Second, the targets' grouping can change over time. For example, a group of four targets can split into two groups of two targets each. Third, the assignment of a target to a group affects the probabilistic properties of the target dynamics. Fourth, the group statistics belong to a second hidden layer. The

Algorithm	RMSE	Distinct particles sampled	Joint proposal acceptance rate	Particle refinement acceptance rate
SIR particle filter	0.212	5.07%	–	–
SIR particle filters with resample-move	0.196	4.88%	–	–
Auxiliary particle filter	0.138	2.71%	–	–
MCMC-particles algorithm	0.093	1.81%	0.76%	1.51%
MCMC-particles-auxiliary algorithm	0.069	3.65%	3.28%	9.81%
MCMC-particles-auxiliary algorithm with independent chains	0.046	8.02%	3.32%	8.04%
MCMC-particles-auxiliary algorithm with likelihood tempering	0.055	7.38%	3.91%	8.78%
SIR particle filters (independent)	0.017	65.35%	–	–

Table 12.7 This table summarises the results of the seven different algorithms applied to the toy example, as well as the independent SIR particle filters. It compares the RMSE, the proportion of distinct particles sampled, the acceptance rate for the joint proposal step (page 252 Step 1), as well as the acceptance rate for the particle refinement step (page 252 Step 2(a)).

target statistics belong to the first hidden layer and the observation process usually depends only on the targets. Finally, the number of targets is typically unknown.

We introduce a general probabilistic framework for group models [30, 31] that incorporates these ideas. At time t, let X_t represent all the individual targets' states, and G_t the group structure or configuration with function similar to the cluster label used in static clustering problems. Finally let Z_t represent the observations (described in more detail in later sections). The dynamic group tracking model described above can then be written as

$$p(X_{1:t}, G_{1:t}, Z_{1:t}) = p(X_1|G_1)p(G_1)p(Z_1|X_1)$$

$$\times \prod_{t'=2}^{t} p(X_{t'}|X_{t'-1}, G_{t'}, G_{t'-1})p(G_{t'}|G_{t'-1}, X_{t'-1})p(Z_{t'}|X_{t'}), \quad (12.9)$$

where the observations, targets and grouping of targets are assumed Markovian as in standard tracking problems. The main components of the group tracking model involve the following two dynamical models, the group dynamical model $p(X_t|X_{t-1}, G_t, G_{t-1})$ and the group structure transition model $p(G_t|G_{t-1}, X_{t-1})$.

The group dynamical model describes the motion of members in a group. It accounts for the interactions that exist between different members. These can be interactions that keep a group together, as well as other repulsive mechanisms that prevent members from occupying the same physical space. Since many physical phenomena can be well described using continuous time stochastic processes, ideally, such models should be developed from a continuous time basis and put into an equivalent discrete time formulation. Owing to the linear and Gaussian form of the group dynamical model which will be presented in the following chapter, an exact equivalent discrete time solution exists. However, many other stochastic processes may not have analytical solutions, which means that obtaining an exact equivalent discrete time formulation from the continuous time model may not be possible.

The group structure transition model describes the way the group membership or group structure G_t changes over time. This process can be dependent or independent of the kinematic states X_t. However, to design a suitable model is not straightforward. This chapter will explore both state-dependent and state-independent models. The general group model given by Eq. (12.9) can be used to model a rich set of group tracking problems. The following sections will describe two such problems.

12.4 Ground target tracking

12.4.1 Basic group dynamical model

This section develops a new group dynamical model [30, 31], conditional upon the group structure, using stochastic differential equations (SDEs) and Itô stochastic calculus. The idea here is to adopt a behavioural model in which each member of a group reacts to the behaviour of other members of that group, typically making its velocity and position more like that of other members in the group. This idea can conveniently be formulated in continuous time through a multivariate SDE, which will later be placed in discrete time without approximation error, owing to the assumed linear and Gaussian form of the model. The acceleration of each target in a group at a particular time t is calculated based on the positions and velocities of surrounding targets in the group. A fairly general linear structure for this can be written, for the ith target in a group. Suppose $s_{t,i} \in \mathcal{R}^d$ is the spatial position of the ith target (where $d = 2$ or 3), then

$$d\dot{s}_{t,i} = \{-\alpha [s_{t,i} - h(s_t)] - \gamma \dot{s}_{t,i} - \beta [\dot{s}_{t,i} - g(\dot{s}_t)]\} dt + dW_{t,i}^s + dB_t^s. \quad (12.10)$$

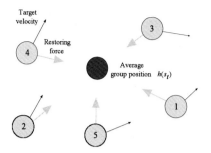

Figure 12.3 Illustration of the restoring forces $-\alpha(s_{t,i} - h(s_t))$ for a five target group. Here $h(s_t)$ is taken as the group mean position vector. Restoring forces are shown as grey arrows, while velocities are shown as black arrows.

Here $s_{t,i}$ is the Cartesian position of the ith target in a group at time t, with $\dot{s}_{t,i}$ the corresponding velocity; B_t^s is a d-dimensioned Brownian motion common to all targets, while $W_{t,i}^s$ is another d-dimensioned Brownian motion assumed to be independently generated for each target i in the group. The term B_t^s, then, models overall randomness in the motion of the group as a whole, while $W_{t,i}^s$ models the individual randomness of each target in the group. Functions $h(\cdot)$ and $g(\cdot)$ are state dependent functions as discussed below, and $s_t = [s_{t,1}, \cdots , s_{t,N}]$ and $\dot{s}_t = [\dot{s}_{t,1}, \cdots , \dot{s}_{t,N}]$ are the collection of all N targets' positions and velocities within a particular group, respectively.[1]

A Newtonian dynamics interpretation of Eq. (12.10) is that there are restoring forces which adjust at each time instant to make, on average, the target position closer to the value $h(s_t)$, the velocity closer to $g(\dot{s}_t)$ and the velocity closer to zero. These three terms comprise the so-called 'drift' function of the SDE. The inclusion of the group and individual Brownian motion terms $W_{t,i}^s$ and B_t^s then serves to model the randomness expected in the behaviour of individuals and of the group as a whole. These latter two terms form the so-called 'diffusion' part of the SDE. Figure 12.3 gives a graphical illustration of the restoring forces towards the average group position $h(s_t)$ for a small group of objects. The whole system, when all targets within a group are coupled with similar equations to Eq. (12.10), forms a multivariate SDE. In order to keep the system linear, the functions $h(\cdot)$ and $g(\cdot)$ are chosen to be linear. In the simplest case, which has been experimented with successfully, $h(\cdot)$ and $g(\cdot)$ are the mean of the position and velocity of the group, respectively, that is

$$h(s_t) = \frac{1}{N} \sum_{j=1}^{N} s_{t,j}, \quad g(\dot{s}_t) = \frac{1}{N} \sum_{j=1}^{N} \dot{s}_{t,j},$$

where N is the group size. This form is used in the simulations. Other forms which have been experimented with success include the leave-one-out average which simply averages over the $N - 1$ remaining members of the group. The parameters α, β and γ are positive, and reflect the strength of the pull towards the group means. Since this is essentially a continuous-time stochastic feedback system, the stability of the system has to be carefully monitored to prevent unstable oscillations from developing. The 'mean reversion' term $\gamma \dot{s}_{t,i}$ prevents the velocities drifting up to very large values with time. A linear SDE for the joint target state can be written as

$$dX_t = AX_t dt + B dW_t + C dB_t. \tag{12.11}$$

---

[1]One single group is assumed here for the sake of notational simplicity. This is generalised straightforwardly for more than one group later.

Here, $S_{t,i} = (x_{t,i}, y_{t,i})^2$ and $X_t = [x_{t,1}, \dot{x}_{t,1}, y_{t,1}, \dot{y}_{t,1}, \ldots, x_{t,N}, \dot{x}_{t,N}, y_{t,N}, \dot{y}_{t,N}, x_{t,N}]^\mathsf{T}$. The matrix $A \in \mathcal{R}^{4N \times 4N}$ is defined as

$$
A = \begin{bmatrix}
A_1 & A_3 & \cdots & A_3 & A_3 \\
A_3 & A_1 & & & \vdots \\
\vdots & & \ddots & & \vdots \\
\vdots & & & A_1 & A_3 \\
A_3 & \cdots & \cdots & A_3 & A_1
\end{bmatrix},
$$

where $A_1 = \mathrm{blkdiag}[A_2, A_2]$ with $A_2 = [0\ 1; (-\alpha + \frac{\alpha}{N})\ (-\beta - \gamma + \frac{\beta}{N})]$, and $A_3 = \mathrm{blkdiag}[A_4, A_4]$ with $A_4 = [0\ 0; \frac{\alpha}{N}\ \frac{\beta}{N}]$. The matrices $B \in \mathcal{R}^{4N \times 2N}$ and $C \in \mathcal{R}^{4N \times 2}$ are defined as $B = \mathrm{blkdiag}[B_1, \ldots, B_1]$ with $B_1 = [0\ 0; 1\ 0; 0\ 0; 1\ 0]$ and $C = [B_1^\mathsf{T}, B_1^\mathsf{T}, \cdots, B_1^\mathsf{T}]^\mathsf{T}$. The multi-dimensional Brownian motions W_t and B_t are given by

$$
W_t = [W_{t,1}^x, W_{t,1}^y, \ldots, W_{t,N}^x, W_{t,N}^y]^\mathsf{T}, \quad B_t = [B_t^x, B_t^y]^\mathsf{T},
$$

with covariance matrices $Q_W = \mathrm{diag}[\sigma_x^2, \sigma_y^2, \ldots, \sigma_x^2, \sigma_y^2]$ and $Q_B = \mathrm{diag}[\sigma_g^2, \sigma_g^2]$ respectively. Equation (12.11) can also be equivalently written as

$$
dX_t = AX_t dt + D dM_t,
$$

where $D = [B\ C]$ and M_t is a Brownian motion with covariance matrix $Q_M = \mathrm{diag}[\sigma_x^2, \sigma_y^2, \ldots, \sigma_x^2, \sigma_y^2, \sigma_g^2, \sigma_g^2]$. The above SDE can be solved exactly using Itô's stochastic calculus [29]. The transition matrix F_N for N targets is defined as $F_N = F_\tau = \exp(A\tau)$. Here, τ is typically set to be the time between successive observations. However, more generally, τ need not be constrained by the observation interval, but evolves with its own dynamics. This can be done in a more flexible model based on variable rate formulation [18, 19]. The corresponding covariance matrix of the above model is given by

$$
Q_N = Q_\tau = \int_{s=t}^{s=t+\tau} \exp(A(t + \tau - s)) D Q_M D^\mathsf{T} \exp(A(t + \tau - s))^\mathsf{T} ds.
$$

The covariance matrix can be obtained using matrix fraction decomposition [36, 39]. Hence the transition density of X_t is given by

$$
p_u(X_t | X_{t-1}) = \mathcal{N}(X_t | F_N X_{t-1}, Q_N).
$$

Basic group dynamical model with repulsive force

A way of preventing targets from becoming too spatially close or colliding is to introduce repulsive forces between targets if they approach each other too closely. This is similar to models in particle physics where two of protons experience a strong repulsive force if they come too close to one another. A direct discrete time version of a related idea has also been implemented by [12]. Here a similar model can be developed by including piecewise constant repulsive force. The SDE that describes the forces acting on a target in a group can be written as

$$
d\dot{s}_{t,i} = \{-\alpha [s_{t,i} - h(s_t)] - \gamma \dot{s}_{t,i} - \beta [\dot{s}_{t,i} - g(\dot{s}_t)] + r_i\} dt + dW_{t,i}^s + dB_t^s.
$$

---

[2] Note that here only a planar (2D) motion is considered. The models do readily extend to 3D motion if required.

Here, r_i can be any suitably chosen piecewise constant force that depends only on the states at $t - 1$. The distribution of X_t is then given by a normal distribution

$$p_u(X_t|X_{t-1}) = \mathcal{N}(X_t|F_N X_{t-1} + R_N H, Q_N). \tag{12.12}$$

The mean of $X_{t+\tau}$ has to take into account the extra term due to the vector of the repulsive force terms r_i for all targets, H. The matrix $R_N = \int_{s=t}^{s=t+\tau} \exp(A(t+\tau-s))ds$ can be calculated using direct matrix exponential expansion or via eigenvalue decomposition.

Group model with virtual leader

The above framework can model targets moving with interacting velocities and positions over an extended period of time. It can be contrasted with models such as the bulk velocity model [21, 34] and the virtual leader-follower model [28], in which an additional state variable is introduced to model the bulk or group parameter. This framework can be adapted to include a latent virtual leader parameter too. This approach to group modelling is closer in spirit to the work of [34, 28], although again the novel spatio-temporal structure above is adopted for individuals within the group. The SDE for the virtual leader model is

$$d\dot{s}_{t,i} = \{-\alpha[s_{t,i} - v_t^s] - \gamma_1 \dot{s}_{t,i} - \beta[\dot{s}_{t,i} - \dot{v}_t^s]\}dt + dW_{t,i}^s,$$
$$d\dot{v}_t^s = -\gamma_2 \dot{v}_t^s dt + dB_t^v,$$

where v_t^s is the unobserved 'virtual leader'. The method outlined in the previous section can also be used to solve this model. This formulation once again leads to a simple analytic solution owing to the linear Gaussian structure, and hence may be embedded efficiently into Kalman filter or Rao–Blackwellised schemes. The properties of this virtual-leader model are unexplored as yet, but more flexible behaviour may be expected since the virtual leader is no longer a deterministic function of the group state. For example, the virtual leader need not be directly part of the group. Instead, it can model the destination point of a group of targets, which they will move towards. This model is introduced here as a variant of the basic group model, which is currently the subject of further studies by [37].

12.4.2   Bayesian model for group target tracking

First, a basic probabilistic framework will need to be established for the problem. For each target i, its state is represented at time t by $X_{t,i} = [x_{t,i}\ \dot{x}_{t,i}\ y_{t,i}\ \dot{y}_{t,i}]^\mathsf{T}$ and $X_t = [X_{t,i}, \cdots, X_{t,N_{max}}]^\mathsf{T}$ is the joint states of all the N_{max} individual targets. As described in the previous section, G_t is used to represent the group structure of the targets at time t.

The aim of inference is to compute the posterior probability distribution $p(X_t, G_t|Z_{1:t})$. From this, one can infer estimates and confidence values for all desired quantities such as number of targets, their positions and velocities X_t, and their group configuration G_t. Note that X_t is a variable-dimensional quantity since targets can be added or deleted from the scene randomly over time. Of course there is no reason either theoretically or computationally why a variable dimension quantity such as this should not be maintained throughout the model as is routinely done in problems of Bayesian model choice. However, in this chapter, this is equivalent to formulating the existence process of targets explicitly in terms of a set of existence variables e_t (see [17] for a more general treatment of model selection using the composite model space formulation). Each $e_{t,i} \in \{0, 1\}$ models the existence process of individual targets, where $e_{t,i} = 1$ models an active target, and $e_{t,i} = 0$ models an inactive target. In this formulation, X_t is regarded as a fixed-dimensional quantity with N_{max}

elements, with each of them being active or inactive according to $e_{t,i}$. This is a reasonable framework given that practical systems have computational and storage limitations.

Assuming a Markovian state transition, the standard Bayesian filtering prediction and update steps are given by

$$p(X_t, e_t, G_t | Z_{1:t}) = \frac{p(Z_t | X_t, e_t, G_t) p(X_t, e_t, G_t | Z_{1:t-1})}{p(Z_t | Z_{1:t-1})},$$

$$p(X_t, e_t, G_t | Z_{1:t-1})$$
$$= \int p(X_t, e_t, G_t | X_{t-1}, e_{t-1}, G_{t-1}) p(X_{t-1}, e_{t-1}, G_{t-1} | Z_{1:t-1}) dX_{t-1} de_{t-1} dG_{t-1},$$

where $Z_{1:t} = [Z_1 \cdots Z_t]$ and $Z_{t'}$ are all the observations collected at time t'. The transition probability model $p(X_t, e_t, G_t | X_{t-1}, e_{t-1}, G_{t-1})$ is written as

$$p(X_t, e_t, G_t | X_{t-1}, e_{t-1}, G_{t-1}) = p(X_t, e_t | G_t, X_{t-1}, e_{t-1}) p(G_t | X_{t-1}, e_{t-1}, G_{t-1}),$$

where $p(G_t | X_{t-1}, e_{t-1}, G_{t-1})$ is the group structure transition model, which will be described in the following section, and $p(X_t, e_t | G_t, X_{t-1}, e_{t-1})$ is the target dynamical model given its group structure G_t designed such that it is unaffected by the group structure at time $t-1$. The motion of different groups are assumed mutually independent. Hence,

$$p(X_t, e_t | G_t, X_{t-1}, e_{t-1}) = \prod_{k=1}^{N_\gamma(G_t)} p(X_{t,\Lambda(k,G_t)}, e_{t,\Lambda(k,G_t)} | X_{t-1,\Lambda(k,G_t)}, e_{t-1,\Lambda(k,G_t)}), \qquad (12.13)$$

where $\{X_{t,\Lambda(k,G_t)}, e_{t,\Lambda(k,G_t)}\}$ represents the joint target states for targets that belong to group k (see the following section for the definition of $\Lambda(k, G_t)$). Each of the densities at the right-hand side of the above equation can be further partitioned into birth, death and update scenarios. The group dynamic update will be given by Eq. (12.12). While the groups are assumed to evolve *a priori* independently of one another, one could also envisage repulsive or attractive force mechanisms between group centroids. This can model higher-level group interactions and could be incorporated into the general formulation above as required.

12.4.3   State-dependent group structure transition model

The group structure transition model depends very much on the type of group targets that are being tracked. Generally, only 'small' changes in group structure are expected over short time intervals. Certain group structure changes would also be considered highly unlikely. In some scenarios, for example, two targets that are widely separated are perhaps unlikely to join together within one group. One possible model for such transitions is described in the sequel.

At each time t, the group structure is represented by a variable G_t. For example, for five targets, the group structure representation $G_t = [1\ 1\ 2\ 2\ 3]^T$ means that Targets 1 and 2 are in Group 1, Targets 3 and 4 are in Group 2, and Target 5 is in Group 3 (see Fig. 12.4). Note that $\gamma_5(11) = [1\ 1\ 2\ 2\ 3]^T$ is the notation for the example of group structure above. This representation will be called the base group representation. The complete list of the base group representation for four and five members can be found in Appendix 12.A.

The first target is always labelled as Group 1. A single target is also considered as a group. Hence, the maximum number of possible groups is five. In this way, the number of possible group structures for five targets is given by the fifth Bell number $B_5 = 52$. Bell numbers [5] can also be viewed as the number of distinct possible ways of putting N_{max} distinguishable balls into one or more indistinguishable boxes. This is exactly equivalent to partitioning a set of N_{max} targets into the various possible groups.

The total number of groups for each group structure is given by $N_\gamma(G_t) = \max(G_t)$. Let $\Lambda(g, G_t)$ be the set of targets that belong to group g of group structure G_t, and let $N_\Lambda(g, G_t)$ be the corresponding number of targets in the group. A transition probability $p(G_t|G_{t-1})$ represents the probability of group structure changes from G_{t-1} at time $t-1$ to G_t at time t.

For example, using the group structure $\gamma_5(11)$ in Fig. 12.4, the total number of groups is $N_\gamma(\gamma_5(11)) = 3$, the set of targets in Group 1 is $\Lambda(1, \gamma_5(11)) = \{1, 2\}$, and it contains $N_\Lambda(1, \gamma_5(11)) = 2$ members in total. The following is a general structure for the group transition probability,

$$p(G_t|X_{t-1}, e_{t-1}, G_{t-1}) = \begin{cases} P_{NC} & \text{if } G_t = G_{t-1}, \\ (1 - P_{NC})\hat{p}(G_t|G_{t-1}, X_{t-1}, e_{t-1}) & \text{otherwise.} \end{cases}$$

Here, the group structure is expected to remain unchanged with probability P_{NC} and to change with probability $(1 - P_{NC})$. The probability of change to a structure where $G_t \neq G_{t-1}$ is denoted with $\hat{p}(G_t|G_{t-1}, X_{t-1}, e_{t-1})$. Specifying $\hat{p}(G_t|G_{t-1}, X_{t-1}, e_{t-1})$ will be an important consideration in the model. In simple cases this probability can be state-independent, i.e. $\hat{p}(G_t|G_{t-1}, X_{t-1}, e_{t-1}) = p(G_t|G_{t-1})$, and the probabilities can be assigned on the basis of a metric that measures how 'similar' G_t is to G_{t-1}, with higher probabilities assigned to more similar configurations. (Another method of designing a state-independent group structure transition model based on the dynamic Dirichlet distribution will be described later in Section 12.5.) In the simulations here, however, a flexible state-dependent model is used in which $\hat{p}(G_t|G_{t-1}, X_{t-1}, e_{t-1}) = \hat{p}(G_t|X_{t-1}, e_{t-1})$, i.e. it depends only on the state and existence variables; $\hat{p}(G_t|X_{t-1}, e_{t-1})$ determines how information from X_{t-1} and e_{t-1} is used to guide group changes. For two targets i and j, suppose a quantity $q_{i,j} \in [0, 1]$ can be used to give an indication of how likely they are to be in the same group at time t. For each group structure h, let Δ be the set of all pairs of targets that belong to the same group. Then, a scoring function such as the one below can be used

$$s(G_t = h|X_{t-1}, e_{t-1}) = \prod_{i,j \in \Delta} q_{i,j} \prod_{i,j \notin \Delta}(1 - q_{i,j}).$$

The advantage of the product form of this scoring function is that it tends to favour smaller changes in group structure. The pseudo transition density $\hat{p}(G_t = h|X_{t-1}, e_{t-1})$ is defined as

$$\hat{p}(G_t = h|X_{t-1}, e_{t-1}) = \frac{s(G_t = h|X_{t-1}, e_{t-1})}{\sum_{\forall\, h', h' \neq G_{t-1}} s(G_t = h'|X_{t-1}, e_{t-1})},$$

while $q_{i,j}$ is defined as

$$q_{i,j} = \begin{cases} P_Q & \text{if } e_{t-1,i} = 0 \text{ or } e_{t-1,j} = 0; \\ k(X_{t-1,i}, X_{t-1,j}) & \text{otherwise.} \end{cases}$$

$$G_t = \gamma_5(11) = \begin{bmatrix} 1 \\ 1 \\ 2 \\ 2 \\ 3 \end{bmatrix}$$

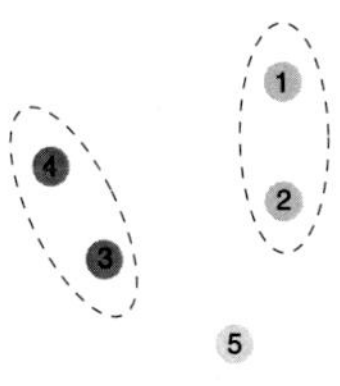

Figure 12.4 This is an example of a group structure variable for five targets split into three groups. Using the base group representation (Appendix 12.A), it is also denoted as $\gamma_5(11)$.

Here, P_Q is a small number between 0 and 1 (e.g. 0.02) such that it allows for an inactive target to be grouped with active targets. This gives the ability to add targets to groups; $k(X_{t-1,i}, X_{t-1,j})$ is a function that assigns values between 0 and 1 measuring the similarity between the kinematics of the pair of active targets. Those with similar kinematics are judged more likely to form part of the same group. The following equation shows an example of the function, which will be used later in the simulations

$$k(X_{t-1,i}, X_{t-1,j}) = \exp\left(-\frac{R_v^2}{2\sigma_{R_v}^2}\right) \exp\left(-\frac{R_d^2}{2\sigma_{R_d}^2}\right),$$

$$R_v = ((\dot{x}_{t-1,i} - \dot{x}_{t-1,j})^2 + (\dot{y}_{t-1,i} - \dot{y}_{t-1,j})^2)^{\frac{1}{2}},$$

$$R_d = \max(0, ((x_{t-1,i} - x_{t-1,j})^2 + (x_{t-1,i} - x_{t-1,j})^2)^{\frac{1}{2}} - D_{sep}).$$

Here, R_v and R_d are the relative speed and distance of the pair of targets $X_{t-1,i}$ and $X_{t-1,j}$ respectively; σ_{R_v} and σ_{R_d} are the corresponding standard deviations; D_{sep} describes the extent of a group.

12.4.4 Observation model

The observation model for the ground vehicle tracking analysed in the next section is based on a discretised grid obtained with the association free or track-before-detect (TBD) approach in [34, 26]. This permits the computation of the likelihood function without first requiring full enumeration of the association hypotheses. Here, each grid point or pixel observation is modelled using simplified position only Rayleigh-distributed measurements [26]. Thresholded measurements that return 1 or 0 for each pixel are employed. The probability of detection $P_{d,n}$ for n targets in a single pixel space, given that the background false alarm probability is set at P_{fa}, is $P_{d,n} = P_{fa}^{\frac{1}{1+n \times SNR}}$.

12.4.5 Simulation results

Tracking scenario

The group tracking algorithm will now be used to track a set of simulation data. For the simulation, a single discretized sensor model is used which scans a fixed rectangular region of 100 by 100 pixels, where each pixel is 50m by 50m. Thresholded measurements are used with $P_{d,1} = 0.7$ for a single target. The false alarm probability for each pixel is $P_{fa} = 0.002$. The sensor returns a set of observations every 5s. The group dynamical model (12.12) is used to generate the simulation. The scenario (see Fig. 12.5(a)) consists of two groups of two targets moving towards each other from time step 1 to 50, and then merging to form a combined group from time step 51 to 100. Figure 12.5(b) shows one realisation of the observation of the tracks. The parameters used to generate the motion of the group are shown in Table 12.8.

    The filtering distribution for the dynamical model coupled with the observation model is complex and highly non-linear. Section 12.2 illustrated that the MCMC-particles algorithm and its various extensions can be effective in high-dimensional problems. Therefore the MCMC-particles algorithm will be used to design the inference algorithm. Using the probabilistic framework from previous sections, the joint distribution of $S_t = \{X_t, e_t, G_t\}$

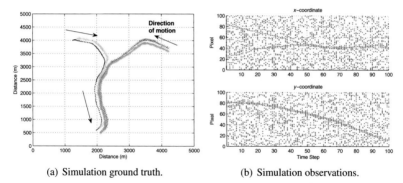

(a) Simulation ground truth.   (b) Simulation observations.

Figure 12.5 These figures show the ground truth and one realisation of the observations ($P_{d,1}$ = 0.7 and P_{fa} = 0.002) for simulation scenario 1. In this scenario, there are two groups of two targets each merging into a single group. See plate section for colour version.

Simulation parameter	Symbol	Value
Time interval between measurements	τ	5 s
Actual number of targets	N	4
Number of simulation time steps		100
Centroid control parameter	α	$0.0006\,\mathrm{s}^{-2}$
Group velocity control parameter	β	$0.050\,\mathrm{s}^{-1}$
Individual velocity control parameter	γ	$0.001\mathrm{s}^{-1}$
Individual motion noise	σ_x	$0.2\,\mathrm{m\,s}^{-1}$
Group motion noise	σ_g	$0.5\,\mathrm{m\,s}^{-1}$
Repulsive force constants	R_1	$4\,\mathrm{m}^2\,\mathrm{s}^{-2}$
	R_2	$10\,\mathrm{m}$

Table 12.8 Track simulation parameters for moving ground vehicles.

and $S_{t-1} = \{X_{t-1}, e_{t-1}, G_{t-1}\}$ is given by

$$p(S_t, S_{t-1}|Z_{1:t}) = p(X_t, e_t, G_t, X_{t-1}, e_{t-1}, G_{t-1}|Z_{1:t})$$
$$\propto p(X_{t-1}, e_{t-1}, G_{t-1}|Z_{1:t-1})p(X_t, e_t, G_t|X_{t-1}, e_{t-1}, G_{t-1})p(Z_t|X_t, e_t).$$

The MCMC-particles algorithm is used to detect and track the group targets. A Monte Carlo run of N_{run} = 30 sets of the observations are generated for each of the scenarios. For each run, all the particles are initialised as inactive ('dead') in order to allow the algorithm to detect all targets unaided. At each time step, N_{MCMC} = 25 000 MCMC iterations of both the joint and individual proposals are performed. The initial N_{burn} = 1000 iterations are used for burn-in. A chain thinning of N_{thin} = 6 is used and N_p = 4000 MCMC output are kept as particle approximation to $p(X_t, e_t, G_t|Z_{1:t})$. The parameters used for tracking can be found in Table 12.9. They are selected to facilitate smoother tracks.

For four targets, Table 12.13 in Appendix 12.A lists all the possible group combinations. Note that many of the group structures are equivalent representations under the permutation invariance of the targets, e.g. $[1\ 1\ 2\ 2]^T = [1\ 2\ 2\ 1]^T = [1\ 2\ 1\ 2]^T$.

The existence variable can be used to declare a legitimate target being tracked. In addition, the variance of the state estimate can also help to indicate if a good track has been achieved. The target track declaration method used here relies on little or no permutation switching of target labels, hence the individual tracks can be identified and colour coded. It is easy to envisage scenarios where this might break down. A systematic way to deal with

Tracking parameter	Symbol	Value
Time interval between measurements	τ	5 s
Maximum number of targets	N_{max}	4
Centroid control parameter	α	$0.0006\,\text{s}^{-2}$
Group velocity control parameter	β	$0.3\,\text{s}^{-1}$
Individual velocity control parameter	γ	$0.001\,\text{s}^{-1}$
Individual motion noise	σ_x, σ_y	$0.8\,\text{m s}^{-1}$
Group motion noise	σ_g	$0.5\,\text{m s}^{-1}$
Repulsive force constants	R_1	$6\,\text{m}^2\,\text{s}^{-2}$
	R_2	$10\,\text{m}$
Grouping constant for inactive target	P_Q	0.02
Probability of group structure remains unchanged	P_{NC}	0.4
Grouping velocity standard deviation	σ_{R_v}	$6\,\text{m s}^{-1}$
Grouping distance standard deviation	σ_{R_d}	$150\,\text{m}$
Grouping distance extent	D_{sep}	$150\,\text{m}$
Target birth probability	P_B	0.3
Target death probability	P_D	0.05
Probability of detection for one target	$P_{d,1}$	0.5
Probability of false alarm	P_{fa}	0.0014

Table 12.9 Tracking parameters for simulation results.

this issue is to use a relabelling algorithm [40]. In general, the scenarios used here pose little or no problem with the posterior estimation of summary statistics.

Results

The estimated track for one set of results is shown in Fig. 12.6(a). The MCMC-particles algorithm can be seen to have successfully detected and tracked the four targets. The ellipse shows the mode of the group configuration and the number indicates the number of targets in the group. Quite clearly, the algorithm is able to infer the correct group structure. This can also be seen in Fig. 12.7(a), which shows the time evolution of the group structure probability. The change of grouping structure from $[1\ 1\ 2\ 2]^{\mathsf{T}}$ to $[1\ 1\ 1\ 1]^{\mathsf{T}}$ at $t = 50$ can be seen clearly in the figure.

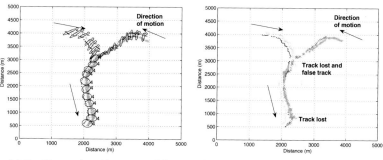

(a) Tracking results with group models.   (b) Tracking results without group models.

Figure 12.6 These figures show one run of the result of the group tracking algorithm compared with a tracking result with independent targets for simulation scenario 1. The ellipse shows the mode of the group configuration, labelled with the number of objects detected in the group. The results without group models show more erratic behaviour in estimation. See plate section for colour version.

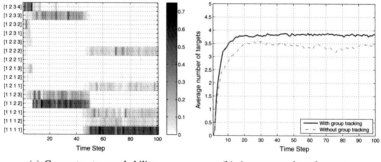

(a) Group structure probability.   (b) Average number of targets.

Figure 12.7 These figures show the group structure probability over time and the average number of targets over 30 runs ($P_{d,1} = 0.7$ and $P_{fa} = 0.002$) for simulation scenario 1. The merging of the two groups can be seen in the changes in group structure probabilities at time step 50. The average number of targets shows the non-group based model's tendency to miss targets in the detection process.

Another 30 Monte Carlo sets of the observations are generated. For these data, the MCMC-particles algorithm is used without any group tracking. The targets are treated as independent targets and there are no group structure transition or any group based interactions. However, the posterior distribution is still a joint distribution due to the observations and repulsive force model.

Figure 12.6(b) shows the estimated track of one set of the results. From the figure, it can be seen that the tracks are less reliably initialised, the track estimates are noisier, and the tracks are more prone to being lost. To achieve better detection and tracking performance in the case without group tracking, the number of MCMC iterations has to be increased significantly. Even then, tracks can still be lost due to the large amount of uncertainty generated when the targets are closed together and measurements are missing. This illustrates the benefit of exploiting group information to improve tracking performance. For each run, the average number of targets N_{X_t} at each time t is estimated by

$$E(N_{X_t}|Z_{1:t}) \approx \frac{1}{N_p} \sum_{p=1}^{N_p} \sum_{i=1}^{N_{max}} e_{t,i,p}.$$

Figure 12.7(b) shows the average number of targets detected for both sets of 30 Monte Carlo runs, i.e. with and without the group tracking. The average number of correctly detected-targets is higher for the runs with the group tracking enabled. It shows that the algorithm is able to detect all the four targets consistently with group tracking.

12.5 Group stock selection

In financial trading, pairs trading is an investment strategy that exploits market instruments that are out of equilibrium. It is a form of market neutral statistical arbitrage. A brief history and discussion of pairs trading can be found in [13]. Pairs trading is a non-directional strategy that identifies two financial instruments with similar characteristics whose price relationship is outside of its historical range. The strategy simply buys one instrument and sells the other in the hope that their price relationship tends to fluctuate around its average in the short term, while remaining stable over the long term. In [11], pairs trading is modelled by using a mean reverting Gaussian Markov chain model for the spread between two securities. Predictions from the calibrated model are then compared with subsequent observations of the spread to determine appropriate investment decisions such as time to buy and sell. To identify suitable pairs of market instruments a common approach is to analyse the matrix of pairwise correlations between all instruments.

In [7] a class of Bayesian models was introduced to model structured, conditional independence relationships in the time-varying, cross-sectional covariance matrices of multiple time series. This can be used to model groups of stocks by specifying a static graph (or equivalently the group structure) G representing the pairwise relationships of the multiple time series, and directly modifying the individual entries of the covariance matrix. The model can be extended to deal with time-varying changes to the group structure.

In this section, we introduce a new model for identifying groups of stocks that might be suitable for a more general version of pairs trading. This will be achieved through writing explicit SDE expressions of the stock prices with group behaviour. The main assumptions here are that stocks in the same group have similar long-term return, they are all affected by a common group noise, and they have mean reversion tendency towards a group mean.

As this approach analyses stocks as a group, it can potentially create a portfolio of stocks which exploit the correlation amongst them to achieve investment returns. This is in contrast to normal portfolio construction where the aim is to reduce correlation between stocks to achieve the same return with lower risk. It is hoped that this may result in better risk return profile, compared to just simple pairs trading, which relies only on a pair rather than a group of stocks.

12.5.1 Group stock mean reversion model

In stock markets, it is possible for market participants to identify and exploit highly correlated stocks which might be priced away from the long-run return μ_r. This might result in 'forced' changes to stock prices that bring them back into equilibrium. To model this behaviour more explicitly,

$$\frac{dX_{t,1}}{X_{t,1}} = (\mu_{r,1} - f_1(X_t))dt + \sigma_{X,1}dB_{t,1} + \sigma_{X,g}dB_{t,g}, \tag{12.14}$$

where $f_1(X_t)$ is some function of the stock prices within the same group. Here, $f_1(X_t)$ models a force term which brings the stock price back to equilibrium faster by temporarily reducing the drift component $\mu_{r,1}$; $B_{t,1}$, $B_{t,2}$ and $B_{t,g}$ are standard Brownian motions, $\sigma_{X,g}$ is the volatility of the group and $\sigma_{X,1}$ and $\sigma_{X,2}$ are the volatilities of the individual stocks.

Solving Eq. (12.14) explicitly in closed form is not easy. One possibility is to simulate it using Euler discretisation. Inference can be done using data imputation techniques such as those of [20]. Another possibility is to consider that from time t to $t+\tau$, the term $f_1(X_t) \approx F_1$ is nearly constant. In this case, the following SDE can be solved exactly,

$$\frac{dX_{t,1}}{X_{t,1}} = (\mu_{r,1} - F_1)dt + \sigma_{X,1}dB_{t,1} + \sigma_{X,g}dB_{t,g}.$$

The solution of the above equation is given by

$$X_{t+\tau,1} = X_{t,1}e^{\left(\mu_{r,1} - F_1 - \frac{1}{2}(\sigma_{X,1}^2 + \sigma_{X,g}^2)\right)\tau + \sigma_{X,1}(B_{t+\tau,1} - B_{t,1}) + \sigma_{X,g}(B_{t+\tau,g} - B_{t,g})}. \tag{12.15}$$

A set of stocks can be modelled using Eq. (12.15). There are many possible methods of constructing $f_1(X_t)$. One method, which is successfully applied, is to use the difference

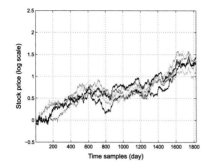

Figure 12.8 Seven simulated stock price time series with common group volatility and group mean reversion. See plate section for colour version.

Simulation parameter	Symbol	Value
Time interval between measurements	τ	$\frac{1}{365}$ year
Number of stocks	N_{max}	7
Individual stock annual volatility	$\sigma_{X,i}$	0.20
Group annual volatility	$\sigma_{X,g}$	0.20
Group mean reversion parameter	η	1
Individual stock annual mean return	$\mu_{r,i}$	0.10

Table 12.10 Parameters for group stock model with group volatility and group mean reversion.

between the stock price and the group average of the stock prices, that is

$$f_1(X_t) = \eta\left(1 - \frac{1}{NX_{t,1}}\sum_{i=1}^{N} X_{t,i}\right), \tag{12.16}$$

where η is a control parameter which determines how strongly the stock prices will tend towards the group mean, and N is the number of stocks that belong to the same group. Another possible method of constructing $f_1(X_t)$ is to use the exponentially weighted mean return for the stock.

Figure 12.8 shows a set of stock prices generated using Eqs. (12.15) and (12.16) with the parameters shown in Table 12.10. The stock prices exhibit strongly clustered behaviour. The group mean reversion stock model will be used for the group stock selection problem in the next section.

12.5.2 State-independent group structure model

In this section, a different representation model for the group structure G_t is used. Assuming that there are K possible groups, then for each target i an assignment variable $g_{t,i} \in \{1,\dots,K\}$ can be defined such that it indicates which group the target is in. The new group structure representation G_t is given by $G_t = [g_{t,1}\ g_{t,2}\ \cdots\ g_{t,N_{max}}]$. It is straightforward to map the new representation using the assignment variable to the base group representation in Appendix 12.A, for example

$$G_t = [1\ 1\ 3\ 3\ 5] \mapsto \gamma_5(11).$$

This mapping provides a way to study the changes in group structure probability. There is a many-to-one mapping from the new representation described above to the Base Group representation. For example, different combinations of the group assignment variables such as $G_t = [2\ 1\ 2\ 1\ 4]$ map to the same base group representation $\gamma_5(11)$.

Now, a state-independent group structure transition model $p(G_t, \pi_t|G_{t-1}, \pi_{t-1})$ will be developed. Here, $G_t = [g_{t,1}\ g_{t,2}\ \cdots\ g_{t,N_{max}}]$, where $g_{t,i} \in \{1,\dots,K\}$ is the group assignment of target i, and π_t models the underlying proportion of targets in various groups at time t. The main aim is to define a reasonable model for $p(G_t, \pi_t | G_{t-1}, \pi_{t-1})$. Consider the general state-independent group structure transition model where

$$p(G_t, \pi_t | G_{t-1}, \pi_{t-1}) = p(\pi_t | \pi_{t-1}) p(G_t | G_{t-1}, \pi_t) = p(\pi_t | \pi_{t-1}) \prod_{i=1}^{N_{max}} p(g_{t,i} | g_{t-1,i}, \pi_t), \quad (12.17)$$

where $p(\pi_t | \pi_{t-1})$ is a distribution that describes the way the underlying proportion of the targets in various groups changes over time (this distribution will be defined later in this section, and termed the dynamic Dirichlet distribution), and $p(g_{t,i} | g_{t-1,i}, \pi_t)$ is the probability model for the changes in group assignment, defined as

$$p(g_{t,i} = k | g_{t-1,i} = l, \pi_t) = \begin{cases} P_G + (1 - P_G) \pi_{t,k} & \text{if } g_{t,i} = g_{t-1,i}, \\ (1 - P_G) \pi_{t,k} & \text{otherwise.} \end{cases}$$

If $\pi_t = \pi_0$ is some fixed quantity, then it is also straightforward to show that the distribution of $g_{t,1:N_{max}}$ over the different groups tends to π_0 after some time.

The main idea of a dynamic Dirichlet distribution is to induce reasonable dependency between successive proportions π_t over time. This can be useful in modelling time-varying proportions of topics in a set of documents [4, 42, 38], as well as changes in group structure or group membership over time.

Here, we use a dynamic Dirichlet distribution that has the form of a simple Dirichlet distribution (written as $\text{Dir}(\cdot | \alpha_0)$ with parameters α_0) as the time marginal. While there is no particular reason for this, it is hoped that by doing so many results that exist for the Dirichlet distribution in the literature can be used. At time $t = 0$, let K be the number of groups, $\alpha_0 = \{\alpha_{0,1}, \ldots, \alpha_{0,K}\}$, $\alpha_{0,i} = \alpha_{0,C}/K$ and $\alpha_{0,C} = \sum_{i=1}^{K} \alpha_{0,i}$. The initial proportion π_0 is given by $\pi_0 \sim \text{Dir}(\pi_0 | \alpha_0)$. There are many possible ways of inducing dependence between successive proportions π_t. To achieve the desired grouping effect, the dependence is induced using a correlated version of the parameter vector α_t

$$\alpha_t = \zeta \alpha_{0,C} \pi_{t-1} + (1 - \zeta) \alpha_0,$$

where $0 \le \zeta \le 1$ is a control parameter to determine the amount of correlation that exists between Dirichlet distributions at time t and $t-1$. If $\zeta = 1$, we recover the dynamic Dirichlet distribution in [42], if $\zeta = 0$ we have an independent Dirichlet distribution. Hence, this distribution will be written as

$$\pi_t | \pi_{t-1} \sim \text{Dir}(\pi_t | \alpha_t) \sim \text{DDD}(\pi_t | \pi_{t-1}, \alpha_0, \zeta), \quad (12.18)$$

where $\text{DDD}(\cdot | \pi_{t-1}, \alpha_0, \zeta)$ is the dynamic Dirichlet distribution with parameters α_0 and ζ. Note that the precision parameter $\alpha_{t,C} = \sum_{i=1}^{K} \alpha_{t,i}$ is constant at each time step t.

12.5.3 Bayesian model for group structure analysis

Given a set of stocks, the task is to analyse how the different stocks are grouped together over time. The grouping is represented by the group structure variable G_t. A simple Bayesian model for the group stocks will be introduced in this section. For N_{max} stocks, let $Z_t = [Z_{t,1} \ Z_{t,2} \cdots Z_{t,N_{max}}]$ be the logarithm of the stock price $X_{t,i}$ given by Eq. (12.15), i.e. $Z_{t,i} = \ln(X_{t,i})$. Then, the joint distribution can be written as

$$p(G_{1:t}, \pi_{1:t}, Z_{1:t}) = p(G_1, \pi_1) p(Z_1 | G_1) \prod_{t'=2}^{t} p(G_{t'}, \pi_{t'} | G_{t'-1}, \pi_{t'-1}) p(Z_{t'} | Z_{t'-1}, G_{t'}),$$

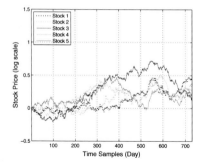

Figure 12.9 Stock price time series of simulation scenario 1 with two groups of two (Stocks 1 and 2) and three stocks (Stocks 3, 4 and 5) each. See plate section for colour version.

where the group structure transition model $p(G_t, \pi_t|G_{t-1}, \pi_{t-1})$ is the state-independent dynamic Dirichlet distribution given by Eq. (12.17), with $G_t = [g_{t,1} \; g_{t,2} \cdots g_{t,N_{max}}]$. The group structure G_1 is initialised where all the stocks are assumed independent, and each stock price starts at $Z_{1,i} = 0$.

Similarly to Eq. (12.13), different groups of stocks are assumed to be mutually independent, and stocks in the same group will be modelled by the group mean reversion model(12.15). For example, if G_t indicates that five stocks are grouped into two groups where $g_1 = \{1, 3\}$ and $g_2 = \{2, 4, 5\}$, then the stock prices are given by

$$p(Z_t|Z_{t-1}, G_t) = p(Z_{t,g_1}|Z_{t-1,g_1})p(Z_{t,g_2}|Z_{t-1,g_2}),$$

and the transition $p(Z_{t,g_1}|Z_{t-1,g_1})$ is obtained from the log-distribution of Eq. (12.15).

12.5.4 Simulation results

In this section, one simulated scenario will be used to study the ability of the group stock models introduced in Section 12.5.3 to identify correct stock groupings. This scenario consists of two groups of stocks with two and three stocks respectively. They begin as separate groups, and after 365 days, the five stocks merge to behave as a single group. The simulated stock prices are generated using the parameters in Table 12.10. Figure 12.9 shows the simulated stock prices. The correct group structure is $\gamma_5(10) = [1\ 1\ 2\ 2\ 2]^T$ before merging, and $\gamma_5(1) = [1\ 1\ 1\ 1\ 1]^T$ after merging.

Inference of the group structure $\{G_t, \pi_t\}$ is achieved using a MCMC-particles algorithm (Algorithm 12.2). The joint distribution of $S_t = \{G_t, \pi_t\}$ and $S_{t-1} = \{G_{t-1}, \pi_{t-1}\}$ is given by

$$p(G_t, \pi_t, G_{t-1}, \pi_{t-1}|Z_{1:t}) \propto p(Z_t|Z_{t-1}, G_t)p(G_t, \pi_t|G_{t-1}, \pi_{t-1})p(G_{t-1}, \pi_{t-1}|Z_{1:t-1}).$$

The parameters in Table 12.11 are used for the group structure inference. It is assumed that the mean return $\mu_{r,i}$ and the volatilities $\sigma_{X,i}$ and $\sigma_{X,g}$ are known. A more complex model can treat these quantities as unknowns, and infer them jointly with the group structure variables. For analysis purposes, the output of the group structure model is mapped to the base group representation used in the previous sections and Appendix 12.A.

Figure 12.10(a) shows the posterior distribution of the group structure $p(G_t|Z_{1:t})$. From the figure it can be seen that the correct group structures are clearly identified with a change in group structure to a single group after 365 days. The average number of groups over time N_t^g can be estimated from the posterior distribution of the group structure. For five stocks and using the base group representation in Appendix 12.A, N_t^g is given as

$$N_t^g = \sum_{k=1}^{52} N_\gamma(\gamma_5(k))p(G_t = \gamma_5(k)|Z_{1:t}),$$

Tracking parameter	Symbol	Value
Time interval between measurements	τ	$\frac{1}{365}$ year
Number of stocks	N_{max}	5
Individual stock annual volatility	$\sigma_{X,i}$	0.20
Group annual volatility	$\sigma_{X,g}$	0.20
Group mean reversion parameter	η	1
Individual stock annual mean return	$\mu_{r,i}$	0.10
Number of groups	K	5
Precision parameter	$\alpha_{0,C}$	35
Correlation parameter	ζ	0.95
Probability of staying in the same group	P_G	0.96

Table 12.11 Tracking parameters for group stock simulation.

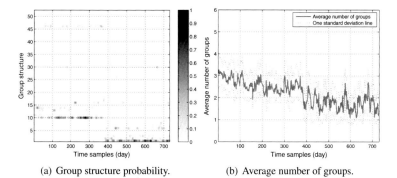

(a) Group structure probability.   (b) Average number of groups.

Figure 12.10 These figures shows the posterior distribution of the group structure and average number of groups N_t^g for Simulation Scenario 1. There is a clear change in group structure to a single group after 365 days. This is also indicated by a change in average group number.

where $N_\gamma(\gamma_5(k))$ refers to the total number of groups in group structure $\gamma_5(k)$. Figure 12.10(b) shows the average number of groups over time. These models can therefore identify groupings of stocks based only on their stock price behaviour.

12.6   Conclusions

This chapter has presented a new approach to model dynamically evolving groups of objects. This is achieved by casting the problem in a general probabilistic framework, and modelling the group interactions of dynamic objects and the evolving group structure over time. The approach permits a unified treatment to various inference goals involving dynamic groupings, from group target detection and tracking to group structure inference.

A novel dynamical model for group target tracking is developed using SDEs with coupled dynamics. The model, named as the basic group dynamical model, is based on the interactions of group targets with each other. Owing to the linear and Gaussian formulation, the group model can be solved exactly to give a Gaussian transition density for the equivalent discrete time model. With appropriately chosen parameters, it can generate realistic group tracks for ground vehicles. A complete Bayesian model for group target detection and tracking is then developed. A general state-dependent group structure transition model is developed to model the changes in group structure over time. The group model is then

γ_4	1	2	3	4	5	6	7	8	9	10	11	12	13	14	15
Target 1	1	1	1	1	1	1	1	1	1	1	1	1	1	1	1
Target 2	1	1	1	1	1	2	2	2	2	2	2	2	2	2	2
Target 3	1	1	2	2	2	1	1	1	2	2	2	3	3	3	3
Target 4	1	2	1	2	3	1	2	3	1	2	3	1	2	3	4

Table 12.12 Unique group representations for four targets.

used to track vehicles in a simulated scenario. It is able to successfully detect and track simulated vehicles, as well as to infer the correct group structures. The results also demonstrate the improvement in performance through exploiting group information.

The use of complex group models in a high-dimensional setting poses significant challenges to joint inference using simulation based methods such as sequential Monte Carlo. This is illustrated in a simple high-dimensional toy example. To overcome this problem, this chapter has introduced a sequential MCMC algorithm called the MCMC-particles algorithm to approximate the posterior distribution of the high-dimensional states under the Bayesian inference framework. This algorithm can be considered to be a generalisation of some existing sequential MCMC algorithms, which allows for further extensions and insights. As the algorithm is based on MCMC, it is very flexible and some of the most powerful methods in Monte Carlo inference, such as parallel chain tempering and local state exploration, can be brought to bear on sequential state estimation problems. The results shown in a toy example demonstrate the effectiveness of this method.

This chapter has also presented an alternative method to model group structure transition which is based on the dynamic Dirichlet distribution and is state independent. An advantage of this state-independent group structure transition model is that it does not require complete enumeration of the group structure in order to compute the transition probabilities or to propose from the distribution. This is applied to a different application taken from finance. The problem here is to identify groups of stocks that might be suitable for trading. This is achieved through writing explicit SDE expressions of the stock prices with group behaviour. The main assumptions here are that stocks in the same group have a similar long term return, they are all affected by a common group noise, and they have

γ_5	1	2	3	4	5	6	7	8	9	10	11	12	13	14	15	16	17	18
Target 1	1	1	1	1	1	1	1	1	1	1	1	1	1	1	1	1	1	1
Target 2	1	1	1	1	1	1	1	1	1	1	1	1	1	1	1	2	2	2
Target 3	1	1	1	1	1	2	2	2	2	2	2	2	2	2	2	1	1	1
Target 4	1	1	2	2	2	1	1	1	2	2	2	3	3	3	3	1	1	1
Target 5	1	2	1	2	3	1	2	3	1	2	3	1	2	3	4	1	2	3
γ_5	19	20	21	22	23	24	25	26	27	28	29	30	31	32	33	34	35	36
Target 1	1	1	1	1	1	1	1	1	1	1	1	1	1	1	1	1	1	1
Target 2	2	2	2	2	2	2	2	2	2	2	2	2	2	2	2	2	2	2
Target 3	1	1	1	1	1	1	2	2	2	2	2	2	2	2	2	2	2	3
Target 4	2	2	2	3	3	3	3	1	1	1	2	2	2	3	3	3	3	1
Target 5	1	2	3	1	2	3	4	1	2	3	1	2	3	1	2	3	4	1
γ_5	37	38	39	40	41	42	43	44	45	46	47	48	49	50	51	52		
Target 1	1	1	1	1	1	1	1	1	1	1	1	1	1	1	1	1		
Target 2	2	2	2	2	2	2	2	2	2	2	2	2	2	2	2	2		
Target 3	3	3	3	3	3	3	3	3	3	3	3	3	3	3	3	3		
Target 4	1	1	1	2	2	2	2	3	3	3	3	4	4	4	4	4		
Target 5	2	3	4	1	2	3	4	1	2	3	4	1	2	3	4	5		

Table 12.13 Unique group representations for five targets.

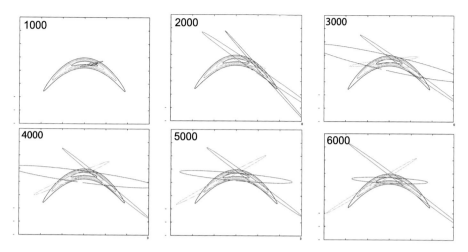

Figure 2.4 Adaptive fit of a mixture of three Gaussian distributions with arbitrary means and covariance using the maximum likelihood approach developed in [2].

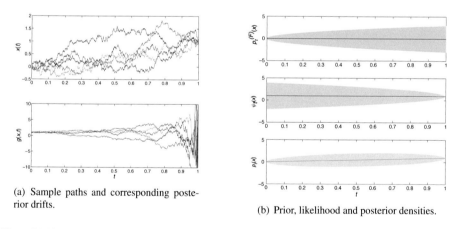

(a) Sample paths and corresponding posterior drifts.

(b) Prior, likelihood and posterior densities.

Figure 6.1 Illustration of a one-dimensional diffusion process without drift and unit diffusion coefficient, starting at the origin and with a noise free observation $y = 1$ at $t = 1$. The posterior process is a Brownian bridge. Note how the drift increases drastically when getting close to the final time. (a) shows five sample paths with their corresponding posterior drift functions. (b) shows the mean and variance (shaded region) of the prior, the likelihood and the posterior marginals. Observe how the variance of the posterior $p_t(x)$ is largest in the middle of the time interval and eventually decreases to 0 at $t = 1$.

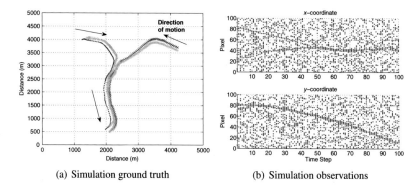

(a) Simulation ground truth   (b) Simulation observations

Figure 11.5 These figures show the ground truth and one realisation of the observations ($P_{d,1}$ = 0.7 and P_{fa} = 0.002) for simulation scenario 1. In this scenario, there are two groups of two targets each merging into a single group.

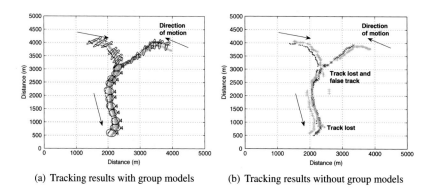

(a) Tracking results with group models   (b) Tracking results without group models

Figure 11.6 These figures show one run of the result of the group tracking algorithm compared with a tracking result with independent targets for Simulation Scenario 1. The ellipse shows the mode of the group configuration, labelled with the number of objects detected in the group. The results without group models show more erratic behaviour in estimation.

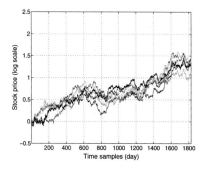

Figure 11.8 Seven simulated stock price time series with common group volatility and group mean reversion.

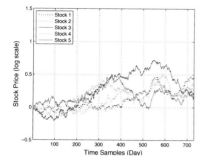

Figure 11.9 Stock price time series of Simulation Scenario 1 with two groups of two (Stocks 1 and 2) and three stocks (Stocks 3, 4 and 5) each.

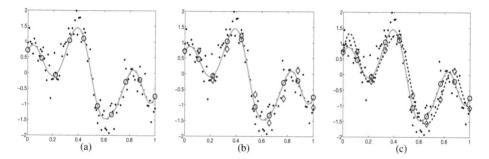

(a) (b) (c)

Figure 14.2 Illustration of sampling using control variables. (a) shows the current GP function $\mathbf{f}^{(t)}$ with green, the data and the current location of the control points (red circles). (b) shows the proposed new positions for the control points (diamonds in magenta). (c) shows the proposed new function values $\mathbf{f}^{(t+1)}$ drawn from the conditional GP prior (blue dotted line).

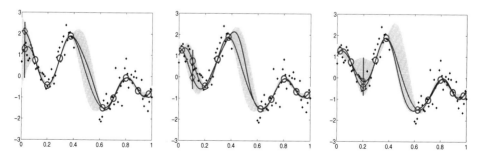

Figure 14.3 Visualisation of iterating between control variables. The red solid line is the current $\mathbf{f}^{(t)}$, the blue line is the proposed $\mathbf{f}^{(t+1)}$, the red circles are the current control variables $\mathbf{f}_c^{(t)}$ while the diamond (in magenta) is the proposed control variable $f_{c_i}^{(t+1)}$. The blue solid vertical line represents the distribution $p(f_{c_i}^{(t+1)}|\mathbf{f}_{c_{\backslash i}}^{(t)})$ (with two standard error bars) and the shaded area shows the effective proposal $p(\mathbf{f}^{t+1}|\mathbf{f}_{c_{\backslash i}}^{(t)})$.

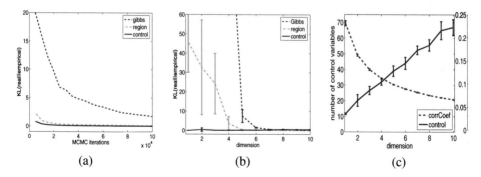

Figure 14.4 (a) shows the evolution of the KL divergence (against the number of MCMC iterations) between the true posterior and the empirically estimated posteriors for a five-dimensional regression dataset. (b) shows the mean values with one-standard error bars of the KL divergence (against the input dimension) between the true posterior and the empirically estimated posteriors. (c) plots the number of control variables used together with the average correlation coefficient of the GP prior.

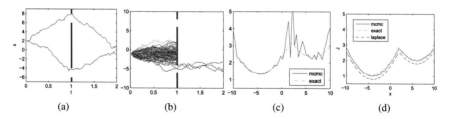

Figure 17.5 Double slit experiment. (a) Setup of the experiment. Particles travel from $t = 0$ to $t = 2$ under dynamics (17.38). A slit is placed at time $t = t_1$, blocking all particles by annihilation. Two trajectories are shown under optimal control. (b) Naive Monte Carlo sampling trajectories to compute $J(x = -1, t = 0)$ through Eq. (17.35). Only trajectories that pass through a slit contribute to the estimate. (c) Comparison of naive MC estimates with $N = 100\,000$ trajectories and exact result for $J(x, t = 0)$ for all x. (d) Comparison of Laplace approximation (dotted line) and Monte Carlo importance sampling (solid jagged line) of $J(x, t = 0)$ with exact result (17.39) (solid smooth line). The importance sampler used $N = 100$ trajectories for each x.

mean reversion tendency towards a group mean. Simulation results show that the group stock models can identify groupings of stocks based on their price behaviour.

12.A   Appendix: Base group representation

Tables (12.12) and (12.13) list the unique group structure γ for four and five targets. For example, $\gamma_5(11) = [1\ 1\ 2\ 2\ 3]^\mathsf{T}$ represents that Targets 1 and 2 are in a group, Targets 3 and 4 are in another group and Target 5 is independent and not grouped.

Bibliography

[1] C. Andrieu, A. Doucet and R. Holenstein. Particle Markov chain Monte Carlo methods. *Journal of Royal Statistical Society Series B*, **72**:1–33, 2010.

[2] C. Berzuini, N. G. Best, W. R. Gilks and C. Larizza. Dynamic conditional independence models and Markov chain Monte Carlo methods. *Journal of the American Statistical Association*, **440**:1403–1412, 1997.

[3] S. S. Blackman and R. Popoli. *Design and Analysis of Modern Tracking Systems*. Artech House, 1999.

[4] D. M. Blei, A. Y. Ng and M. I. Jordan. Latent Dirichlet allocation. *Journal of Machine Learning Research*, **3**:993–1022, March 2003.

[5] P. J. Cameron. *Combinatorics: Topics, Techniques, Algorithms*. Cambridge University Press, 1994.

[6] O. Cappé, S. J. Godsill and E. Moulines. An overview of existing methods and recent advances in sequential Monte Carlo. *Proceedings of the IEEE*, **95**:899–924, May 2007.

[7] C. M. Carvalho and M. West. Dynamic matrix-variate graphical models. *Bayesian Analysis*, **2**:69–98, 2007.

[8] T. C. Clapp and S. J. Godsill. Fixed-lag smoothing using sequential importance sampling. In J. M. Bernardo, J. O. Berger, A. P. Dawid and A. F. M. Smith, editors, *Bayesian Statistics VI*, pages 743–752. 1998.

[9] F. E. Daum and M. Krichman. Meshfree adjoint methods for nonlinear filtering. In *Proceedings of the IEEE Aerospace Conference*, page 16, 2006.

[10] A. Doucet, S. J. Godsill and C. Andrieu. On sequential Monte Carlo sampling methods for Bayesian filtering. *Statistics and Computing*, **10**:197–208, 2000.

[11] R. J. Elliott, J. V. D. Hoek and W. P. Malcolm. Pairs trading. *Quantitative Finance*, **5**:271–276, 2005.

[12] M. Fallon and S. J. Godsill. Multi target acoustic source tracking using track before detect. In *Proceedings of the IEEE Workshop on Applications of Signal Processing to Audio and Acoustics*, pages 102–105, 2007.

[13] E. G. Gatev, W. N. Goetzmann and K. G. Rouwenhorst. Pairs trading: performance of a relative average arbitrage rule. *NBER Working Paper 7032*, 1999. http://www.nber.org/papers/w7032.

[14] C. Geyer. Markov chain Monte Carlo maximum likelihood. In E. Keramigas, editor, *Computing Science and Statistics: The 23rd symposium on the interface*, pages 156–163, 1991.

[15] W. R. Gilks and C. Berzuini. Following a moving target: Monte Carlo inference for dynamic Bayesian models. *Journal of the Royal Statistical Society. Series B (Statistical Methodology)*, **63**:127–146, 2001.

[16] W. R. Gilks, S. Richardson and D. J. Spiegelhalter. *Markov Chain Monte Carlo in Practice*. Chapman and Hall/CRC, 1996.

[17] S. J. Godsill. On the relationship between Markov chain Monte Carlo methods for model uncertainty. *Journal of Computational and Graphical Statistics*, **10**(2):230–248, 2001.

[18] S. J. Godsill and J. Vermaak. Models and algorithms for tracking using trans-dimensional sequential Monte Carlo. In *Proceedings of the IEEE International Conference on Acoustics, Speech and Signal Processing*, volume 3, pages 976–979, 2004.

[19] S. J. Godsill, J. Vermaak, W. Ng and J. Li. Models and algorithms for tracking of manoeuvring objects using variable rate particle filters. *Proceedings of the IEEE*, 95(5):925–952, 2007.

[20] A. Golightly and D. J. Wilkinson. Bayesian sequential inference for nonlinear multivariate diffusions. *Statistics and Computing*, pages 323–338, 2006.

[21] N. J. Gordon, D. J. Salmond and D. Fisher. Bayesian target tracking after group pattern distortion. In O. E. Drummond, editor, *Signal and Data Processing of Small Targets*, volume 3163, pages 238–248. SPIE, 1997.

[22] N. J. Gordon, D. J. Salmond and A. F. M. Smith. Novel approach to nonlinear/non-Gaussian Bayesian state estimation. In *IEEE Proceedings of Radar and Signal Processing*, volume 140, pages 107–113, 1993.

[23] M. I. Jordan, Z. Ghahramani, T. S. Jaakkola and L. K. Saul. An introduction to variational

methods for graphical models. In M. I. Jordan, editor, *Learning in Graphical Models*, pages 183–233. MIT Press, 1999.

[24] Z. Khan, T. Balch and F. Dellaert. MCMC-based particle filtering for tracking a variable number of interacting targets. *IEEE Transactions on Pattern Analysis and Machine Intelligence*, **27**:1805–1819, 2005.

[25] A. Kong, J. S. Liu and W. H. Wong. Sequential imputation and Bayesian missing data problems. *Journal of the American Statistical Association*, **89**:278–288, March 1994.

[26] C. Kreucher, M. Morelande, K. Kastella and A. O. Hero. Particle filtering for multitarget detection and tracking. *IEEE Transactions on Aerospace and Electronic Systems*, **41**:1396–1414, 2005.

[27] J. Liu and M. West. Combined parameter and state estimation in simulation-based filtering. In A. Doucet, N. Freitas, and N. Gordon, editors, *Sequential Monte Carlo in Practice*, pages 197–217. Springer-Verlag, 2001.

[28] R. P. S. Mahler. *Statistical Multisource-Multitarget Information Fusions*. Artech House, 2007.

[29] B. Øksendal. *Stochastic Differential Equations: An Introduction with Applications (Sixth Edition)*. Springer-Verlag, 2003.

[30] S. K. Pang, J. Li and S. J. Godsill. Models and algorithms for detection and tracking of coordinated groups. In *Proceedings of the IEEE Aerospace Conference*, 2008.

[31] S. K. Pang, J. Li and S. J. Godsill. Detection and tracking of coordinated groups. *IEEE Transactions on Aerospace and Electronic Systems*, **47**(1):472–502, 2011.

[32] M. K. Pitt and N. Shephard. Filtering via simulation: Auxiliary Particle Filter. *Journal of the American Statistical Association*, **94**:590–599, 1999.

[33] N. G. Polson, J. R. Stroud and P. Müller. Practical filtering with sequential parameter learning. *Journal of the Royal Statistical Society*, pages 413–428, 2008.

[34] B. Ristic, S. Arulampalam and N. Gordon. *Beyond the Kalman Filter – Particle Filters for Tracking Applications*. Artech House, 2004.

[35] C. P. Robert and G. Casella. *Monte Carlo Statistical Methods – Second Edition*. Springer, 2004.

[36] S. Sarkka. Recursive Bayesian inference on stochastic differential equations. PhD Thesis, Helsinki University of Technology, 2006.

[37] F. Septier, S. K. Pang, A. Carmi and S. J. Godsill. Tracking of coordinated groups using marginalised MCMC-based Particle Algorithm. In *Proceedings of the IEEE Aerospace Conference*, 2009.

[38] N. Srebro and S. Roweis. Time-varying topic models using dependent Dirichlet processes. *The University of Chicago Technical Report UTML-TR-2005-003*, March 2005.

[39] R. F. Stengel. *Optimal Control and Estimation*. Dover Publications, 1994.

[40] M. Stephens. Dealing with label switching in mixture models. *Journal of the Royal Statistical Society. Series B (Statistical Methodology)*, **62**:795–809, 2000.

[41] L. Tierney. Markov chains for exploring posterior distributions. *Annals of Statistics*, **22**:1701–1786, 1994.

[42] X. Wei, J. Sun and X. Wang. Dynamic mixture models for multiple time series. In *Proceedings of the International Joint Conference on Artificial Intelligence*, pages 2909–2914, 2007.

Contributors

Sze Kim Pang, Signal Processing Laboratory, Department of Engineering, University of Cambridge

Simon J. Godsill, Signal Processing Laboratory, Department of Engineering, University of Cambridge

Jack Li, Signal Processing Laboratory, Department of Engineering, University of Cambridge

François Septier, Institut TELECOM/TELECOM Lille 1, France

Simon Hill, Signal Processing Laboratory, Department of Engineering, University of Cambridge

13

Non-commutative harmonic analysis in multi-object tracking

Risi Kondor

13.1 Introduction

Simultaneously tracking n targets in space involves two closely coupled tasks: estimating the current positions $x_1, x_2, \ldots, x_n$ of their tracks, and estimating the assignment $\sigma\colon \{1, 2, \ldots, n\} \to \{1, 2, \ldots, n\}$ of targets to tracks. While the former is often a relatively straightforward extension of the single target case, the latter, called identity management or data association, is a fundamentally combinatorial problem, which is harder to fit in a computationally efficient probabilistic framework.

Identity management is difficult because the number of possible assignments grows with $n!$. This means that for n greater than about 10 or 12, representing the distribution $p(\sigma)$ explicitly as an array of $n!$ numbers is generally not possible.

In this chapter we discuss a solution to this problem based on the generalisation of harmonic analysis to non-commutative groups, specifically, in our case, the group of permutations. According to this theory, the Fourier transform of p takes the form

$$\widehat{p}(\lambda) = \sum_{\sigma \in \mathbb{S}_n} p(\sigma) \rho_\lambda(\sigma),$$

where $\mathbb{S}_n$ denotes the group of permutations of n objects, λ is a combinatorial object called an integer partition, and ρ_λ is a special matrix-valued function called a representation. These terms are defined in our short primer on representation theory in Section 13.2.

What is important to note is that, since ρ_λ is matrix-valued, each Fourier component $\widehat{p}(\lambda)$ is a matrix, not just a scalar. Apart from this surprising feature, non-commutative Fourier transforms are very similar to their familiar commutative counterparts.

In particular, we argue that there is a well-defined sense in which some of the $\widehat{p}(\lambda)$ matrices are the 'low-frequency' components of p, and approximating p with this subset of components is optimal. A large part of this chapter is focused on how to define such a notion of 'frequency', and how to find the corresponding Fourier components. We describe two seemingly very different approaches to answering this question, and find, reassuringly, that they give exactly the same answer.

Of course, in addition to a compact way of representing p, efficient inference also demands fast algorithms for updating p with observations. Section 13.6 gives an overview of the fast Fourier methods that are employed for this purpose.

13.1.1   Related work

The generalisation of harmonic analysis to non-commutative groups is based on representation theory, which, sprouting from the pioneering work of Frobenius, Schur and others at the turn of the twentieth century, has blossomed into one of the most prominent branches of algebra. The symmetric group (as the group of permutations is known) occupies a central position in this theory. For a general introduction to representation theory the reader is referred to [19], while for information on the symmetric group and its representations we recommend [18].

For much of the twentieth century, generalised Fourier transforms were the exclusive domain of pure mathematicians. It was not until the 1980s that connections to statistics and applied probability became widely recognised, thanks in particular to the work of Persi Diaconis and his collaborators. The well-known book [3] covers a wealth of topics ranging from ranking to card shuffling, and presages many of the results that we describe below, in particular with regard to spectral analysis on permutations.

Also towards the end of the 1980s a new field of computational mathematics started emerging, striving to develop fast Fourier transforms for non-commutative groups. The first such algorithm for the symmetric group is due to Clausen [2]. Later improvements and generalizations can be found in [15] and [16]. For an overview of this field, including applications, see [17].

The first context in which non-commutative harmonic analysis appeared in machine learning was multi-object tracking. This chapter is based on [12], where this idea was first introduced. Huang *et al.* [7] extended the model by deriving more general Fourier space updates, and later introduced an alternative update scheme exploiting independence [5]. The journal article [6] is a tutorial quality overview of the subject.

Besides tracking, Fourier transforms on the symmetric group can also be used to construct permutation invariant representations of graphs [11, 14], define characteristic kernels on groups [4, 9], and solve hard optimisation problems [10]. An analogue of compressed sensing for permutations is discussed in [8].

13.2   Harmonic analysis on finite groups

This section is intended as a short primer on representation theory and harmonic analysis on groups. The reader who is strictly only interested in identity management might wish to skip to Section 13.3 and refer back to this section as needed for the definitions of specific terms.

A **finite group** G is a finite set endowed with an operation $G \times G \rightarrow G$ (usually denoted multiplicatively) obeying the following axioms:

G1. For any $x, y \in G$, $xy \in G$ (closure).

G2. For any $x, y, z \in G$, $x(yz) = (xy)z$ (associativity).

G3. There is a unique $e \in G$, called the **identity** of G, such that $ex = xe = x$ for any $x \in G$.

G4. For any $x \in G$, there is a corresponding element $x^{-1} \in G$ called the **inverse** of x, such that $xx^{-1} = x^{-1}x = e$.

One important property that is missing from these axioms is commutativity, $xy = yx$. Groups that do satisfy $xy = yx$ for all x and y are called **commutative** or **Abelian** groups. A simple example of a finite commutative group is $\mathbb{Z}_n = \{0, 1, \ldots, n-1\}$, the group operation being addition modulo n. The group of permutations that appears in tracking problems, however, is not commutative.

Finite groups are quite abstract objects. One way to make them a little easier to handle is to 'model' them by square matrices that multiply the same way as the group elements do. Such a system of matrices $(\rho(x))_{x \in G}$ obeying $\rho(x)\rho(y) = \rho(xy)$ for all $x, y \in G$ is called a **representation** of G. In general, we allow representation matrices to be complex valued. Abstractly, a representation ρ is then a function $\rho \colon G \to \mathbb{C}^{d_\rho \times d_\rho}$, where d_ρ is called the **degree** or the **dimensionality** of ρ.

Once we have found one representation ρ of G, it is fairly easy to manufacture other representations. For example, if T is an invertible d_ρ-dimensional matrix, then $\rho'(x) = T^{-1}\rho(x)T$ is also a representation of G. Pairs of representations related to each other in this way are said to be **equivalent**.

Another way to build new representations is by taking direct sums: if ρ_1 and ρ_2 are two representations of G, then so is $\rho_1 \oplus \rho_2$, defined

$$(\rho_1 \oplus \rho_2)(x) = \rho_1(x) \oplus \rho_2(x) = \begin{pmatrix} \rho_1(x) & 0 \\ 0 & \rho_2(x) \end{pmatrix}.$$

Just as ρ' is essentially the same as ρ, $\rho_1 \oplus \rho_2$ is also not a truly novel representation. Representations which cannot be reduced into a direct sum of smaller representations (i.e., for which there is no matrix T and smaller representations ρ_1 and ρ_2 such that $\rho(x) = T^{-1}(\rho_1(x) \oplus \rho_2(x))T$ for all $x \in G$) are called **irreducible**.

A key goal in developing the representation theory of a given finite group is to find a **complete set of inequivalent irreducible representations**. We will denote such a system of representations by $\mathcal{R}_G$, and call its members **irreps** for short. Just as any natural number can be expressed as a product of primes, once we have $\mathcal{R}_G$ any representation of G can be expressed as a direct sum of irreps from $\mathcal{R}_G$, possibly conjugated by some matrix T. By a basic theorem of representation theory, if G is a finite group then $\mathcal{R}_G$ is of finite cardinality, and is well defined in the sense that if $\mathcal{R}'_G$ is a different system of irreps then there is a bijection between $\mathcal{R}_G$ and $\mathcal{R}'_G$ mapping each ρ to a ρ' with which it is equivalent. Abelian groups are special in that all their irreps are one-dimensional, so they can be regarded as just scalar functions $\rho \colon G \to \mathbb{C}$.

The concept of irreps is exactly what is needed to generalise Fourier analysis to groups. Indeed, the exponential factors $e^{-2\pi i k x}$ appearing in the discrete Fourier transform

$$\widehat{f}(k) = \sum_{x \in \{0,\dots,n-1\}} e^{-2\pi i k x} f(x)$$

are nothing but the irreps of $\mathbb{Z}_n$. This suggests that the **Fourier transform** on a non-commutative finite group should be

$$\widehat{f}(\rho) = \sum_{x \in G} f(x)\rho(x), \qquad \rho \in \mathcal{R}_G. \tag{13.1}$$

At first sight it might seem surprising that f is a function on G, whereas $\widehat{f}$ is a sequence of matrices. It is also strange that the Fourier components, instead of corresponding to different frequencies, are now indexed by irreps. In other respects, however, Eq. (13.1) is very similar to the familiar commutative Fourier transforms. For example, we have an inverse transform

$$f(x) = \frac{1}{|G|} \sum_{\rho \in \mathcal{R}_G} d_\rho \, \mathrm{tr}\left[\rho(x)^{-1} \widehat{f}(\rho)\right], \tag{13.2}$$

and Eq. (13.1) also satisfies a generalised form of Parseval's theorem (more generally referred to as Plancherel's theorem), stating that with respect to the appropriate matrix norms, $f \mapsto \hat{f}$ is a unitary transformation.

Another important property inherited from ordinary Fourier analysis is the **convolution theorem**. On a non-commutative group, the convolution of two functions f and g is defined

$$(f * g)(x) = \sum_{y \in G} f(xy^{-1}) g(y). \tag{13.3}$$

The convolution theorem states that each component of the Fourier transform of $f * g$ is just the matrix product of the corresponding components of $\hat{f}$ and $\hat{g}$, that is

$$\widehat{(f * g)}(\rho) = \hat{f}(\rho) \cdot \hat{g}(\rho). \tag{13.4}$$

The translation and correlation theorems have similar non-commutative analogues.

13.2.1 The symmetric group

The mapping $\sigma: \{1, 2, \ldots, n\} \to \{1, 2, \ldots, n\}$ from targets to tracks is effectively a **permutation** of the set $\{1, 2, \ldots, n\}$. The product of two permutations is usually defined as their composition, i.e., $(\sigma_2 \sigma_1)(i) = \sigma_2(\sigma_1(i))$ for all $i \in \{1, 2, \ldots, n\}$. It is easy to check that with respect to this notion of multiplication the $n!$ different permutations of $\{1, 2, \ldots, n\}$ form a non-commutative finite group. This group is called the **symmetric group** of degree n, and is denoted $\mathbb{S}_n$.

To compute the Fourier transform of the assignment distribution $p(\sigma)$, we need to study the representation theory of the symmetric group. Fortunately, starting with the pioneering work of the Rev Alfred Young at the turn of the twentieth century, mathematicians have invested a great deal of effort in exploring the representation theory of the symmetric group, and have discovered a wealth of beautiful and powerful results. Some of the questions to ask are the following: (1) How many irreps does $\mathbb{S}_n$ have and how shall we index them? (2) What is the dimensionality of each irrep ρ and how shall we index the rows and columns of $\rho(\sigma)$? (3) What are the actual $[\rho(\sigma)]_{i,j}$ matrix entries? To answer these questions Young introduced a system of combinatorial objects, which in his honour we now call Young diagrams and Young tableaux.

A **partition** of n, denoted $\lambda \vdash n$, is a k-tuple $\lambda = (\lambda_1, \lambda_2, \ldots, \lambda_k)$ satisfying $\sum_{i=1}^{k} \lambda_i = n$ and $\lambda_{i+1} \leq \lambda_i$ for $i = 1, 2, \ldots k-1$. The **Young diagram** (Ferrers diagram) of λ just consists of $\lambda_1, \lambda_2, \ldots, \lambda_k$ boxes laid down in consecutive left-justified rows. For example,

is the Young diagram of $\lambda = (4, 3, 1)$. A **Young tableau** is a Young diagram in which the boxes are bijectively filled with the numbers $1, 2, \ldots, n$, and a **standard Young tableau** is a Young tableau in which in each row the numbers increase from left to right and in each column they increase from top to bottom. For example,

1	2	5	8
3	4	7	
6			

is a standard Young tableau of shape $\lambda = (4, 3, 1)$. The set of all Young tableaux of shape λ we denote $\mathcal{T}_\lambda$.

Young discovered that there are exactly as many irreps in $\mathcal{R}_{\mathbb{S}_n}$ as there are partitions of n. Thus, instead of frequencies, in the case of the symmetric group we use partitions to index the irreps. Even more remarkably, if we employ the correct bijection between irreps and partitions, the dimensionality $d_\lambda := d_{\rho_\lambda}$ of ρ_λ is the same as the number of standard tableaux of shape λ. This suggests indexing the rows and columns of $\rho_\lambda(\sigma)$ by standard tableaux: instead of talking about the (i, j)-element of the matrix $\rho_\lambda(\sigma)$, where i and j are integers, we will talk about the (t, t')-element, where t and t' are standard tableaux of shape λ.

As regards defining the values of the actual $[\rho_\lambda(\sigma)]_{t,t'}$ matrix entries, a number of different alternatives are described in the literature, of which the most convenient one for our present purposes is **Young's orthogonal representation**, which we will abbreviate as **YOR**. In the following, whenever we refer to irreps of $\mathbb{S}_n$, we will implicitly always be referring to this system of irreducible representations.

To define YOR we need a more compact way to denote individual permutations than just writing $\sigma = [s_1, s_2, \ldots, s_n]$, where $s_1 = \sigma(1), \ldots, s_n = \sigma(n)$. The usual solution is **cycle notation**. A **cycle** $(c_1, c_2, \ldots, c_k)$ in σ is a sequence such that $\sigma(c_1) = c_2, \ldots, \sigma(c_{n-1}) = c_n$ and $\sigma(c_n) = c_1$. The cycle notation for σ consists of listing its constituent cycles, for example $\sigma = [2, 3, 1, 5, 4]$ would be written $(1, 2, 3)(4, 5)$. Clearly, this uniquely defines σ. Any i that are fixed by σ form single-element cycles by themselves, but these trivial cycles are usually omitted from cycle notation. The **cycle type** $\mu = (\mu_1, \mu_2, \ldots, \mu_\ell)$ of σ is the length of its cycles, listed in weakly decreasing order.

The notion of cycles and cycle type suggest some special classes of permutations. The simplest permutation is the **identity** e, which is the unique permutation of cycle type $(1, 1, \ldots, 1)$. Next, we have the class of **transpositions**, which are the permutations of cycle type $(2, 1, \ldots, 1)$. Thus, a transposition is a single two-cycle $\sigma = (i, j)$, exchanging i with j and leaving everything else fixed. **Adjacent transpositions** are special transpositions of the form $\tau_i = (i, i+1)$.

We define YOR by giving explicit formulae for the representation matrices of adjacent transpositions. Since any permutation can be written as a product of adjacent transpositions, this defines YOR on the entire group. For any standard tableau t, letting $\tau_i(t)$ be the tableau that we get from t by exchanging the numbers i and $i + 1$ in its diagram, the rule defining $\rho_\lambda(\tau_i)$ in YOR is the following: if $\tau_i(t)$ is *not* a standard tableau, then the column of $\rho_\lambda(\tau_i)$ indexed by t is zero, except for the diagonal element $[\rho_\lambda(\tau_i)]_{t,t} = 1/d_t(i, i+1)$; if $\tau_i(t)$ is a standard tableau, then in addition to this diagonal element, we also have a single non-zero off-diagonal element $[\rho_\lambda(\tau_i)]_{\tau_k(t),t} = (1 - 1/d_t(i, i+1)^2)^{1/2}$. All other matrix entries of $\rho_\lambda(\tau_i)$ are zero. In the above $d_t(i, i+1) = c_t(i+1) - c_t(i)$, where $c(j)$ is the column index minus the row index of the cell where j is located in t.

Young's orthogonal representation has a few special properties that are worth noting at this point. First, despite having stressed that representation matrices are generally complex-valued, the YOR matrices are, in fact, all real. It is a special property of $\mathbb{S}_n$ that it admits a system of irreps which is purely real. The second property is that, as the name suggests, the YOR matrices are orthogonal. In particular, $\rho_\lambda(\sigma^{-1}) = \rho_\lambda(\sigma)^\top$. Third, as is apparent from the definition, the $\rho_\lambda(\tau_i)$ matrices are extremely sparse, which will turn out to be critical for constructing fast algorithms. Finally, and this applies to all commonly used systems of irreps for $\mathbb{S}_n$, not just YOR, the representation corresponding to the partition (n) is the trivial representation $\rho_{(n)}(\sigma) = 1$ for all $\sigma \in \mathbb{S}_n$.

13.3 Band-limited approximations

Combining Eq. (13.1) with the representation theory of $\mathbb{S}_n$ tells us that the Fourier transform of the assignment distribution p is the sequence of matrices

$$\widehat{p}(\lambda) := \widehat{p}(\rho_\lambda) = \sum_{\sigma \in \mathbb{S}_n} p(\sigma)\rho_\lambda(\sigma), \qquad \lambda \vdash n.$$

Regarding p as a vector $\mathbf{p} \in \mathbb{R}^{\mathbb{S}_n}$, this can also be written componentwise as

$$[\widehat{p}(\lambda)]_{t,t'} = \langle \mathbf{p}, \mathbf{u}^\lambda_{t,t'} \rangle, \quad \text{where} \quad \mathbf{u}^\lambda_{t,t'} = \sum_{\sigma \in \mathbb{S}_n} [\rho_\lambda(\sigma)]_{t,t'}\, \mathbf{e}_\sigma,$$

and $(\mathbf{e}_\sigma)_{\sigma \in \mathbb{S}_n}$ is the canonical orthonormal basis of $\mathbb{R}^{\mathbb{S}_n}$. From this point of view, the Fourier transform is a series of projections to the subspaces

$$V_\lambda = \operatorname{span}\{\, \mathbf{u}^\lambda_{t,t'} \mid t, t' \in \mathcal{T}_\lambda \,\},$$

called the **isotypics** of $\mathbb{R}^{\mathbb{S}_n}$. By the unitarity of the Fourier transform, the isotypics are pairwise orthogonal and together span the entire space.

The key idea of this chapter is to approximate $\mathbf{p}$ by its projection to some subspace W, expressible as a sum of isotypics $W = \bigoplus_{\lambda \in \Lambda} V_\lambda$. The question is how we should choose W so as to retain as much useful information about $p(\sigma)$ as possible.

In the following we discuss two alternative approaches to answering this question. In the first approach, presented in Section 13.4, we define a Markov process governing the evolution of p, and argue that W should be the subspace least affected by stochastic noise under this model. We find that under very general conditions this subspace is indeed a sum of isotypics, specifically, in the most natural model for identity management, $W = \bigoplus_{\lambda \in \Lambda_k} V_\lambda$, where $\Lambda_k = \{\, \lambda \vdash n \mid \lambda_1 \geq n - k \,\}$. The integer parameter k plays a role akin to the cutoff frequency in low-pass filtering.

In the second approach, in Section 13.5, we ask the seemingly very different question of what sequence of subspaces $U_1, U_2, \ldots$ of $\mathbb{R}^{\mathbb{S}_n}$ capture the first-order marginals $p(\sigma(i) = j)$, second-order marginals $p(\sigma(i_1) = j_1,\ \sigma(i_2) = j_2)$, and so on, up to order k. Surprisingly, we find that the answer is again $U_k = \bigoplus_{\lambda \in \Lambda_k} V_\lambda$.

13.4 A hidden Markov model in Fourier space

Just as in tracking a single target, the natural graphical model to describe the evolution of the assignment distribution $p(\sigma)$ in identity management is a hidden Markov model. According to this model, assuming that at time t the distribution is $p_t(\sigma)$, in the absence of any observations, at time $t + 1$ it will be

$$p_{t+1}(\sigma') = \sum_{\sigma \in \mathbb{S}_n} p(\sigma'|\sigma)\, p_t(\sigma), \tag{13.5}$$

where $p(\sigma'|\sigma)$ is the probability of transitioning from assignment σ to σ'. For example, if a pair of targets i_1 (assigned to track j_1) and i_2 (assigned to track j_2) come very close to each other, there is some probability that due to errors in our sensing systems their assignment might be flipped. This corresponds to transitioning from σ to $\sigma' = \tau\sigma$, where τ is the transposition (j_1, j_2).

When we do have an observation O at $t + 1$, by Bayes' rule the update takes on the slightly more complicated form

$$p_{t+1}(\sigma') = \frac{p(O|\sigma') \sum_{\sigma \in \mathbb{S}_n} p(\sigma'|\sigma) \, p_t(\sigma)}{\sum_{\sigma'' \in \mathbb{S}_n} p(O|\sigma'') \sum_{\sigma \in \mathbb{S}_n} p(\sigma''|\sigma) \, p_t(\sigma)}.$$

As an example, if we observe target i at track j with probability π, then

$$p(O|\sigma') = \begin{cases} \pi & \text{if } \sigma(i) = j, \\ (1 - \pi)/(n - 1) & \text{if } \sigma(i) \neq j. \end{cases} \tag{13.6}$$

Generally, in identity management we are interested in scenarios where observations are relatively infrequent, or the noise introduced by the transition process is relatively strong. Hence, the natural criterion for choosing the right form of band-limiting should be stability with respect to Eq. (13.5).

13.4.1 A random walk on $\mathbb{S}_n$

Equation (13.5) describes a random walk on $\mathbb{S}_n$ with transition matrix $P_{\sigma',\sigma} = p(\sigma'|\sigma)$. In particular, starting from an initial distribution $\mathbf{p}_0$, in the absence of observations, after t time steps the assignment distribution will be

$$\mathbf{p}_t = P^t \mathbf{p}_0. \tag{13.7}$$

As for random walks in general, the evolution of this process is governed by the spectral structure of P. Assuming that P is symmetric and its eigenvalues are $\alpha_1 \geq \alpha_2 \geq \ldots \geq \alpha_{n!} \geq 0$ with corresponding orthonormal eigenvectors $\mathbf{v}_1, \mathbf{v}_2, \ldots, \mathbf{v}_{n!}$ and $\mathbf{p}_0 = \sum_{i=1}^{n!} p_0^{(i)} \mathbf{v}_i$, at time t,

$$\mathbf{p}_t = \sum_{i=1}^{n!} \alpha_i^t p_0^{(i)} \mathbf{v}_i. \tag{13.8}$$

Clearly, the modes of $\mathbf{p}$ corresponding to low values of α will rapidly decay. To make predictions about $\mathbf{p}$, we should concentrate on the more robust, high α modes. Hence, ideally, the approximation subspace W should be spanned by these components.

In most cases we of course do not know the exact form of P. However, there are some general considerations that can still help us find W. First of all, it is generally reasonable to assume that the probability of a transition $\sigma \mapsto \sigma'$ should only depend on σ' relative to σ. In algebraic terms, letting $\sigma' = \tau\sigma$, $p(\tau\sigma|\sigma)$ must only be a function of τ, or equivalently, $p(\sigma'|\sigma) = q(\sigma\sigma^{-1})$ for some function $q \colon \mathbb{S}_n \to \mathbb{R}$. Plugging this into Eq. (13.5) gives

$$p_{t+1}(\sigma') = \sum_{\sigma \in \mathbb{S}_n} q(\sigma'\sigma^{-1}) \, p_t(\sigma),$$

which is exactly the convolution of p_t with q, as defined in Eq. (13.3). Thus, by Eq. (13.4), in Fourier space $\widehat{p}_{t+1}(\lambda) = \widehat{q}(\lambda) \cdot \widehat{p}_t(\lambda)$, and, in particular,

$$\widehat{p}_t(\lambda) = \widehat{q}(\lambda)^t \cdot \widehat{p}_0(\lambda). \tag{13.9}$$

Thus, the Fourier transform effectively block-diagonalises Eq. (13.7). From a computational point of view this is already very helpful: raising the $\widehat{q}(\lambda)$ matrices to the tth power is much cheaper than doing the same to the $n!$-dimensional P.

13.4.2 Relabelling invariance

Continuing the above line of thought, $q(\tau)$ must not depend on how we choose to label the tracks. More explicitly, if prior to a transition $\sigma \mapsto \tau\sigma$ we relabel the tracks by permuting their labels by some $\mu \in \mathbb{S}_n$, then apply τ, and finally apply μ^{-1} to restore the original labelling, then the probability of this composite transition should be the same as that of τ, i.e.,

$$q(\mu^{-1}\tau\mu) = q(\tau) \qquad \forall \mu \in \mathbb{S}_n. \tag{13.10}$$

Expressing the left-hand side by the inverse Fourier transform (13.2) and using the orthogonality of YOR gives

$$q(\mu^{-1}\tau\mu) = \frac{1}{n!} \sum_{\lambda} d_\lambda \operatorname{tr}[\rho_\lambda(\mu^{-1}\tau^{-1}\mu) \cdot \widehat{q}(\lambda)]$$

$$= \frac{1}{n!} \sum_{\lambda} d_\lambda \operatorname{tr}[\rho_\lambda(\mu^{-1}) \cdot \rho_\lambda(\tau^{-1}) \cdot \rho_\lambda(\mu) \cdot \widehat{q}(\lambda)]$$

$$= \frac{1}{n!} \sum_{\lambda} d_\lambda \operatorname{tr}[\rho_\lambda(\tau^{-1}) \cdot \rho_\lambda(\mu) \cdot \widehat{q}(\lambda) \cdot \rho_\lambda(\mu)^\top].$$

It is relatively easy to see that for this to equal

$$q(\tau) = \frac{1}{n!} \sum_{\lambda} d_\lambda \operatorname{tr}[\rho_\lambda(\tau^{-1}) \cdot \widehat{q}(\lambda)]$$

for all τ and μ, we must have $T^\top \widehat{q}(\lambda) T = \widehat{q}(\lambda)$ for all orthogonal matrices T, which in turn implies that each $\widehat{q}(\lambda)$ is a multiple of the identity. This result is summarised in the following theorem.

Theorem 13.1 *If the transition probabilities $p(\sigma'|\sigma) = q(\sigma'\sigma^{-1})$ are relabelling-invariant in the sense of Eq. (13.10), then the Fourier transform of q is of the form*

$$\widehat{q}(\lambda) = q_\lambda I_{d_\lambda}, \qquad \lambda \vdash n,$$

where $(q_\lambda)_{\lambda \vdash n}$ are scalar coefficients and I_{d_λ} denotes the d_λ-dimensional identity matrix.

Theorem 13.1 puts a very severe restriction on the form of q. Plugging into Eq. (13.9) it tells us that in Fourier space the equation governing our random walk is simply

$$\widehat{p}_t(\lambda) = q_\lambda^t \, \widehat{p}_0(\lambda).$$

At a more abstract level, Theorem 13.1 establishes a connection between the different subspaces of $\mathbb{R}^n$ corresponding to the different Fourier components (the isotypics) and the eigenspectrum of P.

Theorem 13.2 *If $p(\sigma'|\sigma) = q(\sigma'\sigma^{-1})$ is relabelling-invariant, then the eigenvectors $\mathbf{v}_1, \mathbf{v}_2, \ldots, \mathbf{v}_{n!}$ of P can be re-indexed by $\{\lambda \vdash n\}$ and $i = 1, 2, \ldots, d_\lambda^2$ so that $\{\mathbf{v}_i^\lambda\}_{i=1}^{d_\lambda^2}$ all share the same eigenvalue q_λ, and together span the isotypic V_λ.*

Hence, the different 'modes' of $\mathbf{p}$ referred to in connection with Eq. (13.8) are exactly its Fourier components! In this sense, approximating p by retaining its high q_λ Fourier components is an optimal approximation, just as in ordinary Fourier analysis low-pass filtering is optimal in the presence of high frequency noise.

13.4.3 Walks generated by transpositions

To find which Fourier components have high q_λ values, we need to be more specific about our random walk. In particular, we make the observation that while in a given finite interval of time many different subsets of targets and tracks may get exchanged, in most real-world tracking scenarios it is reasonable to assume that by making the interval between subsequent time steps sufficiently short, in each interval at most a single pair of targets will get swapped. Thus, there is no loss in restricting the set of allowable transitions to just single transpositions. Since any two transpositions τ_1 and τ_2 are related by $\tau_2 = \mu^{-1}\tau_1\mu$ for some μ, by relabelling invariance the probability of each transposition is the same, reducing the random walk to

$$p(\sigma'|\sigma) = \begin{cases} \beta & \text{if } \sigma' = (i, j) \cdot \sigma \text{ for some } 1 \le i < j \le n, \\ 1 - \binom{n}{2}\beta & \text{if } \sigma' = \sigma, \\ 0 & \text{otherwise,} \end{cases}$$

governed by the single (generally small) scalar parameter β. Now, by the argument leading to Theorem 13.1, we know that $\sum_{1 \le i < j \le n} \rho_\lambda((i, j))$ is a multiple of the identity, in particular,

$$\sum_{1 \le i < j \le n} \rho_\lambda((i, j)) = \frac{1}{d_\lambda} \sum_{1 \le i < j \le n} \text{tr}\left[\rho_\lambda((i, j))\right] I_{d_\lambda}.$$

In general, the function $\chi_\lambda(\sigma) = \text{tr}\left[\rho_\lambda(\sigma)\right]$ is called a **character** of $\mathbb{S}_n$, and obeys

$$\chi_\lambda(\mu^{-1}\sigma\mu) = \text{tr}\left[\rho_\lambda(\mu^{-1}) \cdot \rho_\lambda(\sigma) \cdot \rho_\lambda(\mu)\right] = \text{tr}\left[\rho_\lambda(\sigma) \cdot \rho_\lambda(\mu) \cdot \rho_\lambda(\mu)^{-1}\right] = \text{tr}\left[\rho_\lambda(\sigma)\right] = \chi_\lambda(\sigma)$$

for any μ and σ. Hence, $\chi_\lambda(\tau)$ is the same for all transpositions τ, and choosing $(1, 2)$ as the archetypal transposition, we can write

$$\sum_{1 \le i < j \le n} \rho_\lambda((i, j)) = \binom{n}{2}\frac{\chi_\lambda((1, 2))}{d_\lambda} I_{d_\lambda}.$$

Plugging into the Fourier transform and using the fact that for the identity permutation e, $\rho_\lambda(e) = I_{d_\lambda}$ for all λ yields that

$$q_\lambda = 1 - \beta \binom{n}{2}\left(1 - \frac{\chi_\lambda((1, 2))}{d_\lambda}\right).$$

This type of expression appears in various discussions of random walks over $\mathbb{S}_n$, and, as derived in [3], it may be written explicitly as

$$q_\lambda = 1 - \beta\binom{n}{2}(1 - r(\lambda)) \quad \text{where} \quad r(\lambda) = \binom{n}{2}^{-1} \sum_i \binom{\lambda_i}{2} - \binom{\lambda_i'}{2}, \tag{13.11}$$

where λ' is the transpose of λ, which we get by flipping its rows and columns.

In general, we find that q_λ is highest for 'flat' partitions, which have all their squares concentrated in the first few rows. The exact order in which q_λ drops starts out as follows:

$$1 = q_{(n)} \ge q_{(n-1,1)} \ge q_{(n-2,2)} \ge q_{(n-2,1,1)} \ge q_{(n-3,3)} \ge$$

$$q_{(n-3,2,1)} \ge q_{(n-3,1,1,1)} \ge q_{(n-4,4)} \ge \cdots \tag{13.12}$$

For a principled band-limited approximation to p we cut off this sequence at some point and only retain the Fourier matrices of p up to that point. It is very attractive that we can freely choose where that cutoff should be, establishing an optimal compromise between accuracy and computational expense.

Unfortunately, this freedom is somewhat limited by the fact that the dimensionality of the representations (and hence, of the Fourier matrices) grows very steeply as we move down the sequence (13.12). As we mentioned, $\rho_{(n)}$ is the trivial representation, which is one-dimensional. To find the dimensionality of the next representation, $\rho_{(n-1,1)}$, we must consider all standard tableaux of shape

.

Here and in the following we draw Young diagrams as if $n = 8$, but it should be understood that it is the general pattern that matters, not the exact number of boxes. In standard tableaux of the above shape, any of the numbers $2, 3, \ldots, n$ can occupy the single box in the second row. Once we have chosen this number, the rest of the standard tableau is fully determined by the 'numbers increase from left to right and top to bottom' rule. Hence, in total, there are $n - 1$ standard tableaux of this shape, so $\widehat{p}((n-1,1))$ is an $n-1$-dimensional matrix.

Similarly, standard tableaux of shapes

and

are determined by the numbers that occupy the two boxes in the second (and third) rows, so there are $O(n^2)$ standard tableaux of each of these two shapes.

In general, the number of standard tableaux of a given shape is given by the so-called **hook rule** (see, e.g., [18]), stating that

$$d_\lambda = \frac{n!}{\prod_b \ell(b)},$$

where the product extends over all boxes of the diagram, and $\ell(b)$ is the number of boxes to the right of b plus the number of boxes beneath b plus one. The dimensionalities given by this formula for the first few partitions in the sequence (13.12) are displayed in Table 13.1.

More important than the actual d_λ values in the table is the observation that in general, d_λ grows with $n^{n-\lambda_1}$. Thus, in practice, it makes sense to cut off the Fourier expansion after

(a) the first two Fourier components $\{\widehat{p}_{(n)}, \widehat{p}_{(n-1,1)}\}$; or

(b) the first four Fourier components $\{\widehat{p}_{(n)}, \widehat{p}_{(n-1,1)}, \widehat{p}_{(n-2,2)}, \widehat{p}_{(n-2,1,1)}\}$; or

λ		d_λ	λ		d_λ
(n)		1			
$(n-1,1)$		$n-1$	$(n-3,1,1,1)$		$\frac{(n-1)(n-2)(n-3)}{6}$
$(n-2,2)$		$\frac{n(n-3)}{2}$	$(n-4,4)$		$\frac{n(n-1)(n-2)(n-7)}{24}$
$(n-2,1,1)$		$\frac{(n-1)(n-2)}{2}$			
$(n-3,3)$		$\frac{n(n-1)(n-5)}{6}$	$(n-4,3,1)$		$\frac{n(n-1)(n-3)(n-6)}{8}$
$(n-3,2,1)$		$\frac{n(n-2)(n-4)}{3}$	$(n-4,2,2)$		$\frac{n(n-1)(n-4)(n-5)}{12}$

Table 13.1 The size of the first few irreps of $\mathbb{S}_n$. For concreteness the diagrams are drawn as if $n = 8$.

(c) the first seven Fourier components $\{\widehat{P}_{(n)}, \widehat{P}_{(n-1,1)}, \widehat{P}_{(n-2,2)}, \widehat{P}_{(n-2,1,1)}, \widehat{P}_{(n-3,3)},$ $\widehat{P}_{(n-3,2,1)}, \widehat{P}_{(n-3,1,1,1)}\}$.

Going beyond these first, second and third 'order' Fourier matrices would involve $O(n^4)$-dimensional matrices, which for n in the mid teens or greater is infeasible.

13.4.4   The continuous time limit

The random walk analysis that we just presented is a somewhat simplified version of the account given in [12]. One of the differences is that the derivations in that paper were framed in terms of the **graph Laplacian**

$$\Delta_{\sigma',\sigma} = \begin{cases} -\frac{1}{\beta} p(\sigma'|\sigma) & \text{if } \sigma' \neq \sigma, \\ \frac{1}{\beta} \sum_{\tau \neq \sigma} p(\tau|\sigma) & \text{if } \sigma' = \sigma, \end{cases}$$

of the weighted graph corresponding to the random walk. The transition matrix P is expressed in terms of the graph Laplacian as $P = I - \beta\Delta$. In particular, for the transposition-induced random walk of Section 13.4.3,

$$\Delta_{\sigma',\sigma} = \begin{cases} -1 & \text{if } \sigma' = (i, j) \cdot \sigma \text{ for some } 1 \leq i < j \leq n, \\ \binom{n}{2} & \text{if } \sigma' = \sigma, \\ 0 & \text{otherwise.} \end{cases}$$

The eigenvalues and eigenvectors of the graph Laplacian are also referred to as the spectrum of the corresponding graph.

In general, given a subset S of a finite group G, the graph with vertex set G in which x and y are adjacent if and only if $x^{-1}y \in S$ is called the **Cayley graph** of G generated by S. Thus, by our earlier results, we have the following theorem.

Theorem 13.3 *The eigenvalues of the Cayley graph of $\mathbb{S}_n$ generated by transpositions are*

$$\alpha_\lambda = \binom{n}{2}\left(1 - \frac{\chi_\lambda((1, 2))}{d_\lambda}\right) = \binom{n}{2}(1 - r(\lambda)), \qquad \lambda \vdash n,$$

where $r(\lambda)$ is defined as in Eq. (13.11), and each α_λ is d_λ^2-fold degenerate.

In recent years spectral graph theory has become popular in machine learning in a variety of contexts from dimensionality reduction [1], through constructing kernels [13], to semi-supervised learning. The Laplacian of the Cayley graph establishes a connection to this literature. A detailed account of kernels on finite groups is given in [9], and [4] investigates the properties of kernels on groups in general.

An important advantage of the Laplacian formulation is that it lets us take the continuous time limit of the random walk. Dividing the interval from t to $t+1$ into k equal time steps,

$$\mathbf{p}_{t+1} = \left(I - \frac{\beta\Delta}{k}\right)^k \mathbf{p}_t.$$

In the limit $k \to \infty$, where in any finite interval of time there are an infinite number of opportunities for a given transition to take place, but the probability of it taking place in any specific infinitesimal sub-interval is infinitesimally small, the expression in parentheses becomes the **matrix exponential** $e^{-\beta\Delta}$, and we arrive at the equation describing **diffusion** on our graph,

$$\mathbf{p}'_t = e^{-(t'-t)\beta\Delta}\,\mathbf{p}(t), \tag{13.13}$$

where t and t' are now real numbers. By analogy with Eq. (13.9),

$$\widehat{p}_{t'}(\lambda) = e^{-\alpha_\lambda\beta(t'-t)}\,\widehat{p}_t(\lambda),$$

so in Fourier space diffusion just amounts to rescaling the $\widehat{p}(\lambda)$ Fourier matrices.

In most real-world scenarios transitions happen in continuous time, so the diffusion model is, in fact, more appropriate than the discrete time random walk, and this is the model that we implemented in our experiments.

13.5 Approximations in terms of marginals

The random walk analysis of the previous section is mathematically compelling, but sheds no light on what information is captured by the different Fourier components. Leaving the Fourier formalism aside for the moment, let us ask what other, more intuitive ways we could find an appropriate subspace W for approximating $\mathbf{p}$.

One traditional approach to identity management is to just keep track of the $n{\times}n$ matrix of probabilities

$$M^{(1)}_{j,i} = \text{Prob}\,(\,\text{target } i \text{ is assigned to track } j\,) = \sum_{\sigma(i)=j} p(\sigma).$$

Clearly, this is a very impoverished representation for p, but it does have the merit of being fast to update. Huang *et al.* [6] demonstrate the limitations of such a first-order approach on a specific example. A more refined approach is to look at the $n(n-1)$-dimensional matrix of second-order marginals

$$M^{(2)}_{(j_1,j_2),(i_1,i_2)} = \text{Prob}\,(\,i_1 \text{ is at } j_1 \text{ and } i_2 \text{ is at } j_2\,) = \sum_{\sigma(i_1)=j_1,\,\sigma(i_2)=j_2} p(\sigma),$$

and so on, to higher orders. In general, kth order marginals can be expressed as an inner product

$$M^{(k)}_{(j_1,\ldots,j_k),(i_1,\ldots,i_k)} = \langle \mathbf{p}, \mathbf{u}_{(i_1,\ldots,i_k),(j_1,\ldots,j_k)}\rangle,$$

where $\mathbf{u}_{(i_1,\ldots,i_k),(j_1,\ldots,j_k)} = \sum_{\sigma(i_1)=j_1,\ldots,\sigma(i_k)=j_k} \mathbf{e}_\sigma$, and representing $p(\sigma)$ by $M^{(k)}$ corresponds to approximating it by its projection to

$$U_k = \text{span}\Big\{\mathbf{u}_{(i_1,\ldots,i_k),(j_1,\ldots,j_k)} \mid i_1,\ldots,i_k,j_1,\ldots,j_k \in \{1,2,\ldots,n\}\Big\}. \tag{13.14}$$

The natural question to ask is how the hierarchy of subspaces $U_1 \subset U_2 \subset \ldots \mathbb{R}^{\mathbb{S}_n}$ is related to the $(V_\lambda)_{\lambda\vdash n}$ isotypics. To answer this, the first thing to note is that in matrix form

$$M^{(1)} = \sum_{\sigma\in\mathbb{S}_n} p(\sigma)\,P^{(1)}(\sigma),$$

where $P^{(1)}(\sigma)$ are the usual permutation matrices

$$[P^{(1)}(\sigma)]_{j,i} = \begin{cases} 1 & \text{if } \sigma(i) = j, \\ 0 & \text{otherwise.} \end{cases}$$

Similarly, the matrix of kth order marginals can be written as

$$M^{(k)} = \sum_{\sigma \in \mathbb{S}_n} p(\sigma)\, P^{(k)}(\sigma), \tag{13.15}$$

where $P^{(k)}$ is the kth order permutation matrix

$$[P^{(k)}(\sigma)]_{(j_1,\dots,j_k),(i_1,\dots,i_k)} = \begin{cases} 1 & \text{if } \sigma(i_1) = j_1,\ \sigma(i_2) = j_2,\ \dots,\ \sigma(i_k) = j_k, \\ 0 & \text{otherwise,} \end{cases}$$

which is $n!/(n-k)!$-dimensional.

Such generalised permutation matrices map the basis vector labelled $(i_1, i_2, \dots, i_k)$ to the basis vector labelled $(\sigma(i_1), \dots, \sigma(i_k))$. It follows that $P^{(k)}(\sigma_2) P^{(k)}(\sigma_1)$ maps $(i_1, i_2, \dots, i_k)$ to $(\sigma_2 \sigma_1(i_1), \dots, \sigma_2 \sigma_1(i_k))$. In other words, $P^{(k)}$ is a representation of $\mathbb{S}_n$, and hence it must be expressible as a sum of irreps in the form

$$P^{(k)}(\sigma) = T_k^{-1} \left[\bigoplus_{\lambda \vdash n} \bigoplus_{m=1}^{K_{k,\lambda}} \rho_\lambda(\sigma) \right] T_k \qquad \forall\, \sigma \in \mathbb{S}_n,$$

for some appropriate choice of multiplicities $K_{k,\lambda}$ and invertible matrix T_k (if a particular irrep does not feature in this sum, then we just set the corresponding $K_{k,\lambda}$ to zero). Plugging this into Eq. (13.15) expresses $M^{(k)}$ directly in terms of the Fourier components of p as

$$M^{(k)} = T_k^{-1} \left[\bigoplus_{\lambda \vdash n} \bigoplus_{m=1}^{K_{k,\lambda}} \widehat{p}(\lambda) \right] T_k,$$

implying that the subspace of kth order marginals is the sum of isotypics

$$U_k = \bigoplus_{\substack{\lambda \vdash n \\ K_{k,\lambda} \geq 1}} V_\lambda.$$

The general answer to what the $K_{k,\lambda}$ and T are is given by a result called James' Submodule Theorem, as explained in [6]. Stating the theorem verbatim would require introducing additional notation and terminology. Instead, we just state its specialisation to the case of interest to us.

Theorem 13.4 *The space (13.14) of kth order marginals is the direct sum of isotypics*

$$U_k = \bigoplus_{\substack{\lambda \vdash n \\ \lambda_1 \geq n-k}} V_\lambda.$$

Thus, the intuitive notion of approximating p by its first, second, third, etc. order marginals leads to exactly the same approximation as the random walk analysis did. From this point of view, which is discussed extensively in [3, 6], and elsewhere, the significance of the Fourier formalism is that it provides a canonical basis for the U_k subspaces, eliminating the otherwise non-trivial linear dependencies between marginals. In addition, as we shall see in the next section, the structure of the Fourier transform is also the key to devising fast algorithms for updating p with observations.

13.6   Efficient computation

The previous two sections have made a strong case for approximating p in a particular way, by discarding all but a small number of specific Fourier components. A compact way to store p is only one half of the story, however: if any of the computations required to run the hidden Markov model demanded full Fourier transforms, our approach would still be infeasible. At a minimum, we need to be able to efficiently perform the following three operations:

1. **Rollup**, which is updating p between observations by the noise model, as expressed in Eq. (13.13).

2. **Conditioning**, which is the word used for updating p with observations, such as Eq. (13.6).

3. **Prediction**, which typically involves returning the maximum a posteriori permutation, or computing some set of marginals, such as $p_i(j) = p(\sigma(i) = j)$.

Each of these operations is to be applied to the kth order band-limited approximation described in the previous sections, consisting of the Fourier components

$$\widehat{p}(\lambda), \qquad \lambda \in \Lambda_k = \{\, \lambda \vdash n \mid \lambda_1 \geq n - k \,\}.$$

As we have seen, the largest of these matrices are $O(n^k)$-dimensional, so the total storage complexity is $O(n^{2k})$. We assume that at time zero the correct assignment is known, and that without loss of generality it is the identity permutation, so we initialise our model with $\widehat{p}(\lambda) = I_{d_\lambda}$, since $\rho_\lambda(e) = I_{d_\lambda}$. An alternative way to seed the model would be to set $\widehat{p}((n)) = 1$ and $\widehat{p}(\lambda) = 0$ for all $\lambda \neq (n)$, corresponding to the uniform distribution.

Of the three operations above, rollup is very easy to perform in Fourier space, since as we have seen, it just corresponds to rescaling the individual Fourier matrices according to $\widehat{p}_{t'}(\lambda) = e^{-\alpha_\lambda \beta(t'-t)} \widehat{p}_t(\lambda)$. This takes only $O(n^{2k})$ time.

Deriving algorithms for conditioning and prediction that run similarly fast is somewhat more involved, and requires considering projections of $\mathbf{p}$ to yet another system of subspaces, namely

$$R_{(i_1,\dots,i_\ell),(j_1,\dots,j_\ell)} = \mathrm{span}\{\, \mathbf{e}_\sigma \mid \sigma(i_1) = j_1, \dots, \sigma(i_\ell) = j_\ell \,\}, \quad i_1 < i_2 < \dots < i_e$$

if we are interested in conditioning on or predicting marginals up to order ℓ. Clearly, for any choice of ℓ and $i_1, \dots, i_\ell$,

$$\mathbb{R}^{\mathbb{S}_n} = \bigoplus_{j_1,\dots,j_\ell} R_{(i_1,\dots,i_\ell),(j_1,\dots,j_\ell)},$$

where the sum extends over all choices of mutually distinct $j_1, \dots, j_\ell$. Moreover, $\{\, \sigma \mid \sigma(i_1) = j_1, \dots \sigma(i_\ell) = j_\ell \,\}$ is a structure very similar to $\mathbb{S}_{n-\ell}$ (technically, it is an $\mathbb{S}_{n-\ell}$-coset), since it is a set of $(n-\ell)!$ permutations that map any i which is not one of $i_1, \dots, i_\ell$ to any position j, as long as it is not $j_1, \dots, j_\ell$. This implies that each $R_{(i_1,\dots,i_\ell),(j_1,\dots,j_\ell)}$ subspace has its own Fourier transform with respect to $\mathbb{S}_{n-\ell}$. Our key computational trick is to relate the individual components of these $\mathbb{S}_{n-\ell}$-transforms to the global $\mathbb{S}_n$-transform. For simplicity we only derive these relationships for the 'first-order' subspaces $R_{i,j} \equiv R_{(i),(j)}$. The higher-order relations ($\ell > 1$) can be derived by recursively applying the first-order ones.

Identifying $\mathbb{S}_{n-1}$ with the subgroup of permutations that fix n and defining $[\![a, b]\!]$ as the permutation

$$[\![a, b]\!](i) = \begin{cases} i+1 & \text{if } i = a, \ldots, b-1, \\ a & \text{if } i = b, \\ i & \text{otherwise}, \end{cases}$$

any σ satisfying $\sigma(i) = j$ can be uniquely written as $\sigma = [\![j, n]\!] \tau [\![i, n]\!]^{-1}$ for some $\tau \in \mathbb{S}_{n-1}$. Thus, the projection of a general vector $p \in \mathbb{R}^{\mathbb{S}_n}$ to $R_{i,j}$ is identified with $p_{i,j} \in \mathbb{R}^{\mathbb{S}_{n-1}}$ defined $p_{i,j}(\tau) = p([\![j, n]\!] \tau [\![i, n]\!]^{-1})$. Writing the full Fourier transform as

$$\widehat{p}(\lambda) = \sum_{j=1}^{n-1} \sum_{\tau \in \mathbb{S}_{n-1}} p([\![j, n]\!] \tau [\![i, n]\!]^{-1}) \rho_\lambda([\![j, n]\!] \tau [\![i, n]\!]^{-1})$$

$$= \sum_{j=1}^{n-1} \rho_\lambda([\![j, n]\!]) \left[\sum_{\tau \in \mathbb{S}_{n-1}} p([\![j, n]\!] \tau [\![i, n]\!]^{-1}) \rho_\lambda(\tau) \right] \rho_\lambda([\![i, n]\!])^{-1},$$

the expression in brackets is seen to be almost the same as the Fourier transform of $p_{i,j}$, except that ρ_λ is an irrep of $\mathbb{S}_n$ and not of $\mathbb{S}_{n-1}$. By complete reducibility we know that if τ is restricted to $\mathbb{S}_{n-1}$, then $\rho_\lambda(\tau)$ must be expressible as a sum of $\mathbb{S}_{n-1}$-irreps, but in general the exact form of this decomposition can be complicated. In YOR, however, it is easy to check that the decomposition is just

$$\rho_\lambda(\tau) = \bigoplus_{\lambda^- \in \lambda \downarrow_{n-1}} \rho_{\lambda^-}(\tau), \qquad \tau \in \mathbb{S}_{n-1},$$

where $\lambda \downarrow_{n-1}$ denotes the set of all partitions of $n-1$ that can be derived from λ by removing one box. Thus, $\widehat{p}$ can be computed from $(\widehat{p}_{i,j})_{j=1}^n$ by

$$\widehat{p}(\lambda) = \sum_{j=1}^{n} \rho_\lambda([\![j, n]\!]) \left[\bigoplus_{\lambda^- \in \lambda \downarrow_{n-1}} \widehat{p}_{i,j}(\lambda^-) \right] \rho_\lambda([\![i, n]\!])^\top. \tag{13.16}$$

A short computation shows that the inverse of this transformation is

$$\widehat{p}_{i,j}(\lambda^-) = \frac{1}{n d_{\lambda^-}} \sum_{\lambda \in \lambda^- \uparrow^n} d_\lambda \left[\rho_\lambda([\![j, n]\!])^\top \widehat{p}(\lambda) \rho_\lambda([\![i, n]\!]) \right]_{\lambda^-}, \tag{13.17}$$

where $\lambda^- \uparrow^n$ denotes the set of those partitions of n that we can get by adding a single box to λ, and $[M]_{\lambda^-}$ denotes the block of M corresponding to λ^-. In [12] we explain that thanks to the special structure of YOR, these computations can be performed very fast: for kth-order band-limited functions the complexity of Eqs. (13.16) and (13.17) is just $O(n^{2k+2})$. If we are only interested in a single projection $\widehat{p}_{i,j}$, then this is further reduced to $O(n^{2k+1})$. We remark that these operations are a modified form of the elementary steps in Clausen's FFT [2].

Conditioning on the assignment of individual targets and computing marginals can both be expressed in terms of the forward (13.16) and backward (13.17) transforms. For example, if at a given moment in time target i is observed to be at track j with probability π, then by Bayes' rule, p is to be updated to

$$p'(\sigma) = p(\sigma|O) = \frac{p(O|\sigma)\, p(\sigma)}{\sum_{\sigma' \in \mathbb{S}_n} p(O|\sigma')\, p(\sigma')},$$

where

$$p(O|\sigma) = \begin{cases} \pi & \text{if } \sigma(i) = j, \\ (1-\pi)/(n-1) & \text{if } \sigma(i) \neq j. \end{cases} \tag{13.18}$$

In terms of vectors this is simply $\mathbf{p}' \propto \frac{1-\pi}{n-1}\mathbf{p} + \frac{\pi n - 1}{n-1}\mathbf{p}_{i \to j}$, where $\mathbf{p}_{i \to j}$ is the projection of $\mathbf{p}$ to $R_{i,j}$. Thus, the update can be performed by computing $\mathbf{p}_{i \to j}$ by Eq. (13.17), rescaling by the respective factors $\frac{1-\pi}{n-1}$ and $\frac{\pi n - 1}{n-1}$, transforming back by Eq. (13.16), and finally normalising. All this can be done in time $O(n^{2k+1})$. Higher-order observations of the form $\sigma(i_1) = j_1, \ldots, \sigma(i_\ell) = j_\ell$ would involve projecting to the corresponding $R_{(i_1,\ldots,i_\ell),(j_1,\ldots,j_\ell)}$ subspace and would have the same time complexity.

Prediction in the simplest case consists of returning estimates of the probabilities $p(\sigma(i) = j)$. Computing these probabilities is again achieved by transforming to the $R_{i,j}$ subspaces. In particular, since $\rho_{(n-1)}$ is the trivial representation of $\mathbb{S}_{n-1}$, the one-dimensional Fourier component $\widehat{p}_{i,j}((n-1)) = \sum_{\tau \in \mathbb{S}_{n-1}} p_{i,j}(\tau)$ is exactly $p(\sigma(i) = j)$. In computing this single component, the sum in Eq. (13.17) need only extend over $\lambda = (n)$ and $(n-1)$, thus $p(\sigma(i) = j)$ can be computed from $\widehat{p}$ in $O(n^3)$ time. Naturally, computing $p(\sigma(i) = j)$ for all j then takes $O(n^4)$ time.

13.6.1 Truncation and positivity

In the above discussion we implicitly made the assumption that if p is initialised to be kth order band-limited, then as it evolves in time, it will preserve this structure. This is indeed true of the rollup update, but in the conditioning step adding the rescaled $\mathbf{p}_{i \to j}$ back onto $\mathbf{p}$ will generally activate additional Fourier components. Thus, conditioning must involve truncation in the Fourier domain.

To ensure that $\mathbf{p}$ still remains a probability distribution, we need to normalise and enforce pointwise positivity. Normalisation is relatively easy, since, as for $p_{i \to j}$, the total weight $\sum_{\sigma \in \mathbb{S}_n} p(\sigma)$ can be read off from $\widehat{p}((n))$. If this value strays from unity, all we need to do is divide all the $\widehat{p}(\lambda)$ matrices by it to renormalise.

Positivity is more difficult to enforce. In [12] we argued that in most cases even when $p(\sigma)$ becomes negative for some permutations, this does not seem to be a serious problem for predicting the marginals that we are ultimately interested in. An alternative approach introduced in [7], which seems to do somewhat better, is to use a quadratic program to project $\mathbf{p}$ back onto an appropriate marginal polytope after each conditioning step.

13.6.2 Kronecker conditioning

Our fast, $O(n^{2k+1})$ complexity method for conditioning in Fourier space relies heavily on the specific form (13.18) of the likelihood in our observation model. It is interesting to ask how the posterior might be computed in Fourier space if $g(\sigma) = p(O|\sigma)$ was a general function on permutations. In [6] it is shown this is related to the so called Clebsch–Gordan decomposition, which tells us how the tensor (or Kronecker) product of two representations decomposes into a direct sum:

$$C_{\lambda_1,\lambda_2}^\dagger \left[\rho_{\lambda_1}(\sigma) \otimes \rho_{\lambda_2}(\sigma)\right] C_{\lambda_1,\lambda_2} = \bigoplus_{\lambda \vdash n} \overset{z_{\lambda_1,\lambda_2\lambda}}{\underset{i=1}{\bigoplus}} \rho_\lambda(\sigma), \qquad \forall\, \sigma \in \mathbb{S}_n, \tag{13.19}$$

where the $d_{\lambda_1} d_{\lambda_2}$-dimensional constant matrix C_{λ_1,λ_2}, and the $z_{\lambda_1,\lambda_2\lambda}$ multiplicities are universal (albeit not easily computable) constants. In particular, they show that the Fourier transform of the unnormalised posterior $p'(\sigma) = g(\sigma)\, p(\sigma)$ is

$$\widehat{p}'(\lambda) = \frac{1}{n!\, d_\lambda} \sum_{\lambda_1,\lambda_2 \vdash n} d_{\lambda_1} d_{\lambda_2} \sum_{i=1}^{z_{\lambda_1,\lambda_2,\lambda}} \left[C^\dagger_{\lambda_1,\lambda_2} \left[\widehat{g}(\lambda_1) \otimes \widehat{p}(\lambda_2) \right] C_{\lambda_1,\lambda_2} \right]_{\lambda,i}, \qquad (13.20)$$

where $[\,\cdot\,]_{\lambda,i}$ corresponds to the 'ith λ-block' of the matrix in brackets according to the decomposition (13.19).

The price to pay for the generality of this formula is its computational expense: in contrast to the $O(n^{2k+1})$ complexity of conditioning with Eq. (13.18), if we assume that g is mth order band-limited, the complexity of computing Eq. (13.20) is $O(n^{3k+2m})$. Huang et al. [6] argue that in practice the C_{λ_1,λ_2} matrices are sparse, which somewhat reduces this computational burden, and manage to get empirical results using their approach for $n = 11$.

13.6.3 Empirical performance

Both our group and the Huang–Guestrin–Guibas group have performed experiments to validate the Fourier approach to identity management, but side-by-side comparisons with traditional algorithms are difficult for lack of standard benchmark datasets. Our group culled data from an online source of flight paths of commercial aircraft, while Huang et al. collected data of people moving around in a room, and later of ants in an enclosed space.

All experiments bore out the general rule that the more Fourier components that an algorithm can maintain, the better its predictions will be. Using the fast updates described above our algorithms can afford to maintain second-order Fourier components up to about $n = 30$, and third-order components up to about $n = 15$. Typically, each update takes only a few seconds on an ordinary desktop computer.

In contrast, more traditional identity management algorithms generally either store the entire distribution explicitly, which is only feasible for $n \le 12$, or in some form work with first-order marginals. Thus, Fourier algorithms have a definite edge in the intermediate $12 < n \le 30$ range.

Of course, all these statements relate to the scenario described in the introduction, where observations are relatively rare and p becomes appreciably spread out over many permutations. If the uncertainty can be localised to a relatively small set of permutations or a subset of the targets, then a particle filter method or the factorisation approach in [5] might be more appropriate. For more information on the experiments the reader is referred to [12] and [7].

13.7 Conclusions

Identity management is a hard problem because it involves inference over a combinatorial structure, namely the group of permutations. We argued that the right way to approach this problem is by Fourier analysis on the symmetric group.

While at first sight the Fourier transform on the symmetric group seems like a rather abstract mathematical construction, we have shown that the individual Fourier components of the assignment distribution $p(\sigma)$ can be interpreted in terms of both the modes of a random walk on permutations and in terms of the natural hierarchy of marginal probabilities. In particular, there is a sense in which certain Fourier components capture the 'low-frequency' information in $p(\sigma)$, and estimating $p(\sigma)$ in terms of these components is optimal.

In addition to discussing this principled way of approximating distributions over permutations, we also derived algorithms for efficiently updating it in a Bayesian way with observations. In general, we find that the kth order Fourier approximation to p has space complexity $O(n^{2k})$ and time complexity $O(n^{2k+1})$.

While the present chapter discussed identity management in isolation, in many real-world settings one would want to couple such a system to some other model describing the position of the individual targets, so that the position information can help disambiguate the identity information and vice versa. This introduces a variety of interesting issues, which are still the subject of research.

Acknowledgments   The author thanks Andrew Howard and Tony Jebara for their contributions to [12], the original paper that this chapter is largely based on. He is also indebted to Jonathan Huang, Carlos Guestrin and Leonidas Guibas for various discussions.

Bibliography

[1] M. Belkin and P. Niyogi. Laplacian eigenmaps for dimensionality reduction and data representation. In *Neural Information Processing Systems (NIPS)*, 2001.

[2] M. Clausen. Fast generalized Fourier transforms. *Theoretical Computer Science*, **67**:55–63, 1989.

[3] P. Diaconis. *Group Representations in Probability and Statistics*. IMS Lecture Series. Institute of Mathematical Statistics, 1988.

[4] K. Fukumizu, B. K. Sriperumbudur, A. Gretton and B. Schölkopf. Characteristic kernels on groups and semigroups. In *Neural Information Processing Systems (NIPS)*, 2008.

[5] J. Huang, C. Guestrin, X. Jiang and L. Guibas. Exploiting probabilistic independence for permutations. In *Proceedings of the International Conference on Artificial Intelligence and Statistics (AISTATS)*, 2009.

[6] J. Huang, C. Guestrin and L. Guibas. Fourier theoretic probabilistic inference over permutations. *Journal of Machine Learning Research*, **10**:997–1070, 2009.

[7] J. Huang, C. Guestrin and L. Guibas. Efficient inference for distributions on permutations. In *Neural Information Processing Systems (NIPS)*, 2007.

[8] S. Jagabathula and D. Shah. Inferring rankings under constrained sensing. In *Neural Information Processing Systems (NIPS)*, 2008.

[9] R. Kondor. *Group theoretical methods in machine learning*. PhD thesis, Columbia University, 2008.

[10] R. Kondor. A Fourier space algorithm for solving quadratic assignment problems. In *Proceedings of the ACM-SIAM Symposium on Discrete Algorithms (SODA)*, 2010.

[11] R. Kondor and K. M. Borgwardt. The skew spectrum of graphs. In *Proceedings of the International Conference on Machine Learning (ICML)*, 2008.

[12] R. Kondor, A. Howard, and T. Jebara. Multi-object tracking with representations of the symmetric group. In *Proceedings of the International Conference on Artificial Intelligence and Statistics (AISTATS)*, 2007.

[13] R. Kondor and J. Lafferty. Diffusion kernels on graphs and other discrete structures. In *Proceedings of the International Conference on Machine Learning (ICML) 2002*, 2002.

[14] R. Kondor, N. Shervashidze and K. M. Borgwardt. The graphlet spectrum. In *Proceedings of the International Conference on Machine Learning (ICML)*, 2009.

[15] D. K. Maslen. The efficient computation of Fourier transforms on the symmetric group. *Mathematics of Computation*, **67**(223):1121–1147, 1998.

[16] D. K. Maslen and D. N. Rockmore. Double coset decompositions and computational harmonic analysis on groups. *Journal of Fourier Analysis and Applications*, **6**(4), 2000.

[17] D. N. Rockmore. Some applications of generalized FFTs. *Proceedings of the DIMACS workshop on groups and computation 1995*, 1997.

[18] B. E. Sagan. *The Symmetric Group. Representations, combinatorial algorithms and symmetric functions*, volume 203 of Graduate Texts in Mathematics. Springer, 2001.

[19] J.-P. Serre. *Linear Representations of Finite Groups*, volume 42 of Graduate Texts in Mathematics. Springer-Verlag, 1977.

Contributor

Risi Kondor, Center for the Mathematics of Information, California Institute of Technology, USA

14

Markov chain Monte Carlo algorithms for Gaussian processes

Michalis K. Titsias, Magnus Rattray and Neil D. Lawrence

14.1 Introduction

Gaussian processes (GPs) have a long history in statistical physics and mathematical probability. Two of the most well-studied stochastic processes, Brownian motion [12, 47] and the Ornstein–Uhlenbeck process [43], are instances of GPs. In the context of regression and statistical learning, GPs have been used extensively in applications that arise in geostatistics and experimental design [26, 45, 7, 40]. More recently, in the machine learning literature, GPs have been considered as general estimation tools for solving problems such as non-linear regression and classification [29]. In the context of machine learning, GPs offer a flexible nonparametric Bayesian framework for estimating latent functions from data and they share similarities with neural networks [23] and kernel methods [35].

In standard GP regression, where the likelihood is Gaussian, the posterior over the latent function (given data and hyperparameters) is described by a new GP that is obtained analytically. In all other cases, where the likelihood function is non-Gaussian, exact inference is intractable and approximate inference methods are needed. Deterministic approximate methods are currently widely used for inference in GP models [48, 16, 8, 29, 19, 34]. However, they are limited by an assumption that the likelihood function factorises. In addition, these methods usually treat the hyperparameters of the model (the parameters that appear in the likelihood and the kernel function) in a non full Bayesian way by providing only point estimates. When more complex GP models are considered that may have non-factorising and heavily parameterised likelihood functions, the development of useful deterministic methods is much more difficult. Complex GP models can arise in time series applications, where the association of the latent function with the observed data can be described, for instance, by a system of ordinary differential equations. An application of this type has recently been considered in systems biology [3] where the latent function is a transcription factor protein that influences through time the mRNA expression level of a set of target genes [5, 32, 20]. In this chapter, we discuss Markov chain Monte Carlo (MCMC) algorithms for inference in GP models. An advantage of MCMC over deterministic approximate inference is that it provides an arbitrarily precise approximation to the posterior distribution in the limit of long runs. Another advantage is that the sampling scheme will often not depend on details of the likelihood function, and is therefore very generally applicable.

In order to benefit from the advantages of MCMC it is necessary to develop efficient sampling strategies. This has proved to be particularly difficult in many GP applications that involve the estimation of a smooth latent function. Given that the latent function is represented by a discrete set of values, the posterior distribution over these function values can be highly correlated. The more discrete values used to represent the function, the worse the problem of high correlation becomes. Therefore, simple MCMC schemes such as Gibbs sampling can often be very inefficient. In this chapter, we introduce two MCMC algorithms for GP models that can be more effective in sampling from highly correlated posterior GPs. The first algorithm is a block-based Metropolis–Hastings technique, where the latent function variables are partitioned into disjoint groups corresponding to different function regions. The algorithm iteratively samples each function region by conditioning on the remaining part of the function. The construction of the proposal distribution requires the partitioning of the function points into groups. This is achieved by an adaptive process performed in the early stage of MCMC. The block-based Metropolis–Hastings scheme can improve upon the Gibbs sampler, but it is still not so satisfactory in dealing with highly correlated posterior GPs. Therefore, we introduce a more advanced scheme that uses control variables. These variables are auxiliary function points which are chosen to provide an approximate low-dimensional summary of the latent function. We consider Metropolis–Hastings updates that firstly propose moves in the low-dimensional representation space and then globally sample the function. The design parameters of the control variables, i.e. their input locations, are found by minimising an objective function which is the expected least squares error of reconstructing the function values from the control variables, where the expectation is under the GP prior. The number of control variables required to construct the proposal distribution is found automatically by an adaptive process performed during the early iterations of the Markov chain. This sampling algorithm has previously been presented in [42].

Furthermore, we review other sampling algorithms that have been applied to GP models such as schemes based on variable transformation and Hybrid Monte Carlo [11]. In the context of sampling, we also discuss the problem of inference over large datasets faced by all GP models due to an unfavourable time complexity $O(n^3)$ where n is the number of function values needed in the GP model.

In our experimental study, we firstly demonstrate the MCMC algorithms on regression and classification problems. As our main application, we consider a problem in systems biology where we wish to estimate the concentration function of a transcription factor protein that regulates a set of genes. The relationship between the protein and the target genes is governed by a system of ordinary differential equations in which the concentration of the protein is an unobserved time-continuous function. Given a time series of observed gene expression mRNA measurements and assuming a GP prior over the protein concentration, we apply Bayesian inference using MCMC. This allows us to infer the protein concentration function together with other unknown kinetic parameters that appear in the differential equations.

The remainder of this chapter is organised as follows. Section 14.2 gives an introduction to GP models used in statistical learning, while Section 14.3 gives a brief overview of deterministic approximate inference algorithms applied to GP models. Section 14.4 describes sampling algorithms and Section 14.5 discusses related work. Section 14.6 demonstrates the sampling methods on regression and classification problems, while Section 14.7 gives a detailed description of the application to the regulation of gene transcription. Section 14.8

deals with sampling methods for large GP models. The chapter concludes with a discussion in Section 14.9.

14.2 Gaussian process models

A Gaussian process is a stochastic process, that is a set of random variables $\{f(\mathbf{x})|\mathbf{x} \in X\}$, where X is an index set, for which any finite subset follows a Gaussian distribution. To describe a GP, we only need to specify the mean function $m(\mathbf{x})$ and a covariance or kernel function $k(\mathbf{x}, \mathbf{x}')$

$$m(\mathbf{x}) = \mathsf{E}(f(\mathbf{x})), \tag{14.1}$$

$$k(\mathbf{x}, \mathbf{x}') = \mathsf{E}((f(\mathbf{x}) - m(\mathbf{x}))(f(\mathbf{x}') - m(\mathbf{x}'))), \tag{14.2}$$

where $\mathbf{x}, \mathbf{x}' \in X$. Gaussian processes naturally arise in the study of time-continuous stochastic processes [10, 46]. In the context of statistical learning, the practical use of GPs stems from the fact that they provide flexible ways of specifying prior distributions over real-valued functions that can be used in a Bayesian estimation framework. In this section, we give a brief introduction to GP models in the context of statistical learning. For extensive treatments see, for example, [29].

Suppose we wish to estimate a real-valued function $f(\mathbf{x})$. We assume that $\mathbf{x} \in \mathbb{R}^D$ and D is the dimensionality of the input space. We consider a GP model as the prior over the latent function $f(\mathbf{x})$, where for simplicity the mean function $m(\mathbf{x})$ is set to be equal to zero. This prior imposes stronger preferences for certain types of functions compared to others which are less probable. For instance, the prior may favour smooth or stationary functions, or functions with certain lengthscales. All this is reflected in the choice of the kernel $k(\mathbf{x}, \mathbf{x}')$, which essentially captures our prior beliefs about the function we wish to estimate. The kernel $k(\mathbf{x}, \mathbf{x}')$ must be positive definite and can be chosen to fall within a parametric family so as the values of the hyperparameters $\boldsymbol{\theta}$ further specify a member in this family. A common choice is the squared-exponential kernel

$$k(\mathbf{x}, \mathbf{x}') = \sigma_f^2 \exp\left\{-\frac{1}{2}(\mathbf{x} - \mathbf{x}')^T \Sigma^{-1}(\mathbf{x} - \mathbf{x}')\right\}, \tag{14.3}$$

where σ_f^2 is the kernel variance parameter and Σ is a positive definite matrix. Special cases of this kernel are often used in practice. For instance, Σ can be chosen to be diagonal, $\Sigma = \mathrm{diag}[\ell_1^2, \ldots, \ell_D^2]$, where each diagonal element is the lengthscale parameter for a given input dimension. This can be useful in high-dimensional input spaces, where by estimating the lengthscales we can learn to ignore irrelevant input dimensions that are uncorrelated with the output signal [29, 23]. The above type of kernel function defines a GP model that generates very smooth (infinitely many times differentiable) functions. This can be particularly useful for general purpose learning problems such as those that arise in machine learning applications. Other types of kernel function such as the Matérn class are often used [1, 40, 29]. There are also operations such as addition, multiplication and convolution that allow us to create new valid kernels from old ones.

Having chosen a GP prior over the latent function we would like to combine this with observed data, through a Bayesian formalism, and obtain a posterior over this function. When the data consist of noisy realisations of the latent function and the noise is Gaussian, the above framework has an analytical solution. In particular, let $(X, \mathbf{y}) = \{(\mathbf{x}_i, y_i)\}_{i=1}^n$ be a set of data where $\mathbf{x}_i \in \mathbb{R}^D$ and $y_i \in \mathbb{R}$. Each y_i is produced by adding Gaussian noise to the latent function at input $\mathbf{x}_i$

$$y_i = f_i + \epsilon_i, \quad \epsilon_i \sim N(0, \sigma^2),$$

where $f_i = f(\mathbf{x}_i)$. This defines a Gaussian likelihood model $p(\mathbf{y}|\mathbf{f}) = N(\mathbf{y}|\mathbf{f}, \sigma^2 I)$, where $\mathbf{f} = (f_1, \ldots, f_n)$. The marginalisation property of GPs allows simplification of the prior over the latent function which initially is an infinite-dimensional object. After marginalisation of all function points not associated with the data, we obtain a n-dimensional Gaussian distribution, $p(\mathbf{f}) = N(\mathbf{f}|\mathbf{0}, K_{f,f})$, where $\mathbf{0}$ denotes the n-dimensional zero vector and $K_{f,f}$ is the $n \times n$ covariance matrix obtained by evaluating the kernel function on the observed inputs. Overall, the joint probability model takes the form

$$p(\mathbf{y}, \mathbf{f}) = p(\mathbf{y}|\mathbf{f})p(\mathbf{f}).$$

Notice that this model is nonparametric as the dimension of the (parameter) $\mathbf{f}$ grows linearly with the number of data points. By applying Bayes' rule we can obtain the posterior over $\mathbf{f}$

$$p(\mathbf{f}|\mathbf{y}) = \frac{p(\mathbf{y}|\mathbf{f})p(\mathbf{f})}{\int p(\mathbf{y}|\mathbf{f})p(\mathbf{f})d\mathbf{f}}, \tag{14.4}$$

which can be used to obtain the prediction of any quantity of interest. For instance, the function values $\mathbf{f}_*$ at any set of unseen inputs X_* are computed according to

$$p(\mathbf{f}_*|\mathbf{y}) = \int p(\mathbf{f}_*|\mathbf{f})p(\mathbf{f}|\mathbf{y})d\mathbf{f}, \tag{14.5}$$

where $p(\mathbf{f}_*|\mathbf{f})$ is the conditional GP prior given by

$$p(\mathbf{f}_*|\mathbf{f}) = N(\mathbf{f}_*|K_{f_*,f}K_{f,f}^{-1}\mathbf{f}, K_{f_*,f_*} - K_{f_*,f}K_{f,f}^{-1}K_{f_*,f}^{\top}). \tag{14.6}$$

Here, the covariance matrix K_{f_*,f_*} is obtained by evaluating the kernel function on the inputs X_* and the cross-covariance matrix $K_{f_*,f}$ is obtained by evaluating for X_* and X. The prediction of the values $\mathbf{y}_*$ of the output signal corresponding to the latent points $\mathbf{f}_*$ is given by $p(\mathbf{y}_*|\mathbf{y}) = \int p(\mathbf{y}_*|\mathbf{f}_*)p(\mathbf{f}_*|\mathbf{y})d\mathbf{f}_*$. In the regression case, where the likelihood is Gaussian, all the above computations are analytically tractable and give rise to Gaussian distributions. Furthermore, the posterior over the latent function can be expressed as a new GP with an updated mean and kernel function. Thus, the counterparts of Eqs. (14.1) and (14.2) for the posterior GP are given by

$$m_{\mathbf{y}}(\mathbf{x}) = k(\mathbf{x}, X)(\sigma^2 I + K_{f,f})^{-1}\mathbf{y}, \tag{14.7}$$

$$k_{\mathbf{y}}(\mathbf{x}, \mathbf{x}') = k(\mathbf{x}, \mathbf{x}') - k(\mathbf{x}, X)(\sigma^2 I + K_{f,f})^{-1}k(X, \mathbf{x}'), \tag{14.8}$$

where $k(\mathbf{x}, X)$ is a n-dimensional row vector of kernel function values between $\mathbf{x}$ and X, while $k(X, \mathbf{x}) = k(\mathbf{x}, X)^{\top}$. The above functions fully specify our posterior GP and we can use them directly to compute any quantity of interest. For instance, the mean and the covariance matrix of the predictive Gaussian $p(\mathbf{f}_*|\mathbf{y})$ in Eq. (14.5) is simply obtained by evaluating the above at the inputs X_*.

The posterior GP depends on the values of the kernel parameters θ as well as the likelihood parameters. To make our notation explicit, we write the likelihood as $p(\mathbf{y}|\mathbf{f}, \alpha)$, with α being the parameters of the likelihood,[1] and the GP prior as $p(\mathbf{f}|\theta)$. The quantities (α, θ) are

---

[1] For the regression case α consists only of σ^2.

the hyperparameters of the GP model which have to be specified in order to obtain a close fit to the observed data. A common practice in machine learning is to follow an empirical Bayes approach and choose these parameters by maximising the marginal likelihood:

$$p(\mathbf{y}|\alpha, \theta) = \int p(\mathbf{y}|\mathbf{f}, \alpha)p(\mathbf{f}|\theta)\mathrm{df}.$$

When the likelihood is Gaussian this quantity is just a Gaussian distribution which can be maximised over (α, θ) by applying a continuous optimisation method. A full Bayesian treatment of the hyperparameters requires the introduction of corresponding prior distributions and an estimation procedure based on MCMC; see Section 14.4.5 for further discussion of this issue.

14.3 Non-Gaussian likelihoods and deterministic methods

The above framework, while flexible and conceptually simple, is computationally tractable only when the likelihood function $p(\mathbf{y}|\mathbf{f}, \alpha)$ is Gaussian. When the likelihood is non-Gaussian, computations become intractable and quantities such as the posterior $p(\mathbf{f}|\alpha, \theta, \mathbf{y})$ and the marginal likelihood $p(\mathbf{y}|\alpha, \theta)$ are not available in closed form. Clearly, the posterior process over the latent function $f(\mathbf{x})$ is not a GP any more. In such cases we need to consider approximate inference methods. Before describing MCMC methods in Section 14.4, we give a brief overview of deterministic approximate inference methods and highlight some of their limitations.

Deterministic methods are widely used for approximate inference in GP models, especially in the machine learning community. Three different algorithms used are the Laplace approximation [48], the expectation propagation algorithm [22, 8, 21, 19, 36] and the variational Gaussian approximation [27]. For instance, in binary GP classification, the expectation propagation algorithm seems to be accurate [19]. Deterministic methods were also recently discussed in the statistics literature in the context of Gaussian Markov random fields [34]. All these methods rely heavily on GP models that have a factorising likelihood function, i.e. $p(\mathbf{y}|\mathbf{f}, \alpha) = \prod_{i=1}^{n} p(y_i|f_i)$, where each likelihood factor $p(y_i|f_i)$ depends on a single function value f_i, and there is no sharing of function points across factors. Based on these assumptions, the conditional posterior is written in the form

$$p(\mathbf{f}|\alpha, \theta, \mathbf{y}) \propto \exp\left\{\sum_{i=1}^{n} \log p(y_i|f_i) - \frac{1}{2}\mathbf{f}^T K_{f,f}^{-1}\mathbf{f}\right\}.$$

All alternative methods approximate this posterior by a Gaussian distribution. They differ in the way such a Gaussian is obtained. For instance, the Laplace method replaces each factor $\log p(y_i|f_i)$ with a quadratic approximation, based on a Taylor series, and applies continuous optimisation to locate the mode of $p(\mathbf{f}|\alpha, \theta, \mathbf{y})$. The expectation propagation algorithm and the variational method also use iterative procedures, while being somehow more advanced as they minimise some divergence between a Gaussian approximation and the exact posterior. These methods will often be reasonably accurate especially when the conditional posterior $p(\mathbf{f}|\alpha, \theta, \mathbf{y})$ is uni-modal. Note, however, that the marginal posterior $p(\mathbf{f}|\mathbf{y}) = \int p(\mathbf{f}|\alpha, \theta, \mathbf{y})p(\alpha, \theta|\mathbf{y})\mathrm{d}\alpha\mathrm{d}\theta$ will generally be multi modal even for the standard regression case. The hyperparameters (α, θ) are typically estimated based on empirical Bayes, where point estimates are obtained by maximising an approximation to the marginal likelihood $p(\mathbf{y}|\alpha, \theta)$. More recently a deterministic method, the nested Laplace approximation [34], considers a full Bayesian methodology where the hyperparameters are integrated out by applying numerical integration. However, this method can handle only a small number of hyperparameters (less than six).

In complex GP models, with non-factorising likelihood functions, it is not clear how to apply the current deterministic methods.[2] Such a complex form of likelihood arises in the application described in Section 14.7 that concerns inference of transcription factors in gene regulation. This problem involves a dynamical model derived by solving a system of ordinary differential equations (ODEs). Furthermore, in this model the number of likelihood parameters α can be large (84 in one example given in Section 14.7) and it is of great importance to estimate confidence intervals for those parameters through a full Bayesian methodology. Note that the method described in [34] that considers full Bayesian inference is not applicable in this case, not only because it assumes a factorising likelihood but also because it assumes a small number of hyperparameters.

Instead of using deterministic inference algorithms, we can consider stochastic methods based on MCMC. Efficient MCMC methods can reliably deal with complex GP models, having non-factorising likelihoods, and unlike deterministic methods they benefit from a arbitrarily precise approximation to the true posterior in the limit of long runs. In the next section we discuss MCMC algorithms.

14.4 Sampling algorithms for Gaussian process models

A major concern with the development of MCMC algorithms in GP models is how to efficiently sample from the posterior conditional $p(\mathbf{f}|\alpha, \theta, \mathbf{y})$. This posterior involves a high-dimensional random variable, consisting of function values that can be highly correlated with one another.

In this section, we describe several sampling schemes that can simulate from $p(\mathbf{f}|\alpha, \theta, \mathbf{y})$ given that the hyperparameters obtain some arbitrary, but fixed, values. In order for our presentation to be instructive, we start with simple schemes such as Gibbs sampling (Section 14.4.1) and move to more advanced schemes using block-based Metropolis–Hastings (Section 14.4.2) and control variables (Section 14.4.3). All these methods can easily be generalised to incorporate steps that can also simulate from (α, θ) as discussed in Section 14.4.5. To simplify our notation in the next three sections we omit reference to the hyperparameters.

14.4.1 Gibbs sampling and independent Metropolis–Hastings

The MCMC algorithm we consider is the general Metropolis–Hastings (MH) algorithm [30, 14]. Suppose we wish to sample from the posterior (14.4). The MH algorithm forms a Markov chain. We initialise $\mathbf{f}^{(0)}$ and we consider a proposal distribution $Q(\mathbf{f}^{(t+1)}|\mathbf{f}^{(t)})$ that allows us to draw a new state given the current state. The new state is accepted with probability $\min(1, A)$ where

$$A = \frac{p(\mathbf{y}|\mathbf{f}^{(t+1)})p(\mathbf{f}^{(t+1)})}{p(\mathbf{y}|\mathbf{f}^{(t)})p(\mathbf{f}^{(t)})} \frac{Q(\mathbf{f}^{(t)}|\mathbf{f}^{(t+1)})}{Q(\mathbf{f}^{(t+1)}|\mathbf{f}^{(t)})}.$$

To apply this generic algorithm, we need to choose the proposal distribution Q. For GP models, finding a good proposal distribution is challenging since $\mathbf{f}$ is high dimensional and

---

[2]This is true for the expectation propagation, variational Gaussian approximation and nested Laplace method which seem to depend on the assumption of having a factorising likelihood. The Laplace approximation is, of course, generally applicable.

the posterior distribution can be highly correlated. Despite that, there is a lot of structure in a GP model, specifically in the prior $p(\mathbf{f})$, that can greatly facilitate the selection of a good proposal distribution.

To motivate the algorithms presented in Sections 14.4.2 and 14.4.3, we firstly discuss two extreme options for specifying the proposal distribution Q. One simple way to choose Q is to set it equal to the GP prior $p(\mathbf{f})$ so that the proposed state is independent of the current one. This gives us an independent MH algorithm [30]. However, sampling from the GP prior is very inefficient since it ignores the posterior structure induced by the data leading to a low acceptance rate. Thus the Markov chain will get stuck in the same state for thousands of iterations. On the other hand, sampling from the prior is appealing because any generated sample satisfies the smoothness requirement imposed by the kernel function. Functions drawn from the posterior GP should satisfy the same smoothness requirement as well. It would be interesting to design proposal distributions that can possess this property but simultaneously allow us to increase the acceptance rate.

The other extreme choice for the proposal, that has been considered in [24], is to apply Gibbs sampling where we iteratively draw samples from each posterior conditional density $p(f_i|\mathbf{f}_{\backslash i}, \mathbf{y})$ with $\mathbf{f}_{\backslash i} = \mathbf{f} \setminus f_i$. This scheme is feasible only when each conditional is log-concave and the adaptive rejection sampling method [17] can be used. This will often be the case for models with a factorising likelihood, where $p(f_i|\mathbf{f}_{\backslash i}, \mathbf{y}) \propto p(y_i|f_i)p(f_i|\mathbf{f}_{\backslash i})$. Any sample in the Gibbs algorithm is accepted with probability one. However, Gibbs sampling can be extremely slow for densely discretised or sampled functions, as in the regression problem of Fig. 14.1, where the posterior distribution over $\mathbf{f}$ becomes highly correlated. To clarify this, note that the variance of the posterior conditional $p(f_i|\mathbf{f}_{\backslash i}, \mathbf{y})$ will typically be smaller than the variance of the conditional GP prior $p(f_i|\mathbf{f}_{\backslash i})$. However, $p(f_i|\mathbf{f}_{\backslash i})$ may already have a tiny variance caused by the conditioning on all remaining latent function values. The more densely sampled a function is (relative to the lengthscale of the kernel function), the more inefficient the Gibbs algorithm becomes since the variance of $p(f_i|\mathbf{f}_{\backslash i})$ tends to zero. For the one-dimensional example in Fig. 14.1, Gibbs sampling is practically not useful. We study this issue further in Section 14.6.

To obtain an algorithm similar to Gibbs sampling but without requiring the use of adaptive rejection sampling, we can consider as proposal distribution in the MH algorithm the sequence of the conditional densities $p(f_i|\mathbf{f}_{\backslash i})$. Thus, we replace the posterior conditional $p(f_i|\mathbf{f}_{\backslash i}, \mathbf{y})$ with the prior conditional $p(f_i|\mathbf{f}_{\backslash i})$. We call this algorithm, which has been used in geostatistics [9], the Gibbs-like algorithm. This algorithm can exhibit a high acceptance rate, but it is inefficient to sample from highly correlated functions for the reasons discussed above.

A common technique used to improve the slow mixing of the Gibbs-type of algorithms when sampling from a high-dimensional posterior distribution is to cluster the variables into separate groups and sample all variables of a group within a single MH step based on an appropriately defined proposal distribution. Given that different groups of variables are weakly correlated, such a scheme can be more effective. Next we describe the local region sampling algorithm which is a way of implementing this idea for GP models.

14.4.2 Sampling using local regions

We now introduce a simple generalisation of the Gibbs-like algorithm that is more appropriate for sampling from smooth functions. The idea is to divide the domain of the function into regions and sample the entire function within each region.

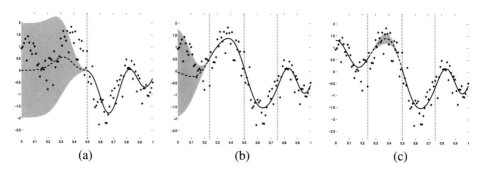

Figure 14.1 Illustration of the hierarchical clustering process. Panel (a) shows the variance (displayed with shaded two standard errors bars) of the initial conditional GP prior where we condition on the right side of the function. Since the variance is high the generated local parts of the function will not fit the data often. Dividing the local input region in (a) into two smaller groups (panels (b) and (c)) results in a decrease of the variance of the newly formed GP conditional priors and gives an increase in the acceptance rate. However, notice that the variance of the proposal distribution in the boundaries between different function regions is always small. This can affect the efficiency of the sampling algorithm.

We wish to divide the domain of the function into local regions and sample these local regions iteratively. Let $\mathbf{f}_k$ denote the function points that belong to the local region k, where $k = 1, \ldots, M$ and $\mathbf{f}_1 \cup \ldots \cup \mathbf{f}_M = \mathbf{f}$. New values for the region k are proposed by drawing from the conditional GP prior $p(\mathbf{f}_k^{t+1}|\mathbf{f}_{\backslash k}^{(t)})$, where $\mathbf{f}_{\backslash k} = \mathbf{f} \setminus \mathbf{f}_k$, by conditioning on the remaining function values; $\mathbf{f}_k^{(t+1)}$ is accepted with probability $\min(1, A)$ where $A = \frac{p(\mathbf{y}|\mathbf{f}_k^{(t+1)}, \mathbf{f}_{\backslash k}^{(t)})}{p(\mathbf{y}|\mathbf{f}_k^{(t)}, \mathbf{f}_{\backslash k}^{(t)})}$. Sampling $\mathbf{f}_k$ is iterated between all different regions $k = 1, \ldots, M$. Note that the terms associated with the GP prior cancel out from the acceptance probability since sampling from the conditional prior ensures that any proposed sample is invariant to the GP prior. Given that the initial state $\mathbf{f}^{(0)}$ is a sample from the prior, any proposed function region leads to a possible sample drawn from the GP prior. Notice that sampling from the GP prior and the Gibbs-like algorithm are two extreme cases of the above scheme.

To apply the algorithm, we need to partition the function values $\mathbf{f}$ into groups. This process corresponds to adaption of the proposal distribution and can be carried out during the early iterations of MCMC. An adaptive scheme can start with a small number of clusters, so that the acceptance rate is very low, and then refine the initial clusters in order to increase the acceptance rate. Following the widely used ideas in the theory of adaptive MCMC [15, 31, 18] (see Chapter 2) according to which desirable acceptance rates of MH algorithms are around $1/4$, we require the algorithm to sample with acceptance rate close to that value.

More specifically, the adaption process is as follows. We obtain an initial partitioning of the vector $\mathbf{f}$ by clustering the inputs X using the k-means algorithm. Then we start the simulation and observe the local acceptance rate r_k associated with the proposal $p(\mathbf{f}_k|\mathbf{f}_{\backslash k})$. Each r_k provides information about the variance of the proposal distribution relative to the local characteristics of the function in region k. A small r_k implies that $p(\mathbf{f}_k|\mathbf{f}_{\backslash k})$ has high variance and most of the generated samples are outside of the support of the posterior GP; see Fig. 14.1 for an illustrative example. Hence, when r_k is small, we split the cluster k into two clusters by locally applying the k-means algorithm using all the inputs previously assigned to the initial cluster k. Clusters that have high acceptance rate are unchanged. This hierarchical partitioning process is recursively repeated until all of the current clusters exhibit a local acceptance rate larger than the predefined threshold $1/4$. Notice that the above partitioning process can be characterised as supervised in the sense that the information provided by the MH steps is used to decide which clusters need to be further split into smaller groups. Figure 14.1 gives an illustration of the adaptive partitioning process in a one-dimensional regression problem.

Once the adaption of the proposal distribution has ended, we can start sampling from the posterior GP model. The final form of the proposal distribution is a partition of the vector $\mathbf{f}$ into M disjoint groups and the conditional GP prior is the proposal distribution for each group.

As shown in Section 14.6, the local region algorithm improves upon the Gibbs sampler. However, this scheme will still be inefficient to sample from highly correlated posteriors since the variance of the proposal distribution can become very small close to the boundaries between neighbouring function regions as illustrated in Fig. 14.1. In such cases, there will be variables belonging to different groups which are highly correlated with respect to the GP prior distribution. Of course, these variables will be also highly correlated in terms of the GP posterior. Therefore, the boundaries between function regions can cause the state vector $\mathbf{f}^{(t)}$ to move with a rather small speed when exploring the probability mass, which will lead the Markov chain to mix poorly. In the sequel we describe a sampling algorithm using auxiliary variables, called control points, which attempts to resolve the problems encountered by the local region sampling method and sample more efficiently from highly correlated posterior GPs.

14.4.3 Sampling using control variables

The algorithm described previously is a local sampler that samples each part of the function by conditioning on the remaining part of the function. As discussed previously, this can result in a slow exploration of the probability density. To resolve the problem of local sampling we would like to sample the function in a more global sense. Below we discuss an algorithm that achieves this by making use of auxiliary variables.

Let $\mathbf{f}_c$ be a set of M auxiliary function values that are evaluated at inputs X_c and drawn from the GP prior. We call $\mathbf{f}_c$ the control variables and their meaning is analogous to the auxiliary inducing variables used in sparse GP models [39, 28]. To compute the posterior $p(\mathbf{f}|\mathbf{y})$ based on control variables we use the expression

$$p(\mathbf{f}|\mathbf{y}) = \int_{\mathbf{f}_c} p(\mathbf{f}|\mathbf{f}_c, \mathbf{y}) p(\mathbf{f}_c|\mathbf{y}) d\mathbf{f}_c. \tag{14.9}$$

Assuming that $\mathbf{f}_c$ is an approximate sufficient statistic for the parameter $\mathbf{f}$, so that $p(\mathbf{f}|\mathbf{f}_c, \mathbf{y}) \simeq p(\mathbf{f}|\mathbf{f}_c)$, we can approximately sample from $p(\mathbf{f}|\mathbf{y})$ in a two-stage manner: firstly sample the control variables from $p(\mathbf{f}_c|\mathbf{y})$ and then generate $\mathbf{f}$ from the conditional prior $p(\mathbf{f}|\mathbf{f}_c)$. This scheme can allow us to introduce an MH algorithm, where we need to specify only a proposal distribution $q(\mathbf{f}_c^{(t+1)}|\mathbf{f}_c^{(t)})$, that will mimic sampling from $p(\mathbf{f}_c|\mathbf{y})$, and always sample $\mathbf{f}$ from the conditional prior $p(\mathbf{f}|\mathbf{f}_c)$. The whole proposal distribution takes the form

$$Q(\mathbf{f}^{(t+1)}, \mathbf{f}_c^{(t+1)}|\mathbf{f}_c^{(t)}) = p(\mathbf{f}^{(t+1)}|\mathbf{f}_c^{(t+1)})q(\mathbf{f}_c^{(t+1)}|\mathbf{f}_c^{(t)}), \tag{14.10}$$

which is used in the MH algorithm in order to sample from the augmented posterior $p(\mathbf{f}, \mathbf{f}_c|\mathbf{y})$. We should emphasise that this proposal distribution does not define an independent Metropolis–Hastings algorithm. However, it satisfies a certain conditional independence relationship according to which each proposed state $(\mathbf{f}^{(t+1)}, \mathbf{f}_c^{(t+1)})$ depends only on the previous state of the control points $\mathbf{f}_c^{(t)}$ and not on $\mathbf{f}^{(t)}$. Figure 14.2 illustrates the

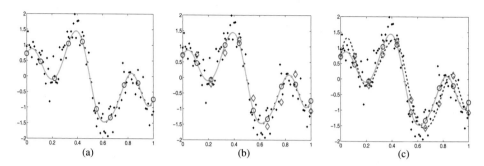

Figure 14.2 Illustration of sampling using control variables. (a) shows the current GP function $\mathbf{f}^{(t)}$ with green, the data and the current location of the control points (red circles). (b) shows the proposed new positions for the control points (diamonds in magenta). (c) shows the proposed new function values $\mathbf{f}^{(t+1)}$ drawn from the conditional GP prior (blue dotted line). See plate section for colour version.

steps of sampling from this proposal distribution. Each proposed sample is accepted with probability $\min(1, A)$ where A is given by

$$
A = \frac{p(\mathbf{y}|\mathbf{f}^{(t+1)})p(\mathbf{f}_c^{(t+1)})}{p(\mathbf{y}|\mathbf{f}^{(t)})p(\mathbf{f}_c^{(t)})}\frac{q(\mathbf{f}_c^{(t)}|\mathbf{f}_c^{(t+1)})}{q(\mathbf{f}_c^{(t+1)}|\mathbf{f}_c^{(t)})},
\tag{14.11}
$$

where the terms involving the conditional GP prior $p(\mathbf{f}|\mathbf{f}_c)$ cancel out. The usefulness of the above sampling scheme stems from the fact that the control variables can form a low-dimensional representation of the function that does not depend much on the size of $\mathbf{f}$, i.e. on how densely the function has been discretised. The control points will tend to be less correlated with one another since the distance between pairs of them can be large as illustrated in Fig. 14.2. The use of the proposal distribution in Eq. (14.10) implies that the speed of the Markov chain, i.e. the ability to perform big moves when sampling $\mathbf{f}$, will crucially depend on how the control variables are sampled from $q(\mathbf{f}_c^{(t+1)}|\mathbf{f}_c^{(t)})$. The other part of the proposal distribution draws an $\mathbf{f}^{(t+1)}$ that interpolates smoothly between the control points. Thus, while Gibbs-sampling will move more slowly as we keep increasing the size of $\mathbf{f}$, the sampling scheme using control variables will remain equally efficient in performing big moves. In Section 14.4.4 we describe how to select the number M of control variables and the inputs X_c using an adaptive MCMC process. In the remainder of this section we discuss how we set the proposal distribution $q(\mathbf{f}_c^{(t+1)}|\mathbf{f}_c^{(t)})$.

A suitable choice for q is to use a Gaussian distribution with diagonal or full covariance matrix. The covariance matrix can be adapted during the burn-in phase of MCMC, for instance using the algorithm of [18] to tune the acceptance rate. Although this scheme is general, it has practical limitations. Firstly, tuning a full covariance matrix is time consuming and in our case this adaption process must be carried out simultaneously with searching for an appropriate set of control variables. Also, since the terms involving $p(\mathbf{f}_c)$ do not cancel out in Eq. (14.11), using a diagonal covariance for the q distribution has the risk of proposing control variables that may not satisfy the GP prior smoothness requirement. To avoid these problems, we define q by using the GP prior. According to Eq. (14.9) a suitable choice for q must mimic the sampling from the posterior $p(\mathbf{f}_c|\mathbf{y})$. Given that the control points are far apart from each other, Gibbs sampling in the control variables space can be efficient. However, iteratively sampling f_{c_i} from the conditional posterior $p(\mathbf{f}_{c_i}|\mathbf{f}_{c_{\backslash i}}, \mathbf{y}) \propto p(\mathbf{y}|\mathbf{f}_c)p(f_{c_i}|\mathbf{f}_{c_{\backslash i}})$, where $\mathbf{f}_{c_{\backslash i}} = \mathbf{f}_c \setminus f_{c_i}$ is intractable for non-Gaussian

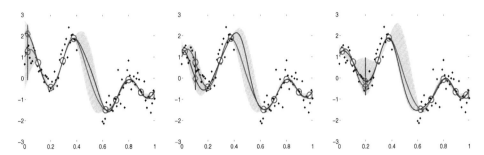

Figure 14.3 Visualisation of iterating between control variables. The red solid line is the current $\mathbf{f}^{(t)}$, the blue line is the proposed $\mathbf{f}^{(t+1)}$, the red circles are the current control variables $\mathbf{f}_c^{(t)}$ while the diamond (in magenta) is the proposed control variable $f_{c_i}^{(t+1)}$. The blue solid vertical line represents the distribution $p(f_{c_i}^{(t+1)}|\mathbf{f}_{c_{\setminus i}}^{(t)})$ (with two standard error bars) and the shaded area shows the effective proposal $p(\mathbf{f}^{t+1}|\mathbf{f}_{c_{\setminus i}}^{(t)})$. See plate section for colour version.

likelihoods.[3] An attractive alternative is to use a Gibbs-like algorithm where each f_{c_i} is drawn from the conditional GP prior $p(\mathbf{f}_{c_i}^{(t+1)}|\mathbf{f}_{c_{\setminus i}}^{(t)})$ and is accepted using the MH step. More specifically, the proposal distribution draws a new $f_{c_i}^{(t+1)}$ for a certain control variable i from $p(f_{c_i}^{(t+1)}|\mathbf{f}_{c_{\setminus i}}^{(t)})$ and generates the function $\mathbf{f}^{(t+1)}$ from $p(\mathbf{f}^{(t+1)}|f_{c_i}^{(t+1)},\mathbf{f}_{c_{\setminus i}}^{(t)})$. The sample $(f_{c_i}^{(t+1)},\mathbf{f}^{(t+1)})$ is accepted using the MH step. This scheme of sampling the control variables one-at-a-time and resampling $\mathbf{f}$ is iterated between different control variables. A complete iteration of the algorithm consists of a full scan over all control variables. The acceptance probability A in Eq. (14.11) becomes the likelihood ratio and the prior smoothness requirement is always satisfied. The detailed iteration of this sampling method is given in Algorithm 14.1 and is illustrated in Fig. 14.3.

Although the control variables are sampled one-at-a-time, $\mathbf{f}$ can still be drawn with a considerable variance which does not shrink to zero in certain regions of the input space as happened for the local region sampling algorithm. To clarify this, note that when the control variable f_{c_i} changes, the effective proposal distribution for $\mathbf{f}$ is

$$p(\mathbf{f}^{t+1}|\mathbf{f}_{c_{\setminus i}}^{(t)}) = \int_{f_{c_i}^{(t+1)}} p(\mathbf{f}^{t+1}|f_{c_i}^{(t+1)},\mathbf{f}_{c_{\setminus i}}^{(t)})p(f_{c_i}^{(t+1)}|\mathbf{f}_{c_{\setminus i}}^{(t)})\mathrm{d}f_{c_i}^{(t+1)},$$

which is the conditional GP prior given all the control points apart from the current point f_{c_i}. This conditional prior can have considerable variance close to f_{c_i} and in all regions that are not close to the remaining control variables. As illustrated in Fig. 14.3, the iteration over different control variables allows $\mathbf{f}$ to be drawn with a considerable variance everywhere in the input space whilst respecting the smoothness imposed by the GP prior.

14.4.4 Selection of the control variables

To apply the previous algorithm we need to select the number, M, of the control points and the associated inputs X_c. Here X_c must be chosen so that knowledge of $\mathbf{f}_c$ can determine $\mathbf{f}$ with small error. The prediction of $\mathbf{f}$ given $\mathbf{f}_c$ is equal to $K_{f,f_c}K_{f_c,f_c}^{-1}\mathbf{f}_c$ which is the mean of the conditional prior $p(\mathbf{f}|\mathbf{f}_c)$. A suitable way to search over X_c is to minimise the reconstruction error $\|\mathbf{f} - K_{f,f_c}K_{f_c,f_c}^{-1}\mathbf{f}_c\|^2$ averaged over any possible value of $(\mathbf{f},\mathbf{f}_c)$:

---

[3]This is because we need to integrate out $\mathbf{f}$ in order to compute $p(\mathbf{y}|\mathbf{f}_c)$.

Algorithm 14.1 Control-points MCMC

Input: Initial state of control points $\mathbf{f}_c^{(0)}$ and $\mathbf{f}^{(0)}$.
repeat
    for $i = 1$ **to** M **do**
        Sample the ith control point: $\mathbf{f}_{c_i}^{(t+1)} \sim p(\mathbf{f}_{c_i}^{(t+1)}|\mathbf{f}_{c_{\backslash i}}^{(t)})$.
        Sample $\mathbf{f}^{(t+1)}$: $\mathbf{f}^{(t+1)} \sim p(\mathbf{f}^{t+1}|f_{c_i}^{(t+1)}, \mathbf{f}_{c_{\backslash i}}^{(t)})$.
        Accept or reject $(\mathbf{f}^{(t+1)}, f_{c_i}^{(t+1)})$ with the MH probability (likelihood ratio).
    end for
until Convergence of the Markov chain is achieved.

$$G(X_c) = \int_{\mathbf{f},\mathbf{f}_c} \|\mathbf{f} - K_{f,f_c}K_{f_c,f_c}^{-1}\mathbf{f}_c\|^2 p(\mathbf{f}|\mathbf{f}_c)p(\mathbf{f}_c)\mathrm{d}\mathbf{f}\mathrm{d}\mathbf{f}_c = \mathrm{Tr}(K_{f,f} - K_{f,f_c}K_{f_c,f_c}^{-1}K_{f,f_c}^{\top}).$$

The quantity inside the trace is the covariance of $p(\mathbf{f}|\mathbf{f}_c)$ and thus $G(X_c)$ is the total variance of this distribution. We can minimise $G(X_c)$ w.r.t. X_c using continuous optimisation similarly to the approach in [39]. Note that $G(X_c)$ is non-negative and when it becomes zero, $p(\mathbf{f}|\mathbf{f}_c)$ becomes a delta function, which means that the control variables fully determine $\mathbf{f}$.

To find the number of control points M we start with an initial small value and we follow an adaptive MCMC strategy that increases M until the acceptance rate of the chain reaches a certain value. More precisely, the input locations X_c of the initial set of control points is optimised by minimising $G(X_c)$. Then, we run the Markov chain for a small window of W iterations (e.g. $W = 100$) and compute the acceptance rates $r_i, i = 1, \ldots, M$, associated with each control variable separately. If all these rates satisfy a certain condition, the adaptive process terminates, otherwise we add more control points and the steps above are repeated. The condition we use is that each acceptance rate r_i must obtain a value within the range $[20, 30]/M$ per cent so that a full iteration over all control variables will have an overall acceptance rate (computed as $r = \sum_{i=1}^{M} r_i$) around 25 per cent. This strategy was chosen because it worked well in most problems where we applied our method and we have not attempted so far to develop any theoretical analysis regarding the asymptotically optimal acceptance rate.

14.4.5 Sampling the hyperparameters

Above we discussed algorithms for sampling from the conditional posterior $p(\mathbf{f}|\alpha, \theta, \mathbf{y})$ given a fixed setting of the hyperparameters (α, θ). These parameters, however, are typically unknown and we need to estimate them by using a full Bayesian approach. In particular, we need to assign priors to those parameters, denoted by $p(\alpha)$ and $p(\theta)$, and sample their values during MCMC by adding suitable updates into all previous MH algorithms. In these updates, we simulate from the conditional posterior distribution $p(\alpha, \theta|\mathbf{f}, \mathbf{y})$ which factorises across α and θ, thus yielding two separate conditionals

$$p(\alpha|\mathbf{f}, \mathbf{y}) \propto p(\mathbf{y}|\mathbf{f}, \alpha)p(\alpha), \quad p(\theta|\mathbf{f}) \propto p(\mathbf{f}|\theta)p(\theta).$$

Sampling from any of these distributions is carried out by using some proposal distribution, for instance a Gaussian, in the MH algorithm. The kernel hyperparameters often take positive values and they can be sampled in the log space. In the experiments we use Gaussian proposal distributions which are adapted during the early iterations of MCMC in order to tune the acceptance rate. Furthermore, in the problem of transcriptional gene regulation (see Section 14.7), the likelihood parameters α exhibit additional conditional independencies and thus we can sample them independently in separate blocks. Neal [24] uses Hybrid Monte Carlo [11] to sample the hyperparameters in GP models following his earlier work on Bayesian neural networks [23].

An accepted state for the kernel hyperparameters requires an update of the proposal distribution when sampling $\mathbf{f}$. This holds for all algorithms, described previously, that simulate from the conditional posterior $p(\mathbf{f}|\alpha, \theta)$. For instance, in the algorithm using control variables and for a newly accepted state of the hyperparameters, denoted by $\theta^{(t)}$, the conditional Gaussian $p(\mathbf{f}|\mathbf{f}_c, \theta^{(t)})$ needs to be computed. This requires the estimation of the mean vector of this Gaussian as well as the Cholesky decomposition of the covariance matrix. Finally, we should point out that sampling the kernel hyperparameters can easily become one of the most expensive updates during MCMC, especially when the dimension of the vector $\mathbf{f}$ is large.

14.5   Related work and other sampling schemes

The MCMC algorithms described in Sections 14.4.3 and 14.4.2 use an adaptive process which tunes the proposal distribution in order to fit better the characteristics of the posterior distribution. We can classify these algorithms as instances of adaptive MCMC methods. However, our schemes are specialised to GP models. The most advanced algorithm we presented, that uses control variables, adapts the proposal distribution by finding a set of control variables which somehow provide an approximate low-dimensional representation of the posterior distribution. This way of adaption is rather different to other adaptive MCMC techniques. Perhaps the nearest technique in the literature is the principal directions method [4].

Regarding other sampling algorithms for GP models, several other schemes seem possible and some have been considered in applications. A sampling method often considered is based on the transformation of the vector $\mathbf{f}$ of function values [19]. In particular, since much of the correlation that exists in the posterior conditional distribution $p(\mathbf{f}|\alpha, \theta, \mathbf{y})$ is coming from the GP prior, a way to reduce this correlation is to transform $\mathbf{f}$ so that the GP prior is whitened. If L is the Cholesky decomposition of the covariance matrix $K_{f,f}$ of the GP prior $p(\mathbf{f}|\theta)$, then the transformation $\mathbf{z} = L^{-1}\mathbf{f}$ defines a new random vector that is white with respect to the prior. Sampling in the transformed GP model can be easier as the posterior over $\mathbf{z}$ can be less correlated than the posterior over $\mathbf{f}$. However, since $\mathbf{z}$ is a high-dimensional random variable, the use of a Gaussian proposal distribution in a random walk MH algorithm can be inefficient. This is mainly because of practical difficulties encountered when tuning a full covariance matrix in very high dimensional spaces. Therefore, a more practical approach often considered [19], is to sample $\mathbf{z}$ based on the hybrid Monte Carlo algorithm [11]. This method uses gradient information and has shown to be effective in sampling in high-dimensional spaces [23].

Another common approach to sample the function latent values is to construct a Gaussian approximation to the posterior conditional $p(\mathbf{f}|\alpha, \theta, \mathbf{y})$ and use this as a proposal distribution in the MH algorithm [33, 6, 44]. The authors in [44] further combine this approximation with a transformation of the random variables and a subsequent use of Hybrid Monte Carlo. A Gaussian approximation can be constructed, for instance, by using one of the techniques discussed in Section 14.3. This method can be appropriate for specialised problems in which the likelihood function takes a simple factorising form and the number of the hyperparameters is rather small. Notice that the Gaussian approximation is obtained by fixing the hyperparameters (α, θ) to certain values. However, once new values are sampled for those parameters, the Gaussian approximation can become inaccurate. This is rather more likely to occur when the number of hyperparameters is large and varying their values can significantly affect the shape of the conditional posterior $p(\mathbf{f}|\alpha, \theta, \mathbf{y})$. To overcome this, we could update the Gaussian approximation to accommodate the changes made in the values of the hyperparameters. However, this scheme can be computationally very expensive and additionally we need to make sure that such updates do not affect the convergence of the Markov chain to the correct posterior distribution.

Finally, another simple approach for sampling in a GP model is to use the underrelaxation proposal distribution [25, 2] according to which the proposed new state $\mathbf{f}^{(t+1)}$ is produced by $\mathbf{f}^{(t+1)} = \pi \mathbf{f}^{(t)} + \sqrt{1 - \pi^2}\mathbf{u}$, where $\mathbf{u}$ is a sample drawn from the GP prior $p(\mathbf{f})$ and $\pi \in [-1, 1]$. This procedure leaves the GP prior invariant, so that the MH acceptance probability depends only on the likelihood ratio.

14.6   Demonstration on regression and classification

In this section, we demonstrate the sampling algorithms on regression and classification problems. In the first experiment we compare Gibbs sampling (*Gibbs*), sampling using local regions (*region*) and sampling using control variables (*control*) in standard regression problems of varied input dimensions. The performance of the algorithms can be accurately assessed by computing the Kullback–Leibler (KL) divergences between the exact Gaussian posterior $p(\mathbf{f}|\mathbf{y})$ and the Gaussians obtained by MCMC. We fix the number of training points to $N = 200$ and we vary the input dimension d from 1 to 10. The training inputs X were chosen randomly inside the unit hypercube $[0, 1]^d$. This can allow us to study the behaviour of the algorithms with respect to the amount of correlation in the posterior GP which is proportional to how densely the function is sampled. The larger the dimension, the sparser the function is sampled. The outputs $\mathbf{y}$ were chosen by randomly producing a GP function using the squared-exponential kernel $\sigma_f^2 \exp(-\frac{\|\mathbf{x}_m - \mathbf{x}_n\|^2}{2\ell^2})$, where $(\sigma_f^2, \ell^2) = (1, 0.01)$ and then adding noise with variance $\sigma^2 = 0.09$. The burn-in period was 10^4 iterations.[4] For a certain dimension d the algorithms were initialised to the same state obtained by randomly drawing from the GP prior. The parameters $(\sigma_f^2, \ell^2, \sigma^2)$ were fixed to the values that generated the data. The experimental setup was repeated 10 times so as to obtain confidence intervals. We used thinned samples (by keeping one sample every 10 iterations) to calculate the means and covariances of the 200-dimensional posterior Gaussians. Figure 14.4(a) shows the KL divergence against the number of MCMC iterations for the five-dimensional input dataset. It seems that for 200 training points and five dimensions, the function values are still highly correlated and thus *Gibbs* takes much longer for the KL divergence to drop to zero. Figure 14.4(b) shows the KL divergence against the input dimension after fixing the number of iterations to be 3×10^4. Clearly *Gibbs* is very inefficient in low dimensions because of the highly correlated posterior. As dimension increases and the functions become sparsely sampled, *Gibbs* improves and eventually the KL divergence approaches zero. The *region* algorithm works better than *Gibbs* but in low dimensions it also suffers from the problem of high correlation. For the *control* algorithm we observe that the KL divergence is very close to zero for all dimensions. Note also that as we increase the number of dimensions *Gibbs* eventually becomes slightly better than the *control* algorithm (for $d = 8$ and onwards) since the function values tend to be independent

---

[4]For *Gibbs* we used 2×10^4 iterations since the *region* and *control* algorithms require additional iterations during the adaption phase.

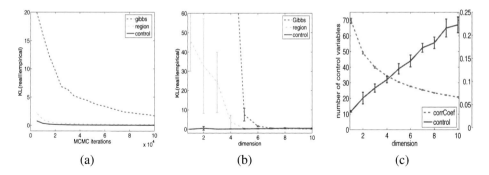

Figure 14.4 (a) shows the evolution of the KL divergence (against the number of MCMC iterations) between the true posterior and the empirically estimated posteriors for a five-dimensional regression dataset. (b) shows the mean values with one-standard error bars of the KL divergence (against the input dimension) between the true posterior and the empirically estimated posteriors. (c) plots the number of control variables used together with the average correlation coefficient of the GP prior. See plate section for colour version.

from one another. Figure 14.4(c) shows the increase in the number of control variables used as the input dimension increases. The same plot shows the decrease of the average correlation coefficient of the GP prior as the input dimension increases. This is very intuitive, since one should expect the number of control variables to increase as the function values become more independent. In the limit when the function values are independent, there will be no accurate low-dimensional representation of the function values and the optimal number of control variables will tend to the number of function values sampled.

Next we consider two GP classification problems for which exact inference is intractable. Gaussian processes classification involves a factorising likelihood function. For the binary classification problem each factor $p(y_i|f_i)$ in the likelihood is defined based on the probit or logit model. Deterministic inference methods for GP classification are widely used in machine learning [48, 8, 21]. Among these approaches, the expectation-propagation (EP) algorithm of [22] is found to be the most efficient [19]. Our MCMC implementation confirms these findings since sampling using control variables gave similar classification accuracy to EP. We used the Wisconsin Breast Cancer (WBC) and the Pima Indians Diabetes (PID) binary classification datasets. The first consists of 683 examples (9 input dimensions) and the second of 768 examples (8 dimensions). Twenty per cent of the examples were used for testing in each case. The MCMC samplers were run for 5×10^4 iterations (thinned to one sample every five iterations) after a burn-in of 10^4 iterations. The hyperparameters were fixed to those obtained by EP. Figure 14.5(a)–(b) shows the log-likelihood for MCMC samples on the WBC dataset, for the *Gibbs* and *control* algorithms respectively. It can be observed that mixing is far superior for the *control* algorithm and it has also converged to a much higher likelihood. In Fig. 14.5(c) we compare the test error and the average negative log-likelihood in the test data obtained by the two MCMC algorithms with the results from EP. The proposed *control* algorithm shows similar classification performance to EP, while the Gibbs algorithm performs significantly worse on both datasets.

14.7 Transcriptional regulation

We consider a small biological sub-system where a set of target genes are regulated by one transcription factor (TF) protein. Ordinary differential equations (ODEs) can provide a useful framework for modelling the dynamics in these biological networks

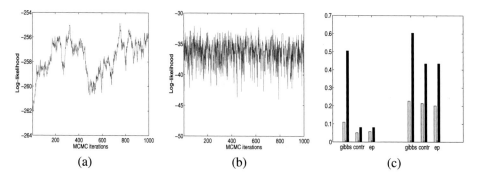

Figure 14.5 We show results for GP classification. Log-likelihood values are shown for MCMC samples obtained from (a) *Gibbs* and (b) *control* applied to the WBC dataset. In (c) we show the test errors (grey bars) and the average negative log-likelihoods (black bars) on the WBC (left) and PID (right) datasets and compare with EP.

[3, 5, 32, 20, 13]. The concentration of the TF and the gene-specific kinetic parameters are typically unknown and need to be estimated by making use of a time series of observed gene expression levels. We use a GP prior to model the unobserved TF activity, as proposed in [20], and apply full Bayesian inference based on the MCMC. Next we discuss in detail this method.

Barenco *et al.* introduce a linear ODE model for gene activation from TF [5] and this approach was further extended to account for non-linear models [32, 20]. The general form of the ODE model for transcription regulation with a single TF has the form

$$\frac{dy_j(t)}{dt} = B_j + S_{j}g(f(t)) - D_jy_j(t),$$ (14.12)

where the changing level of a gene j's expression, $y_j(t)$, is given by a combination of basal transcription rate, B_j, sensitivity, S_j, to its governing TF's activity, $f(t)$, and the decay rate of the mRNA. The function g is typically a non-linear activation function that accounts for phenomena such as gene activation, gene repression and saturation effects. Later in this section, we give specific examples of g functions. Notice also that the TF protein concentration function $f(t)$ takes positive values. The differential equation can be solved for $y_j(t)$ giving

$$y_j(t) = \frac{B_j}{D_j} + \left(A_j - \frac{B_j}{D_j}\right)e^{-D_jt} + S_je^{-D_jt}\int_0^t g(f(u))e^{D_ju}du,$$

where the A_j term arises from the initial condition. Due to the non-linearity of the g function that transforms the TF, the integral in the above expression is not analytically obtained. However, numerical integration can be used to accurately approximate the integral with a dense grid $(u_i)_{i=1}^P$ of points in the time axis and evaluate the function at the grid points $f_p = f(u_p)$. In this case the above equation can be written as

$$y_j(t) = \frac{B_j}{D_j} + \left(A_j - \frac{B_j}{D_j}\right)e^{-D_jt} + S_je^{-D_jt}\sum_{p=1}^{P_t} w_pg(f_p)e^{D_ju_p},$$ (14.13)

where the weights w_p arise from the numerical integration method used and, for example, can be given by the composite Simpson rule. Notice that the dense grid of function values $\{f_p\}_{p=1}^P$ does not have associated observed output data. As discussed shortly the number of discrete time points in which gene expression measurements are available is much sparser than the set of function points.

The TF concentration $f(t)$ in the above system of ODEs is a latent function that needs to be estimated. Additionally, the kinetic parameters of each gene $\alpha_j = (B_j, D_j, S_j, A_j)$ are unknown and also need to be estimated. To infer these quantities we use mRNA measurements (obtained from microarray experiments) of N target genes at T different time steps. Let y_{jt} denote the observed gene expression level of gene j at time t and let $\mathbf{y} = \{y_{jt}\}$ collect together all these observations. Assuming a Gaussian noise for the observed gene expressions the likelihood of our data has the form

$$p(\mathbf{y}|\mathbf{f}, \{\alpha_j\}_{j=1}^N) = \prod_{j=1}^N \prod_{t=1}^T p(y_{jt}|\mathbf{f}_{1 \le p \le P_t}, \alpha_j, \sigma_j^2), \tag{14.14}$$

where each probability density in the above product is a Gaussian with mean given by Eq. (14.13), $\mathbf{f}_{1 \le p \le P_t}$ denotes the TF values up to time t and σ_j^2 is a gene-specific variance parameter. Notice that there are five parameters per gene and thus overall there are $5 \times N$ likelihood parameters. The above likelihood function is non-Gaussian due to the non-linearity of g. Further, the above likelihood does not have a factorised form, as in the regression and classification cases, since an observed gene expression depends on the protein concentration activity in all previous time points. Also note that the discretisation of the TF in P time points corresponds to a very dense grid, while the gene expression measurements are sparse, i.e. $P \gg T$.

To apply full Bayesian inference in the above model, we need to define prior distributions over all unknown quantities. The protein concentration $\mathbf{f}$ is a positive quantity, thus a suitable prior is to consider a GP prior for $\log \mathbf{f}$. The kernel function of this GP prior is chosen to be the squared-exponential kernel, $\exp(-\frac{1}{2\ell^2}(t - t')^2)$, where the variance of this kernel, the σ_f^2 in Eq. (14.3), is fixed to one, which helps to avoid identifiability problems when interacting with the sensitivity parameter S_j. The lengthscale ℓ^2 is assigned a gamma prior. The kinetic parameters of each gene are all positive scalars and are represented in the log space. These parameters are given vague Gaussian priors. Each noise variance σ_j^2 is given a conjugate gamma prior. Sampling the GP function is done exactly as described in Section 14.4; we have only to plug in the likelihood (14.14) in the MH step. Sampling from the kinetic parameters is carried out using Gaussian proposal distributions with diagonal covariance matrices that sample the positive kinetic parameters in the log space. Notice also that the kinetics parameters α_j for gene j are sampled independently from the corresponding parameters of all other genes. This is because the conditional $p(\alpha_1, \ldots, \alpha_N|\mathbf{f})$ factorises across different α_js. Finally each noise variance σ_j^2 is sampled from its gamma conditional posterior distribution.

We now consider two experiments where we apply the algorithm that uses control variables (see Section 14.4.3) to infer the protein concentration of TFs that activate or repress a set of target genes. The latent function in these problems is always one dimensional and densely discretised. We first consider the TF p53 which is a tumour repressor activated during DNA damage. According to [5], irradiation is performed to disrupt the equilibrium of the p53 network and the transcription of p53 target genes are then stimulated. Seven samples of the expression levels of five target genes in three replicas are collected as the raw time course data. The non-linear activation of the protein follows the Michaelis Menten kinetics inspired response [3] that allows saturation effects to be taken into account so the g function in Eq. (14.12) takes the form $g(f(t)) = \frac{f(t)}{\gamma_j + f(t)}$, where the Michaelis constant for the jth gene, given by γ_j, is an additional likelihood parameter that is inferred by MCMC.

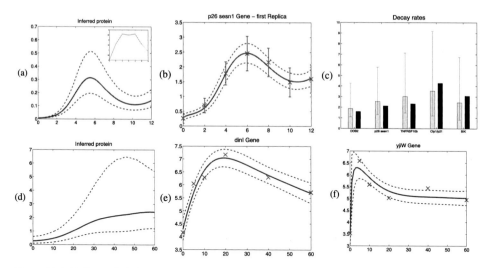

Figure 14.6 (a) Shows the inferred TF concentration for p53; the small plot on top-right shows the ground-truth protein concentration obtained by a *Western blot* experiment [5]. (b) Shows the predicted expression of a gene obtained by the estimated ODE model; red crosses correspond to the actual gene expression measurements. (c) Shows the estimated decay rates for all five target genes used to train the model. Grey bars display the parameters found by MCMC and black bars the parameters found in [5] using a linear ODE model. (d) Shows the inferred TF for LexA. Predicted expressions of two target genes are shown in (e) and (f). Error bars in all plots correspond to 95 per cent credibility intervals.

Notice that since $f(t)$ is positive the GP prior is placed on the log $f(t)$. Gene expressions for the genes are available for $T = 7$ different times. To apply MCMC we discretise $\mathbf{f}$ using a grid of $P = 121$ points. During sampling, seven control variables were needed to obtain the desirable acceptance rate. Running time was 4 hours for 5×10^5 sampling iterations plus 5×10^4 burn-in iterations. Acceptance rate for $\mathbf{f}$ after burns in was between 15%–25%. The first row of Fig. 14.6 summarises the estimated quantities obtained from MCMC simulation.

Next we consider the TF LexA in E.Coli that acts as a repressor. In the repression case there is an analogous Michaelis Menten model [3] where the non-linear function g takes the form $g(f(t)) = \frac{1}{\gamma_j + f(t)}$. Again the GP prior is placed on the log of the TF activity. We applied our method to the same microarray data considered by [32] where mRNA measurements of 14 target genes are collected over six time points. The amount of LexA is reduced after UV irradiation, decreasing for a few minutes and then recovering to its normal level. For this dataset, the expression of the 14 genes were available for $T = 6$ times. Notice that the number of likelihood parameters in this model is $14 \times 6 = 84$. The GP function $\mathbf{f}$ was discretised using 121 points. The result for the inferred TF profile along with predictions of two target genes are shown in the second row of Fig. 14.6. Our inferred TF profile and reconstructed target gene profiles are similar to those obtained in [32]. However, for certain genes, our model provides a better fit to the gene profile.

14.8   Dealing with large datasets

The application of GP models becomes intractable when the dimension of the vector of function values $\mathbf{f}$ needed to specify the likelihood is very large. This is because we need to store a large matrix of size $n \times n$ and invert this matrix (see Eqs. (14.5) and (14.6)) which scales as $O(n^3)$. For regression and classification problems, where the dimension of $\mathbf{f}$ grows linearly with the number of training examples, this is the well-known problem of large datasets [8, 38, 37, 39, 28]. Notice that GP models become intractable for large datasets not only in the case of non-Gaussian likelihood functions but also for the standard regression problem; observe that the posterior GP described by Eqs. (14.7) and (14.8) requires the inversion of an $n \times n$ matrix. Next we discuss how we can deal with the problem of large datasets in the context of MCMC inference. The same problem has also been addressed in [44].

A simple way to reduce the complexity of the GP model is to decrease the dimension of $\mathbf{f}$. In problems having factorising likelihoods, this implies that we have to ignore the large majority of the training examples and use only a small subset of the data. A more advanced strategy is to construct a sparse approximation based on a carefully chosen set of support or inducing variables [8, 38, 37, 39, 28, 41]. In the context of MCMC, this framework fits naturally within the sampling scheme that uses control variables which are exactly analogous to the inducing variables. One way to construct an approximate GP model that can deal with a very large dimension of $\mathbf{f}$ is to modify the prior $p(\mathbf{f})$. By using a set of auxiliary control variables $\mathbf{f}_c$, which are function points drawn from the GP, we can write $p(\mathbf{f})$ as

$$p(\mathbf{f}) = \int p(\mathbf{f}|\mathbf{f}_c)p(\mathbf{f}_c)d\mathbf{f}_c.$$

The intractable term in this expression is the conditional distribution $p(\mathbf{f}|\mathbf{f}_c)$ which has an $n \times n$ full covariance matrix: $K_{f,f} - K_{f,f_c}K_{f_c,f_c}^{-1}K_{f,f_c}^{\top}$. Clearly, we cannot simulate from this conditional Gaussian, because of the prohibitively large full covariance matrix. Therefore, the algorithm using control variables is not computationally tractable. To overcome this problem, we can modify the GP prior by replacing $p(\mathbf{f}|\mathbf{f}_c)$ with a simpler distribution. The simplest choice is to use a delta function centred at the mean of $p(\mathbf{f}|\mathbf{f}_c)$, given by $K_{f,f_c}K_{f_c,f_c}^{-1}\mathbf{f}_c$. This allows us to analytically marginalise out $\mathbf{f}$ and obtain the joint probability model:

$$q(\mathbf{y}, \mathbf{f}_c) = \int p(\mathbf{y}|\mathbf{f})\delta(\mathbf{f} - K_{f,f_c}K_{f_c,f_c}^{-1}\mathbf{f}_c)p(\mathbf{f}_c)d\mathbf{f} = p(\mathbf{y}|K_{f,f_c}K_{f_c,f_c}^{-1}\mathbf{f}_c)p(\mathbf{f}_c).$$

This modified GP model corresponds to the projected process approximation [8, 37]. An MCMC algorithm applied to this model requires only sampling $\mathbf{f}_c$. Further, notice that the control points algorithm (see Algorithm 14.1) in this case reduces to the Gibbs-like algorithm. A more advanced approximation to the GP prior is obtained by the sparse pseudo-inputs GP method of [39] which is also referred to as fully independent training conditional (FITC) in [28]. Here, $q(\mathbf{f}|\mathbf{f}_c) = \prod_{i=1}^{n} p(f_i|\mathbf{f}_c)$, where each $p(f_i|\mathbf{f}_c)$ is a marginal conditional prior with mean $K(\mathbf{x}_i, X_c)K_{f_c,f_c}^{-1}\mathbf{f}_c$ and variance $k(\mathbf{x}_i, \mathbf{x}_i) - K(\mathbf{x}_i, X_c)K_{f_c,f_c}^{-1}K(X_c, \mathbf{x}_i)$. This approximation keeps only the diagonal elements of the covariance matrix of $p(\mathbf{f}|\mathbf{f}_c)$. The algorithm using control points can be applied exactly as described in Algorithm 14.1. Notice that for factorising likelihoods, the step of sampling $\mathbf{f}$ given $\mathbf{f}_c$ simplifies to n independent problems since the posterior $p(\mathbf{f}|\mathbf{f}_c, \mathbf{y})$ factorises across the dimensions of $\mathbf{f}$, exactly as the prior. This implies that we could also marginalise out $\mathbf{f}$ numerically in such case. Extensions of the FITC approximation can be considered by representing exactly only small blocks of the covariance matrix of $p(\mathbf{f}|\mathbf{f}_c)$ [28].

A different approach for sampling in large GP models, is to follow the variational framework [41, 8, 37]. In this method, the GP prior $p(\mathbf{f})$ is not modified, but instead a variational distribution is fitted to the exact posterior $p(\mathbf{f}, \mathbf{f}_c|\mathbf{y})$. The variational distribution factorises as follows

$$q(\mathbf{f}, \mathbf{f}_c) = p(\mathbf{f}|\mathbf{f}_c)\phi(\mathbf{f}_c), \tag{14.15}$$

where the conditional prior $p(\mathbf{f}|\mathbf{f}_c)$ is one part of the variational distribution, while the other part, $\phi(\mathbf{f}_c)$, is an unknown (generally non-Gaussian) distribution that is defined optimally through the minimisation of the KL divergence between $q(\mathbf{f}, \mathbf{f}_c)$ and the exact posterior $p(\mathbf{f}, \mathbf{f}_c|\mathbf{y})$. The optimal setting for $\phi(\mathbf{f}_c)$ is given by

$$\phi(\mathbf{f}_c) \propto p(\mathbf{f}_c) \exp\left\{\int p(\mathbf{f}|\mathbf{f}_c) \log p(\mathbf{f}|\mathbf{y})d\mathbf{f}\right\}, \tag{14.16}$$

where we assume that the integral inside the exponential can be either computed analytically or approximated accurately using some numerical integration method. For instance, for a log Gaussian Cox model [9, 34] this integral can be obtained analytically and generally for factorising likelihoods the computations involve n independent one-dimensional numerical integration problems. Given that we can integrate out $\mathbf{f}$ in Eq. (14.16), we can then apply MCMC and sample from $\phi(\mathbf{f}_c)$ using, for instance, the Gibbs-like algorithm. The whole representation of the variational distribution in Eq. (14.15) will have an analytic part, the conditional prior $p(\mathbf{f}|\mathbf{f}_c)$, and a numerical part expressed by a set of samples drawn from $\phi(\mathbf{f}_c)$.

14.9   Discussion

Gaussian processes allow for inference over latent functions using a Bayesian nonparametric framework. In this chapter, we discussed MCMC algorithms that can be used for inference in GP models. The more advanced algorithm that we presented uses control variables which act as approximate low-dimensional summaries of the function values that we need to sample from. We showed that this sampling scheme can efficiently deal with highly correlated posterior distributions.

Markov chain Monte Carlo allows for full Bayesian inference in the transcription factor networks application. An important direction for future research will be scaling the models used to much larger systems of ODEs with multiple interacting transcription factors. In such cases the GP model becomes much more complicated and several latent functions need to be estimated simultaneously.

Regarding deterministic versus stochastic inference, in simple GP models with factorising likelihoods and a small number of hyperparameters, deterministic methods, if further developed, can lead to reliable inference methods. However, in more complex GP models having non-factorising likelihood functions and a large number of hyperparameters, we believe that MCMC is currently the only reliable way of carrying out accurate full Bayesian inference.

Acknowledgments   This work is funded by EPSRC Grant No EP/F005687/1 'Gaussian Processes for Systems Identification with Applications in Systems Biology'.

Bibliography

[1] P. Abrahamsen. A review of Gaussian random fields and correlation functions. Technical Report 917, Norwegian Computing Center, 1997.

[2] R. P. Adams, I. Murray and D. J. C. MacKay. The Gaussian process density sampler. In D. Koller, D. Schuurmans, Y. Bengio and L. Bottou, editors, *Advances in Neural Information Processing Systems 21*, pages 9–16. 2009.

[3] U. Alon. *An Introduction to Systems Biology: Design Principles of Biological Circuits.* Chapman and Hall/CRC, 2006.

[4] C. Andrieu and J. Thoms. A tutorial on adaptive MCMC. *Statistics and Computing*, **18**:343–373, 2008.

[5] M. Barenco, D. Tomescu, D. Brewer, J. Callard, R. Stark and M. Hubank. Ranked prediction of p53 targets using hidden variable dynamic modeling. *Genome Biology*, **7**(3), 2006.

[6] O. F. Christensen, G. O. Roberts and Sköld. Robust Markov chain Monte Carlo methods for spatial generalized linear mixed models. *Journal of Computational and Graphical Statistics*, **15**:1–17, 2006.

[7] N. A. C. Cressie. *Statistics for Spatial Data*. John Wiley & Sons, 1993.

[8] L. Csato and M. Opper. Sparse online Gaussian processes. *Neural Computation*, **14**:641–668, 2002.

[9] P. J. Diggle, J. A. Tawn and R. A. Moyeed. Model-based Geostatistics (with discussion). *Applied Statistics*, **47**:299–350, 1998.

[10] J. L. Doob. *Stochastic Processes*. John Wiley & Sons, 1953.

[11] S. Duane, A. D. Kennedy, B. J. Pendleton and D. Roweth. Hybrid Monte Carlo. *Physics Letters B*, **195**(2):216–222, 1987.

[12] A. Einstein. On the movement of small particles suspended in a stationary liquid by the molecular kinetic theory of heat. Dover Publications, 1905.

[13] P. Gao, A. Honkela, N. Lawrence and M. Rattray. Gaussian process modelling of latent chemical species: Applications to inferring transcription factor activities. In *ECCB08*, 2008.

[14] A. Gelman, J. Carlin, H. Stern and D. Rubin. *Bayesian Data Analysis*. Chapman and Hall, 2004.

[15] A. Gelman, G. O. Roberts and W. R. Gilks. Efficient metropolis jumping rules. In *Bayesian statistics*, 5, 1996.

[16] M. N. Gibbs and D. J. C. MacKay. Variational Gaussian process classifiers. *IEEE Transactions on Neural Networks*, **11**(6):1458–1464, 2000.

[17] W. R. Gilks and P. Wild. Adaptive rejection sampling for Gibbs sampling. *Applied Statistics*, **41**(2):337–348, 1992.

[18] H. Haario, E. Saksman and J. Tamminen. An adaptive metropolis algorithm. *Bernoulli*, **7**:223–240, 2001.

[19] M. Kuss and C. E. Rasmussen. Assessing approximate inference for binary Gaussian process classification. *Journal of Machine Learning Research*, **6**:1679–1704, 2005.

[20] N. D. Lawrence, G. Sanguinetti and M. Rattray. Modelling transcriptional regulation using Gaussian processes. In *Advances in Neural Information Processing Systems, 19*. MIT Press, 2007.

[21] N. D. Lawrence, M. Seeger and R. Herbrich. Fast sparse Gaussian process methods: the informative vector machine. In *Advances in Neural Information Processing Systems, 13*. MIT Press, 2002.

[22] T. Minka. Expectation propagation for approximate Bayesian inference. In *UAI*, pages 362–369, 2001.

[23] R. M. Neal. *Bayesian Learning for Neural Networks*. Lecture Notes in Statistics 118. Springer, 1996.

[24] R. M. Neal. Monte Carlo implementation of Gaussian process models for Bayesian regression and classification. Technical report, Dept. of Statistics, University of Toronto, 1997.

[25] R. M. Neal. Suppressing random walks in Markov chain Monte Carlo using ordered overrelaxation. In M. I. Jordan, editor, *Learning in Graphical Models*, pages 205–225. Kluwer Academic Publishers, 1998.

[26] A. O'Hagan. Curve fitting and optimal design for prediction. *Journal of the Royal Statistical Society, Series B*, **40**(1):1–42, 1978.

[27] M. Opper and C. Archambeau. The variational Gaussian approximation revisited. *Neural Computation*, **21**(3), 2009.

[28] J. Quiñonero Candela and C. E. Rasmussen. A unifying view of sparse approximate Gaussian process regression. *Journal of Machine Learning Research*, **6**:1939–1959, 2005.

[29] C. E. Rasmussen and C. K. I. Williams. *Gaussian Processes for Machine Learning*. MIT Press, 2006.

[30] C. P. Robert and G. Casella. *Monte Carlo Statistical Methods*. Springer-Verlag, 2nd edition, 2004.

[31] G. O. Roberts, A. Gelman and W. R. Gilks. Weak convergence and optimal scaling of random walk metropolis algorithms. *Annals of Applied Probability*, **7**:110–120, 1996.

[32] S. Rogers, R. Khanin and M. Girolami. Bayesian model-based inference of transcription factor activity. *BMC Bioinformatics*, **8**(2), 2006.

[33] H. Rue and L. Held. *Gaussian Markov Random Fields: Theory and Applications*. Monographs on Statistics and Applied Probability. Chapman & Hall, 2005.

[34] H. Rue, S. Martino and N. Chopin. Approximate Bayesian inference for latent Gaussian models using integrated nested Laplace approximations. *Journal of the Royal Statistical Society: Series B: Statistical Methodology*, **71**(2):319–392, 2009.

[35] B. Schölkopf and A. Smola. *Learning with Kernels*. MIT Press, 2002.

[36] M. Seeger. Bayesian Gaussian process models: PAC-Bayesian generalisation error bounds and sparse approximations. PhD thesis, University of Edinburgh, July 2003.

[37] M. Seeger, C. K. I. Williams and N. D. Lawrence. Fast forward selection to speed up sparse Gaussian process regression. In C.M. Bishop and B. J. Frey, editors, *Proceedings of the Ninth International Workshop on Artificial Intelligence*. MIT Press, 2003.

[38] A. J. Smola and P. Bartlett. Sparse greedy Gaussian process regression. In *Advances in Neural Information Processing Systems, 13*. MIT Press, 2001.

[39] E. Snelson and Z. Ghahramani. Sparse Gaussian process using pseudo inputs. In *Advances in Neural Information Processing Systems, 13*. MIT Press, 2006.

[40] M. L. Stein. *Interpolation of Spatial Data*. Springer, 1999.

[41] M. K. Titsias. Variational learning of inducing variables in sparse Gaussian processes. In *Twelfth International Conference on Artificial Intelligence and Statistics, JMLR: W and CP*, volume 5, pages 567–574, 2009.

[42] M. K. Titsias, N. D. Lawrence and M. Rattray. Efficient sampling for Gaussian process inference using control variables. In D. Koller, D. Schuurmans, Y. Bengio, and L. Bottou, editors, *Advances in Neural Information Processing Systems 21*, pages 1681–1688. 2009.

[43] G. E. Uhlenbeck and L. S. Ornstein. On the theory of Brownian motion. *Physics Review*, **36**:823–841, 1930.

[44] J. Vanhatalo and A. Vehtari. Sparse log Gaussian processes via MCMC for spatial epidemiology. *Journal of Machine Learning Research: Workshop and conference proceedings*, **1**:73–89, 2007.

[45] G. Wahba. Spline models for observational data. *Society for Industrial and Applied Mathematics*, **59**, 1990.

[46] M. C. Wang and G. E. Uhlenbeck. On the Theory of the Brownian motion II. *Reviews of Modern Physics*, **17**(2-3):323–342, 1945.

[47] N. Wiener. Differential space. *Journal of Mathematical Physics*, **2**:131–174, 1923.

[48] C. K. I. Williams and D. Barber. Bayesian classification with Gaussian processes. *IEEE Transactions on Pattern Analysis and Machine Intelligence*, **20**(12):1342–1351, 1998.

Contributors

Michalis K. Titsias, School of Computer Science, University of Manchester
Magnus Rattray, School of Computer Science, University of Manchester
Neil D. Lawrence, School of Computer Science, University of Manchester

15

Nonparametric hidden Markov models

Jurgen Van Gael and Zoubin Ghahramani

15.1 Introduction

Hidden Markov models (HMMs) are a rich family of probabilistic time series models with a long and successful history of applications in natural language processing, speech recognition, computer vision, bioinformatics, and many other areas of engineering, statistics and computer science. A defining property of HMMs is that the time series is modelled in terms of a number of discrete hidden states. Usually, the number of such states is specified in advance by the modeller, but this limits the flexibility of HMMs. Recently, attention has turned to Bayesian methods which can automatically infer the number of states in an HMM from data. A particularly elegant and flexible approach is to assume a countable but unbounded number of hidden states; this is the nonparametric Bayesian approach to hidden Markov models first introduced by Beal *et al.* [4] and called the *infinite HMM* (iHMM). In this chapter, we review the literature on Bayesian inference in HMMs, focusing on nonparametric Bayesian models. We show the equivalence between the Polya urn interpretation of the infinite HMM and the hierarchical Dirichlet process interpretation of the iHMM in Teh *et al.* [35]. We describe efficient inference algorithms, including the beam sampler which uses dynamic programming. Finally, we illustrate how to use the iHMM on a simple sequence labelling task and discuss several extensions.

Sequential data are at the core of many statistical modelling and machine learning problems. For example, text consists of sequences of words, financial data are often sequences of prices, speech signals are represented as sequences of short-term power-spectra coefficients, proteins are sequences of amino acids, DNA are sequences of nucleotides and video is a sequence of still images. Although it is possible to directly model the relationships between subsequent elements of a time series, e.g. using autoregressive or n-gram models, in many cases we believe the data has some underlying hidden structure. For example, the observed pixels in a video might correspond to objects, the power-spectra coefficients in a speech signal might correspond to phones, and the price movements of financial instruments might correspond to underlying economic and political events. Models that explain sequential data in terms of such underlying hidden variables can be more interpretable and have better predictive properties than models that try to directly relate observed variables.

The hidden Markov model is an influential model for sequential data that captures such hidden structure; [2, 8, 26]. An HMM describes a probability distribution over a sequence

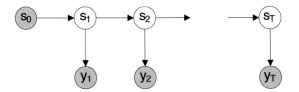

Figure 15.1 Belief network representation of the hidden Markov model.

of observations $y_1, y_2, \cdots, y_T$ of length T. The HMM assumes there exists a Markov chain denoted by $s_1, s_2, \cdots, s_T$ where each s_t is in one of K possible states. The distribution of the state at time t only depends on the states before it, through the state at time $t - 1$ by a K by K stochastic transition matrix π, where $\pi_{ij} = P(s_t = j | s_{t-1} = i)$. This is the first-order *Markov property*, which gives the HMM its middle name. Although it is straightforward to generalise the HMM to higher order, for simplicity we only consider first-order Markov models in this chapter. We refer to the variable that indexes sequences as time, and assume discrete time steps. However, the models described are readily applicable to sequences indexed by any other scalar variable. Generally, we do not directly observe the Markov chain, but rather an observation y_t which only depends on an observation model F parameterised by a state-dependent parameter θ_{s_t}. For example, if we model an object moving through a video using an HMM, we could assume that the position of the object at time t (s_t), is only dependent on its position at time $t - 1$. Moreover, we don't directly observe this position but rather we observe pixels y_t whose configuration is dependent on the state at time t. We can write the probability distribution induced by the HMM as follows:[1]

$$p(y_{1:T}, s_{1:T} | K, \pi, \theta) = \prod_{t=1}^{T} p(s_t | s_{t-1}) p(y_t | s_t) = \prod_{t=1}^{T} \pi_{s_{t-1}, s_t} F(y_t; \theta_{s_t}). \tag{15.1}$$

Figure 15.1 shows the belief network representation of the HMM. The observation model F can be made arbitrarily complex: in a natural language processing application [12] used a multinomial output distribution, [19] describe how in speech recognition a Normal distribution or mixture of Normal distributions is commonly used.

When designing HMMs a key question is how many states K to choose. If we have prior knowledge about the underlying physical process generating the observed sequence, and we know the number of states in that process, then we can set K to that value. For example, HMMs have been used to model ion channel currents, where it is known that the ion channel protein can be in some discrete number of physical conformations. In speech recognition, we could impose the constraint that the hidden states correspond to known phones of a language. However, in many applications the number of underlying states is not known a priori and must be inferred from data.

In Section 15.2 we review HMM parameter learning in detail and describe several Bayesian approaches to learning the number of states. Unfortunately, these Bayesian approaches have both statistical and computational limitations. The main statistical limitation is the assumption that a (usually small) finite number of states provides an adequate

---

[1]To make notation more convenient, we assume that for all our time series models, all latent chains start in a dummy state that is the 1 state: e.g. for the HMM $s_0 = 1$.

model of the sequence. In many settings, it is unlikely one can bound a priori the number of states needed. For example, if the states correspond to political and economic circumstances affecting financial variables, it's hard to say how many such discrete circumstances are needed, and to be confident that new, as yet unobserved circumstances won't arise in the future. The computational limitation is that these approaches have to compare different finite numbers of states, and each such comparison requires some method of approximating intractable marginal likelihoods.

The main focus in this chapter is on nonparametric Bayesian approaches to hidden Markov modelling as introduced by [4]. Their model, known as the *infinite hidden Markov model*, is reviewed in Section 15.3. We show how it overcomes the statistical and computational limitations of the Bayesian approach to the HMM by defining a Markov chain which has a countably infinite (i.e. unbounded) number of hidden states. For any finite observed sequence, only a finite number of these states can be visited. Moreover, as the sequence length is extended and new 'circumstances' arise, new states can be recruited from the unbounded pool of states. In Section 15.4 we describe how to design tractable inference algorithms that avoid the computation of intractable marginal likelihoods that plague the Bayesian treatment of the HMM. Finally, we conclude this chapter with an application of the iHMM in a natural language processing setting and describe various existing and new extensions to the iHMM.

15.2 From HMMs to Bayesian HMMs

In practice we often use the HMM in a setting where the sequence $y_{1:T}$ is given and we want to learn something about the hidden representation $s_{1:T}$, and perhaps about the parameters π, θ and K. The form of the observation model F is also important, but for this chapter we assume that F is fixed and any flexibility in F is captured by its parameterisation through θ. As an example of learning in HMMs, consider speech recognition: we can use an HMM where the hidden state sequence corresponds to phones and the observations correspond to acoustic signals. The parameters π, θ might come from a physical model of speech or be learned from recordings of speech. Depending on how much domain knowledge is available, we distinguish three computational questions.

- π, θ, K **given.** With full knowledge of the parameters π, θ and K we only need to infer $s_{1:T}$ given the observations $y_{1:T}$. We can apply Bayes' rule to Eq. (15.1) to find the posterior distribution over $s_{1:T}$

$$p(s_{1:T}|K, \pi, \theta, y_{1:T}) = \frac{p(y_{1:T}, s_{1:T}|K, \pi, \theta)}{p(y_{1:T}|K, \pi, \theta)} \propto \prod_{t=1}^{T} p(s_t|s_{t-1})p(y_t|s_t).$$

The last line follows from the fact that $p(y_{1:T}|K, \pi, \theta)$ is a constant that is independent of $s_{1:T}$. Computing this distribution can be done using a beautiful application of dynamic programming which is called the forward-backward algorithm in the context of HMMs. Reference [26] gives an excellent overview of this algorithm.

- K **given,** π, θ **learned.** If only the number of hidden states K and observations $y_{1:T}$ are known, we often want to learn the best parameters θ and π in addition to the hidden representation $s_{1:T}$. This problem is underspecified: we need a criterion to decide what the 'best parameters' are. Common criteria are the maximum likelihood and maximum a posteriori objectives. The former finds θ, π which maximise $p(y_{1:T}|\theta, \pi)$ while the latter introduces a prior distribution for θ, π and finds the θ, π which maximise $p(y_{1:T}|\theta, \pi)p(\theta, \pi)$. Algorithms like expectation maximisation [7] can search for the maximum likelihood and maximum a posteriori solutions but will generally only find locally optimal estimates.

- π, θ, K **learned.** Finally, given observations $y_{1:T}$, consider the problem of discovering a statistically meaningful value for K in addition to the hidden representation $s_{1:T}$ and the other parameters π, θ. Using the maximum likelihood criterion turns out to be a bad idea as more states always lead to a better fit of the data: the nonsensical solution where $K = T$ and each state s_t has its own emission and transition parameters, maximises the likelihood. The Akaike Information Criterion [1] and Bayesian Information Criterion [28] can be used to adjust the maximum likelihood estimate by penalising the number of parameters.

A more principled approach to learning π, θ or K is to consider a fully Bayesian analysis of the model. The Bayesian analysis considers the parameters π, θ as unknown quantities and introduces them as random variables in the model. This requires adding a prior distribution, e.g. $p(\theta|H)$ and $p(\pi|\alpha)$, and extending the full joint distribution to

$$p(y_{1:T}, s_{1:T}, \pi, \theta|K) = p(\pi|\alpha)p(\theta|H)\left(\prod_{t=1}^{T} p(s_t|s_{t-1})p(y_t|s_t)\right)$$

$$= p(\pi|\alpha)p(\theta|H)\left(\prod_{t=1}^{T} \pi_{s_{t-1},s_t} F(y_t; \theta_{s_t})\right).$$

A common choice for the prior on π is to use a symmetric Dirichlet distribution on each row: if we denote with π_k the kth row of π then $\pi_k \overset{iid}{\sim} \text{Dirichlet}(\alpha/K, \alpha/K, \cdots, \alpha/K)$ for all $k \in \{1, K\}$. Similarly, a common prior on θ factorises for each state k: $\theta_k \overset{iid}{\sim} H$ for all $k \in \{1, K\}$, where θ_k denotes the parameter for state k; H can be any distribution but will frequently be chosen to be conjugate to the observation model F. Figure 15.2 shows the belief network for a Bayesian analysis of the HMM.

We can now compute the quantities $p(\pi, \theta|y_{1:T}, \alpha, H)$ or $p(s_{1:T}|y_{1:T}, \alpha, H)$ by integrating over respectively $s_{1:T}$ or π, θ. By integrating over unknown variables, the posterior distribution will concentrate around parameter settings which give high probability *on average*. This reduces the overfitting problems that plague maximum likelihood approaches.

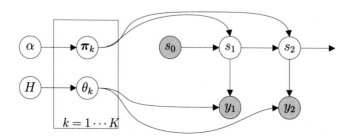

Figure 15.2 Belief network representation of the Bayesian hidden Markov model.

Moreover, in a Bayesian analysis of the HMM we can compute the marginal likelihood or evidence $p(y_{1:T}|K) = \int p(y_{1:T}|K, \theta, \pi)p(\theta, \pi|K)$. This marginal likelihood can be used for *comparing, choosing or averaging* over different values of K. Unfortunately, analytically computing the marginal likelihood for an HMM is intractable. We briefly review three different methods to deal with this intractability.

- There is a large body of literature in statistics on how to use *Markov Chain Monte Carlo* (MCMC) techniques to learn the number of states in HMMs and related models. We can distinguish two main approaches: MCMC methods which estimate the marginal likelihood explicitly and methods which switch between different K. Examples of the former are Annealed Importance Sampling by [23] and Bridge Sampling by [11] which have been successfully applied in practice. The disadvantage of these methods is that it can be computationally expensive to find an accurate estimate of the marginal likelihood for a particular K. If one needs to run the estimation procedure for each different K, the computational overhead becomes high. Reversible jump MCMC methods pioneered by [16] are a family of methods which 'jump' between models of different size. In the context of HMMs, [27] have implemented this idea to jump between HMM models of different K.

- A very elegant approximation to the exact marginal likelihood is the approach developed by [32]. Note that in the belief network in Fig. 15.2, if the hidden states $s_{1:T}$ were observed, the parameters π and θ become independent and assuming that the prior and likelihood are conjugate, we can compute the marginal likelihood analytically. By choosing a good state sequence, one can integrate out the other parameters and compute an approximation to the marginal likelihood. The authors in [32] devise a state-merging algorithm based on this idea.

- A third technique to approximate the marginal likelihood is based on *variational Bayesian* (VB) inference. This computes a lower bound on the marginal likelihood; [20] and [3] describe VB inference algorithms that bound the marginal likelihood of an HMM. The technique generalises EM as it doesn't use a point estimate of the parameters π, θ but rather an approximate posterior of these parameters. Moreover, VB also generalises the idea in [32] as it doesn't use a point estimate of the state sequence $s_{1:T}$ but rather a full distribution on this quantity.

15.3 The infinite hidden Markov model

Whether we choose a particular value for K or average over K, the Bayesian treatment of HMMs requires us to define a large number of HMMs: one for each value of K. The authors in [4] introduced a probabilistic model similar to the HMM but where K is infinite and any finite sequence $s_{1:T}$ only visits a finite fraction of states. This model is attractive because it implicitly defines a distribution over the number of visited states in the HMM rather than define K different HMMs. The authors also describe how the distribution over $s_{1:T}$ can be used to generate observations $y_{1:T}$. This model is called the *infinite hidden Markov model* or iHMM.

In [35], the hierarchical Polya urn model in [4] was re-interpreted as a hierarchical Dirichlet process (HDP).[2] This interpretation embeds the iHMM into the Dirichlet process formalism, leading to a deeper theoretical understanding. The HDP interpretation

---

[2]For this reason, some authors also use the name HDP-HMM for the infinite HMM model.

gives the iHMM new measure-theoretic, Chinese Restaurant Franchise and stick-breaking representations.

In the following section we introduce the hierarchical Polya urn scheme construction of the iHMM. The scheme makes clear the generative procedure for the hidden representation $s_{1:T}$ and allows us to better understand the effect of the hyperparameters. Section 15.3.2 introduces the HDP-based description of the iHMM. This interpretation will turn out to be useful when we want to design inference methods for the iHMM.

15.3.1 A hierarchical Polya urn scheme

Polya urn schemes are a family of algorithms which define a discrete probability distribution through the metaphor of filling an urn with coloured balls. For our purposes we consider a Polya urn scheme that is parameterised by a single real number $\alpha > 0$. We will count the total amount of balls with colour i in the urn as n_i. Initially the urn is empty (all $n_i = 0$) but at each time step, with probability $\frac{n_i}{\alpha + \sum_i n_i}$ we add a ball with colour i to the urn and with probability $\frac{\alpha}{\alpha + \sum_i n_i}$ we add a ball with a new colour to the urn. Depending on the colour we augment the appropriate n_i variable by one. First note that if we execute this recipe N times there will be N balls in the urn. The amount of different colours that are represented in the urn can be anything between 1 and N. Also, if there are a lot of balls with colour j in the urn the probability of adding an extra ball with colour j is high. The parameter α controls the growth of the number of colours: if α is large with respect to $\sum_i n_i$ then it is very likely that a new colour will be added to the urn. A Polya urn scheme can be interpreted as a nonparametric prior for a clustering: each datapoint corresponds to a ball and each cluster to a colour. It is clear from our description above that in this setting the number of clusters is a random quantity, that grows with the number of data points.

The hierarchical Polya urn model introduced in [4] describes how to extend the Polya urn scheme in a time series setting. We review this model below and illustrate a sample draw from the hierarchical Polya urn in Fig. 15.3.

Consider a countably infinite number of Polya urns with parameter α, one for each possible state the iHMM can be in. We refer to this set as the set of transition urns. In addition to having coloured balls, we also colour the urns and identify both the colours of the urns and balls with states. We draw balls from the hierarchical Polya urn and keep track of their colours: s_t refers to the colour of the tth ball drawn from the hierarchical Polya urn. For bookkeeping purposes, we also keep track of the quantity n_{ij}: the number of balls of colour j in the transition urn with colour i.

Initially, all urns are empty and we assume we observed a dummy ball with arbitrary colour s_0. At each time step t, we record the colour s_{t-1} of the previously drawn ball and then draw according to the Polya urn scheme from the urn with colour s_{t-1}. We set s_t to the colour of the extra ball which we added to urn s_{t-1}. We interpret the number of balls with colour j in the urn with colour i as being proportional to the transition probability of a Markov chain

$$p(s_t = j | s_{t-1} = i, \alpha) = \frac{n_{ij}}{\sum_{j'} n_{ij'} + \alpha}. \tag{15.2}$$

Note that these probabilities do not sum to one: under the Polya urn scheme there is a probability $\frac{\alpha}{\sum_{j'} n_{ij'} + \alpha}$ of adding a ball with a new colour to the urn. To determine the colour of the new ball we introduce an extra *oracle* Polya urn with parameter γ. We denote with c_i the number of balls in the oracle urn with colour i. When we need a ball with a new colour, we draw a ball from the oracle urn, record its colour s_t and replace that ball with two balls of the same colour back into the oracle urn and one ball with the same colour to the transition urn with colour s_{t-1}. Formally, when we draw a ball with colour j from the oracle urn we set $c_j \leftarrow c_j + 1$ and $n_{s_{t-1},j} \leftarrow n_{s_{t-1},j} + 1$. Conditional on drawing from the oracle, the transition probability is

$$p(s_t = j | s_{t-1} = i, \gamma) = \begin{cases} \frac{c_j}{\sum_{j'} c_{j'} + \gamma} & \text{if } j \text{ represents an existing colour,} \\ \frac{\gamma}{\sum_{j'} c_{j'} + \gamma} & \text{if } j \text{ represents a } \textit{new} \text{ colour.} \end{cases}$$

In other words, when we query the oracle, with probability proportional to γ we introduce an entirely new colour. The combination of transition and oracle urns explains why this

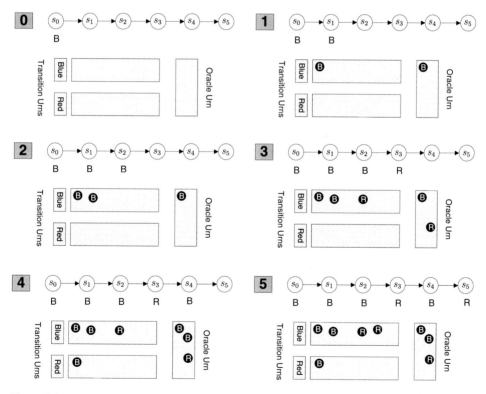

Figure 15.3 Hierarchical Polya urn example: we initialise ($t = 0$) our hierarchical Polya urn with both the transition and oracle urns empty and assume our first dummy state carries the colour blue. In the first step we check the blue urn and find that there are no balls. This means that with probability $\alpha/\alpha = 1$ we should query the oracle. In the oracle urn, the probabilities of drawing a blue ball is $\gamma/\gamma = 1$ so we put a blue ball in both the blue urn and the oracle urn. Next, we generate the state for time step 2: now, with probability $1/(1 + \alpha)$ we draw a blue ball and with probability $\alpha/(1 + \alpha)$ we query the oracle urn. In our example we draw a blue ball implying that we add an extra blue ball to the blue transition urn. For time step 3, our example shows that the oracle urn was queried (with probability $\alpha/(2+\alpha)$) and that in the oracle a new red ball was drawn which was added to the blue transition urn as well as to the oracle urn. This means that in time step 4 we first query the red urn and since there are no balls in it, with probability 1 we query the oracle urn; this time returning a blue ball moving us back to the blue urn. Finally in step 5, a red ball is drawn from the blue transition urn without querying the oracle. The resulting sequence of colours *blue, blue, red, blue, red* corresponds to the state sequence $s_1 = 1, s_2 = 1, s_3 = 2, s_4 = 1, s_5 = 2$.

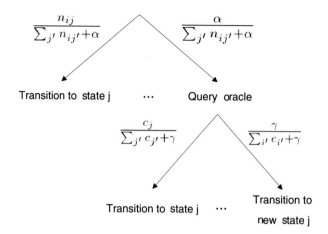

Figure 15.4 Hierarchical Polya urn transition scheme as a decision tree.

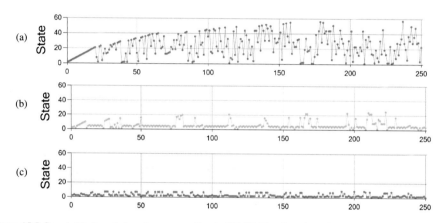

Figure 15.5 Sample Markov chain paths generated by the iHMM. The plots show the state sequence for an iHMM with parameters (a) $\gamma = 20, \alpha = 20$; (b) $\gamma = 20, \alpha = 2$; (c) $\gamma = 2, \alpha = 20$.

scheme is called the *hierarchical Polya urn*[3] scheme: we stack the transition urn and oracle urns on top of each other in a decision hierarchy illustrated in Fig. 15.4. To conclude the hierarchical Polya urn algorithm, we interpret the s_t as the states of a Markov chain. It is clear that the number of possible states is a random quantity and can grow arbitrarily large. Figure 15.3 illustrates a draw from the hierarchical Polya urn scheme.

The hyperparameters γ and α play an important role in determining the number of states in an iHMM; this is illustrated in Fig. 15.5. The hyperparameter γ controls how frequently we are going to add a ball with a completely new colour to the urns, in other words, the probability of visiting a new state. The top and bottom plots in Fig. 15.5 show what happens when we change from $\gamma = 20$ to $\gamma = 2$: the number of states grows much more slowly in the bottom plot than in the top plot. The hyperparameter α on the other hand controls how frequently we query the oracle. The top and middle plots in Fig. 15.5 illustrate the difference between $\alpha = 20$ and $\alpha = 2$. We see that in the middle plot, once a particular

---

[3]In [4] this was originally called a hierarchical Dirichlet process but that term has subsequently been used by [35] to refer to the closely related Dirichlet process with base measure drawn from another Dirichlet process.

transition accumulates a lot of counts it becomes more and more likely that we take that transition again. For example, the $4 \rightarrow 3$ and $3 \rightarrow 4$ transitions are taken frequently. In the limit of $\alpha \rightarrow \infty$, we always query the oracle and the distribution of ball colours for each transition urn is going to be very close to the distribution implied by the oracle urn. In this limiting case, we can think of the oracle urn as specifying the expected number of times we visit each state which is the stationary distribution of the Markov chain.

Completing the iHMM The hierarchical Polya urn scheme defines a nonparametric distribution on the hidden state sequence $s_{1:T}$. In order to complete it to a full hidden Markov model we need to introduce a mechanism to generate observations conditional on the state sequence $s_{1:T}$. For that we introduce

- a base distribution H from which we draw the output likelihood parameters θ_k for each state $k \in \{1, \ldots, \infty\}$,

- a likelihood model F which takes a state s_t and its parameter θ_{s_t} and generates a datapoint y_t.

In [4] there was an additional parameter reinforcing self transitions. This idea was revisited by [10] as the sticky HDP-HMM. We will review this in Section 15.6.2.

15.3.2 The hierarchical Dirichlet process

The Polya urn scheme is an intuitive procedure for generating state sequences with arbitrarily large state space. In this section, we review the interpretation of the iHMM using the hierarchical Dirichlet process framework by [35]. Using this representation we will be able to more easily design inference schemes for the iHMM.

We briefly review the theory of Dirichlet processes first, but refer to [34] and [17] for more background on the basic theory of nonparametric Bayesian methods. A draw from a Dirichlet process $G \sim \text{DP}(\alpha, H)$ is a discrete distribution that puts probability mass on a countable number of atoms in the domain of H. The atoms are iid draws from the base distribution H and the parameter α controls how concentrated the mass of the DP is. We can write

$$G = \sum_{i=1}^{\infty} \beta_i \delta_{\theta_i}, \tag{15.3}$$

where $\beta_i = \hat{\beta}_i \prod_{l=1}^{i-1}(1 - \hat{\beta}_l)$ with $\hat{\beta}_l \overset{iid}{\sim} \text{Beta}(1, \alpha)$, $\theta_i \overset{iid}{\sim} H$ and δ_{θ_i} is a point mass at θ_i. We refer to this construction of β as the stick-breaking distribution [30], $\beta \sim \text{Stick}(\alpha)$.

The idea behind the hierarchical Dirichlet process in [35] is that the base distribution of a DP is itself a draw from a DP.

$$G_0 | \gamma, H \sim \text{DP}(\gamma, H),$$

$$G_j | \alpha, G_0 \overset{iid}{\sim} \text{DP}(\alpha, G_0).$$

Thus there are a set of distributions G_j coupled through a common G_0. This construction has some interesting properties that make it suitable to build nonparametric hidden Markov models. The first important property of this construction, illustrated in Fig. 15.6, is the fact that G_0 and all G_j share the same atoms. This is not too hard to see from the perspective of drawing a G_j: since G_j is a draw from a DP, its atoms are draws from the DP's base distribution. This is G_0 in our case: since G_0 is discrete, G_j and G_0 share the same atoms.

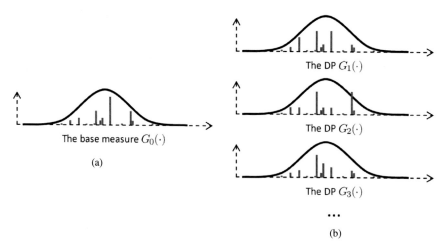

Figure 15.6 Visualisation of the hierarchical Dirichlet process. (a) The stick-breaking representation of the base measure. (b) The stick-breaking representations of the child Dirichlet processes. The solid line is the base measure H which was chosen to be Gaussian in this example.

Next, we focus on the distribution of probability mass for G_0 and all G_j's. Equation (15.3) illustrates the stick-breaking representation of a DP. The theory of HDPs shows us that the mass of the G_j's is distributed according to a stick *rebreaking* process. If $\beta_{1:\infty}$ represent the sticks for G_0 and $\hat{\pi}_{ij} \overset{iid}{\sim} \text{Beta}(\alpha\beta_j, \alpha(1 - \sum_{l=1}^{j} \beta_j))$ then the jth stick for G_i is $\pi_{ij} = \hat{\pi}_{ij} \prod_{l=1}^{j-1}(1 - \hat{\pi}_{il})$, or more intuitively, the rebreaking process for any finite subset of the sticks can be written as

$$\left(\pi_{i1}, \pi_{i2}, \ldots, \pi_{ik}, \sum_{l=i+1}^{\infty} \pi_{il} \right) \overset{iid}{\sim} \text{Dirichlet}\left(\alpha\beta_1, \alpha\beta_2, \ldots, \alpha\beta_k, \alpha(\sum_{l=i+1}^{\infty} \beta_l) \right).$$

The previous paragraph hints at how we can use the HDP construction to build an iHMM: we set the rows of an infinite-dimensional transition matrix equal to the sticks of a countably infinite number of G_j. We start a Markov chain in a dummy state $s_0 = 1$ and then transition according to π_{ij}. When we transition into state i, we use atom θ_i as the parameter for the output distribution F. The key enabler in this scenario is the fact that all states share the same set of likelihood model parameters θ. Figure 15.7 shows the belief network underlying the iHMM in the HDP representation, defined by

$$\beta|\gamma \sim \text{Stick}(\gamma)$$

$$\pi_{k\cdot}|\alpha, \beta \overset{iid}{\sim} \text{Stick}(\alpha\beta) \qquad \forall k \in \{1 \ldots \infty\},$$

$$s_t|s_{t-1}, \pi \sim \pi_{s_{t-1}, \cdot} \qquad \text{with} \quad s_0 = 1,$$

$$\theta_k|H \overset{iid}{\sim} H \qquad \forall k \in \{1 \ldots \infty\},$$

$$y_t|s_t, \theta \sim F(\theta_{s_t}).$$

Although it is not immediately obvious, the hierarchical Polya urn model and hierarchical Dirichlet process define the same distribution over the Markov chain $s_{1:T}$. In Appendix 15.A we sketch a proof for this equivalence.

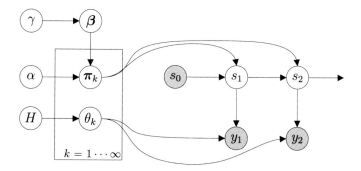

Figure 15.7 The belief network for the iHMM.

15.4 Inference

When the iHMM was introduced in [4] it was presented with two different inference algorithms: a Gibbs sampler with a per iteration time complexity of $O(KT^2)$ and an approximate Gibbs sampler with a time complexity of $O(KT)$; where K is the number of represented states in that iteration. The re-interpretation of the iHMM in the HDP framework by [35] slightly modified the approximate Gibbs sampler from [4] to make it exact, whilst retaining the $O(KT)$ complexity. We describe this linear time inference scheme in Section 15.4.1.

The linear time Gibbs sampler updates the hidden state at each time step conditioned on all other states in the Markov chain. Typically, the state sequence variables in a Markov chain are strongly correlated. As is well known, Gibbs sampling tends to mix slowly when there are strong correlations between variables. Unfortunately, strong correlations are common when modelling sequential data: e.g. when we know a stock's price today we have a good guess about the stock's price tomorrow.

A Markov chain Monte Carlo method for the Bayesian treatment of the HMM that works around the correlation problem is reviewed in [29]. We will refer to this dynamic programming based algorithm which resamples the whole state sequence at once, as the forward-filtering backward-sampling (FF-BS) algorithm.

Because the iHMM has a potentially infinite number of states, we cannot naively apply the FF-BS algorithm. In Section 15.4.2 we describe the *beam sampler* introduced by [36]. The beam sampler is an auxiliary variable MCMC algorithm which adaptively truncates the iHMM so we can run a variant of the FF-BS algorithm. It resamples the whole Markov chain at once and hence suffers less from slow mixing than the Gibbs sampling.

15.4.1 The collapsed Gibbs sampler

When we inspect the belief network in Fig. 15.7 we see that the unobserved random variables corresponding to the rows of the transition matrix π_k have observed descendants: the observations $y_{1:T}$. Following the standard rules for belief networks we conclude that the π_k are conditionally dependent given $y_{1:T}$. If we observe β and $s_{1:T}$ however, the rows of the transition matrix become conditionally independent. We can consider each transition as a draw from a Polya urn scheme and use our knowledge of Polya urns to resample the state sequence. Moreover, if the output distribution F is conjugate to the HDP base distribution H we will show how we can also analytically integrate out the likelihoods involved. One iteration of the collapsed Gibbs sampler will consist of two steps: resampling the states $p(s_{1:T}|y_{1:T}, \alpha, \beta, \gamma, H, F)$ and resampling the base distribution $p(\beta|y_{1:T}, s_{1:T}, \alpha, \gamma, H, F)$.

Sampling s_t

If we condition on β and $s_{1:T}$, the DPs for each of the transitions become independent. Hence, for all $k \in \{1, 2, \ldots\}$ we can treat all the transitions out of state k as draws from a Polya urn. Since they form an exchangeable sequence we can resample $s_{1:T}$ by taking out one s_t at a time (essentially removing two transitions) and resampling it from the posterior

$$p(s_t|y_{1:T}, s_{-t}, \alpha, \beta, \gamma, H, F) \propto p(y_t|s_t, s_{-t}, y_{-t}, H, F)p(s_t|s_{-t}, \alpha, \beta, \gamma),$$

where s_{-t} denotes all states except s_t. The first factor is the conditional likelihood of y_t given $s_{1:T}, y_{-t}$ and H

$$p(y_t|s_t, s_{-t}, y_{-t}, H, F) = \int p(y_t|\theta_{s_t})p(\theta|s_{-t}, y_{-t}, H)d\theta, \tag{15.4}$$

where y_{-t} denotes all observations except y_{-t}. If the output likelihood F is conjugate to the HDP base distribution H, this quantity can generally be analytically computed. In non-conjugate scenarios one can use techniques in [24] to approximate this computation.

In order to compute the factor $p(s_t|s_{-t}, \alpha, \beta, \gamma)$, we first use the property that conditional on β the Polya urns for each row are independent. This means that the transition in and the transition out of s_t can be considered draws from a Markov exchangeable sequence (that is, the in-transition is a draw from the exchangeable sequence out of urn s_{t-1} and the out-transition is a draw from the exchangeable sequence out of urn s_t). If we denote with n_{ij}^{-t} the number of transitions from state i to state j excluding the transitions involving time step t, similarly let $n_{\cdot i}^{-t}, n_{i \cdot}^{-t}$ be the number of transitions in and out of state i excluding time step t and K be the number of distinct states in s_{-t} then we can write

$$p(s_t = k|s_{-t}, \alpha, \beta, \gamma) \propto \begin{cases} (n_{s_{t-1},k}^{-t} + \alpha\beta_k)\frac{n_{k,s_{t+1}}^{-t} + \alpha\beta_{s_{t+1}}}{n_{k\cdot}^{-t} + \alpha} & \text{if } k \leq K, k \neq s_{t-1} \\[2mm] (n_{s_{t-1},k}^{-t} + \alpha\beta_k)\frac{n_{k,s_{t+1}}^{-t} + 1 + \alpha\beta_{s_{t+1}}}{n_{k\cdot}^{-t} + 1 + \alpha} & \text{if } k = s_{t-1} = s_{t+1} \\[2mm] (n_{s_{t-1},k}^{-t} + \alpha\beta_k)\frac{n_{k,s_{t+1}}^{-t} + \alpha\beta_{s_{t+1}}}{n_{k\cdot}^{-t} + 1 + \alpha} & \text{if } k = s_{t-1} \neq s_{t+1} \\[2mm] \alpha\beta_k\beta_{s_{t+1}} & \text{if } k = K+1. \end{cases}$$

We resample the whole state sequence $s_{1:T}$ by resampling each s_t in turn, conditional on all other states.

Sampling β

Recall that β is the distribution on the atoms for the base distribution of the HDP. If we had kept track of the Polya urn representation of the base distribution (that is, the counts of each ball type c_i in the oracle urn) then we could resample from the posterior $\beta \sim$ Dirichlet$(c_1, c_2, \cdots, c_K, \gamma)$. Although we don't have the representation $c_{1:K}$ we can introduce an auxiliary variable m_{ij} with the following interpretation: m_{ij} denotes the number of oracle calls that returned a ball with label j when we queried the oracle from state i.

Since the total number of type j balls in the oracle urn must equal $\sum_i m_{ij}$, if we can sample m_{ij} then we have implicitly sampled $c_j = \sum_i m_{ij}$ and hence we can resample β.

First note that if the number of transitions from state i to j is non-zero ($n_{ij} > 0$) then we know that we must have queried the oracle at least once when we were in state i. Moreover, we also know that $m_{ij} \leq n_{ij}$ since we can query the oracle at most once for every transition. Let $S_{ij} = \{s_{(ij_1)}, s_{(ij_2)}, \cdots, s_{(ij_{n_{ij}})}\}$ be the set of states that transitioned from state i to state j. The exchangeability of the transitions out of state i implies that the sequence S_{ij} is exchangeable as well. Note that m_{ij} is the number of elements in S_{ij} that were obtained from querying the oracle. Because S_{ij} is an exchangeable sequence, we compute the probability

$$p(s_{ij_{n_{ij}}} = j | S_{ij}^{-n_{ij}}) \propto \begin{cases} n_{ij} - 1 & \text{if we didn't query the oracle,} \\ \alpha \beta_j & \text{if we queried the oracle.} \end{cases}$$

These equations form the conditional distribution of a Gibbs sampler whose equilibrium distribution is the distribution of a Polya urn scheme with parameter $\alpha \beta_j$. In other words, in order to sample m_{ij}, we sample n_{ij} elements from a Polya urn with parameter $\alpha \beta_j$ and count the final number of ball types.[4]

Complexity

We can break down the computational complexity for an iteration where the sample uses at most K states in two different parts. When sampling the hidden state sequence, for each time step $1 \leq t \leq T$ we need to compute $O(K)$ probabilities; this results in a $O(TK)$ contribution to the computational cost. On the other hand, when sampling the β variables, for each of the K^2 entries of the transition matrix, we need to sample n_{ij} random variables. Since $\sum_{ij} n_{ij} = T$ this leads to an extra $O(K^2 + T)$ complexity. In summary, one iteration of the collapsed Gibbs sampler has an $O(TK + K^2)$ computational complexity.

Discussion

First, note that non-conjugate models can be handled using the sampling methods in [24]. An example can be found in [36] who experimented with a collapsed Gibbs sampler with normal base distribution and Student-t distributed likelihood for a changepoint detection problem.

As we discussed above, the collapsed Gibbs sampler suffers from one major limitation: sequential data are likely to be strongly correlated. In other words, it is unlikely that the Gibbs sampler which makes individual updates to s_t can cause large blocks within $s_{1:T}$ to change state. We will now introduce the beam sampler which does not suffer from this slow mixing behaviour by sampling the whole sequence $s_{1:T}$ in one go.

15.4.2 The beam sampler

As we argued above, we would like to use a method that resamples the whole state sequence of the iHMM at once. Methods that achieve this for finite HMMs, e.g. the forward-filtering backward-sampling algorithm, efficiently enumerate all possible state trajectories (using

---

[4]Thanks to Emily Fox for bringing this to our attention; a previous implementation computed Stirling numbers of the second kind which are rather expensive to compute for large-scale applications.

dynamic programming), compute their corresponding probabilities and sample from this set. Unfortunately, the forward-filtering backward-sampling algorithm does not apply to the iHMM because the number of states, and hence the number of potential state trajectories, is infinite.

The core idea of the beam sampling [36] is to introduce auxiliary variables $u_{1:T}$ such that conditioned on $u_{1:T}$ the number of trajectories with positive probability is finite. Then, dynamic programming can be used to compute the conditional probabilities of each of these trajectories and efficiently sample whole state trajectories. These auxiliary variables do not change the marginal distribution over other variables and hence MCMC sampling still converges to the true posterior. The idea of using auxiliary variables to limit computational cost is inspired by [38] who applied it to limit the number of components in a DP mixture model that need to be considered during sampling.

Sampling π and θ   Since the auxiliary variable and dynamic program below need the transition and likelihood model parameters, we can think of them as another set of auxiliary variables which we sample just prior to sampling $u_{1:T}$. Let n_{ij} be the number of times state i transitions to state j in the state sequence $s_{1:T}$, where $i, j \in \{1 \ldots K\}$, K is the number of distinct states in $s_{1:T}$, and these states have been relabelled $1 \ldots K$. Merging the infinitely many states not represented in $s_{1:T}$ into one state, the conditional distribution of $(\pi_{k1} \ldots \pi_{kK}, \sum_{k'=K+1}^{\infty} \pi_{kk'})$ given its Markov blanket $s_{1:T}, \beta, \alpha$ is

$$\text{Dirichlet}(n_{k1} + \alpha\beta_1 \ldots n_{kK} + \alpha\beta_K, \alpha \sum_{i=K+1}^{\infty} \beta_i).$$

Each θ_k is independent of others conditional on $s_{1:T}, y_{1:T}$ and their prior distribution H, i.e. $p(\theta|s_{1:T}, y_{1:T}, H) = \prod_k p(\theta_k|s_{1:T}, y_{1:T}, H)$. When the base distribution H is conjugate to the data distribution F, each θ_k can generally be sampled efficiently. Otherwise Metropolis–Hastings or other approaches may be applied. Note that beam sampling in the non-conjugate case is simpler than for Gibbs sampling: we only need to sample from a non-conjugate posterior rather than use Monte Carlo integration to compute the integral in Eq. (15.4).

Sampling $u_{1:T}$ For each time step t we introduce an auxiliary variable u_t with conditional distribution $u_t \sim \text{Uniform}(0, \pi_{s_{t-1}s_t})$.

Sampling $s_{1:T}$ The key observation is the distribution over state sequences $s_{1:T}$ conditional on the auxiliary variables $u_{1:T}$ will only have non-zero probability where $\pi_{s_{t-1}s_t} \geq u_t$. Other paths are not consistent with the conditional distribution $p(u_t|s_{1:T}, \pi)$. Moreover, there are only finitely many such trajectories with this property: since $\pi_{kk'} > 0$ with probability 1, $u_t > 0$ with probability 1; given the auxiliary variable u_t, note further that for each possible value of s_{t-1}, u_t partitions the set of transition probabilities out of state s_{t-1} into two sets: a finite set with $\pi_{s_{t-1}k} > u_t$ and an infinite set with $\pi_{s_{t-1}k} < u_t$. Thus we can recursively show that for $t = 1, 2 \ldots T$ the set of trajectories $s_{1:t}$ with all $\pi_{s_{t'-1}s_{t'}} > u_t$ is finite. The mathematics below makes this more clear and will also show how dynamic programming can compute the conditional distribution over all such trajectories.

First note that the probability density for u_t is

$$p(u_t|s_{t-1}, s_t, \pi) = \frac{\mathbb{I}(0 < u_t < \pi_{s_{t-1},s_t})}{\pi_{s_{t-1},s_t}}, \tag{15.5}$$

where $\mathbb{I}(C) = 1$ if condition C is true and 0 otherwise. We compute $p(s_t|y_{1:t}, u_{1:t})$ for all time steps t as follows (we omit the additional conditioning variables π and θ for clarity):

$$
\begin{aligned}
p(s_t|y_{1:t}, u_{1:t}) &\propto p(s_t, u_t, y_t|y_{1:t-1}, u_{1:t-1}), \\
&= \sum_{s_{t-1}} p(y_t|s_t)p(u_t|s_t, s_{t-1})p(s_t|s_{t-1})p(s_{t-1}|y_{1:t-1}, u_{1:t-1}), \\
&= p(y_t|s_t) \sum_{s_{t-1}} \mathbb{I}(u_t < \pi_{s_{t-1}, s_t})p(s_{t-1}|y_{1:t-1}, u_{1:t-1}), \\
&= p(y_t|s_t) \sum_{s_{t-1}: u_t < \pi_{s_{t-1}, s_t}} p(s_{t-1}|y_{1:t-1}, u_{1:t-1}). \quad (15.6)
\end{aligned}
$$

Note that we only need to compute Eq. (15.6) for the finitely many s_t values belonging to some trajectory with positive probability. Furthermore, although the sum over s_{t-1} is technically a sum over an infinite number of terms, the auxiliary variable u_t truncates this summation to the finitely many s_{t-1}'s that satisfy both constraints $\pi_{s_{t-1}, s_t} > u_t$ and $p(s_{t-1}|y_{1:t-1}, u_{1:t-1}) > 0$. Finally, to sample the whole trajectory $s_{1:T}$, we sample s_T from $p(s_T|y_{1:T}, u_{1:T})$ and perform a backward pass where we sample s_t given the sample for s_{t+1}: $p(s_t|s_{t+1}, y_{1:T}, u_{1:T}) \propto p(s_t|y_{1:t}, u_{1:t})p(s_{t+1}|s_t, u_{t+1})$.

Sampling β We discard the transition matrix π and sample β using the same algorithm as the Gibbs sampler in Section 15.4.1.

Complexity For each time step and each state assignment we need to sum over all represented previous states. If K states are represented, the worst case complexity is $O(TK^2)$. However, the sum in Eq. (15.6) is only over previous states for which the transition probability is larger than u_t. In practice this means that we might only need to sum over much less states.

Figure 15.8 shows the empirical complexity of the beam sampler on the application which we introduce in Section 15.5. As we can see from the plot, initially the beam sampler considers about $K^2/2$ transitions per state but very quickly this number decreases to about 10 per cent of K^2. This means that the beam sampler will run approximately 10 times faster than the dynamic program which considers all transitions. This increase doesn't come for free: by considering less potential transitions, the chain might mix slower.

Discussion A practical point of attention is that after sampling u_t, we need to make sure that *all* possible transition probabilities in $\pi_{s_{t-1}} > u_t$ are represented. This might involve extending our representation of $\pi_{s_{t-1}}$ and θ with new states sampled from their posterior distribution. Since there are no observations associated with these new states, the posterior distribution equals the prior distribution.

To conclude our discussion of the beam sampler, it is useful to point out that u_t need not be sampled from the uniform distribution on $[0, \pi_{s_{t-1}, s_t}]$. We can choose $u_t \sim \pi_{s_{t-1} s_t} \text{Beta}(a, b)$ which with the appropriate choice of a and b could bias our auxiliary variable closer to 0 or closer to $\pi_{s_{t-1} s_t}$. Smaller auxiliary variables imply that we consider more transitions in the dynamic program, hence mixing can be faster, at a larger computational cost. Larger auxiliary variables imply that the dynamic program is sparser, hence mixing can be slower, at a smaller computational cost. Note that we need to adjust the dynamic program in Eq. (15.6)

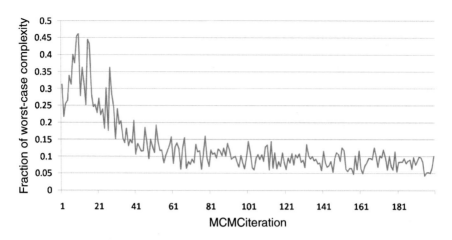

Figure 15.8 This plot shows an example of how efficient the beam sampler is in practice. On the *x*-axis we plot the iteration; on the *y*-axis we plot the fraction of the worst case complexity per state. Recall that if the sampler currently represents K states, the worst-case complexity for a particular state will be K^2.

slightly to take into account the density of the Beta distribution rather than the uniform distribution.

15.5   Example: unsupervised part-of-speech tagging

Part-of-speech tagging (PoS-tagging) is the task of annotating the words in a sentence with their appropriate part-of-speech tag: e.g. for the sentence 'The man sat', 'The' is a *determiner*, 'man' is a *noun* and 'sat' is a *verb*. Part-of-speech-tagging is a standard component in many linguistic processing pipelines so any improvement on its performance is likely to impact a wide range of tasks.

Hidden Markov models are commonly used to model PoS-tags [21]: more specifically, they are generally applied by setting the words in the corpus to correspond to the observations $y_{1:T}$ and the hidden representation $s_{1:T}$ is then interpreted as the unknown PoS-tag. This parameterisation is particularly useful as the Markov chain allows the model to disambiguate between PoS-tags. For example in the sentence 'The man sat', the word 'man' could be a verb (as in 'man your posts'). Because it appears after a determiner and before a verb, it is more likely to be a noun. Most often, a PoS-tagger is trained in a supervised fashion using a corpus of annotated sentences. Building this corpus is quite expensive; hence [18], [14] and [12] explored the possibility of using unsupervised methods to learn a good PoS-tagger. Using either EM, variational Bayes or MCMC methods, the authors explored how well the states of an HMM that is trained purely unsupervised, correspond to what humans typically consider as PoS-tags.

Choosing the number of hidden states is hard, as was carefully discussed in [18]. First of all, there are many different sets of PoS-tag classes of different granularity resulting in different labelled corpora using different PoS-tag classes. Secondly, even if we would choose a particular number of PoS-classes, our HMM might decide that there is enough statistical evidence to merge or split certain classes.

In this section we describe our experiments using the iHMM for learning the number of PoS-tags automatically from data. We only discuss a very simple model as an illustration of the concepts reviewed in this chapter. For a more complete overview of using the iHMM for unsupervised PoS-tagging we refer to [37].

Our setup is to use an iHMM with $\gamma = 5$ and $\alpha = 0.8$. A commonly used likelihood in natural language applications is a simple multinomial distribution. We choose a symmetric Dirichlet distribution as our base distribution H so it is conjugate to our likelihood. To enforce a sparse output distribution for each state, we choose the symmetric Dirichlet with parameters 0.1. We trained on section 0 of the Wall Street Journal (WSJ) part of the Penn Treebank [22]. This dataset contains 1917 sentences with a total of 50 282 word tokens (observations) and 7904 word types (dictionary size). We initialised the sampler with 50 states and assigned each s_t to one out of 50 states uniformly at random and ran the sample for 50 000 iterations. Figure 15.9 shows the evolution of the number of states for the first 10 000 iterations. As this plot clearly shows, the iHMM sampler seamlessly switches between models of different size between iterations.

As we already discussed in Section 15.4.2, when a sample of length T in the iHMM uses K states, the beam sampler has a worst case complexity of $O(TK^2)$. However, in Fig. 15.8 we show how in our example after only 200 iterations only 10 per cent of the worst case computations need to be done. In our example with $T = 50\,000$ and $K \sim 30$, one iteration takes about 1 second on a quad core CPU.

To investigate whether the output of the iHMM-based PoS-tagger correlates with our notion of PoS-tags, we consider the top five words for the five most common states; see Table 15.1. The first column, a.k.a. state 9 shows that the iHMM assigns a lot of weight

9 (8699)	12 (4592)	8 (4216)	18 (3502)	17 (3470)
of (1152)	the (1943)	, (2498)	company (93)	it (204)
to (1000)	a (944)	and (260)	year (85)	that (117)
in (829)	its (173)	's (146)	market (52)	he (112)
and (439)	an (157)	said (136)	U.S. (46)	" (110)
for (432)	this (77)	– (95)	time (32)	they (101)

Table 15.1 This table analyses a sample after 40 000 iterations of the beam sampler. Each column in the table describes a particular state and its five most frequent words in the sample we analysed. The top line of each column is the state ID in the iHMM and its frequency in brackets. The following rows list the top five words with their frequency in the sample.

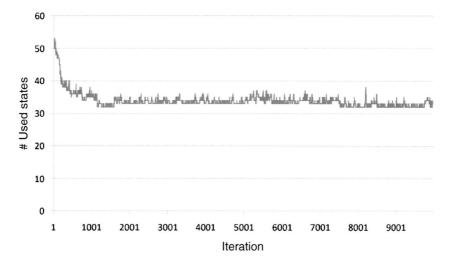

Figure 15.9 This plot illustrates the evolution of the number of represented states in the beam sampler.

to the words 'of,to,in,and,for'. This corresponds well to the class of prepositions (**IN** in the ground truth annotation scheme). When we look at the ground truth labelling of the corpus, we find that the annotators put 'to' in its own PoS-class (**TO**). The iHMM does not find any statistical reason to do so. Skimming over the other states we see that state 12 is a mix of determiners (**DT**) and possessive pronouns (**PRP\$**), state 8 takes care of punctuation together with some coordinating conjunction words (**CC**), state 18 captures many nouns (**NN,NNS,NNP,NNPS**) and state 17 captures personal pronouns (**PRP**).

15.6   Beyond the iHMM

In this section we discuss a number of extensions to the iHMM which we have found useful in practice.

15.6.1   The input–output iHMM

The iHMM, like the HMM assumes that the Markov chain evolves completely autonomously and the observations are conditionally independent given the Markov chain. In many real scenarios, the Markov chain can be affected by external factors: a robot is driving around in an interior environment while taking pictures. The sequence of pictures could be modelled by an iHMM where the latent chain represents the robot's location (e.g. a room index). If our robot doesn't perform a random walk through the environment but uses a particular policy, we can integrate the robot's actions as inputs to the iHMM. We call this model the input–output iHMM (IO-iHMM) in analogy to its finite counterpart the IO-HMM by [5]. Fig. 15.10 illustrates the belief network of the IO-iHMM. A different way to think about the IO-iHMM is as a conditional sequence model: it predicts the sequence of observations $y_{1:T}$ from inputs $e_{1:T}$ through a hidden representation $s_{1:T}$. This model can be useful for structured sequence prediction problems.

   We can think of the IO-iHMM where the transition probabilities depend on the inputs e_t as an iHMM with a three-dimensional transition matrix: for each input symbol e and each previous state s, the probabilities for moving to the next state is $p(s_t|s_{t-1}, e_t) = \pi_{e_t, s_{t-1}, s_t}$. The vectors $\pi_{e,s,\cdot}$ can be constructed similarly to the rows of the transition matrix in the iHMM, by drawing $\pi_{e,s,\cdot} \overset{iid}{\sim} \mathrm{Stick}(\alpha\beta)$. One effect of introducing a dependency on input variables is that the number of parameters increases. If we train a finite sequence of length T with the iHMM and find an effective number of states equal to K then we have to learn $O(K^2)$

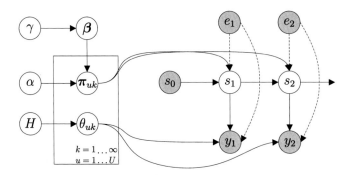

Figure 15.10 Belief network of the IO-iHMM. The dotted lines denote the fact that we can choose to make either the Markov chain or the observations (or both) dependent on a set of inputs.

transition matrix parameters. If we train the same sequence with the IO-iHMM using an input sequence with E possible input symbols and find K effective states, then we have to learn $O(EK^2)$ transition matrix parameters. Similarly, if we introduce a dependency of the observation model on the input sequence, $y_t \sim F(\theta_{s_t, e_t})$, we augment the number of parameters of the observation model with a factor of E. This suggests that either: (a) more data will be needed to learn a model with the same capacity as the iHMM; (b) with the same amount of data a model with smaller capacity will be learned or (c) the model complexity must be reduced by coupling the parameters.

15.6.2   The sticky and block-diagonal iHMM

In many applications, it is useful to explicitly model the time scale of transitions between states. For an HMM or iHMM, the weight on the diagonal of the transition matrix controls the frequency of state transitions. The probability that we stay in state i for g time steps is a geometric distribution $p(g) = \pi_{ii}^{g-1}(1 - \pi_{ii})$.

As we noted in the introduction to the iHMM, the original hierarchical Polya urn description in [4] introduced a self-transition hyperparameter in the iHMM adding prior probability mass to the diagonal of the transition matrix π. The authors in [10] further elaborated this idea in the hierarchical Dirichlet process representation of the iHMM. They also developed a dynamic programming based inference algorithm for a truncated version of the model. They coined it the *sticky iHMM* (or sticky HDP-HMM). The sticky iHMM is particularly appropriate for segmentation problems where the number of segments is not known a priori. Fox *et al.* [10] show impressive results on a speaker diarisation task.

Formally, the sticky iHMM still draws the base measure $\beta \sim \mathsf{Stick}$ but then draws the rows of the transition matrix from the following distribution

$$\pi_{ij} \overset{iid}{\sim} \mathsf{Dirichlet}(\frac{\alpha}{\alpha + \kappa}\beta_1, \frac{\alpha}{\alpha + \kappa}\beta_2, \cdots, \frac{\alpha\beta_i + \kappa}{\alpha + \kappa}, \cdots).$$

The effect of this change is that for all states the diagonal entry carries more weight. The parameter κ controls the switching rate or lengthscale of the process.

A more general model which allows grouping of states into a block-diagonal structure is given by the *block-diagonal infinite HMM* in [31]. When the blocks are of size one, this is a sticky iHMM, but larger blocks allow unsupervised clustering of states. The block-diagional iHMM is used for unsupervised learning of view-based object models from video data, where each block or cluster of states corresponds to an object and the model assumptions capture the intuition that temporally contiguous video frames are more likely to correspond to different views of the same object than to different objects.

Another approach to introduce more control over the self-transition probability is to have an explicit duration model for the time spent in a particular state. This type of model is known as a hidden semi-Markov model. Inference in these models is more costly than in HMM's and nonparametric versions have not yet been explored.

15.6.3   iHMM with Pitman–Yor base distribution

From the Polya urn scheme, we know that the base process (a.k.a. the oracle urn) behaves like an average distribution over the states. In other words, the base process influences the expected number of states visited for a given sequence length. The left plot in Fig. 15.11 plots the frequency of colours in a Polya urn for a Dirichlet process against the colour's rank. From this plot, we can see that the Dirichlet process is quite specific about the distribution implied in the Polya urn: because the right tail of the plot drops off sharply, we know

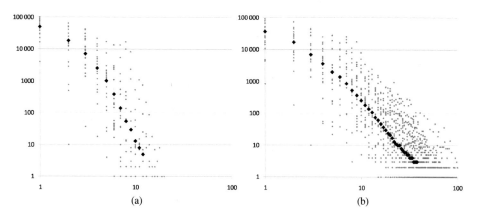

Figure 15.11 In this plot we show (on a log-log scale) the frequency versus rank of colours in the Polya urn for both the Dirichlet process (a) and the Pitman–Yor process (b). We see that the data from the Pitman–Yor process can be fitted with a straight line implying that it follows a power-law behaviour; this is not the case for the Dirichlet process.

that the amount of colours that appear only once or twice is very small. A two-parameter generalisation of the Dirichlet process, known as the Pitman–Yor process ([25]) introduces more flexibility in this behaviour. The right plot in Fig. 15.11 shows that the frequency-rank for draws from a Pitman–Yor process *can* be more specific about the tails. More in particular, the Pitman–Yor process fits a power-law distribution; [15] and [33] showed how in the context of language modelling the Pitman–Yor distribution encodes more realistic priors. Analogous to the Dirichlet process, the Pitman–Yor process has a stick-breaking constructing: the sticks for the Pitman–Yor distribution with parameters d and α can be constructed by drawing $\hat{\beta}_i \overset{iid}{\sim} \text{Beta}(1 - d, \alpha + id)$ and $\beta_i = \hat{\beta}_i \prod_{l=1}^{i-1}(1 - \hat{\beta}_l)$. Note that the Pitman–Yor process with $d = 0$ is exactly the Dirichlet process.

In the context of the iHMM, it is fairly straightforward to replace the Dirichlet process base distribution by a Pitman–Yor distribution allowing the iHMM to use more states. Although the collapsed Gibbs sampler and beam sampler work with only minor adjustments, it is critical that the beam sampler be implemented with great care. As we mentioned in the discussion of the beam sampler, we need to consider all transitions ij where $\pi_{ij} > u_t$. Unfortunately, the quantity π_{ij} decreases much faster for the Pitman–Yor process stick-breaking construction than the Dirichlet process stick-breaking construction. The advantage is that it allows for many small transition probabilities, unfortunately it also means that the quantity $\sum_l \pi_{il}$ decreases very slowly. Since the beam sampler must consider all $\pi_{ij} > u_t$, it will need to expand the transition matrix to K states so that $\sum_{l>K} \pi_{il} < u_t$ and it is sure it considered all possible states. This means when running the forward-filtering backward-sampling algorithm that we potentially end up with a very large transition matrix. Luckily most of the entries in π will be quite small (otherwise the remaining mass $\sum_{j>K} \pi_{ij}$ can't decrease slowly). Hence, while expanding the transition matrix we can keep a sorted list of matrix entries and when we run the forward-filtering step, at each time step we walk down this list until u_t becomes larger than the elements in the list.

15.6.4 The auto-regressive iHMM and switching linear dynamical system

Many time series are modelled using auto-regressive (AR) models or linear dynamical systems (LDSs) which assume that the dynamics of the process are linear. More powerful non-linear generalisations can be obtained by switching between a fixed set of linear

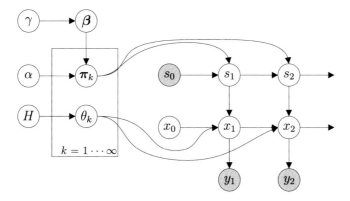

Figure 15.12 The belief network for a switching linear dynamical system with a potentially infinitely large state space.

dynamics. A model where the switching is driven by an HMM is often called a switching linear dynamical system (SLDS)[5]; [13] review a number of variants of the SLDS all of whom share the property that there are a fixed finite number of dynamics.

An extension of the SLDS in [9] allows for an arbitrary large number of dynamics to be learned from data by replacing the finite Markov chain underlying the SLDS with an iHMM. They explored two prototypical variants of the SLDS. The first model assumes the observations follow auto-regressive dynamics; this model is referred to as the AR-iHMM. The second model assumes that only part of the continuous variables are observed and the unobserved variables follow linear dynamics; this model is referred to as the infinite SLDS. The inference in [9] is implemented on a finite truncation of the nonparametric model. In this incarnation, the model is similar to the Bayesian SLDS from [6], except that the nonparametric model introduces an additional 'prior on the prior' for the rows of the transition matrix.

Figure 15.12 illustrates the belief network for the SLDS with a potentially infinitely large state space. Inference in both models can be done efficiently using the beam sampler. For the AR model, a collapsed Gibbs sampler is possible while for the LDS we are only aware of algorithms that explicitly represent the hidden state of the LDS.

15.7 Conclusions

We reviewed both the hierarchical Polya urn construction and the hierarchical Dirichlet process construction for the iHMM and showed a proof that both formalisations are equivalent. Building on these different representations of the iHMM, we described a collapsed Gibbs sampler and a dynamic programming based beam sampler. Both inference methods are only marginally harder to implement than their HMM based counterparts. We believe this makes the iHMM an attractive solution to the problems one faces when learning the number of states for an HMM.

As we have described, there are a number of interesting ways of extending iHMMs. We can allow inputs and outputs, sticky self-transitions, block-structured models, Pitman–Yor base distributions, autoregressive and switching linear structure. Given the important role

---

[5]Also known as a Markov-switching model, Markov jump system or switching state space model.

of hidden Markov models in time series and sequence modelling, and the flexibility of non-parametric approaches, there is great potential for many future applications and extensions of the infinite hidden Markov model.

15.A Appendix: Equivalence of the hierarchical Polya urn and hierarchical Dirichlet process

In this appendix, we sketch a proof that the hierarchical Polya urn scheme from [4] and the hierarchical Dirichlet process formulations of the iHMM from [35] define equivalent distributions over the hidden state sequence $s_{1:T}$. We will refer to the distribution over $s_{1:T}$ defined by the hierarchical Polya urn scheme as $p_{urn}(s_{1:T})$ and the distribution defined by the hierarchical Dirichlet process as $p_{hdp}(s_{1:T})$.

Although we didn't introduce the Chinese Restaurant Franchise representation of the HDP, our proof relies on this representation. We refer to [35] for a detailed description of this representation. We first introduce two different sets of statistics that will be used in the proof:

- for the Polya urn we keep track of the numbers n_{ij} specifying the number of balls in transition urn i of colour j and the number c_i specifying the number of balls of colour i in the oracle urn;

- for the hierarchical Dirichlet process we keep track of the number of customers in the Chinese Restaurant Franchise (CRF) representation ([35]): m_{ijl} is the number of customers sitting in restaurant i at the lth table that serves dish j and b_l is the number of customers sitting at the table serving dish l in the base restaurant (or in other words: the number of tables serving dish l in all restaurants together).

Theorem 15.1 *The distribution over the sequence of states $s_{1:T}$ defined by the hierarchical Polya urn scheme, $p_{urn}(s_{1:T})$ is the same as the distribution defined by the hierarchical Dirichlet process $p_{hdp}(s_{1:T})$.*

The core idea of the inductive proof is that the CRF representation keeps track of a bit more information than the Polya urn: in the CRF, m_{ijl} keeps track of who sits at which table serving a particular dish, while in the Polya urn n_{ij} only keeps track of the total number of people who are sitting at a table serving dish j. Since the exact configuration doesn't matter for the predictive probability $p(s_t|s_{1:t-1})$, the two schemes define the same distribution over the sequence $s_{1:T}$. We formalise this idea in the proof sketch below.

Sketch of proof The proof follows an inductive argument. For the base case of the induction we note that $p_{urn}(s_1) = p_{hdp}(s_1) = 1$ because initially there are no customers in the CRF nor are there balls in the Polya urn and hence we can always initialise the first state to be the state with identifier 1. After this assignment, note that we called the oracle once. Hence $c_1 = 1$ and we have set $n_{11} = 1$, analogously, $m_{111} = 1$ since there is one person sitting in the whole CRF and he must be in restaurant 1 eating dish 1 and $b_1 = 1$ since there is only one table serving dish 1 in the whole CRF.

Next we describe the inductive argument: after generating state s_{t-1}, we assume $b_i = c_i$ for *all* i and for *any* configuration $m_{ijl} : n_{ij} = \sum_l m_{ijl}$. Note that we don't assume a particular configuration for m_{ijl} but any configuration that satisfies $n_{ij} = \sum_l m_{ijl}$. We now prove that $p_{urn}(s_t|s_{1:t-1}) = p_{hdp}(s_t|s_{1:t-1})$. If we are in state s_{t-1} under the Polya urn scheme there are two possibilities: either we query the oracle or we don't. We query the oracle with probability $\frac{\alpha}{\sum_j n_{s_{t-1},j}+\alpha}$ and if we do so, we either go to state i with probability $\frac{c_i}{\sum_k c_k+\gamma}$ or to a new state with probability $\frac{\gamma}{\sum_k c_k+\gamma}$. Under the HDP, the probability that we choose to sit at a new table in restaurant s_{t-1} is $\frac{\alpha}{\sum_{jl} m_{s_{t-1},j,l}+\alpha}$. If we do choose to sit at a new table, we choose an existing dish i with probability $\frac{b_i}{\sum_k b_k+\gamma}$ and a new dish with probability $\frac{\gamma}{\sum_k b_k+\gamma}$. Since choosing a dish in the HDP representation corresponds to transition to a particular state in the iHMM, we can see that under the induction hypothesis conditioned on the fact that we query the oracle (or sit at a new table) the probabilities are exactly the same. Similarly, if under the Polya urn scheme, we decide not to query the oracle, we transition to state i with probability $\frac{n_{s_{t-1},i}}{\sum_j n_{s_{t-1},j}+\alpha}$. Under the CRF, we will sit at a table serving dish i with probability $\frac{\sum_l m_{s_{t-1},i,l}}{\sum_{jl} m_{s_{t-1},j,l}+\alpha}$. Under the induction hypothesis, these two probabilities are again the same. QED.

Acknowledgments We would like to thank Finale Doshi-Velez, Andreas Vlachos and Sébastien Bratières for their helpful comments on the manuscript. We thank the two anonymous reviewers for valuable suggestions. Jurgen Van Gael is supported by a Microsoft Research Scholarship.

Bibliography

[1] H. Akaike. A new look at the statistical model identification. *IEEE Transactions on Automatic Control*, **19**(6):716–723, 1974.

[2] L. E. Baum, T. Petrie, G. Soules and N. Weiss. A maximization technique occurring in the statistical analysis of probabilistic functions of Markov chains. *Annals of Mathematical Statistics*, **41**(1):164–171, 1970.

[3] M. J. Beal. Variational algorithms for approximate Bayesian inference. PhD thesis, University of London, 2003.

[4] M. J. Beal, Z. Ghahramani and C. E. Rasmussen. The infinite hidden Markov model. In *Advances in Neural Information Processing Systems*, pages 577–584, 2002.

[5] Y. Bengio and P. Frasconi. An input output HMM architecture. In *Advances in Neural Information Processing Systems*, pages 427–434, 1995.

[6] S. Chiappa. A Bayesian approach to switching linear Gaussian state-space models for unsupervised time-series segmentation. In *Proceedings of the International Conference on Machine Learning and Applications*, pages 3–9, 2008.

[7] A. P Dempster, N. M Laird and D. B Rubin. Maximum likelihood from incomplete data via the EM algorithm. *Journal of the Royal Statistical Society. Series B (Methodological)*, **39**(1):1–38, 1977.

[8] L. E. Baum and T. Petrie. Statistical inference for probabilistic functions of finite state Markov chains. *Annals of Mathematical Statistics*, **37**(6):1554–1563, 1966.

[9] E. B. Fox, E. B. Sudderth, M. I. Jordan and A. S. Willsky. Nonparametric Bayesian learning of switching linear dynamical systems. In *Advances in Neural Information Processing Systems*, pages 457–464, 2009.

[10] E. B. Fox, E. B. Sudderth, M. I. Jordan and A. S. Willsky. An HDP-HMM for systems with state persistence. In *Proceedings of the International Conference on Machine learning*, volume 25, Helsinki, 2008.

[11] S. Fruhwirth-Schnatter. Estimating marginal likelihoods for mixture and Markov switching models using bridge sampling techniques. *Econometrics Journal*, **7**(1):143–167, 2004.

[12] J. Gao and Johnson. M. A comparison of Bayesian estimators for unsupervised hidden Markov model POS taggers. In *Proceedings of the 2008 Conference on Empirical Methods in Natural Language Processing*, pages 344–352, 2008.

[13] Z. Ghahramani and G. E. Hinton. Variational learning for switching state-space models. *Neural Computation*, **12**(4):831–864, 2000.

[14] S. Goldwater and T. Griffiths. A fully Bayesian approach to unsupervised part-of-speech tagging. In *Proceedings of the Association for Computational Linguistics*, volume 45, page 744, 2007.

[15] S. Goldwater, T. Griffiths and M. Johnson. Interpolating between types and tokens by estimating power-law generators. In *Advances in Neural Information Processing Systems*, pages 459–466, 2006.

[16] P. J. Green. Reversible jump Markov chain Monte Carlo computation and Bayesian model determination. *Biometrika*, **82**(4):711–732, 1995.

[17] N. Hjort, C. Holmes, P. Muller and S. Walker, editors. *Bayesian Nonparametrics*. Cambridge University Press, 2010.

[18] M. Johnson. Why doesnt EM find good HMM POS-taggers. In *Proceedings of the Joint Conference on Empirical Methods in Natural Language Processing and Computational Natural Language Learning*, pages 296–305, 2007.

[19] D. Jurafsky and J. H. Martin. *Speech and Language Processing*. Pearson Prentice Hall, 2008.

[20] D. J. C. MacKay. Ensemble learning for hidden Markov models. Technical report, Cavendish Laboratory, University of Cambridge, 1997.

[21] C. D. Manning and H. Schütze. *Foundations of Statistical Natural Language Processing*. MIT Press.

[22] M. P. Marcus, M. A. Marcinkiewicz and B. Santorini. Building a large annotated corpus of English: the Penn Treebank. *Computational Linguistics*, **19**(2):313–330, June 1993.

[23] R. M. Neal. Annealed importance sampling. *Statistics and Computing*, **11**:125–139, 1998.

[24] R. M. Neal. Markov chain sampling methods for Dirichlet process mixture models. *Journal of Computational and Graphical Statistics*, **9**(2):249–265, 2000.

[25] J. Pitman. *Combinatorial stochastic processes*, volume 1875 of Lecture Notes in Mathematics. Springer-Verlag, 2006.

[26] L. R. Rabiner. A tutorial on hidden Markov models and selected applications in speech recognition. *Proceedings of the IEEE*, **77**(2):257–286, 1989.

[27] C. P. Robert, T. Ryden and D. M. Titterington. Bayesian inference in hidden Markov models through the reversible jump Markov chain Monte Carlo method. *Journal of the Royal Statistical Society. Series B, Statistical Methodology*, pages 57–75, 2000.

[28] G. Schwarz. Estimating the dimension of a model. *Annals of Statistics*, **6**(2):461–464, 1978.

[29] S. L. Scott. Bayesian methods for hidden Markov models: Recursive computing in the 21st century. *Journal of the American Statistical Association*, **97**(457):337–351, 2002.

[30] J. Sethuraman. A constructive definition of Dirichlet priors. *Statistica Sinica*, **4**:639–650, 1994.

[31] T. Stepleton, Z. Ghahramani, G. Gordon and T-S. Lee. The block diagonal infinite hidden Markov model. In *Proceedings of the International Conference on Artificial Intelligence and Statistics*, pages 552–559, 2009.

[32] A. Stolcke and S. Omohundro. Hidden Markov model induction by Bayesian model merging. *Advances in Neural Information Processing Systems*, **5**: pages 11-18, 1993.

[33] Y. W. Teh. A hierarchical Bayesian language model based on Pitman-Yor processes. In *Proceedings of the 21st International Conference on Computational Linguistics and 44th Annual Meeting of the Association for Computational Linguistics*, pages 985–992, 2006.

[34] Y. W. Teh. Dirichlet processes. *Encyclopedia of Machine Learning*, to appear.

[35] Y. W. Teh, M. I. Jordan, M. J. Beal and D. M. Blei. Hierarchical Dirichlet processes. *Journal of the American Statistical Association*, **101**(476):1566–1581, 2006.

[36] J. Van Gael, Y. Saatci, Y. W. Teh and Z. Ghahramani. Beam sampling for the infinite hidden Markov model. In *Proceedings of the International Conference on Machine Learning*, pages 1088–1095, 2008.

[37] J. Van Gael, A. Vlachos and Z. Ghahramani. The infinite HMM for unsupervised POS tagging. In *Proceedings of the Conference on Empirical Methods in Natural Language Processing*, pages 678–687, 2009.

[38] S. G. Walker. Sampling the Dirichlet mixture model with slices. *Communications in Statistics – Simulation and Computation*, **36**(1):45, 2007.

Contributors

Jurgen Van Gael, Department of Engineering, University of Cambridge
Zoubin Ghahramani, Department of Engineering, University of Cambridge

16

Bayesian Gaussian process models for multi-sensor time series prediction

Michael A. Osborne, Alex Rogers, Stephen J. Roberts,
Sarvapali D. Ramchurn and Nick R. Jennings

16.1   Introduction

Sensor networks have recently generated a great deal of research interest within the computer and physical sciences, and their use for the scientific monitoring of remote and hostile environments is increasingly commonplace. While early sensor networks were a simple evolution of existing automated data loggers, that collected data for later offline scientific analysis, more recent sensor networks typically make current data available through the Internet, and thus, are increasingly being used for the real-time monitoring of environmental events such as floods or storm events (see [10] for a review of such environmental sensor networks).

Using real-time sensor data in this manner presents many novel challenges. However, more significantly for us, many of the information processing tasks that would previously have been performed offline by the owner or single user of an environmental sensor network (such as detecting faulty sensors, fusing noisy measurements from several sensors, and deciding how frequently readings should be taken), must now be performed in real-time on the mobile computers and PDAs carried by the multiple different users of the system (who may have different goals and may be using sensor readings for very different tasks). Importantly, it may also be necessary to use the trends and correlations observed in previous data to predict the value of environmental parameters into the future, or to predict the reading of a sensor that is temporarily unavailable (e.g. due to network outages). Finally, we note that the open nature of the network (in which additional sensors may be deployed, and existing sensors may be removed, repositioned or updated at any time) means that these tasks may have to be performed with only limited knowledge of the precise location, reliability and accuracy of each sensor.

Many of the information processing tasks described above have previously been tackled by applying principled Bayesian methodologies from the academic literature of geospatial statistics and machine learning, specifically, kriging [4] and Gaussian processes [22]. However, due to the computational complexity of these approaches, to date they have largely been used offline in order to analyse and re-design existing sensor networks (e.g. to reduce maintenance costs by removing the least informative sensors from an existing sensor network [7], or to find the optimum placement of a small number of sensors, after a trial deployment of a larger number has collected data indicating their spatial correlation

[13]). Thus, there is a clear need for more computationally efficient algorithms, that can be deployed on the mobile computers and PDAs carried by our first responders, in order to perform this information processing in real-time.

Against this background, this chapter describes our work developing just such an algorithm. More specifically, we present a novel iterative formulation of a Gaussian process (GP) that uses a computationally efficient implementation of *Bayesian Monte Carlo* to marginalise hyperparameters, efficiently re-uses previous computations by following an online update procedure as new data sequentially arrives, and uses a principled 'windowing' of data in order to maintain a reasonably sized (active) dataset. We use our algorithm to build a probabilistic model of the environmental variables being measured by sensors within the network, tolerant to data that may be missing, delayed, censored and/or correlated. This model allows us to perform information processing tasks including: modelling the accuracy of the sensor readings, predicting the value of missing sensor readings, predicting how the monitored environmental variables will evolve in the near future, and performing active sampling by deciding when and from which sensor to acquire readings. We validate our multi-output Gaussian process formulation using data from networks of weather sensors, and we demonstrate its effectiveness by benchmarking it against alternative methods. Our results are promising, and represent a step towards the deployment of real-time algorithms that use principled machine learning techniques to autonomously acquire and process data from sensor networks.

The remainder of this chapter is organised as follows: Section 16.2 describes the information processing problem that we face. Section 16.3 presents our Gaussian process formulation, and Section 16.4 describes the sensor networks used to validate this formulation. In Section 16.5 we present experimental results using data from these networks, and in Section 16.6 we discuss the computational cost of our algorithm. Finally, related work is discussed in Section 16.7, and we conclude in Section 16.8.

16.2   The information processing problem

As discussed above, we require that our algorithm be able to autonomously perform data acquisition and information processing despite having only limited specific knowledge of each of the sensors in their local neighbourhoods (e.g. their precise location, reliability and accuracy). To this end, we require that the algorithm explicitly represents:

1. The uncertainty in the estimated values of environmental variables being measured, noting that sensor readings will always incorporate some degree of measurement noise.

2. The correlations or delays that exist between sensor readings; sensors that are close to one another, or in similar environments, will tend to make similar readings, while many physical processes involving moving fields (such as the movement of weather fronts) will induce delays between sensors.

We then require that it uses this representation in order to:

1. Perform regression and prediction of environmental variables; that is, interpolate between sensor readings to predict variables at missing sensors (i.e. sensors that have failed or are unavailable due to network outages), and perform prediction in order to support decision making.

2. Perform efficient active sampling by selecting when to take a reading, and which sensor to read from, such that the minimum number of sensor readings are used to maintain the estimated uncertainty in environmental variables below a specified threshold (or similarly, to minimise uncertainty given a constrained number of sensor readings). Such constraints might reflect either the computational cost of processing an additional reading or the energy cost associated with the sensor acquiring a new observation.

More specifically, the problem that we face can be cast as a multivariate regression and decision problem in which we have $l = 1, \ldots, L$ environmental variables $y_l \in \mathbb{R}$ of interest (such as air temperature, wind speed or direction specified at different sensor locations). We assume a set of N potentially noisy sensor readings, $\{[[l_1, t_1], z_1], \ldots, [[l_N, t_N], z_N]\}$, in which we, for example, observe the value z_1 for the l_1th variable at time t_1, whose true unknown value is y_1. Where convenient, we may group the inputs as $x = [l, t]$. Note that we do not require that all the variables are observed at the same time, nor do we impose any discretisation of our observations into regularly spaced time steps. Given this data, we are interested in inferring the vector of values $y_\star$ for any other vector of variables labelled by $l_\star$ at times $t_\star$.

16.3 Gaussian processes

Multivariate regression problems of the form described above have often been addressed using multi-layer neural networks. However, Gaussian processes (GPs) are increasingly being applied in this area. They represent a powerful way to perform Bayesian inference about functions; we consider our environmental variables as just such a function [22]. This function takes as inputs the variable label and time pair x and produces as output the variable's value y. In this work, we will assume that our inputs are always known (e.g. our data is time-stamped), and will incorporate them into our background knowledge, or context, I. A GP is then a generalised multivariate Gaussian prior distribution over the (potentially infinite number of) outputs of this function

$$ p(y \mid \mu, K, I) \triangleq \mathrm{N}(y; \mu, K) \triangleq \frac{1}{\sqrt{\det(2\pi K)}} \, \exp\left(-\frac{1}{2}(y - \mu)^\mathsf{T} K^{-1}(y - \mu)\right). $$

It is specified by prior mean and covariance functions, which generate μ and K. We emphasise that we use a single GP to express a probability distribution over all our environmental variables, the correlations amongst which are expressed by our covariance function. The multivariate Gaussian distribution is qualified for this role due to the fact that both its marginal and conditional distributions are themselves Gaussian. This allows us to produce analytic posterior distributions for any variables of interest, conditioned on whatever sensor readings have been observed. These distributions have both an analytic mean, which we use as our best estimate of the output, as well as an analytic variance, which we use as an indication of our uncertainty.

While the fundamental theory of GPs is well established (see [22] for example), there is much scope for the development of computationally efficient implementations. To this end, in this work we present a novel online formalism of a multi-dimensional GP that allows us to model the correlations between sensor readings, and to update this model online as new observations are sequentially available. Space precludes a full description of this algorithm (see [19] for further details), however, in the next sections we describe the covariance functions that we use to represent correlations and delays between sensor readings, the *Bayesian Monte Carlo* method that we use to marginalise the hyperparameters of these covariance functions, and how we efficiently update the model as new data is received, by reusing the results of previous computations, and applying a principled 'windowing' of our data series.

16.3.1 Covariance functions

The prior mean of a GP represents whatever we expect for our function before seeing any data. We take this as a function constant in time, such that $\mu([l, t]) = \mu_l$. The *covariance function* of a GP specifies the correlation between any pair of outputs. This can then be used to generate a covariance matrix over our set of observations and predictants. Fortunately, there exist a wide variety of functions that can serve in this purpose [1, 25], which can then be combined and modified in a further multitude of ways. This gives us a great deal of flexibility in our modelling of functions, with covariance functions available to model periodicity, delay, noise and long-term drifts.

As an example, consider a covariance given by the Hadamard product of a covariance function over time alone and a covariance function over environmental variable labels alone, such that

$$K([l, t], [l', t']) \triangleq K_{\text{label}}(l, l') \, K_{\text{time}}(t - d_l, t' - d_{l'}),$$

where d allows us to express the delays between environmental variables. We will often use the completely general *spherical parameterisation*, s, such that

$$K_{\text{label}}(l, l') \triangleq \text{diag}(g) \, s^{\mathsf{T}} s \, \text{diag}(g), \tag{16.1}$$

where g gives an intuitive lengthscale for each environmental variable, and $s^{\mathsf{T}} s$ is the correlation matrix [20]. This parameterisation allows us to represent any potential degree of correlation between our variables. As a less general alternative, we might instead use a term dependent on the spatial separation between sensors.

Similarly, we can represent correlations over time with a wide variety of covariance functions, permitting the incorporation of what domain knowledge we have. For example, we use the additive combination of a periodic and a non-periodic disturbance term

$$K_{\text{time}}(t, t') \triangleq K_{\text{time},1}(t, t') + K_{\text{time},2}(t, t'),$$

where we expect our variable to be well represented by the superposition of an oscillatory and a non-oscillatory component. We represent both terms using the Matérn class [22] (with $\nu = 5/2$), given by

$$K_{\text{time},i}(t, t') \triangleq h^2 \left(1 + \sqrt{5}r_i + \frac{5r_i^2}{3}\right) \exp\left(-\sqrt{5}r_i\right), \tag{16.2}$$

for $i \in \{1, 2\}$, where $r_1 = \sin \pi \left|\frac{t-t'}{w}\right|$ for periodic terms, and $r_2 = \left|\frac{t-t'}{w}\right|$ for non-periodic terms. The Matérn class allows us to empirically select a degree of smoothness, given by the choice of ν, appropriate for the functions we are trying to track. Finally, to represent measurement noise, we further extend the covariance function to

$$V([l, t], [l', t']) \triangleq K([l, t], [l', t']) + \sigma^2 \, \delta([l, t] - [l', t']),$$

where $\delta(-)$ is the Kronecker delta and σ^2 represents the variance of additive Gaussian noise.

This choice of covariance is intended to model correlated periodic variables subject to local disturbances which may themselves be correlated amongst variables. This general model describes many environmental variables that are subject to some daily cycle (e.g. the 12-hour cycle of the tide, or the 24-hour cycle seen in most temperature readings), but we reiterate that, given different domain knowledge, a variety of other covariance functions can be chosen. For example, a more suitable covariance for air temperature was found to include an additional additive covariance term over time. This allows for the possibility of both long-term drifts in temperature occurring over the course of a week, as well as more high-frequency, hourly changes. We might also multiply periodic terms (like $K_{\text{time},1}(t,t')$) by another non-periodic term (like $K_{\text{time},2}(t,t')$) to express a short-term periodicity, whose relevance tails off with time. With such a covariance, we can model periodic patterns that may gradually change over time.

Given these examples of the plethora of possibilities for including additional terms to our covariance, a natural question is when to stop. The answer is, in principle, never. The 'Occam's razor' action of Bayesian inference [16] will automatically lead us to select the simplest sub-model that still explains the data. Note this is true even if our prior is flat over the model complexity.

In practice, however, the flexibility of our model comes at the cost of the introduction of a number of hyperparameters, which we collectively denote as ϕ. These include correlation hyperparameters (i.e. g, s and d), along with others such as the periods and amplitudes of each covariance term (i.e. w and h) and the noise deviation σ. The constant prior means $\mu_1, \ldots, \mu_M$ are also included as additional hyperparameters. Taking these hyperparameters as given and using the properties of the Gaussian distribution, we are able to write our predictive equations as

$$p(y_\star \mid z_{1:N}, \phi, I) = N(y_\star; m_\star, C_\star), \tag{16.3}$$

where, collecting our inputs as $x_\star \triangleq [l_\star, t_\star]$ and $x_{1:N} \triangleq [l_{1:N}, t_{1:N}]$, we have

$$m_\star = \mu_\phi(x_\star) + K_\phi(x_\star, x_{1:N})V_\phi(x_{1:N}, x_{1:N})^{-1}(z_{1:N} - \mu_\phi(x_{1:N})), \tag{16.4}$$

$$C_\star = K_\phi(x_\star, x_\star) - K_\phi(x_\star, x_{1:N})V_\phi(x_{1:N}, x_{1:N})^{-1}K_\phi(x_{1:N}, x_\star). \tag{16.5}$$

16.3.2 Marginalisation

Of course, it is rare that we can be certain a priori about the values of our hyperparameters. Rather than Eq. (16.3), we must consider

$$p(y_\star \mid z_{1:N}, I) = \frac{\int d\phi\, p(y_\star \mid z_{1:N}, \phi, I)\, p(z_{1:N} \mid \phi, I)\, p(\phi \mid I)}{\int d\phi\, p(z_{1:N} \mid \phi, I)\, p(\phi \mid I)},$$

in which we have marginalised ϕ. Unfortunately, both our likelihood $p(z_{1:N} \mid \phi, I)$ and predictions $p(y_\star \mid z_{1:N}, \phi, I)$ exhibit non-trivial dependence upon ϕ and so our integrals are non-analytic. As such, we resort to quadrature, which inevitably involves evaluating the two quantities

$$q(\phi) \triangleq p(y_\star \mid z_{1:N}, \phi, I), \quad r(\phi) \triangleq p(z_{1:N} \mid \phi, I)$$

at a set of η sample points $\phi_s = \{\phi_1, \ldots, \phi_\eta\}$, giving $q_s \triangleq q(\phi_s)$ and $r_s \triangleq r(\phi_s)$. Of course, this evaluation is a computationally expensive operation. Dense sampling over the space of all possible sets of hyperparameters is clearly infeasible. Note that the more complex

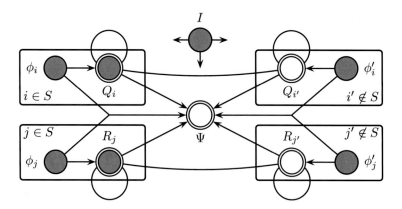

Figure 16.1 Belief network for marginalising hyperparameters using Bayesian Monte Carlo. Shaded nodes are known and double-circled nodes are deterministic given all their parents. All Q nodes are correlated with one another, as are all R nodes, and the context I is correlated with all nodes.

our model, and hence the greater the number of hyperparameters, the higher the dimension of the hyperparameter space we must sample in. As such, the complexity of models we can practically consider is limited by the curse of dimensionality. We can view our sparse sampling as introducing a form of uncertainty about the functions q and r, which we can again address using Bayesian probability theory.

To this end, we apply *Bayesian Monte Carlo*, and thus, assign further GP priors to q and r [18, 21]. This choice is motivated by the fact that variables over which we have a multivariate Gaussian distribution are joint Gaussian with any projections of those variables. Given that integration is a projection, we can hence use our computed samples q_s in order to perform Gaussian process regression about the value of integrals over $q(\phi)$, and similarly for r. Note that the quantity we wish to perform inference about,

$$\psi \triangleq p(y_\star \mid q, r, z_{1:N}, I) = \frac{\int q(\phi_\star) r(\phi_\star) p(\phi_\star \mid I) \, d\phi_\star}{\int r(\phi_\star) p(\phi_\star \mid I) \, d\phi_\star},$$

possesses richer structure than that previously considered using Bayesian Monte Carlo techniques. In our case, $r(\phi)$ appears in both our numerator and denominator integrals, introducing correlations between the values we estimate for them. The correlation structure of this probabilistic model is illustrated in Fig. 16.1.

In considering any problem of inference, we need to be clear about both what information we have and which uncertain variables we are interested in. In our case, both function values, q_s and r_s, and their locations, ϕ_s, represent valuable pieces of knowledge.[1] As with our convention above, we will take knowledge of sample locations ϕ_s to be implicit within I. We respectively define $m^{(q)}$ and $m^{(r)}$ as the means for q and r conditioned on q_s and r_s from Eq. (16.4), $C^{(q)}$ and $C^{(r)}$ the similarly conditional covariances from Eq. (16.5). The ultimate quantity of our interest is then

$$p(y_\star \mid q_s, r_s, z_{1:N}, I)$$
$$= \iiint p(y_\star \mid q, r, z_{1:N}, I) \, p(\psi \mid q, r, I) \, p(q \mid q_s, I) \, p(r \mid r_s, I) \, d\psi \, dq \, dr$$

---

[1] As discussed by [17], traditional, frequentist Monte Carlo effectively ignores the information content of ϕ_s, leading to several unsatisfactory features.

$$= \iiint \psi \, \delta \left(\psi - \frac{\int q_\star \, r_\star \, p(\phi_\star \mid I) \, d\phi_\star}{\int r_\star \, p(\phi_\star \mid I) \, d\phi_\star} \right) N\big(q; m^{(q)}, C^{(q)}\big) \, N\big(r; m^{(r)}, C^{(r)}\big) \, d\psi \, dq \, dr$$

$$= \int \frac{\int m_\star^{(q)} \, r_\star \, p(\phi_\star \mid I) \, d\phi_\star}{\int r_\star \, p(\phi_\star \mid I) \, d\phi_\star} \, N\big(r; m^{(r)}, C^{(r)}\big) \, dr.$$

Here, unfortunately, our integration over r becomes non-analytic. However, we can employ a Laplace approximation by expanding the integrand around an assumed peak at $m^{(r)}$. Before we can state its result, to each of our hyperparameters we assign a Gaussian prior distribution (or if our hyperparameter is restricted to the positive reals, we instead assign a Gaussian distribution to its log) given by

$$p(\phi \mid I) \triangleq N\big(\phi; \nu, \lambda^\mathsf{T} \lambda\big).$$

Note that the intuitive spherical parameterisation (16.1) assists with the elicitation of priors over its hyperparameters. We then assign *squared exponential* covariance functions for the GPs over both q and r, given by $K(\phi, \phi') \triangleq N\big(\phi; \phi', w^\mathsf{T} w\big)$.

Finally, using the further definition for $i, j \in \{1, \dots, \eta\}$

$$\mathfrak{N}_s(i, j) \triangleq N\left(\begin{bmatrix} \phi_i \\ \phi_j \end{bmatrix}; \begin{bmatrix} \nu \\ \nu \end{bmatrix}, \begin{bmatrix} \lambda^\mathsf{T}\lambda + w^\mathsf{T} w & \lambda^\mathsf{T}\lambda \\ \lambda^\mathsf{T}\lambda & \lambda^\mathsf{T}\lambda + w^\mathsf{T} w \end{bmatrix} \right),$$

our Laplace approximation gives us

$$p(y_\star \mid z_{1:N}, I) \simeq q_s^\mathsf{T} \rho, \tag{16.6}$$

where the weights of this linear combination are

$$\rho \triangleq \frac{K(\phi_s, \phi_s)^{-1} \, \mathfrak{N}_s \, K(\phi_s, \phi_s)^{-1} \, r_s}{1_{s,1}^\mathsf{T} \, K(\phi_s, \phi_s)^{-1} \, \mathfrak{N}_s \, K(\phi_s, \phi_s)^{-1} \, r_s}, \tag{16.7}$$

and $1_{s,1}$ is a vector containing only ones of dimensions equal to q_s. With a GP on $p(y_\star \mid \phi, I)$, each $q_i = p(y_\star \mid z_{1:N}, \phi_i, I)$ will be a slightly different Gaussian. Hence we effectively approximate $p(y_\star \mid z_{1:N}, I)$ as a Gaussian (process) mixture; Bayesian Monte Carlo returns a weighted sum of our predictions evaluated at a sample set of hyperparameters. The assignment of these weights is informed by the best use of all pertinent information. As such, it avoids the risk of overfitting that occurs when applying a less principled technique such as likelihood maximisation [16].

16.3.3 Censored observations

In the work above, we have assumed that observations of our variables of interest were corrupted by simple Gaussian noise. However, in many contexts, we instead observe *censored* observations. That is, we might observe that a variable was above or below certain thresholds, but no more. Examples are rich within the weather sensor networks considered. Float sensors are prone to becoming lodged on sensor posts, reporting only that the water level is below that at which it is stuck. Other observations are problematically rounded to the nearest integer – if we observe a reading of x, we can say only that the true value was between $x - 0.5$ and $x + 0.5$. We extend our sequential algorithms to allow for such a noise model.

More precisely, we assume that we actually observe bounds b_c that constrain Gaussian-noise-corrupted versions z_c of the underlying variables of interest y_c at x_c. This framework allows for imprecise censored observations. We may additionally possess observations z_d that are, as previously considered, Gaussian-noise-corrupted versions of the underlying variables of interest y_d at x_d. Note that the noise variance for censored observations may differ from the noise variance associated with other observations. Conditioned on this combination of censored and uncensored observations, the distribution for our variables of interest is

$$p(y_\star \mid z_d, b_c, I) = \frac{\int d\phi \int_{b_c} dz_c \, p(y_\star \mid z_d, z_c, \phi, I) \, p(z_c \mid z_d, \phi, I) \, p(z_d \mid \phi, I) \, p(\phi \mid I)}{\int d\phi \int_{b_c} dz_c \, p(z_c \mid z_d, \phi, I) \, p(z_d \mid \phi, I) \, p(\phi \mid I)}.$$

While we cannot determine this full, non-Gaussian distribution easily, we can analytically determine its mean and covariance. We use the abbreviations $m_{c|d} \triangleq m(z_c \mid z_d, \phi, I)$ and $C_{c|d} \triangleq C(z_c \mid z_d, \phi, I)$. To reflect the influence of our censored observations, the first required modification to our previous results is to incorporate a new term into our likelihoods,

$$r^{(cd)}(\phi) = N(z_d; m(z_d \mid \phi, I), C(z_d \mid \phi, I)) \int_{b_c} dz_c \, N(z_c; m_{c|d}, C_{c|d}),$$

reflecting this new knowledge that z_c is constrained by bounds b_c. This gives us the new weights over hyperparameter samples

$$\rho^{(cd)} \triangleq \frac{K(\phi_s, \phi_s)^{-1} \, \mathfrak{N}_s \, K(\phi_s, \phi_s)^{-1} \, r_s^{(cd)}}{1_{s,1}^\mathsf{T} \, K(\phi_s, \phi_s)^{-1} \, \mathfrak{N}_s \, K(\phi_s, \phi_s)^{-1} \, r_s^{(cd)}}.$$

We can then write our predictive mean as

$$m(y_\star \mid z_d, b_c, I) = \sum_{i \in s} \rho_i^{(cd)} \bigg(\mu_{\phi_i}(x_\star) + K_{\phi_i}(x_\star, [x_c, x_d])$$

$$\times V_{\phi_i}([x_c, x_d], [x_c, x_d])^{-1} \left[\begin{array}{c} \frac{\int_{b_c} dz_c \, z_c \, N(\,;\,,z_c) m_{c|d} C_{c|d}}{\int_{b_c} dz_c \, N(\,;\,,z_c) m_{c|d} C_{c|d}} - \mu_{\phi_i}(x_c) \\ y_d - \mu_{\phi_i}(x_d) \end{array} \right] \bigg), \quad (16.8)$$

noting that a censored observation is intuitively treated as an uncensored observation equal to the conditional mean of the GP over the bounded region. We have also the predictive covariance

$$C(y_\star \mid z_d, b_c, I) = \sum_{i \in s} \rho_i^{(cd)} \Big(K_{\phi_i}(x_\star, x_\star)$$

$$- K_{\phi_i}(x_\star, [x_c, x_d]) V_{\phi_i}([x_c, x_d], [x_c, x_d])^{-1} K_{\phi_i}([x_c, x_d], x_\star) \Big). \quad (16.9)$$

We now have the problem of approximating the integrals $\int_{b_c} dz_c \, N(z_c; m_{c|d}, C_{c|d})$ and $\int_{b_c} dz_c \, z_c \, N(z_c; m_{c|d}, C_{c|d})$, which are non-analytic. Fortunately, there exists an efficient Monte Carlo algorithm [8] for exactly this purpose. This does, however, introduce a practical limit to the number of censored observations we can simultaneously consider.

16.3.4   Efficient implementation

In order to evaluate Eqs. (16.4), (16.5), (16.8) and (16.9), we must determine the product of various matrices with the inverse of the relevant covariance matrix V. The most stable means of doing so involves the use of the Cholesky decomposition, R, of V. Performing this Cholesky decomposition represents the most computationally expensive operation we must perform; its cost scaling as $O(N^3)$ in the number of data points N. However, as discussed earlier, we do not intend to use our GP with a fixed set of data, but rather, within an online algorithm that receives new observations over time. As such, we must be able to iteratively update our predictions in as little time as possible. Fortunately, we can do so by exploiting the special structure of our problem. When we receive new data, our V matrix is changed only in the addition of a few new rows and columns. Hence most of the work that went into computing its Cholesky decomposition at the last iteration can be recycled to produce the new Cholesky decomposition (see Appendix 16.A.1 for details of the relevant rank-1 updates). Another problematic calculation required by Eqs. (16.4) and (16.8) is the computation of the data-dependent term $R^{-1}(y - \mu(x))$, in which $y - \mu(x)$ is also only changing due to the addition of new rows. As such, efficient updating rules are also available for this term (see Appendix 16.A.2). As such, we are able to reduce the overall cost of an update from $O(N^3)$ to $O(N^2)$.

However, we can further increase the efficiency of our updates by making a judicious assumption. In particular, experience shows that our GP requires only a very small number of recent observations in order to produce good estimates. Indeed, most (non-periodic) covariance functions have very light tails such that only points within a few multiples of the time scale are at all relevant to the point of interest. Hence we seek sensible ways of discarding information once it has been rendered 'stale', to reduce both memory usage and computational requirements.

One pre-eminently reasonable measure of the value of data is the uncertainty we still possess after learning it. In particular, we are interested in how uncertain we are about $x_\star$; as given by the covariance of our Gaussian mixture (16.6). Our approach is thus to drop our oldest data points (those which our covariance deems least relevant to the current predictant) until this uncertainty exceeds some predetermined threshold.

Just as we were able to efficiently update our Cholesky factor upon the receipt of new data, so we can downdate to remove data (see Appendix 16.A.3 for the details of this operation). This allows us to rapidly remove the least informative data, compute our uncertainty about $y_\star$, and then repeat as required; the GP will retain only as much data as necessary to achieve a pre-specified degree of accuracy. This allows a principled way of 'windowing' our data series.

Finally, we turn to the implementation of our marginalisation procedure. Essentially, our approach is to maintain an ensemble of GPs, one for each hyperparameter sample, running in parallel, each of which we update and downdate according to the proposals above. Their predictions are then weighted and combined according to Eq. (16.6). Note that the only computations whose computational cost grows at greater than a quadratic rate in the number of samples, η, are the Cholesky decomposition and multiplication of covariance matrices in Eq. (16.6), and these scale rather poorly as $O(\eta^3)$. To address this problem, we take our Gaussian priors for each different hyperparameter $\phi_{(e)} \in \phi$ as independent. We further take a covariance structure given by the product of terms over each hyperparameter, the common *product correlation rule* (e.g. [23])

$$K(\phi, \phi') = \prod_e K_e\big(\phi_{(e)}, \phi'_{(e)}\big).$$

If we additionally consider a simple grid of samples, such that ϕ_s is the tensor product of a set of samples $\phi_{(e),s}$ over each hyperparameter, then the problematic term in Eq. (16.6) reduces to the Kronecker product of the equivalent term over each individual hyperparameter,

$$K(\phi_s, \phi_s)^{-1} \mathfrak{N}_s K(\phi_s, \phi_s)^{-1} = K(\phi_{(1),s}, \phi_{(1),s})^{-1} \mathfrak{N}_s(\phi_{(1),s}, \phi_{(1),s}) K(\phi_{(1),s}, \phi_{(1),s})^{-1}$$
$$\otimes K(\phi_{(2),s}, \phi_{(2),s})^{-1} \mathfrak{N}_s(\phi_{(2),s}, \phi_{(2),s}) K(\phi_{(2),s}, \phi_{(2),s})^{-1}$$
$$\otimes \ldots \tag{16.10}$$

This means that we only have to perform the expensive Cholesky factorisation and multiplication with matrices whose size equals the number of samples for each hyperparameter, rather than on a matrix of size equal to the total number of hyperparameter samples. This hence represents an effective way to avoid the 'curse of dimensionality'.

Applied together, these features provide us with an efficient online algorithm that can be applied in real-time as data is sequentially collected from the sensor network.

16.3.5   Active data selection

Finally, in addition to the regression and prediction problem described in Section 16.2, we are able to use the same algorithm to perform active data selection. This is a decision problem concerning which observations should be taken. In this, we once again take a utility that is a function of the uncertainty in our predictions given the current set of observations. We specify a utility of negative infinity if our uncertainty about any variable is greater than a pre-specified threshold, and a fixed negative utility is assigned as the cost of an observation (in general, this cost could be different for different sensors). Note that the uncertainty increases monotonically in the absence of new data, and shrinks in the presence of an observation. Hence our algorithm is simply induced to make a reading whenever the uncertainty grows beyond a pre-specified threshold.

Our algorithm can also decide which observation to make at this time, by determining which sensor will allow it the longest period of grace until it would be forced to observe again. This clearly minimises the number of costly observations. Note that the uncertainty of a GP, as given by Eq. (16.5), is actually dependent only on the location of a observation, not its actual value. Hence the uncertainty we imagine remaining after taking an observation from a sensor can be quickly determined without having to speculate about what data we might possibly collect. However, this is true only so long as we do not consider the impact of new observations on our hyperparameter sample weights (16.7). Our approach is to take the model, in particular the weights over samples, as fixed[2], and investigate only how different schedules of observations affect our predictions within it. With this proviso, we are guaranteed to maintain our uncertainty below a specified threshold, while taking as few observations as possible.

16.4   Trial implementation

In order to empirically evaluate the information processing algorithm described in the previous section, we have used two sensor networks.

---

[2]Our model, of course, is updated after our scheduled observations are actually made; we consider it fixed only within the context of deciding upon this scheduling.

Bramblemet. The first is a network of weather sensors located on the south coast of England.[3] This network consists of four sensors (named Bramblemet, Sotonmet, Cambermet and Chimet), each of which measures a range of environmental variables (including wind speed and direction, air temperature, sea temperature and tide height) and makes up-to-date sensor measurements available through separate web pages (see www.bramblemet.co.uk). The use of such weather sensors is attractive since they exhibit challenging correlations and delays whose physical processes are well understood, and they are subject to network outages that generate instances of missing sensor readings on which we can evaluate our information processing algorithms.

Wannengrat. We additionally tested our methods on a network of weather sensors located at Wannengrat near Davos, Switzerland. Data from and more details about the network are available at http://sensorscope.epfl.ch.

16.5   Empirical evaluation

In this section we empirically evaluate our information processing algorithm on real weather data collected from the sensor networks described above. We compare our multi-output GP formalism against conventional independent GPs in which each environmental variable is modelled separately (i.e. correlations between these parameters are ignored). We also perform a comparison against a Kalman filter [11, 14]. In particular, we compare against a dynamic auto-regressive model, in the form of a state space model, giving a simple implementation of a Kalman filter to perform sequential predictions. We also test against the naïve algorithm that simply predicts that the variable at the next time step will be equal to that most recently observed at that sensor.

In our comparison, we present results for three different sensor types: tide height, air temperature and air pressure. Tide height was chosen since it demonstrates the ability of the GP to learn and predict periodic behaviour, and more importantly, because this particular dataset contains an interesting period in which extreme weather conditions (a Northerly gale) cause both an unexpectedly low tide and a failure of the wireless connection between several of the sensors and the shore that prevents our algorithm acquiring sensor readings. Air temperature was chosen it exhibits a very different noise and correlation structure to the tide height measurements, and thus demonstrate that the generic approach described here is still able to perform reliable regression and prediction. Finally, air pressure was chosen as a demonstration of our effectiveness in processing censored observations, as all air pressure readings are subject to (the reasonably severe) rounding to the nearest Pascal.

We plot the sensor readings acquired by our algorithm (shown as markers) and the true fine-grained sensor readings (shown as bold) that were downloaded directly from the sensor (rather than through the website) after the event. Note that the acquired readings are a rounded version of the true data. The true data also contains segments that are missing from the acquired readings. We additionally plot the mean and standard deviation of our algorithm's predictions (shown as a solid line with plus or minus a single standard deviation shown as shading). Note that both quantities are derived by combining the GP predictions from each hyperparameter sample set, as described in Section 16.3.2.

---

[3]The network is maintained by the Bramblemet/Chimet Support Group and funded by organisations including the Royal National Lifeboat Institution, Solent Cruising and Racing Association and Associated British Ports.

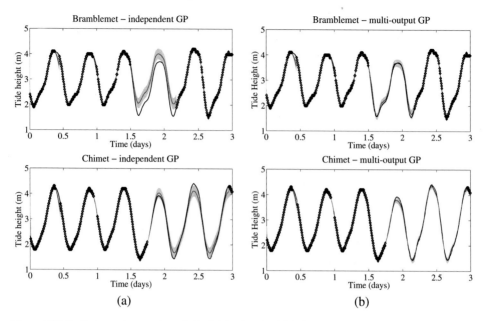

Figure 16.2 Prediction and regression of tide height data for (a) independent and (b) multi-output Gaussian processes.

16.5.1   Regression and prediction

Figures 16.2 and 16.3 illustrate the efficacy of our GP formalism in this scenario. Note that we present just two sensors for reasons of space, but we use readings from all four sensors in order to perform inference. At time t, Fig. 16.2 depicts the posterior distribution of the GP, conditioned on all observations prior to and inclusive of t. Figure 16.3 demonstrates our algorithm's one-step ahead predictive performance, depicting the posterior distribution at time t conditioned on all observations prior to and inclusive of $t - 5$ mins.

We first consider Fig. 16.2 showing the tide predictions, and specifically, we note the performance of our multi-output GP formalism when the Bramblemet sensor drops out at $t = 1.45$ days. In this case, the independent GP quite reasonably predicts that the tide will repeat the same periodic signal it has observed in the past. However, the GP can achieve better results if it is allowed to benefit from the knowledge of the other sensors' readings during this interval of missing data. Thus, in the case of the multi-output GP, by $t = 1.45$ days, the GP has successfully determined that the sensors are all very strongly correlated. Hence, when it sees an unexpected low tide in the Chimet sensor data (caused by the strong Northerly wind), these correlations lead it to infer a similarly low tide in the Bramblemet reading. Hence, the multi-output GP produces significantly more accurate predictions during the missing data interval, with associated smaller error bars. Exactly the same effect is seen in the later predictions of the Chimet tide height, where the multi-output GP predictions use observations from the other sensors to better predict the high tide height at $t = 2.45$ days.

Figure 16.3 shows the air temperature sensor readings where a similar effect is observed. Again, the multi-output GP is able to accurately predict the missing air temperature readings from the Chimet sensor having learnt the correlation with other sensors, despite the fact that the dataset is much noisier and the correlations between sensors are much weaker. In this, it demonstrates a significant improvement in performance over

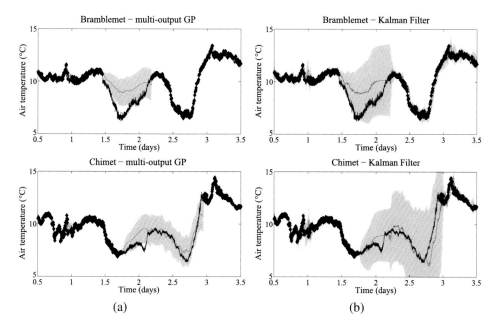

Figure 16.3 One-step lookahead prediction of air temperature data for (a) a multi-output Gaussian process and (b) a Kalman filter.

Kalman filter predictions on the same data. The root mean square errors (RMSEs) are 0.7395 °C for our multi-output GP, 0.9159 °C for the Kalman filter and 3.8200 °C for the naïve algorithm. Note that the Kalman filter also gives unreasonably large error bars in its predictions.

16.5.2 Censored observations

Figure 16.4 demonstrates regression and prediction over the rounded air pressure observations from the Bramblemet censor alone. Here we can demonstrate a dramatic improvement over Kalman filter prediction. The RMSEs are 0.3851 Pa for the GP, 3.2900 Pa for the Kalman filter and 3.6068 Pa for the naïve algorithm. Both the GP and Kalman filter have an order of 16; that is, they store only up to the 16 most recent observations.

16.5.3 Active data selection

We now demonstrate our active data selection algorithm. Using the fine-grained data (downloaded directly from the sensors), we can simulate how our GP would have chosen its observations had it been in control. Results from the active selection of observations from all the four tide sensors are displayed in Fig. 16.5, and for three wind speed sensors in Fig. 16.6. Again, these plots depict dynamic choices; at time t, the GP must decide when next to observe, and from which sensor, given knowledge only of the observations recorded prior to t, in an attempt to maintain the uncertainty in tide height below 10 cm.

   Consider first the case shown in Fig. 16.5(a), in which separate independent GPs are used to represent each sensor. Note that a large number of observations are taken initially as the dynamics of the sensor readings are learnt, followed by a low but constant rate of observation.

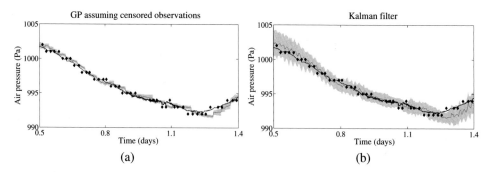

Figure 16.4 Prediction and regression of air pressure data for (a) a Gaussian process employing censored observations and (b) a Kalman filter.

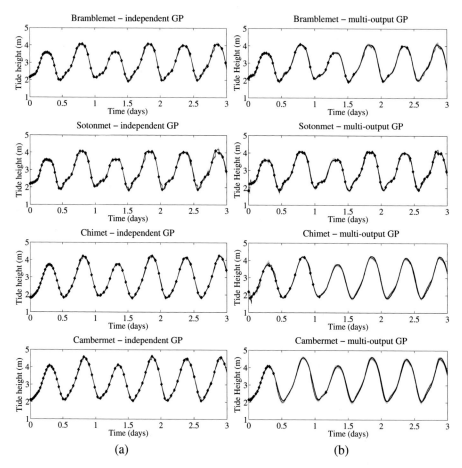

Figure 16.5 Comparison of active sampling of tide data using (a) independent and (b) multi-output Gaussian processes.

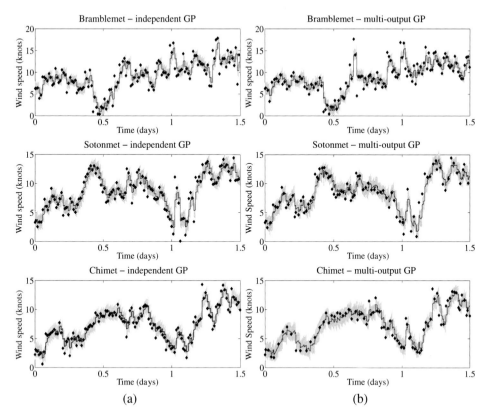

Figure 16.6 Comparison of active sampling of wind speed using (a) independent and (b) multi-output Gaussian processes.

In contrast, for the multi-output case shown in Fig. 16.5(b), the GP is allowed to explicitly represent correlations and delays between the sensors. This dataset is notable for the slight delay of the tide heights at the Chimet and Cambermet sensors relative to the Sotonmet and Bramblemet sensors, due to the nature of tidal flows in the area. Note that after an initial learning phase as the dynamics, correlations and delays are inferred, the GP chooses to sample predominantly from the undelayed Sotonmet and Bramblemet sensors.[4] Despite no observations of the Chimet sensor being made within the time span plotted, the resulting predictions remain remarkably accurate. Consequently only 119 observations are required to keep the uncertainty below the specified tolerance, whereas 358 observations were required in the independent case. This represents another clear demonstration of how our prediction is able to benefit from the readings of multiple sensors.

Figure 16.6 shows similar results for the wind speed measurements from three of the four sensors (the Cambermet sensor being faulty during this period) where the goal was to maintain the uncertainty in wind speed below 1.5 knots. In this case, for purposes of clarity, the fine-grained data is not shown on the plot. Note that the measurement noise is much greater in this case, and this is reflected in the uncertainty in the GP predictions.

---

[4]The dynamics of the tide height at the Sotonmet sensor are more complex than the other sensors due to the existence of a 'young flood stand' and a 'double high tide' in Southampton. For this reason, the GP selects Sotonmet as the most informative sensor and samples it most often.

Furthermore, note that while the Sotonmet and Chimet sensors exhibit a noticeable correlation, Bramblemet appears to be relatively uncorrelated with both. This observation is
reflected in the sampling that the GP performs. The independent GPs sample the Bramblemet, Sotonmet and Chimet sensors 126, 120 and 121 times respectively, while over
the same period, our multi-output GP samples the same sensors 115, 88 and 81 times.
Our multi-output GP learns online that the wind speed measurements of the Sotonmet and
Chimet sensors are correlated, and then exploits this correlation in order to reduce the number of times that these sensors are sampled (inferring the wind speed at one location from
observations of another). However, there is little or no correlation between the Bramblemet
sensor and the other sensors, and thus, our multi-output GP samples Bramblemet almost as
often as the independent GPs.

Figure 16.7 shows the results of an active sampling experiment over the Wannengrat
data. Given the larger number of sensors in this dataset, it was impractical to use the arbitrary parameterisation (16.1), which requires a hyperparameter for every distinct pair of
sensors. Instead, we express the covariance between sensors as a function of the spatial
distance between the known sensor locations. We used the Matérn covariance function
(16.2) for this purpose, with the spatial distance being used to fill the role of r. This spatial

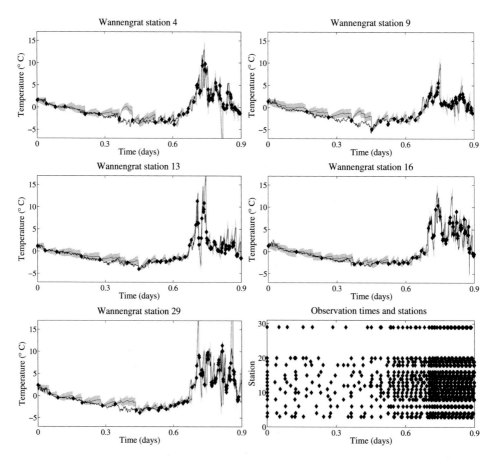

Figure 16.7 Active sampling of ambient temperatures at 16 Wannengrat sensor stations.

distance was specified by a single isotropic scale hyperparameter, which was marginalised along with the other hyperparameters. It can be seen that there is a dramatic increase in sampling frequency coincident with the volatile fluctuations in temperature that begin at about $t = 0.7$ days.

16.6   Computation time

As described earlier, a key requirement of our algorithm is computational efficiency, in order that it can be used to represent multiple correlated sensors, and hence, used for real-time information processing. Here we consider the computation times involved in producing the results presented in the previous section. To this end, Table 16.1 tabulates the computation times required in order to update the algorithm as a new observation is received. This computation time represents the cost of updating the weights of Eq. (16.6) and the Cholesky factor of V (as described in Section 16.3.4). Once this calculation has been performed, making predictions at any point in time is extremely fast (it is simply a matter of adding another element in $z_\star$).

Note that we expect the cost of computation to grow as $O(N^2)$ in the number of stored data points. Our proposed algorithm will automatically determine the quantity of data to store in order to achieve the desired level of accuracy. In the problems we have studied, a few hundred points were typically sufficient (the largest number we required was 750, for the multi-output wind speed data), although of course this will depend critically on the nature of the variables under consideration. For example, our use of a model that explicitly considers the correlations amongst sensors allows us to eliminate much redundant information, reducing the quantity of data we are required to store.

We also have the cost of computing Eq. (16.10), which will grow in the cube of the number of samples in each hyperparameter. However, we consider only a fixed set of samples in each hyperparameter, and thus, Eq. (16.10) needs only be computed once, offline. In this case, our online costs are limited by the multiplication of that term by the likelihoods r_s to give the weights of Eq. (16.6), and this only grows as $O(\eta^2)$. Furthermore, note that this cost is independent of how the η samples are distributed amongst the hyperparameters.

The results in Table 16.1 indicate that real-time information processing is clearly feasible for the problem sizes that we have considered. In general, limiting the number of hyperparameter samples is of critical importance to achieving practical computation. As such, we should exploit any and all prior information that we possess about the system to limit the volume of hyperparameter space that our GP is required to explore online. For example, an informative prior expressing that the tidal period is likely to be around half a day will greatly reduce the number of samples required for this hyperparameter. Similarly, an offline analysis of any available training data will return sharply peaked posteriors over our hyperparameters that will further restrict the required volume to be searched over online. For example, we represent the tidal period hyperparameter with only a single sample online, so certain does training data make us of its value. Finally, a simpler and less flexible covariance model, with fewer hyperparameters, could be chosen if computational limitations become particularly severe. Note that the use of the completely general spherical parameterisation requires a correlation hyperparameter for each pair of variables, an approach which is clearly only feasible for moderate numbers of variables. A simple alternative, of course, would be to assume a covariance over variable label which is a function

		Data points (N)		
		10	100	500
Hyperparameter samples (η)	1	< 0.01	< 0.01	0.04
	10	0.02	0.02	0.20
	100	0.14	0.22	2.28
	1000	1.42	2.22	29.73

Table 16.1 Required computation time (seconds) per update, over N the number of stored data points and η the number of hyperparameter samples. Experiments performed using MATLAB on a 3.00GHz processor with 2GB of RAM.

of the spatial separation between the sensors reading them – sensors that are physically close are likely to be strongly correlated – in which case we would require only enough hyperparameters to define this measure of separation. While a more complicated model will return better predictions, a simple one or two hyperparameter covariance may supply accuracy sufficient for our needs.

16.7   Related work

Gaussian process regression has a long history of use within geophysics and geospatial statistics (where the process is known as kriging [4]), but has only recently been applied within sensor networks. Examples here include the use of GPs to represent spatial correlations between sensors in order that they may be positioned to maximise mutual information [13], and the use of multivariate Gaussians to represent correlations between different sensors and sensor types for energy efficient querying of a sensor network [5].

Our work differs in that we use GPs to represent temporal correlations, and represent correlations and delays between sensors with additional hyperparameters. It is thus closely related to other work using GPs to perform regression over multiple responses [2, 26]. However, our focus is to derive a computationally efficient algorithm, and thus, we use a number of novel computational techniques to allow the re-use of previous calculations as new sensor observations are made. We additionally use a novel Bayesian Monte Carlo technique to marginalise the hyperparameters that describe the correlations and delays between sensors. Finally, we use the variance of the GP's predictions in order to perform active data selection.

Our approach has several advantages relative to sequential state space models [9, 11]. Firstly, these models require the discretisation of the time input, representing a discarding of potentially valuable information. Secondly, their sequential nature means they must necessarily perform difficult iterations in order to manage missing or late data, or to produce long-range forecasts. In our GP approach, what observations we have are readily managed, regardless of when they were made. Equally, the computation cost of all our predictions is identical, irrespective of the time or place we wish to make them about. Finally, a sequential framework requires an explicit specification of a transition model. In our approach, we are able to learn a model from data even if our prior knowledge is negligible. The benefits of our approach are empirically supported by Fig. 16.3.

Previous work has also investigated the use of censored sensor readings within a GP framework [6], or the similar problems involved in classification and ordinal regression [3]. Our approach differs in a number of respects. Firstly, we consider the potential combination of both censored and uncensored observations. Our work also proposes a principled Bayesian Monte Carlo method for adapting our models to the data, considering the contributions from a number of samples in hyperparameter space, rather than simply taking a single sample. Monte Carlo techniques are also used to evaluate our other integrals, in comparison to the Laplace or expectation propagation approximations present in other work. This allows a more accurate assessment of the likelihoods of our hyperparameter samples and more accurate predictions.

Active data selection has been the topic of much previous research [15, 24]. Our problem, of active data selection for tracking, is simplified relative to much of that work owing to the fact that we have a well-defined point of interest. This will either be the current value of our environmental variables, or some future value according to the degree of lookahead. Note also that our uncertainty in this value reflects our underlying uncertainty about the correct model, due to our principled marginalisation. More observations will be scheduled if there is a significant degree of uncertainty about the model. Previous work has also considered the intelligent discarding of data [12]. Again, our task is made relatively easier by our well-defined utility: the uncertainty in our point of interest.

16.8   Conclusions

In this chapter we addressed the need for algorithms capable of performing real-time information processing of sensor network data, and we presented a novel computationally efficient formalism of a multi-output Gaussian process. Using weather data collected from two sensor networks, we demonstrated that this formalism could effectively predict missing sensor readings caused by network outages, and could perform active sampling to maintain estimation uncertainty below a pre-specified threshold.

There are many possibilities for further work to build upon that presented in this chapter. Firstly, as a potential replacement for the fixed hyperparameter samples used in this work, we would like to investigate the use of a moving set of hyperparameter samples. In such a scheme, both the weights and positions of samples would be adjusted according to data received, and as the posterior distributions of these hyperparameters become more sharply peaked, we would reduce the number of samples to further increase the computational efficiency of our algorithm.

Secondly, we intend to investigate the use of correlations between different sensor types (rather than between different sensors of the same type as presented here) to perform regression and prediction within our weather sensor network. In addition, we would like to introduce more flexible covariance functions, able to cope with abrupt changes in the characteristics of data known as *changepoints*. Such covariance functions would, for example, allow the automatic detection of changepoints due to sensor failures.

Acknowledgments   This research was undertaken as part of the ALADDIN (Autonomous Learning Agents for Decentralised Data and Information Networks) project and is jointly funded by a BAE Systems and EPSRC strategic partnership (EP/C548051/1). We would like to thank B. Blaydes of the Bramblemet/Chimet Support Group, and W. Heaps of Associated British Ports (ABP) for allowing us access to the weather sensor network, hosting our RDF data on the sensor websites, and for providing raw sensor data as required. We would also like to thank an anonymous reviewer for many helpful comments.

16.A   Appendix

16.A.1   Cholesky factor update

We have a positive definite matrix, represented in block form as $\begin{bmatrix} V_{1,1} & V_{1,3} \\ V_{1,3}^{\mathsf{T}} & V_{3,3} \end{bmatrix}$ and its

Cholesky factor, $\begin{bmatrix} R_{1,1} & R_{1,3} \\ 0 & R_{3,3} \end{bmatrix}$. Given a new positive definite matrix, which differs from

the old only in the insertion of some new rows and columns, $\begin{bmatrix} V_{1,1} & V_{1,2} & V_{1,3} \\ V_{1,2}^{\mathsf{T}} & V_{2,2} & V_{2,3} \\ V_{1,3}^{\mathsf{T}} & V_{2,3}^{\mathsf{T}} & V_{3,3} \end{bmatrix}$, we wish

to efficiently determine its Cholesky factor, $\begin{bmatrix} S_{1,1} & S_{1,2} & S_{1,3} \\ 0 & S_{2,2} & S_{2,3} \\ 0 & 0 & S_{3,3} \end{bmatrix}$. For A triangular, we define

$x = A \setminus b$ as the solution to the equations $A x = b$ as found by the use of backwards or forwards substitution. The following rules are readily obtained

$$S_{1,1} = R_{1,1}, \quad S_{1,2} = R_{1,1}^{\mathsf{T}} \setminus V_{1,2}, \quad S_{1,3} = R_{1,3}, \quad S_{2,2} = \mathrm{chol}(V_{2,2} - S_{1,2}^{\mathsf{T}} S_{1,2}),$$
$$S_{2,3} = S_{2,2}^{\mathsf{T}} \setminus (V_{2,3} - S_{1,2}^{\mathsf{T}} S_{1,3}), \quad S_{3,3} = \mathrm{chol}(R_{3,3}^{\mathsf{T}} R_{3,3} - S_{2,3}^{\mathsf{T}} S_{2,3}).$$

By setting the appropriate row and column dimensions (to zero if necessary), this allows us to efficiently determine the Cholesky factor given the insertion of rows and columns in any position.

16.A.2   Data term update

We have all terms defined in Appendix 16.A.1, in addition to $\begin{bmatrix} Y_1 \\ Y_2 \\ Y_3 \end{bmatrix}$ and the product $\begin{bmatrix} C_1 \\ C_3 \end{bmatrix} \triangleq$

$\begin{bmatrix} R_{1,1} & R_{1,3} \\ 0 & R_{3,3} \end{bmatrix}^{-\mathsf{T}} \begin{bmatrix} Y_1 \\ Y_3 \end{bmatrix}$. To efficiently determine $\begin{bmatrix} D_1 \\ D_2 \\ D_3 \end{bmatrix} \triangleq \begin{bmatrix} S_{1,1} & S_{1,2} & S_{1,3} \\ 0 & S_{2,2} & S_{2,3} \\ 0 & 0 & S_{3,3} \end{bmatrix}^{-\mathsf{T}} \begin{bmatrix} Y_1 \\ Y_2 \\ Y_3 \end{bmatrix}$, we have

$$D_1 = C_1, \quad D_2 = S_{2,2}^{-\mathsf{T}}(Y_2 - S_{1,2}^{\mathsf{T}} C_1), \quad D_3 = S_{3,3}^{-\mathsf{T}}(R_{3,3}^{\mathsf{T}} C_3 - S_{2,3}^{\mathsf{T}} D_2).$$

16.A.3   Cholesky factor downdate

We have a positive definite matrix, represented in block form as $\begin{bmatrix} V_{1,1} & V_{1,2} & V_{1,3} \\ V_{1,2}^{\mathsf{T}} & V_{2,2} & V_{2,3} \\ V_{1,3}^{\mathsf{T}} & V_{2,3}^{\mathsf{T}} & V_{3,3} \end{bmatrix}$ and

its Cholesky factor, $\begin{bmatrix} S_{1,1} & S_{1,2} & S_{1,3} \\ 0 & S_{2,2} & S_{2,3} \\ 0 & 0 & S_{3,3} \end{bmatrix}$. Given a new positive definite matrix, which differs

from the old only in the deletion of some new rows and columns, $\begin{bmatrix} V_{1,1} & V_{1,3} \\ V_{1,3}^{\mathsf{T}} & V_{3,3} \end{bmatrix}$, we wish

to efficiently determine its Cholesky factor $\begin{bmatrix} R_{1,1} & R_{1,3} \\ 0 & R_{3,3} \end{bmatrix}$. The following rules are readily obtained

$$R_{1,1} = S_{1,1}, \quad R_{1,3} = S_{1,3}, \quad R_{3,3} = \mathrm{chol}(S_{2,3}^{\mathsf{T}} S_{2,3} + S_{3,3}^{\mathsf{T}} S_{3,3}).$$

Note that the special structure of $R_{3,3}$ can be exploited for the efficient resolution of the required Cholesky operation, as, for example, in the MATLAB function cholupdate [27]. By setting the appropriate row and column dimensions (to zero if necessary), this allows us to efficiently determine the Cholesky factor given the deletion of rows and columns in any position.

Bibliography

[1] P. Abrahamsen. A review of Gaussian random fields and correlation functions. Technical Report 917, Norwegian Computing Center, Box 114, Blindern, N-0314 Oslo, Norway, 1997. 2nd edition.

[2] P. Boyle and M. Frean. Dependent Gaussian processes. In *Advances in Neural Information Processing Systems 17*, pages 217–224. The MIT Press, 2005.

[3] W. Chu and Z. Ghahramani. Gaussian processes for ordinal regression. *Journal of Machine Learning Research*, **6**(1):1019, 2006.

[4] N. A. C. Cressie. *Statistics for Spatial Data*. John Wiley & Sons, 1991.

[5] A. Deshpande, C. Guestrin, S. Madden, J. Hellerstein and W. Hong. Model-driven data acquisition in sensor networks. In *Proceedings of the Thirtieth International Conference on Very Large Data Bases (VLDB 2004)*, pages 588–599, 2004.

[6] E. Ertin. Gaussian process models for censored sensor readings. In *Statistical Signal Processing, 2007. SSP'07. IEEE/SP 14th Workshop on*, pages 665–669, 2007.

[7] M. Fuentes, A. Chaudhuri and D. H. Holland. Bayesian entropy for spatial sampling design of environmental data. *Environmental and Ecological Statistics*, **14**:323–340, 2007.

[8] A. Genz. Numerical computation of multivariate normal probabilities. *Journal of Computational and Graphical Statistics*, **1**(2):141–149, 1992.

[9] A. Girard, C. Rasmussen, J. Candela and R. Murray-Smith. Gaussian process priors with uncertain inputs – application to multiple-step ahead time series forecasting. In *Advances in Neural Information Processing Systems 16*. MIT Press, 2003.

[10] J. K. Hart and K. Martinez. Environmental Sensor Networks: A revolution in the earth system science? *Earth-Science Reviews*, **78**:177–191, 2006.

[11] A. H. Jazwinski. *Stochastic Processes and Filtering Theory*. Academic Press, 1970.

[12] A. Kapoor and E. Horvitz. On discarding, caching, and recalling samples in active learning. In *Uncertainty in Artificial Intelligence*, 2007.

[13] A. Krause, C. Guestrin, A. Gupta and J. Kleinberg. Near-optimal sensor placements: maximizing information while minimizing communication cost. In *Proceedings of the Fifth International Conference on Information Processing in Sensor Networks (IPSN '06)*, pages 2–10, Nashville, Tennessee, USA, 2006.

[14] S. M. Lee and S. J. Roberts. Multivariate time series forecasting in incomplete environments. Technical Report PARG-08-03. Available at www.robots.ox.ac.uk/~parg/publications.html, University of Oxford, December 2008.

[15] D. J. C. MacKay. Information-based objective functions for active data selection. *Neural Computation*, **4**(4):590–604, 1992.

[16] D. J. C. MacKay. *Information Theory, Inference and Learning Algorithms*. Cambridge University Press, 2002.

[17] A. O'Hagan. Monte Carlo is fundamentally unsound. *The Statistician*, **36**:247–249, 1987.

[18] A. O'Hagan. Bayes-Hermite quadrature. *Journal of Statistical Planning and Inference*, **29**:245–260, 1991.

[19] M. Osborne and S. J. Roberts. Gaussian processes for prediction. Technical Report PARG-07-01. Available at www.robots.ox.ac.uk/~parg/publications.html, University of Oxford, September 2007.

[20] J. Pinheiro and D. Bates. Unconstrained parameterizations for variance-covariance matrices. *Statistics and Computing*, **6**:289–296, 1996.

[21] C. E. Rasmussen and Z. Ghahramani. Bayesian Monte Carlo. In *Advances in Neural Information Processing Systems 15*, pages 489–496. The MIT Press, 2003.

[22] C. E. Rasmussen and C. K. I. Williams. *Gaussian Processes for Machine Learning*. MIT Press, 2006.

[23] M. J. Sasena. Flexibility and efficiency enhancements for constrained global design optimization with Kriging approximations. PhD thesis, University of Michigan, 2002.

[24] S. Seo, M. Wallat, T. Graepel and K. Obermayer. Gaussian process regression: active data selection and test point rejection. In *Neural Networks, 2000. IJCNN 2000, Proceedings of the IEEE-INNS-ENNS International Joint Conference on*, volume 3, 2000.

[25] M. L. Stein. Space-time covariance functions. *Journal of the American Statistical Association*, **100**(469):310–322, 2005.

[26] Y. W. Teh, M. Seeger and M. I. Jordan. Semiparametric latent factor models. In *Proceedings of the Conference on Artificial Intelligence and Statistics*, pages 333–340, 2005.

[27] The MathWorks. MATLAB R2007a, 2007.

Contributors

Michael A. Osborne, Department of Engineering Science, University of Oxford, Oxford, OX1 3PJ

Alex Rogers, School of Electronics and Computer Science, University of Southampton, Southampton, SO17 1BJ

Stephen J. Roberts, Department of Engineering Science, University of Oxford, Oxford, OX1 3PJ

Sarvapali D. Ramchurn, School of Electronics and Computer Science, University of Southampton, Southampton, SO17 1BJ

Nick R. Jennings, School of Electronics and Computer Science, University of Southampton, Southampton, SO17 1BJ

17

Optimal control theory and the linear Bellman equation

Hilbert J. Kappen

17.1 Introduction

Optimising a sequence of actions to attain some future goal is the general topic of control theory [26, 9]. It views an agent as an automaton that seeks to maximise expected reward (or minimise cost) over some future time period. Two typical examples that illustrate this are motor control and foraging for food.

As an example of a motor control task, consider a human throwing a spear to kill an animal. Throwing a spear requires the execution of a motor program that is such that at the moment that the hand releases the spear it has the correct speed and direction to hit the desired target. A motor program is a sequence of actions, and this sequence can be assigned a cost that consists generally of two terms: a path cost that specifies the energy consumption to contract the muscles to execute the motor program, and an end cost that specifies whether the spear will kill the animal, just hurt it, or miss it altogether. The optimal control solution is a sequence of motor commands that results in killing the animal by throwing the spear with minimal physical effort. If x denotes the state space (the positions and velocities of the muscles), the optimal control solution is a function $u(x, t)$ that depends both on the actual state of the system at each time t and also explicitly on time.

When an animal forages for food, it explores the environment with the objective to find as much food as possible in a short time window. At each time t, the animal considers the food it expects to encounter in the period $[t, t + T]$. Unlike the motor control example, the time horizon recedes into the future from the current time and the cost consists now only of a path contribution and no end cost. Therefore, at each time the animal faces the same task, but possibly from a different location in the environment. The optimal control solution $u(x)$ is now time-independent and specifies for each location in the environment x the direction u in which the animal should move.

The general stochastic control problem is intractable to solve and requires an exponential amount of memory and computation time. The reason is that the state space needs to be discretised and thus becomes exponentially large in the number of dimensions. Computing the expectation values means that all states need to be visited and requires exponentially large sums. The same intractabilities are encountered in reinforcement learning.

In this chapter, we aim to give a pedagogical introduction to control theory. For simplicity, we will first consider in Section 17.2 the case of discrete time and discuss the dynamic programming solution. This gives us the basic intuition about the Bellman equations in

continuous time that are considered later on. In Section 17.3 we consider continuous time
control problems. In this case, the optimal control problem can be solved in two ways:
using the Hamilton–Jacobi–Bellman (HJB) equation which is a partial differential equation
[2] and is the continuous time analogue of the dynamic programming method, or using the
Pontryagin minimum principle (PMP) [23] which is a variational argument and results in
a pair of *ordinary* differential equations. We illustrate the methods with the example of a
mass on a spring.

In Section 17.4 we generalise the control formulation to stochastic dynamics. In the
presence of noise, the PMP formalism has no obvious generalisation (see however [39]).
In contrast, the inclusion of noise in the HJB framework is mathematically quite straightforward. However, the numerical solution of either the deterministic or stochastic HJB
equation is in general difficult due to the curse of dimensionality.

There are some stochastic control problems that can be solved efficiently. When the
system dynamics is linear and the cost is quadratic (LQ control), the solution is given in
terms of a number of coupled ordinary differential (Riccati) equations that can be solved
efficiently [26]. Linear quadratic control is useful to maintain a system such as a chemical
plant, operated around a desired point in state space, and is therefore widely applied in
engineering. However, it is a linear theory and too restricted to model the complexities of
intelligent behaviour encountered in agents or robots.

The simplest control formulation assumes that all model components (the dynamics,
the environment, the costs) are known and that the state is fully observed. Often, this is
not the case. Formulated in a Bayesian way, one may only know a probability distribution
of the current state, or over the parameters of the dynamics or the costs. This leads us to
the problem of partial observability or the problem of joint inference and control. We discuss two different approaches to learning: adaptive control and dual control. Whereas in
the adaptive control approach the learning dynamics is exterior to the control problem, in
the dual control approach it is recognised that learning and control are interrelated and the
optimal solution for the combined learning and control problem is computed. We illustrate
the complexity of joint inference and control with a simple example. We discuss the concept of certainty equivalence, which states that for particular linear quadratic problems the
inference and control problems disentangle and can be solved separately. We will discuss
these issues in Section 17.5.

Recently, we have discovered a class of continuous non-linear stochastic control problems that can be solved more efficiently than the general case [16, 17]. These are control
problems with a finite time horizon, where the control acts additively on the dynamics and
is in some sense proportional to the noise. The cost of the control is quadratic in the control variables. Otherwise, the path cost, end cost and the intrinsic dynamics of the system
are arbitrary. These control problems can have both time-dependent and time-independent
solutions of the type that we encountered in the examples above. For these problems, the
Bellman equation becomes a linear equation in the exponentiated cost-to-go (value function). The solution is formally written as a path integral. We discuss the path integral control
method in Section 17.6. The path integral can be interpreted as a free-energy, or as the normalisation of a probabilistic time series model (Kalman filter, hidden Markov model). One
can therefore consider various well-known methods from the machine learning community
to approximate this path integral, such as the Laplace approximation and Monte Carlo sampling [17], variational approximations or belief propagation [34]. In Section 17.7.2 we show
an example of an n joint arm where we compute the optimal control using the variational
approximation for large n.

Non-linear stochastic control problems display features not shared by deterministic control problems nor by linear stochastic control. In deterministic control, only the globally optimal solution is relevant. In stochastic control, the optimal solution is typically a weighted mixture of suboptimal solutions. The weighting depends in a non-trivial way on the features of the problem, such as the noise and the horizon time and on the cost of each solution. This multimodality leads to surprising behaviour in stochastic optimal control. For instance, the optimal control can be qualitatively very different for high and low noise levels. In [16] it was shown that, in a stochastic environment, optimally the choice to move to one of two targets should be delayed in time. The decision is formally accomplished by a dynamical symmetry breaking of the cost-to-go function.

17.2 Discrete time control

We start by discussing the most simple control case, which is the finite horizon discrete time deterministic control problem. In this case the optimal control explicitly depends on time. See also [36] for further discussion. Consider the control of a discrete time dynamical system

$$x_{t+1} = x_t + f(t, x_t, u_t), \quad t = 0, 1, \ldots, T - 1,$$ (17.1)

where x_t is an n-dimensional vector describing the *state* of the system and u_t is an m-dimensional vector that specifies the *control* or *action* at time t. Note that Eq. (17.1) describes a noiseless dynamics. If we specify x at $t = 0$ as x_0 and we specify a sequence of controls $u_{0:T-1} = u_0, u_1, \ldots, u_{T-1}$, we can compute future states of the system $x_{1:T}$ recursively from Eq. (17.1). Define a cost function that assigns a cost to each sequence of controls

$$C(x_0, u_{0:T-1}) = \phi(x_T) + \sum_{t=0}^{T-1} R(t, x_t, u_t).$$ (17.2)

Here $R(t, x, u)$ is the cost associated with taking action u at time t in state x, and $\phi(x_T)$ is the cost associated with ending up in state x_T at time T. The problem of optimal control is to find the sequence $u_{0:T-1}$ that minimises $C(x_0, u_{0:T-1})$. The problem has a standard solution, which is known as dynamic programming. Introduce the *optimal cost-to-go*

$$J(t, x_t) = \min_{u_{t:T-1}} \left(\phi(x_T) + \sum_{s=t}^{T-1} R(s, x_s, u_s) \right), \quad t \leq T - 1,$$

which solves the optimal control problem from an intermediate time t until the fixed end time T, starting at an arbitrary location x_t. The minimum of Eq. (17.2) is given by $J(0, x_0)$. One can recursively compute $J(t, x)$ from $J(t + 1, x)$ for all x in the following way. Given $J(T, x) = \phi(x)$, then

$$J(t, x_t) = \min_{u_{t:T-1}} \left(\phi(x_T) + \sum_{s=t}^{T-1} R(s, x_s, u_s) \right)$$

$$= \min_{u_t} \left(R(t, x_t, u_t) + \min_{u_{t+1:T-1}} \left[\phi(x_T) + \sum_{s=t+1}^{T-1} R(s, x_s, u_s) \right] \right)$$

$$= \min_{u_t} \left(R(t, x_t, u_t) + J(t + 1, x_{t+1}) \right)$$

$$= \min_{u_t} \left(R(t, x_t, u_t) + J(t + 1, x_t + f(t, x_t, u_t)) \right). \tag{17.3}$$

The minimisation over the whole path $u_{0:T-1}$ has reduced to a sequence of minimisations over u_t due to the Markovian nature of the problem: the future depends on the past and vice versa only through the present. Also note that in the last line the minimisation is done for each x_t separately. The algorithm to compute the optimal control $u^*_{0:T-1}$, the optimal trajectory $x^*_{1:T}$ and the optimal cost is given by

1. Initialisation: $J(T, x) = \phi(x)$.

2. Backwards: For $t = T - 1, \ldots, 0$ and for all x compute

$$u^*_t(x) = \arg \min_u \{ R(t, x, u) + J(t + 1, x + f(t, x, u)) \},$$

$$J(t, x) = R(t, x, u^*_t) + J(t + 1, x + f(t, x, u^*_t)).$$

3. Forwards: For $t = 0, \ldots, T - 1$ compute

$$x^*_{t+1} = x^*_t + f(t, x^*_t, u^*_t(x^*_t)).$$

The execution of the dynamic programming algorithm is linear in the horizon time T.

17.3   Continuous time control

In the absence of noise, the optimal control problem in continuous time can be solved in two ways: using the Pontryagin minimum principle (PMP) [23], which is a pair of *ordinary* differential equations or the Hamilton–Jacobi–Bellman (HJB) equation which is a *partial* differential equation [2]. The latter is very similar to the dynamic programming approach that we have treated above. The HJB approach also allows for a straightforward extension to the noisy case. We will first treat the HJB description and subsequently the PMP description. For further reading see [26, 14].

17.3.1   The HJB equation

Consider the dynamical system (17.1) where we take the time increments to zero, i.e. we replace $t + 1$ by $t + dt$ with $dt \to 0$:

$$x_{t+dt} = x_t + f(x_t, u_t, t)dt. \tag{17.4}$$

In the continuous limit we will write $x_t = x(t)$. The initial state is fixed to $x(0) = x_0$ and the final state is free. The problem is to find a control signal $u(t), 0 < t < T$, which we denote as $u(0 \to T)$, such that

$$C(x_0, u(0 \to T)) = \phi(x(T)) + \int_0^T d\tau R(x(\tau), u(\tau), \tau) \tag{17.5}$$

is minimal. Here C consists of an end cost $\phi(x)$ that gives the cost of ending in a configuration x, and a path cost that is an integral over time that depends on the trajectories $x(0 \to T)$ and $u(0 \to T)$. Equation (17.3) becomes

$$J(t, x) = \min_u \left(R(t, x, u)dt + J(t + dt, x + f(x, u, t)dt) \right),$$

$$\approx \min_u \left(R(t, x, u)dt + J(t, x) + \partial_t J(t, x)dt + \partial_x J(t, x)f(x, u, t)dt \right),$$

$$-\partial_t J(t, x) = \min_u \left(R(t, x, u) + f(x, u, t)\partial_x J(x, t) \right), \qquad (17.6)$$

where in the second line we have used the Taylor expansion of $J(t + dt, x + dx)$ around x, t to first order in dt and dx and in the third line have taken the limit $dt \rightarrow 0$. We use the shorthand notation $\partial_x J = \partial J/\partial x$. Equation (17.6) is a partial differential equation, known as the *Hamilton–Jacobi–Bellman (HJB) equation*, that describes the evolution of J as a function of x and t and must be solved with boundary condition $J(x, T) = \phi(x)$; ∂_t and ∂_x denote partial derivatives with respect to t and x, respectively. The optimal control at the current x, t is given by

$$u(x, t) = \arg\min_u \left(R(x, u, t) + f(x, u, t)\partial_x J(t, x) \right). \qquad (17.7)$$

Note that in order to compute the optimal control at the current state $x(0)$ at $t = 0$ one must compute $J(x, t)$ for all values of x and t.

17.3.2 Example: mass on a spring

To illustrate the optimal control principle consider a mass on a spring. The spring is at rest at $z = 0$ and exerts a force proportional to $F = -z$ towards the rest position. Using Newton's law $F = ma$ with $a = \ddot{z}$ the acceleration and $m = 1$ the mass of the spring, the equation of motion is given by $\ddot{z} = -z + u$, with u an unspecified control signal with $-1 < u < 1$. We want to solve the control problem: Given initial position and velocity z_i and $\dot{z}_i$ at time 0, find the control path $u(0 \rightarrow T)$ such that $z(T)$ is maximal. Introducing $x_1 = z$, $x_2 = \dot{z}$, then

$$\dot{x} = Ax + Bu, \qquad A = \begin{pmatrix} 0 & 1 \\ -1 & 0 \end{pmatrix}, \qquad B = \begin{pmatrix} 0 \\ 1 \end{pmatrix},$$

and $x = (x_1, x_2)^T$. The problem is of the above type, with $\phi(x) = C^T x$, $C^T = (-1, 0)$, $R(x, u, t) = 0$ and $f(x, u, t) = Ax + Bu$. Equation (17.6) takes the form

$$-J_t = (\partial_x J)^T Ax - |(\partial_x J)^T B|.$$

We try $J(t, x) = \psi(t)^T x + \alpha(t)$. The HJB equation reduces to two ordinary differential equations $\dot{\psi} = -A^T \psi$, $\dot{\alpha} = |\psi^T B|$. These equations must be solved for all t, with final boundary conditions $\psi(T) = C$ and $\alpha(T) = 0$. Note that the optimal control in Eq. (17.7) only requires $\partial_x J(x, t)$, which in this case is $\psi(t)$ and thus we do not need to solve α. The solution for ψ is $\psi_1(t) = -\cos(t - T)$, $\psi_2(t) = \sin(t - T)$ for $0 < t < T$. The optimal control is $u(x, t) = -\text{sign}(\psi_2(t)) = -\text{sign}(\sin(t - T))$. As an example consider $x_1(0) = x_2(0) = 0$, $T = 2\pi$. Then, the optimal control is

$$u = -1, \quad 0 < t < \pi, \qquad u = 1, \quad \pi < t < 2\pi.$$

The optimal trajectories are, for $0 < t < \pi$, $x_1(t) = \cos(t) - 1$, $x_2(t) = -\sin(t)$ and, for $\pi < t < 2\pi$, $x_1(t) = 3\cos(t) + 1$, $x_2(t) = -3\sin(t)$. The solution is drawn in Fig. 17.1(a). We see that in order to excite the spring to its maximal height at T, the optimal control is to first push the spring down for $0 < t < \pi$ and then to push the spring up between $\pi < t < 2\pi$, taking maximal advantage of the intrinsic dynamics of the spring. Note that, since there is no cost associated with the control u and u is hard limited between -1 and 1, the optimal control is always either -1 or 1. This is known as bang-bang control.

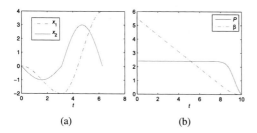

Figure 17.1 (a) Optimal control of mass on a spring such that at $t = 2\pi$ the amplitude is maximal; x_1 is position of the spring, x_2 is velocity of the spring. (b) Stochastic optimal control in the case of a linear system with quadratic cost; $T = 10$, time discretisation $dt = 0.1$, $\nu = 0.05$. The optimal control is to steer towards the origin with $-P(t)x$, where P is roughly constant until $T \approx 8$. Afterward control weakens because the expected diffusion is proportional to the time-to-go.

(a)   (b)

17.3.3 Pontryagin minimum principle

In the previous section, we solved the optimal control problem as a partial differential equation, with a boundary condition at the end time. The numerical solution requires a discretisation of space and time and is computationally expensive. The solution is an optimal cost-to-go function $J(x, t)$ for all x and t. From this we compute the optimal control sequence (17.7) and the optimal trajectory.

An alternative to the HJB approach is a variational approach that directly finds the optimal trajectory and optimal control and bypasses the expensive computation of the cost-to-go. This approach is known as the Pontryagin minimum principle. We can write the optimal control problem as a constrained optimisation problem with independent variables $u(0 \to T)$ and $x(0 \to T)$. We wish to minimise

$$\min_{u(0 \to T), x(0 \to T)} \phi(x(T)) + \int_0^T dt R(x(t), u(t), t)$$

subject to the constraint that $u(0 \to T)$ and $x(0 \to T)$ are compatible with the dynamics

$$\dot{x} = f(x, u, t) \tag{17.8}$$

and the boundary condition $x(0) = x_0$. Here $\dot{x}$ denotes the time derivative dx/dt. We can solve the constrained optimization problem by introducing the Lagrange multiplier function $\lambda(t)$ that ensures the constraint (17.8) for all t:

$$C = \phi(x(T)) + \int_0^T dt \left[R(t, x(t), u(t)) - \lambda(t)(f(t, x(t), u(t)) - \dot{x}(t)) \right]$$

$$= \phi(x(T)) + \int_0^T dt[-H(t, x(t), u(t), \lambda(t)) + \lambda(t)\dot{x}(t)], \tag{17.9}$$

$$-H(t, x, u, \lambda) = R(t, x, u) - \lambda f(t, x, u).$$

The solution is found by extremising C. If we vary the action C w.r.t. to the trajectory x, the control u and the Lagrange multiplier λ, we get

$$\delta C = \phi_x(x(T))\delta x(T) + \int_0^T dt[-H_x \delta x(t) - H_u \delta u(t) + (-H_\lambda + \dot{x}(t))\delta \lambda(t) + \lambda(t)\delta \dot{x}(t)]$$

$$= (\phi_x(x(T)) + \lambda(T))\,\delta x(T) + \int_0^T dt \left[(-H_x - \dot{\lambda}(t))\delta x(t) - H_u \delta u(t) + (-H_\lambda + \dot{x}(t))\delta \lambda(t) \right]$$

where the subscripts x, u, λ denote partial derivatives, e.g. $H_x = \frac{\partial H(t, x(t), u(t), \lambda(t))}{\partial x(t)}$. In the second line above we have used partial integration:

$$\int_0^T dt \lambda(t) \delta \dot{x}(t) = \int_0^T dt \lambda(t) \frac{d}{dt} \delta x(t) = -\int_0^T dt \frac{d}{dt} \lambda(t) \delta x(t) + \lambda(T) \delta x(T) - \lambda(0) \delta x(0)$$

and $\delta x(0) = 0$. The stationary solution ($\delta C = 0$) is obtained when the coefficients of the independent variations $\delta x(t), \delta u(t), \delta \lambda(t)$ and $\delta x(T)$ are zero. Thus,

$$\begin{aligned}
\dot{\lambda} &= -H_x(t, x(t), u(t), \lambda(t)), & 0 &= H_u((t, x(t), u(t), \lambda(t)), \\
\dot{x} &= H_\lambda(t, x, u, \lambda), & \lambda(T) &= -\phi_x(x(T)).
\end{aligned} \qquad (17.10)$$

We can solve Eq. (17.10) for u and denote the solution as $u^*(t, x, \lambda)$. This solution is unique if H is convex in u. The remaining equations are

$$\dot{x} = H_\lambda^*(t, x, \lambda), \qquad \dot{\lambda} = -H_x^*(t, x, \lambda) \qquad (17.11)$$

where we have defined $H^*(t, x, \lambda) = H(t, x, u^*(t, x, \lambda), \lambda)$ and with boundary conditions

$$x(0) = x_0, \qquad \lambda(T) = -\phi_x(x(T)). \qquad (17.12)$$

The solution provided by Eq. (17.11) with boundary conditions Eq. (17.12) are coupled ordinary differential equations that describe the dynamics of x and λ over time with a boundary condition for x at the initial time and for λ at the final time. Compared to the HJB equation, the complexity of solving these equations is low since only time discretisation and no space discretisation is required. However, due to the mixed boundary conditions, finding a solution that satisfies these equations is not trivial and requires sophisticated numerical methods. The most common method for solving the PMP equations is called (multiple) shooting [11, 13].

Equations (17.11) are also known as the so-called Hamilton equations of motion that arise in classical mechanics, but then with initial conditions for both x and λ, [12]. In fact, one can view control theory as a generalisation of classical mechanics. In classical mechanics H is called the Hamiltonian. Consider the time evolution of H

$$\dot{H} = H_t + H_u \dot{u} + H_x \dot{x} + H_\lambda \dot{\lambda} = H_t, \qquad (17.13)$$

where we have used the dynamical equations (17.11) and (17.10). In particular, when f and R in Eq. (17.9) do not explicitly depend on time, neither does H and $H_t = 0$. In this case we see that H is a constant of motion: the control problem finds a solution such that $H(t = 0) = H(t = T)$.

17.3.4 Again mass on a spring

We consider again the example of the mass on a spring that we introduced in Section 17.3.2 where we had

$$\begin{aligned}
\dot{x}_1 &= x_2, & \dot{x}_2 &= -x_1 + u, \\
R(x, u, t) &= 0, & \phi(x) &= -x_1.
\end{aligned}$$

The Hamiltonian (17.9) becomes $H(t, x, u, \lambda) = \lambda_1 x_2 + \lambda_2(-x_1 + u)$. Using Eq. (17.10) we obtain $u^* = -\text{sign}(\lambda_2)$ and $H^*(t, x, \lambda) = \lambda_1 x_2 - \lambda_2 x_1 - |\lambda_2|$. The Hamilton equations are

$$\begin{aligned}
\dot{x} &= \frac{\partial H^*}{\partial \lambda} & \Rightarrow & & \dot{x}_1 &= x_2, & \dot{x}_2 &= -x_1 - \text{sign}(\lambda_2), \\
\dot{\lambda} &= -\frac{\partial H^*}{\partial x} & \Rightarrow & & \dot{\lambda}_1 &= -\lambda_2, & \dot{\lambda}_2 &= \lambda_1,
\end{aligned}$$

with $x(t = 0) = x_0$ and $\lambda(t = T) = (1, 0)$.

17.3.5 Comments

The HJB method gives a sufficient (and often necessary) condition for optimality. The solution of the PDE is expensive. The PMP method provides a necessary condition for optimal control. This means that it provides candidate solutions for optimality. The PMP method is computationally less complicated than the HJB method because it does not require discretisation of the state space. The PMP method can be used when dynamic programming fails due to lack of smoothness of the optimal cost-to-go function.

The subject of optimal control theory in continuous space and time has been well studied in the mathematical literature and contains many complications related to the existence, uniqueness and smoothness of the solution, particularly in the absence of noise. See [14] for a clear discussion and further references. In the presence of noise and in particular in the path integral framework, as we will discuss below, it seems that many of these intricacies disappear.

17.4 Stochastic optimal control

In this section, we consider the extension of the continuous control problem to the case that the dynamics is subject to noise and is given by a stochastic differential equation. First, we give a very brief introduction to stochastic differential equations.

17.4.1 Stochastic differential equations

Consider the random walk on the line

$$x_{t+1} = x_t + \xi_t, \qquad \xi_t = \pm\sqrt{\nu},$$

with $x_0 = 0$. The increments ξ_t are iid random variables with mean zero, $\langle\xi_t^2\rangle = \nu$ and ν is a constant. We can write the solution for x_t in closed form as $x_t = \sum_{i=1}^t \xi_i$. Since x_t is a sum of random variables, x_t becomes Gaussian in the limit of large t. We can compute the evolution of the mean and covariance

$$\langle x_t\rangle = \sum_{i=1}^t \langle\xi_i\rangle = 0,$$

$$\langle x_t^2\rangle = \sum_{i,j=1}^t \langle\xi_i\xi_j\rangle = \sum_{i=1}^t \langle\xi_i^2\rangle + \sum_{i,j=1,j\neq i}^t \langle\xi_i\rangle\langle\xi_j\rangle = \nu t.$$

Note that the fluctuations $\sigma_t = \sqrt{\langle x_t^2\rangle} = \sqrt{\nu t}$ increase with the square root of t. This is a characteristic of diffusion, such as for instance ink in water or warm air in a room. In the continuous time limit we define

$$dx_t = x_{t+dt} - x_t = d\xi, \tag{17.14}$$

with $d\xi$ an infinitesimal mean zero Gaussian variable. In order to get the right scaling with t we must choose $\langle d\xi^2\rangle = \nu dt$. Then in the limit of $dt \to 0$ we obtain

$$\frac{d}{dt}\langle x\rangle = \lim_{dt\to 0}\left\langle\frac{x_{t+dt} - x_t}{dt}\right\rangle = \lim_{dt\to 0}\frac{\langle d\xi\rangle}{dt} = 0 \quad \Rightarrow \quad \langle x\rangle(t) = 0,$$

$$\frac{d}{dt}\langle x^2\rangle = \nu \quad \Rightarrow \quad \langle x^2\rangle(t) = \nu t.$$

The conditional probability distribution of x at time t given x_0 at time 0 is Gaussian and specified by its mean and variance. Thus

$$p(x, t|x_0, 0) = \frac{1}{\sqrt{2\pi vt}} \exp\left(-\frac{(x - x_0)^2}{2vt}\right).$$

The process (17.14) is called a Wiener process.

17.4.2 Stochastic optimal control theory

Consider the stochastic differential equation which is a generalisation of Eq. (17.4)

$$dx = f(x(t), u(t), t)dt + d\xi; \qquad (17.15)$$

$d\xi$ is a Wiener process with $\langle d\xi_i d\xi_j \rangle = v_{ij}(t, x, u)dt$ and v is a symmetric positive definite matrix. Because the dynamics is stochastic, it is no longer the case that when x at time t and the full control path $u(t \to T)$ are given, we know the future path $x(t \to T)$. Therefore, we cannot minimise Eq. (17.5), but can only hope to be able to minimise its expected value over all possible future realisations of the Wiener process

$$C(x_0, u(0 \to T)) = \left\langle \phi(x(T)) + \int_0^T dt R(x(t), u(t), t) \right\rangle_{x_0}. \qquad (17.16)$$

The subscript x_0 on the expectation value is to remind us that the expectation is over all stochastic trajectories that start in x_0. The solution of the control problem proceeds in a similar manner to the deterministic case, with the only difference that we must add the expected value over trajectories. Equation (17.3) becomes

$$J(t, x_t) = \min_{u_t} R(t, x_t, u_t)dt + \langle J(t + dt, x_{t+dt}) \rangle_{x_t}.$$

We must again make a Taylor expansion of J in dt and dx. However, since $\langle dx^2 \rangle$ is of order dt because of the Wiener process, we must expand up to order dx^2:

$$\langle J(t + dt, x_{t+dt}) \rangle = \int dx_{t+dt} \mathcal{N}(x_{t+dt}|x_t, vdt) J(t + dt, x_{t+dt})$$

$$= J(t, x_t) + dt \partial_t J(t, x_t) + \langle dx \rangle \partial_x J(t, x_t) + \frac{1}{2} \langle dx^2 \rangle \partial_x^2 J(t, x_t),$$

$$\langle dx \rangle = f(x, u, t)dt,$$

$$\langle dx^2 \rangle = v(t, x, u)dt.$$

Thus we obtain the *stochastic Hamilton–Jacobi–Bellman equation*

$$-\partial_t J(t, x) = \min_u \left(R(t, x, u) + f(x, u, t)\partial_x J(x, t) + \frac{1}{2} v(t, x, u)\partial_x^2 J(x, t)\right), \qquad (17.17)$$

with boundary condition $J(x, T) = \phi(x)$. Equation (17.17) reduces to the deterministic HJB equation (17.6) in the limit $v \to 0$.

17.4.3   Linear quadratic control

In the case that the dynamics is linear and the cost is quadratic one can show that the optimal cost-to-go J is also a quadratic form and one can solve the stochastic HJB equation in terms of 'sufficient statistics' that describe J. Here x is n-dimensional and u is p-dimensional. The dynamics is linear

$$dx = [A(t)x + B(t)u + b(t)]dt + \sum_{j=1}^{m}(C_j(t)x + D_j(t)u + \sigma_j(t))d\xi_j,$$

with dimensions: $A = n \times n, B = n \times p, b = n \times 1, C_j = n \times n, D_j = n \times p, \sigma_j = n \times 1$ and $\langle d\xi_j d\xi_{j'} \rangle = \delta_{jj'}dt$. The cost function is quadratic

$$\phi(x) = \frac{1}{2}x^T G x,$$

$$f_0(x, u, t) = \frac{1}{2}x^T Q(t)x + u^T S(t)x + \frac{1}{2}u^T R(t)u,$$

with $G = n \times n, Q = n \times n, S = p \times n, R = p \times p$. We parameterise the optimal cost-to-go function as

$$J(t, x) = \frac{1}{2}x^T P(t)x + \alpha^T(t)x + \beta(t), \tag{17.18}$$

which should satisfy the stochastic HJB equation (17.17) with $P(T) = G$ and $\alpha(T) = \beta(T) = 0$. The function $P(t)$ is an $n \times n$ matrix, $\alpha(t)$ is an n-dimensional vector and $\beta(t)$ is a scalar. Substituting this form of J in Eq. (17.17), this equation contains terms quadratic, linear and constant in x and u. We can thus do the minimisation with respect to u exactly and the result is

$$u(t) = -\Psi(t)x(t) - \psi(t),$$

with

$$\hat{R} = R + \sum_{j=1}^{m} D_j^T P D_j \quad (p \times p), \qquad \hat{S} = B^T P + S + \sum_{j=1}^{m} D_j^T P C_j \quad (p \times n),$$

$$\Psi = \hat{R}^{-1}\hat{S} \quad (p \times n), \qquad\qquad \psi = \hat{R}^{-1}(B^T \alpha + \sum_{j=1}^{m} D_j^T P \sigma_j) \quad (p \times 1).$$

The stochastic HJB equation then decouples as three ordinary differential equations (Riccati equations)

$$-\dot{P} = PA + A^T P + \sum_{j=1}^{m} C_j^T P C_j + Q - \hat{S}^T \hat{R}^{-1}\hat{S}, \tag{17.19}$$

$$-\dot{\alpha} = [A - B\hat{R}^{-1}\hat{S}]^T \alpha + \sum_{j=1}^{m}[C_j - D_j\hat{R}^{-1}\hat{S}]^T P \sigma_j + Pb, \tag{17.20}$$

$$\dot{\beta} = \frac{1}{2}\left| \sqrt{\hat{R}}\psi \right|^2 - \alpha^T b - \frac{1}{2}\sum_{j=1}^{m}\sigma_j^T P \sigma_j. \tag{17.21}$$

The way to solve these equations is to first solve Eq. (17.19) for $P(t)$ with end condition $P(T) = G$. Use this solution in Eq. (17.20) to compute the solution for $\alpha(t)$ with end condition $\alpha(T) = 0$. Finally, $\beta(s) = -\int_s^T \dot{\beta}dt$ can be computed from Eq. (17.21).

17.4.4 Example of LQ control

Find the optimal control for the dynamics

$$\mathrm{d}x = (x + u)\mathrm{d}t + \mathrm{d}\xi, \qquad \left\langle \mathrm{d}\xi^2 \right\rangle = v\mathrm{d}t,$$

with end cost $\phi(x) = 0$ and path cost $R(x, u) = \frac{1}{2}(x^2 + u^2)$. The Riccati equations reduce to

$$-\dot{P} = 2P + 1 - P^2, \qquad -\dot{\alpha} = 0, \qquad \dot{\beta} = -\frac{1}{2}vP,$$

with $P(T) = \alpha(T) = \beta(T) = 0$ and $u(x, t) = -P(t)x$. We compute the solution for P and β by numerical integration. The result is shown in Fig. 17.1(b). The optimal control is to steer towards the origin with $-P(t)x$, where P is roughly constant until $T \approx 8$. Afterwards control weakens because the total future state cost reduces to zero when t approaches the end time. Note that in this example the optimal control is independent of v. It can be verified from the Riccati equations that this is true in general for 'non-multiplicative' noise ($C_j = D_j = 0$).

17.5 Learning

So far, we have assumed that all aspects that define the control problem are known. But in many instances this is not the case. What happens if (part of) the state is not observed? For instance, as a result of measurement error we do not know x_t but only a probability distribution $p(x_t|y_{0:t})$ given some previous observations $y_{0:t}$. Or, we observe x_t, but do not know the parameters of the dynamical equation (17.15). Or, we do not know the cost/rewards functions that appear in Eq. (17.16).

Using a Bayesian point of view, the agent can represent the uncertainty as beliefs, i.e. probability distributions over the hidden states, parameters or rewards. The optimal behaviour is then a trade-off between two objectives: choosing actions that optimise the expected future reward given the current beliefs and choosing actions that improve the accuracy of the beliefs. In other words, the agent faces the problem of finding the right compromise between learning and control, a problem which is known in control theory as dual control and was originally introduced by [6] (see [7] for a recent review). In addition to the observed state variables x, there are an additional number of variables θ that specify the belief distributions. The dual control solution is the ordinary control solution in this extended (x, θ) state space. The value function becomes a function of the extended state space and the Bellman equation describes the evolution in this extended state space. Some approaches to partially observed MDPs (POMDPs) [25, 15, 24] are an example of dual control problems.

A typical solution to the dual control problem for a finite time horizon problem is a control strategy that first chooses actions that explore the state space in order to learn a good model and use it at later times to maximise reward. In other words, the dual control problem solves the exploration exploitation problem by making explicit assumptions about the belief distributions. This is very reminiscent of our own life. Our life is finite and we have only one life. Our aim is to maximise accumulated reward during our lifetime, but in order to do so we have to allocate some resources to learning as well. It requires that we plan our learning and the learning problem becomes an integral part of the control problem. At $t = 0$, there is no knowledge of the world and thus making optimal control actions is impossible. At $t = T$, learning has become useless, because we will have no more opportunity to make use of it. So we should learn early in life and act later in life, as

Figure 17.2 When life is finite and is executed only one time, we should first learn and then act.

is schematically shown in Fig. 17.2. See [3] for a further discussion. We discuss a simple example in Section 17.5.1.

Note that reinforcement learning is typically defined as an adaptive control problem rather than a dual control problem. These approaches use beliefs that are specified in terms of hyperparameters θ, but the optimal cost-to-go is still a function of the original state x only. The Bellman equation is an evolution equation for $J(x)$ where unobserved quantities are given in terms of their expected values that depend on θ. This control problem is then in principle solved for fixed θ (although in reinforcement learning often a sample-based approach is taken and no strict convergence is enforced): θ is adapted as a result of the samples that are collected. In this formulation, the exploration exploitation dilemma arises since the control computation will propose actions that are only directed towards exploitation assuming the wrong θ (its optimal value still needs to be found). As a result, the state space is not fully explored and the updates for θ thus obtained are biased. The common heuristic to improve the learning is to mix these actions with 'exploratory actions' that explore the state space in directions that are not dictated by exploitation. Well-known examples of this approach are Bayesian reinforcement learning [5] and some older methods that are reviewed in [31]. Nevertheless, the principled solution is to explore all space, for instance by using a dedicated exploration strategy such as proposed in the E^3 algorithm [20].

In the case of finite time control problems the difference between the dual control formulation and the adaptive control formulation becomes particularly clear. The dual control formulation requires only one trial of the problem. It starts at $t = 0$ with its initial belief θ_0 and initial state x_0 and computes the optimal solution by solving the Bellman equation in the extended state space for all intermediate times until the horizon time T. The result is a single trajectory $(x_{1:T}, \theta_{1:T})$. The adaptive control formulation requires many trials. In each trial i, the control solution is computed by solving the Bellman equation in the ordinary state space where the beliefs are given by θ^i. The result is a trajectory $(x_{1:T}, \theta^i)$. Between trials, θ is updated using samples from the previous trial(s). Thus, in the adaptive control approach the learning problem is not solved as part of the control problem but rather in an 'outer loop'. The time scale for learning is unrelated to the horizon time T. In the dual control formulation, learning must take place in a single trial and is thus tightly related to T. Needless to say, the dual control formulation is more attractive than the adaptive control formulation, but is computationally significantly more costly.

17.5.1 Inference and control

As an example [10, 21], consider the LQ control problem

$$dx = \alpha u dt + d\xi$$

with α *unobserved* and x observed. The path cost $R(x, u, t)$, end cost $\phi(x)$ and noise variance ν are given. Although α is unobserved, we have a means to observe α indirectly through the sequence $x_t, u_t, t = 0, \dots$. Each time step we observe dx and u and we can thus update our belief about α using Bayes formula

$$p_{t+dt}(\alpha | dx, u) \propto p(dx | \alpha, u) p_t(\alpha) \tag{17.22}$$

with $p(dx|\alpha, u)$ a Normal distribution in dx with variance vdt and $p_t(\alpha)$ a probability distribution that expresses our belief at time t about the values of α. The problem is that the future information that we receive about α depends on u: if we use a large u, the term $\alpha u dt$ is larger than the noise term $d\xi$ and we will get reliable information about α. However, large u values are more costly and also may drive us away from our target state $x(T)$. Thus, the optimal control is a balance between optimal inference and minimal control cost. The solution is to augment the state space with parameters θ_t (sufficient statistics) that describe $p_t(\alpha) = p(\alpha|\theta_t)$ and θ_0 known, which describes our initial belief in the possible values of α. The cost that must be minimised is

$$C(x_0, \theta_0, u(0 \to T)) = \left\langle \phi(x(T)) + \int_0^T dt R(x, u, t) \right\rangle,$$

where the average is with respect to the noise $d\xi$ as well as the uncertainty in α.

For simplicity, consider the example that α attains only two values $\alpha = \pm 1$. Then $p_t(\alpha|\theta) = \sigma(\alpha\theta)$, with the sigmoid function $\sigma(x) = \frac{1}{2}(1 + \tanh(x))$. The update equation (17.22) implies a dynamics for θ:

$$d\theta = \frac{u}{v}dx = \frac{u}{v}(\alpha u dt + d\xi).$$

With $z_t = (x_t, \theta_t)$ we obtain a standard HJB (Eq. (17.17))

$$-\partial_t J(t, z)dt = \min_u \left(R(x, u, t)dt + \langle dz \rangle_z \partial_z J(z, t) + \frac{1}{2}\langle dz^2 \rangle_z \partial_z^2 J(z, t) \right)$$

with boundary condition $J(z, T) = \phi(x)$. The expectation values appearing in this equation are conditioned on (x_t, θ_t) and are averages over $p(\alpha|\theta_t)$ and the Gaussian noise. We compute $\langle dx \rangle_{x,\theta} = \bar{\alpha} u dt$, $\langle d\theta \rangle_{x,\theta} = \frac{\bar{\alpha} u^2}{v}dt$, $\langle dx^2 \rangle_{x,\theta} = vdt$, $\langle d\theta^2 \rangle_{x,\theta} = \frac{u^2}{v}dt$, $\langle dxd\theta \rangle = udt$, with $\bar{\alpha} = \tanh(\theta)$ the expected value of α for a given value θ. The result is

$$-\partial_t J = \min_u \left(R(x, u, t) + \bar{\alpha} u \partial_x J + \frac{u^2 \bar{\alpha}}{v} \partial_\theta J + \frac{1}{2} v \partial_x^2 J + \frac{1}{2} \frac{u^2}{v} \partial_\theta^2 J + u \partial_x \partial_\theta J \right)$$

with boundary conditions $J(x, \theta, T) = \phi(x)$. Thus the dual control problem (joint inference on α and control problem on x) has become an ordinary control problem in x, θ. Quoting [10]: 'It seems that any systematic formulation of the adaptive control problem leads to a meta-problem which is not adaptive.' Note also that the dynamics for θ is non-linear (due to the u^2 term) although the original dynamics for dx was linear. The solution to this non-linear stochastic control problem requires the solution of this PDE and was studied in [19]. An example of the optimal control solution $u(x, \theta, t)$ for $x = 2$ and different θ and t is given in Fig. 17.3. Note the 'probing' solution with u is much larger when α is uncertain (θ small) than when α is certain ($\theta = \pm\infty$). This exploration strategy is optimal in the dual control formulation. In [19] we further demonstrate that exploration is achieved through symmetry breaking in the Bellman equation; that optimal actions can be discontinuous in the beliefs (as in Fig. 17.3); and that the optimal value function is typically non-differentiable. This poses a challenge for the design of value function approximations for POMDPs, which typically assumes a smooth class of functions.

17.5.2 Certainty equivalence

Although in general adaptive control is much more complex than non-adaptive control, there exists an exception for a large class of linear quadratic problems, such as the Kalman filter [27]. Consider the dynamics

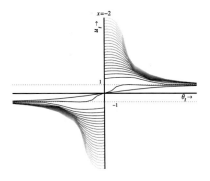

Figure 17.3 Dual control solution with end cost $\phi(x) = x^2$ and path cost $\int_t^{t_f} dt' \frac{1}{2} u(t')^2$ and $\nu = 0.5$. Plot shows the deviation of the control from the certain case: $u_t(x, \theta)/u_t(x, \theta = \pm\infty)$ as a function of θ for different values of t. The curves with the larger values are for larger times-to-go.

$$dx = (x + u)dt + d\xi, \quad y = x + \eta,$$

where now x is not observed, but y is observed and all other model parameters are known. When x is observed, we assume a quadratic cost

$$C(x_t, t, u_{t:T}) = \left\langle \sum_{\tau=t}^{T} \frac{1}{2}(x_\tau^2 + u_\tau^2) \right\rangle.$$

We denote the optimal control solution by $u(x, t)$. When x_t is not observed, we can compute $p(x_t|y_{0:t})$ using Kalman filtering and the optimal control minimises

$$C_{KF}(y_{0:t}, t, u_{t:T}) = \int dx_t p(x_t|y_{0:t}) C(x_t, t, u_{t:T}), \tag{17.23}$$

with C as above. Since $p(x_t|y_{0:t}) = \mathcal{N}(x_t|\mu_t, \sigma_t^2)$ is Gaussian, Eq. (17.23) becomes

$$\int dx_t C(x_t, t, u_{t:T}) \mathcal{N}(x_t|\mu_t, \sigma_t^2) = \sum_{\tau=t}^{T} \frac{1}{2} u_\tau^2 + \sum_{\tau=t}^{T} \left\langle x_\tau^2 \right\rangle_{\mu_t, \sigma_t},$$

which is

$$\sum_{\tau=t}^{T} \frac{1}{2} u_\tau^2 + \frac{1}{2}(\mu_t^2 + \sigma_t^2) + \frac{1}{2} \int dx_t \left\langle x_{t+dt}^2 \right\rangle_{x_t, \nu dt} \mathcal{N}(x_t|\mu_t, \sigma_t^2) + \cdots$$

$$= \sum_{\tau=t}^{T} \frac{1}{2} u_\tau^2 + \frac{1}{2}(\mu_t^2 + \sigma_t^2) + \frac{1}{2} \left\langle x_{t+dt}^2 \right\rangle_{\mu_t, \nu dt} + \frac{1}{2} \sigma_t^2 + \cdots$$

$$= C(\mu_t, t, u_{t:T}) + \frac{1}{2}(T - t)\sigma_t^2.$$

The first term is identical to the observed case with $x_t \to \mu_t$. The second term does not depend on u and thus does not affect the optimal control. Thus, the optimal control for the Kalman filter $u_{KF}(y_{0:t}, t)$ computed from C_{KF} is identical to the optimal control function $u(x, t)$ that is computed for the observed case C, with x_t replaced by μ_t: $u_{KF}(y_{0:t}, t) = u(\mu_t, t)$. This property is known as certainty equivalence [27], and implies that for these systems the control computation and the inference computation can be done separately, without loss of optimality.

17.6 Path integral control

As we have seen, the solution of the general stochastic optimal control problem requires the solution of a partial differential equation. This is for many realistic applications not an attractive option. The alternative considered often, is to approximate the problem somehow by a linear quadratic problem which can then be solved efficiently using the Riccati equations. In this section, we discuss a special class of non-linear, non-quadratic control problems for which some progress can be made [16, 17]. For this class of problems, the non-linear Hamilton–Jacobi–Bellman equation can be transformed into a linear equation by a log transformation of the cost-to-go. The transformation stems back to the early days of quantum mechanics and was first used by Schrödinger to relate the Hamilton–Jacobi formalism to the Schrödinger equation (a linear diffusion-like equation). The log transform was first used in the context of control theory by [8] (see also [9]).

Due to the linear description, the usual backward integration in time of the HJB equation can be replaced by computing expectation values under a forward diffusion process. The computation of the expectation value requires a stochastic integration over trajectories that can be described by a path integral. This is an integral over all trajectories starting at x, t, weighted by $\exp(-S/\lambda)$, where S is the cost of the path (also known as the action) and λ is a constant that is proportional to the noise.

The path integral formulation is well known in statistical physics and quantum mechanics, and several methods exist to compute path integrals approximately. The Laplace approximation approximates the integral by the path of minimal S. This approximation is exact in the limit of $v \to 0$, and the deterministic control law is recovered. In general, the Laplace approximation may not be sufficiently accurate. A very generic and powerful alternative is Monte Carlo (MC) sampling. The theory naturally suggests a naive sampling procedure, but it is also possible to devise more efficient samplers, such as importance sampling.

We illustrate the control method on two tasks: a temporal decision task, where the agent must choose between two targets at some future time; and a simple n joint arm. The decision task illustrates the issue of spontaneous symmetry breaking and how optimal behavior is qualitatively different for high and low noise. The n joint arm illustrates how the efficient approximate inference methods (the variational approximation in this case) can be used to compute optimal controls in very high dimensional problems.

17.6.1 Path integral control

Consider the special case of Eqs. (17.15) and (17.16) where the dynamic is linear in u and the cost is quadratic in u

$$dx_i = f_i(x, t)dt + \sum_{j=1}^{p} g_{ij}(x, t)(u_j dt + d\xi_j), \qquad (17.24)$$

$$R(x, u, t) = V(x, t) + \frac{1}{2}u^T R u \qquad (17.25)$$

with R a non-negative matrix. The functions $f_i(x, t)$, $g_{ij}(x, t)$ and $V(x, t)$ are arbitrary functions of x and t, and $\left\langle d\xi_j d\xi_{j'} \right\rangle = v_{jj'} dt$. In other words, the system to be controlled can be arbitrarily complex and subject to arbitrary complex costs. The control instead, is restricted to the simple linear-quadratic form when $g_{ij} = 1$ and in general must act in the same subspace as the noise. We will suppress all component notation from now on. Quantities such as f, u, x, dx are vectors and R, g, v are matrices. The stochastic HJB equation (17.17) becomes

$$-\partial_t J = \min_u \left(\frac{1}{2} u^T R u + V + (\nabla J)^T (f + gu) + \frac{1}{2} \mathrm{Tr} v g^T \nabla^2 J g \right).$$

Due to the linear-quadratic appearance of u, we can minimise with respect to u explicitly which yields

$$u = -R^{-1} g^T \nabla J, \tag{17.26}$$

which defines the optimal control u for each x, t. The HJB equation becomes

$$-\partial_t J = V + (\nabla J)^T f + \frac{1}{2} \mathrm{Tr} \left(-g R^{-1} g^T (\nabla J)(\nabla J)^T + g v g^T \nabla^2 J \right).$$

Note that after performing the minimisation with respect to u, the HJB equation has become non-linear in J. We can, however, remove the non-linearity which will help us to solve the HJB equation. Define $\psi(x, t)$ through $J(x, t) = -\lambda \log \psi(x, t)$. We further assume that there exists a constant λ such that the matrices R and v satisfy: $\lambda R^{-1} = v$.[1] This relation basically says that directions in which control is expensive should have low noise variance. It can also be interpreted as saying that all noise directions are controllable (in the correct proportion). Then the HJB becomes

$$-\partial_t \psi(x, t) = \left(-\frac{V}{\lambda} + f^T \nabla + \frac{1}{2} \mathrm{Tr} \left(g v g^T \nabla^2 \right) \right) \psi. \tag{17.27}$$

Equation (17.27) must be solved backwards in time with $\psi(x, T) = \exp(-\phi(x)/\lambda)$. The linearity allows us to reverse the direction of computation, replacing it by a diffusion process, in the following way. Let $\rho(y, \tau | x, t)$ describe a diffusion process for $\tau > t$ defined by the Fokker–Planck equation

$$\partial_\tau \rho = -\frac{V}{\lambda} \rho - \nabla^T (f\rho) + \frac{1}{2} \mathrm{Tr} \left(\nabla^2 (g v g^T \rho) \right) \tag{17.28}$$

with initial condition $\rho(y, t | x, t) = \delta(y - x)$. Note that when $V = 0$, Eq. (17.28) describes the evolution of diffusion process (17.24) with $u = 0$. Define $A(x, t) = \int dy \rho(y, \tau | x, t) \psi(y, \tau)$. It is easy to see by using the equations of motion (17.27) and 17.28 that $A(x, t)$ is independent of τ. Evaluating $A(x, t)$ for $\tau = t$ yields $A(x, t) = \psi(x, t)$. Evaluating $A(x, t)$ for $\tau = T$ yields $A(x, t) = \int dy \rho(y, T | x, t) \psi(x, T)$. Thus,

$$\psi(x, t) = \int dy \rho(y, T | x, t) \exp(-\phi(y)/\lambda). \tag{17.29}$$

The important conclusion is that the optimal cost-to-go $J(x, t) = -\lambda \log \psi(x, t)$ can be computed either by backward integration using Eq. (17.27) or by forward integration of a diffusion process given by Eq. (17.28). The optimal control is given by Eq. (17.26). Both Eq. (17.27) and Eq. (17.28) are partial differential equations and, although being linear, still suffer from the curse of dimensionality. However, the great advantage of the forward diffusion process is that it can be simulated using standard sampling methods which can efficiently approximate these computations. In addition, as is discussed in [17], the forward diffusion process $\rho(y, T | x, t)$ can be written as a path integral and in fact (17.29) becomes a path integral. This path integral can then be approximated using standard methods, such as the Laplace approximation.

---

[1] Strictly, the weaker condition $\lambda g(x, t) R^{-1} g^T (x, t) = g(x, t) v g^T (x, t)$ should hold.

Example: linear quadratic case

The class of control problems contains both additive and multiplicative cases. We give an example of both. Consider the control problem (17.24) and (17.25) for the simplest case of controlled free diffusion:

$$V(x, t) = 0, \quad f(x, t) = 0, \quad \phi(x) = \frac{1}{2}\alpha x^2.$$

In this case, the forward diffusion described by Eqs. 17.28 can be solved in closed form and is given by a Gaussian with variance $\sigma^2 = v(T - t)$:

$$\rho(y, T|x, t) = \frac{1}{\sqrt{2\pi}\sigma} \exp\left(-\frac{(y - x)^2}{2\sigma^2}\right).$$

Since the end cost is quadratic, the optimal cost-to-go (17.29) can be computed exactly as well. The result is

$$J(x, t) = vR \log\left(\frac{\sigma}{\sigma_1}\right) + \frac{1}{2}\frac{\sigma_1^2}{\sigma^2}\alpha x^2 \tag{17.30}$$

with $1/\sigma_1^2 = 1/\sigma^2 + \alpha/vR$. The optimal control is computed from Eq. (17.26):

$$u = -R^{-1}\partial_x J = -R^{-1}\frac{\sigma_1^2}{\sigma^2}\alpha x = -\frac{\alpha x}{R + \alpha(T - t)}.$$

We see that the control attracts x to the origin with a force that increases with t getting closer to T. Note that the optimal control is independent of the noise v as we also saw in the previous LQ example in Section 17.4.4.

Example: multiplicative case

Consider as a simple example of a multiplicative case, $f = 0, g = x, V = 0$ in one dimension and $R = 1$. Then the forward diffusion process reduces to

$$dx = x(u dt + d\xi) \tag{17.31}$$

and $x(t_i) = x_0$ for initial time t_i. If we define $y = \log x$ then

$$dy = \frac{dy}{dx}dx + \frac{1}{2}\frac{d^2y}{dx^2}dx^2 = u dt + d\xi - \frac{v}{2}dt$$

with $y(t_i) = \log x_0$ and the solution in terms of y is simply a Gaussian distribution

$$\tilde{\rho}(y', t|y, t_i) = \frac{1}{\sqrt{2\pi}\sigma} \exp(-(y' - y - (u - v/2)(t - t_i))^2/2\sigma^2)$$

with $\sigma^2 = (t - t_i)v$. In terms of x the solution becomes

$$\rho(x', t|x, t_i) = \frac{1}{x'}\tilde{\rho}(\log x', t|\log x, t_i). \tag{17.32}$$

The solution is shown in Fig. 17.4(a) for $u = 0$ and final time $t_f = 0.1, 0.5$ and $t_f = 2$. For $t_f = 0.5$ the solution is compared with forward simulation of Eq. (17.31). Note that the diffusion drifts towards the origin, which is caused by the state-dependent noise. The

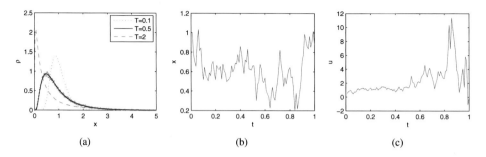

Figure 17.4 Optimal control for the one-dimensional multiplicative process (17.31) with quadratic control cost $\int_{t_1}^{t_f} dt \frac{1}{2} u(t)^2$ to reach a fixed target $x' = 1$, starting from an initial position $x = 1$. (a) $p(x', t_f | x = 1, t_i = 0)$ vs. x' for $t_f = 0.1, 0.5, 2$ and shows the forward diffusion solution in the absence of control (17.32) which is used to compute the optimal control solution (17.33). (b) Optimal trajectory $x(t)$. (c) Optimal control $u(t)$.

noise is proportional to x and therefore the conditional probability $p(x_{\text{small}} | x_{\text{large}})$ is greater than the reverse probability $p(x_{\text{large}} | x_{\text{small}})$. This results in a net drift towards small x. From Eq. (17.32), we can compute the optimal control. Consider the control task to steer to a fixed end point x' from an arbitrary initial point x. Then,

$$\psi(x,t) = p(x', t_f | x, t) = \frac{1}{\sqrt{2\pi vT}} \frac{1}{x'} \exp\left(-(\log(x') - \log(x) + vT/2)^2 / 2vT\right),$$

$$J(x,t) = -v \log \psi(x,t) = v \log \sqrt{2\pi vT} + v \log x' + (\log(x') - \log(x) + vT/2)^2 / 2T,$$

$$u(x,t) = -x \frac{dJ(x,t)}{dx} = \frac{1}{T} \log\left(\frac{x'}{x}\right) + v/2, \tag{17.33}$$

with $T = t_f - t$. The first term attracts x to x' with strength increasing in $1/T$ as usual. The second term is a constant positive drift, to counter the tendency of the uncontrolled process to drift towards the origin. An example of the solution for a task to steer from $x = 1$ at $t = 0$ to $x = 1$ at $t = 1$ is shown in Fig. 17.4(b) and Fig. 17.4(c).

17.6.2 The diffusion process as a path integral

The diffusion equation (17.28) contains three terms. The second and third terms describe drift $f(x,t)dt$ and diffusion $g(x,t)d\xi$ as in Eq. (17.24) with $u = 0$. The first term describes a process that kills a sample trajectory with a rate $V(x,t)dt/\lambda$. This term does not conserve the probability mass. Thus, the solution of Eq. (17.28) can be obtained by sampling the following process

$$dx = f(x,t)dt + g(x,t)d\xi,$$
$$x = x + dx, \quad \text{with probability } 1 - V(x,t)dt/\lambda,$$
$$x_i = \dagger, \quad \text{with probability } V(x,t)dt/\lambda. \tag{17.34}$$

We can thus obtain a sampling estimate of

$$\psi(x,t) = \int dy \rho(y, T | x, t) \exp(-\phi(y)/\lambda) \approx \frac{1}{N} \sum_{i \in \text{alive}} \exp(-\phi(x_i(T))/\lambda) \tag{17.35}$$

by computing N trajectories $x_i(t \to T), i = 1, \ldots, N$. Each trajectory starts at the same value x and is sampled using the dynamics (17.35). 'Alive' denotes the subset of trajectories that do not get killed along the way by the † operation. The diffusion process can formally be 'solved' as a path integral. We restrict ourselves to the simplest case $g_{ij}(x, t) = \delta_{ij}$. The general case can also be written as a path integral, but is somewhat more involved. The argument follows simply by splitting the time interval $[t, T]$ into a large number n of infinitesimal intervals $[t, t + dt]$. For each small interval, $\rho(y, t + dt | x, t)$ is a product of a Gaussian distribution due to the drift f and diffusion $gd\xi$, and the annihilation process $\exp(-V(x, t)dt/\lambda)$: $\rho(y, t + dt | x, t) = \mathcal{N}(y | x + f(x, t)dt, v)$. We can then compute $\rho(y, T | x, t)$ by multiplying all these infinitesimal transition probabilities and integrating the intermediate variables y. The result is

$$\rho(y, T | x, t) = \int [dx]_x^y \exp\left(-\frac{1}{\lambda} S_{\text{path}}(x(t \to T))\right),$$

$$S_{\text{path}}(x(t \to T)) = \int_t^T d\tau \frac{1}{2} (\dot{x}(\tau) - f(x(\tau), \tau))^T R(\dot{x}(\tau) - f(x(\tau), \tau)) + \int_t^T d\tau V(x(\tau), \tau).$$

(17.36)

Combining Eq. (17.36) and Eq. (17.29), we obtain the cost-to-go as

$$\psi(x, t) = \int [dx]_x \exp\left(-\frac{1}{\lambda} S(x(t \to T))\right),$$

$$S(x(t \to T)) = S_{\text{path}}(x(t \to T)) + \phi(x(T)).$$

(17.37)

Note that ψ has the general form of a partition sum, S is the energy of a path and λ the temperature. The corresponding probability distribution is

$$p(x(t \to T) | x, t) = \frac{1}{\psi(x, t)} \exp\left(-\frac{1}{\nu} S(x(t \to T))\right).$$

The function $J = -\lambda \log \psi$ can be interpreted as a free-energy. See [17] for details. Although we have solved the optimal control problem formally as a path integral, we are still left with the problem of computing the path integral. Here one can resort to various standard methods such as Monte Carlo sampling [17] of which the naive forward sampling (17.34) is an example. One can however, improve on this naive scheme using importance sampling where one changes the drift term such as to minimise the annihilation of the diffusion by the $-V(x, t)dt/\lambda$ term.

A particularly cheap approximation is the Laplace approximation, that finds the trajectory that minimises S in Eq. (17.37). This approximation is exact in the limit of $\lambda \to 0$ which is the noiseless limit. The Laplace approximation gives the classical path. One particular effective forward importance sampling method is to use the classical path as a drift term. We will give an example of the naive and importance forward sampling scheme below for the double slit problem.

One can also use a variational approximation to approximate the path integral using the variational approach for diffusion processes [1], or use the EP approximation [22]. An illustration of the variational approximation to a simple n joint arm is presented in Section 17.7.2.

17.7 Approximate inference methods for control

17.7.1 Monte Carlo sampling

In this section, we illustrate the path integral control method for the simple example of a double slit. The example is sufficiently simple that we can compute the optimal control solution in closed form. We use this example to compare the Monte Carlo and Laplace approximations to the exact result. Consider a stochastic particle that moves with constant velocity from t to T in the horizontal direction and where there is deflecting noise in the x direction:

$$dx = udt + d\xi. \tag{17.38}$$

The cost is given by Eq. (17.25) with $\phi(x) = \frac{1}{2}x^2$ and $V(x, t_1)$ implements a slit at an intermediate time t_1, $t < t_1 < T$:

$$V(x, t_1) = 0, \quad a < x < b, \quad c < x < d,$$
$$= \infty, \quad \text{otherwise.}$$

The problem is illustrated in Fig. 17.5(a) where the constant motion is in the t (horizontal) direction and the noise and control is in the x (vertical) direction. The cost-to-go can be solved in closed form. The result for $t > t_1$ is a simple linear quadratic control problem for which the solution is given by Eq. (17.30) and for $t < t_1$ is [17]:

$$J(x, t) = vR \log\left(\frac{\sigma}{\sigma_1}\right) + \frac{1}{2}\frac{\sigma_1^2}{\sigma^2}x^2 - vR \log\frac{1}{2}\left(F(b, x) - F(a, x) + F(d, x) - F(c, x)\right) \tag{17.39}$$

$$F(x_0, x) = \text{Erf}\left(\sqrt{\frac{A}{2v}}\left(x_0 - \frac{B(x)}{A}\right)\right), \quad A = \frac{1}{t_1 - t} + \frac{1}{R + T - t_1}, \quad B(x) = \frac{x}{t_1 - t}.$$

The solution (17.39) is shown for $t = 0$ in Fig. 17.5(b). We can compute the optimal control from Eq. (17.26).

We assess the quality of the naive MC sampling scheme, as given by Eqs. (17.34) and (17.35) in Fig. 17.5(b) and Fig. 17.5(c). Figure 17.5(b) shows the sampling trajectories of

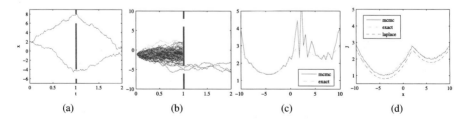

Figure 17.5 Double slit experiment. (a) Setup of the experiment. Particles travel from $t = 0$ to $t = 2$ under dynamics (17.38). A slit is placed at time $t = t_1$, blocking all particles by annihilation. Two trajectories are shown under optimal control. (b) Naive Monte Carlo sampling trajectories to compute $J(x = -1, t = 0)$ through Eq. (17.35). Only trajectories that pass through a slit contribute to the estimate. (c) Comparison of naive MC estimates with $N = 100\,000$ trajectories and exact result for $J(x, t = 0)$ for all x. (d) Comparison of Laplace approximation (dotted line) and Monte Carlo importance sampling (solid jagged line) of $J(x, t = 0)$ with exact result (17.39) (solid smooth line). The importance sampler used $N = 100$ trajectories for each x. See plate section for colour version.

the naive MC sampling procedure for one particular value of x. Note the inefficiency of the sampler because most of the trajectories are killed at the infinite potential at $t = t_1$. Figure 17.5(c) shows the accuracy of the naive MC sampling estimate of $J(x, 0)$ for all x between -10 and 10 using $N = 100\,000$ trajectories. We note that the number of trajectories that are required to obtain accurate results strongly depends on the initial value of x due to the annihilation at $t = t_1$. As a result, low values of the cost-to-go are more easy to sample accurately than high values. In addition, the efficiency of the sampling procedures depends strongly on the noise level. For small noise, the trajectories spread less by themselves and it is harder to generate trajectories that do not get annihilated. In other words, sampling becomes more accurate for high noise, which is a well-known general feature of sampling.

The sampling is particularly difficult in this example because of the infinite potential that annihilates most of the trajectories. However, similar effects will be observed in general due to the multi-modality of the Action. We can improve the importance sampling procedure using the Laplace approximation (see [17]). The Laplace approximation in this case are the two piece-wise linear trajectories that pass through one of the slits to the goal. The Laplace approximation and the results of the importance sampler are given in Fig. 17.5(d). The Laplace approximation is quite good for this example, in particular when one takes into account that a constant shift in J does not affect the optimal control. The MC importance sampler dramatically improves over the naive MC results in Fig. 17.5, in particular since 1000 times less samples are used and is also significantly better than the Laplace approximation.

17.7.2 The variational method

We consider a particularly simple realisation of an n joint arm in two dimensions, each joint having length 1. The location of the ith joint in the 2d plane is

$$x_i = \sum_{j=1}^{i} \cos \theta_i, \quad y_i = \sum_{j=1}^{i} \sin \theta_i$$

with $i = 1, \ldots, n$. Each of the joint angles is controlled by a variable u_i. The dynamics of each joint is, for independent Gaussian noise $d\xi_i$ with $\langle d\xi_i^2 \rangle = \nu dt$,

$$d\theta_i = u_i dt + d\xi_i, \quad i = 1, \ldots, n.$$

Denote by θ the vector of joint angles, and u the vector of controls. The expected cost for control path $u_{t:T}$ is

$$C(\theta, t, u_{t:T}) = \left\langle \phi(\theta(T)) + \int_t^T \frac{1}{2} u^T(t)\, u(t) \right\rangle,$$

$$\phi(\theta) = \frac{\alpha}{2} \left((x_n(\theta) - x_{\text{target}})^2 + (y_n(\theta) - y_{\text{target}})^2 \right),$$

with $x_{\text{target}}, y_{\text{target}}$ the target coordinates of the end joint. Because the state-dependent path cost V and the intrinsic dynamics of f are zero, the solution to the diffusion process (17.34) that starts with the arm in the configuration θ^0 is a Gaussian so that Eq. (17.29) becomes[2]

---

[2]This is not exactly correct because θ is a periodic variable. One should use the solution to diffusion on a circle instead. We can ignore this as long as $\sqrt{\nu(T - t)}$ is small compared to 2π.

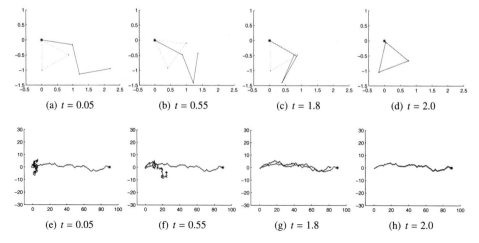

(a) $t = 0.05$ (b) $t = 0.55$ (c) $t = 1.8$ (d) $t = 2.0$

(e) $t = 0.05$ (f) $t = 0.55$ (g) $t = 1.8$ (h) $t = 2.0$

Figure 17.6 (a)–(d) Path integral control of a $n = 3$ joint arm. The objective is that the end joint reaches a target location at the end time $T = 2$. Solid line: current joint configuration in Cartesian coordinates (x, y) corresponding to the angle state θ_0 at time t. Dashed: expected joint configuration computed at the horizon time $T = 2$ corresponding to the expected angle state $\langle \theta \rangle$ from Eq. (17.41) with θ^0 the current joint position. Target location of the end effector is at the origin, resulting in a triangular configuration for the arm. As time t increases, each joint moves to its expected target location due to the control law (17.40). At the same time the expected configuration is recomputed, resulting in a different triangular arm configuration. (e)–(h). Same, with $n = 100$.

$$\psi(\theta^0, t) = \int d\theta \left(\frac{1}{\sqrt{2\pi \nu(T-t)}} \right)^n \exp\left(-\sum_{i=1}^{n} (\theta_i - \theta_i^0)^2 / 2\nu(T-t) - \phi(\theta)/\nu \right).$$

The control at time t for all components i is computed from Eq. (17.26) and is

$$u_i = \frac{1}{T-t} \left(\langle \theta_i \rangle - \theta_i^0 \right), \tag{17.40}$$

where $\langle \theta_i \rangle$ is the expectation value of θ_i computed w.r.t. the probability distribution

$$p(\theta) = \frac{1}{\psi(\theta^0, t)} \exp\left(-\sum_{i=1}^{n} (\theta_i - \theta_i^0)^2 / 2\nu(T-t) - \phi(\theta)/\nu \right). \tag{17.41}$$

Thus the stochastic optimal control problem reduces the inference problem to computing $\langle \theta_i \rangle$. There are several ways to compute this. One can use a simple importance sampling scheme, where the proposal distribution is the n-dimensional Gaussian centred on θ^0 (first term in Eq. (17.41)) and where samples are weighted with $\exp(-\phi(\theta)/\nu)$. This does not work very well (results not shown). One can also use a Metropolis Hastings method with a Gaussian proposal distribution. This works quite well (results not shown). One can also use a very simple variational method which we will now discuss.

The expectations $\langle \theta \rangle$ are found using a factorised Gaussian variational approximation $q(\theta) = \prod_{i=1}^{n} \mathcal{N}(\theta_i | \mu_i, \sigma_i)$ to $p(\theta)$ in Eq. (17.41). We compute μ_i and σ_i by minimising the divergence $KL(q|p) \equiv \langle \log q(\theta)/p(\theta) \rangle_{q(\theta)}$, which equals, up to a constant,

$$-\sum_{i=1}^{n} \log \sqrt{2\pi \sigma_i^2} + \log \psi(\theta^0, t) + \frac{1}{2\nu(T-t)} \sum_{i=1}^{n} \left(\sigma_i^2 + (\mu_i - \theta_i^0)^2 \right) + \frac{1}{\nu} \langle \phi(\theta) \rangle_q.$$

Because ϕ is quadratic in x_n and y_n and these are defined in terms of sines and cosines, the $\langle \phi(\theta) \rangle$ can be computed in closed form. The computation of the variational equations result from setting the derivative of the KL with respect to μ_i and σ_i^2 equal to zero. The result is, for $\Delta x \equiv \langle x_n \rangle - x_{\text{target}}$, $\Delta y \equiv \langle y_n \rangle - y_{\text{target}}$,

$$\mu_i \leftarrow \theta_i^0 + \alpha(T - t)\left(\sin \mu_i e^{-\sigma_i^2/2} - \cos \mu_i e^{-\sigma_i^2/2}\Delta y\right)$$

$$\frac{1}{\sigma_i^2} \leftarrow \frac{1}{\nu}\left(\frac{1}{(T-t)} + \alpha e^{-\sigma_i^2} - \alpha\Delta x \cos \mu_i e^{-\sigma_i^2/2} - \alpha\Delta y \sin \mu_i e^{-\sigma_i^2/2}\right).$$

The converged estimate for $\langle \theta_i \rangle$ is μ_i. The problem is illustrated in Fig. 17.6.

Note that the computation of $\langle \theta_i \rangle$ solves the coordination problem between the different joints. Once $\langle \theta_i \rangle$ is known, each θ_i is steered independently to its target value $\langle \theta_i \rangle$ using the control law (17.40). The computation of $\langle \theta_i \rangle$ in the variational approximation is very efficient and can be used to control arms with hundreds of joints.

17.8 Discussion

We have given a basic introduction to some notions in optimal deterministic and stochastic control theory and have discussed recent work on the path integral methods for stochastic optimal control. We would like to mention a few additional issues.

One can extend the path integral control formalism to multiple agents that jointly solve a task. In this case the agents need to coordinate their actions not only through time, but also among each other to maximise a common reward function. The approach is very similar to the *n*-joint problem that we studied in the last section. The problem can be mapped to a graphical model inference problem and the solution can be computed exactly using the junction tree algorithm [37, 38] or approximately [35, 34].

There is a relation between the path integral approach discussed and the linear control formulation proposed in [32]. In that work the discrete space and time case is considered and it is shown, that if the immediate cost can be written as a KL divergence between the controlled dynamics and a passive dynamics, the Bellman equation becomes linear in a very similar way as we derived for the continuous case in Eq. (17.27). In [33] it was further observed that the linear Bellman equation can be interpreted as a backward message passing equation in a HMM. In [18] we have taken this analogy one step further. When the immediate cost is a KL divergence between transition probabilities for the controlled and passive dynamics, the total control cost is also a KL divergence between probability distributions describing controlled trajectories and passive trajectories. Therefore, the optimal control solution can be directly inferred as a Gibbs distribution. The optimal control computation reduces to the probabilistic inference of a marginal distribution on the first and second time slice. This problem can be solved using efficient approximate inference methods. We also show how the path integral control problem is obtained as a special case of this KL control formulation.

The path integral approach has recently been applied to the control of character animation [4]. In this work the linearity of the Bellman equation (17.27) and its solution (17.29) is exploited by noting that if ψ_1 and ψ_2 are solutions for end costs ϕ_1 and ϕ_2, then $\psi_1 + \psi_2$ is a solution to the control problem with end cost $-\lambda \log \left(\exp(-\phi_1/\lambda) + \exp(-\phi_2/\lambda)\right)$. Thus, by computing the control solution to a limited number of archetypal tasks, one can efficiently obtain solutions for arbitrary combinations of these tasks. In robotics, [30, 28, 29] have shown that the path integral method has great potential for application in robotics. They have compared the path integral method with some state-of-the-art reinforcement learning methods, showing very significant improvements. In addition, they have successfully implemented the path integral control method to a walking robot dog.

Acknowledgments   This work is supported in part by the Dutch Technology Foundation and the BSIK/ICIS project.

Bibliography

[1] C. Archambeau, M. Opper, Y. Shen, D. Cornford and J. Shawe-Taylor. Variational inference for diffusion processes. In D. Koller and Y. Singer, editors, *Advances in Neural Information Processing Systems 19*. MIT Press, 2008.

[2] R. Bellman and R. Kalaba. *Selected Papers on Mathematical Trends in Control Theory*. Dover, 1964.

[3] D. P. Bertsekas. *Dynamic Programming and Optimal Control*. Second edition Athena Scientific, 2000.

[4] M. da Silva, F. Durand and J. Popović. Linear Bellman combination for control of character animation. In *SIGGRAPH '09: ACM SIGGRAPH 2009 papers*, pages 1–10, New York, 2009. ACM.

[5] R. Dearden, N. Friedman and D. Andre. Model based bayesian exploration. In *Proceedings of the Fifteenth Conference on Uncertainty in Artificial Intelligence*, pages 150–159, 1999.

[6] A. A. Feldbaum. Dual control theory. I–IV. *Automation remote control*, **21–22**:874–880, 1033–1039, 1–12, 109–121, 1960.

[7] N. M. Filatov and H. Unbehauen. *Adaptive Dual Control*. Springer-Verlag, 2004.

[8] W. H. Fleming. Exit probabilities and optimal stochastic control. *Applied Mathematics and Optimization*, **4**:329–346, 1978.

[9] W. H. Fleming and H. M. Soner. *Controlled Markov Processes and Viscosity solutions*. Springer-Verlag, 1992.

[10] J. J. Florentin. Optimal, probing, adaptive control of a simple Bayesian system. *International Journal of Electronics*, **13**:165–177, 1962.

[11] G. Fraser-Andrews. A multiple-shooting technique for optimal control. *Journal of Optimization Theory and Applications*, **102**:299–313, 1999.

[12] H. Goldstein. *Classical Mechanics*. Addison Wesley, 1980.

[13] M. T. Heath. *Scientific Computing: An Introductory Survey*. McGraw-Hill, 2002. 2nd edition.

[14] U. Jönsson, C. Trygger and P. Ögren. Lectures on optimal control. Unpublished, 2002.

[15] L. P. Kaelbling, M. L. Littman and A. R. Cassandra. Planning and acting in partially observable stochastic domains. *Artificial Intelligence*, **101**:99–134, 1998.

[16] H. J. Kappen. A linear theory for control of non-linear stochastic systems. *Physical Review Letters*, **95**:200201, 2005.

[17] H. J. Kappen. Path integrals and symmetry breaking for optimal control theory. *Journal of Statistical Mechanics: Theory and Experiment*, page P11011, 2005.

[18] H. J. Kappen, V. Gómez and M. Opper. Optimal control as a graphical model inference problem. http://arxiv.org/abs/0901.0633.

[19] H. J. Kappen and S. Tonk. Optimal exploration as a symmetry breaking phenomenon. Technical report, 2010.

[20] M. Kearns and S. Singh. Near-optimal reinforcement learning in polynomial time. *Machine Learning*, pages 209–232, 2002.

[21] P. R. Kumar. Optimal adaptive control of linear-quadratic-Gaussian systems. *SIAM Journal on Control and Optimization*, **21**(2):163–178, 1983.

[22] T. Mensink, J. Verbeek and H. J. Kappen. EP for Efficient Stochastic Control with Obstacles. In *ECAI*, pages 1–6 2010.

[23] L. S. Pontryagin, V. G. Boltyanskii, R. V. Gamkrelidze and E. F. Mishchenko. *The Mathematical Theory of Optimal Processes*. Interscience, 1962.

[24] P. Poupart and N. Vlassis. Model-based Bayesian reinforcement learning in partially observable domains. In *Proceedings International Symposium on Artificial Intelligence and Mathematics (ISAIM)*, 2008.

[25] E. J. Sondik. The optimal control of partially observable Markov processes. PhD thesis, Stanford University, 1971.

[26] R. Stengel. *Optimal Control and Estimation*. Dover publications, 1993.

[27] H. Theil. A note on certainty equivalence in dynamic planning. *Econometrica*, **25**:346–349, 1957.

[28] E. Theodorou, J. Buchli and S. Schaal. Learning policy improvements with path integrals. In *International Conference on Artificial Intelligence and Statistics*, 2010.

[29] E. Theodorou, J. Buchli and S. Schaal. Reinforcement learning of motor skills in high dimensions: a path integral approach. In *International Conference of Robotics and Automation*, 2010.

[30] E. A. Theodorou, J. Buchli and S. Schaal. Path integral-based stochastic optimal control for rigid body dynamics. In *Adaptive Dynamic Programming and Reinforcement Learning, 2009. ADPRL '09. ieee symposium on*, pages 219–225, 2009.

[31] S. B. Thrun. The role of exploration in learning control. In D. A. White and D. A. Sofge, editors, *Handbook of Intelligent Control*. Multiscience Press, 1992.

[32] E. Todorov. Linearly-solvable Markov decision problems. In B. Schölkopf, J. Platt, and T. Hoffman, editors, *Advances in Neural Information Processing Systems 19*, pages 1369–1376. MIT Press, 2007.

[33] E. Todorov. General duality between optimal control and estimation. In *47th IEEE Conference on Decision and Control*, pages 4286–4292, 2008.

[34] B. van den Broek, W. Wiegerinck, and H. J. Kappen. Graphical model inference in optimal control of stochastic multi-agent systems. *Journal of AI Research*, **32**:95–122, 2008.

[35] B. van den Broek, W. Wiegerinck and H. J. Kappen. Optimal control in large stochastic multi-agent systems. In *Adaptive Agents and Multi-Agent Systems III. Adaptation and Multi-Agent Learning*, volume 4865/2008, pages 15–26. Springer, 2008.

[36] R. Weber. Lecture notes on optimization and control. Lecture notes of a course given autumn 2006, 2006.

[37] W. Wiegerinck, B. van den Broek and H. J. Kappen. Stochastic optimal control in continuous space-time multi-agent systems. In *Uncertainty in Artificial Intelligence. Proceedings of the 22th conference*, pages 528–535. Association for UAI, 2006.

[38] W. Wiegerinck, B. van den Broek and H. J. Kappen. Optimal on-line scheduling in stochastic multi-agent systems in continuous space and time. In *Proceedings AAMAS*, page 8, 2007.

[39] J. Yong and X.Y. Zhou. *Stochastic Controls. Hamiltonian Systems and HJB Equations.* Springer, 1999.

Contributor

Hilbert J. Kappen, Donders' Institute for Neuroscience, Radboud University, 6525 EZ Nijmegen, The Netherlands

18

Expectation maximisation methods for solving (PO)MDPs and optimal control problems

Marc Toussaint, Amos Storkey and Stefan Harmeling

18.1 Introduction

As this book demonstrates, the development of efficient probabilistic inference techniques has made considerable progress in recent years, in particular with respect to exploiting the structure (e.g., factored, hierarchical or relational) of discrete and continuous problem domains. In this chapter we show that these techniques can be used also for solving Markov decision processes (MDPs) or partially observable MDPs (POMDPs) when formulated in terms of a structured dynamic Bayesian network (DBN).

The problems of planning in stochastic environments and inference in state space models are closely related, in particular in view of the challenges both of them face: scaling to large state spaces spanned by multiple state variables, or realising planning (or inference) in continuous or mixed continuous-discrete state spaces. Both fields developed techniques to address these problems. For instance, in the field of planning, they include work on factored Markov decision processes [5, 17, 9, 18], abstractions [10], and relational models of the environment [37]. On the other hand, recent advances in inference techniques show how structure can be exploited both for exact inference as well as for making efficient approximations. Examples are message-passing algorithms (loopy belief propagation, expectation propagation), variational approaches, approximate belief representations (particles, assumed density filtering, Boyen–Koller) and arithmetic compilation (see, e.g., [22, 23, 7]).

In view of these similarities one may ask whether existing techniques for probabilistic inference can directly be translated to solving stochastic planning problems. From a complexity theoretic point of view, the equivalence between inference and planning is well known (see, e.g., [19]). Inference methods have been applied before to optimal decision making in influence diagrams [8, 25, 29]. However, contrary to MDPs, these methods focus on a finite number of decisions and a non-stationary policy, where optimal decisions are found by recursing backward starting from the last decision (see [4] and [31] for a discussion of MDPs versus influence diagrams). More recently, [6] have used inference on abstract hidden Markov models for policy recognition, i.e., for reasoning about executed behaviours, but do not address the problem of computing optimal policies from such inference. Reference [2] proposed a framework which suggests a straightforward way to translate the problem of planning to a problem of inference: A Markovian state-action model is assumed, which is conditioned on a start state s_0 and a goal state s_T. Here, however, the total time T has to be fixed ad hoc and the MAP action sequence that is proposed as a solution is not optimal in the sense of maximising an expected future reward. The authors in [28] introduced the same idea independently in the context of continuous state stochastic control and called this optimistic inference control. The authors in [35] used inference to compute plans (considering the maximal probable explanation (MPE) instead of the MAP action sequence) but again the total time has to be fixed and the plan is not optimal in the expected return sense.

We provide a framework that translates the problem of maximising the discounted expected future return in the infinite-horizon MDP (or general DBN) into a problem of likelihood maximisation in a related mixture of finite-time MDPs. This allows us to use expectation maximisation (EM) for computing optimal policies, utilising arbitrary inference techniques in the E-step. We can show that this optimises the discounted expected future return for arbitrary reward functions and without assuming an ad hoc finite total time. The approach is generally applicable on any DBN-description of the problem whenever we have efficient inference techniques for this structure. Dynamic Bayesian networks allow us to consider structured representations of the environment (the world state) as well as the agent (or multiple agents, in fact).

The next section introduces our likelihood maximisation approach for solving Markov decision processes. This will involve the introduction of a mixture of variable length DBNs for which we can show equivalence between likelihood maximisation and maximisation of expected future return. Section 18.3 in detail derives an EM algorithm. Here, the key is efficient inference algorithms that handle the mixture of variable length processes. The derived algorithms are applicable on arbitrary structured DBNs. In Section 18.4 we reconsider the basic MDP case, explain the relation of the EM algorithm to policy and value iteration, and demonstrate the approach using exact inference on a discrete maze and Gaussian belief state propagation in non-linear stochastic optimal control problems.

In Section 18.5 we consider a non-trivial DBN representation of a POMDP problem. We propose a certain model of an agent (similar to finite state controllers, FSCs) that uses an internal memory variable as a sufficient representation of history which gates a reactive policy. We use this to learn sufficient memory representations (e.g., counting aisles) and primitive reactive behaviours (e.g., aisle or wall following) in some partially observable maze problems. This can be seen by analogy to the classical machine learning paradigm of learning latent variable models of data for bootstrapping interesting internal representations (e.g., independent components analysis) – but here generalised to the learning of latent variable models of successful behaviour. Section 18.6 will conclude this chapter and discuss existing follow-up work and future directions of research.

18.2 Markov decision processes and likelihood maximisation

A Markov decision process ([15]) is a stochastic process on the random variables of state s_t, action a_t, and reward r_t, as defined by the

initial state distribution	$P(s_0 = s)$,
transition probability	$P(s_{t+1} = s' \mid a_t = a, s_t = s)$,
reward probability	$P(r_t = r \mid a_t = a, s_t = s)$,
policy	$P(a_t = a \mid s_t = s; \pi) =: \pi_{as}$.

We assume the process to be stationary (none of these quantities explicitly depends on time) and call the expectation $\mathcal{R}(a, s) = \mathrm{E}\{r \mid a, s\} = \sum_r r \, P(r \mid a, s)$ the reward function. In

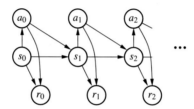

Figure 18.1 Dynamic Bayesian network for an MDP. The x states denote the state variables, a the actions and r the rewards.

model-based reinforcement learning the transition and reward probabilities are estimated from experience (see, e.g., [1]). In Section 18.6.1 we discuss follow-up work that extends our framework to the model-free case. The random variables s_t and a_t can be discrete or continuous whereas the reward r_t is a real number. Figure 18.1 displays the dynamic Bayesian network for an infinite-horizon Markov decision process.

The free parameter of this DBN is the policy π with numbers $\pi_{as} \in [0, 1]$ normalised w.r.t. a. The problem we address is *solving the MDP*:

Definition 18.2.1. *Solving an MDP means to find a parameter π of the infinite-horizon DBN in Fig. 18.1 that maximises the expected future return $V^\pi = \mathrm{E}\{\sum_{t=0}^{\infty} \gamma^t r_t; \pi\}$, where $\gamma \in [0, 1)$ is a discount factor.*

The classical approach to solving MDPs is anchored in Bellman's equation, which simply reflects the recursive property of the future discounted return

$$\sum_{t=0}^{\infty} \gamma^t r_t = r_0 + \gamma \left[\sum_{t=0}^{\infty} \gamma^t r_{t+1} \right],$$

and consequently of its expectation conditioned on the current state,

$$V^\pi(s) = \mathrm{E}\{\sum_{t=0}^{\infty} \gamma^t r_t \mid s_0 = s; \pi\} = \sum_{s',a} P(s'|a, s) \pi_{as} \left[\mathcal{R}(a, s) + \gamma V^\pi(s') \right].$$

Standard algorithms for computing value functions can be viewed as iterative schemes that converge towards the Bellman equation or as directly solving this linear equation w.r.t. V by matrix inversion.

In contrast, our general approach is to translate the problem of solving an MDP into a problem of likelihood maximisation. There are different approaches for such a translation. One issue to be considered is that the quantity we want to maximise (the expected future return) is a *sum* of expectations in every time slice, whereas the likelihood in Markovian models is the *product* of observation likelihoods in each time slice. A first idea for achieving equivalence is to introduce exponentiated rewards as observation likelihoods – but that turns out non-equivalent (see Remark (iii) in Appendix 18.A).

The authors in [34, 33] introduced an alternative based on a mixture of finite-length processes. Intuitively, the key argument for this approach is perhaps the question *Where do I start the backward sweep?* In all EM approaches we need to compute a posterior over trajectories in the E-step so that we can update the policy in the M-step. In finite-length Markov processes, such inference can efficiently be done by a forward-backward sweep (Baum–Welch). If the process is infinite it is unclear where in the future to start (anchor) the backward sweep. However, when introducing a binary reward event there is a very

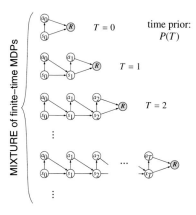

MIXTURE of finite-time MDPs

Figure 18.2 Mixture of finite-time MDPs.

intuitive solution to this: Let us simply declare that the reward event occurs at some time T in the future, without knowing what T is, and we start the backward sweep from that time T backward. In that way we can start computing backward and forward messages in parallel without having to estimate some horizon ad hoc, and decide when to stop if there is sufficient overlap between the forward and backward propagated messages [34]. When we choose a geometric prior $P(T) = (1 - \gamma)\gamma^t$ this turns out to implement the discounting correctly.

The mixture model is in some respects different to the original MDP but the likelihood of 'observing reward' in this mixture model is proportional to the expected future return in the original MDP. The reasons for this choice of approach are related to inference (performing a backward pass) without pre-fixing a finite time horizon T, the handling of discounting rewards, and also to the resulting relations to standard policy and value iteration, as it will later become more clear.

We define the mixture model as follows. Let $\xi = (s_{0:T}, a_{0:T})$ denote a state-action sequence of length T, and let R be a random event (binary variable) with $P(R|a, s)$ proportional to the reward function $\mathcal{R}(a, s)$, for instance as in [8],

$$P(R|a, s) = \frac{\mathcal{R}(a, s) - \min(\mathcal{R})}{\max(\mathcal{R}) - \min(\mathcal{R})}.$$

Each finite-time MDP defines the joint

$$P(R, \xi | T; \pi) = P(R | a_T, s_T) \, P(a_T | s_T; \pi) \left[\prod_{t=0}^{T-1} P(s_{t+1} | a_t, s_t) \, P(a_t | s_t; \pi) \right] P(s_0). \quad (18.1)$$

That is, each finite-time MDP has the same initialisation, transition and reward probabilities as the original MDP but (i) it ends at a finite time T and (ii) it emits a single binary reward R only at the final time step.

Now let T be a random variable with prior $P(T)$. The mixture of finite-time MDPs is given by the joint

$$P(R, \xi, T; \pi) = P(R, \xi | T; \pi) \, P(T).$$

Note that this defines a distribution over the random variable ξ in the space of variable length trajectories. Figure 18.2 illustrates the mixture. We find

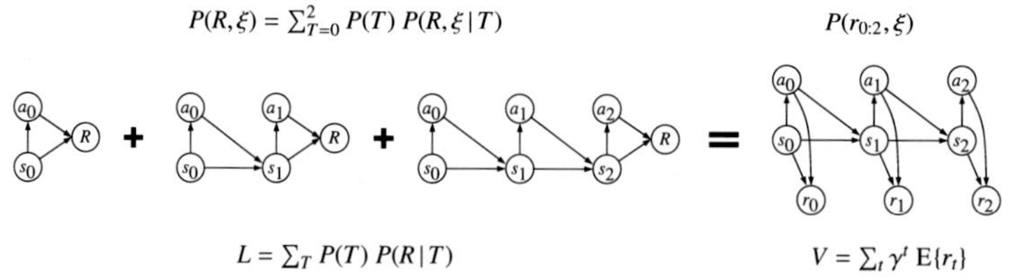

$$P(R,\xi) = \sum_{T=0}^{2} P(T)\, P(R,\xi\,|\,T) \qquad\qquad\qquad P(r_{0:2},\xi)$$

$$L = \sum_T P(T)\, P(R\,|\,T) \qquad\qquad\qquad V = \sum_t \gamma^t\, E\{r_t\}$$

Figure 18.3 Illustration of the equivalence between the mixture and the original MDP.

Theorem 18.2.1. *When introducing binary rewards R such that $P(R\,|\,a,s) \propto \mathcal{R}(a,s)$ and choosing the geometric time prior $P(T) = \gamma^T(1-\gamma)$, maximising the likelihood*

$$L(\pi) = P(R; \pi)$$

of observing reward in the mixture of finite-time MDPs is equivalent to solving the original MDP.

Given the way we defined the mixture, the proof is straightforward and illustrated in Fig. 18.3.

Proof. Let H be some horizon for which we later take the limit to ∞. We can rewrite the value function of the original MDP as

$$V^\pi = \sum_{a_{0:H},s_{0:H}} \left[P(s_0)\,\pi(a_0\,|\,s_0) \prod_{t=1}^{H} \pi(a_t\,|\,s_t)\, P(s_t\,|\,a_{t-1},s_{t-1}) \right]\left[\sum_{T=0}^{H} \gamma^T \mathcal{R}(a_T, s_T) \right]$$

$$= \sum_{T=0}^{H} \gamma^T \sum_{a_{0:H},s_{0:H}} \mathcal{R}(a_T, s_T) P(s_0)\,\pi(a_0\,|\,s_0) \prod_{t=1}^{H} \pi(a_t\,|\,s_t)\, P(s_t\,|\,a_{t-1},s_{t-1})$$

$$= \sum_{T=0}^{H} \gamma^T \sum_{a_{0:T},s_{0:T}} \mathcal{R}(a_T, s_T) P(s_0)\,\pi(a_0\,|\,s_0) \prod_{t=1}^{T} \pi(a_t\,|\,s_t)\, P(s_t\,|\,a_{t-1},s_{t-1})$$

$$= \sum_{T=0}^{H} \gamma^T\, E_{a_{0:T},s_{0:T}\,|\,\pi}\{\mathcal{R}(a_T, s_T)\}.$$

In the second line we pulled the summation over T to the front. Note that the second and third line are really different: the product is taken to the limit T instead of H since we eliminated the variables $a_{T+1:H}$, $s_{T+1:H}$ with the summation. The last expression has already the form of a mixture model, where T is the mixture variable, γ^T is the mixture weight ($P(T) = \gamma^T(1-\gamma)$ the normalized geometric prior), and the last term is the expected reward in the final time slice of a *finite-time* MDP of length T (since the expectation is taken over $a_{0:T}$, $s_{0:T}\,|\,\pi$).

The likelihood in our mixture model can be written as

$$L(\pi) = P(R; \pi)$$

$$= (1-\gamma) \sum_{T=0}^{\infty} \gamma^T P(R\,|\,T; \pi)$$

$$\propto (1-\gamma)\, E_{a_{0:T},s_{0:T}\,|\,\pi}\{\mathcal{R}(a_T, s_T)\}$$

$$= (1-\gamma)\, V^\pi.$$

The proportionality stems from the definition $P(R\,|\,a_t, s_t) \propto \mathcal{R}(a_T, s_T)$ of R.   □

In Appendix 18.A we remark on the following points in some more detail:

(i) the interpretation of the mixture with death probabilities of the agent,

(ii) the difference between the models w.r.t. the correlation between rewards,

(iii) approaches to consider exponentiated rewards as observation likelihoods.

18.3 Expectation maximisation in mixtures of variable length dynamic Bayesian networks

The algorithms we will derive in this section are independent from the context of MDPs. We investigate the general case of a variable length stationary Markov process where we have observations only at the start and the final time. The length of the process is unknown and we assume a mixture of variable length processes where the length prior is the geo-metric distribution $P(T) = \gamma^T (1 - \gamma)$ for $\gamma \in [0, 1)$. We first derive EM algorithms for an unstructured Markov process on one random variable which is then easily generalised to structured DBNs.

18.3.1 Single variable case

Let ξ be a random variable in the domain $\mathcal{X}^* = \bigcup_{T=0}^{\infty} \mathcal{X}^{T+1}$, that is, a variable length trajec-tory in $\mathcal{X}$ (in other terms, a finite but arbitrary length string over the alphabet $\mathcal{X}$). We use the notation $\xi = (x_0, \dots, x_T)$ for a length-T trajectory and write $|\xi| = T$. We consider T a random variable and assume an auxiliary binary random variable R depending on the final state x_T which represents some generic observation. Specifically, we consider the joint

$$P(R, \xi, T; \theta) = P(R \mid \xi; \theta) \, P(\xi \mid T; \theta) \, P(T)$$

$$= P(R \mid x_T; \theta) \left[\prod_{t=0}^{T-1} P(x_{t+1} \mid x_t; \theta) \right] P(x_0; \theta) \, \delta_{|\xi|T} \, P(T).$$

Here, $\delta_{|\xi|T}$ is one for $|\xi| = T$ and zero otherwise; $P(T)$ is a prior over the length of the process; $P(x_0; \theta)$ is the start distribution of the process; $P(x_{t+1} \mid x_t; \theta)$ is the transition prob-ability; and $P(R \mid x_T; \theta)$ is the probability of the R-event which depends only on the final state. The joint is normalised since, when summing over all $\xi \in \mathcal{X}^*$ with all lengths $L = |\xi|$,

$$\sum_{\xi \in \mathcal{X}^*} P(\xi \mid T; \theta) = \sum_{L=0}^{\infty} \sum_{x_0, \dots, x_L} \left[\prod_{t=0}^{L-1} P(x_{t+1} \mid x_t; \theta) \right] P(x_0; \theta) \, \delta_{LT}$$

$$= \sum_{x_0, \dots, x_T} \left[\prod_{t=0}^{T-1} P(x_{t+1} \mid x_t; \theta) \right] P(x_0; \theta) = 1.$$

For expectation maximisation (EM) we assume R is observed and we want to find parameters θ of the joint that maximise the likelihood $P(R; \theta) = \sum_{T, \xi} P(R, \xi, T; \theta)$. The length T of the process and the whole trajectory ξ itself are latent (non-observed) variables. Let $q(\xi, T)$ be a distribution over the latent variables. Consider

$$F(\theta, q) := \log P(R; \theta) - D\big(q(\xi, T) \,\big|\, P(\xi, T \mid R; \theta)\big) \tag{18.2}$$

$$= \log P(R; \theta) - \sum_{\xi,T} q(\xi, T) \log \frac{q(\xi, T)}{P(\xi, T \mid R; \theta)}$$

$$= \sum_{\xi,T} q(\xi, T) \log P(R; \theta) + \sum_{\xi,T} q(\xi, T) \log P(\xi, T \mid R; \theta) + H(q)$$

$$= \sum_{\xi,T} q(\xi, T) \log P(R, \xi, T; \theta) + H(q). \tag{18.3}$$

Expectation maximisation will start with an initial guess of θ, then iterate finding a q that maximises F for fixed θ in the form of Eq. (18.2), and then finding a new θ that maximises F for fixed q in the form of Eq. (18.3). Let us first address the M-step. This will clarify which quantities we actually need to compute in the E-step.

The M-step computes $\arg\max_\theta$ of

$$F(\theta, q) = \sum_{\xi,T} q(\xi, T) \log P(R, \xi, T; \theta) + H(q)$$

$$= \sum_{\xi,T} q(\xi, T) \Big[\log P(R \mid x_T; \theta) + \log P(\xi \mid T; \theta) + \log P(T) \Big] + H(q)$$

$$= \sum_{\xi,T} q(\xi, T) \Big[\log P(R \mid x_T; \theta) + \log P(\xi \mid T; \theta) \Big] + \text{terms indep of } \theta$$

$$= \sum_{\xi} \sum_{T=0}^{\infty} q(\xi, T) \Big[\log P(R \mid x_T; \theta) + \sum_{t=0}^{T-1} \log P(x_{t+1} \mid x_t; \theta) \Big]$$

$$= \sum_{\xi} \sum_{T=0}^{\infty} q(\xi, T) \log P(R \mid x_T; \theta) + \sum_{\xi} \sum_{t=0}^{\infty} \sum_{T=t+1}^{\infty} q(\xi, T) \log P(x_{t+1} \mid x_t; \theta)$$

$$= \sum_{x} \Big[\sum_{T=0}^{\infty} q(x_T = x, T) \Big] \log P(R \mid x_T = x; \theta)$$

$$+ \sum_{x',x} \Big[\sum_{t=0}^{\infty} \sum_{T=t+1}^{\infty} q(x_{t+1} = x', x_t = x, T) \Big] \log P(x_{t+1} = x' \mid x_t = x; \theta). \tag{18.4}$$

The last line uses the fact that the process and the reward are stationary (i.e., $P(x_{t+1} = x' \mid x_t = x; \theta)$ does not explicitly depend on t and $P(R \mid x_T = x; \theta)$ does not depend explicitly on T). The last equation clarifies that the E-step actually only needs to return the quantities in the brackets. The exact E-step is

$$q^*(\xi, T) = P(\xi, T \mid R; \theta^{\text{old}}) = \frac{P(R \mid \xi, T; \theta^{\text{old}}) \, P(\xi \mid T; \theta^{\text{old}}) \, P(T)}{P(R; \theta^{\text{old}})}.$$

Let us investigate the bracket terms in Eq. (18.4) for the exact E-step in more detail:

$$\sum_{T=0}^{\infty} q^*(x_T, T) = \frac{1}{P(R; \theta^{\text{old}})} P(R \mid x_T; \theta^{\text{old}}) \sum_{T=0}^{\infty} P(x_T; \theta^{\text{old}}) \, P(T)$$

$$\sum_{t=0}^{\infty} \sum_{T=t+1}^{\infty} q^*(x_{t+1}, x_t, T) = \frac{1}{P(R; \theta)} \sum_{t=0}^{\infty} \sum_{T=t+1}^{\infty} P(R \mid x_{t+1}, T; \theta^{\text{old}})$$

$$\times P(x_{t+1} \mid x_t; \theta^{\text{old}}) \, P(x_t; \theta^{\text{old}}) \, P(T).$$

At this point we use the property of the geometric length prior

$$P(T = t + \tau) = \frac{1}{1 - \gamma} P(T = t) \, P(T = \tau)$$

$$\sum_{t=0}^{\infty} \sum_{T=t+1}^{\infty} q^*(x_{t+1}, x_t, T) = \frac{1}{P(R; \theta)(1 - \gamma)} \sum_{t=0}^{\infty} \sum_{\tau=1}^{\infty} P(R \,|\, x_{t+1}, T = t + \tau; \theta^{\text{old}})$$

$$\times \, P(T = \tau) \, P(x_{t+1} \,|\, x_t; \theta^{\text{old}}) \, P(x_t; \theta^{\text{old}}) \, P(T = t)$$

$$= \frac{1}{P(R; \theta)(1 - \gamma)} \Big[\sum_{\tau=1}^{\infty} P(R \,|\, x_{t+1}, T = t + \tau; \theta^{\text{old}}) \, P(T = \tau) \Big]$$

$$\times \, P(x_{t+1} \,|\, x_t; \theta^{\text{old}}) \Big[\sum_{t=0}^{\infty} P(x_t; \theta^{\text{old}}) \, P(T = t) \Big].$$

In the last line we used that $P(R \,|\, x_{t+1}, T = t + \tau; \theta^{\text{old}})$ does not explicitly depend on t but only on the time-to-go τ. We finally define quantities

$$\alpha(x_t) := \sum_{t=0}^{\infty} P(x_t; \theta^{\text{old}}) \, P(T = t) \tag{18.5}$$

$$\beta(x_{t+1}) := \frac{1}{1 - \gamma} \sum_{\tau=1}^{\infty} P(R \,|\, x_{t+1}, T = t + \tau; \theta^{\text{old}}) \, P(T = \tau)$$

$$= \frac{1}{1 - \gamma} \sum_{\tau=0}^{\infty} P(R \,|\, x_t', T = t + \tau; \theta^{\text{old}}) \, P(T = \tau + 1) \tag{18.6}$$

such that the relevant parts of $F(\theta, q^*)$ for the M-step can be written more compactly. Eq. (18.4) now reads

$$F(\theta, q^*) = \sum_x \Big[P(R \,|\, x_T; \theta^{\text{old}}) \, \alpha(x) \Big] \log P(R \,|\, x_T; \theta)$$

$$+ \sum_{x',x} \Big[\beta(x') \, P(x' \,|\, x; \theta^{\text{old}}) \, \alpha(x) \Big] \log P(x_{t+1} \,|\, x_t; \theta). \tag{18.7}$$

Note, $\alpha(x)$ and $\beta(x)$ are just quantities that are defined in Eqs. (18.5) and (18.6) and useful for the EM algorithm, but have no explicit interpretation yet. They are analogous to the typical forward and backward messages in Baum–Welch, but different in that there are no observations and that they incorporate the whole mixture over variable length processes and exploit the geometric length prior. If one likes, α can be interpreted as the last-state-occupancy-probability averaged over the mixture of all length processes; and β can be interpreted as (is proportional to) the probability of observing R in the future (not immediately) averaged over the mixture of all length processes. The explicit M-step depends on the kind of parameterisation of $P(R \,|\, x_T; \theta)$ and $P(x_{t+1} \,|\, x_t; \theta)$ but is straightforward to derive from Eq. (18.7). We will derive explicit M-steps in the (PO)MDP context in the next section.

18.3.2 Explicit E-step algorithms

In the remainder of this section we describe efficient algorithms to compute $\alpha(x)$ and $\beta(x)$ as defined in Eqs. (18.5) and (18.6). For brevity we write $\boldsymbol{P} \equiv P(x' \,|\, x; \theta^{\text{old}})$ as a matrix and $\alpha \equiv \alpha(x)$ and $S \equiv P(x_0 = x)$ as vectors. The α quantity can be computed iteratively in two ways: We define another quantity a_t (which directly corresponds to the typical forward message) and from Eq. (18.5) get

$$a_t := P(x_t = x) = P \, a_{t-1}, \quad a_0 = S, \tag{18.8}$$

$$\alpha_h = \sum_{t=0}^{h} a_t \, P(T = t) = \alpha_{h-1} + (1 - \gamma)\gamma^h \, a_h, \quad \alpha_0 = (1 - \gamma) \, S.$$

Iterating both equations together can be used to compute α approximately as α_h in the limit $h \to \infty$. Alternatively we can use

$$\alpha_h = \sum_{t=0}^{h} a_t \, P(T = t) = (1 - \gamma) \Big[a_0 + \sum_{t=1}^{h} a_t \, \gamma^t \Big]$$

$$= (1 - \gamma) \Big[S + \sum_{t=1}^{h} P \, a_{t-1} \, \gamma^t \Big] = (1 - \gamma) \Big[S + P \sum_{t=0}^{h-1} a_t \, \gamma^{t+1} \Big]$$

$$= (1 - \gamma) \, S + \gamma \, P \, \alpha_{h-1} \tag{18.9}$$

as a direct recursive equation for α_h. Analogously we have two ways to compute β (a row vector). With $R \equiv P(R \mid x_T = x)$ the direct computation of Eq. (18.6) is

$$b_\tau := P(R \mid x_t = x, T = t + \tau) = b_{\tau-1} \, P, \quad b_0 = R, \tag{18.10}$$

$$\beta_h = \frac{1}{1 - \gamma} \sum_{\tau=0}^{h} b_\tau \, P(T = \tau + 1) = \beta_{h-1} + \gamma^{h+1} \, b_h(x), \quad \beta_0 = \gamma \, b_0.$$

And a second way to compute β is

$$\beta_h = \frac{1}{1 - \gamma} \sum_{\tau=0}^{h} b_\tau \, P(T = \tau + 1) = \gamma b_0 + \sum_{\tau=1}^{h} b_\tau \, \gamma^{\tau+1}$$

$$= \gamma R + \sum_{\tau=1}^{h} b_{\tau-1} \, P \gamma^{\tau+1} = \gamma R + \gamma \Big[\sum_{\tau=0}^{h-1} b_\tau \, \gamma^{\tau+1} \Big] P$$

$$= \gamma R + \gamma \, \beta_{h-1} \, P \tag{18.11}$$

in the limit $h \to \infty$. Note that, in the context of MDPs, this equation is exactly equivalent to *policy evaluation*, i.e., the computation of the value function for a fixed policy. We will discuss this in more detail in Section 18.4.2.

When choosing to compute also the a_t and b_t quantities we can use them to compute the length posterior and likelihood,

$$P(R \mid T = t + \tau) = \sum_x P(R \mid x_t = x, T = t + \tau) \, P(x_t = x) = b_\tau^{\mathsf{T}} \, a_t,$$

$$P(R) = \sum_T P(R \mid T) \, P(T), \tag{18.12}$$

$$P(T \mid R) = P(R \mid T) \, P(T) / P(R), \tag{18.13}$$

$$E\{T \mid R\} = \sum_T T \, P(T \mid R).$$

In particular, Eqs. (18.12) and (18.13) can be computed while iterating Eqs. (18.8) and (18.10) and thereby provide a heuristic to choose the horizon (stopping criterion of the iteration) on the fly. On the other hand Eqs. (18.9) and (18.11) are update equations for α and β which can be used in an incremental E-step: we can reuse the α and β of the previous EM-iterations as an initialisation and iterate Eqs. (18.9) and (18.11) only a few steps. This corresponds to computing parts of α and β with old parameters θ^{old} from previous EM-iterations and only the most recent updates with the current parameters. The horizon h implicitly increases in each EM-iteration. Algorithms 18.1 and 18.2 explicitly describe the standard E-step and the incremental version.

Algorithm 18.1 Standard E-step

Input: vectors S, R, matrix P, scalars γ, H
Output: vectors α, β, $P(T|R)$, scalars $P(R)$, $E\{T|R\}$

1: initialise $a = S$, $b = R$, $\alpha = a$, $\beta = \gamma\, b$, $L(0) = a^\top b$
2: **for** $h = 1$ **to** H **do**
3:    $a \leftarrow P\, a$
4:    $L(2h - 1) = \gamma^{2h-1}\, a^\top b$
5:    $b \leftarrow b\, P$
6:    $L(2h) = \gamma^{2h}\, a^\top b$
7:    $\alpha \mathrel{+}= \gamma^h\, a$
8:    $\beta \mathrel{+}= \gamma^{h+1}\, b$
9: **end for**
10: $L\mathrel{*}= 1 - \gamma$
11: $\alpha \mathrel{*}= 1 - \gamma$
12: $P(R) = \sum_{t=0}^{2H} L(t)$
13: $P(T = t|R) = L(t)/P(R)$
14: $E\{T|R\} = [\sum_{t=0}^{2H} tL(t)]/P(R)$

Algorithm 18.2 Incremental E-step

Input: vectors α, β, S, R, matrix P, scalars γ, H
Output: vector α, β, scalar $P(R)$

1: **for** $h = 1$ **to** H **do**
2:    $\alpha \leftarrow (1 - \gamma)\, S + \gamma\, P\, \alpha$
3:    $\beta \leftarrow \gamma\, [R + \beta\, P]$
4: **end for**
5: $P(R) = a^\top R$

18.3.3 Structured DBN case

In the case of a structured DBN the process is defined on more than one variable. Generally the transition probability $P(x_{t+1}|x_t; \theta)$ is then replaced by a set of factors (or conditional probability tables) that describes the coupling between two consecutive time slices. It is straightforward to generalise Algorithms 18.1 and 18.2 to exploit the structure in such a DBN: In each time slice we now have several random variables $s_t^1, \ldots, s_t^k, a_t^1, \ldots, a_t^l$. We choose the notation $s_t^1, \ldots, s_t^k$ for a set of variables which are a separator of the Markov process and $a_t^1, \ldots, a_t^l$ are the remaining variables in a time slice. For exact inference we have to maintain quantities $\alpha(s)$ and $\beta(s)$ over the separator clique. To exploit the DBN structure we need to replace the transition matrix multiplications (lines 3 and 5 in Algorithm 18.1, and lines 2 and 3 in Algorithm 18.2) with other inference techniques. The simplest solution is to use the elimination algorithm. For instance, instead of the matrix multiplication $a \leftarrow Pa$ (line 3 of Algorithm 18.1), we think of P as a list of factors over the variables (s_t, a_t, s_{t+1}) that couple two time slices, a is a factor over the 'left' separator clique (s_t), we pass the list of factors $\{P, a\}$ to the elimination algorithm and query for the marginal over the 'right' separator clique (s_{t+1}). This yields the new assignment to a. When we choose a good elimination order this procedure is equivalent to the Junction Tree method described in [23].

Concerning the M-step, the energy expression (18.7) generalises to

$$F(\theta, q^*) = \sum_{a,s} \left[P(R \mid a, s; \theta^{\text{old}}) \, P(a \mid s; \theta^{\text{old}}) \, \alpha(s) \right] \log P(R \mid a, s; \theta) \, P(a \mid s; \theta)$$

$$+ \sum_{s',a,s} \left[\beta(s') \, P(s' \mid a, s; \theta^{\text{old}}) \, P(a \mid s; \theta^{\text{old}}) \, \alpha(s) \right] \log P(s' \mid a, s; \theta) \, P(a \mid s; \theta). \quad (18.14)$$

18.4   Application to MDPs

18.4.1   Expectation maximisation with a tabular policy

A standard MDP is a DBN with random variables s_t and a_t in each time slice where the state s_t is a separator. In the simplest case we parameterise the policy $P(a_t \mid s_t; \theta)$ using a full CPT,

$$P(a_t = a \mid s_t = s; \theta) = \pi_{as}.$$

The energy $F(\theta, q^*)$ (Eq. (18.14)) reads (neglecting terms independent of π)

$$\sum_{a,s} \left[P(R|a, s) \, \pi_{as}^{\text{old}} \, \alpha(s) \right] \log \pi_{as} + \sum_{s',a,s} \left[\beta(s') \, P(s'|a, s) \, \pi_{as}^{\text{old}} \, \alpha(s) \right] \log \pi_{as}.$$

Since π_{as} is constrained to normalise over a for each s this energy is maximised by

$$\pi_{as}^{\text{new}} = \pi_{as}^{\text{old}} \left[P(R|a, s) + \sum_{s'} \beta(s') \, P(s'|a, s) \right]. \quad (18.15)$$

The two terms in the brackets correspond to the expected immediate reward plus the expected future reward as predicted by β – the brackets are exactly equivalent to the classical Q-function.

In the case of a plain unstructured MDP we can also derive a greedy and usually faster version of the M-step, given as

$$\forall_s : \pi_{as}^{\text{new}} = \delta(a, a^*(s)), \quad a^*(s) = \arg\max_a \left[P(R|a, s) + \sum_{s'} \beta(s') \, P(s'|a, s) \right]. \quad (18.16)$$

This update corresponds to a greedy version of the previous M-step. If we were to iterate Eq. (18.15) without recomputing the bracket term each time (skipping intermediate E-steps) we would converge to this greedy M-step. Further, as we know from reinforcement learning, the greedy M-step can be thought of as exploiting our knowledge that the optimal policy must be a deterministic one (in the fully observable case).

Note however that this does not generalise to arbitrarily structured DBNs. In fact, in the POMDP case that we investigate later we are not aware of such a greedy version of the M-step.

18.4.2 Relation to policy iteration and value iteration

So far we have developed our approach for a plain unstructured MDP. It turns out that in this case the E- and M-step are very closely related to the policy evaluation and update steps in standard policy iteration.

We introduced the mixture of MDPs in a way such that the likelihood is proportional to the expected future return. Hence, for the unstructured MDP, $b(s) := P(R \mid s_t = s, T = t + \tau; \pi)$ as defined in Eq. (18.10) is proportional to the expected reward in τ time steps in the future conditioned on the current state. This is also the value function of the finite-time MDP of length τ. Hence, the $\beta(s)$ defined in Eq. (18.6) is proportional to the value function $V^\pi(s)$ of the original MDP. Analogously, the bracket term in the M-step (Eq. (18.15)) is proportional to the Q-function $Q^\pi(a, s)$ in the original MDP.

We conclude that the E-step in an unstructured MDP is a form of policy evaluation since it also yields the value function. However, quite different to traditional policy evaluation, the E-step also computes α's, i.e., probabilities to visit states given the current policy, which may be compared to previous approaches like diverse densities (in the context of subgoal analysis [20]) or policy search by density estimation [24]. The full E-step provides us with posteriors over actions, states and the total time. In practice we can use the α's in an efficient heuristic for pruning computations during inference (see Section 18.4.3 and Appendix 18.B). Further, the E-step generalises to arbitrarily structured DBNs and thereby goes beyond standard policy evaluation, particularly when using approximate inference techniques like message passing or approximate belief representations.

Concerning the M-step, in the unstructured MDP the greedy M-step is *identical* to the policy update in policy iteration. That means that one iteration of the EM will yield exactly the same policy update as one iteration of policy iteration (provided one does exact inference and exact value function computation without time horizon cutoffs). Again, the M-step goes beyond a standard policy update in the generalised case. This becomes particularly apparent when in structured DBNs (e.g. the POMDP case in Section 18.5) the full posteriors computed via inference (including forward propagated messages analogous to α's) are necessary for the M-step.

In summary,

Lemma 18.1. *The EM algorithm on an unstructured MDP using exact inference and the greedy M-step is equivalent to policy iteration in terms of the policy updates performed.*

Interestingly, this also means they are equivalent w.r.t. convergence. (Recall that policy iteration is guaranteed to converge to the global optimum whereas EM algorithms are only guaranteed to converge to local optima.) The computational costs of both methods may differ depending on the implementation (see below).

Finally, the incremental E-step of Algorithm 18.2 only updates the β and α functions by propagating them for H steps. For $H = 1$ and when using the greedy M-step this is equivalent to value iteration. In a structured (but fully observable) MDP, we have the same equivalence with structured value iteration.

18.4.3 Discrete maze examples

Efficiency

We first tested the EM algorithm with standard E-step and greedy M-step on a discrete maze of size 100×100 and compared it to standard value iteration (VI) and policy iteration (PI). Walls of the maze are considered to be trap states (leading to unsuccessful trials) and

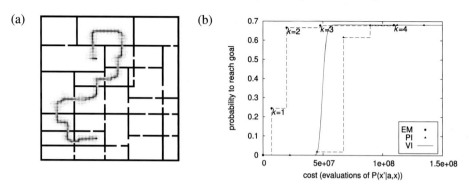

Figure 18.4 (a) State visiting probability calculated by EM for some start and goal state. The radii of the dots are proportional to $P(s \in \xi | R)$. (b) The probability of reaching the goal (for EM) and the value calculated for the start state (PS) against the cost of the planning algorithms (measured by evaluations of $P(s' | a, s)$).

actions (north, south, east, west, stay) are highly noisy in that with a probability of 0.2 they lead to random transitions. In the experiment we chose a uniform time prior (discount factor $\gamma = 1$), initialised π uniformly, and iterated the policy update $k = 5$ times. To increase computational efficiency we exploited that the algorithm explicitly calculates posteriors which can be used to prune unnecessary computations during inference as explained in Appendix 18.B. For policy evaluation in PI we performed 100 iterations of standard value function updates.

Figure 18.4(a) displays the posterior state visiting probabilities $P(s \in \xi | R)$ of the optimal policy computed by the EM for a problem where a reward of 1 is given when the goal state g is reached and the agent is initialised at a start state s. Computational costs are measured by the number of evaluations of the environment $P(s' | a, s)$ needed during the planning procedure. Figure 18.4(b) displays the probability of reaching the goal $P(R; \pi)$ against these costs. Note that for EM (and PI) we can give this information only after a complete E- and M-step cycle (policy evaluation and update) which are the discrete dots (triangles) in the graph. The graph also displays the curve for VI, where the currently calculated value V_A of the start state (which converges to $P(R)$ for the optimal policy) is plotted against how often VI evaluated $P(s' | a, s)$.

In contrast to VI and PI, the inference approach takes considerable advantage of knowing the start state in this planning scenario: the forward propagation allows for the pruning and the early decision on cutoff times in the E-step as described in Appendix 18.B. It should thus not surprise and not be overstated that the EM is more efficient in this specific scenario. Certainly, a similar kind of forward propagation could also be introduced for VI or PI to achieve equal efficiency. Nonetheless, our approach provides a principled way of pruning by exploiting the computation of proper posteriors. The policies computed by all three methods are equal for states which have significantly non-zero state visiting probabilities.

Multimodal time posteriors

The total time T plays a special role as a random variable in our mixture model. We use another simple experiment to illustrate this special role by considering the total time posteriors. Modelling walls as trap states leads to interesting trade-offs between staying away from walls in favour of security and choosing short paths. Fig. 18.5 displays a 15×20 maze with three possible pathways from the start (bottom left) to the goal (bottom right)

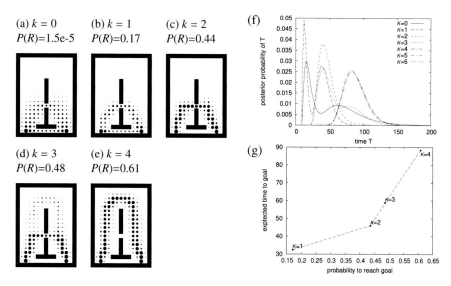

Figure 18.5 (a)–(e) State visiting probabilities for various EM-iterations k. The start and goal states are to the bottom left and right, respectively. The radii of the dots are proportional to $P(s \in \xi | R)$. (f) The different possible pathways lead to a multimodal time posterior $P(T | R)$. (g) The trade-off between the expected time to goal (mean of $P(T | R)$) and the probability to reach the goal. The dots corresponds to $k = 1, ..., 4$ (from left to right).

state. The direct pathway is a narrow aisle clinched between two walls and thus highly risky. The next one up requires a step through a narrow doorway. The top one is secure but longest. The five figures illustrate the state visiting probability $P(s \in \xi | R)$ for random walks ($k = 0$) and the policies calculated by EM for $k = 1, ..., 4$ iterations. Also the success probability $P(R)$ is indicated. Figure 18.5(f) displays the corresponding time posteriors $P(T | R)$ for the different k's. Interesting is the multimodality of these time posteriors in that specific environment. The multimodality in some way reflects the topological properties of the environment: that there exist multiple possible pathways from the start to the goal with different typical lengths (maxima of the time posterior) and different success probabilities (area (integral) of a mode of the time posterior). Already for $k = 0$ the multimodality exhibits that, besides the direct pathway (of typical length ≈ 15), there exist alternative, longer routes which comprise significant success probability. One way to exploit this insight could be to choose a new time prior for the next inference iteration that explicitly favours these longer routes. Figure 18.5(g) nicely exhibits the trade-off between the expected time to goal and the probability to reach the goal.

18.4.4 Stochastic optimal control

Gaussian belief state propagation

Next we want to show that the framework naturally allows us to transfer other inference techniques to the problem of solving MDPs. We address the problem of stochastic optimal control in the case of a continuous state and control space. A standard inference technique in continuous state spaces is to assume Gaussian belief states as representations for a's and b's and propagate forward-backward and using the unscented transform to handle also non-linear transition dynamics (see [23] for an overview on inference techniques in DBNs). Note that using Gaussian belief states implies that the effective value function (Section 18.4.2) becomes a mixture of Gaussians.

All the equations we derived remain valid when reinterpreted for the continuous case (summations become integrations, etc.) and the exact propagations (Eqs. (18.8) and (18.10)) are replaced by propagations of Gaussian belief states using the unscented transform. In more detail, let $N(x, a, A)$ be the normal distribution over x with mean a and covariance A and let $\overline{N}(x, a, A)$ be the respective *non-normalised* Gaussian function with $\overline{N}(a, a, A) = 1$. As a transition model we assume

$$P(x'|u, x) = N(x', \phi(u, x), Q(u)), \quad Q(u) = C + \mu|u|^2 I,$$

where $\phi(u, x)$ is a non-linear function depending on the current state x and the control signal u, C is a constant noise covariance, and we introduced a parameter μ for an additional noise term that is squared in the control signal. With the parameterisation $a_t(x) = N(x, a_t, A_t)$ and $b_\tau(x) = \overline{N}(x, b_\tau, B_\tau)$ (note that b's always remain non-normalised Gaussian likelihoods during propagation), forward and backward propagation read

$$(a_t, A_t) = UT_\phi(a_{t-1}, A_{T-1}), \quad (b_\tau, B_\tau) = UT_{\phi^{-1}}(b_{\tau-1}, B_{\tau-1}),$$

where $UT_\phi(a, A)$ denotes the unscented transform of a mean and covariance under a non-linear function. In brief, this transform deterministically considers $2n + 1$ points (say with standard deviation distance to the mean) representing the Gaussian. In the forward case (the backward case) it maps each point forward using ϕ (backward using ϕ^{-1}), associates a covariance $Q(u)$ (a covariance $\phi'^{-1} Q(u) \phi'^{-1T}$, where ϕ'^{-1} is the local inverse linearisation of ϕ at each point) with each point, and returns the Gaussian that approximates this mixture of Gaussians. Further, for any t and τ we have

$$P(R|T = t + \tau) = N(a_t, b_\tau, A_t + B_\tau),$$
$$P(x_t = x|R, T = t + \tau) = N(x, c_{t\tau}, C_{t\tau}),$$
$$C_{t\tau}^{-1} = A_t^{-1} + B_\tau^{-1}, \quad c_{t\tau} = C_{t\tau} (A_t^{-1} a_t + B_\tau^{-1} b_\tau).$$

The policy and the M-step

In general, the policy is given as an arbitrary non-linear function $\pi : x \mapsto u$. Clearly, we cannot store such a function in memory. However, via the M-step the policy can always be implicitly expressed in terms of the b-quantities of the previous E-step and numerically evaluated at specific states x. This is particularly feasible in our case because the unscented transform used in the belief propagation (of the next E-step) only needs to evaluate the transition function ϕ (and thereby π) at some states; and we have the advantage of not needing to approximate the function π in any way. For the M-step (Eq. (18.16)) we need to maximise the mixture of Gaussians (see Eq. (18.6))

$$\hat{q}_\tau(u, x) := \left[P(R|u, x) + \int_{x'} P(x'|u, x) \beta(x') \right],$$

$$\beta(x') = \frac{1}{1 - \gamma} \sum_{\tau=0}^{\infty} P(T = \tau + 1) \overline{N}(x', b_{\tau-1}, B_{\tau-1}).$$

We use a gradient ascent. The gradient for each component of the mixture of Gaussians is:

$$q_\tau(u, x) := \int_{x'} P(x'|u, x) \overline{N}(x', b_{\tau-1}, B_{\tau-1}) = |2\pi B_{\tau-1}|^{1/2} N(b_{\tau-1}, \phi(u, x), B_{\tau-1} + Q(u)),$$

$$\partial_u q_\tau(u, x) = -q_\tau(u, x) \left[h^T \left(\partial_u \phi(u, x) \right) - \mu u \left(tr(A^{-1}) - h^T h \right) \right],$$

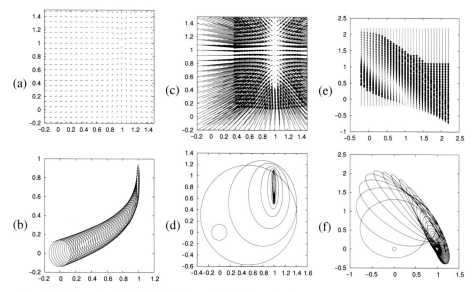

Figure 18.6 Learned policies (left) and forward simulation (*a*'s) of these policies (right) for aspheric Gaussian-shaped targets. (a)–(b) are for the case of restricted action amplitude (the walker model). (c)–(d) are for unconstrained amplitude (the golfer model). And (e)–(f) are for the approach to a new position under phase space dynamics.

$$A := B_{\tau-1} + Q(u), \quad h := A^{-1}(\phi(u, x) - b).$$

We perform this gradient ascent whenever we query the policy at a specific state x.

Examples

Consider a simple two-dimensional problem where the start state is distributed around zero via $a_0(x) = \mathcal{N}(x, (0,0), .01I)$ and the goal region is determined by $P(R \mid x) = \overline{\mathcal{N}}(x, (1,1),$ diag$(.0001, .1))$. Note that this goal region around $(1, 1)$ is heavily skewed in that rewards depend more on the precision along the x-dimension than the y-dimension. We first consider a simple control law $\phi(u, x) = x + 0.1\, u$ and the discount factor $\gamma = 1$. When choosing $\mu = 0$ (no control-dependent noise), the optimal control policy will try to jump directly to the goal $(1, 1)$. Hence we first consider the solution when manually constraining the norm of $|u|$ to be small (effectively following the gradient of $P(r = 1 \mid u_t = u, x_t = x; \pi)$). Figures 18.6(a) and 18.6(b) show the learned control policy π and the forward simulation given this policy by displaying the covariance ellipses for $a_{0:T}(x)$ after $k = 3$ iterations. What we find is a control policy that reduces errors in the x-dimension more strongly than in the y-dimension, leading to the tangential approach to the goal region. This is related to studies on redundant control or the so-called uncontrolled manifold.

Next we can investigate what the effect of control-dependent noise is without a constraint on the amplitude of u. Figures 18.6(c) and 18.6(d) display results (after $k = 3$ iterations) for $\mu = 1$ and no additional constraints on u. The process actually resembles a golf player: the stronger the hit, the more noise. The optimal strategy is to hit fairly hard in the beginning, hopefully coming closer to the goal, such that later a number of smaller and more precise hits can be made. The reason for the small control signals around the goal region is that small steps have much more accuracy and reward expectation is already fairly large for just the x-coordinate being close to 1.

Finally we think of x being a phase space and consider the dynamics $\phi(u, x) = (x_1 + 0.1x_2, x_2 + 0.1u)$ where u is the one-dimensional acceleration of the velocity x_2, and x_1 is a position. This time we set the start and goal to $(0, 0)$ and $(1, 0)$ respectively, both with variance 0.001 and choose $\mu = 10$. Figures 18.6(e) and 18.6(f) display the result and show nicely how the learned control policy approaches the new position on the x-axis by first gaining and then reducing velocity.

18.5   Application to POMDPs

A stationary, partially observable Markov decision process (POMDP, see e.g. [14]) is given by four time-independent probability functions,

the initial world state distribution	$P(s_0 = s)$,
the world state transitions	$P(s_{t+1} = s' \mid a_t = a, s_t = s)$,
the observation probabilities	$P(y_t = y \mid s_t = s)$,
the reward probabilities	$P(r_t = r \mid a_t = a, s_t = s)$.

These functions are considered known. We assume the world states, actions and observations (s_t, y_t, a_t) are discrete random variables while the reward r_t is a real number.

The POMDP only describes one 'half' of the process to be described as a DBN – the other half is the agent interacting with the environment. Our point of view is that the agent could use an arbitrary 'internal machinery' to decide on actions. Finite state controllers are a simple example. However, a general DBN formulation of the agent's internal machinery allows us to consider much more structured ways of behaviour organisation, including factorised and hierarchical internal representations (see, e.g., [30, 32]). In the remainder of this section we investigate a policy model that is slightly different to finite state controllers but still rather simple. However, the approach is generally applicable to any DBN formulation of the POMDP and the agent.

To solve a given POMDP challenge an agent needs to maintain some internal memory variable (if not the full belief state) that represents information gained from previous observations and actions. We assume that this variable is updated depending on the current observation and used to *gate* reactive policies rather than to directly emit actions. More precisely, the dynamic Bayesian network in Fig. 18.7(a) captures the POMDP and the agent model which is defined by the

initial internal memory distribution	$P(b_0 = b) =: \nu_b$
internal memory transition	$P(b_{t+1} = b' \mid b_t = b, y_t = y) =: \lambda_{b'by}$
reactive policies	$P(a_t = a \mid b_t = b, y_t = y) =: \pi_{aby}$.

Here we introduced b_t as the agent's internal memory variable. It is comparable to the 'node state' in finite state controllers (Fig. 18.7(b)), but differs in that it does not directly emit actions but rather gates reactive policies: for each internal memory state b the agent uses a different 'mapping' π_{aby} (i.e. a different reactive policy) from observations to actions.

As for the MDP case, solving the POMDP in this approach means to find parameters $\theta = (\nu, \lambda, \pi)$ of the DBN in Fig. 18.7 that maximise the expected future return $V^\theta = \mathrm{E}\{\sum_{t=0}^\infty \gamma^t r_t; \theta\}$ for a discount factor $\gamma \in [0, 1)$.

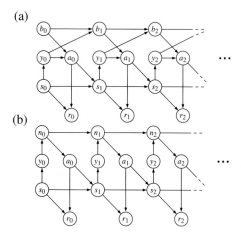

Figure 18.7 (a) DBN of the POMDP and policy with internal memory b_t; the time is unbounded and rewards are emitted at every time step. (b) For comparison: the DBN of a POMDP with a standard FSC, with 'node state' n_t.

M-step

The M-steps for the parameters can directly be derived from the free-energy in the form (Eq. (18.14)). We have:

$$\pi_{aby}^{\text{new}} = \frac{\pi_{aby}^{\text{old}}}{C_{by}} \sum_{s} \left[P(R|a, s) + \sum_{b's'} \beta(b', s') \lambda_{b'by} P(s'|a, s) \right] P(y|s)\, \alpha(b, s),$$

$$\lambda_{b'by}^{\text{new}} = \frac{\lambda_{b'by}^{\text{old}}}{C'_{by}} \sum_{s',a,s} \beta(b', s')\, P(s'|a, s)\, \pi_{aby}\, P(y|s)\, \alpha(b, s),$$

$$v_b^{\text{new}} = \frac{v_b^{\text{old}}}{C''_b} \sum_{x} \beta(b, s)\, P(s_0 = s),$$

where C_{by}, C'_{by} and C''_b are normalisation constants. Note that in these updates the α's (related to state visiting probabilities) play a crucial role. Also we are not aware of a greedy version of these updates that proved efficient (i.e. without immediate convergence to a local minimum).

Complexity

Let S, B, A and Y momentarily denote the cardinalities of random variables s, b, a, y, respectively. The main computational cost accumulates during $\boldsymbol{a}$- and $\boldsymbol{b}$-propagation; with the separator (b_t, s_t) both of which have complexity $O(H B^2 S^2)$. Here and below, S^2 scales with the number of non-zero elements in the transition matrix $P(s'|s)$ (assuming non-zero action probabilities). We always use sparse matrix representations for transition matrices. The number of propagations H scales with the expected time of reward (for a simple start-goal scenario this is the expected time to goal). Sparse vector representations of α's and β's further reduce the complexity depending on the topological dimensionality of $P(s'|s)$. The computational complexity of the M-step scales with $O(AYB^2S^2)$; in total this adds to $O((H + AY)B^2S^2)$ for one EM iteration.

For comparison, let N denote the number of nodes in an FSC. The computation of a policy gradient w.r.t. a *single* parameter of an FSC scales with $O((H + AY)N^2S^2)$ (taken

(a)   (b)

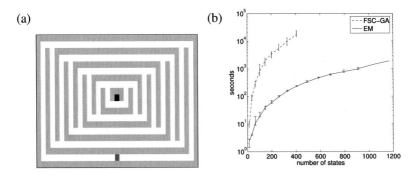

Figure 18.8 (a) A simple scalable maze from [21], here with 330 states. The start (goal) position is marked grey (black). The robot has five actions (north, south, east, west, stay) and his observation is a 4 bit number encoding the presence of adjacent walls. (b) Running times of EM-learning and FSC gradient ascent that show how both methods scale with the maze size. The lines are medians, the errorbars min and max of 10 independent runs for each of the various maze sizes. (For maze sizes beyond 1000 we display only 1 run.)

from [21], top of page 7). A fully parameterised FSC has $NA + N^2Y$ parameters, bearing a total complexity of $O((H + AY)N^4S^2Y)$ to compute a full policy gradient.

For EM learning as well as gradient ascent, the complexity additionally multiplies with the number k of EM iterations respectively gradient updates.

18.5.1 POMDP Experiments

Scaling

The POMDP EM algorithm has no free parameters except for the initialisations of $\lambda_{b'by}$, π_{aby} and ν_b. Roughly, we initialised ν_b and π_{aby} approximately uniformly, while $\lambda_{b'by}$ was initialised in a way that favours not to switch the internal memory state, i.e., the diagonal of the matrix $\lambda_{b'b}$ was initialised larger than the off-diagonal terms. More precisely, we first draw non-normalised numbers

$$\pi_{aby} \sim 1 + 0.1\,\mathcal{U}([0,1])\,, \quad \lambda_{b'by} \sim 1 + 5\,\delta_{b'b} + 0.1\,\mathcal{U}([0,1])\,, \quad \nu_b = 1, \qquad (18.17)$$

where $\mathcal{U}([0,1])$ is the uniform distribution over $[0,1]$, and then normalise these parameters.

To start with, we test the scaling behaviour of our EM algorithm and compare it with that of gradient ascent for a FSC (FSC-GA). We tried three options for coping with the problem that the simple policy gradient in [21] ignores the normalisation constraints of the parameters: (1) projecting the gradient on the simplex, (2) using a step-size-adaptive gradient ascent (RPROP) with added soft-constraint gradients towards the simplex, (3) using MATLAB's gradient-based constraint optimisation method 'fmincon'. The second option gave the best results and we refer to those in the following. Note that our algorithm does not have such problems: the M-step assigns correctly normalised parameters. Figure 18.8 displays the results for the simple maze considered in [21] for various maze sizes. Our policy model needs $B = 2$ internal memory states, the FSC $N = 5$ graph nodes to solve these problems. The discount factor was chosen $\gamma = 0.99$. The results confirm the differences we noticed in the complexity analysis.

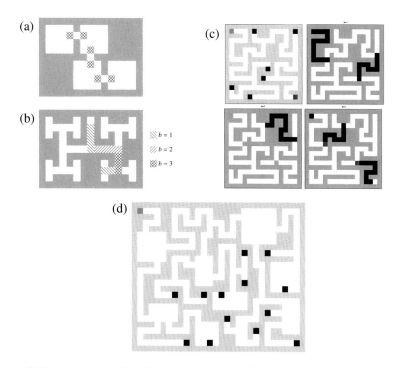

Figure 18.9 Further mazes considered in the experiments. (c) Top left is the maze with the start (light grey), goal (bottom right) and drain-states (dark). The other three illustrations display the internal memory state b (grey value $\propto \widehat{\alpha}(b, s)$ for $b = 1, 2, 3$) at different locations in the maze. (d) Large maze with 1516 turtle states.

Training the memory to gate primitive reactive behaviours

To exemplify the approach's ability to learn an appropriate memory representation for a given task we investigate further maze problems. We consider a *turtle*, which can move forward, turn right or left, or wait. With probability $1 - \epsilon$ this action is successful; with probability $\epsilon = 0.1$ the turtle does not respond. The state space is the cross product of positions and four possible orientations, and the observations are a 4 bit number encoding the presence of adjacent walls relative to the turtle's orientation. Further, whenever the agent reaches the goal (or a zero-reward drain state, see below) it is instantly reset to the start position.

Figures 18.9(a) and 18.9(b) display two small mazes with two specific difficulties: The interior states, entries and exits (cross-shaded) of the halls in Fig. 18.9(a) all have the same observation 0000. These halls are therefore places when the agent is likely to get lost. For $B = 2$ (that is, when the latent variable b has two possible values), the turtle learns a wall-following strategy as a basic reactive behaviour, while the internal memory is used only at the exits and entrances to halls: for internal state $b = 1$ and observation $y = 0000$ the turtle turns left and switches to $b = 2$, while for $b = 2$ and $y = 0000$ the turtle goes straight and switches back to $b = 1$. The maze in Fig. 18.9(b) is a binary-decision maze and poses the problem of remembering how many junctions have passed already: To reach the goal, the turtle has to follow aisles and at T-junctions make decisions [left, right, right, left]. For $B = 3$ the algorithm finds the obvious solution: Each internal memory state is associated with simple reactive behaviours that follows aisles and, depending on b, turns left or right at a T-junction. A finite state controller would certainly find a very similar

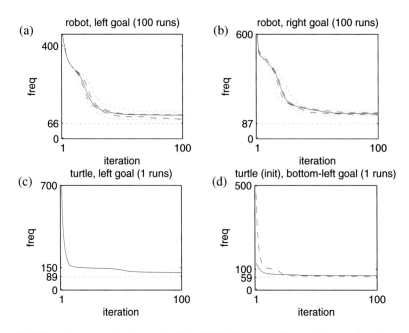

Figure 18.10 Learning curves for the maze in Fig. 18.9(d). The expected reward interval (see footnote) is given over the number of EM iterations. Solid: median over 100 independent trial runs (with noisy initialisations (Eq. (18.17))), dashed and dotted: 2.5, 25, 75 and 97.5 percentiles, dotted baseline: shortest path to the goal in the respective environment which *were* possible in the noise-free case. The optimal controller in our stochastic case is necessarily above this baseline.

solution. However, in our case this solution generalises to situations when the corridors are not straight: Figure 18.9(c) (top left) displays a maze with 30 locations (number of states is 480), where the start state is in the top left corner and the goal state in the bottom right. Again, the turtle has to make decisions [left, right, right, left] at T-junctions to reach the goal, but additionally has to follow complex aisles in-between. Unlike with FSCs, our turtle needs again only $B = 3$ internal memory states to represent the current corridor. The shading in Fig. 18.9(c) displays the probability of visiting a location on a trajectory while being in memory state $b = 1, 2$ or 3.

Finally, we investigate the maze in Fig. 18.9(d) with 379 locations (1516 turtle states). The maze is a complex combination of corridors, rooms and junctions. On this maze we also tested a normal robot (north, south, west, east actions with noise $\epsilon = 0.1$), learning curves for $B = 3$ for the left and rightmost goals are given in Fig. 18.10(a) and Fig. 18.6(b) and exhibit reliable convergence.[1] We also investigated single runs in the turtle case for the leftmost goal (Fig. 18.10(c)) and the second left goal (Fig. 18.10(d) dashed line). Again, the turtle utilises that aisle following can be implemented with a simple reactive behaviour; the internal memory is only used for decision making in halls and at junctions.

---

[1] As a performance measure we define the *expected reward interval* which is directly linked to $P(R)$. Consider a cyclic process that receives a reward of 1 every d time steps; the expected future reward of this process is $P(R) = \sum_{T=1}^{\infty} P(dT) = (1 - \gamma) \sum_{T=1}^{\infty} \gamma^{dT} = \frac{\gamma^d (1-\gamma)}{1-\gamma^d}$. Inverting this relation, we translate a given expected future reward into an expected reward interval via $d = \frac{\log P(R) - \log(P(R)+1-\gamma)}{\log \gamma}$. This measure is rather intuitive: The performance can directly be compared with the shortest path length to the goal. Note though that in the stochastic environment even an optimal policy has an expected reward interval larger than the shortest path to goal.

Since the aisle following behaviour can readily be generalised to all goal settings we performed another experiment: we took the final policy π_{aby} learned for the leftmost goal as an initialisation for the task of finding the second left goal. Note that the start-to-goal paths are largely disjoint. Still, the algorithm converges, particularly in the beginning, much faster (Fig. 18.10(d) solid line), showing that such generalisation is indeed possible.

To conclude these experiments, we can summarise that the agent learned internal memory representations to switch between reactive behaviours. In the experiments they mainly turned out to represent different corridors. Generalisation of the reactive behaviours to new goal situations is possible. Further, memorisation is not time bounded, e.g., independent of the length of an aisle the turtle agent can sustain the current internal memory while executing the reactive aisle following behaviour.

18.6 Conclusion

We introduced a framework for solving (PO)MDPs by translating the problem of maximising expected future return into a problem of likelihood maximisation. One ingredient for this approach is the mixture of finite-time models we introduced in Section 18.2. We have shown that this approach establishes equivalence for arbitrary reward functions, allows for an efficient inference procedure, propagating synchronously forward and backward without pre-fixing a finite time horizon H, and allows for the handling of discounting rewards. We also showed that in the case of an unstructured MDP the resulting EM algorithm using exact inference and a greedy M-step is closely related to standard policy iteration.

However, unlike policy iteration, the EM algorithm generalises to arbitrary DBNs and the aim of this approach is to transfer the full variety of existing inference techniques to the problem of solving (PO)MDPs. This refers especially to structured problem domains, where DBNs allow us to consider structured representations of the environment (the world state, e.g. factorisation or hierarchies) as well as the agent (e.g. hierarchical policies or multiple agents). Inference techniques like variational approaches, message-passing algorithms, or approximate belief representations in DBNs can be used to exploit such structure in (PO)MDPs.

18.6.1 Follow-up and related work

We exemplified the approach for exact inference on unstructured MDPs, using Gaussian belief state propagation on a non-linear stochastic optimal control problem, and on a more complex DBN formulation of a POMDP problem. Recently there have been a series of papers based on or closely related to the general framework that we presented here. In [32] we extended the approach to learning hierarchical controllers for POMDPs. In [36] we presented a model-free reinforcement learning version of our EM approach. The authors in [12, 13] use MCMC methods for approximate inference in this context and generalise the EM algorithm for continuous MDPs [11]. Finally, [26, 16] developed similar EM techniques in a robotics and model-free context.

An interesting issue for future research is to consider max-product BP (a generalisation of Viterbi) for planning. In the POMDP context, further aspects to consider are: Can we use inference techniques also to estimate the number of internal states we need to solve a problem (cf. infinite hidden Markov models [3] as a method to learn the number of hidden states needed to model the data)? Or are there efficient heuristics to add hidden states in a DBN, e.g., analogous to how new nodes are added to bounded FSCs [27]?

We hope that our approach lays new ground for a whole family of new, inference-based techniques being applicable in the realm of (PO)MDPs.

Acknowledgments   M.T. is grateful to the German Research Foundation (DFG) for the Emmy Noether fellowship TO 409/1-3.

18.A   Appendix: Remarks

(i) The mixture of finite-time MDPs may be compared to a classical interpretation of reward discounting: Assume the agent has a probability $(1 - \gamma)$ of dying after each time step. Then the distribution over his life span is the geometric distribution $P(T) = \gamma^T(1 - \gamma)$. In our mixture of finite-time MDPs we treat each possible life-span T separately. From the agent's perspective, he knows that he has a finite life span T but he does not know what it is – he lives in a mixture of possible worlds. Each finite life span is terminated by a single binary reward (say, going to heaven or hell). The agent's behaviour must reflect his uncertainty about his life span and act by accounting for the probability that he might die now or later on, i.e., he must 'average' over the mixture of possible worlds he might live in.

(ii) In the original MDP, the rewards at two different time slices, say r_t and r_{t+1}, are strongly correlated. The mixture of finite-time MDPs does not include such correlations because the observations of reward at $T = t$ and $T = t + 1$ are treated by separate finite-time MDPs. However, since the expected future return V^π is merely a *sum* of reward expectations at different time slices such correlations are irrelevant for solving the MDP and computing optimal policies.

(iii) Do exponentiated rewards as observation likelihoods lead to equivalence? Let us introduce modified binary reward variables $\hat{r}_t$ in every time slice with probabilities

$$P(\hat{r}_t = 1 \mid a_t, s_t) = e^{\gamma^t \mathcal{R}(a_t, s_t)} , \quad \mathcal{R}(a_t, s_t) := \mathrm{E}\{r_t \mid a_t, s_t\}.$$

Then
$$\log P(\hat{r}_{0:T} = 1; \pi) = \log \mathrm{E}_{a_{0:T}, s_{0:T}} \Big\{ \prod_{t=0}^{T} P(\hat{r}_t = 1 \mid a_t, s_t) \Big\}$$

$$\geq \mathrm{E}_{a_{0:T}, s_{0:T}} \Big\{ \log \prod_{t=0}^{T} P(\hat{r}_t = 1 \mid a_t, s_t) \Big\}$$

$$= \mathrm{E}_{a_{0:T}, s_{0:T}} \Big\{ \sum_{t=0}^{T} \gamma^t \mathcal{R}(a_t, s_t) \Big\}$$

$$= V^\pi.$$

That is, maximisation of $P(\hat{r}_{0:T} = 1; \pi)$ is *not* equivalent to maximisation of V^π. However, this points to a formulation in terms of a Kullback–Leibler divergence minimisation

$$V^\pi = \mathrm{E}_{a_{0:T}, s_{0:T}} \Big\{ \log \prod_{t=0}^{T} P(\hat{r}_t = 1 \mid a_t, s_t) \Big\}$$

$$= \sum_{a_{0:T}, s_{0:T}} \Big[P(s_0) \, \pi(a_0 \mid s_0) \prod_{t=1}^{T} \pi(a_t \mid s_t) \, P(s_t \mid a_{t-1}, s_{t-1}) \Big] \log \Big[\prod_{t=0}^{T} \exp\{\gamma^t \mathcal{R}(a_t, s_t)\} \Big]$$

$$= \sum_{a_{0:T}, s_{0:T}} p(a_{0:T}, s_{t:T} \mid \pi) \log q(a_{0:T}, s_{t:T}),$$

where we defined

Figure 18.11 Only the envelopes emanating from the start distribution $(P(s))$ and rewards $(P(R|a, s))$ contribute to the propagation. They are chopped where they do not overlap with the other envelope after $T_M/2$ iterations.

$$p(a_{0:T}, s_{t:T} \mid \pi) = P(s_0)\, \pi(a_0 \mid s_0) \prod_{t=1}^{T} \pi(a_t \mid s_t)\, P(s_t \mid a_{t-1}, s_{t-1}),$$

$$q(a_{0:T}, s_{t:T}) = \prod_{t=0}^{T} \exp\{\gamma^t \mathcal{R}(a_t, s_t)\}.$$

The first distribution p is the prior trajectory defined by the policy π disregarding any rewards. The second 'distribution' (if one normalises it) $q(a_{0:T}, s_{0:T})$ has a very simple form, it fully factorises over time and in each time slice we have the exponentiated reward with 'temperature' γ^{-t}. If $q(s_{0:T})$ is normalised, we can also write the value in terms of a Kullback–Leibler divergence $V^\pi = -D(p \mid q) + H(p)$.

18.B   Appendix: Pruning computations

Consider a finite state space and assume that we fixed the maximum allowed time T by some upper limit T_M (e.g., by deciding on a cutoff time based on the time posterior computed on the fly, see below). Then there are potentially large regions of the state space on which we may prune computations, i.e., states s for which the posterior $P(s_t = s \mid T = t + \tau) = 0$ for any t and τ with $t + \tau \le T_M$. Figure 18.11 illustrates the idea. Let us consider the a-propagation (Eq. (18.8)) first (all statements apply conversely for the b-propagation). For iteration time t we define a set of states

$$S_a(t) = \{s \mid a_t(s) \ne 0 \ \wedge \ (t < T_M/2 \ \vee \ b_{T_M-t}(s) \ne 0)\}.$$

Under the assumption that $b_\tau(s) = 0 \Rightarrow \forall \tau' \le \tau : b_{\tau'}(s) = 0$ it follows

$$i \in S_a(t) \Leftarrow a_t(s) \ne 0 \ \wedge \ b_{T_M-t}(s) \ne 0$$
$$\Leftarrow \exists_{\tau \le T_M-t} : a_t(s) \ne 0 \ \wedge \ b_\tau(s) \ne 0$$
$$\Longleftrightarrow \exists_{\tau \le T_M-t} : \gamma_{t\tau}(s) \ne 0.$$

Thus, every state that is potentially visited at time t (for which $\exists_{\tau:t+\tau \le T_M} : \gamma_{t\tau}(s) \ne 0$) is included in $S_a(t)$. We will exclude all states $s \notin S_a(t)$ from the a-propagation procedure and not deliver their messages. The constraint $t < T_M/2$ concerning the b's was inserted in the definition of $S_a(t)$ only because of the feasibility of computing $S_a(t)$ at iteration time t. Initialising $S_a(0) = \{s \mid P(s) \ne 0\}$, we can compute $S_a(t)$ recursively via

$$S_a(t) = \begin{cases} S_a(t-1) \cup \mathsf{OUT}(S_a(t-1)) & \text{for } t < T_M/2, \\ \left[S_a(t-1) \cup \mathsf{OUT}(S_a(t-1))\right] \cap \{s \mid b_{T_M-t}(s) \ne 0\} & \text{for } t \ge T_M/2, \end{cases}$$

where $\mathsf{OUT}(S_a(t-1))$ is the set of states which have non-zero probability transitions from states in $S_a(t-1)$. Analogously, the bookkeeping for states that participate in the b-propagation is

$$S_b(0) = \{s \mid P(R|a, s) \ne 0\}$$

$$S_b(\tau) = \begin{cases} S_b(\tau-1) \cup \mathrm{IN}(S_b(\tau-1)) & \text{for } \tau < T_M/2, \\ \left[S_b(\tau-1) \cup \mathrm{IN}(S_b(\tau-1))\right] \cap \{s \mid a_{T_M-\tau}(s) \neq 0\} & \text{for } \tau \geq T_M/2. \end{cases}$$

For the discount prior, we can use a time cutoff T_M for which we expect further contributions to be insignificant. The choice of this cutoff involves a payoff between computational cost and accuracy of the E-step. Let T_0 be the minimum T for which the finite-time likelihood $P(R \mid T; \pi) \neq 0$. It is clear that the cutoff needs to be greater than T_0. In the experiment in Section 18.4.3 we used an increasing schedule for the cutoff time, $T_M = (1 + 0.2\,k)\,T_0$, depending on the iteration k of the EM algorithm to ensure that with each iteration we become more accurate.

Bibliography

[1] C. G. Atkeson and J. C. Santamaría. A comparison of direct and model-based reinforcement learning. In *International Conference on Robotics and Automation*, 1997.

[2] H. Attias. Planning by probabilistic inference. In Christopher M. Bishop and Brendan J. Frey, editors, *Proceedings of the 9th International Workshop on Artificial Intelligence and Statistics*, 2003.

[3] M. J. Beal, Z. Ghahramani and C. E. Rasmussen. The infinite hidden Markov model. In T. Dietterich, S. Becker, and Z. Ghahramani, editors, *Advances in Neural Information Processing Systems 14*. MIT Press, 2002.

[4] C. Boutilier, T. Dean, and S. Hanks. Decision theoretic planning: structural assumptions and computational leverage. *Journal of Artificial Intelligence Research*, **11**:1–94, 1999.

[5] C. Boutilier, R. Dearden and M. Goldszmidt. Exploiting structure in policy construction. In *Proceedings of the 14th International Joint Conference on Artificial Intelligence (IJCAI 1995)*, pages 1104–1111, 1995.

[6] H. Bui, S. Venkatesh and G. West. Policy recognition in the abstract hidden Markov models. *Journal of Artificial Intelligence Research*, **17**:451–499, 2002.

[7] M. Chavira, A. Darwiche, and M. Jaeger. Compiling relational Bayesian networks for exact inference. *International Journal of Approximate Reasoning*, **42**:4–20, 2006.

[8] G. F. Cooper. A method for using belief networks as influence diagrams. In *Proceedings of the Fourth Workshop on Uncertainty in Artificial Intelligence*, pages 55–63, 1988.

[9] C. Guestrin, D. Koller, R. Parr and S. Venkataraman. Efficient solution algorithms for factored MDPs. *Journal of Artificial Intelligence Research*, **19**: 399–468, 2003.

[10] M. Hauskrecht, N. Meuleau, L. P. Kaelbling, T. Dean and C. Boutilier. Hierarchical solution of Markov decision processes using macro-actions. In *Proceedings of Uncertainty in Artificial Intelligence*, pages 220–229, 1998.

[11] M. Hoffman, N. de Freitas, A. Doucet and J. Peters. An expectation maximization algorithm for continuous Markov decision processes with arbitrary rewards. In *Twelfth International Conference on Artificial Intelligence and Statistics*, 2009.

[12] M. Hoffman, A. Doucet, N. de Freitas and A. Jasra. Bayesian policy learning with trans-dimensional MCMC. In *Advances in Neural Information Processing Systems 20*. MIT Press, 2008.

[13] M. Hoffman, H. Kueck, A. Doucet and N. de Freitas. New inference strategies for solving Markov decision processes using reversible jump MCMC. In *Uncertainty in Artificial Intelligence*, 2009.

[14] L. P. Kaelbling, M. L. Littman and A. R. Cassandra. Planning and acting in partially observable stochastic domains. *Artificial Intelligence*, **101**:99–134, 1998.

[15] L. P. Kaelbling, M. L. Littman and A. W. Moore. Reinforcement learning: A survey. *Journal of Artificial Intelligence Research*, **4**:237–285, 1996.

[16] J. Kober and J. Peters. Policy search for motor primitives in robotics. In D. Koller, D. Schuurmans and Y. Bengio, editors, *Advances in Neural Information Processing Systems 21*. MIT Press, 2009.

[17] D. Koller and R. Parr. Computing factored value functions for policies in structured MDPs. In *Proceedings of the 16th International Joint Conference on Artificial Intelligence*, pages 1332–1339, 1999.

[18] B. Kveton and M. Hauskrecht. An MCMC approach to solving hybrid factored MDPs. In *Proceedings of the 19th International Joint Conference on Artificial Intelligence*, volume 19, pages 1346–1351, 2005.

[19] M. L. Littman, S. M. Majercik and T. Pitassi. Stochastic Boolean satisfiability. *Journal of Automated Reasoning*, **27**(3):251–296, 2001.

[20] A. McGovern and A. G. Barto. Automatic discovery of subgoals in reinforcement learning using diverse density. In *Proceedings of the 18th International Conference on Machine Learning*, pages 361–368, 2001.

[21] N. Meuleau, L. Peshkin, K.-E. Kim and L. P. Kaelbling. Learning finite-state controllers for partially observable environments. In *Proceedings of Fifteenth Conference on Uncertainty in Artificial Intelligence*, pages 427–436, 1999.

[22] T. Minka. A family of algorithms for approximate Bayesian inference. PhD thesis, MIT, 2001.

[23] K. Murphy. Dynamic Bayesian networks: Representation, inference and learning. PhD Thesis, UC Berkeley, Computer Science Division, 2002.

[24] A. Y. Ng, R. Parr and D. Koller. Policy search via density estimation. In *Advances in Neural Information Processing Systems*, pages 1022–1028, 1999.

[25] J. Pearl. *Probabilistic Reasoning In Intelligent Systems: Networks of Plausible Inference*. Morgan Kaufmann, 1988.

[26] J. Peters and S. Schaal. Reinforcement learning by reward-weighted regression for operational space control. In *Proceedings of the International Conference on Machine Learning*, 2007.

[27] P. Poupart and C. Boutilier. Bounded finite state controllers. In *Advances in Neural Information Processing Systems 16 (NIPS 2003)*, volume 16. MIT Press, 2004.

[28] T. Raiko and M. Tornio. Learning nonlinear state-space models for control. In *Proceedings of International Joint Conference on Neural Networks*, 2005.

[29] R. D. Shachter. Probabilistic inference and influence diagrams. *Operations Research*, **36**:589–605, 1988.

[30] G. Theocharous, K. Murphy and L. Kaelbling. Representing hierarchical POMDPs as DBNs for multi-scale robot localization. In *International Conference on Robotics and Automation*, 2004.

[31] M. Toussaint. Lecture note: Influence diagrams. http://ml.cs.tu-berlin.de/~mtoussai/notes/, 2009.

[32] M. Toussaint, L. Charlin and P. Poupart. Hierarchical POMDP controller optimization by likelihood maximization. In *Uncertainty in Artificial Intelligence*, 2008.

[33] M. Toussaint, S. Harmeling and A. Storkey. Probabilistic inference for solving (PO)MDPs. Technical Report EDI-INF-RR-0934, University of Edinburgh, School of Informatics, 2006.

[34] M. Toussaint and A. Storkey. Probabilistic inference for solving discrete and continuous state Markov Decision Processes. In *Proceedings of the 23nd International Conference on Machine Learning*, pages 945–952, 2006.

[35] D. Verma and R. P. N. Rao. Goal-based imitation as probabilistic inference over graphical models. In *Advances in Neural Information Processing Systems*, 2006.

[36] N. Vlassis and M. Toussaint. Model-free reinforcement learning as mixture learning. In *Proceedings of the 26th International Conference on Machine Learning*, 2009.

[37] L. Zettlemoyer, H. Pasula and L. P. Kaelbling. Learning planning rules in noisy stochastic worlds. In *Proceedings of the Twentieth National Conference on Artificial Intelligence*, 2005.

Contributors

Marc Toussaint, Technische Universität Berlin, Franklinstr. 28/29 FR6-9, 10587 Berlin.
Amos Storkey, Institute for Adaptive and Neural Computation, University of Edinburgh
Stefan Harmeling, MPI for Biological Cybernetics, Dept. Schölkopf, Tübingen.

Index

Printed in the United States
By Bookmasters